MW01620871

CASPAR DAVID FRIEDRICH

WERNER HOFMANN

CASPAR DAVID FRIEDRICH

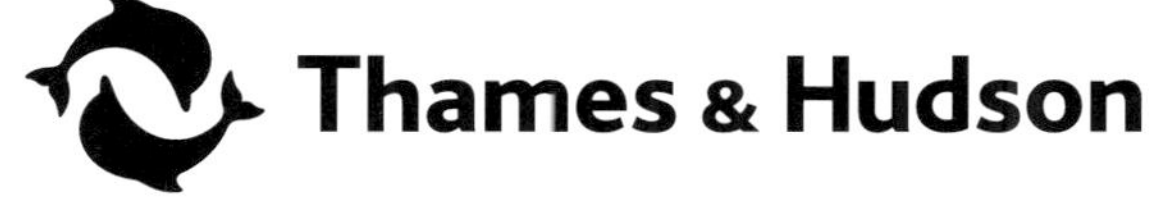

Three years ago, Eric Hazan wanted a monograph on Caspar David Friedrich for his publishing house. I thank him for his initiative, and also thank Jean-François Barrielle, who later pursued the project so vigorously.

Stéphanie Grégoire was responsible for overseeing the production of the book. In the finished product, the author finds the flow of his text complemented by a seductive visual rhythm, and he is very grateful.

W. H.

Translated from the German by Mary Whittall

Any copy of this book issued by the publisher as a paperback is sold subject to the condition that it shall not by way of trade or otherwise be lent, resold, hired out or otherwise circulated without the publisher's prior consent in any form of binding or cover other than that in which it is published and without a similar condition including these words being imposed on a subsequent purchaser.

This edition first published in the United Kingdom in 2000 by
Thames & Hudson Ltd, 181A High Holborn, London WC1V 7QX

This edition first published in hardcover in the United States of America in 2000
by Thames & Hudson Inc., 500 Fifth Avenue, New York, New York 10110

© 2000 Thames & Hudson Ltd, London

Original edition © 2000 Éditions Hazan, Paris

All Rights Reserved. No part of this publication may be reproduced or transmitted in any form or by any means, electronic or mechanical, including photocopy, recording or any other information storage and retrieval system, without prior permission in writing from the publisher.

British Library Cataloguing-in-Publication Data
A catalogue record for this book is available from the British Library

Library of Congress Catalog Card Number: 00-101621

ISBN 0-500-09295-8

Printed and bound in Italy

CONTENTS

For Jacqueline

Art may be a game, but it is a serious game.

C. D. F.

THE PAINTER AND THE ZEITGEIST

Nowadays an artist's standing depends on his visibility in the media. The more his work is seen on T-shirts and album covers, the more firmly he stamps himself on the public consciousness. But commerce is not the only test of the possible multiple meanings of an artist, a symbol or an image. A few years ago Caspar David Friedrich's *The Wanderer above a Sea of Mists* (ill. 1; the title is apocryphal) was conscripted by the editors of Germany's biggest-circulation news magazine, *Der Spiegel*, 'to translate the complexity of events surrounding the collapse of the Third Reich [1945] and ways of dealing with the burden of history'. The result was a cover illustration (ill. 2) that placed the mountaineer in his city clothes on the edge of the precipice of the German horror. Apparently calm and collected, he looks into an abyss, and out of the mist, children stare up at him from behind the barbed wire of a concentration camp, while a unit of the National People's Army marches out of the picture and out of history. To the left is a Nazi swastika, to the right the flag of the German Democratic Republic, and above that a border guard jumping over a barbed-wire barrier into the freedom of the West, an image borrowed from a famous photograph. Meanwhile Hitler, the originator of this collective disaster, gazes into the distance, an unshakeably determined visionary. The designer carefully positioned the Brandenburg Gate on the central axis of his 'composition' so as both to form a bridge between the two halves of the narrative and to provide the Wanderer with a foil which simultaneously crowns the figure and bears down on it.

The man is contemplating the German inferno. Yet he does not possess any obvious qualities that would predestine him to searching the national conscience. In Friedrich's painting he partially hides a view of rocks stacked below and a distant chain of mountain peaks. A covering of mist lies over bizarre rock formations, like the ones Friedrich had seen during his own wanderings in the sandstone hills that flank the Elbe, east of Dresden. The Wanderer, a Rousseauesque *promeneur solitaire*, has come to the physical end of his explorations. He cannot go a step further; only his thoughts can carry him from 'here' to an uncertain 'there', from the height he has reached into the inaccessible distance. He stands on the brink, confronting a void which might just as easily fulfil expectations as arouse fears. Seen only from behind, the questioning posture of the figure remains open, not predisposed to one answer more than any other. Perhaps the man is concerned less with external experiences than with internal ones, examined under the gaze of the 'inner eye' to which the painter himself was so fond of referring. Because of this, the Wanderer lends himself to being projected – or co-opted – into different contexts. One of these is the succession of German catastrophes in the twentieth century, which forced the nation once again to question its own identity: hence the creation of an everyday icon of German consciousness for the cover of *Der Spiegel*.

However, when the anonymous Wanderer was set down on a horizon of German expectation, that is to say, in a specific situation for which the painting provided no justification, then the connection between the Wanderer and the sensibility of his own time was lost. When a case is made today claiming (and co-opting) his affinity to the music and literature of that era, there are often good grounds for it. Friedrich's painting has been used on the cover of a recording of Schubert's *'Wanderer' Fantasy* and on the jacket of Benjamin Constant's 1806 novel, *Adolphe*. This is not inappropriate, for Constant describes his hero as follows: 'He used to walk out in the evenings, always alone, and often passed whole days seated, without moving, supporting his head on his two hands.'

There is an even stronger connection with René de Chateaubriand; in *Génie du Christianisme* (1802), the French writer uses the same metaphor for man's journey through life that Friedrich's figure expresses in visual terms: 'Man is suspended in the present, between the past and the future, as if on a rock between two chasms. Behind and ahead, all is darkness; he can scarcely make out the phantoms that rise up from the bottom of both abysses, float for a moment on the surface and then dive back down again.' What the poet's words share with the painter's image is their climate of uncertainty and isolation. Both are placed firmly within the Christian tradition which gave a new emphasis to solitude: 'When it peopled the universe with elegant phantoms, mythology robbed creation of its gravity, its grandeur and its solitude. It took Christianity to chase away this population of fauns, satyrs and nymphs, to give caves their silence and woods their reveries once more.' Chateaubriand proposed a new iconography of landscape, and argued indirectly for the hitherto humble genre to be revalued. But the painters of his own country paid little or no attention to him. They had no time for a Christianized view of nature, being at first far too caught up in the events of the Revolution and then committed by Napoleonic art policy to the affirmations of history painting. Neither of these periods of upheaval needed the private man at his meditations; they called for the hero triumphant, or suffering as he fell. The tragic creed of *romantisme* is based on this exertion of all man's energies, and is centred on an image of mankind roused by ambition and danger; this image finds its most imposing embodiments in the works of Théodore Géricault and Eugène Delacroix.

A few comparisons will illustrate how little this *romantisme* has to do with the kind of Romanticism associated with Friedrich. Delacroix painted wanderers too, but they are given clear and definite goals: *Dante and Virgil traverse the lake surrounding the walls of the infernal city of Dis.* Meanwhile, Friedrich's married couples and pairs of friends are not seeking adventures but are poised in contemplation of natural phenomena. Alternatively, compare two popular icons: Friedrich's Wanderer adopted as a stylized representative by a nation in search of itself, and Delacroix's *Liberty Leading the People*, demonstrating how the role of hero is played. Her triumphant figure is also open to multiple interpretations. On the one hand she is the radiant epiphany of the bellicose patron goddess of revolutionary iconography. On the other hand she is not only 'the savage power of the people, casting off a deadly burden', as Heine saw her, but also the *femme Messie* of the Saint-Simonists, in whom the Christian Queen of Heaven lives on in secularized form. By this token, Delacroix's early work *The Virgin of the Sacred Heart* is a prototype for his Liberty, who carries a gun and a flag in place of the heart of Jesus and a cross. Right up into the present

1. *The Wanderer above a Sea of Mists*, 1818, oil on canvas, 74.8 × 94.8 cm (29½ × 37⅜ in.). Hamburger Kunsthalle, Hamburg.

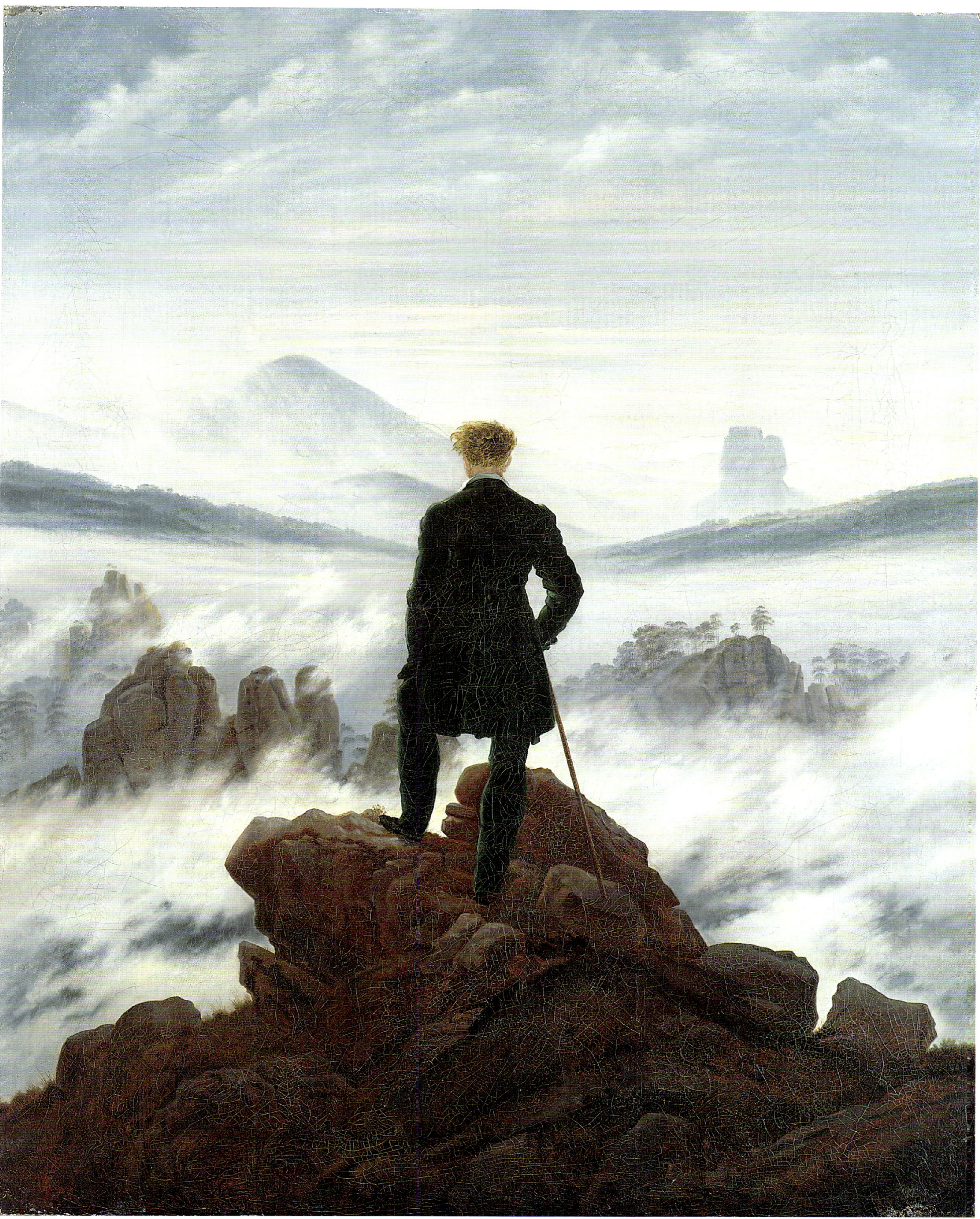

day, the figure of Liberty storming the barricades has proved itself a matrix that can be adapted to many different situations, unmasking politicians' hypocrisy in the hands of caricaturists and personifying the ideals of left-wing pamphleteers.

Liberty is a latter-day angelic messenger, who owes her dramatic appeal to the iconography of Catholic history painting. As the incarnation of her own objective, she elicits the polarized reactions peculiar to programmatic images and challenges the viewer to make either/or decisions. Friedrich, unlike Delacroix, did not paint the proclamation of an ideal or a cut-and-dried statement of belief. His painting is neither the expression of a Christian-Catholic message of salvation nor its secular equivalent in the democratic concept of freedom. The invitation to identify with the figure whose back we see involves neither collective action nor revolutionary commitment to a party, but rather entry into a realm of stillness, encouraging reflection remote from mundane concerns. The painter leaves it to the viewer to find different dimensions of meaning for the Wanderer and for himself. The appeal is addressed in good Protestant fashion to the individual's sense of personal responsibility – the source, as we shall see, of a new subjective freedom in dealing with works of art.

Of course, this comparison of Friedrich and Delacroix is valid only for a few specific examples of their work. It is not meant to extend to generalizations or to support conclusions about the ethnic traits of German and French painters. Instead it represents a first attempt – which will be followed by others in these pages – to break open the homogeneous outlines of European 'Romanticism', strip its content of any national characteristics, and relate that content to individuals. Within it, we find some differences, which are often sociologically determined, but we also come across surprising similarities and agreement. For example, Chateaubriand's term *l'oeil de l'âme* has much in common with Friedrich's oft-cited advice: 'Close your physical eye, so that you see your picture first with the spiritual eye. Then bring what you saw in the dark into the light, so that it may have an effect on others, shining inwards from outside.' Note that it is the Frenchman who speaks of 'the eye of the soul', supposedly a German domain, while Friedrich is content to speak of the 'spiritual eye'. Unfortunately the affinity was never enhanced by actual contact between the two men. It is a pity that Chateaubriand, as French ambassador to the Prussian court in 1821, evidently had no opportunity to see two major works by Friedrich, *The Monk by the Sea* (ill. 22) and *The Abbey in the Oak Wood* (ill. 23). Both had been bought by Frederick William III in 1810 following an exhibition at the Berlin Academy.

It was left to another Frenchman, the sculptor David d'Angers, to coin a phrase that encapsulated Friedrich's contribution to landscape painting. He went to see the painter in Dresden in 1834, when the sixty-year-old's fame was long past its zenith, and wrote detailed accounts of his visit in his diary and later in a letter (6 December) to his friend Victor Paire: 'Friedrich! The only landscape painter who has so far had the power to move all the faculties of my soul, the painter who has invented a new genre: the tragedy of landscape.' This phrase, *la tragédie du paysage*, struck a note that was to resonate and grow more profound in the French response to Friedrich. In February 1938 Albert Béguin published his pioneering study *L'âme romantique et le rêve*, in which Friedrich was accorded several appreciative pages. Béguin invoked the figure of Rousseau's *promeneur solitaire*, whose solitude often turns into desolation: 'To the isolation and anguish of the human being in his lowliness comes life's response of nature in perpetual metamorphosis.... In this sympathy between the soul and the world around it, we may ultimately perceive a religious overtone, even when there is no Christian symbol to specify it.' Béguin may have had in mind the painting of a ship caught in the ice, which at that date was still known as *The Wrecked 'Hope'* (ill. 159).

This painting was central among the reproductions chosen to illustrate an article that appeared around the same time in the periodical *Minotaure*. Written by Madeleine Landsberg, it bore the unambiguous title 'Caspar David Friedrich – peintre de l'angoisse romantique'. Landsberg saw regressive desires in Friedrich's work that were doomed to tragic failure. She concluded that the painter's principal human and exemplary qualities lay in the very impossibility of regression: 'Romantic works such as those of Friedrich are whirlpools attracting that part of us which yearns to drown.' Friedrich was attributed with a sense of existential *Angst* which characterized the sensibility of French intellectuals of the period. (Marie Bonaparte's psychoanalytical study of Edgar Allan Poe had appeared in 1933.)

At the same time, Hitler's Germany was manufacturing an image of Friedrich appropriate to the New Era, although the concept of Romanticism was something of a stumbling block. One shocking simplification brusquely divided Romantic artists into the 'effeminate and cowardly' and the 'manly and brave'. The former were said to take refuge in the universal and the international, while the latter 'attacked national and German questions'; Friedrich was numbered among the attackers. Even in 1938, before the outbreak of war, the raving perpetrator of this nonsense was almost reaching for his gun as he wrote, trying to enlist Romanticism (the manly kind, of course) to his violent cause: 'This type of Romanticism is a German art of strife, an art of self-denial, an art of sacrifice.' Beating the drums of war, he looked into the abyss of suicidal yearning, as Béguin and Landsberg did, but saw with other eyes. He dismissed *angoisse*, ritualized tragic failure as an art of sacrifice, and placed it prophetically on the battlefield at the side of death.

The Third Reich's brutal appropriation of Friedrich still clings in places. Some will not forgive him for the fact that Hitler allegedly held him in high esteem – a fault that also afflicts other masters, without tarnishing their reputations. When paintings and drawings by Friedrich from collections in Moscow and St Petersburg (where they had already gone in the painter's lifetime) were shown in the Metropolitan Museum in New York in the spring of 1991, Hilton Kramer, writing in the *New York Observer*, found that the paintings 'offer not much in the way of pictorial nourishment'. Another critic, by contrast, was offended by the excellence of Friedrich's technique and accused the landscapes of being dead and frozen.

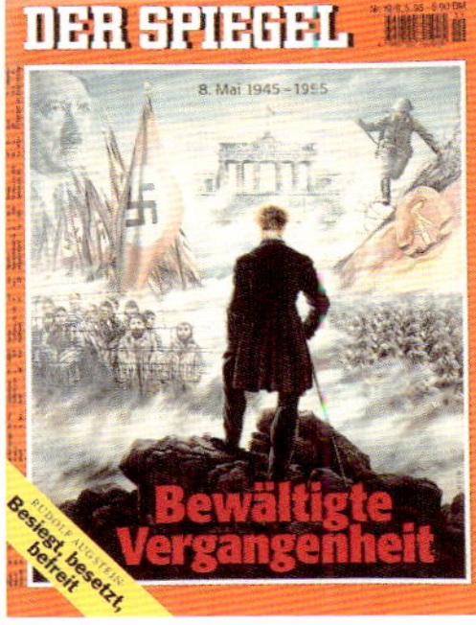

2. Cover of *Der Spiegel*, no. 19, 8 May 1995.

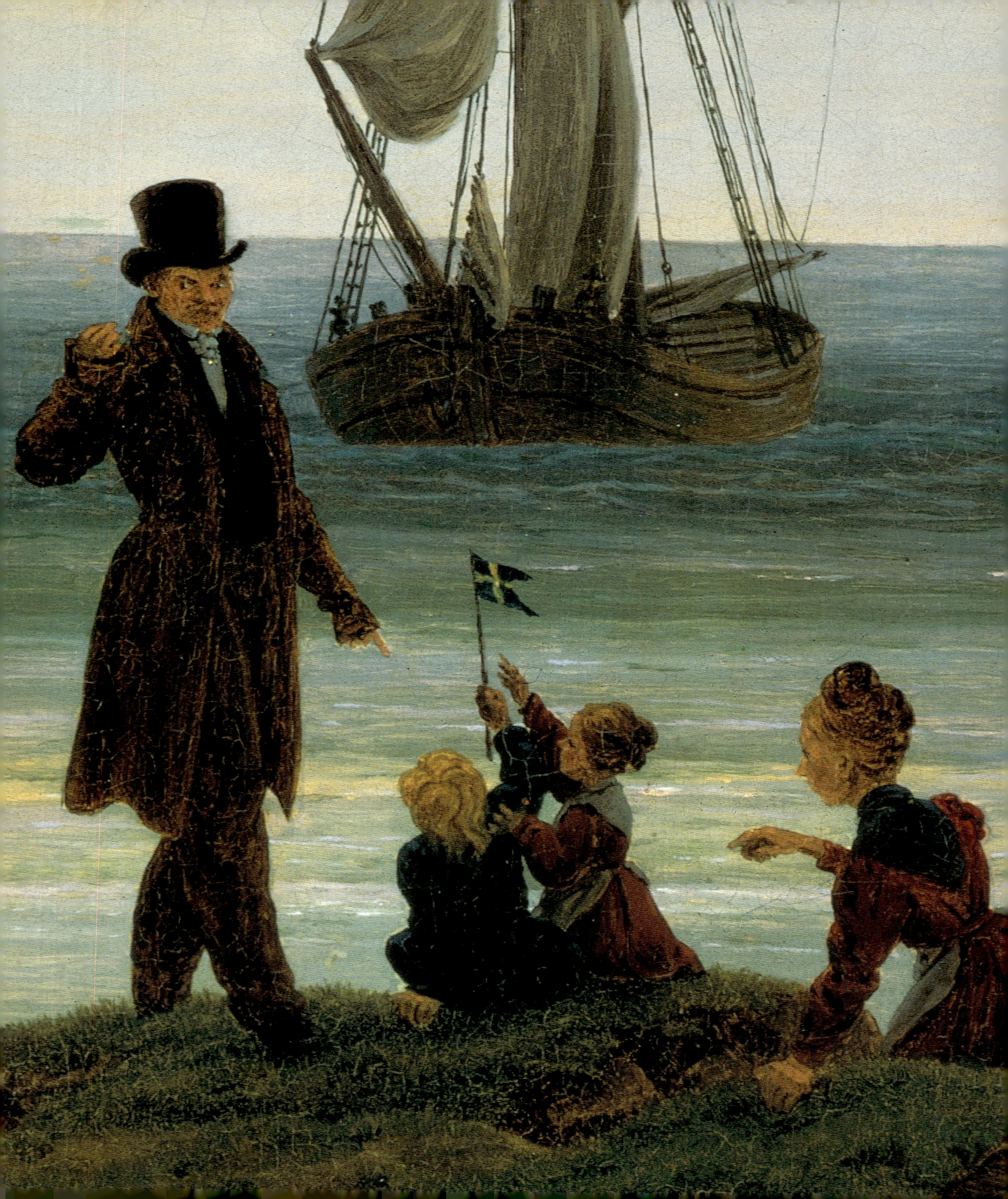

I

FRIEDRICH IN HIS TIME

Where does Friedrich belong? This one question is really several: what in him is German, what is European, and what is personally and inalienably his own? The following pages, explicitly or implicitly, will deal with these questions.

The painter who nowadays embodies the German contribution to European Romantic art, according to Robert Rosenblum, was born on 5 September 1774 as a subject of the King of Sweden. He was one of eight children of a soapboiler and candlemaker. His birthplace, Greifswald, numbered some five thousand inhabitants at the time, and just sixty students were registered at the university, founded in 1456. The little town on the Baltic coast, together with the rest of the province of West Pomerania, had fallen to Sweden during the Thirty Years' War. Later, in 1815, the Congress of Vienna assigned the region to Prussia. Friedrich seems originally to have wanted to dedicate one of his most famous works, *The Tetschen Altar* (1807–8, ill. 21), to 'his king', Gustav IV Adolf of Sweden. A central detail in *The Stages of Life* (ills 3, 163, 165) bears witness to the painter's allegiance to his former sovereign: the two children – one might be his own son Gustav Adolf, born in 1824 – hold aloft the Swedish flag. According to Per Atterbom, Friedrich thought of himself as half Swedish.

The Swedish connection is mentioned here, not with the intention of expatriating the painter, but rather to indicate the looseness of ties to dynastic or political units within the greater German cultural world. As long as there was no national state, cities and provinces were on the one hand commodities to be traded in response to shifts in the balance of power; on the other hand, they enjoyed a certain autonomy, as no central power controlled them. In the north, the tradition of the Free Cities of the Hanseatic League was a further contributory factor. Unification into a centralized state, long ago accomplished in other parts of Europe, was delayed until the nineteenth century in this 'belated nation' (Plessner). The monarchies and principalities, the numerous ecclesiastical territories and the old Free Imperial cities stood in its way, all stubbornly defending their particular structures. The Holy Roman Emperor, from his palace in Vienna, was almost powerless against this coalition of interests, despite its frequent internal dissensions.

The map of the German states looked like a patchwork quilt threatening to come apart at the seams. Only the multinational Habsburg Empire, along with Prussia, Hanover, Saxony and Bavaria stood out as larger, integrated units. The polycentralism of political and administrative power was reflected in spiritual and intellectual life, which was splintered and fragmented but also full of exciting contradictions,

3. *The Stages of Life*, detail,
1834–35, oil on canvas,
72.5 x 94 cm (28½ x 37 in.).
Museum der bildenden Künste, Leipzig.

depending on one's point of view. The absence of a dominant capital city was both a loss and a gain. Events in the intellectual and artistic sphere had to take place without the authority of a centre to set standards, encourage talent and stimulate and speed up the exchange of opinions, but the lack of such a centre allowed subjective inclinations to develop unsupervised, relatively free of codified norms and official conventions of taste. The competition played out on very restricted stages in Paris and London was spread out across several centres within the German cultural realm, and these centres were not only rivals amongst themselves but were also liable to lose the status of centre to other contenders. Even places on the periphery could make their voices heard in this scattered topography. The whole mosaic had many edges, both internal and external, but living near the outside did not necessarily make you an outsider.

This was as true for Friedrich as for anyone else. His first formative steps were taken under the guidance of two teachers in Greifswald itself. Johann Gottfried Quistorp taught him drawing, and the literary scholar Gotthard Ludwig Theobul Kosegarten introduced him to the great literature of the classical and contemporary worlds and also to Ossian. It was most likely on the advice of both that Friedrich went to the Academy in Copenhagen in 1794, where he remained until 1798. The attraction of this institution lay partly in its international reputation but will have been strengthened by the Protestant-engendered unresponsiveness towards the arts that was prevalent in German cities on the North Sea and Baltic coasts. Goethe took a shot at their puritanism in 1800, when he wrote a *Flüchtige Übersicht über die Kunst in Deutschland* (*Cursory Survey of Art in Germany*), summarizing in a few pages the artistic life of Stuttgart, Karlsruhe, Düsseldorf, Hanover, Berlin, Dresden, Leipzig and Vienna, all seats of secular and spiritual princes. He dismissed the German North with the mocking suggestion that it would be a sound commercial venture to import Roman plaster casts to Hamburg and Bremen, so that 'an artistic genius banished to the North would not be deprived of all light'. In fact, young talents were not waiting for imported goods but instead forsaking their 'banishment' for Copenhagen, where they could improve their eyes and hands in the study of classical sculpture.

The German North received attention in the latter part of the eighteenth century, not through the visual arts but through the intellectual advances being made in Riga, Königsberg and Hamburg. These were an important contribution to the ideas circulating in Europe at the time, and became central to the tenets of the age. In their wake, a new definition of artistic creativity emerged; like thought, art was declared to have come of age. Key figures in this process were four men whose writings represented the North – whether under Swedish, Prussian or Hanseatic administration – which was the background to Friedrich's art.

Immanuel Kant (1724–1802), Gotthold Ephraim Lessing (1729–81), Johann Georg Hamann (1730–88) and Johann Gottfried Herder (1744–1803) were in the forefront of German intellectuals dealing with the Enlightenment. The initial appropriation and assimilation of Enlightenment ideas was swiftly followed by their overthrow in the arena of Protestant pietism. The process was set in motion by French and English influences – Montesquieu, Diderot, Rousseau, Shaftesbury and Burke to name but a few – but it then followed a peculiarly German path: theology was reshaped as philosophy and simultaneously subsumed into it.

Hamann, the 'Magus of the North', was born in Königsberg and worked as a private tutor in Riga, then under the rule of imperial Russia. His vehement irrationalism sought to replace Christian dogmatism with a symbolic world-view. This symbolism had aesthetic traits: 'Senses and passions understand only images. The entire treasury of human knowledge and happiness consists of images.' The sensory world carries divine revelation within itself, but at the same time God remains an enigma.

Hamann's ideas were developed by Herder. He too was born in East Prussia, in Mohrungen, and studied theology in Königsberg before becoming a teacher at the cathedral school in Riga, where he was also a popular preacher. According to the diary he wrote on a sea voyage from Riga to Nantes in 1769, he perceived the sensory world, interwoven as it was with symbols and parables, as an ongoing divine revelation. As a philosopher he spoke disparagingly of the 'so-called Enlightenment'. He repudiated received norms of taste, championed the specific against the general and maintained that 'in a certain respect, every human perfection is national, secular, and in the most exact sense individual'. This principle enabled the artist to declare his independence from prescripts: 'No longer practise ... any school, any compulsion; see with new eyes.' This jettisoning of dead weight promoted self-discovery without preconditions: 'When shall I have come far enough that I may destroy in me everything I have learnt, and only invent for myself what I think and learn and believe!'

Lessing's essays and review articles on drama, published as *Hamburgische Dramaturgie* (1767–69), represent the programmatic correlative to Herder's aspirations. 'It is granted to genius', Lessing wrote, 'not to know a thousand things that every schoolboy knows; his spiritual and intellectual treasure is not the acquired contents of his memory but that which he is able to produce from within himself.' Creative freedom is not arbitrary, however. 'Each and every one is entitled to his own taste; and to seek to account to oneself for one's taste is commendable.'

Kant summed up all these ideas succinctly in his *Critique of Pure Reason* (1790): 'There cannot be any objective rule of taste capable of determining what is beautiful by reference to concepts.' This formula was to bring about a Copernican revolution in art and art theory. It was devised and announced at Königsberg University, on the northeastern edge of Prussia, close to the Russian border; Kant's publisher was based in Riga.

We don't know what Friedrich knew of the writings of these philosophers, what he may have heard about them in Copenhagen or even earlier, from Kosegarten. We do know that he was not a speculative thinker, as Philipp Otto Runge was, and neither did he possess Runge's ambitious drive towards self-improvement. Nevertheless, Friedrich's writings contain some important insights into both his own art and that of his contemporaries. They show that both his subjectivity and his religious ethos were based on the self-reliance which Hamann, Herder, Lessing and Kant all granted the creative artist as his right and duty. Friedrich knew that no single person is the 'yardstick for all'; that there are no rules for beauty; that 'judges of art' move only along well-trodden paths; that every natural phenomenon can become art and that the noble human being finds God in everything.

The impact of these beliefs is somewhat diminished by a question mark hanging over them: when were they written down? Certainly not before Friedrich settled in Dresden, when he had made a name for himself and could claim the right to be outspoken in his praise and blame – a judge of art who was scornful about other judges of art. These fundamental principles are not things he picked up from reading. An insistence on the artist's own responsibility, a contempt for the dead weight of accumulated knowledge and a trust in God rooted in the perceptible world – Friedrich must have carried the seeds of all these convictions within himself from the first and as they developed, they may have also made him critical of an institution that tried to teach art. Similar conclusions were drawn by two of his compatriots who also studied in Copenhagen, Asmus Jakob Carstens (from 1776 to 1783) and Philipp Otto Runge (from 1799 to 1801). Critical distancing from the practices and methods of academic tuition set all of them on an arduous journey of self-discovery, and meant that these three very individual artists came to exemplify the artistic upheavals that marked the turn of the eighteenth to the nineteenth century. In simplified terms, this distancing obliged the students to choose between figure and landscape.

The choice reflects the three-stage division of 'modes' set out by Goethe in his 1789 essay *Einfache Nachahmung der Natur, Manier, Stil* (*Simple Imitation of Nature, Manner, Style*). The highest mode, 'style', included history painting legitimized by mythology. This was represented in Copenhagen by Nicolai Abildgaard. The genres that confined themselves to 'simple imitation' – in other words, landscape and portraiture – lay much lower on the list. In Copenhagen these were the province of Jens Juel.

So how did the three North Germans respond in these circumstances? Carstens (1754–98) devoted his short life to seeking the 'essence of things', which for Goethe was the preserve of style, and pursued a figurative ideal inspired by the example of Michelangelo. According to his friend Carl Ludwig Fernow, his life in Rome was spent 'solely amid wars between gods and battles of Titans', but he also sometimes attempted subjects of the kind that Goethe termed 'impossible to depict', such as 'the Birth of Light', using human figures to portray a cosmic event. Runge took up the same challenge in his *Times of Day*, with no prior knowledge of Carstens's works. Inspired by both Abildgaard and Juel, Runge feared that, rather than form, he would attain only 'manner', the middle stage which Goethe placed between style and simple imitation. Runge was fascinated by Homer and Ossian, but historical subjects did not satisfy him; he wanted to go beyond narration to a new iconic dignity. In Dresden, where he settled in 1802, he referred to historical subjects as 'confusion'. Instead, he envisioned a means of escape which he formulated as a question: 'Is it not possible to reach an apex in this new art – call it landscapery, if you will? Might it perhaps be even more beautiful than earlier ones?' Runge gave the most convincing answer to his own question in *Morning* (ill. 20), a profoundly thoughtful, profane altarpiece, which incorporates the theme of landscape into a cosmic scheme, thereby raising it to a higher plane. Runge's art has nothing to do with 'landscapery' as it was generally understood at that time.

Accurately assessing his own abilities and inclination, Caspar David Friedrich decided in favour of landscape from the first. He was not interested in complicated, intellectual-cum-religious systems of reference but in the calm observation for which Schiller praised Goethe so highly. He wanted to imbue the substance of what he saw with deeper significance and to use it to make symbols and parables. The eye with which he registered the concrete world connects him with Jens Juel, whose *Landscape with Northern Lights* (*c.* 1790; ill. 171) seems to be a forerunner to Friedrich's solemn prayers to nature. Friedrich's reformist ambitions were revealed in his remarks on the future and destiny of landscape painting:

'I do not believe that landscape painting has ever yet been understood and represented as worthily as it could and should be, given its intrinsic nature. But I also believe that it has been closer to its goal than it is now. People now begin with lies and end with lies; they overload pictures by piling up objects beside, behind and on top of each other, in the desire, I believe, to depict abundance. What the landscape painters of today see in an arc of 100 degrees in nature, they squeeze mercilessly into a 45 degree angle of vision. Things that are separated in nature by large intervening spaces are crowded together all touching each other, overfilling and oversaturating the eye, and making an unpleasant, disquieting impression on the viewer.'

This critique of his contemporaries – one of the targets was Joseph Anton Koch (ill. 180) – gives an indication of Friedrich's revolutionary concept of picture composition. He rejected the 'restrictive forms' of the 'well-trodden paths', and mocked prettified trees and rocks and the garishness of 'modish colouring'. He has no interest in clangour or formal exaggeration, and he demands from the landscape painter not dazzling feats of clever brushwork but the 'pure will ... to represent Nature simply, nobly and greatly, as she truly is, if one has a mind, disposition and feeling to recognize and understand her'.

Friedrich may have been looking back at his own beginnings when he wrote down his artistic credo, beginnings which contain something of the 'ragout' which he later rejected. Formal charm and atmospheric values are still rather too apparent in the *View of Mountains with Waterfall* (ill. 4), which dates from about 1793. A moon, racing clouds, a waterfall, a rocky ravine and a towering mountainous massif – all these picturesque requisites for a mysterious night-time scene form a stage set on which the figure of a woman seems to be feeling her way. Her arms imploringly hold out an invisible divining rod,

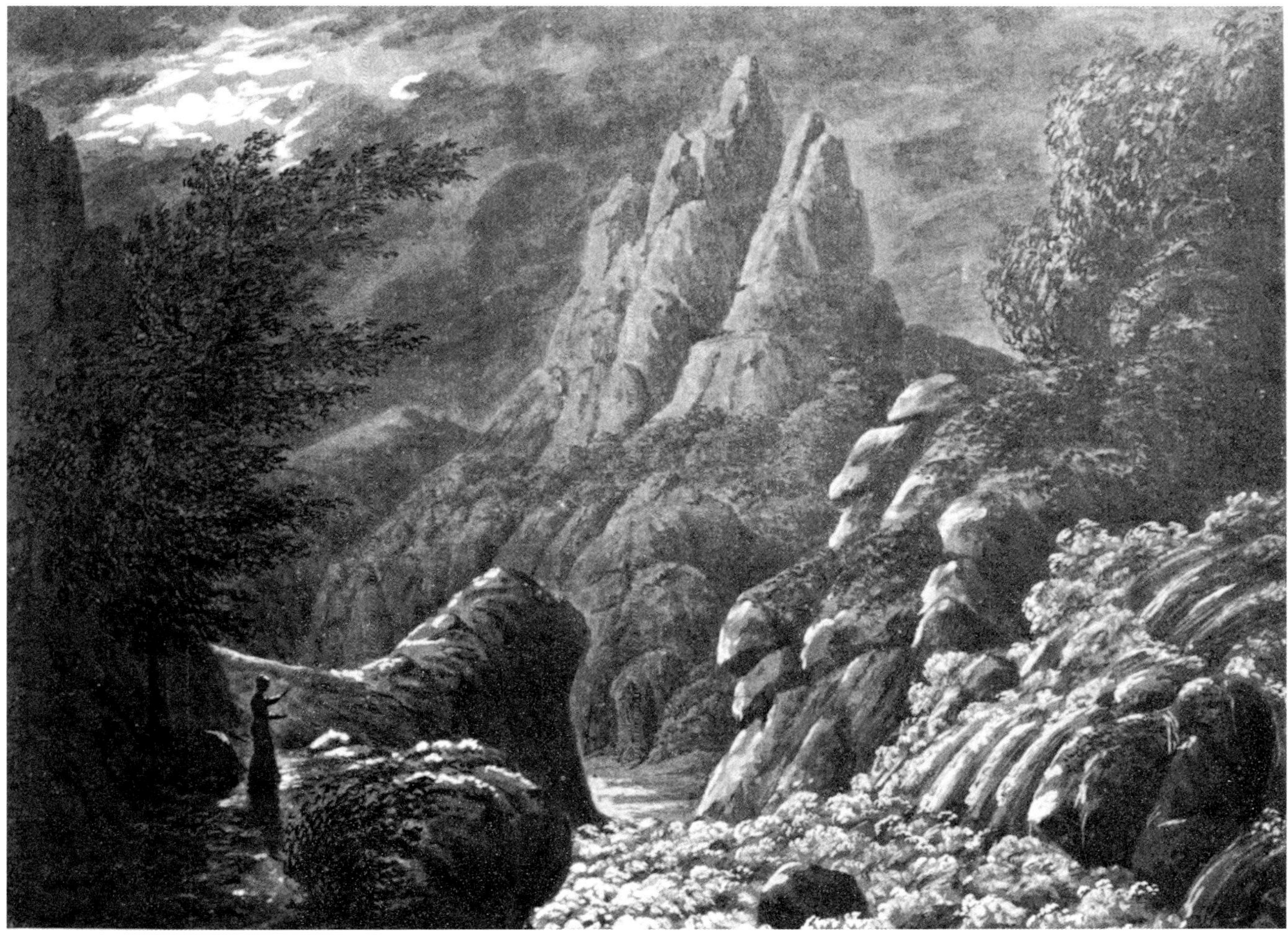

4. ***View of Mountains with Waterfall,***
c. 1793, sepia with watercolour wash on brown paper,
50.1 x 69.8 cm (19¾ x 27⅝ in.).
Private collection, Essen.

suggesting at the same time an attitude of prayer. It is not too fanciful to see it as a scene in a romantic opera. In any case, the woman is not a passive element of staffage but is connected, questioning and expectant, to the events of the natural world; the multiplicity of moods in the picture is at first sight rather bewildering. The 'ragout' we might taste here can already be found in Goethe's *The Sorrows of Werther* (1774), the vade-mecum of the years of *Sturm und Drang* and *Empfindsamkeit*: 'Monstrous mountains surrounded me, abysses lay before me and swollen becks plunged down, rivers streamed below me and forest and mountain rang. And I saw them toiling and working in each other in the depths of the earth, all the forces unfathomable.'

When we first look at the picture we see a melodrama. Then gradually, from the 'ragout' emerges a stabilizing formal idea, one which Friedrich would often return to later in his career. The mountainous massif and the fissure in the rock through which the water forces its way are almost exactly on the central axis. The water streams in the direction of the artist's standpoint, which he yields to the viewer. Yet we do not feel endangered, because the picture space is separated from our experiential space. The distancing device also imposes order on the individual spatial planes. The narrow rock arch acts as an opening (a negative form) within the positive form of the mountain. The upright, physical mass and the compressed intervening space relate to each other on a vertical axis. Here lies the origin of the hieratic solemnity we shall encounter again in Friedrich's sacralized landscapes. The opening forms a 'shrine', which is crowned by distant peaks; the same structure also appears in the Weimar *Mountain Landscape* (1804–5; ill. 5). Friedrich's intention is to transmute nearness into distance, to link the accessible abruptly with the inaccessible beyond it. *The Wanderer above a Sea of Mists* draws its life from the same tension. Formally, the tension is created by the confrontation of foreground and background in the form of planes in silhouette, with no perspectival axes between them that lead into the depth of the picture. Our gaze does

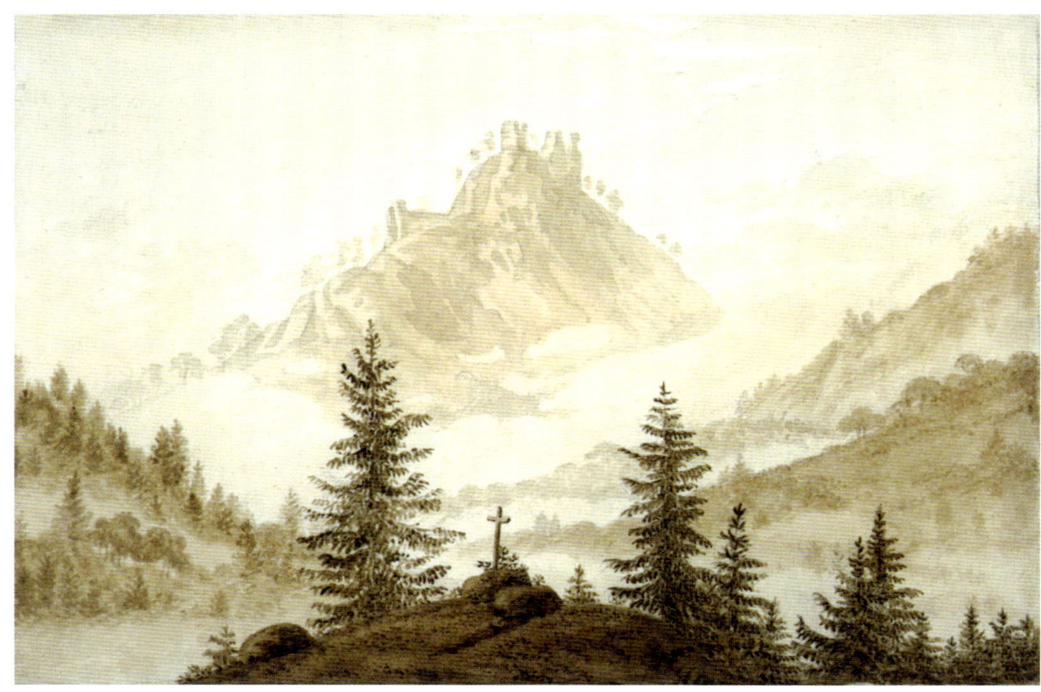

5. ***Mountain Landscape*****,**
1804–5, sepia,
12.2 x 18.2 cm (4¾ x 7⅛ in.).
Goethe Nationalmuseum,
Weimar.

not move into the depths gradually – it plunges headlong. This has led some interpreters to compare *The Wanderer* with the landscape painting of the Far East.

The abrupt conjoining of near and distant nature: that is the new path that Friedrich forged for composition in landscape painting. His means were often modest; we might call them economical, with context being the determining factor. He takes his earlier *Woman beside a Chest* and sets her down, without changing her posture, in a rocky landscape where she becomes *The Woman with the Raven at the Abyss* (1801; ill. 10). Friedrich's brother executed the woodcut from the artist's original. Moved from an interior into the wilds of nature, the woman is unexpectedly monumentalized: we see her as an emblem of 'desolation'. Yet Friedrich achieves this without the rhetorical formulas used by eighteenth-century artists to express desolation. Neither does the scenery seem to be pieced together from ready-made elements. It is credible as the portrayal of a real landscape, even if it is not one. This objective plausibility should not necessarily produce a suggestive form, or a metaphorical dimension, yet that is precisely what Friedrich has achieved. Occupying the centre of the composition, the woman is on the brink of the abyss and at the same time she is unreachable by the viewer towards whom she turns. Like her, nature too shows signs of paralysis. We are witnesses and accomplices to a truly critical moment. We shall soon come to recognize this moment as the central subject of Friedrich's art. It is depicted in the woodcut in language that becomes definitive in later works. The space is stratified, and the standing figure's axis of symmetry gives the whole a sheer verticality. But this rigid immobility contains an element of tension which is almost cinematic. It is as if the woman wants to warn us: One step nearer and I'll throw myself over the edge.

Friedrich used these and other devices with the intention of raising the standing of the landscape genre. He did so, I suspect, with one eye on Goethe's essay *Einfache Nachahmung der Natur, Manier, Stil*, which was yet another summary of what had been laid down since the sixteenth century regarding the relative ranking of the forms and subjects of works of art. Goethe took the rules governing modes from classical rhetoric as a starting point for his reflections; in the belief that Friedrich referred to this tradition of thought in order to reject it, I will outline it briefly.

The theory of modes (*modi*) makes it the painter's duty to give his subjects (*sujets*) the appropriate character. Nicolas Poussin, in a famous letter to Paul Fréart de Chantelou, explains the situation from the point of view of a painter well-schooled in the theory of his art. He sets out the reasons why he resorts sometimes to one means of expression and sometimes to another (he does not distinguish between the terms *manière* and *mode*): 'The subjects that I depict for you must be represented in a different manner' from those he paints for Monsieur Pointel. This modification, or adaptation, of his means takes Poussin back to the inventions of our 'worthy ancient Greeks': 'inventors of all good things, [they] found several modes which they used to produce marvellous effects'. Poussin lists five different modes. 'The Doric mode is steady, serious and severe' and is used for subjects that are 'grave, severe and full of discernment'. 'The Phrygian mode is violent, furious, very severe [and] produces amazement'; it is especially apt for battle scenes. The Lydian mode is appropriate for 'lamentable things', the Hypolydian mode 'contains a certain mellowness and sweetness', which is suitable for 'divine matters, glory and paradise', and the Ionic mode was invented for cheerful themes such as feasts, dances and bacchanals.

Although landscape ranked low as subject matter, it too had its rules. The distinction between the sublime and pastoral modes made by Roger de Piles in his *Cours de peinture par principes* (1709) was even referred to by Beethoven in the *Eroica* and *Pastoral* symphonies, as Ernst Gombrich has shown. In the eighteenth century, these categories were codified in Edmund Burke's polarities of the beautiful and the sublime, supplemented by an intermediate category, the picturesque. Silent mountainous regions, ravines and the uniformity of the sea were sublime to Burke. Uvedal Price judged that the picturesque included surprise effects produced by sudden changes of form, and 'irregularity' in general.

The theory of modes was undeniably directed towards order and regulation. If its stipulations were to take effect, painters had to refrain from mixing modes. The convention was widely observed well into the eighteenth century, ensuring that European painting retained homogeneous traits, but the effect was achieved at the cost of restrictions on the free play of invention. Jonathan Richardson's *Essay on the Theory of Painting* (1715) contains an example of this kind of recommendation which even specifies colour and brushwork: 'If the subject be grave, melancholy or terrible, the general tint of the colouring must incline to brown, black or red, and gloomy; but be gay, and pleasant in subjects of joy, and triumph. Generally, if the character of the picture is greatness, terrible or savage, as battles, robberies, witchcrafts, apparitions, or even the portraits of men of such characters there ought to be employed a rough, bold pencil [brush].' For Richardson, it was no longer the status of the subject matter that determined the choice of artistic means. 'If the subject be grave...' could as easily refer to a history painting as to a landscape. The language is adaptable: the 'character of the picture', its greatness or its terror, could be depicted just as well in a portrait as in a battle scene.

Goethe tried to focus and deepen the theory of modes in his essay, but he also wanted to make room for transitions and combinations in the middle reaches of the scale. His lowest rank was the 'simple imitation of nature'. This represented the 'peaceful existence' of things and therefore required a quiet, introverted disposition in the artist. Goethe knew the value of restraint: 'This kind of reproduction should therefore be undertaken by calm, faithful, contained people, working from so-called dead or still objects. Of its nature, it does not rule out a high degree of perfection.' Artistic endeavours reached their highest level in 'style', which rested 'on the deepest foundations of perception, on the essence of things, in so far as we are permitted to perceive it in visible and tangible shapes'.

Friedrich did not want to restrict landscape to the simple imitation of nature, but nor did he want to ennoble and elevate it to the ideal heights of 'style'. He neither contented himself with what the eye beheld nor wanted to paint 'the essence of things'. He took a third path. Goethe also offered painters a third path, which he called 'manner'. He was thinking of those who found it irksome 'only to spell out, as it were, the letters of nature's signs'. For that reason, this type of painter 'creates a manner for himself, makes a language for himself, in order to re-express in his own way what he has grasped with the soul [!]'. The outcome is 'a language in which the speaker's spirit expresses and describes itself directly. And just as opinions about moral subjects come in a different order and take different shapes in the soul of every thinking person, so each artist of this kind will see, apprehend and reproduce the world differently; he will interpret its phenomena more thoughtfully or more lightly, he will represent them more steadily or more cursorily.' (An astonishing charter from a man who began to consider himself a supreme judge of art only a short time later.)

Goethe next turned his mind to the relationship between the whole and its parts, taking landscape as an example. The many small, 'subordinate' subjects must be sacrificed, 'if the overall expression of the

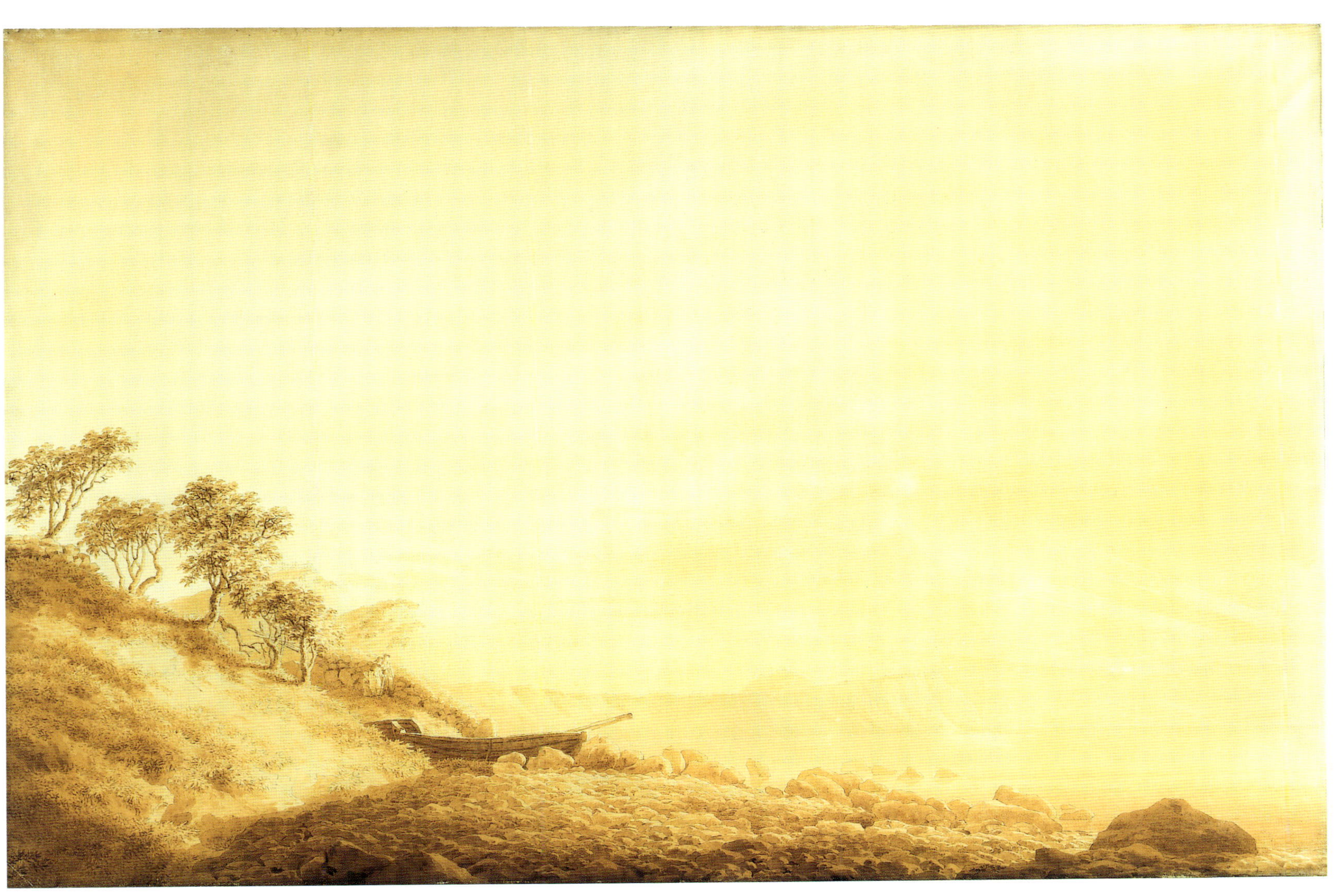

6. *Cape Arkona at Sunrise,*
c. 1803, pencil and sepia,
65 x 98 cm (25⅝ x 38⅝ in.).
Hamburger Kunsthalle, Hamburg.

larger subject is to be achieved.' He thought it wrong for a painter to 'pause anxiously at individual details, instead of holding fast to the concept of the whole'. This squaring of the circle, preserving the individual element and linking it with the whole, is exactly what Friedrich set out to do. While Goethe indicated that the modes might be uncoupled from association with specific iconographic areas, Friedrich wanted to erect a bridge between simple imitation and style, in order to depict nature as a place for subjective experience, while simultaneously conveying a sense of the sacred.

Was Friedrich then a mannerist? Certainly not, unless we remove the negative association the word had around 1800 (something of which still clings to it) and restore the neutral meaning it had for Poussin. This is what Goethe was referring to when he claimed to be using the word 'manner ... in a high and respectable sense', which no one whose work came within the ambit of 'manner' would have any cause to complain about. Goethe both paraphrased and circumvented the coordinates of the modes, for his own modes ran 'delicately' into one another. This flexible concept of manner seems to allow genres, including landscape, to rise in rank, but Friedrich was convinced that the 'judges of art' were opposed to anything of the sort, and excluded certain genres (flower pieces, for example) from their hierarchy of values altogether. Friedrich thought such exclusions were 'barbarous', for 'every genre is surely capable of a higher view and development, sufficient to claim to be a work of art'. But it was precisely his doubt as to 'whether the landscape painting of today can be regarded as an advancing area at this time in art' that strengthened his resolve to win new respectability for landscape.

The issue here is not one of tiresome artistic disputes about status. Goethe's attempts to mediate between the modes and Friedrich's desire for a purified yet unstylized formal language belong in the intellectual field of reference of that moment in history.

In the summer of 1794 – the year in which the twenty-year-old Friedrich began his studies in Copenhagen – a significant discussion took place in Jena. What had begun as a misunderstanding ended by cementing the friendship between Goethe and Schiller, whose acquaintance until then had been fleeting. Finding himself walking away from a meeting of the Natural History society in the same direction as Schiller, Goethe took the opportunity to talk about his favourite topic, the beginnings of plant life and the metamorphosis of plants, which he pictured vividly as a process governed by natural laws. As a strict Kantian in the matter of categories, Schiller remarked that this was not an empirical experience but an 'idea'. Goethe was initially put out, but it was not long before Schiller was acknowledging a debt to him. 'I lacked a drive or inclination for many speculative ideas', Schiller wrote to him on 23 August 1794, 'and you put me on their track.' The ice was broken and a friendship began.

Schiller envied Goethe, whom he believed to be immune to the dangers of 'byways', 'down which both speculation and wilful imagination, heeding only itself, so easily lose themselves'. He also admired Goethe's agility in moving from observation to abstract deduction, and from concepts back to intuitions, forging links between unity and multiplicity. Goethe's morphological way of seeing perceived the drive towards the whole in each individual element, as well as the traces of the initial quest for form in the whole. The outcome was an intimate relationship, in which all the formative stages were combined. Governed by the postulate – almost an ideal – of 'inner necessity', these organic processes were directed towards achieving a complete, self-contained wholeness.

But Friedrich's world-view was quite different. It produced contradictions and conflicts which Goethe, too, probably perceived, but mostly banished from his 'idea' (which he took for empirical experience). The painter invented symbolic means for expressing alienation, distancing and a lack of intimacy in the relationship between human beings and nature. For him, too, the individual was subordinated to a larger whole, but he did not strive towards organic intermingling, or mutual exchange. Instead he constructed networks built from tensions, which could be intensified and developed into polarities. He gave his perception a distance which made the experiential world uncertain and made facts enigmatic, however exactly they were reproduced.

Rock Arch in the Uttewalder Grund (ill. 7), a large sepia drawing of 1801, is a good example. A tourist attraction is drawn with a dual focus, as a literally monstrous place, representing the superior power of nature and yet offering a shelter which contains a possible route of escape. In the gestures of the two tiny figures in the 'cave', oppression is transformed into liberation and the existential 'prison' is subsumed in the frisson that tempted sensation-seeking Sunday excursionists into the wilderness. We would be likely to assume that Friedrich was not such a person even if we did not have this comment from him: 'I once spent a whole week in the Uttewalder Grund among the rocks and the fir trees, and did not encounter a single living soul in all that time; it's true I wouldn't recommend the practice to anyone, it was almost too much even for me.'

Using his experience of solitude in the picture, Friedrich faithfully records the natural scenery, but at the same time he underlines the fundamental motif of inaccessibility by depicting the rocks in silhouette so that they form a vertical wall, in which disturbing 'faces' can be made out. This wall rears up like a barrier, blocking off the space that lies behind it, which is discernable only as a sense of light, offering a kind of promise. The passage from 'here' to that uncertain 'there' seems a risky enterprise, posing a test of courage like a rite of initiation. Friedrich uses a polarizing formal language; in the terminology of his time, it could be said that he 'raises himself above the Real and that he remains within the Sensory'. The combination of these two is essential for 'aesthetic art', wrote Schiller in a letter to Goethe (14 September 1797).

Equipped with this dual vision, Friedrich proceeds to use it to uncover rifts in nature, which he uses to affect the thoughts and actions of his figures. What they seem to feel and convey to the viewer corresponds to what John Dennis called 'delightful horror', the mixture of feelings identified by Burke as characteristic of our experience of the sublime. Schiller drew on the notion in his definition of the sublime, to which the *Rock Arch in the Uttewalder Grund* offers a visual equivalent: 'The feeling of the sublime is a mixed feeling. It is a compound of unease, expressed in the highest degree as terror, and joy, capable of intensifying to delight, and although it is not really pleasure, it is much preferred to any pleasure by fine souls.'

Friedrich's 'manner' is not directed wholly towards either 'simple imitation' or 'style', but looks both ways, simultaneously separating and mediating between the near and the far, the small and the large, outward and inward perceptions. It could be said that the technique is as much of a mixture as the dual sensation it evokes: 'delightful horror'. Traditional concepts such as 'unity in multiformity' are no longer sufficient to describe this procedure, for Friedrich manages to intensify the individuality of his disparate components to such a extent that their relationship resembles that of thesis and antithesis. These structures contain no space for summarization, only for speculation. (For example, Helmut Börsch-Supan's conviction that the rock arch is a symbol of death and the light in the background the promise of paradise.)

Friedrich felt intuitively that his duality originated in the two poles of knowing and of feeling. In one of his maxims he expressed a wish for himself: 'One painter knows what he is doing; another feels what he is doing. If only it were possible to make a single painter from the two!' In this statement he was addressing the two factors, consciousness and unconsciousness, which dominated contemporary discussion of the preconditions and genesis of the creative act. Schiller, for example, invoked them in a letter to Goethe of 27 March 1801, with reference to Friedrich Wilhelm von Schelling's transcendental philosophy. Schiller disagreed with the 'idealist' Schelling's thesis that things in nature 'begin in unconsciousness and are raised to consciousness, whereas in art one proceeds from consciousness towards the unconscious', and asserted the contrary: 'In practice, the poet too begins with the unconscious alone, in fact he must count himself lucky if he succeeds, through the clearest consciousness of his operations, only in getting so far as to find the first, obscure total idea of his work undiminished in the completed artefact. Without an obscure but powerful total idea, which precedes everything technical, no work of poetry can come into being, and poetry, it seems to me, consists of this very ability to express and communicate that which is unconscious; that is to say, to translate it into an object.' For Schiller, what distinguished the poet from the non-poet was the fact that the latter did not start from the unconscious or end there. Goethe agreed with him: 'I believe that everything a genius does, as a genius, happens unconsciously.'

Friedrich expressed the same idea as follows: 'The painter should not paint merely what he sees in front of him but also what he sees within him. If he sees nothing within himself, however, then he should refrain from painting what he sees in front of him.' He too invoked a 'obscure total idea'. It was a matter of bringing 'what you saw in the dark into the light, so that it may have an effect on others as it shines in from outside'.

There had been a dialogue between inner and outer images for centuries, hinging on what Schiller called the 'obscure total idea'. It began when Petrarch climbed Mont Ventoux, inventing mountaineering and giving the external image a new, overpowering presence. After his adventure, the poet wrote that he now turned his inner eye upon himself (26 April 1336). Leonardo da Vinci talked of the eye in passing as the 'window of the soul', but it seems that for him inner perception was contained in outer perception; the two were not separate. Not until the late Renaissance and what art historians call mannerism was authority claimed for 'inward conception' (*disegno interno*), for instance by Federico Zuccaro in his treatise *L'Idea de' pittori, scultori ed architetti* (1607). Erwin Panofsky pointed out that 'idea' in this context meant the imagination, the power of conception, not the thing conceived – or Schiller's 'obscure total idea'.

The images of the world which Friedrich's art helped to bring to light were now marked out on two intersecting planes, so that the subjective elements of lived experience and cultural factors made contact with the objective elements of the intellectual and spiritual climate of the age. The painter's conceptual world – not its formal realizations – fits into the panorama of his time, as seen in terms of the history of art and of that approach to cultural history known as *Geistesgeschichte*, which concerns itself in particular with

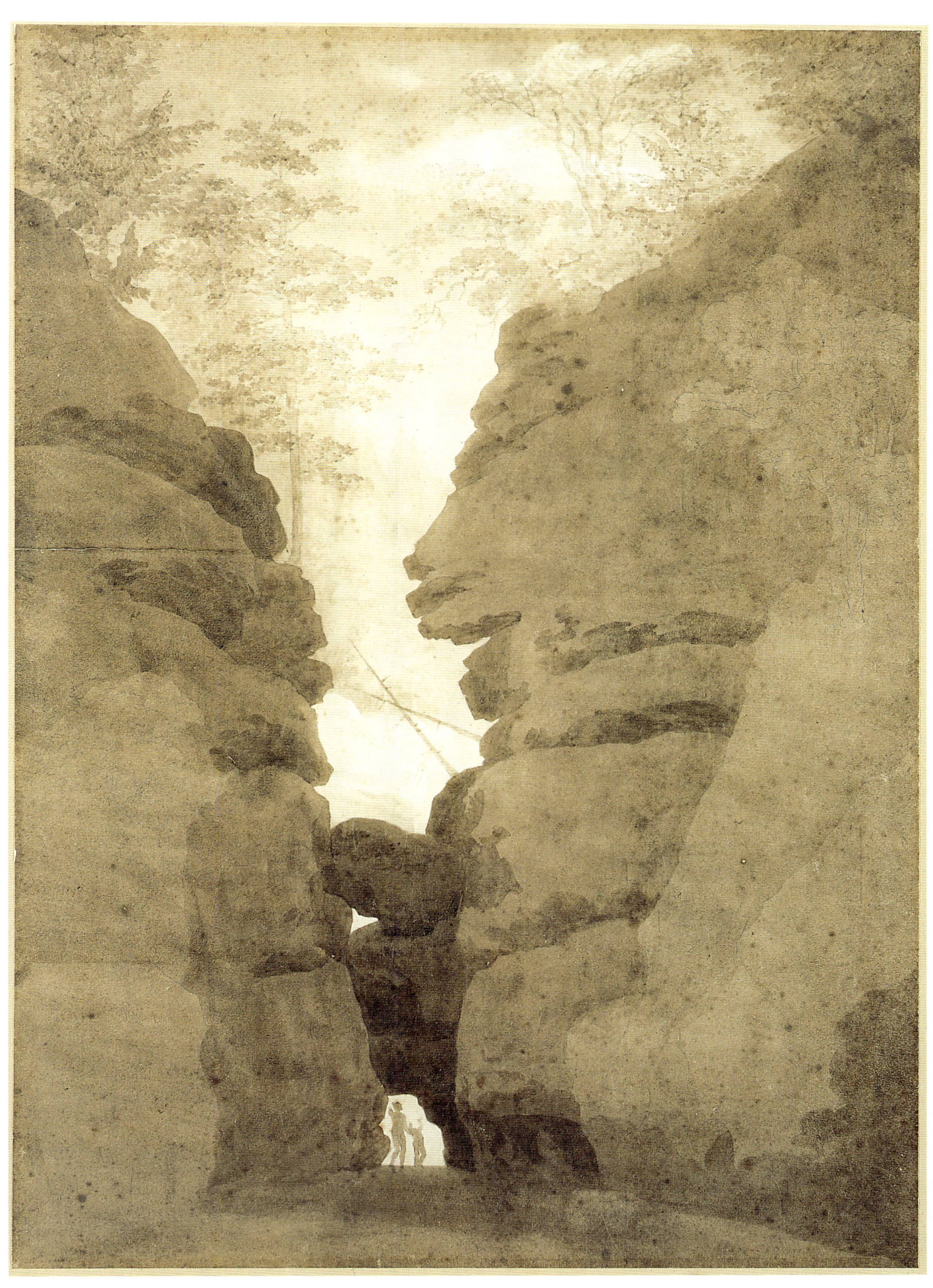

7. Rock Arch in the Uttewalder Grund,
c. 1801, sepia.
70.5 x 50.3 cm (27¾ x 19¾ in.).
Museum Folkwang, Essen.

the changing Zeitgeist. It is not a truism to say that Friedrich's world fit with his time: in 1805 there was a significant encounter between him and the Zeitgeist which could have resulted in a collision.

Among those who aroused Friedrich's displeasure were the 'judges of art' who set subjects for artists to depict, in order to 'give art, or rather artists, a higher direction'. He did not deny the need for this, but he objected to the vanity of 'wanting to lay down prescripts, being able to make public announcements of prize competitions, and preening themselves as guardians and patrons of art'. No good came of it, he wrote, citing the example of an artist 'of profound disposition' whose entry for one such competition was dead and devoid of spirit or intellect, 'because the subject set was completely foreign to his nature. He was only attracted by the prize...'.

Who was he actually talking about? The judge is easily identified. He was enthroned in Weimar, where he had instituted an annual art competition in 1799, inviting entries on a subject chosen by himself with the help of his advisers. Goethe hoped to encourage artists to concentrate their painting and drawing skills on what he regarded as the 'highest purpose of art' (the preserve of 'style'), namely 'to depict human forms with as much sensory meaning and as much beauty as possible'. The subjects were intended to elevate public taste. And who was the artist of pure character, forced into prostitution by Weimar's artistic diktat? Friedrich may have been thinking of Runge, whose entry for the 1801 competition, *Achilles' Battle with the Rivers*, was harshly criticized. Runge condemned 'that whole process' as heading in 'the wrong direction', venting his anger in a letter to his father with a rhetorical question: 'How can we entertain the disastrous idea of wanting to revive the art of antiquity?'

Friedrich went on to challenge Weimar's 'wrong direction' even more boldly. In 1805 he submitted two sepia drawings which ignored the chosen subject matter, the Labours of Hercules. One showed fisherfolk beside a lake and the other a religious procession (ills 8 and 9). As a second Hercules, Friedrich did not undertake to clean the Augean stables or fight dragons, but instead calmly and resolutely presented a different, purer art in response to the Weimar art machine. In his brief accompanying letter to Goethe, he said he was 'brazen enough' to take part in the competition, but gave no reason for his deviation from the theme. He got away with his heresy: Pope Goethe gave him a dispensation and saw that he was awarded first prize jointly with a certain Joseph Hoffmann, sharing the money. The joy and surprise Friedrich expressed in a letter were certainly not feigned.

The significance of the episode was symptomatic. In giving half the prize to a history painter and half to a 'landscaper', the jury sought a compromise to resolve their dilemma. They accepted the intrusion of an uninvited genre, and accorded the monks' devotions equal status with the Greek hero's exploits. The 'diligence and purity' of his execution were in Friedrich's favour, according to their report. Goethe, however, must have recognized that Friedrich had not contributed to his goal of winning the high moral ground for the highest sensory plane. He seems to have detected that his attempt to legislate for art had ended in failure, and withdrew from the exercise; the 1805 competition was the last. 'Feeling is placed above intelligence', he wrote resignedly, looking back on the episode in 1812. That could be a reference to the direction Friedrich had taken in the meantime, which the two sepias had foreshadowed; a direction which led him to work of a kind Goethe accused of affected piety.

In retrospect it is clear that in entering the two drawings for the Weimar competition, Friedrich made a crucial contribution to a change of direction that was to have great historical consequences. He thrust history painting aside and presented the case for an artistic language which had only a limited connection with traditional landscape, for central to its subject matter were human beings found meditating or contemplating nature. The relationship of the figures to the scenery both enhanced the landscape and intensified it to the point where it became a poetic, psychological, religious or philosophical metaphor – though it also became enigmatic and open to multiple interpretations.

The choice of the two sepias (which Goethe presented to the Weimar collection) reveals an obvious programmatic intention, but an encoded one. Friedrich wants them to be read as a pair, but he does not make their interrelationship unambiguously plain. They are not companion pieces, either formally or iconographically, unless perhaps the depiction of the couple by the lake represents an incurious, vegetative existence and the religious procession a spiritual answer to it. If we take into account Friedrich's disenchanted attitude towards Catholic rites and monasticism, however, we might read the two pictures in precisely the opposite sense: the pilgrimage is an act of formulaic piety that has outlived its meaning, while the man and woman beside the lake are thoughtfully active and wholly integrated into God's creation. Perhaps Friedrich also remembered the sermons his mentor Kosegarten used to preach on the shore on the island of Rügen, so that fishermen on their boats could listen without interrupting their fishing. So if worship in the open air stands for the Lutheran-Evangelical creed, not allowing itself to be confined to stone churches and liturgical ceremonies, then the monks' procession is the Catholic equivalent. It too forsakes the church building and makes its way through an 'arch' formed by two trees towards a wayside calvary. Yet what appears to unite the two Christian denominations actually divides them. The monks' collective ritual allows no room for the subjective experience of faith felt by Friedrich's figures. In that light, the monk stands for a mode of faith whose day is past. A dessicated relic, he bears the marks of tragic isolation, even within the collective group, and that makes him a subject to which Friedrich was to return time and time again.

The multiplicity of meaning revealed in the Weimar pair of drawings is encountered constantly in Friedrich's pairings of his pictures. It begins in two early woodcuts; *The Woman with the Cobweb* (ill. 11) definitely belongs with *The Woman with the Raven at the Abyss* (ill. 10). She is seated among thick vegetation, from which two dead trees stand up like torsos. Between them, a cobweb has been spun, perfect and a work of supreme skill. The scene can certainly be viewed from a metaphysical perspective, but it is also possible that Friedrich was thinking only of formal contrast when he set mutely flourishing, earthbound growth against an airy, transparent, geometric shape. (What he presented as contrast was made an organic and geometric common denominator by Runge in his *Times of Day* cycle dating from the same period.)

However we interpret Friedrich's confrontations, they are always part of a dialogue, in which each position entails both questions and answers. One thesis opposes another, and a final resolution is never reached. Each of the two positions relativizes the other, and simultaneously enriches it. Friedrich uses different artistic devices to achieve this. Contrast is one of them, demonstrated in the pair *The Monk by the Sea* and *The Abbey in the Oak Wood* (ills 22 and 23); here the bipolarity of the Weimar pair is restated on an incomparably higher formal level. If we look at these two paintings with dual focus, letting one 'dissolve' into the other, the result is a montage. There is no formal bridge leading from one picture to the other. Such a connection does exist between the two precise *Views from the Artist's Studio* (ills 67 and 68),

8. Pilgrimage at Sunrise,
1805, pencil and sepia,
40.5 × 62 cm (16 × 24⅜ in.).
Staatliche Kunstsammlungen, Weimar.

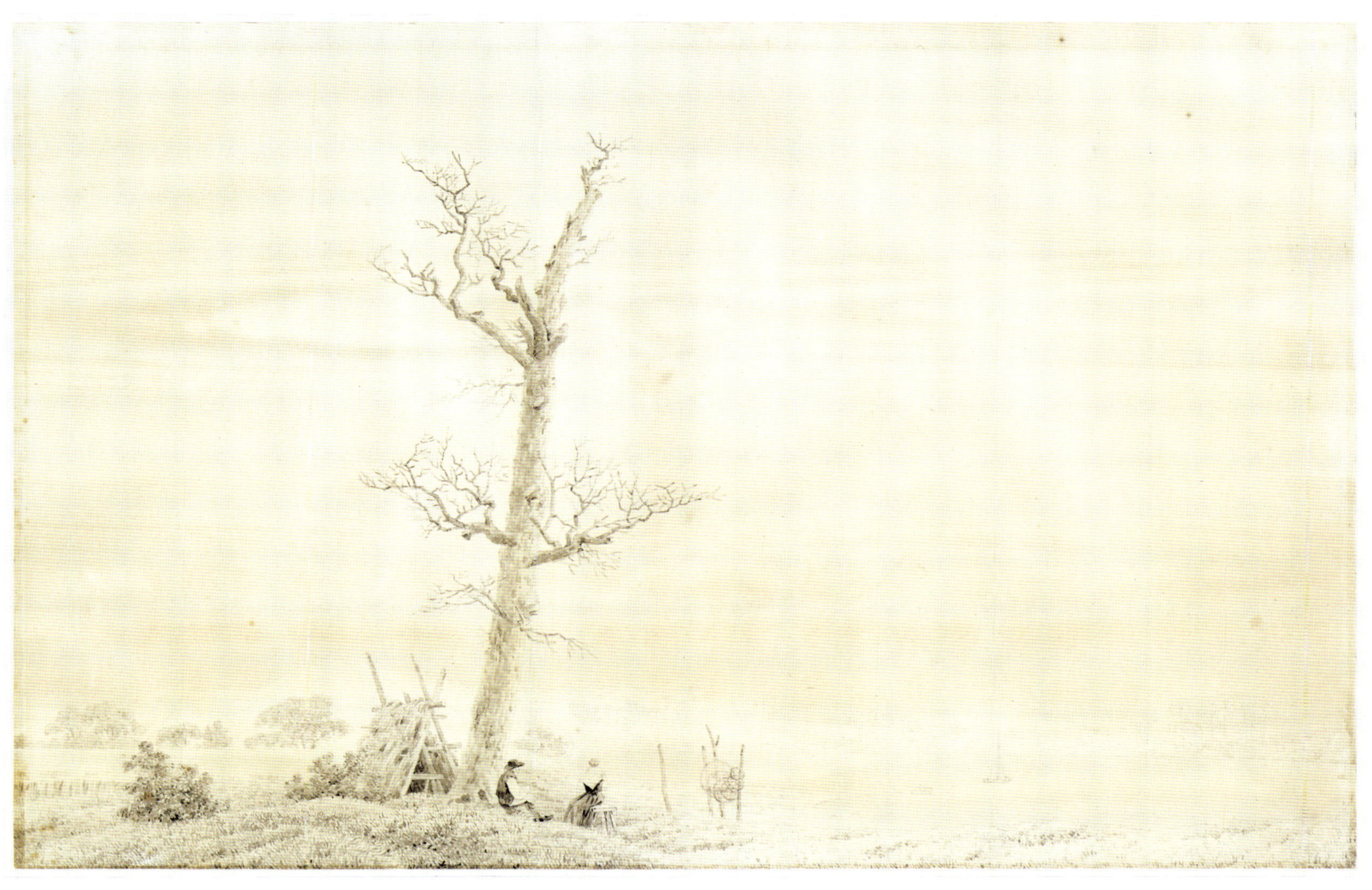

9. ***Summer Landscape with a Dead Oak Tree,***
1805, pencil and sepia,
40.5 x 62 cm (16 x 24⅜ in.).
Staatliche Kunstsammlungen, Weimar.

each of which shows a different aspect, one urban, one rural, of the further shore of the Elbe. The connection becomes even closer when Friedrich depicts the same landscape at two different moments in the same painting. This complementary double vision is achieved through the use of transparent paper painted on both sides. One side shows the landscape by daylight, the other, when lit by a candle, shows it by moonlight (ills 129 and 130). The different spatial experiences are augmented by two different temporal experiences.

This pairing of contrasts gives us a more differentiated view of Friedrich's range, and does something to counter the accusation that he chose to paint 'so much of death, decay and the grave'. He himself refuted this opinion in detail in his *Aphorismen über Kunst und Leben* (*Aphorisms on Art and Life*). Both his outer and inner perceptions tended to make him receptive to polar tensions, which he then turned into a 'collage' in words or images. His dual vision even enabled him to sense the abrupt transformation of a cloudless idyll into a scene of death. The entry in his journal describing a glorious August day in Loschwitz (written in 1803) represents a mood swing of that sort, directly opposing summer with winter: 'Children are playing, kissing and enjoying themselves, and one of them claps his hands to greet the rising sun. Lambs are grazing in the valley and on the hillsides. Not a stone to be seen. Not a sombre twig, not a fallen leaf. All nature breathes peace, joy and innocence and life. You know my house and the wonderful view. But today for the first time the normally glorious countryside cries out to me of decay and death, where before it has only smiled to me of joy and life. The sky is overcast and stormy, and now it casts its

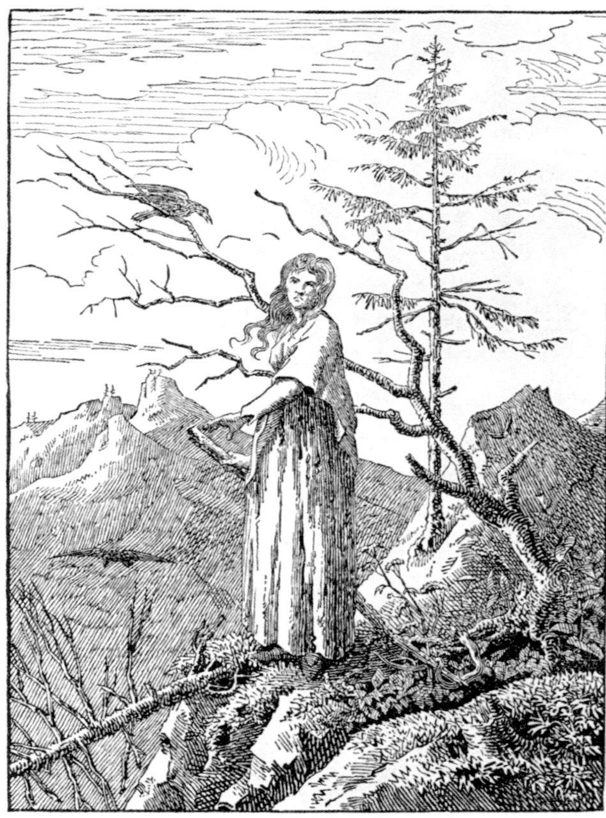

10. *The Woman with the Raven at the Abyss,*
1801, woodcut,
16.9 x 11.9 cm. (6⅝ x 4⅝ in.).
Hamburger Kunsthalle, Hamburg.

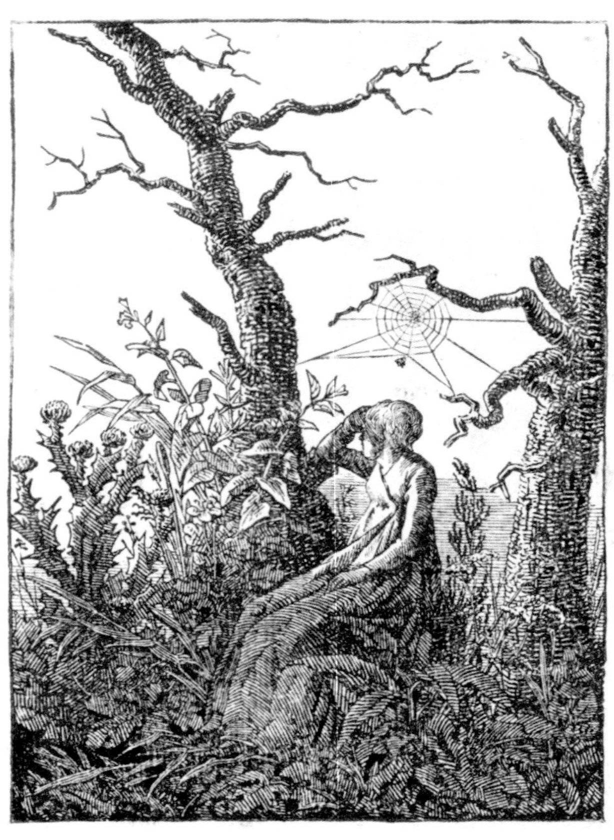

11. *The Woman with the Cobweb,*
1801, woodcut,
17 x 11.9 cm (6⅝ x 4⅝ in.).
Hamburger Kunsthalle, Hamburg.

monochrome winter coat over the lovely coloured mountains and fields for the first time. All nature lies before me drained of colour.'

There is one painting which, viewed in isolation, falls outside the gloomy atmospheric framework that we expect of Friedrich's landscapes. *Summer (Landscape with a Pair of Lovers)* (1807; ill. 14), in the Neue Pinakothek in Munich, reproduces the happy, idyllic landscape of the first part of the journal entry from 1803 quoted above. Friedrich had already used this motif that same year in a cycle of the four seasons, giving reason to believe that the Munich painting also had a wintery pendant (ill. 144, now lost). When Friedrich turned the dual vision with which he regarded the times of day and the seasons of the year to the stages of human life, as the contemporary descriptions of his pictures by Gotthilf Heinrich von Schubert indicate, he appears to have designated an inescapable final chord to winter. Yet following the journey into death, nature prepares new life. Because 'everything moves in an ever-alternating circle', Friedrich's winter journey also contains, albeit hidden, the seed of a new beginning.

The sense that human life hangs between certainty and uncertainty is reflected in the metaphor of Friedrich's contemporary Chateaubriand which was quoted in the first chapter, and to which the German painter's work provides a visual complement: 'Man is suspended in the present, between the past and the future, as if on a rock between two chasms. Behind and ahead, all is darkness.' *The Wanderer above a Sea of Mists* could easily be described in those terms. Space would then become time, and its uncertain dimensions would be transferred from a three-dimensional present into the past and into the future.

It is in his scenes of winter and mist that Friedrich depicts most vividly the state of suspension which Chateaubriand assigns to human existence. On one occasion Friedrich came out in vigorous defence of these categories of landscape, saying that the judges of art were unfair to denigrate winter and mist. They were blind to the 'great white cloth' of winter beneath which nature was preparing new life, and they saw mist as mere greyness. In actual fact, he wrote, the contrary was the case: 'When a region cloaks itself in mist, it appears larger and more sublime, elevating the imagination, and rousing the expectations like a veiled girl.'

Two pictures of misty scenes with which Friedrich began his career as a painter in oils in 1807 provide a definitive example. The mist acts as both wall and space, veil and transparency. It places nature in a state of expectation (one the viewer is made to share) by clothing its three levels – shore, sea and sky – in a momentary stillness that nevertheless contains impulses in contrary motion. In both pictures, everything beyond the narrow zone of the shore seems to disappear in time and space and simultaneously to appear out of them. The veiling and unveiling complement each other and form a state of suspension where a number of uncertainties combine. Friedrich also demonstrates one of his disorientating artistic devices for the first time. Any ground on which we might walk or material we might touch is restricted to the narrow strips of shore. The sea, clouds and mist withhold the spatial depth from our touch and our approach. Beyond question, the picture with the sailing ship and the rowing boat (ills 15 and 16) – which way is it moving, if it is moving at all? – is metaphorically the more mysterious of the two. Any life contained there is hidden in the two constructs which allow man to move on the water, yet there is no movement to be discerned. In Chateaubriand's words: 'Man is suspended....'

In the other picture (ill. 17), the solidity of the ground is the dominant feature and the fisherman takes centre stage. The bushes and hummocks of green grass make the shore a place where a living can be

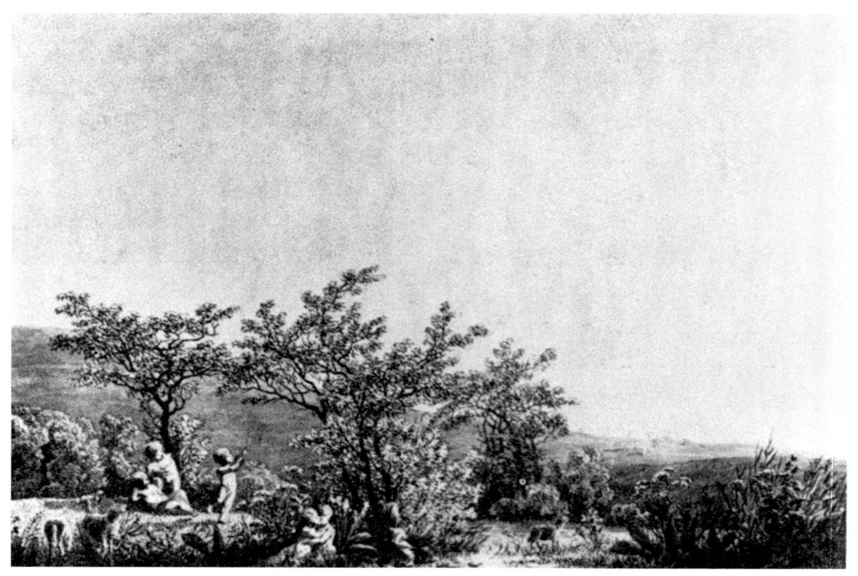

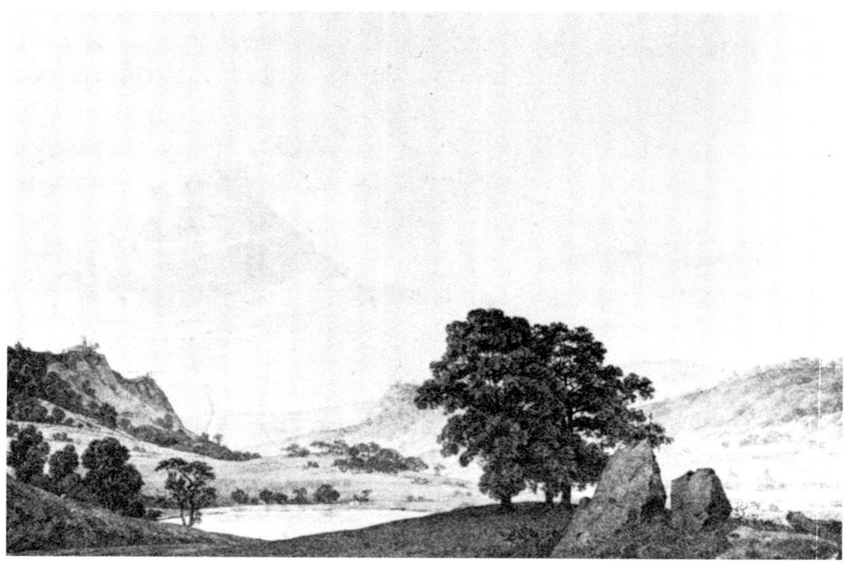

12. *Spring*,
1803, sepia,
19 × 27.5 cm (7½ × 10¾ in.).
Formerly Reichskammer der bildenden Künste, Berlin (destroyed).

13. *Autumn*,
1807, sepia,
19 × 27.5 cm (7½ × 10¾ in.).
Formerly Reichskammer der bildenden Künste, Berlin (destroyed).

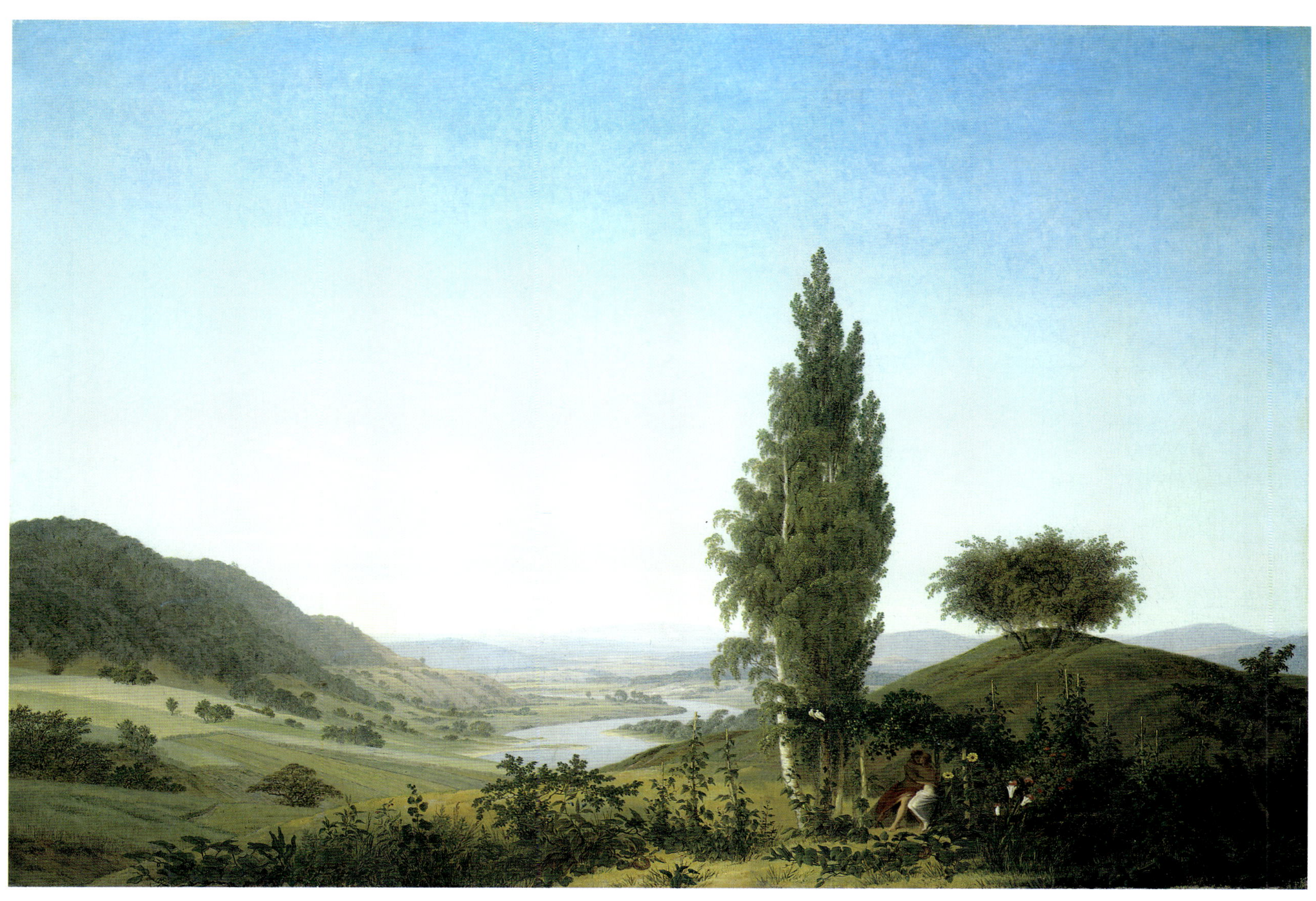

14. ***Summer (Landscape with a Pair of Lovers)*****,**
1807, oil on canvas,
71.4 x 103.6 cm (28⅛ x 40¾ in.).
Neue Pinakothek, Munich.

scraped, as the nets and the structure for drying hay testify. A narrow footbridge crosses a channel. This minimal acknowledgment of human existence on earth accords with the transparent clouds which we might imagine are about to clear.

Friedrich shows a fine artistic judgment in his orchestration of these two situations in which nature and humanity come together. In one case a narrow platform where activity continues, in the other an apparently deserted, stony shore where boatmen's paraphernalia – an anchoring stone and poles (resembling crutches) on which to hang fishing nets – lies unused, suggesting resignation and failure. It is left for us to choose between these two possible states of the human condition. This question is not addressed to our artistic judgment but to our attitude to this life and the life beyond. The issue here is not one of taste but of belief.

15. ***Mist*****, detail,**
1807, oil on canvas,
34.2 x 50.2 cm (13⅜ x 19⅝ in.).
Österreichische Galerie im Belvedere, Vienna.

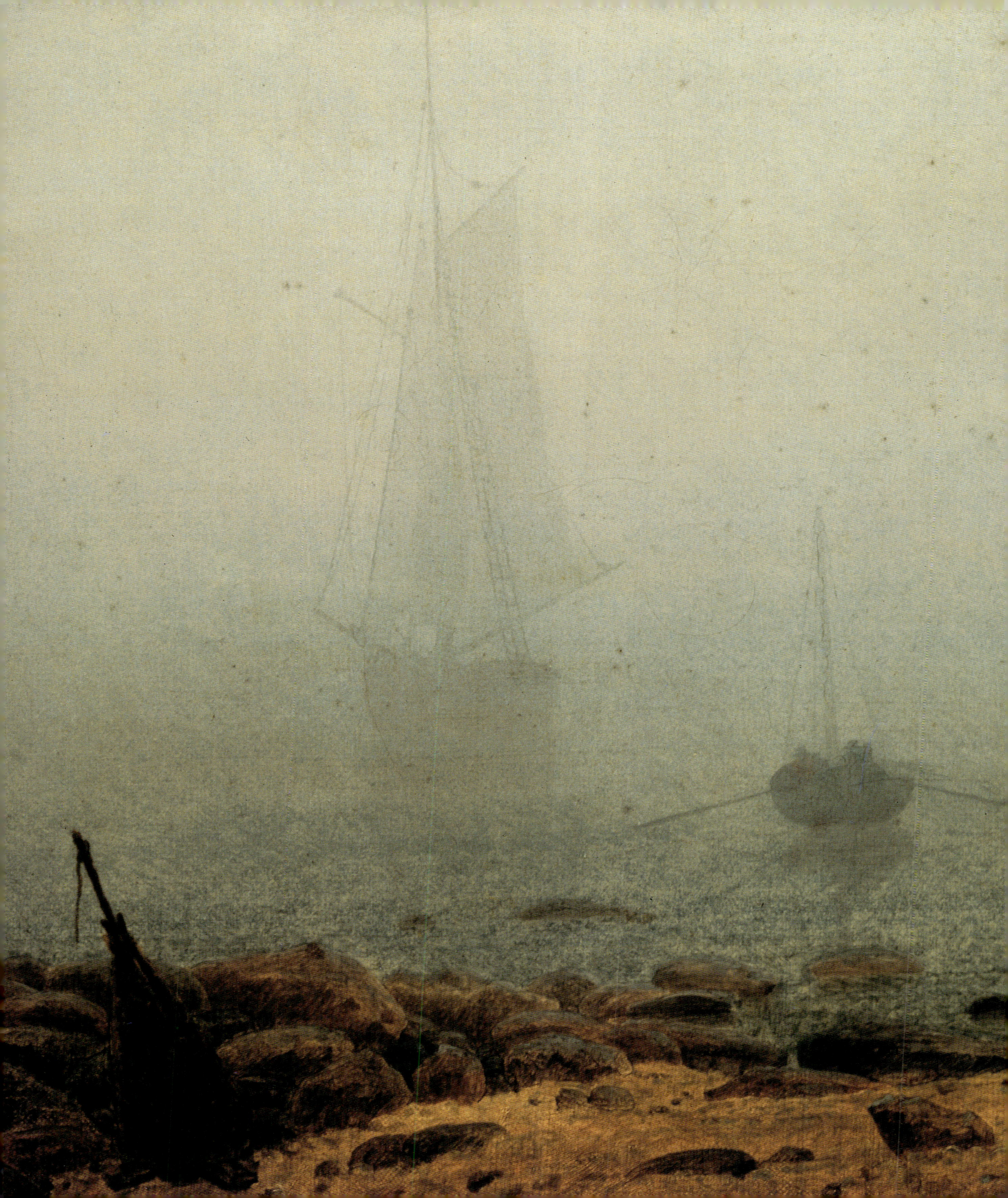

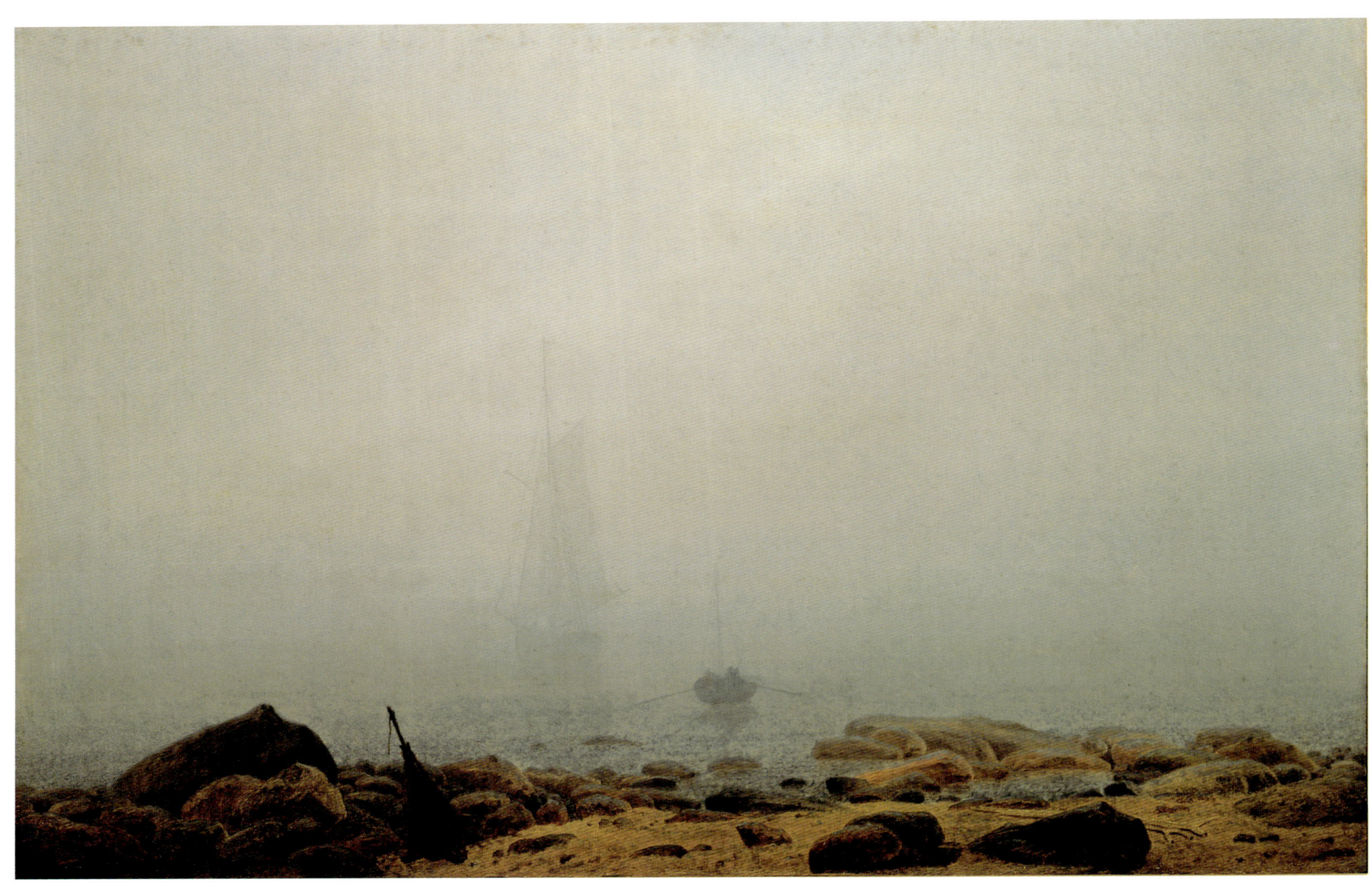

16. *Mist*,
1807, oil on canvas,
34.2 x 50.2 cm (13⅜ x 19¾ in.).
Österreichische Galerie im Belvedere, Vienna.

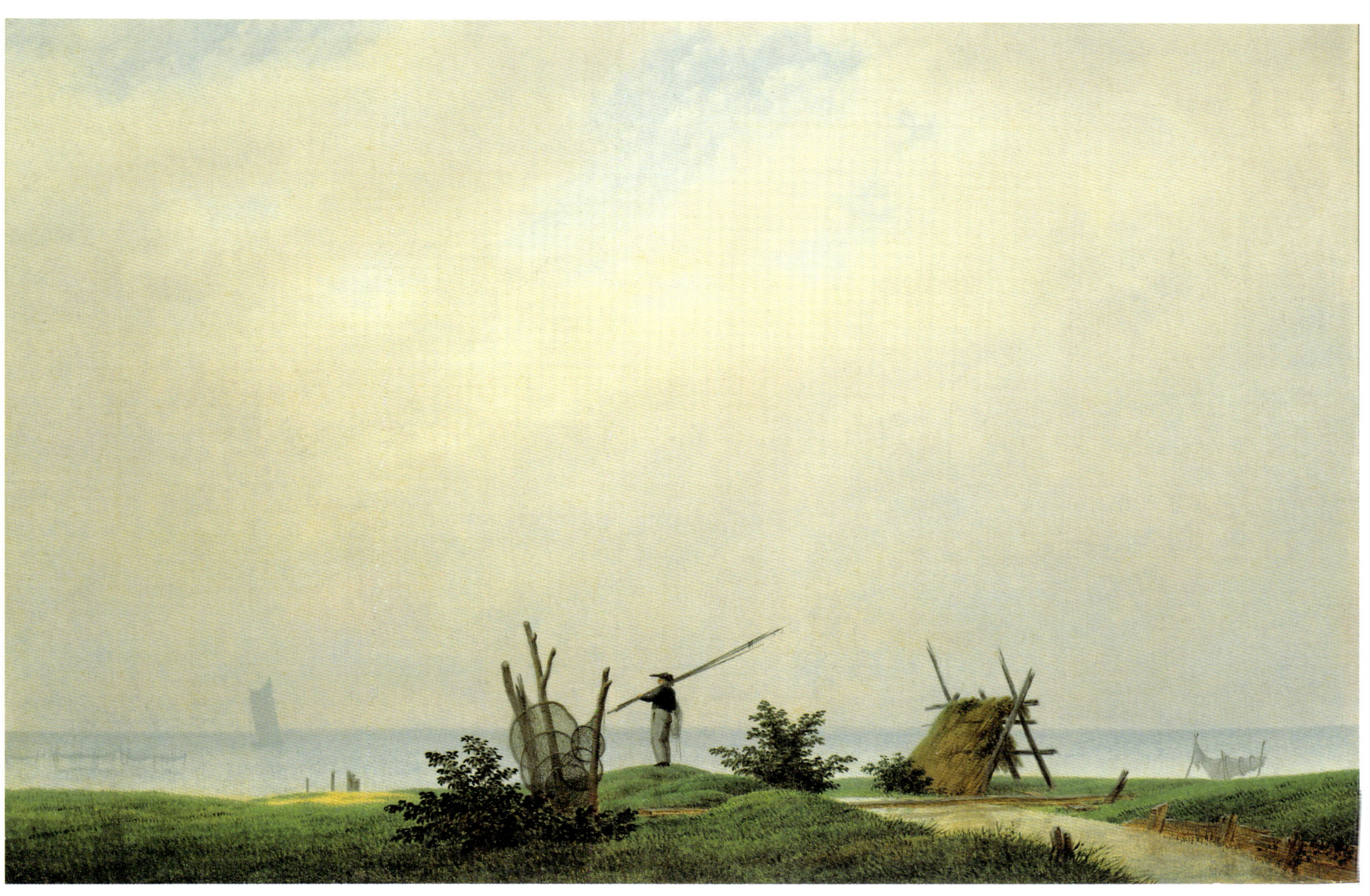

17. ***Seashore with Fisherman*****,**
1807, oil on canvas,
33.5 x 50.8 cm (13¼ x 20 in.).
Österreichische Galerie im Belvedere, Vienna.

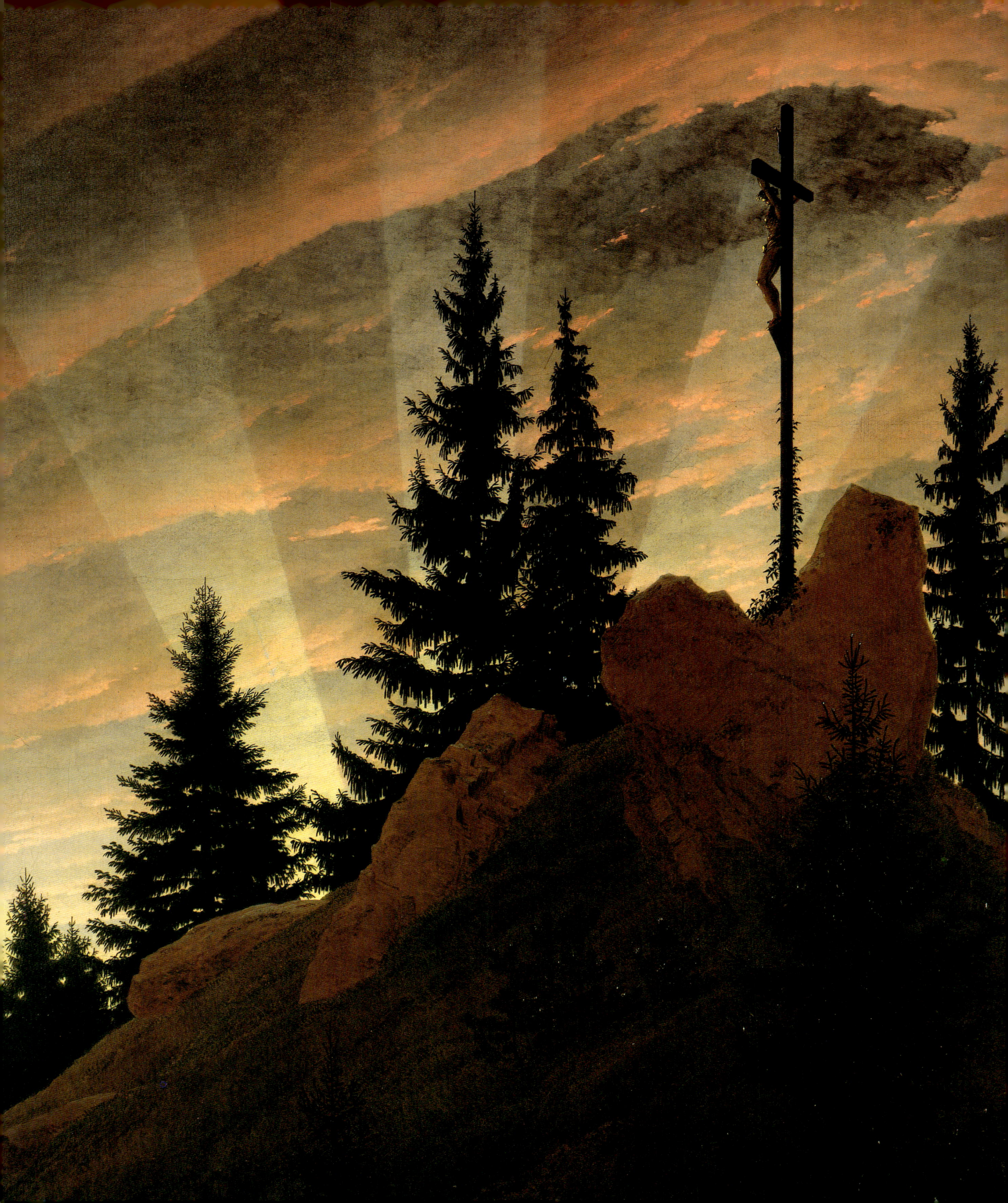

II

THREE KEY WORKS

1. The Tetschen Altar

Chateaubriand's metaphor of man suspended in space does not only have an existential dimension, but also an eschatological one. Friedrich's Dresden *Cross in the Mountains*, also known as *The Tetschen Altar* (ills 18 and 21), serves to illustrate this state. Christ, the carved figure hanging on the cross, seems suspended between heaven and earth, no longer held down by gravity but not yet entirely released from its laws. He is a hybrid, with the dual nature of both the begotten Son of God and the created brother of mankind.

It is not clear how Friedrich came to receive the commission for this picture. The initial motivation seems to have come from Kosegarten, who wanted an altarpiece for a chapel on Rügen, but that was painted by Runge. According to one contemporary account, Countess von Thun-Hohenstein had seen a sepia of a *Cross in the Mountains* at the Dresden Academy exhibition in March 1807, and subsequently commissioned Friedrich to paint a panel for the altar in the private chapel in Schloss Tetschen. (Friedrich had originally intended to dedicate the altar to the King of Sweden.)

Of all the manifestos in paint which Friedrich produced in rapid succession between 1808 and 1810 – his most prolific years – none is more complex or problematic than *The Tetschen Altar*. There is a programmatic consequentiality in the way the concept transforms the empirical landscape into a landscape icon. This was not the first time Friedrich had painted crosses in natural scenery, and he arrived at the composition of the 1808 altar using two different approaches. In the first of these, empirical facts were arranged in a clear order to create a hierarchy of significance; this approach is demonstrated in the Weimar *Mountain Landscape* (ill. 5). In the foreground, a cross is placed symmetrically between two fir trees, forming a triptych. The central axis, occupied by the cross, is crowned by a distant mountain peak rising out of the mist, and offering, perhaps, the promise of salvation. The iconic elements – symmetry and frontality – are extremely conspicuous in this regularized landscape. Friedrich's second route to *The Tetschen Altar* was more discreet, however. *Morning Mist in the Mountains* (ill. 19) is notable for its masterly representation of fleeting natural phenomena, suggesting eyewitness observation. The solid objects distributed in three-dimensional space are to a great extent dematerialized, freed from their

18. *The Cross in the Mountains (The Tetschen Altar)*, detail, 1807–8, oil on canvas, 115 × 110.5 cm (45¼ × 43½ in.). Gemäldegalerie Neue Meister, Dresden.

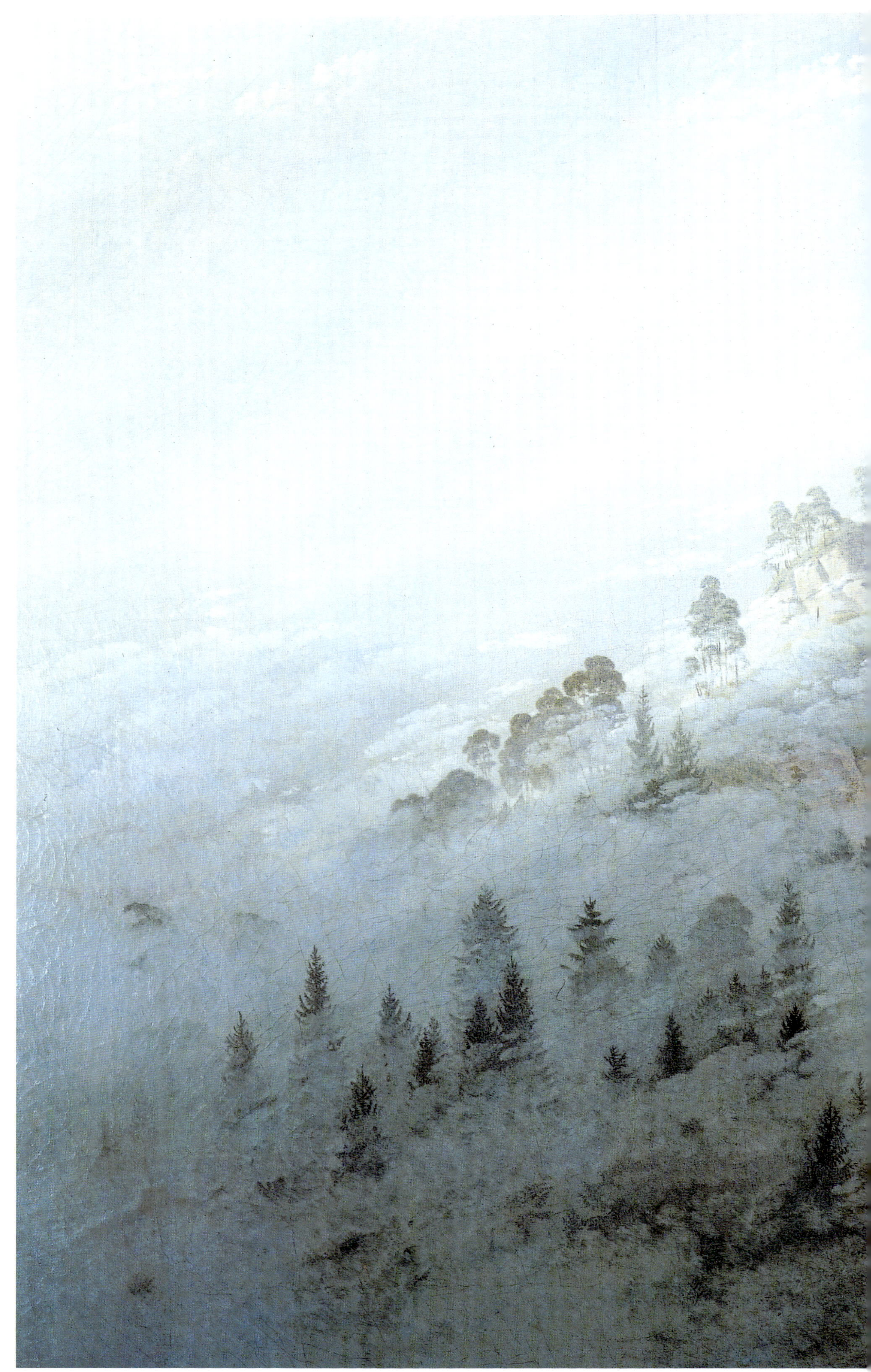

19. *Morning Mist in the Mountains*, 1808, oil on canvas, 71 x 104 cm (28 x 41 in.). Staatliches Museum Schloss Heidecksburg, Rudolstadt.

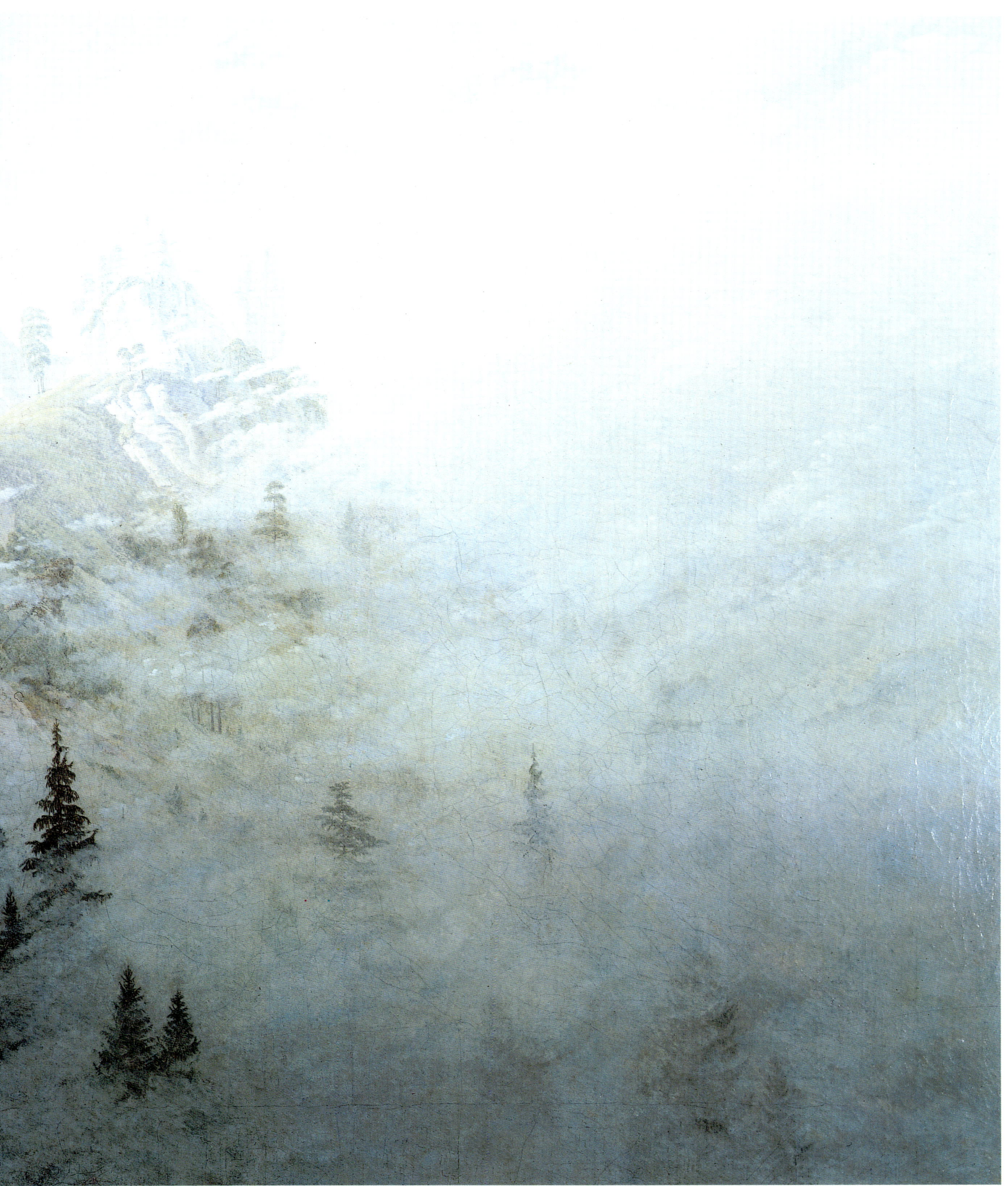

grounding on the earth and withdrawn into the uncertainty created by the mist. On the highest of the rocks stands a modest cross; it is only on second glance that the viewer recognizes that it lies on the painting's central axis.

The Tetschen Altar starts from the same basic elements; it takes the facts of empirical experience and transforms them into an icon. The sunset, a natural event, is stripped of its transitory nature and made transcendent, becoming three or four rays of light. In this way it assumes a symbolic power that is supernatural, even eternal. These sharply defined rays of light avoid the central axis of the canvas, as do the rocks and trees: all are arranged in a markedly asymmetrical way. The cross, too, is placed off the central axis. Friedrich proves himself an accurate observer of clouds, but he also articulates the evening sky and makes it conform discreetly to the rise and fall of the rounded pinnacle of rock. This rears up steeply and in silhouette, so that physical access to the peak appears barred to the viewer. This results in the distancing that is characteristic of icons: the sensory information is withdrawn and made remote.

The curve of the cloud follows that of the semicircular frame, which gives that remoteness power and precision. The frame is meticulously executed, with all the regularity that the picture avoids. Carved by the Dresden sculptor Gottlieb Kühn to Friedrich's specifications, it was described by the painter as follows: 'At the sides, the frame has two Gothic columns. Palm branches rise from them and form a curve above the painting. There are five angels' heads in the branches, all looking down at the cross and worshipping. The evening star stands above the middle angel in purest shining silver. At the bottom, in an oblong panel, is the all-seeing eye of God, enclosed by the holy trigon, surrounded with rays. Ears of corn and vines on either side bow to the all-seeing eye and signify the body and blood of Him who is fixed to the cross.' Friedrich expanded on the Christian aspects of his outlook in his explanation of the picture. 'With the teachings of Jesus, an old world died, the time when God the Father walked directly on earth. The sun went down and the earth could no longer grasp the departing light. The Saviour on the cross shines in the gold of sunset with the purest, noblest metal, and reflects the light onto the earth with a gentler gleam. The cross stands on a rock, as unshakeably firm as our faith in Jesus. Fir trees grow around the cross, evergreen and everlasting, like the hope of men in Him, Christ crucified.'

In the language of modern art historians, the painting might be interpreted as follows: *The Cross in the Mountains* is characterized essentially by the couplings (or confrontations) of different formal strata (modes). These occur, firstly, within the picture, secondly, within the frame, and thirdly, in the interplay between the frame and the picture. All of these are elements which we recognize today as the innovative impulses in the *Altar*. They also entail several obvious breaks with tradition, and this is why Friedrich Wilhelm von Ramdohr, a conservative but astute critic, felt driven to write a long and detailed critique when the painting was exhibited in Friedrich's Dresden studio at Christmas 1808 (see page 276). This led to the famous 'Ramdohr Dispute', to which the painter's friends contributed their differing opinions.

Ramdohr pointed out a series of inconsistencies and offences against the conventions of painterly illusion based on empirical observation and the rules of central perspective. He condemned the detailed, painstaking imitation ('every needle on the fir trees ... is illustrated'), but he also deplored the absence of aerial perspective, and saw the rays of sunlight as a serious offence against 'all the rules of optics'. He was particularly disturbed by the dark mass of the ground – 'without any curvature' – and its relationship to the aerial space: 'It stands in the most strident contrast to the bright sky, without any transition or harmony...'. In his response, Friedrich admitted that the aerial perspective was 'too weakly expressed', also 'that the reddening of the sky is faulty and leaves it uncertain whether it is morning or evening, and that the mountain lacks curvature'. But he claimed the right to paint a landscape that did not contain 'several planes', and consciously dispensed with the contrast between curved and straight lines which Ramdohr demanded.

Discrepancies were also what struck Ramdohr most forcibly in the relationship between the picture and the frame. He could see that they formed a conceptual whole: the frame 'is closely related to the painting and is all the more integral for the fact that without it, the allegory would be utterly incomprehensible.' Yet in spite of that statement, his verdict was: 'The frame has no connection with the picture.' What he meant by this, clearly, was that for all its inconsistencies, the painting is a realistic representation, while the frame contains the sensory information about the picture's meaning in symbolic shorthand. Ramdohr was not prepared to connect these two semiotic planes and for that reason found the frame incomprehensible and described it as if he did not have the first notion of Christian iconography. The eye of God, to him, was just 'an eye inside a triangle surrounded by rays', the angels' heads were 'children's heads with wings', the vines and ears of corn were simply vines and ears of corn.

Ramdohr, a son of the Enlightenment, rested his wholly pragmatic point of view on the principle of central perspective, and the resulting unification of space. The formulation of central perspective in the fourteenth and fifteenth centuries meant loss as well as gain for the religious content of European painting. Erwin Panofsky gave the classic exposition. By locating the content of pictures in the material world, the use of perspective 'sealed off religious art from the realm of the magical, where the work of art itself works the miracle, and from the realm of the dogmatic and symbolic, where the work bears witness to, or foretells, the miraculous'. In compensation, art gained 'something entirely new: the realm of the visionary, where the miraculous becomes a direct experience of the beholder, in that the supernatural events in a sense erupt into his own, apparently natural, visual space...'.

Where does the Ramdohr dispute stand within the framework outlined by Panofsky? Friedrich conceded that he had departed from the conventions of central perspective. As he had painted a conglomerate of heterogeneous sensory data to convey his meaning, instead of a coherent 'natural visual space', he could not take advantage of the illusionism which the painters of Catholic Europe had used since the Counter-Reformation to represent miraculous acts in sensorily evocative terms. The Protestant Friedrich did not invite the viewer to see anything visionary or supernatural in his painting, but compensated for this by transferring the supernatural content that our empirical vision cannot see to the picture frame, where it takes the form of Christian symbols. Friedrich did not paint a collective *Adoration of the Name of God* in an illusionistic space, as his contemporary Francisco de Goya did (Zaragoza, 1772), but the symbol itself, in relation to the meditation of an observer. In this way, Friedrich gave the *Altar* access to 'the realm of the dogmatic and symbolic', although he could not have included it in the picture itself, nor would he have wanted it there. 'The noble human being [the painter] finds God in everything.' He goes on to explain that the sun is to be understood as the 'image of the eternal Father, giver of all life'. The natural event assumes a dimension of spiritual meaning, which is also simultaneously present in the eye of God in the predella, only without the admixture of empirical sensory information. Nevertheless, Friedrich did in fact provide a visible reference to link the frame and the picture, one which Ramdohr refused to see: the gilded triangle continues the articulation of the rock mass, and its rays mutate into those of the setting sun.

All these considerations lead to the conclusion that Friedrich's innovation covertly involved a return to an earlier tradition. Just as he broke with the tradition of central perspective, he also adopted structures taken from medieval pictures and icons. But he did this in a novel way, not in the historicizing spirit of his contemporaries, the Nazarenes, who attempted to revive the world of painting before Raphael. In the interaction of the picture and the frame Friedrich placed different levels of reality in opposition and dismissed the monofocal singularity of meaning ensured by the principle of central perspective and unified space. His innovation was in this respect closer to the complex, polyfocal reality of a modern picture, a characteristic also shared by the structure of medieval pictures.

A pictorial manifesto with the significance of *The Tetschen Altar* could not be repeated. When Friedrich returned to the same concept about ten years later, in his projected *Cross in front of a Rainbow in the Mountains* (ill. 45), he obviously had an altarpiece for a parish church in mind, and the outcome was a less challenging, more conventional version of the Dresden *Cross in the Mountains.* In 1808, the painter had boldly ignored 'the rules of art, acknowledged and hallowed over the centuries', but now, probably with a minister and a congregation to consider, he used a compromised formula that avoided his earlier radicalism. The project was never executed.

However, *The Tetschen Altar* is not an isolated instance of a manifesto proclaiming the iconization or sacralization of landscape. It has a counterpart in Runge's *Morning* (also 1808; ill. 20), an essay in interpreting a time of day as a time in world history and conversely, relating religious revelation to a natural event, enlarged to a cosmic scale. Runge's Aurora, the bringer of light, is a 'symbol of the all-embracing beginning: the day at morning, the year in spring, human life at birth, the world at the creation' (Julius Langner). In order to represent this manifold concept visually, Runge too ignored the central perspective of 'natural experiential space' and arrived – inevitably! – at the same idea as Friedrich did, of linking the picture and its frame. This is done in two ways. Firstly, a vertical central axis rises from the solar eclipse on the bottom of the painted frame, through the newborn babe, Aurora, the lily of light, and the evening star up to the halo of cherubim crowning the whole. Secondly, beginning with the two genii striving to escape the darkness, the centre panel is fully framed by a round dance of genii and plants, which correspond to those in the central field; this finally flows into the halo of cherubim.

We may find that *The Tetschen Altar* both looks back to the Middle Ages before perspective and forward to the modern era and the end of perspective, but these facts of art history should not allow us to forget another field of reference: that of landscape as the occasion for religious meditation. Ramdohr saw in Friedrich's 'swooning adulation of the cross' the desire to 'cripple' art, 'taking it back to its earlier simplicity' – a shrewd observation, if it had been hedged by a different set of prejudices. Ramdohr was shaped by the Enlightenment and to him *The Tetschen Altar* embodied 'an idea of our religion which is worthy of respect in itself, and consoling, but not in the least aesthetic'. The work of art as the object of what Kant called 'disinterested appreciation' should be distinguished, Ramdohr seems to suggest, from the work of art as the stimulus of extra-artistic 'pathological emotion'. Ramdohr concurred with the boundary drawn by Hegel (in *Philosophie der Geschichte*) between a work of art and a 'mere thing' that produces a religious effect, such as a reliquary. 'It is quite different when the spirit has before it a mere thing, such as the host itself, a stone, a piece of wood, or a bad picture, as opposed to an intelligent picture or a good work of sculpture, where soul meets soul, and spirit meets spirit.' Hegel came to the conclusion that religion did not find its satisfaction in the relationship to beauty. For religion, 'quite bad, ugly, commonplace works serve the purpose just as well, in fact *better*'. He was able to cite evidence and testimonies that 'true works of art, such as Raphael's Madonnas, do not enjoy the veneration, and do not receive the quantities of gifts, that the bad pictures do; these are sought out and are objects of greater veneration and generosity'. Hegel summed up: 'Art therefore has already moved away from the principle of the church.'

The Tetschen Altar was not hung in the castle chapel but in one of the bedrooms, across from an engraving of Raphael's *Sistine Madonna* (the painting itself already belonged to the Dresden gallery). At such proximity, the deficiencies deplored by Ramdohr would have affronted anyone who approached the painting armed with the same expectations. Such a person would see it as a retrogression into the mysticism 'which is insinuating itself everywhere' and 'prefers the era of the Middle Ages and its institutes to the age of the Medicis'. Ramdohr's annoyance is understandable if we compare the *Sistine Madonna* with *The Tetschen Altar*.

The *Madonna* adorned the main altar in San Sisto in Piacenza until 1754, when it was bought by Augustus III of Saxony. It therefore lost its original, sacred role and instead came to serve the cult of genius as an example of the very highest artistic mastery. The painting is an open window on the supersensory world, which seems to form a continuum with our 'natural visual space' in the everyday world, so that the

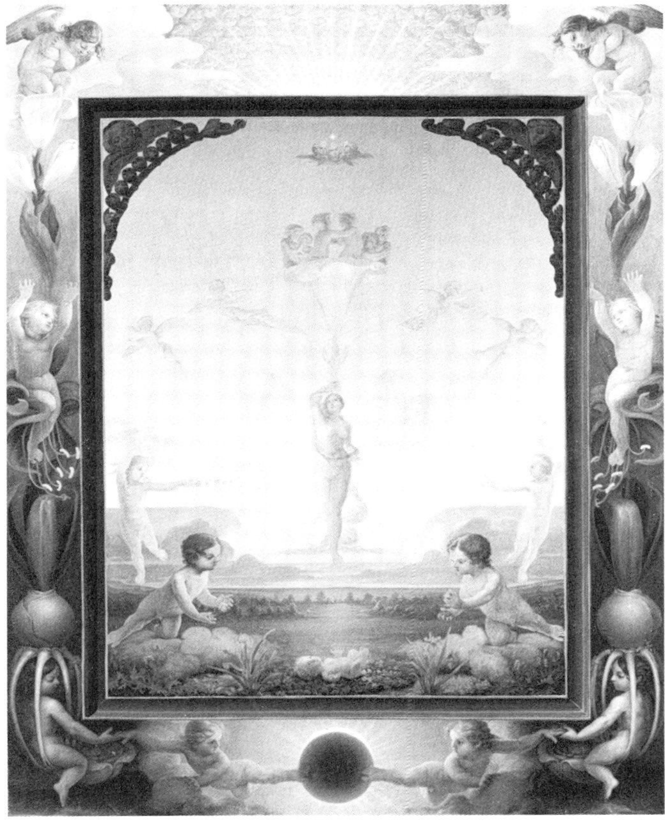

20. Philipp Otto Runge, *Morning*, 1808, oil on canvas, 109 x 85.5 cm (42⅞ x 33¾ in.). Hamburger Kunsthalle, Hamburg.

figure of St Sixtus easily mediates between the place where the viewer is and heaven. Marielene Putscher wrote: 'Like an apparition and yet physically real, the Madonna with her Child stands between the two kneeling saints. The lightness with which she stands or floats and the white light that makes her figure stands out darker strengthen the impression of her having just materialized, while the curtains and the balustrade in front strengthen the impression of physicality.'

Raphael's staging of the picture relies on our sympathetic interest. The verisimilitude of his figures expresses the artistic intention that created them. The easy naturalness made the two winged putti, in particular, universal favourites. They are scarcely involved in the event, and find nothing there to arouse their awe. Friedrich, on the other hand, wanted his five identical angels' heads to be 'worshipping'. Raphael's putti are nonchalant little boys of flesh and blood; Friedrich's angels are elements in a work of art, and as removed as an icon. Where Raphael succeeds in representing the supersensory quality of the vision in sensorily convincing language, so that it draws closer to the real world, Friedrich's intentions strive in exactly the opposite direction. He diminishes the sensory quality of the landscape and uses the picture frame to embed it in a supersensory, symbolic context. Raphael makes the 'realm of the dogmatic and symbolic' withdraw, but for Friedrich it is more important than the illusion of a 'natural visual space'. Viewed thus, Raphael's picture, in Hegel's words, has indeed moved away from the principle of the church. Friedrich's altar, by contrast, turns back towards the iconic dignity which Raphael abandoned. At the same time, however, his icon stands for a faith which has taken its leave from the institutionalized church embodied by Catholicism and given itself over to private, subjective worship.

Framed by curtains, the Madonna resembles a picture and yet preserves the illusion of breathing, abundant life. Friedrich's crucified figure, on the other hand, is plainly a work of art, a substitute intended to awake remembrance of what happened at Golgotha and raise the event into timelessness. Friedrich neither depicts a vision nor concerns himself with religious history. It is his way of expressing the doubt about the credibility of miracle workers and miraculous images that Novalis put into words in *Heinrich von Ofterdingen*. 'Those times are no more', Heinrich's father says, 'when divine visions mixed with dreams, and we cannot understand, even if we try, what it felt like for those chosen men the Bible tells us about. There must have been something different about dreams in those days, as there was about human affairs. Direct communication with heaven [as depicted so convincingly in the *Sistine Madonna*] no longer takes place in the age of the world that we live in now. The old stories and writings are now the only sources to give us any knowledge of the world above, as far as we need it, and instead of those express revelations the Holy Spirit now speaks to us indirectly through the understanding of clever and well-meaning men, and through the lives and destinies of the devout. I have never found the miraculous images of today particularly edifying, and I have never believed the stories of great wonders that our priests tell about them.'

The loss observed with resignation by the old man forms a spiritual and intellectual background which brings into focus the radical nature of *The Tetschen Altar*, and which was itself the subject of close theological scrutiny at the beginning of the nineteenth century. Friedrich certainly did not entertain any idea of painting theology, but his theories and his innovative recoil from traditional formal language converged with the Christian apologetics of a contemporary philosopher, who argued the need for a

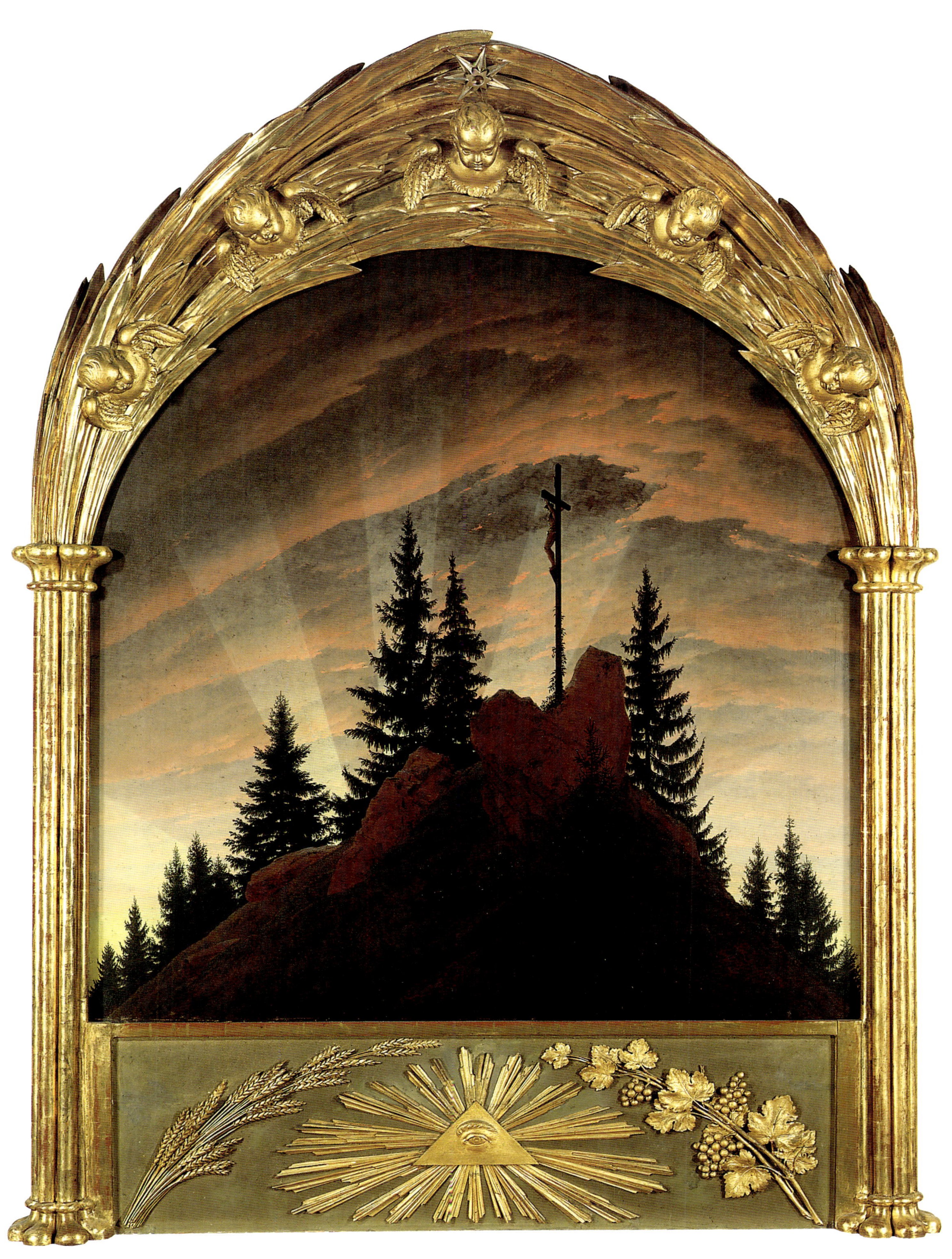

21. *The Cross in the Mountains (The Tetschen Altar)*,
1807–8, oil on canvas, 115 × 110.5 cm (45¼ × 43½ in.).
Gemäldegalerie Neue Meister, Dresden.

religious revival. The philosopher in question was Friedrich Schleiermacher (1768–1834), who was preacher at the Charité Hospital in Berlin and a university professor. He became the first dean of Berlin University's theological faculty, which was founded in 1810 at the instigation of himself and Wilhelm von Humboldt.

In 1799 Schleiermacher attracted a great deal of attention with his treatise *Über die Religion. Reden an die Gebildeten unter ihren Verächtern* (*On Religion: Speeches to its Cultured Despisers*), which Friedrich may have been familiar with. Schleiermacher seems to have visited Friedrich in his studio in Dresden in 1818, but it is idle to speculate about any possible influence the theologian may have had on the painter. It is enough to outline the state of mind which they both shared, each working autonomously in his own field and determined to take on the highest degree of creative responsibility. Just as Schleiermacher attempted to liberate the substance of religion from literalist theologians, so Friedrich wanted to found art uncompromisingly on the artist's conscience and emotions. The painter rejected the rules and norms of the academies, while the theologian discarded historical religion's arcane learning and the dead weight of dogma.

Both eschewed the Enlightenment reliance on 'ratiocination', the process of logical reasoning. Accordingly, Schleiermacher distanced himself from 'natural religion' and sought a faith that would be constantly renewed under the subjective gaze, and that alone. At this point it may be pertinent to look outside the small world of German Protestantism. The thesis that 'there is no Natural Religion' had found an earlier passionate advocate in William Blake (1757–1827), writing in 1788, who concluded that 'All Religions are One' – a heretical proposition that relativized the status of Christianity. Schleiermacher argued much the same. Blake based his authority as a poet and visionary on the belief 'that the poetic Genius is the true Man', and he may well have agreed with Schleiermacher's assertion that 'everyone with eyes to see is a new priest, a new mediator, a new organ'. Just as the church with its institutions and its dogmatic structures had become unnecessary, so its servants and officiants had become superfluous; the same was also true of those teachers of art who held official appointments and devoted themselves to academic regimentation. Like Blake, Friedrich claimed for art the freedom that Schleiermacher saw realized in true religion. Schleiermacher wanted to disentangle religion from theology's patterns of abstract thought and renew it through the act of seeing. For him, the essence of religion was 'neither thinking nor doing but seeing and feeling'. What counted was the individual approach, not the general concept: 'Seeing is and remains something individual'. This meant, necessarily, limiting oneself to specifics. 'Each of us must be aware that his [religion] is only a part of the whole, that there are other opinions about those same objects that bind him to religion: opinions which are equally devout and yet differ entirely from his, and that seeing and feeling may spring from other elements of religion which perhaps mean nothing at all to him.'

When Schleiermacher railed to 'pale imitators' that each should 'see with his own eyes' and bring forth all that lies 'within his innermost being', he was advocating the unconditional spiritual spontaneity that we find again and again in Friedrich's aphorisms. Similarly, some of the painter's maxims could have been penned by the philosopher; the following, for instance:

'The holy Ten Commandments are the pure, lucid statement of what we all know of truth and goodness. Each of us recognizes them unconditionally as the voice of his inner self, no one can rebel against them. So if you wish to dedicate yourself to art, if you feel a calling to consecrate your life to it, oh, pay good heed to the voice of your inner self, for it is the art within us.'

'Beware the superficial knowledge of cold facts, beware sinful ratiocination, for it kills the heart, and when heart and mind have died in a man, there art cannot dwell.'

'Preserve a pure, childlike understanding within yourself and follow the voice of your inner self unconditionally, for it is the Divine in us and does not lead us astray. Regard every pure mental impulse as holy, honour every devout presentiment as holy, for it is the art within us! In the hour of inspiration it takes on visible form, and this form is your picture.'

'Let no man profit from another's abilities and bury his own talent! Only that which you recognize as true and beautiful, good and noble within yourself, is your talent.'

'See with your own eyes, and reproduce things faithfully as they appear to you; reproduce everything in your picture as it affects you.... The spirit of nature reveals itself differently to each of us, and therefore no one should impose his doctrines and rules on another as infallible law. No man is the yardstick for all, each is the yardstick only for himself, and for minds more or less kindred to his.'

'The artist's feeling is his law. Pure sensation can never be contrary to nature, only ever true to nature. But never should the feeling of another be imposed on us as law.'

An artist's 'greatest merit' is 'to stimulate the spirit, and arouse thoughts, feelings and sensations in the viewer, even if they are not his own'.

For Schleiermacher, too, subjectively justified 'seeing' assumed the importance of religious revelation, as it did for Friedrich. 'To me, everything is a miracle. What is revelation? It is any original and new way of seeing the universe, and each of us must surely know best what is original and new for him.... What is inspiration? It is only the religious name for freedom.' On the basis of subjective decisions, art and religion are equal. Friedrich's thinking and the practice of his art were filled with this same interrelatedness of art and religion. In other words, the artist's subjective observation (way of seeing) does not apply to the perceptible world alone but to religion also. The two experiences are interlinked, meaning that works of art can be granted the status of religious statements (revelations) as well as the prestige of artistic quality.

Schleiermacher refused to turn the scriptures into a 'closed codex of religion' and said that the Bible did not 'forbid any other book to be a Bible too'. Once again, this is reminiscent of Blake and his holy books, recounting new creation myths. In view of this freedom, an artist like Friedrich could be expected to paint a picture that functions as a subjective form of altarpiece precisely because it ignores the 'closed codex' of the tradition of Christian altarpieces. The contemplation which *The Cross in the Mountains* encourages in the viewer is a 'new way of seeing the universe' or a revelation as Schleiermacher defined it. In this revelation, religion and art are in accord.

At the very end of *On Religion*, Schleiermacher wrote of the future. He foresaw the decline of Christianity: 'There will come times of ruin, perhaps even divine in origin; new apostles of God will be needed to hold yet faster to that which has fallen away, and to purify with heavenly fire that which has been spoiled.' Once again, he invoked the 'artist's great and remarkable way of seeing', which is denied others. And he confesses 'Gladly would I stand on the ruins of the religion I revere.' Friedrich did not practise his art as an apostle of God, or with heavenly fire (like Blake, for instance), but worked modestly, in tranquil seclusion. Nor was he a prophet of doom, to whom signs of the coming apocalypse had been revealed. Nonetheless, Schleiermacher's metaphor of the ruins of religion, so far as it refers to religion's outer form, can be read in association with a picture concept that Friedrich often used: the depiction of intact churches as ruins. For instance, the building in *Monastery Graveyard in Snow* (ill. 31) resembles the Marienkirche in Stralsund, and two late watercolours (both lost) prophesied the ruin of the Jakobikirche in Greifswald. The painting Friedrich wrote about in the following passage is also lost:

'I am working once again on a big painting.... Like the picture I mentioned in my last letter, it represents the interior of a ruined church. I've based it on the beautiful cathedral in Meissen, which is still in a good state of preservation. The interior is piled high with rubble, out of which soar the mighty pillars with slender, delicate columns that still support some of the lofty vault. The time of the glory of the temple and its servants is past; another time and a new desire for clarity and truth have risen from the ruined whole. Tall, slender, evergreen pines have grown up out of the rubble, and on the rotting images of saints, broken altars and shattered sacred vessels stands an Evangelical [Lutheran] priest. With the Bible in his left hand and his right hand on his heart, he leans on a ruined memorial to a bishop, his eyes raised to the blue sky, thoughtfully contemplating the pale, light clouds.'

This thoughtful contemplation is the very process Schleiermacher called 'seeing and feeling'.

2. The Monk by the Sea and The Abbey in the Oak Wood

The Cross in the Mountains shows art and religion taking up new positions. The painting is not tied to a specific context: although it has some of the traits of an altarpiece, it was not necessarily restricted to a chapel and, as it turned out, could even be hung in a bedroom. Similarly, the characteristics of its form and content are such as to evade categorization in any traditional genre, for it occupies a new area between landscape and sacred picture. The phrase 'landscape as icon' was coined to describe this hybrid role.

The views aired in the public discussion of the painting – in itself an unusual occurrence in the German context – show that his contemporaries recognized the painter's intentions and were as often puzzled by them as they were convinced. Two years later in Berlin, there was another spontaneous response to Friedrich's work, although this time unaccompanied by controversy. In 1810 he sent two works to the annual exhibition of the Prussian Royal Academy, which the catalogue listed laconically as 'Two landscapes in oils'. These were *The Monk by the Sea* and *The Abbey in the Oak Wood*. The exhibition gave Friedrich what today would be called his 'breakthrough'.

The submission of these two paintings needs to be viewed against its historical background. After the annihilating defeats of her army at Jena and Auerstedt in October 1806, Prussia had withdrawn from the continuing trials of strength between the European powers. But inside the defeated state, the forces of renewal stirred. One of the most important was a focus on educational reform, centred on the university in Berlin founded by Wilhelm von Humboldt. As a resident of Dresden, the capital of Saxony, Friedrich was probably not responding to a patriotic urge when he sent his paintings, recognized today as two of his masterworks, to the Prussian capital. However, the act did express the view that it would be wrong to write off Berlin, and the response to it proved he was right. The Crown Prince persuaded his father, Frederick William III, to buy both pictures, and this at a time when Prussia had to find the money to pay the reparations demanded by Napoleon. (Though what are 450 thalers when set against 120 million francs?) The prince may have been fascinated by the sombre atmosphere of the two paintings, which contained neither comfort nor patriotic uplift. They probably offered him a refuge from current events, precisely because their fundamental tone of anchorite isolation was so remote from the world of war and politics. The prince held to this attitude even when he succeeded to the throne. It led to accusations of being blinded to reality, but also earned him the description of 'the Romantic on the throne'.

The Prussian Royal Academy confirmed Friedrich's status when it elected him a member in February 1811. It is true that four out of the nine votes went against him, probably at the instigation of the combative sculptor Gottfried Schadow, but Friedrich's election was a victory within the lion's den of art politics. A decade earlier Goethe had described the Berlin scene as a stronghold of naturalism, where the 'prosaic spirit of the times' had the upper hand: 'Poetry is thrust aside by history, character and personified ideas by portraiture, symbolic representation by allegory, landscape by viewpainting, general human interest by patriotism.' Friedrich had nothing to contribute to any of those sober tendencies.

Along with the official purchases and honours came a journalistic idea which counts as one of the earliest and also most impressive documents of art criticism to emanate from Germany, a country which

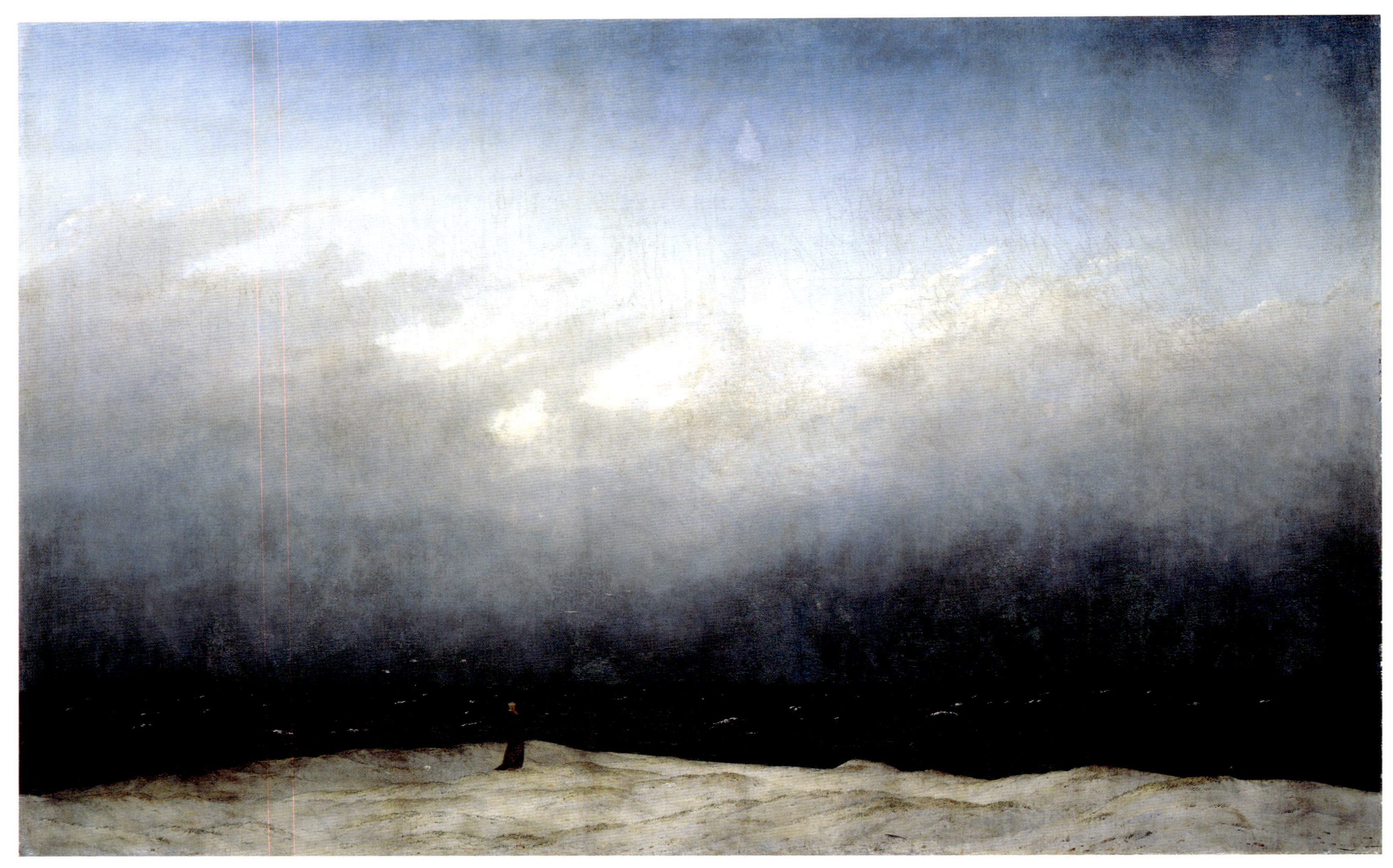

22. *The Monk by the Sea*,
c. 1809, oil on canvas,
110 × 171.5 cm (43¼ × 67½ in.).
Nationalgalerie, Berlin.

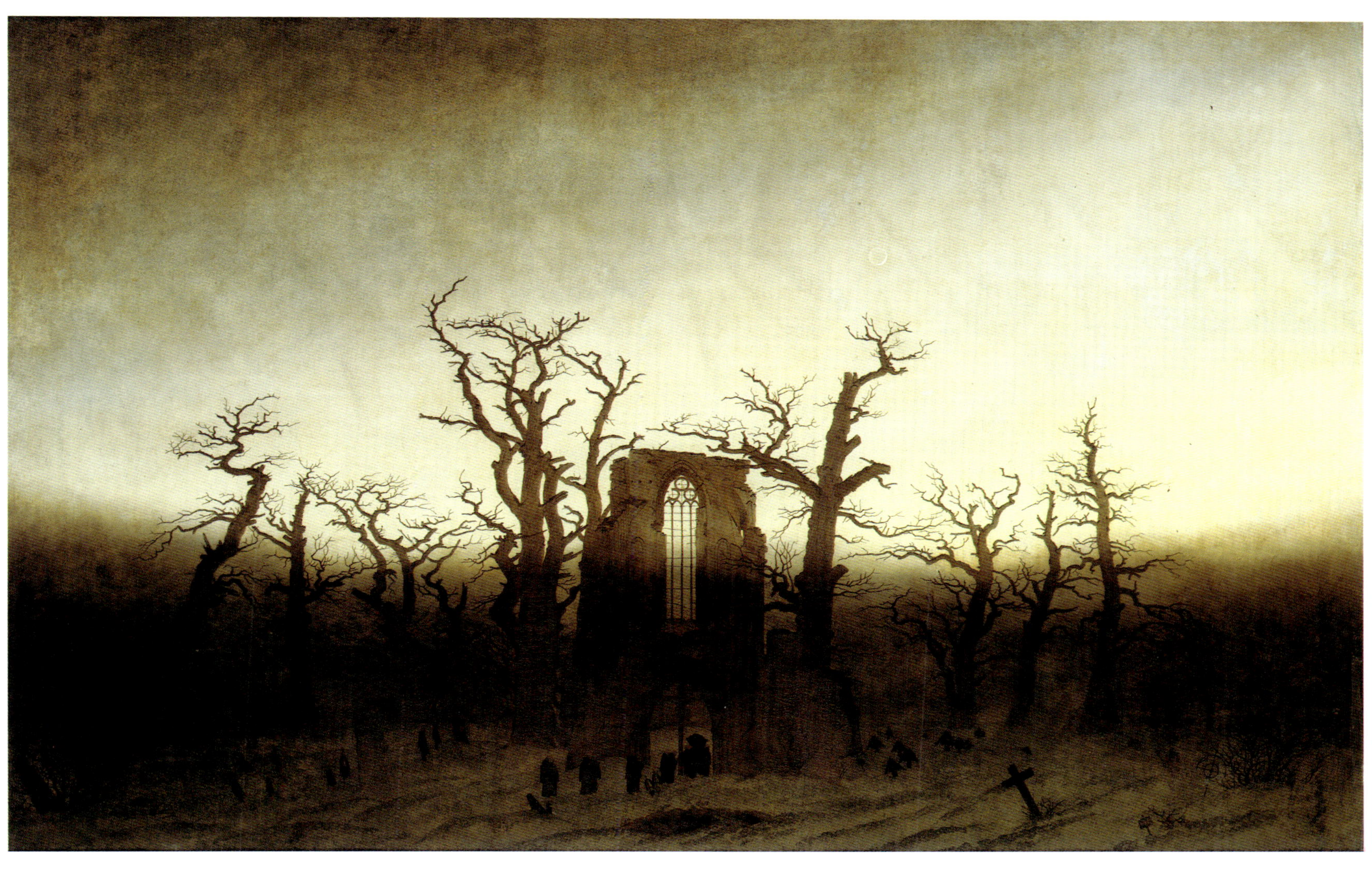

23. *The Abbey in the Oak Wood*,
c. 1809, oil on canvas,
110.4 × 171 cm (43⅝ × 67⅜ in.).
Nationalgalerie, Berlin.

at that time was only just beginning to read newspapers. Three illustrious names from the front rank of the new 'Romantic' literature – Achim von Arnim, Clemens Brentano and Heinrich von Kleist – brought their intelligence and imagination to bear on an everyday newspaper article, which was then coloured by a disagreement between writers and their editor.

The occasion was the showing of Friedrich's *The Monk by the Sea* (ills 22, 25). As editor of the *Berliner Abendblätter*, Kleist commissioned an article from his friends in the style of a Parisian salon review (see complete text, page 282). The piece took the form of conversations which Brentano and Arnim pretended to have overheard in the Academy from various visitors talking as they stood in front of Friedrich's painting. The brief conversations contained platitudes and misunderstandings ('Ossian' was confused with 'ocean') but also some apt associations, as when a lady says: 'It's as if the sea was thinking Young's *Night Thoughts*.' The chatter ran the gamut of the misunderstandings to which Friedrich was exposed. It was no philistine but Goethe himself who said his pictures could 'just as well be looked at upside down'. Friedrich might have disputed that, but he did not argue with the public's reactions if they did not coincide with his own. His friend Christian August Semler said that when it came to 'allegories like this, with many possible meanings, it can easily happen that the artist interprets his picture differently from many of the people who see it. But that does not detract from the value of his picture, so long as it makes others reflect, as he does, on his symbols, and so long as the paths along which they are led do not veer off to a completely different destination but head in a similar direction towards the same general area'. However, Kleist was less tolerant than the painter, and did not know what to make of the plethora of opinions expressed. He suppressed the conversations and interspersed the introductory text with a piece written by himself, with the whole signed 'C.B.' much to the annoyance of Brentano and Arnim.

Kleist's remarks deserve the name of genius, and are among the most penetrating comments ever made about Friedrich's art. 'There can be nothing sadder or more desolate in the world than this place: the only spark of life in the broad domain of death, the lonely centre in the lonely circle. The picture, with its two or three mysterious subjects, lies there like an apocalypse, as if it were thinking Young's *Night Thoughts*, and since it has, in its uniformity and boundlessness, no foreground but the frame, it is as if one's [the viewer's] eyelids had been cut off.

'Yet the painter has undoubtedly broken an entirely new path in the field of his art, and I am convinced that with his spirit, a square mile of the sand of Mark Brandenburg could be represented with a barberry bush, on which a lone crow might sit preening itself, and that such a picture would have an effect that rivalled Ossian or Kosegarten. Why, if the artist painted this landscape using its own chalk and its own water, I believe he would make the foxes and wolves weep: the most powerful praise, without doubt, that could be given to this kind of landscape painting.'

The 'two or three mysterious subjects' are easily identified (what makes them mysterious will be discussed below): they are the dunes, the sea and the sky, and between them the human figure, a vertical line which both separates and connects. The sky occupies a little over four-fifths of the area of the picture. The remainder is divided into the strips of the dark sea and, in strong contrast, the sand dunes, the colour of bleached bone. Never before had a painter juxtaposed aggregate states of matter so soberly, so close together and yet so little connected. At the front lie the immobile waves of sand; behind (and simultaneously above) them, the mobile sea, and above everything the condensed moisture of the clouds.

The stages of liquefaction and dematerialization leave only a narrow zone for man. Sea and sky are both barred to him. But where he stands compensates for his insignificance. He is on the highest point of the dunes, exactly underneath the vivid chiaroscuro conflict of the scraps of cloud which – like him – are directed to the right. Furthermore, his position is given weight by the picture's organization. It is no surprise to discover that the man in the monk's habit divides the width of the picture exactly by the Golden Section. Chance? Intuition? Or calculation? Friedrich spent a long time on this picture and reworked several parts of it, so it may be assumed that his instinct and perhaps also memories of his academic training led him to this generally recognized harmonious proportion.

At the same time, a contradiction is apparent. The man is lost, yet he has a dominant function. He is a well-considered caesura, stabilizing everything that is going on in the picture, and directing the viewer's thoughts to desolation and the 'domain of death'. By interrupting the 'uniformity', which ignores humankind, the vertical axis focuses attention on the oppressive weight of the place's exposure and isolation. With this comes the impression of timelessness. Time seems to have stopped; this is probably the reason Kleist thought of the apocalypse.

Another contradiction lies in the vertical layering of the spatial planes, which are not held together by the sense of depth that axial perspective would give. There is no foreground to stop our gaze travelling directly into the picture, yet it immediately hits a barrier. This is what Kleist meant when he wrote of the viewer's eyelids having been cut off. What is the cause of this? Without the mediation of perspective, nearness is transformed ultimately into inaccessible distance. There is no empirical path from us to the monk. Consequently an aura of something wholly Other extends across the picture; one of Friedrich's contemporaries might have made a comparison with the optical illusion of a panorama and its three-dimensional foregrounds. This is clearly what Kleist was thinking of when he alluded to an imagined landscape painted 'using its own chalk and its own water'. The meticulously detailed reproduction of the real world could not be more true to life, yet the paradoxical outcome is not to feel at home here but to feel distanced – alienated – from a place which is simultaneously in this world and beyond it.

The key to the painter's intended meaning is the fact that the monk is a self-portrait. As if to demonstrate his identification with the monk, in 1810 Friedrich drew himself with monkish attributes in the last of his self-portraits, gazing outwards with mesmeric concentration (ill. 24). One side of the face is in shadow, the other in light. Jens Christian Jensen called this the artist's 'broken' quality and divined the presence of something 'divided, schizoid'. There are indeed some indicators of subjective stresses in Friedrich's life. Carl Gustav Carus told of one formative incident with the tact of a friend: 'Friedrich had a dreadful experience as a boy. He was skating on the ice at Greifswald with an especially beloved brother when, before his eyes, his brother fell through the ice and was swallowed up in the depths. Add to this a very high conception of art, an innately gloomy nature and, proceeding from these, a profound dissatisfaction with his own achievements, and it becomes easy to understand that he may have once attempted suicide. He always wrapped this in deep secrecy.' The most likely date for the attempt was during Friedrich's early years in Dresden.

The biographical information is augmented and given more objective colouring by the context of the sensibilities of the age, which had been developing since the middle of the eighteenth century. As the remarks of Kleist and the chattering visitors to the exhibition purportedly heard by his two friends remind

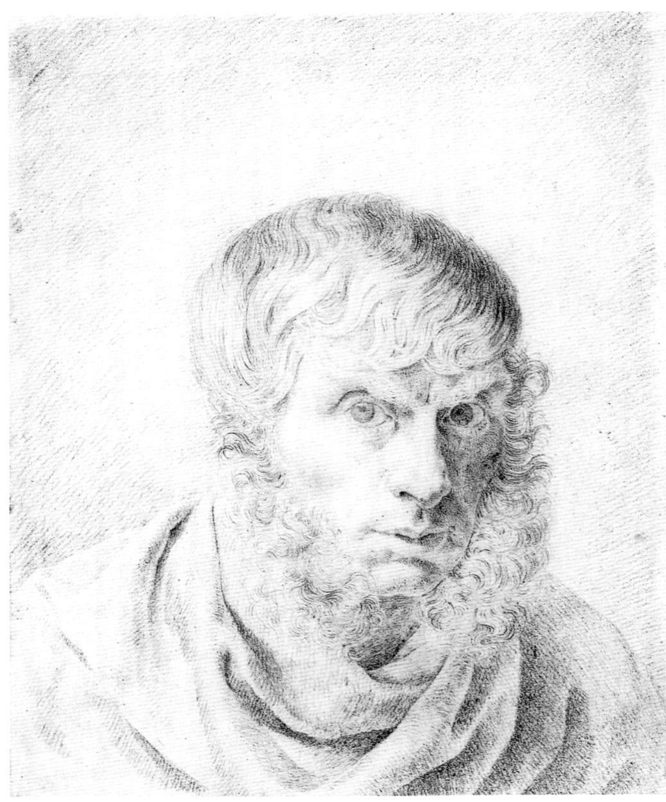

24. ***Self-portrait,***
1810, chalk,
23 × 18.2 cm (9 × 7¼ in.).
Kupferstichkabinett, Berlin.

us, the songs of Ossian, attributed by their real author James Macpherson to a blind third-century bard, had left a permanent impression. The deception was eventually uncovered but in the meantime the poems had swept through Europe: even Napoleon was a devotee. To Goethe's Werther, the songs represented liberation from the taste canonized in artistic rules – by which he meant the writings of theorists like Charles Batteux, Roger de Piles, Johann Joachim Winckelmann and Johann Georg Sulzer. The second part of *The Sorrows of Werther* incorporates Goethe's own prose translations of certain passages from Ossian, including the following: 'It is night: I am alone, forlorn on the hill of storms. The wind is heard in the mountain. The torrent pours down the rock. No hut receives me from the rain; forlorn on the hill of winds!' Nor was Kleist the only one to detect the influence of Ossian on *The Monk by the Sea*. Semler spoke of the world of a 'Christian Ossian', and Karl August Böttiger thought that the artist should 'paint Ossian's cloudy figures in the Scottish Highlands for us'.

If we combine Ossian with Edward Young's *Night Thoughts* (1742–44), and add some gloomy verse about graveyards and hermits, we reach the literary common ground from which Friedrich and his contemporaries learned to think of nature as intensified into something monstrous. The theoretical superstructure came from Edmund Burke's *Philosophical Enquiry into the Origin of our Ideas of the Sublime and the Beautiful* (1757; a German edition was published in Riga in 1773). What Burke says there about the 'uniformity', 'vastness' and endlessness of deserts, seashores and threatening clouds reads like a commentary on *The Monk by the Sea.* It was Kant and Schiller who transmitted Burke's ideas to German readers. Schiller analysed the mixed feeling ('delightful horror') in his essay *Über das Erhabene* (*On the Sublime*; 1802): 'It is a compound of unease, expressed in the highest degree as terror, and joy, capable of intensifying to delight, and although it is not really pleasure, it is much preferred to any pleasure by fine

25. ***The Monk by the Sea*, detail,**
c. 1809, oil on canvas,
110 × 171.5 cm (43¼ × 67½ in.).
Nationalgalerie, Berlin.

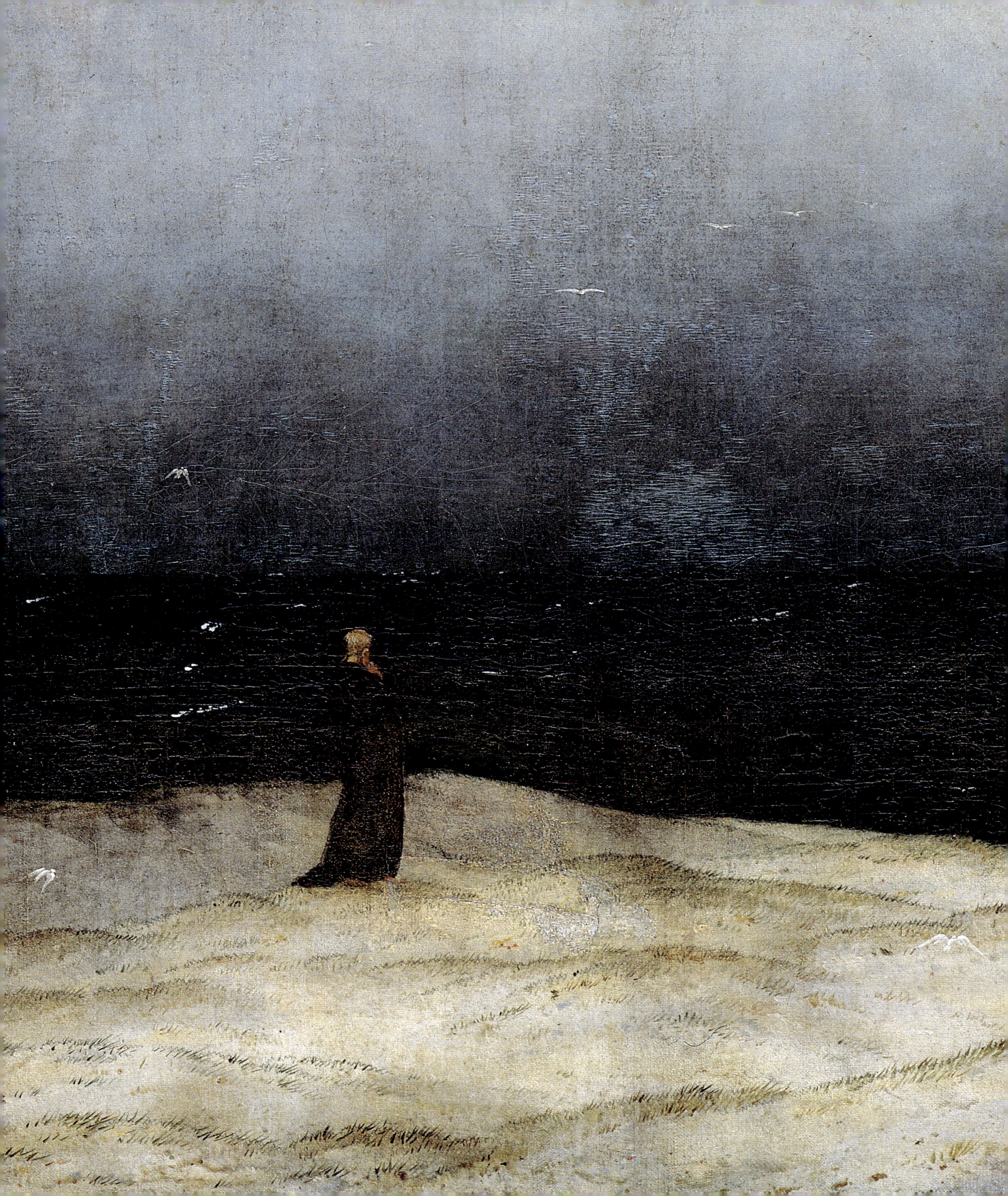

souls. This compounding of two contradictory sensations in one single emotion is an irrefutable proof of our moral independence.' This independence is demonstrated when, instead of experiencing the sublime as a physical threat, we create it as the object of our own imagination, in an act of 'free contemplation'. Friedrich does just this when he paints his alter ego as a monk by the sea, exposed to the dangers of nature. When Schiller says that a person approaching the 'terrifying images of his own imagination' does so 'fearlessly and with horrified pleasure', it applies to Friedrich, both as painter and as monk. And it follows, in Schiller's words, 'that we ourselves stand in two different relationships to the object, and therefore that two opposing natures must be united in us'.

We are well supplied with information about Friedrich's contradictory nature. The sharp-eyed Gotthilf Heinrich von Schubert diagnosed 'a strange pairing of temperamental states, tending to the deepest seriousness and the most lighthearted jesting, which it is not uncommon to find together in the most pronounced melancholics and comedians'. Fishermen on Rügen often saw him 'like one who voluntarily seeking a watery grave, clambering about, on and among the jagged edges of the cliff face and its precipices which dropped straight into the sea.... When a storm approached over the sea with thunder and lightning, he hurried to meet it at the cliff edge, like someone who had made a pact of friendship with those powers, or followed them into the oak wood, where the lightning rent the tall trees, and there he would murmur, half to himself, "How vast, how mighty, how glorious!".' The Russian writer Vasily Andreyevich Zhukovsky recorded something Friedrich said in later years: 'I must remain alone and know that I am alone, in order to see and feel nature completely; I must surrender myself to my surroundings, unite myself with my clouds and rocks, in order to be what I am.'

It is true that no one would ever look at *The Monk by the Sea* and suspect the presence of the 'cheerful good nature' which Schubert also recognized in Friedrich and demonstrated in a number of entertaining anecdotes. But another piece of evidence reveals Friedrich's double life beyond all doubt. It is a drawing which seems to depict a sombre critical moment, but in fact takes on quite a different aspect in the painter's whimsical commentary. On 2 May 1814, Friedrich wrote a letter to the painter Louise Seidler (ill. 26) and sketched himself at the mouth of a dark cave, similar to the one in his painting *Tombs of Ancient Heroes* (ill. 51). Was he gazing into an abyss? Far from it. The letter itself shows the other side of Friedrich's personality:

'I read your letter beside the roaring waterfall in the Plaun'scher Grund, and all the baking and roasting made me want to enjoy the splashing and plashing. If only the rocks had turned into cakes and roast meat at that moment, and the water into wine: a new cave would certainly have come into being and the raging water would have turned into a rippling stream. Then I could have sat down before my work with a full stomach and rendered it eternal. At this very moment it is all so vivid in front of my eyes that I must try to give you a little sketch of it.'

The drawing reproduces the topography exactly, but gives no hint of that land of milk and honey. We may wonder if the watercolour showing a man disappearing behind a tree (ill. 27) is an example of the same mischievous wit.

The 'entirely new path' that Kleist acclaimed in *The Monk by the Sea* points in a different formal direction in *The Abbey in the Oak Wood* (ill. 23). The horizontal layers of *The Monk*, the intensification of three uniformities, generate a paradox: an abundance of emptiness. (Marcel Proust once referred to a *plénitude du silence.*) *The Abbey*, in contrast, offers the viewer a richly varied syntax, the dialogue of several different formal zones. Once again, however, it is a matter of spatial dissociation. Friedrich fills the depths of the space with mysteries, and moreover polarizes the relationship of above and below, sky and earth. The main vertical accent is provided by the ruin of a Gothic church in the dead centre of the picture, which is more like a frail piece of stage scenery than a solid architectural structure. Our recognition that the Gothic belongs to the remote past adds to the phantom-like distance of the ruin. The result is a twofold symbol of transience, underlined by the monks standing there like gravestones muffled up against the cold. They are brought to the crucifix below the pointed arch for a burial (probably of a brother of their order), and also for a ritual conjuration of the past. The ruinous state of the building and the figures is transferred to the religion they both serve. There is no trace of an abbey, as such, to be seen.

The Christian, Gothic past is framed by the heathen past and its faith, symbolized by the bare oak trees. Perhaps they formerly flanked a dolmen as in the Weimar *Dolmen by the Sea* (ill. 28) or the Dresden *Dolmen in the Snow* (ill. 29), or a heathen burial ground on the site later occupied by the church. The bizarrely contorted branches, whose verisimilitude is attested by Friedrich's drawings, conceal a carefully constructed symmetrical equilibrium. The trunks grouped on the left and right relate to the ruin and with it form the rhythm of a triptych. This articulation gives the landscape its distance and its dignity.

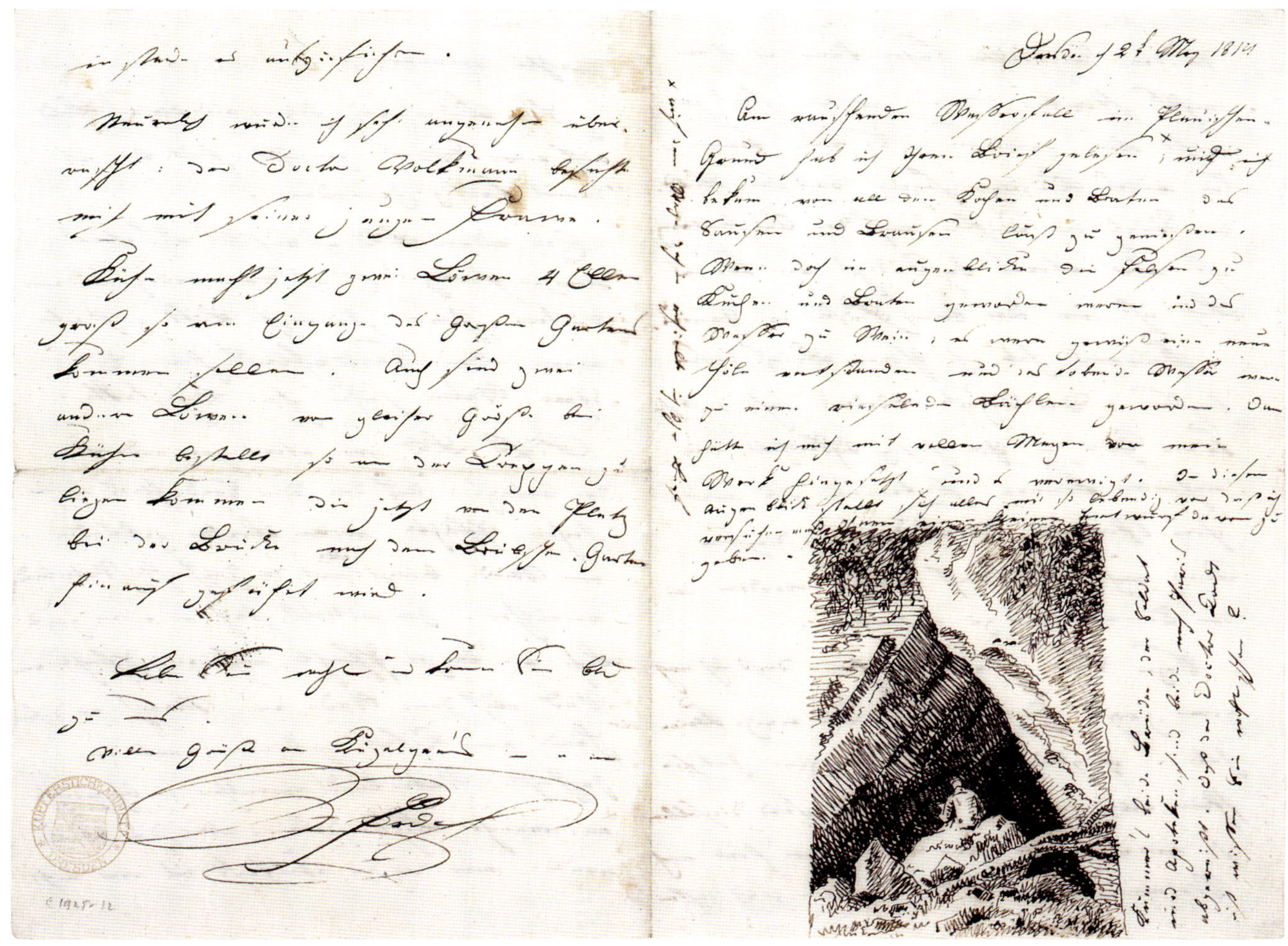

26. Letter to Louise Seidler,
1814, ink,
19.4 x 26.2 cm (7⅝ x 10⅜ in.).
Kupferstichkabinett, Dresden.

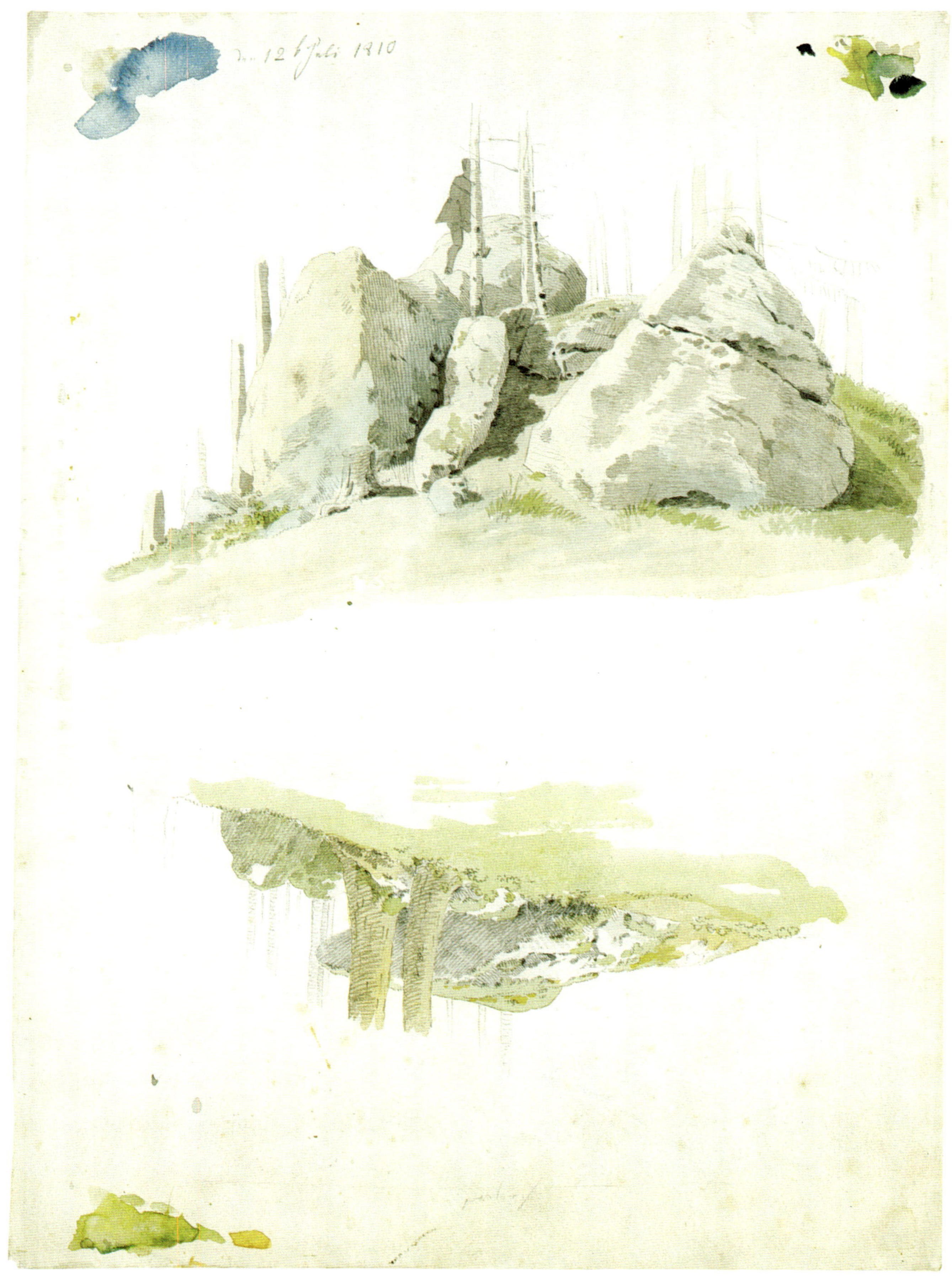

27. *Rocks and Trees,*
12 July 1810, pencil and watercolour,
36 × 26 cm (14⅛ × 10¼ in.).
Hamburger Kunsthalle, Hamburg.

Tree trunks and ruins, the remains of the Germanic heathen past and the Christian past, are not contrasted with each other but come together in a barrier that closes off space. Whatever may lie beyond them is swallowed up in mist and hidden from view. Do the window gratings suggest traditional forms of belief that are closed rather than open? Behind their linearity, in the background comes a separation into upper and lower levels, brought about by colour. A dirty brown blanket of fog bears down on the wintery landscape, the graves, the monks and the ruins. Anyone walking in it will be enfolded in a sunken world. There is nothing to show that the tips of the branches and the top line of the ruin reach up into a cool bright sky. The place where they meet the firmament lies beyond the sight of the monks; it is visible only to the viewer, from his position outside the fog. From there, faced with Friedrich's parable of belief held fast in the grip of decline, and yet able to renew itself, the viewer must make a choice. If he does not want to withdraw into the sheltering darkness he must risk exposing himself to the clarity of the air above, from which no warmth comes.

It would be bold indeed to relate the pale sky to the two things that filled Kant with 'admiration and awe': 'the starry sky above me and the moral law within me'. Kant goes on:

'I must not look for them or merely suppose them to be veiled in darkness, or in transcendence, beyond the range of my sight; I see them in front of me and connect them directly with the consciousness of my existence. The first begins from the place I occupy in the external sensory world and expands the context in which I stand far out beyond the reach of sight, with worlds upon worlds and systems within systems, and still further into the boundless tides of its periodic motion, its beginning and continuation. The second begins from my invisible self, my personality, and places me in a world that is truly infinite, but can be sensed only by the understanding mind, and I recognize that my connection with it (and thereby with all those other visible worlds, simultaneously) is complete and necessary, not merely accidental as with them.' (*Critique of Practical Reason*, 1788.)

Something of the rigour and refusal to accept conditions which shaped Kant's thinking is also discernible in the concept behind Friedrich's picture. A reminder: 'The time of the glory of the temple and its servants is past and another time and a different desire for clarity and truth have arisen out of the ruined whole.' Perhaps the metaphor for this secretly iconoclastic conviction is in the firmament, reaching out into a cosmic infinity which evades any kind of physically formative experience. Where the light of the sky meets the fog, it forms a shallow depression, as if the dazzling clarity is sinking slowly but steadily down on to the darkness and the relics it shelters. If this impression is correct, *The Abbey in the Oak Wood* contains a declaration of the knowing confidence of belief, freed of the dead weight of history, which is as yet unknown in *The Monk by the Sea.*

In *The Monk* and *The Abbey*, Friedrich invented the structures which from then on would embody *la tragédie du paysage.* Both paintings have formal precursors, which illustrate how swiftly and steadily Friedrich intensified and enriched his language and steered it in a new direction. In the two Weimar sepias (ills 8 and 9), the peaceful, self-contained existence of the fisherman and woman is paired with a procession of monks. In one of the two Vienna paintings (ill. 17) the fisherman encounters nature through a mixture of activity and contemplation, although with a practical and professional motivation which is not raised to the status of a 'sentimental' experience. 'Sentimental' is used here in the sense Schiller used to distinguish the naive (intuitive) poet from the sentimental (reflective) one: the former has

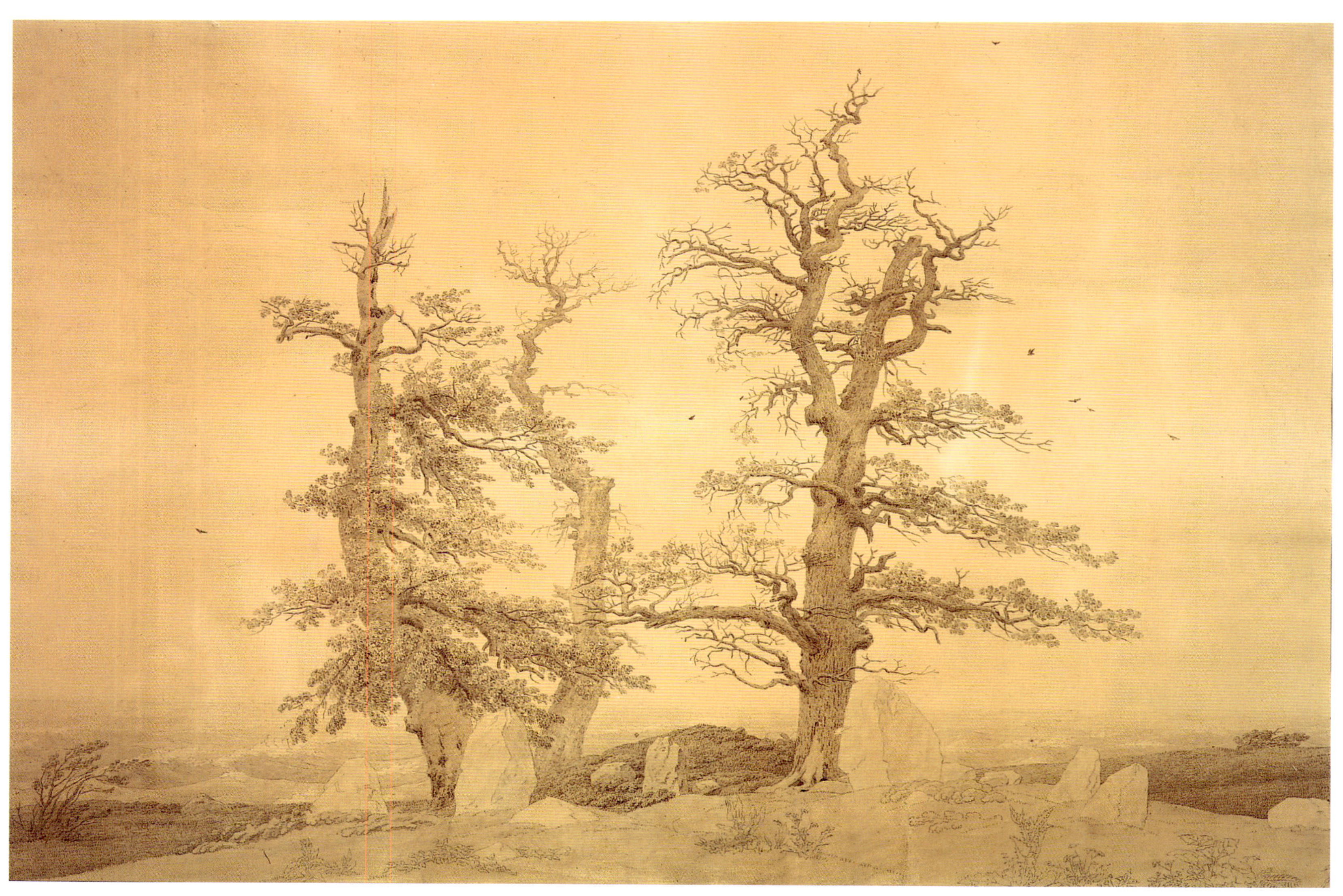

28. ***Dolmen by the Sea,***
1807, pencil and sepia,
64.5 x 95 cm (25½ x 37⅜ in.).
Staatliche Kunstsammlungen, Weimar.

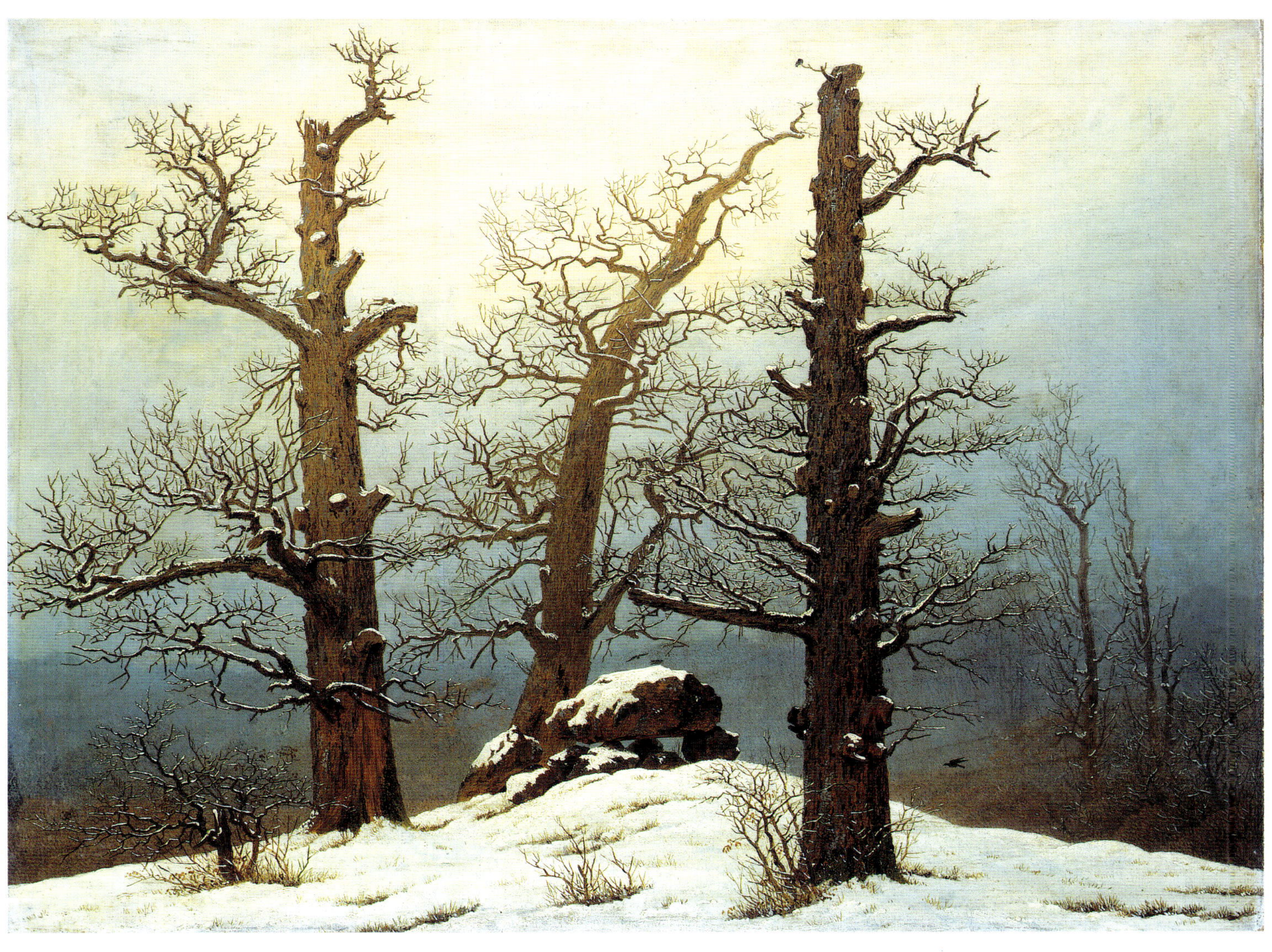

29. ***Dolmen in the Snow,***
1807, oil on canvas,
61.5 x 80 cm (24¼ x 31½ in.).
Gemäldegalerie Neue Meister, Dresden.

what the latter seeks. Applied to Friedrich's fisherman, the word would mean that he still abides in the 'undivided unity' of nature, and knows nothing of the 'mixed feelings' that made Friedrich dress and portray himself as a monk.

Horizontal layers and vertical axes, the fundamentals of *The Monk* and *The Abbey*, had preoccupied the painter in earlier pictures. The deep horizon in both the Vienna beach scenes (ills 16 and 17) already displays emptiness in abundance. A similar direction is suggested in the Rügen landscapes, especially the large sepia in the Albertina in Vienna (ill. 30), where the horizon is every bit as deep as in *The Monk by the Sea*. The beaches are topographically identifiable and always represented at a specific time of day; although empty they invite the viewer to take a walk along the shore. The notes of remoteness and alienation are still absent.

The concern with vertical emphases goes back to the early *View of Mountains with a Waterfall* (ill. 4), which has a triple rhythm made up of two 'funnels'. One is formed by the steep sides of the gulley, the other by the mountain peak seen between them. There is a reciprocal interaction in *The Tetschen Altar*, where the converging axes of the rays of the setting sun respond to the triangular mass of the rock. The frame of oak trees and the ruined church between them in *The Abbey in the Oak Wood* is a comparable structure, and the 'two-funnel' structure is even clearer in *Monastery Graveyard in Snow* (1817–19; ill. 31). The ruin in the background forms a counterpoint to the slanting lines of the two gigantic oak trees; the linear energies converge in the pointed arch, while the tree trunks carry them downwards, again in a funnel formation. Though it is represented with much greater height, the ruined choir is based on the (still intact) Marienkirche in Stralsund, a more explicit rendering of the intimations of decline in *The Abbey in the Oak Wood* (ills 23, 32). Börsch-Supan does not share this opinion: in his view, Friedrich depicted 'three phases in religious history: paganism in the oak trees, medieval Christianity in the nave of the church and present-day Christianity in the choir and in the action in front of the altar'. It is possible to see the three phases as a continuous transition only because *Monastery Graveyard in Snow* lacks the quality that gives *The Abbey in the Oak Wood* its compelling duality and makes it, in Schiller's terminology, a 'sublime object' of a 'twofold kind': that quality is the transformation of befogged consciousness into a new clarity.

In *The Monk by the Sea* and *The Abbey in the Oak Wood*, Friedrich gives religious belief an emphasis that is at once tragic and elitist. He relates it to the artist's position on the fringes of society, and reflects on the dangers lying in wait for those who, like Schleiermacher, have no wish to be a 'pale imitator'. It is not that he places the artist's religion in a special category, but he does claim that art offers radical forms of communication which differ from the traditional confession of a community of faith. But neither this claim, nor the conviction that 'the glory of the temple and its servants' was past, prevented him from including the church in his pictorial conceptions, as a concrete place of prayer and preaching. He did not only paint ruined chancels and abbeys, therefore, but also intact Gothic churches, stylized as the fulfilment of the hope of salvation. By transferring them from the here and now to an imaginary, inaccessible space he made them non-functioning counterparts of real church buildings, symbols of perfection. This is illustrated in a pair of pictures, one now in Schwerin and one in Dortmund, which compare and contrast inconsolability with consolation. In the Schwerin painting (ill. 33), a man stands stooped and bowed in a gap between two trees, which grow away from each other as if separated by a

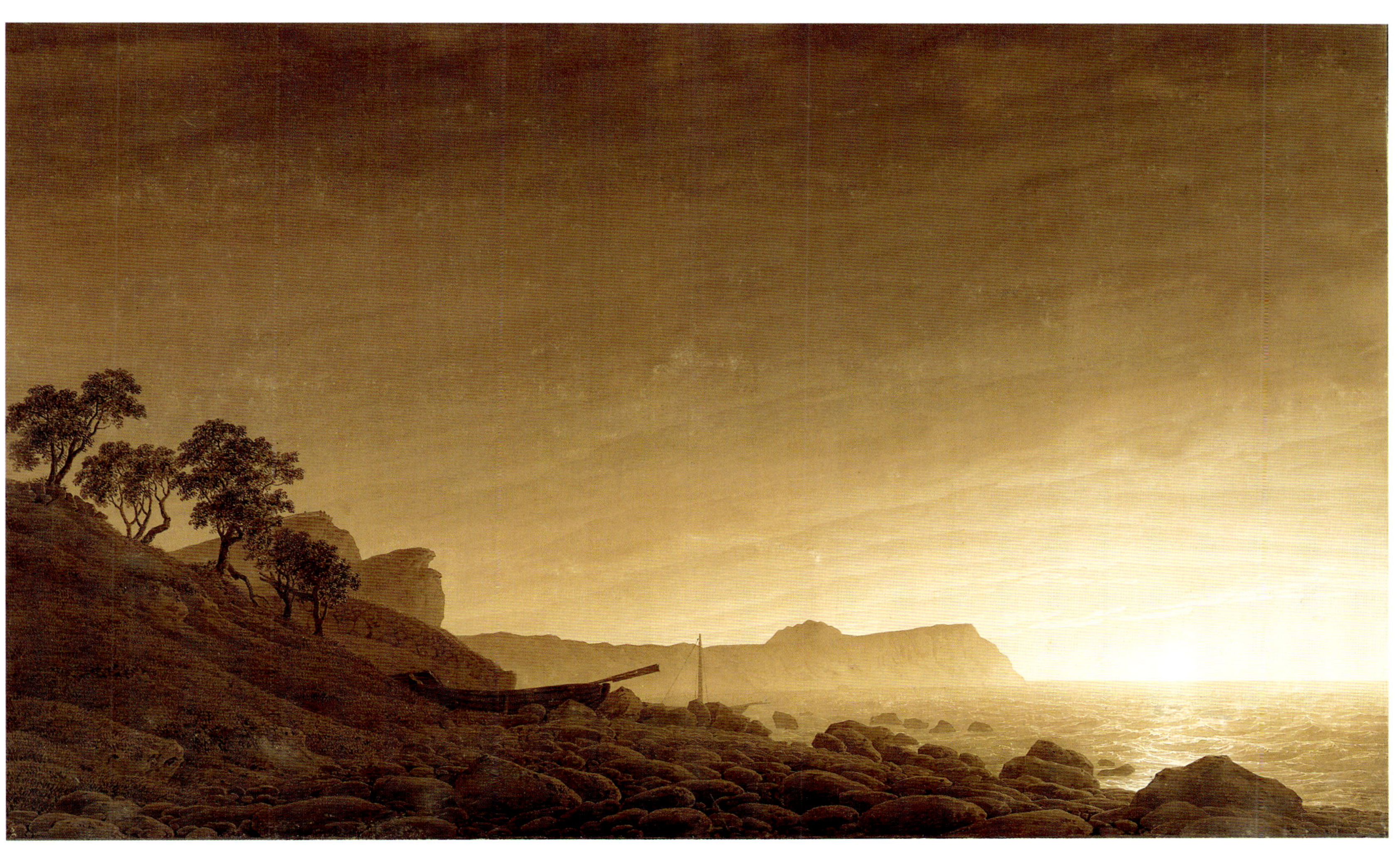

30. *Cape Arkona*,
1805–6, pencil and sepia,
60.9 × 100 cm (24 × 39⅜ in.).
Graphische Sammlung Albertina, Vienna.

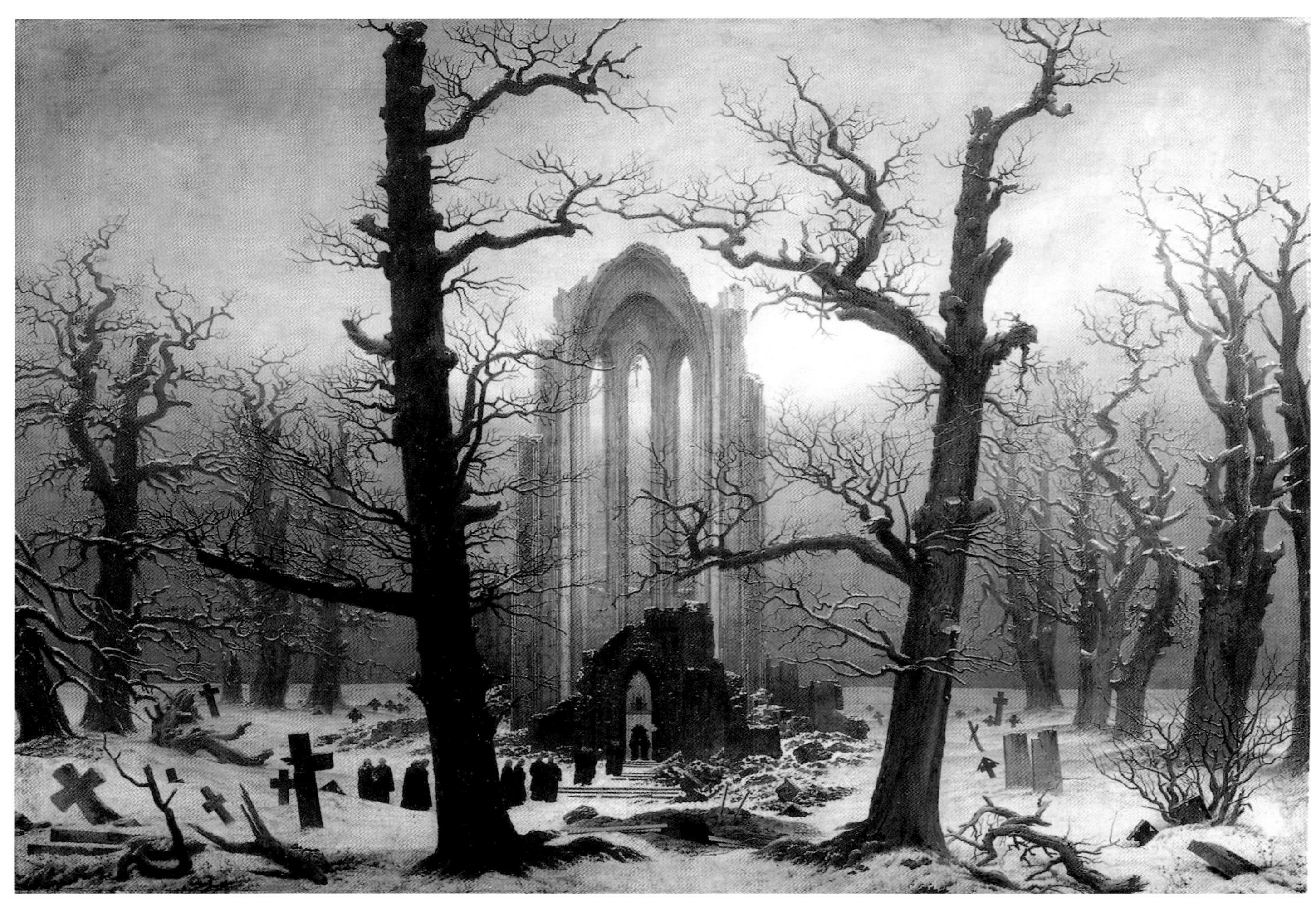

31. *Monastery Graveyard in Snow*,
1817–19, oil on canvas,
121 x 170 cm (47⅝ x 66⅞ in.).
Formerly Nationalgalerie, Berlin.

32. *The Abbey in the Oak Wood*, detail,
c. 1809, oil on canvas,
110.4 x 171 cm (43⅝ x 67⅜ in.).
Nationalgalerie, Berlin.

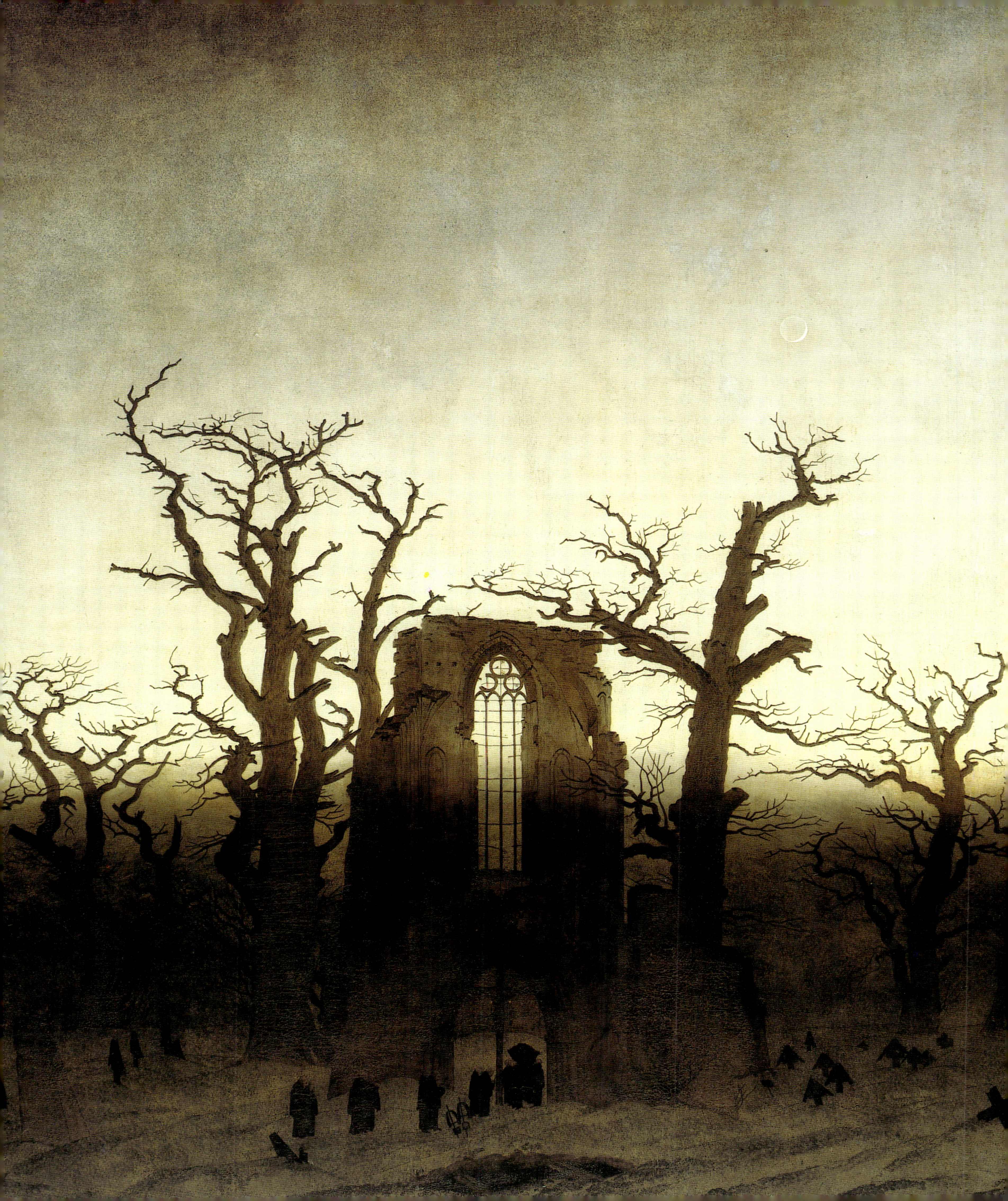

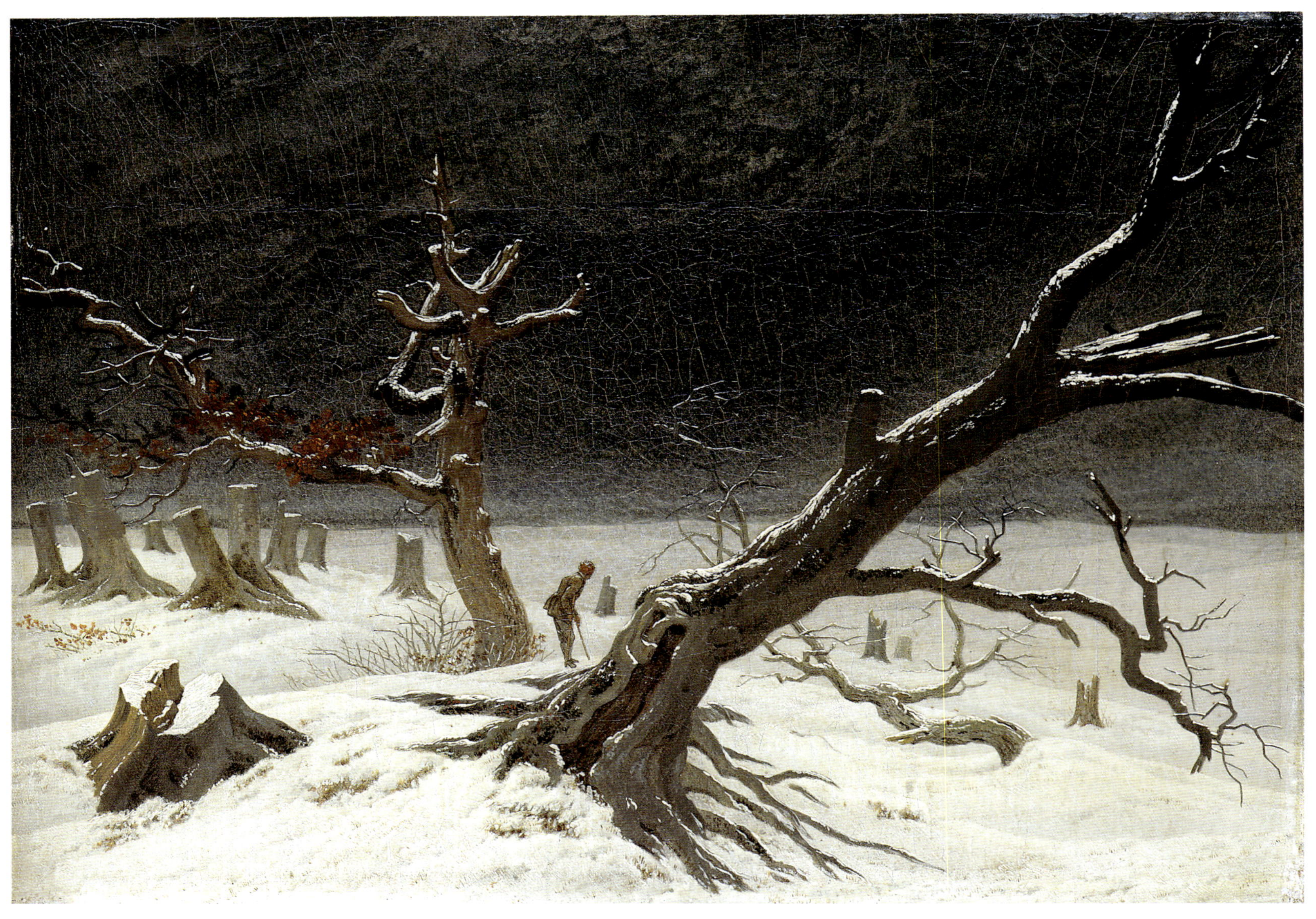

33. *Winter Landscape*,
1811, oil on canvas,
33 x 46 cm (13 x 18⅛ in.).
Staatliches Museum, Schwerin.

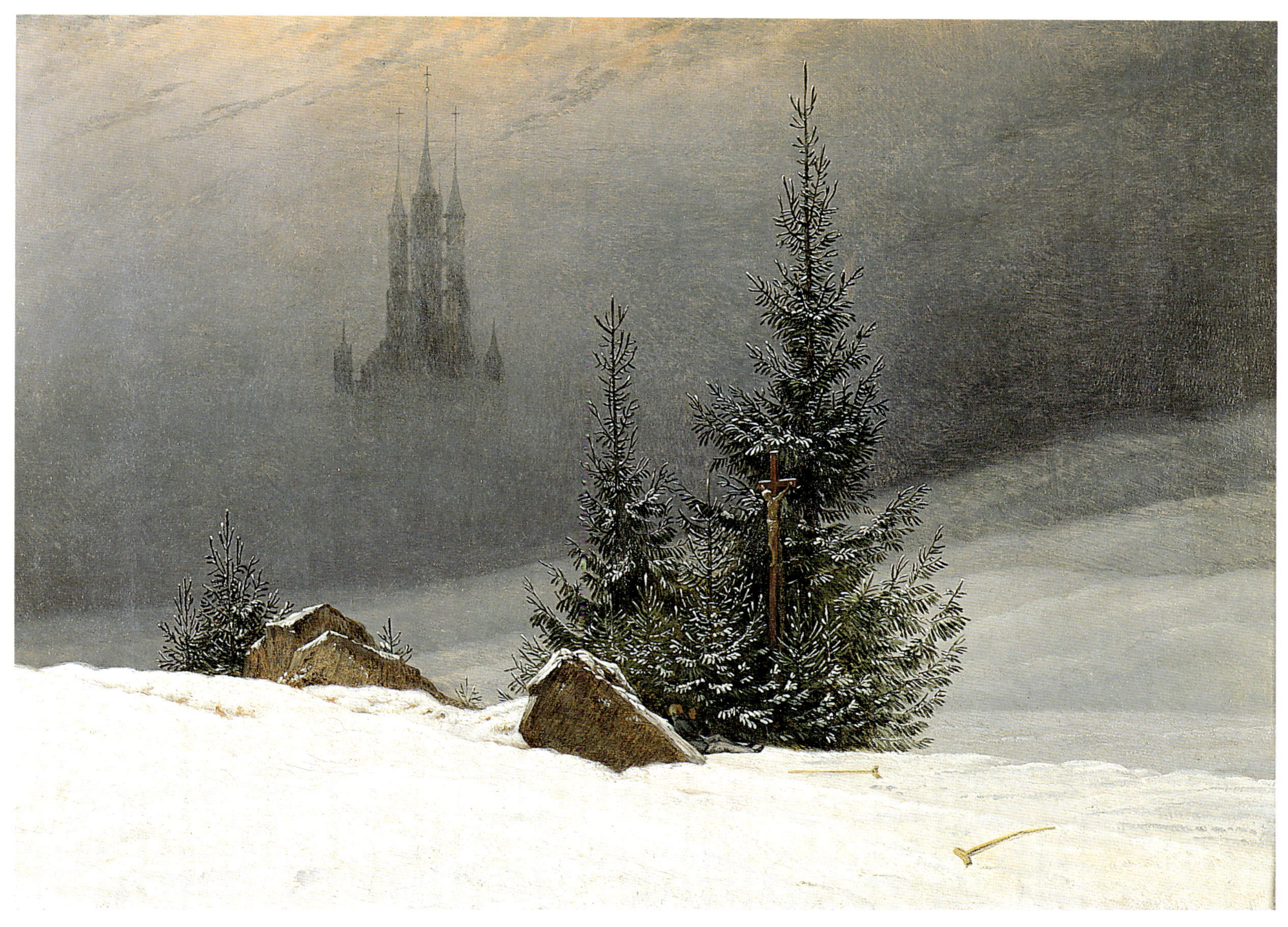

34. *Winter Landscape with Church*,
1811, oil on canvas,
33 x 45 cm (13 x 17⅝ in.).
Museum für Kunst und Kulturgeschichte, Dortmund.

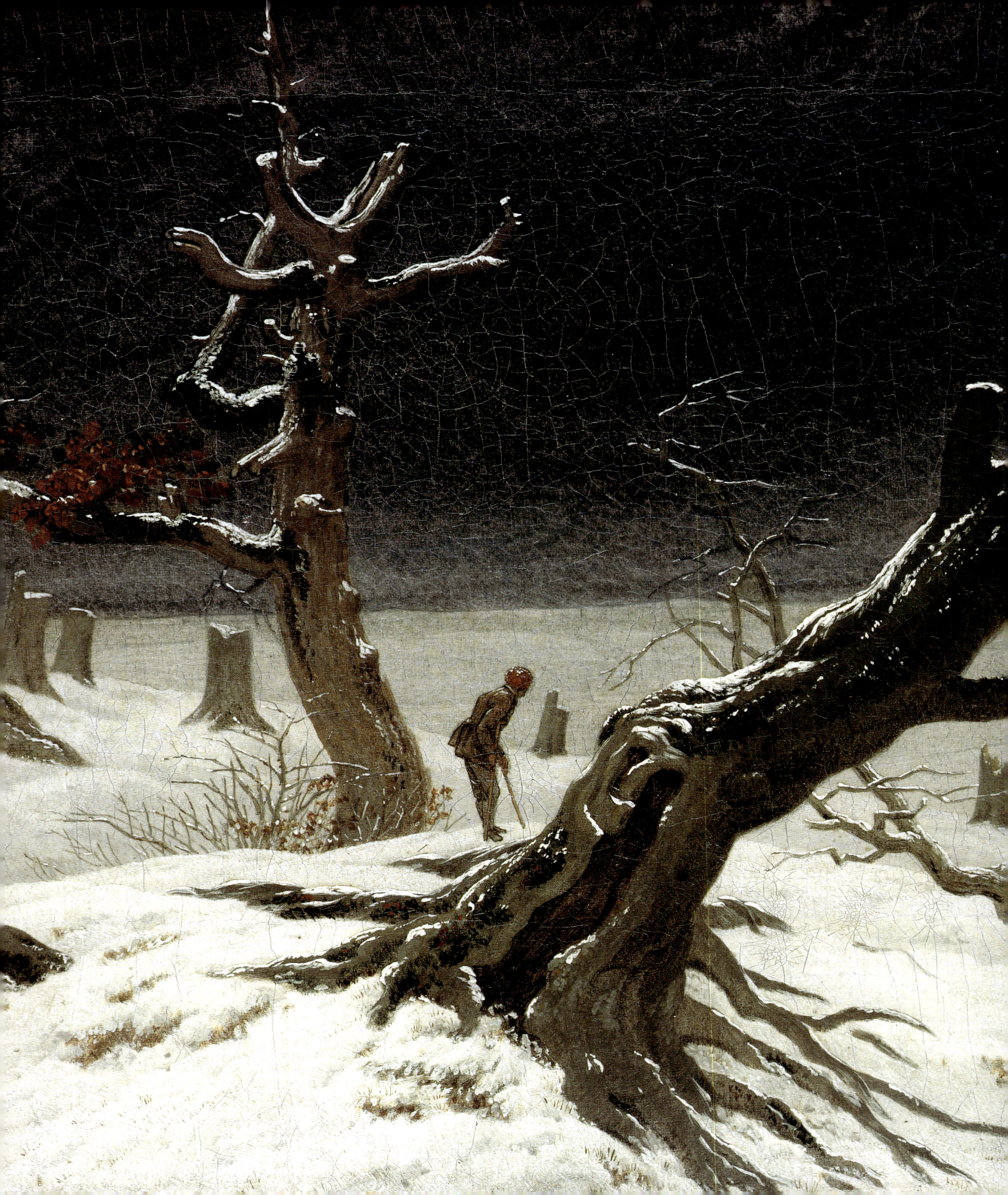

wedge, paraphrasing the curve of the man's body. He appears to have lost not just his way but also every drop of energy. There is no formal mediation between this and the other picture (ill. 34), an almost identical version of which came to the National Gallery in London, where it is claimed to be the original. The change of scene is as complete as a cinematic jump-cut: another landscape, another sky. Only the snow is common to both pictures. Two abandoned crutches set us searching for a human being. We discover him sitting propped against a rock, praying to a crucifix which stands discreetly in a clump of firs. A fantasy church, Gothic and many-spired, rises in the background, balancing the slender verticals of the trees. The praying man does not look at it and does not appear to need it – the rock of faith, the crucifix and the trees are shelter enough. This sense of shelter stems from trust in the power of prayer and from the relinquishing of the church as a mediating institution – two characteristics of Protestant belief.

In the Düsseldorf *Cross in the Mountains* (ill. 36), Friedrich forces the two planes – crucifix and church – together to form a compound hieratic symbol, but so strictly that the iconization of landscape is attained yet at the same time loses something of its tension and risk. The consonance of architecture, cross and nature is taken so far that a continuum is created between the two poles of the accessible and the remote sensory worlds. The carefully calculated symmetry produces a vertical axis which rises seamlessly from the source of life and faith by way of the crucifix (exactly in the centre) to the architectural capriccio of the church façade. Otto Schmitt has demonstrated that this façade is an amalgam of the east front and the west tower of the Marienkirche in the Mecklenburg town of Neubrandenburg. In another painting of almost identical format, *The Cross in the Forest* (Stuttgart, ill. 37), the church is replaced by a bright cross of light in the sky. Even when the forest does not contain any sacred symbol, a religious connotation can be given by a triple structure (ill. 38), which evokes Christ's crucifixion with the two thieves, as well as the Holy Trinity.

Friedrich made no further attempts to force symbols of this world and the world beyond to coincide exactly and so do away with the separation of the planes. His *Vision of the Christian Church* (ill. 41), in which the vision appears to two ecstatic druids, uses a structural pattern with which we are already familiar. The two druids form the base of a funnel which widens in the clouds behind them to frame a church façade. The diaphanous architecture is reminiscent of the palm branches and eye of God from the frame of *The Tetschen Altar*. Meissen Cathedral and the Marienkirche in Neubrandenburg are thought to be the architectural models. The result is an eclectic piece of drawing-board Gothic, comparable to the neo-Gothic spires which Augustus Welby Pugin later used to illustrate his *Apology for the Revival of Christian Architecture* (London, 1843). The Mormon Temple in Salt Lake City, begun in 1853, may also be influenced by Friedrich's *Vision* or by his *Cathedral* (ill. 42). Within its pointed arch frame, the latter picture is wholeheartedly orchestrated as a vision, and the angels hovering around the crucifix leave no doubt as to its intended function as a focus for prayer. The intention significantly narrows the viewer's contribution. He no longer stands in a pictorial space, prayerfully meditating or asking questions to aid his search. Once the painter's partner to some extent, his role is now restricted to a single, affirmative act in front of the painting: worship.

Because they have only one possible interpretation, Friedrich's 'miraculous images' fail to convince. His art is not credible when he deprives it of the realities of this world and uses traditional symbols to depict a unison, a complete concord. This is why his *Allegory of Profane Music* (ill. 39) seems preferable to

35. *Winter Landscape*, detail,
1811, oil on canvas,
33 x 46 cm (13 x 18¼ in.).
Staatliches Museum, Schwerin.

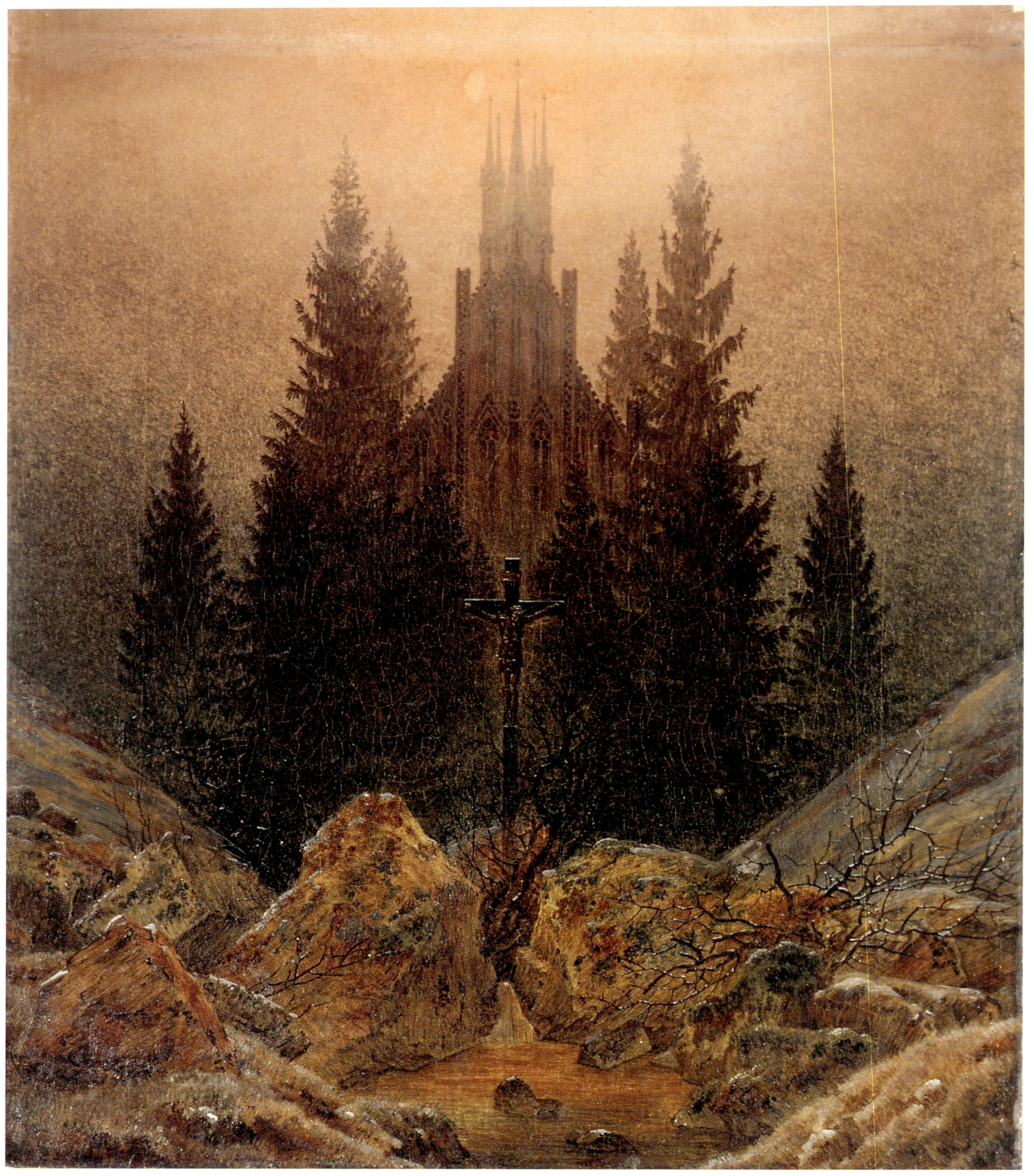

36. *The Cross in the Mountains*,
1811–12, oil on canvas,
44.5 × 37.4 cm (17½ × 14¾ in.).
Kunstmuseum, Düsseldorf.

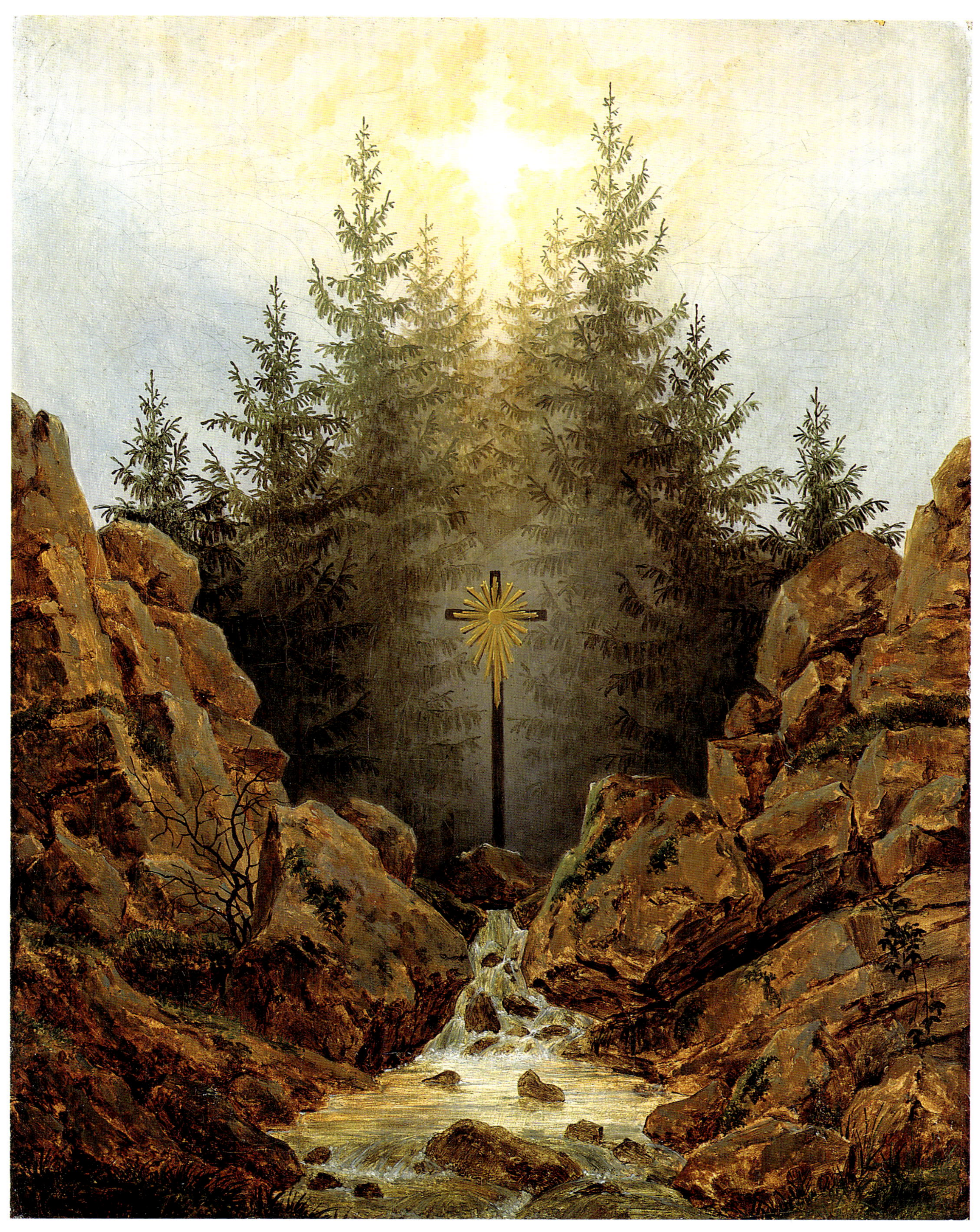

37. ***The Cross in the Forest*,**
c. 1820, oil on canvas,
42 x 32 cm (16½ x 12⅝ in.).
Staatsgalerie, Stuttgart.

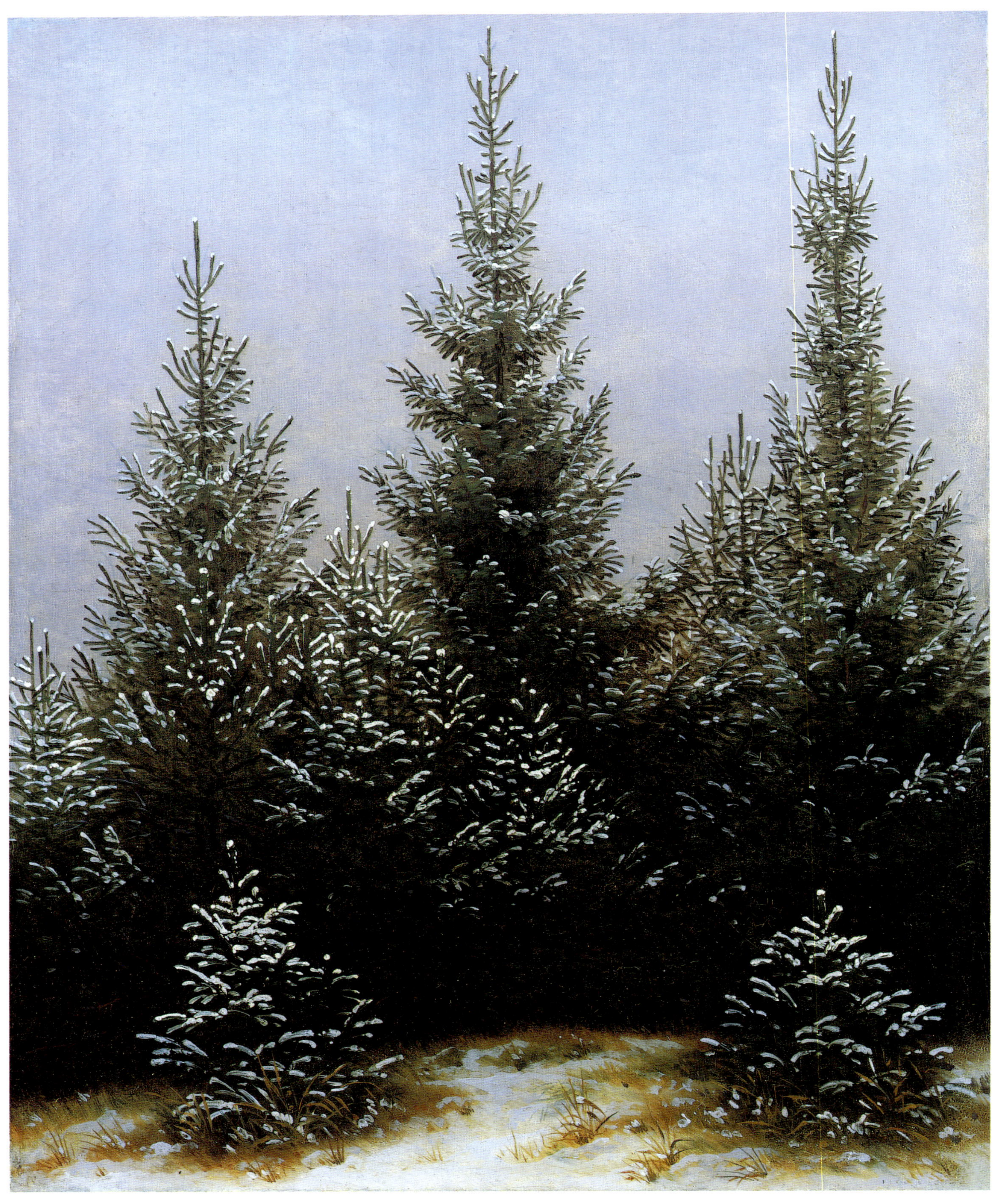

38. *Pine Thicket*,
1828, oil on canvas,
30 × 24 cm (11¾ × 9½ in.).
Neue Pinakothek, Munich.

The Musician's Dream (ill. 40). His subjective failure confirms the objective verdict pronounced on the genre of the 'miraculous image' by Novalis's old man: that its time is past.

While the monk was a figure in which Friedrich could portray himself outside the social community governed by the church on earth, the painter's utopian visions of the Church enabled him to find his way back into an ideal, if abstract community. This change of direction was connected with the historical time in which he lived, and more precisely with the wind of resacralization that began to blow after the wars of liberation from Napoleonic dominance, assisting the restoration of old regimes and institutions. One specific example was the Marienkirche in Stralsund, which the Congress of Vienna handed to Prussia. The church had been used to store hay during the French occupation and its interior needed complete renovation, so the town council commissioned some designs from Friedrich and his brother Christian. The surviving, painstaking drawings (ills 43 and 44) show how seriously the painter approached the work. He explained his intentions to the council in a letter which also sheds light on his democratic attitude towards the church as an institution.

'A building meant to honour God must, in my opinion, be ordered as simply as possible. Those entering must be able to take in everything in a single glance, but this one glance must, wherever possible, lift up the heart and the mind and incline them to humble themselves before Him who sees man's innermost self. He at least who enters God's house with a pure heart must not have his frame of mind disturbed by unharmonious design and formless excesses of decoration. In a building where people gather to humble themselves before God, who is no respecter of individuals, surely all distinctions of rank should

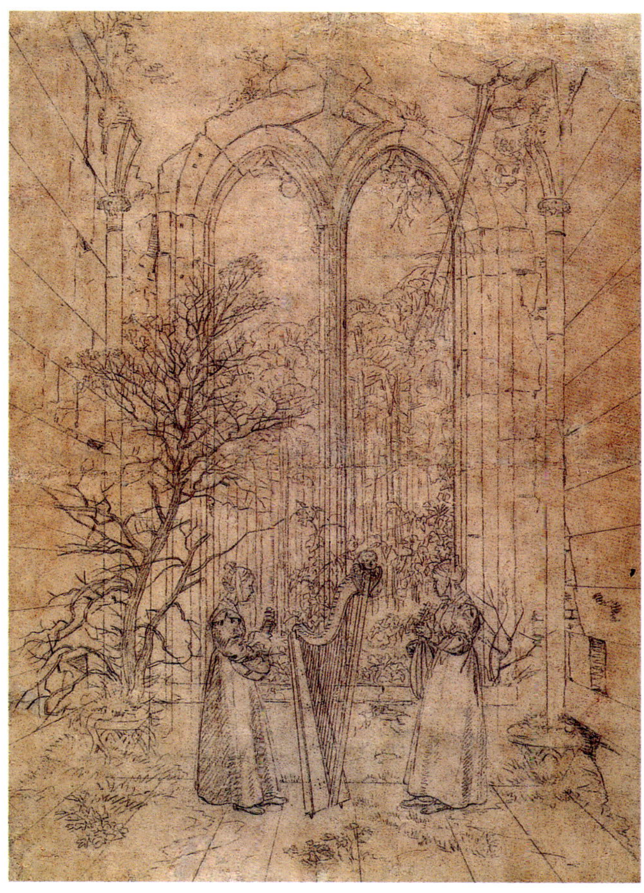

39. *Allegory of Profane Music,*
black chalk,
73.5 x 51.8 cm (29 x 20⅜ in.).
Musée du Louvre, Paris.

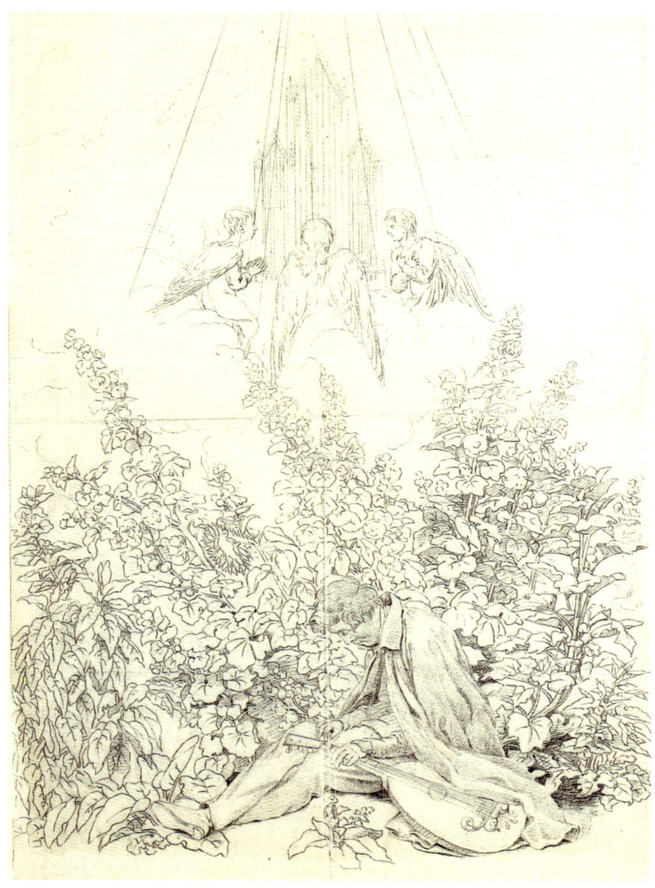

40. *The Musician's Dream,*
c. 1826–27, sepia,
72 x 51 cm (28⅜ x 20⅛ in.).
Hamburger Kunsthalle, Hamburg.

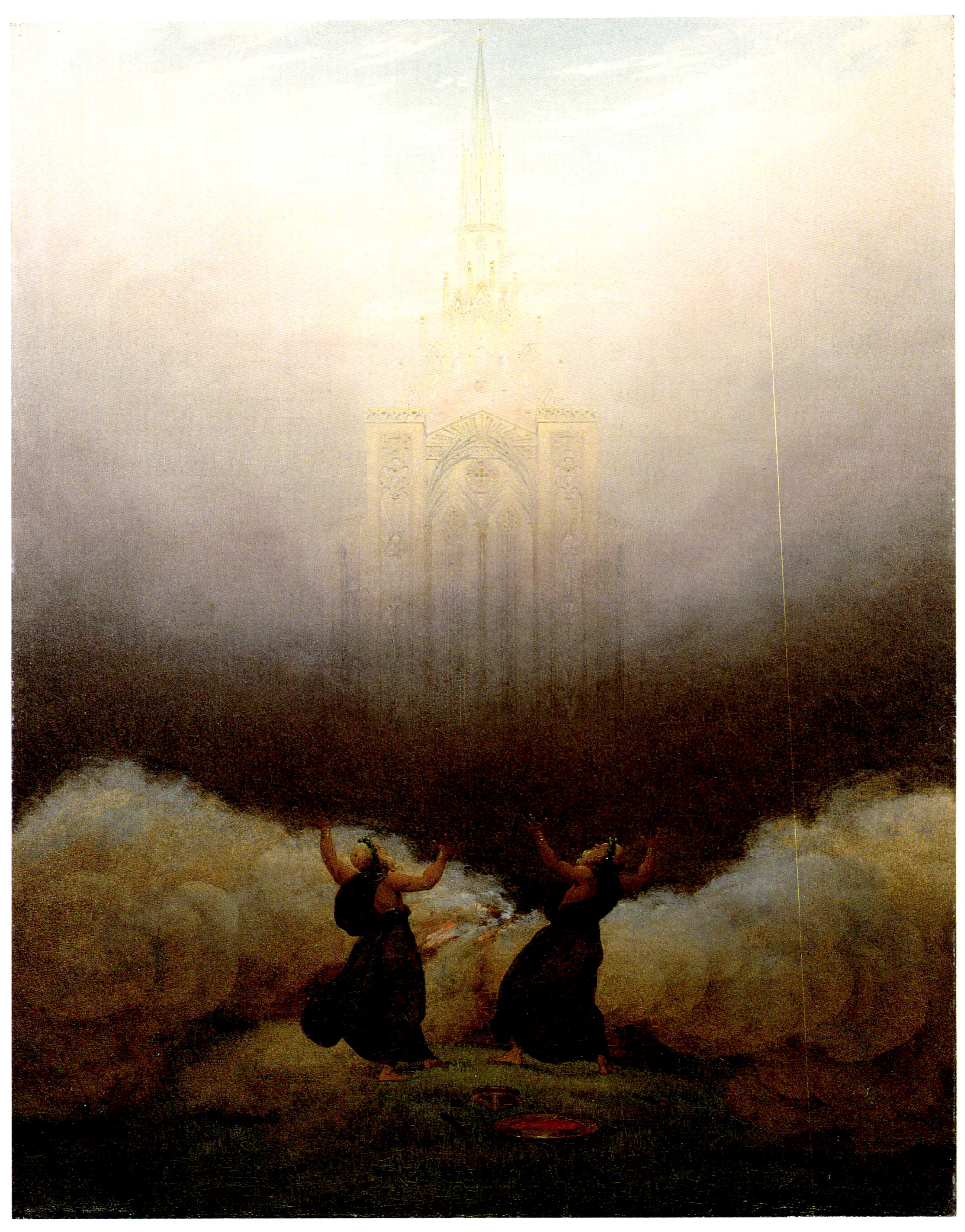

41. *Vision of the Christian Church*, 1813–14, oil on canvas, 66.5 × 51.5 cm (26¼ × 20¼ in.). Georg Schäfer Collection.

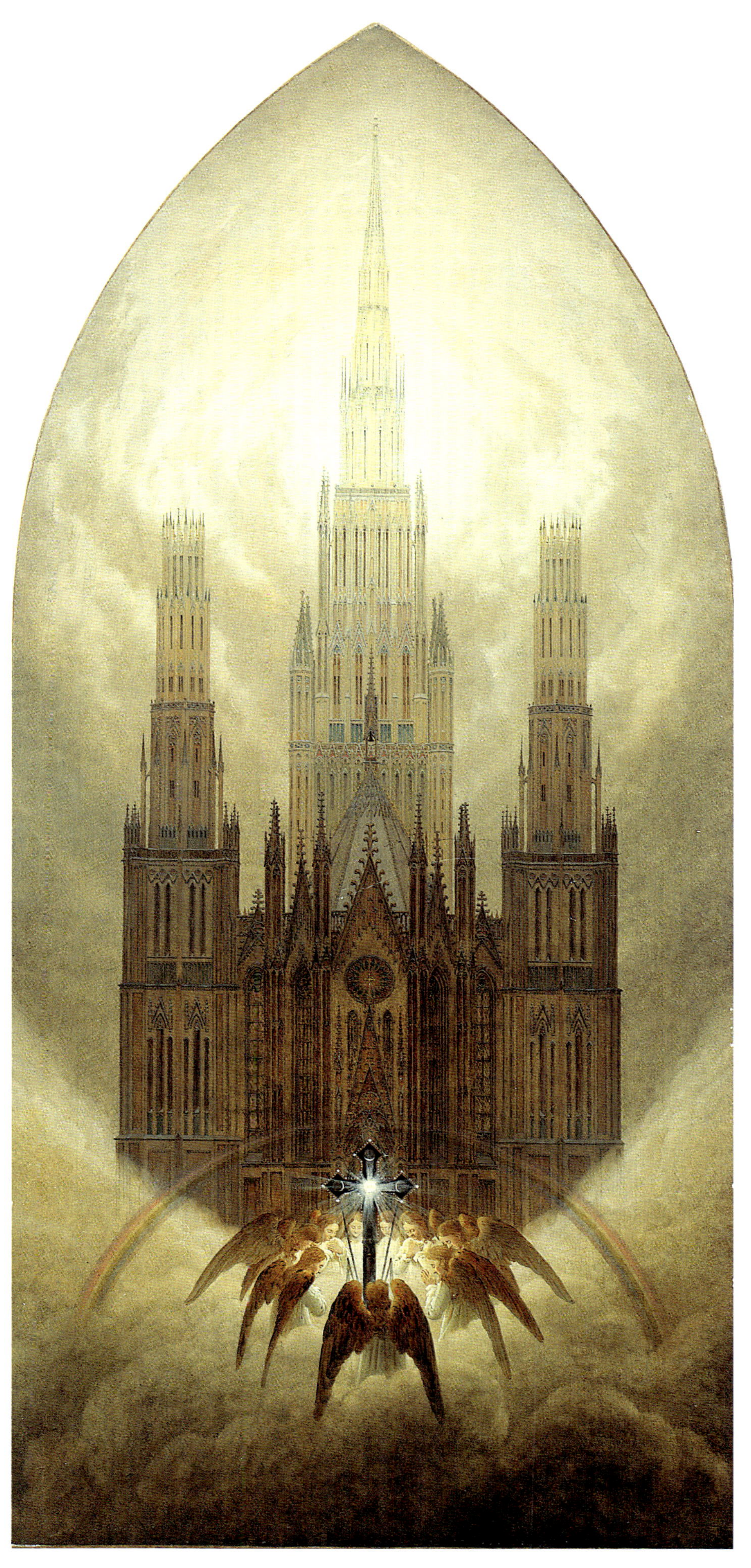

42. *The Cathedral*,
c. 1818, oil on canvas,
152.5 × 70.5 cm (60 × 27¾ in.).
Georg Schäfer Collection.

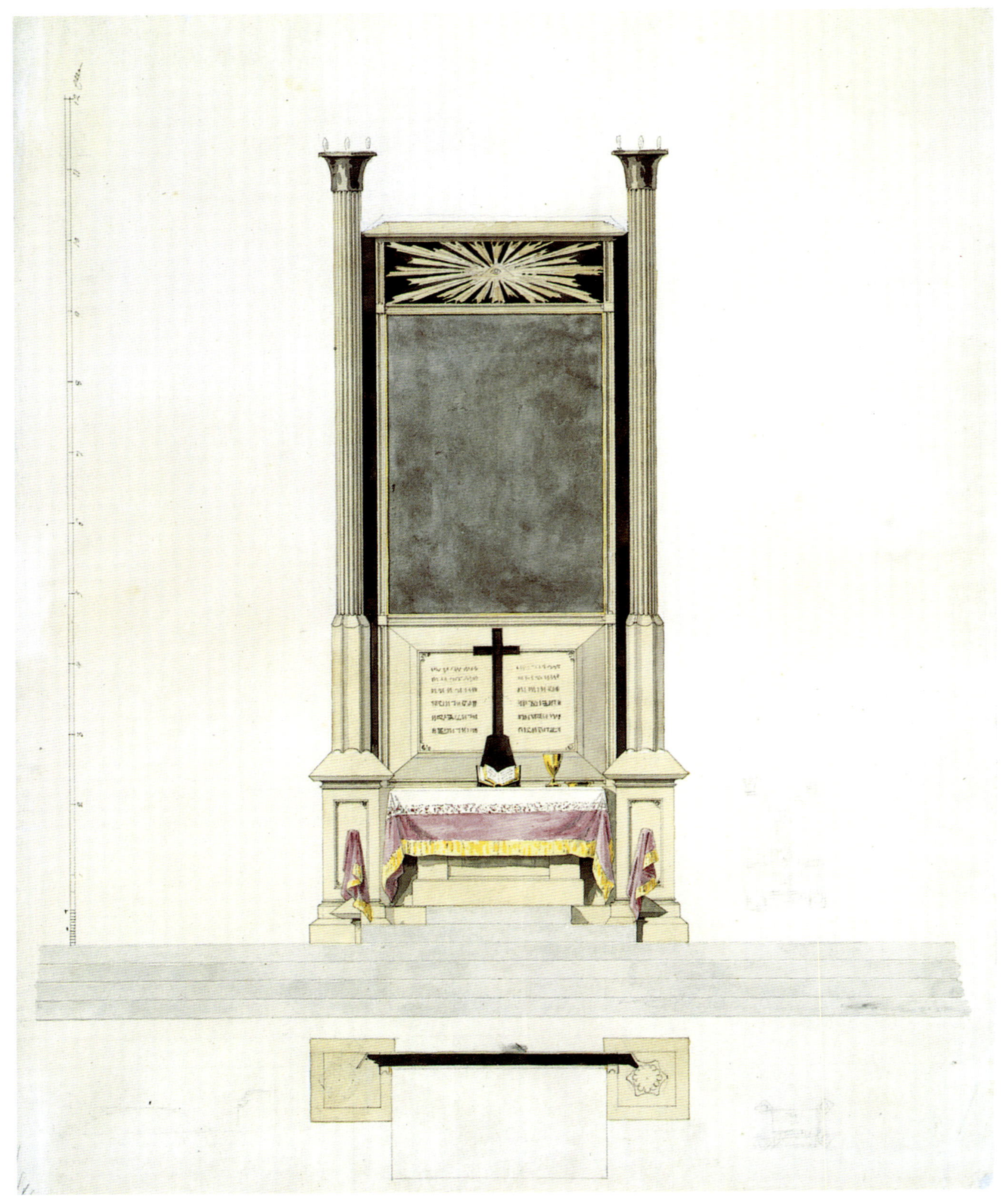

43. Altar design,
1817, pencil, ink and watercolour, 54.8 × 43.7 cm (21½ × 17¼ in.).
Germanisches Nationalmuseum, Nuremberg.

44. Design for the Marienkirche, Stralsund,
1817, pencil, ink and watercolour, 56.6 × 43.7 cm (22¼ × 17¼ in.).
Germanisches Nationalmuseum, Nuremberg.

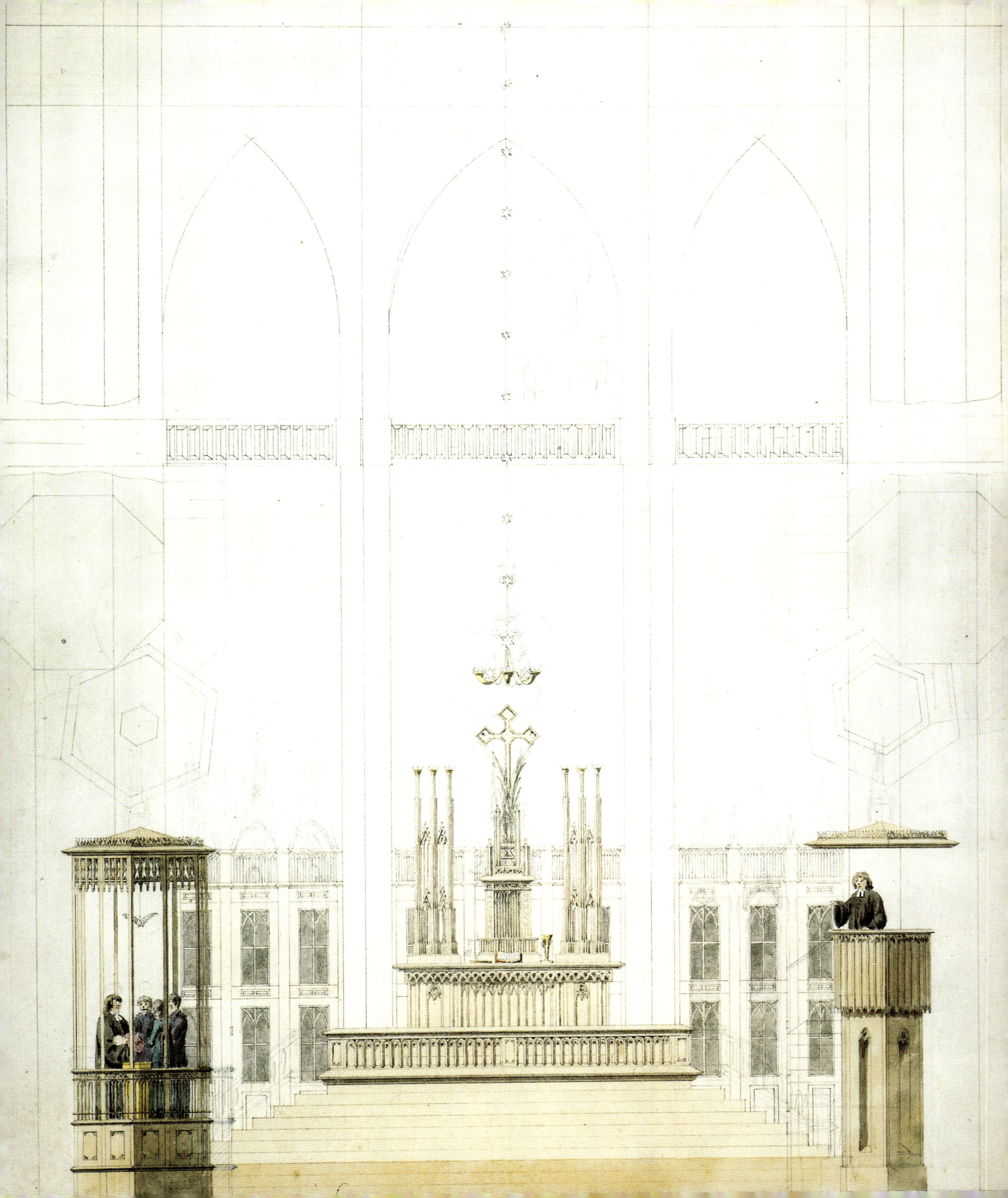

cease; the rich man should feel here, if nowhere else, that he is no greater than the poor man, and the poor man should receive visible consolation that we are all equal in the sight of God.'

Friedrich speaks of the church as he might of a painting: both should lift up the heart and the mind. The 'excesses' that he would like to banish from the church correspond to the 'restrictive forms' and 'clangour' of virtuoso painters that he wished to banish from painting. His designs for Stralsund are in keeping with the views expressed in the letter. Their slender, purist neo-Gothicism shows hints of the Empire style, though the stylization cannot be ascribed to any precise historical model. *The Cathedral* (ill. 42) was probably painted in connection with the Stralsund project and the Dresden *Cross in front of a Rainbow in the Mountains* (ill. 45) may also have been intended for it. However, probably due to lack of money, Friedrich's designs were never realized.

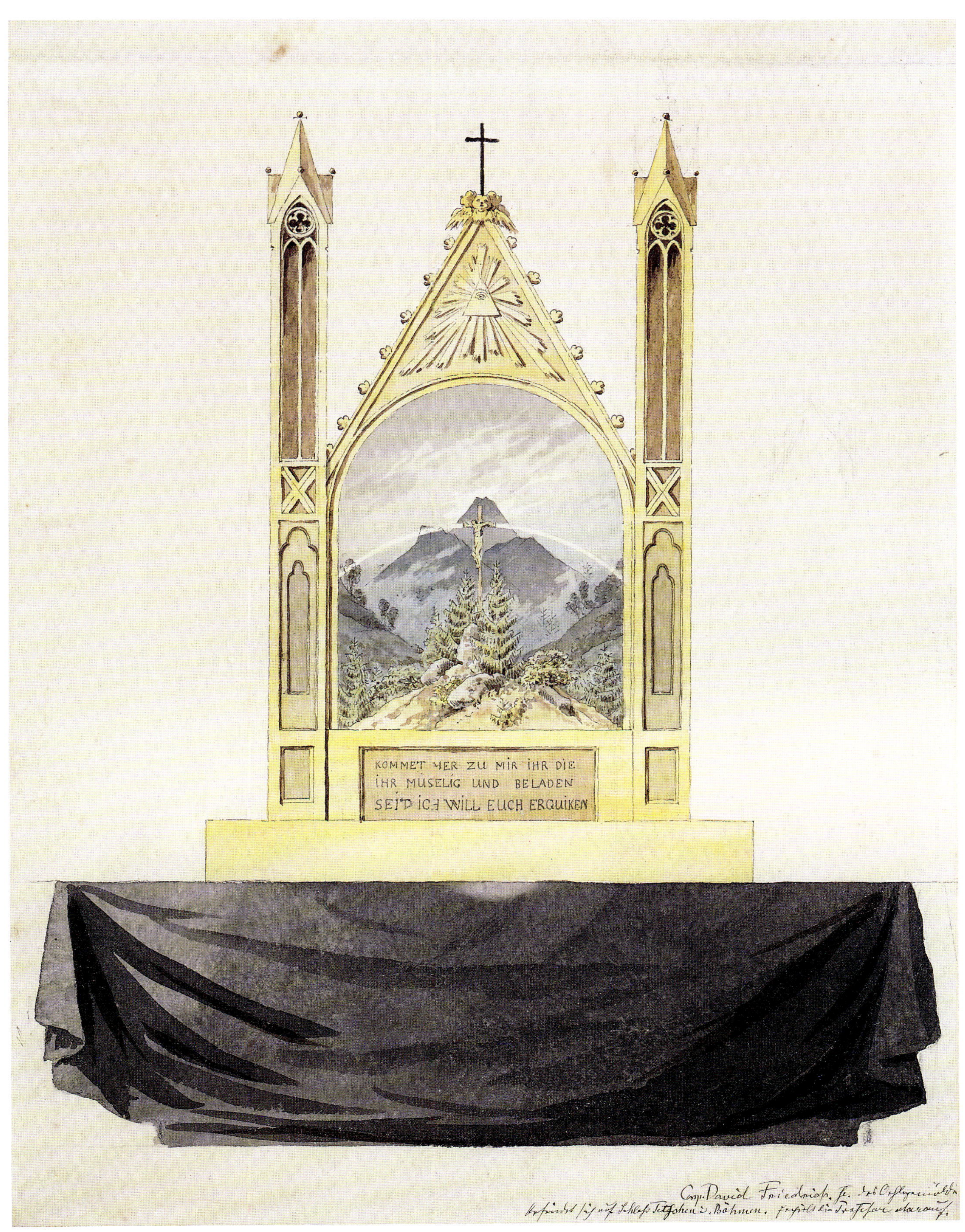

45. *The Cross in front of a Rainbow in the Mountains*,
c. 1817, ink and watercolour,
27.2 × 20.8 cm (10⅝ × 8 in.).
Kupferstichkabinett, Dresden.

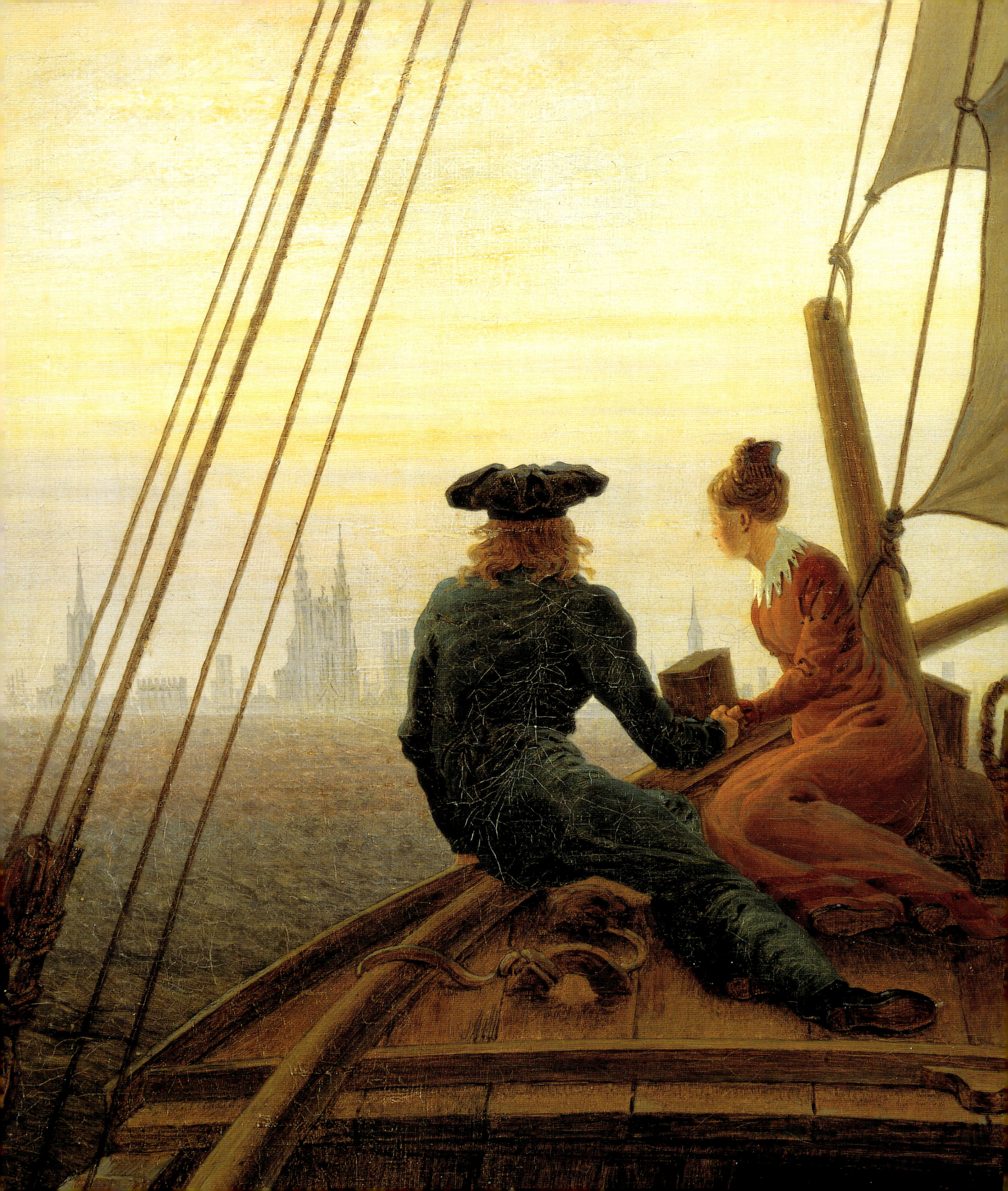

III

PUBLIC LIFE AND PRIVATE LIFE

Resacralization was just part of the comprehensive process of renewal that seemed imminent after the end of Napoleonic rule. Reformers everywhere launched themselves at the body politic, but their zeal was short-lived. The patriotic ideal also made its mark on Friedrich's work; at first with hope, then with disappointment. His patriotism followed the same straight line as his religious convictions; just as his faith knew no servility, so he sided with the people in politics. To him, Prussia's defeats in 1806 and their consequences were a national humiliation. After the Peace of Tilsit (July 1807), the defeated were forced into collaboration; Prussia had to supply Napoleon with 20,000 soldiers for the Russian campaign. The King of Saxony was one of the most compliant allies of Napoleon, and it was in Dresden that the multinational Grande Armée assembled before setting off eastwards on 29 May 1812. It re-entered the city exactly one year later, on 12 May 1813, beaten and driven back to the west by the Russians. After the liberation of Dresden, Friedrich composed a prayer of thanksgiving, praising God's wrath but not overlooking the misery endured by the besieged:

'Tormented by hunger, without shelter or aid,
Without pity or mercy,
They exhale life's last breath.'

At the end he voiced the longing for peace of those who had suffered most under the vicissitudes of the war years:

'So that the worker may rejoice in his labour and enjoy the fullness of Thy blessing in peace,
Give rain and sunshine in its season, that everything may blossom and bring forth fruit.
And no longer allow savage hordes to lay waste our fields and meadows.'

And last of all Friedrich expressed a wish as bluntly as any man in the street:

'O Lord, who hast freed us from the yoke of the French, save us also from the Russians.'

No firebrand himself, Friedrich did number some fanatical patriots among his friends. One was the poet and publicist Ernst Moritz Arndt (1769–1860), another was Friedrich Ludwig Jahn (1778–1852), known as 'the father of gymnastics' for his role as founder of the gymnastics associations that began to spring up in Germany at that time. Friedrich was also close to Heinrich von Kleist (1777–1811) and Theodor Körner (1791–1813). These patriots pinned their hopes on the free and independent Germany promised to the people by the King of Prussia and the Tsar of Russia in the Declaration of Kalisch (25 March 1813). When Napoleon was finally overthrown, and the time came for deeds to follow words,

46. ***On the Sailing Boat*, detail,**
1818–19, oil on canvas,
71 x 56 cm (28 x 22 in.).
Hermitage Museum, St Petersburg.

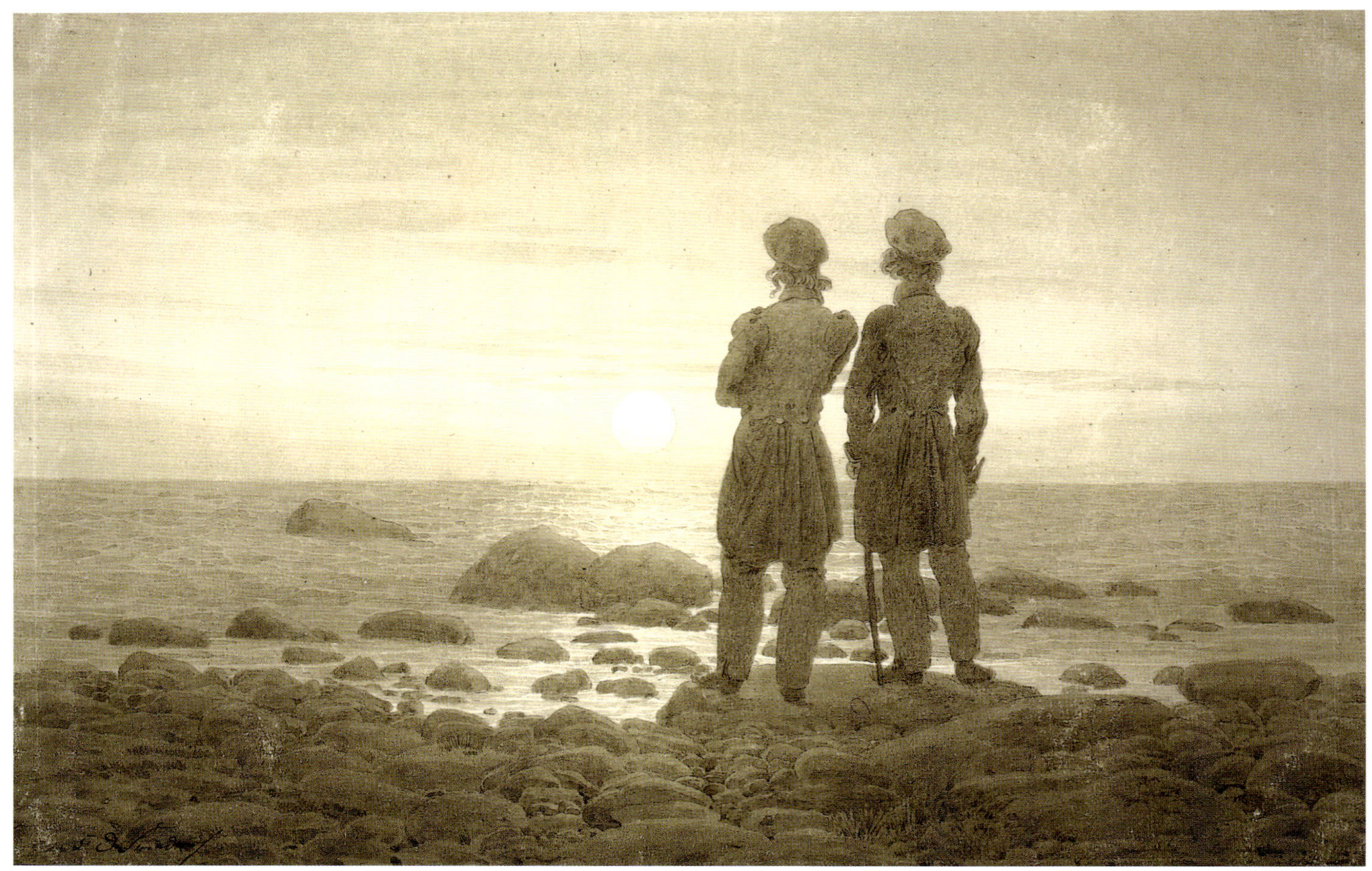

47. *Two Men at Moonrise*,
1835–37, pencil and sepia,
24.5 x 34.5 cm (9¾ x 13½ in.).
Hermitage Museum, St Petersburg.

nothing more was heard of that promise. The Congress of Vienna took a different approach to the creation of a new European order, and made it an instrument for reconciling interests. States, dynasties and territorial claims were on the agenda, but nations were not. One of the results was the German League, a phantom state consisting of thirty-eight sovereign members: thirty-four German states and four Free Cities (Frankfurt, Bremen, Hamburg and Lübeck). Three non-German monarchs belonged to the League: the English as King of Hanover, the Danish as Duke of Holstein and the Dutch as Grand Duke of Luxemburg. In spite of this conglomeration of interests, the preamble spoke pompously of Germany and her security and independence, which would be established in concord with the European balance of power. A contemporary satire, entitled *Trau keinem* (*Trust nobody*), depicted representatives of the powers eyeing each other suspiciously while they carved up the globe. When his brother Christian became embroiled in a minor legal wrangle in 1817, Friedrich remarked that he would not trust any authority for a second.

By then he already ranked among the disappointed, if not embittered. Even at the height of the post-liberation euphoria, he had no illusions, and foresaw the retreat into half measures which would follow the joyful acclamations. He wrote to Arndt (12 March 1814), in answer to the question of why there were no monuments to the 'great cause of the people', or to 'the high-hearted deeds of individual Germans': 'Nothing great of that kind will happen as long as we live in thrall to princes. Where the people have no voice, they are also not allowed to respect or have any sense of themselves as a people.' He himself had chosen the modest compromise of painting a picture that would show a monument to 'noble Scharnhorst' in the 'public square of an imaginary town', and he asked Arndt to come up with an inscription for it. Gerhard David von Scharnhorst, one of the reformist generals in the Prussian army, had been killed in 1813. Friedrich's memorial picture does not survive.

The centre of resistance to restoration of the old institutions was in the *Burschenschaften*, the associations of university students. There, 'medieval dreams of emperor and empire crossed with a Jacobin resentment which threatened perfidious princes and their lieutenants with the revenger's dagger' (Franz Mehring). These words refer to the actions of a theology student, Karl Ludwig Sand, which gave the reactionary forces an excuse to put public life in the member states of the German League under the vigilance of a police state. On 23 March 1819 Sand stabbed to death the playwright and diplomat August von Kotzebue, who had spent decades in the service of Russia and kept Alexander I informed about conditions in Germany. Kotzebue also edited a weekly newspaper, in which he poured scorn on the liberal, intellectual camp. The dominant powers in the League, suspicious at the best of times, took fright at the assassination, and under the pretext that there was a widespread conspiracy to be crushed, they began a wave of house-to-house searches and arrests among intellectuals and in university circles. Jahn was arrested in July 1819, and charged with having 'promoted demagogic politics on the gymnastics ground'. Schleiermacher was put under surveillance in Berlin. Secret information was compiled against Arndt. Joseph Görres (1774–1848), the pugnacious Catholic publicist, escaped arrest only by fleeing to Switzerland by way of Strasbourg.

The immediate hunt for conspirators was soon given a legal foundation. After a meeting called by the Austrian chancellor Metternich, Austria and Prussia issued the Karlsbad Decrees, named after the spa town where the meeting took place (now Karlovy Vary in the Czech Republic); these were intended to put a stop to all future 'demagogic activities'. A new university law regulated disciplinary and surveillance measures; a new press law did away with the 'pernicious principle of press freedom'. Censorship before publication was reintroduced for all printed matter.

'Demagogic activities' obviously became a catchphrase. When Peter von Cornelius, the celebrated history painter and one of the Nazarenes, visited Friedrich in his Dresden studio in 1820, the latter showed him his painting *Two Men Contemplating the Moon* (ill. 95) with the dry but pregnant comment: 'They're engaging in demagogic activities.' Friedrich was seeing his picture through the censor's eyes, and making fun of the guardians of public order to whom everything was suspicious. Such minds would naturally attribute subversive opinions to these two characters, since dark cloaks and velvet berets were distinguishing features of the 'German costume' recommended to patriots by Arndt in 1814 and later condemned as provocative by Metternich and his spies. Men wearing German costume are common in Friedrich's paintings (ills 47, 48 and 49). They carry themselves calmly and thoughtfully – reason enough for some to suspect a hypocritical disguise, and for others to recognize a political affiliation.

How did Friedrich go about turning his patriotism into art? What became of that passionate love of his country when he picked up his brush? Unlike religious subjects, patriotic ones did not inspire him to paint glorificatory 'miraculous images'. He confined himself to what was appropriate to his artistic bent, and depicted grief, pensiveness and solitude in the context of the wars of liberation. The outcome can be seen in landscapes invested with patriotic significance. It says much for his shrewd self-assessment that he avoided stridency, and refrained from emphasis when he felt it was excessive. For example, in 1814 he began a *Stormy Landscape at Dusk with Ravens* but then decided against the extreme nature of the material and abandoned it. 'The design of this picture was quite different: scattered about on the bleak stretch of sand were posts, with boards tied to them, buffeted by the wind, all inscribed "Traitor to his Country". In the very centre a long post was driven into a big hole; on the post was a wheel, on the wheel a man, and tied to his hands was a board inscribed "Traitor to his Country". I had several brutes in mind, but I began to find the picture too disturbing, I wasn't capable of executing it.' Goya could have painted an indictment of that kind, but Friedrich could not.

The three paintings in which Friedrich tackled the subjects of occupation and liberation belong to the genre of commemorative pictures. The scene depicted in *Tombs of Ancient Heroes* (ill. 51) is anything but a neat cemetery. The site seems to have been randomly chosen amidst the wilds of nature. Friedrich wanted to portray a place that was remote and not easily accessible, but where anyone prepared to make the necessary effort to reach it would find much to meditate on. The viewer is also required to make an effort, since the picture's condensed structure constitutes a puzzle, whose content is only revealed to an eye which scans it slowly. Once again, an extreme spatial barrier underlines the sense that there is no escape from this place, which fills the whole picture. The space has become a wall, as it has in the watercolour of a quarry (ill. 50), whose blocks of stone resemble unfinished graves. But the new feature in *Tombs*, as has often been noted, is that the wall of rock does not include any opening into the sky beyond. All that remains is a kind of residual space, the cave in the middle of the picture. Its darkness offers the ultimate seclusion in this secluded place. Anyone who risks approaching its tempting 'interior', as the two French chasseurs do, is not exactly walking into an ambush, but is entering a hiding place that is also a dungeon. The finality of the place is like a magic spell weighing down on both the Germans and the

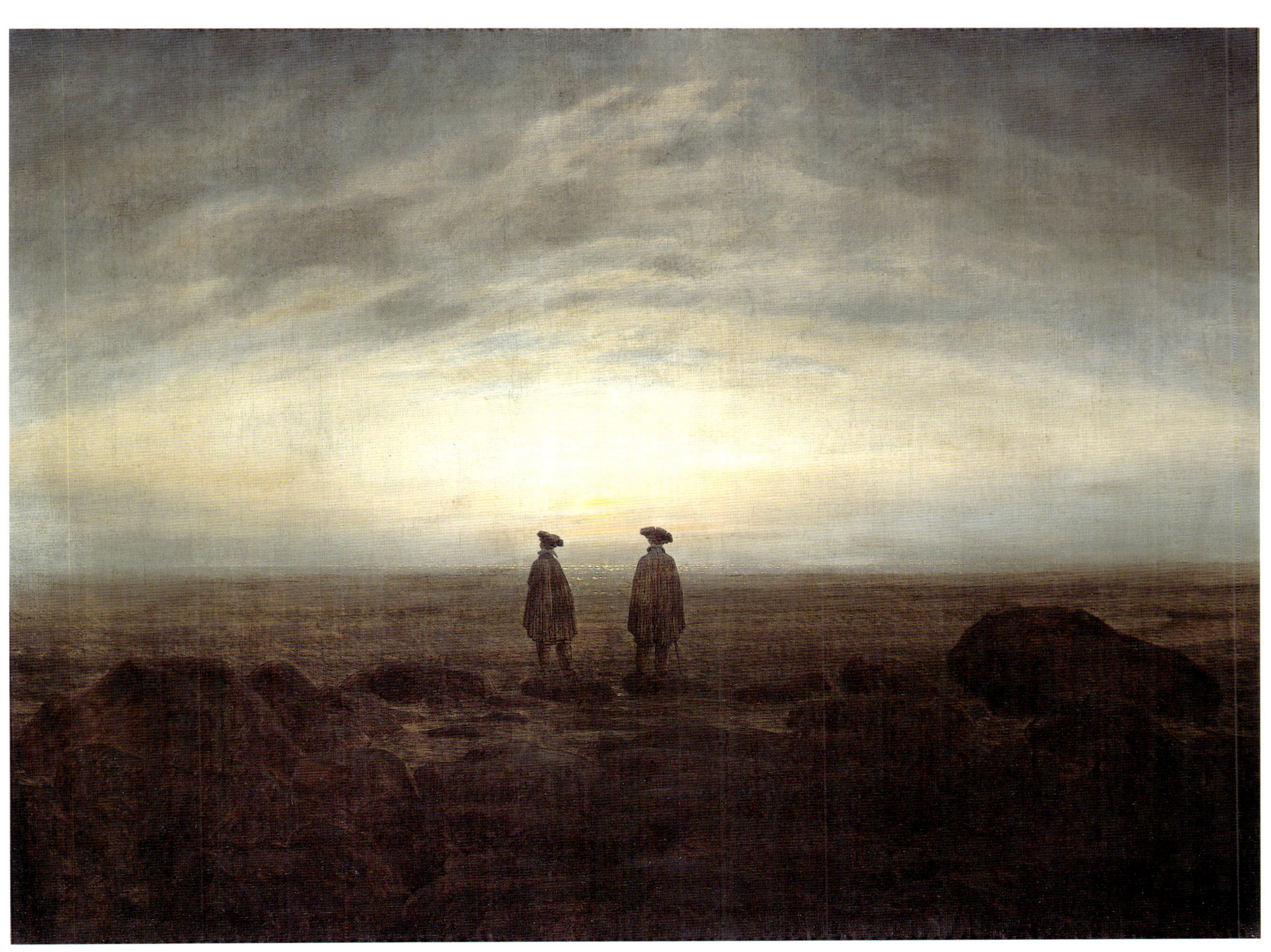

48. *Two Men by the Sea at Moonrise*,
1817, oil on canvas,
51 x 66 cm (20⅛ x 26 in.).
Nationalgalerie, Berlin.

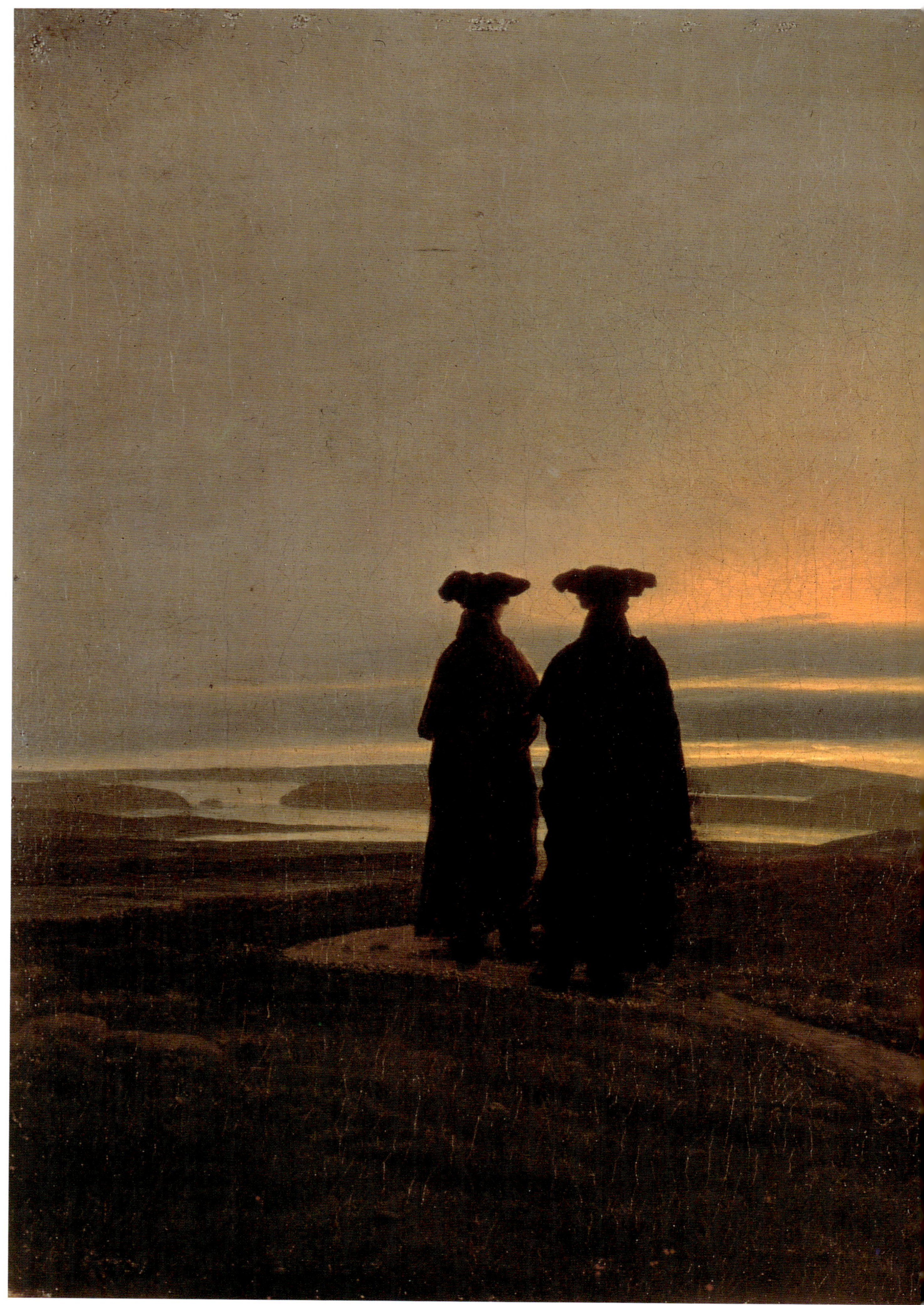

49. *Evening Landscape with Two Men*,
1830–35, oil on canvas,
25 × 31 cm (9⅞ × 12¼ in.).
Hermitage Museum, St Petersburg.

French: on both the fallen warriors in their coffins and the two living dead at the cave entrance, who gaze at a sarcophagus as if it was meant for them.

The inscriptions contain references to contemporary history which rework the theme of honouring past heroes. On the central panel of the sarcophagus on the left are the words 'FRIEDE DEINER GRUFT / RETTER IN NOT' ('Peace be on your grave / Saviour in time of need'). The three capital letters – 'G A F' – on the obelisks could be the initials of the hero apostrophized in the inscription 'EDLER JUINGLING, VATERLANDS-ERRETTER' ('Noble youth, Saviour of the Fatherland'; the spelling is a little erratic). The formal and material flawlessness of the obelisk sounds a contrary signal to those of the other monuments and the cave. The cave, perhaps, embodies the fate that the obelisk opposes. A psychoanalyst would have something to ponder in the contrast.

The most unequivocal political allusion is also the most carefully encoded. The question 'Where is Friedrich's patriotism in this scene?' was answered by Börsch-Supan when he discovered that a snake in the foreground has the colours of the French tricolour. Its weary, perhaps lifeless body is coiled round a broken gravestone inscribed 'ARMINIUS'. In a lost preliminary drawing the name on the stone is 'HERMAN' and various warlike attributes are also carved on it. Hermann (Arminius) was the chief of the German Cherusker tribe (Cherussi) who defeated a Roman army in the Teutoburg Forest in AD 9. In the sketch, the destruction of the grave is clearly meant to make a statement; the way it is drawn exaggerates the loss of form. Two complementary possibilities suggest themselves: has the grave been vandalized, and/or did the dead man leave it in order to stand by his fellow countrymen in the wars of liberation?

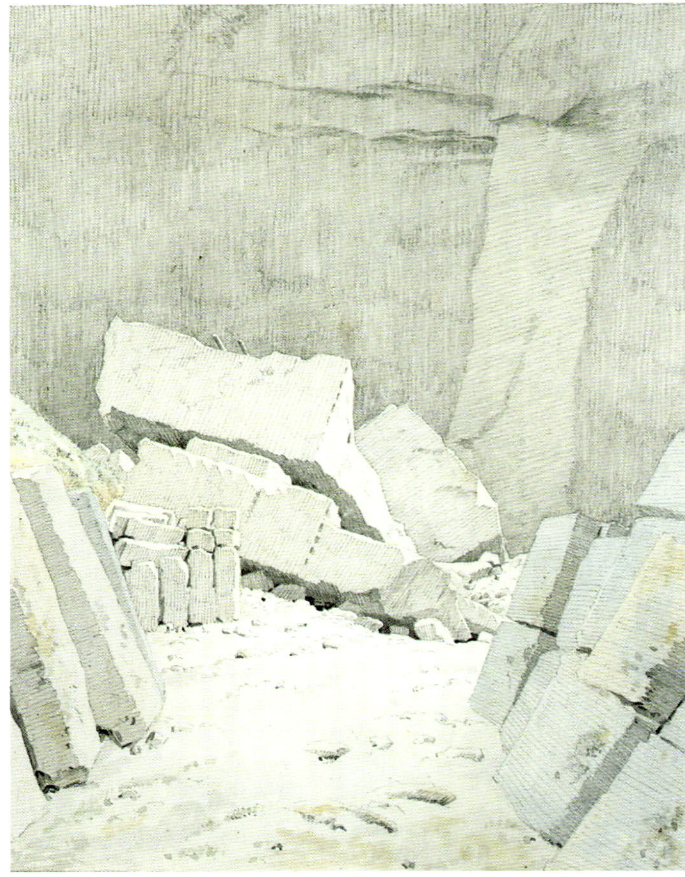

50. *Fallen Rocks*,
19 June 1813, watercolour over pencil,
21 × 17.4 cm (8¼ × 7 in.).
Kupferstichkabinett, Berlin.

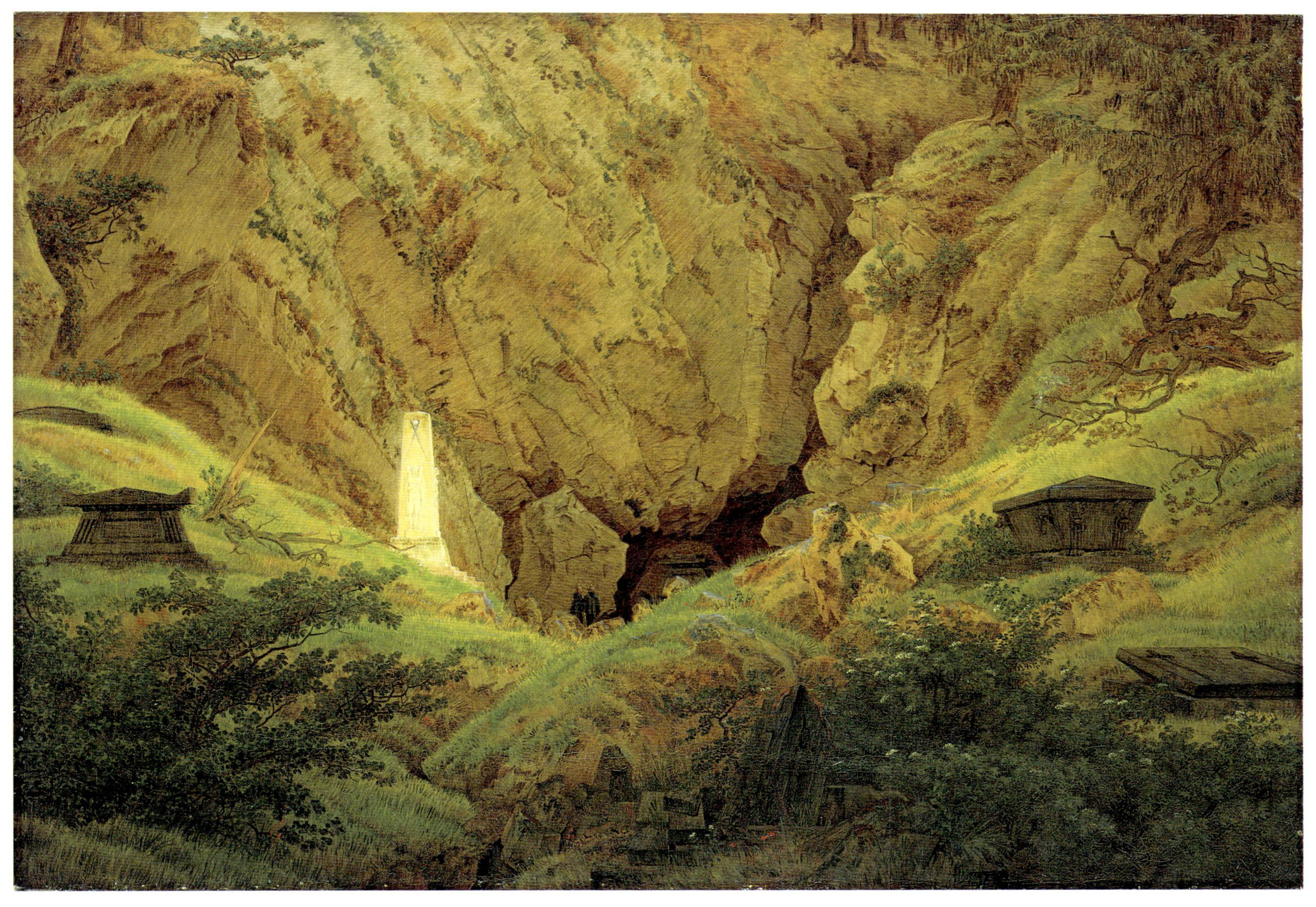

51. *Tombs of Ancient Heroes*,
1812, oil on canvas,
49.5 x 70.5 cm (19½ x 27¾ in.).
Hamburger Kunsthalle, Hamburg.

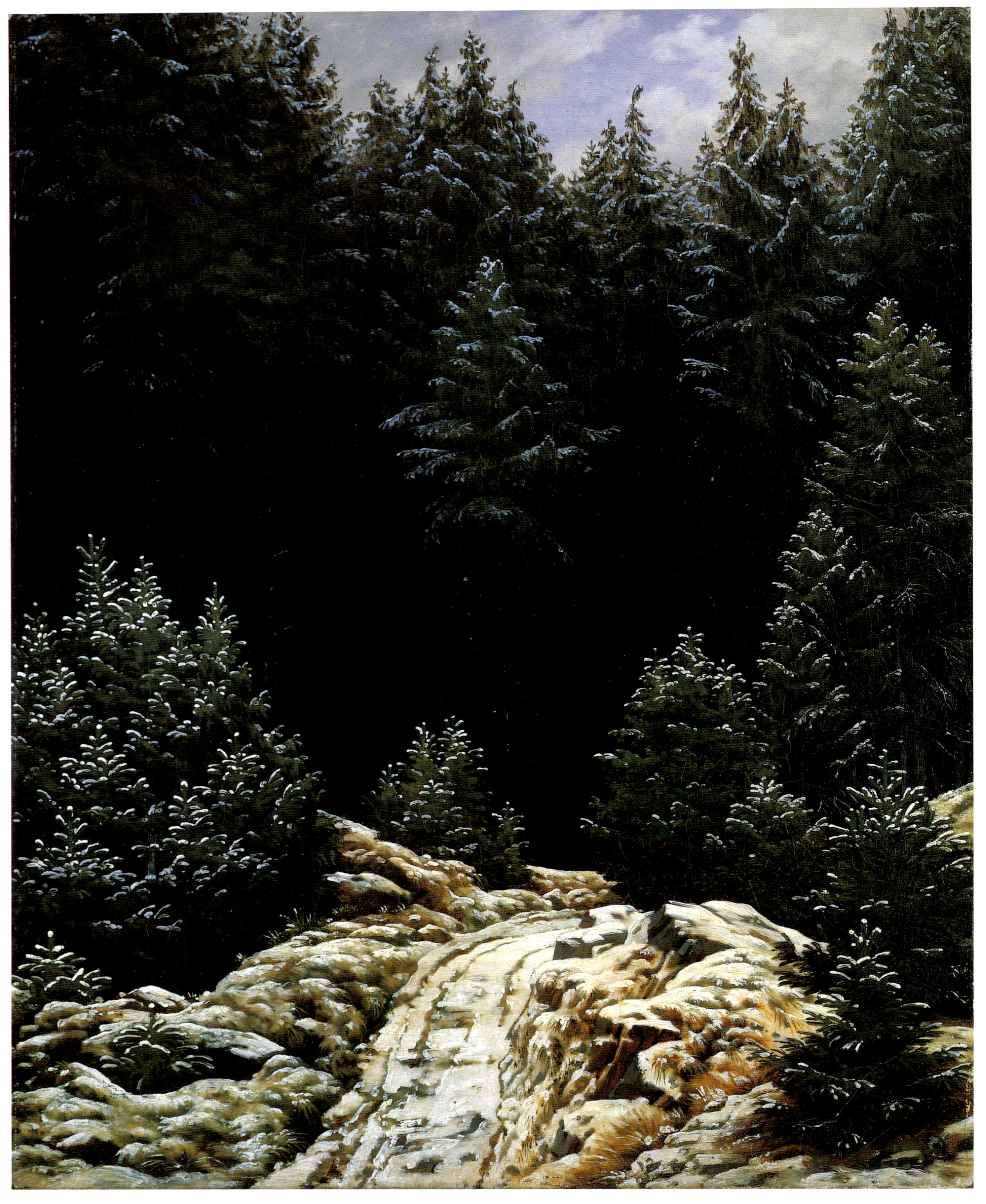

52. *Early Snow*,
1828, oil on canvas,
43.8 x 34.5 cm (17¼ x 13½ in.).
Hamburger Kunsthalle, Hamburg.

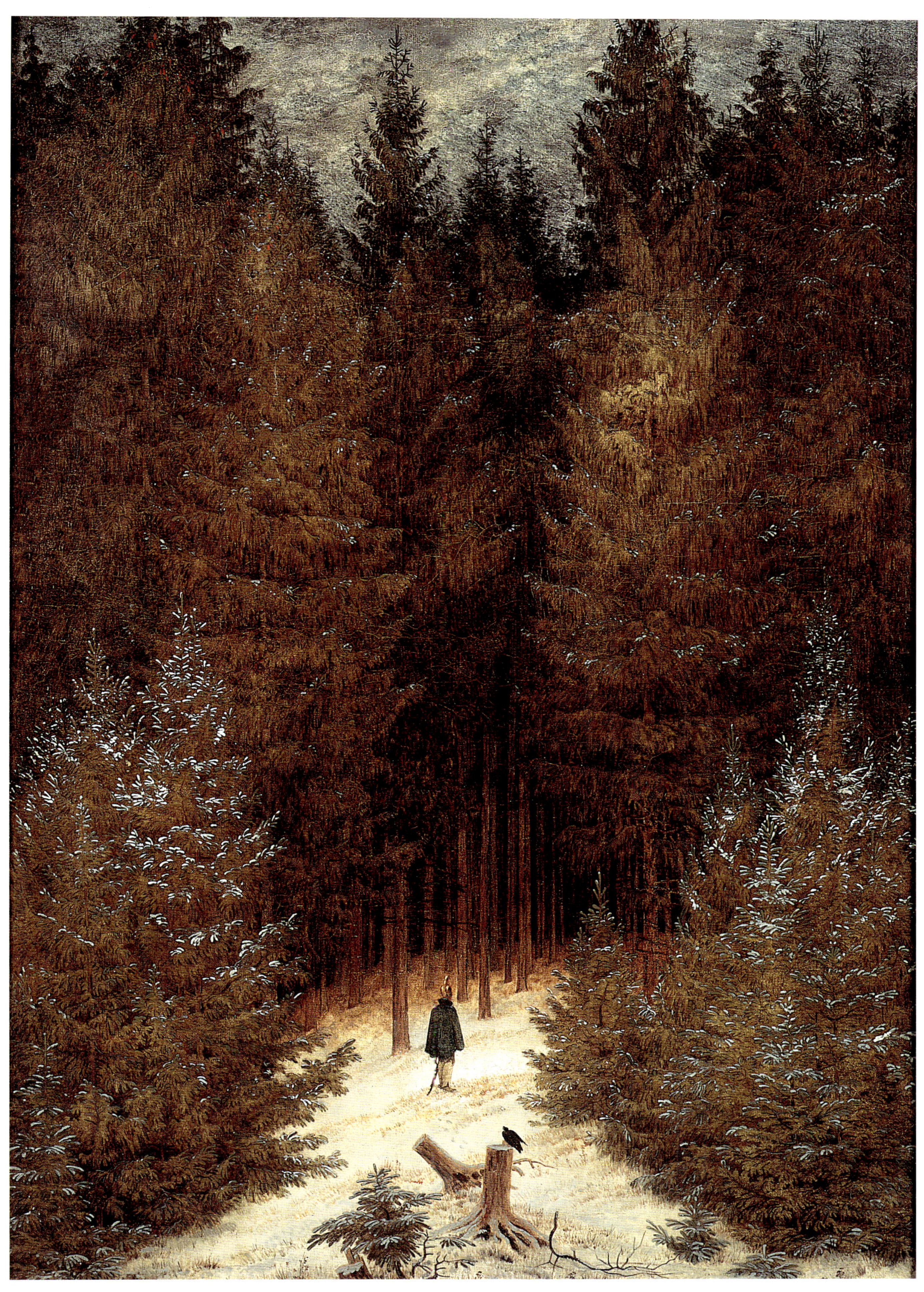

53. *The Chasseur in the Woods,*
1814, oil on canvas,
65.7 x 46.7 cm (25⅞ x 18⅜ in.).
Private collection.

Whichever it is, the tomb of Arminius represents a rallying cry to contemporary Germans to take the past as a model and draw courage from it. Kleist had the same aim when he wrote his fiery anti-French play *Hermannsschlacht* (*Hermann's Battle*, 1808). Anyone reading the text at that time could be in no doubt about what it alluded to. While it was the Romans who had to be driven off Germania's 'sacred soil' eighteen centuries earlier, for Kleist and Friedrich the latterday Romans came from across her western border. Kleist's drama was not published until 1821, however, and we do not know whether Friedrich was familiar with it.

Besides the patriotic message and the reminder of the emerging self-awareness of their Germanic ancestors, Friedrich may also have had religious analogies in mind. As Börsch-Supan says: 'Possibly Friedrich wanted, with the soldiers and the cave ... to make an allusion to the tomb of Christ and the resurrection.' It should be noted, however, that in the final analysis the painter gives nature the decisive power over human destinies: 'Arminius does not repel the invaders, they are swallowed by Nature' (Helmut Leppien).

The same nature metaphor occurs in *The Chasseur in the Woods* (ill. 53), exhibited at the Berlin Academy in October 1814. Now that Napoleon and his army had been defeated, the message did not have to be expressed in code. Anyone who needed help found it in the *Vossische Zeitung*: 'A French chasseur walks alone through the forest of snow-covered fir trees, and a raven on a tree trunk sings him his death song.' Nevertheless, the painting belongs among Friedrich's commemorative pictures. The painter gives the enemy soldier the calm air of a man who awaits his allotted fate with dignity. There is no trace

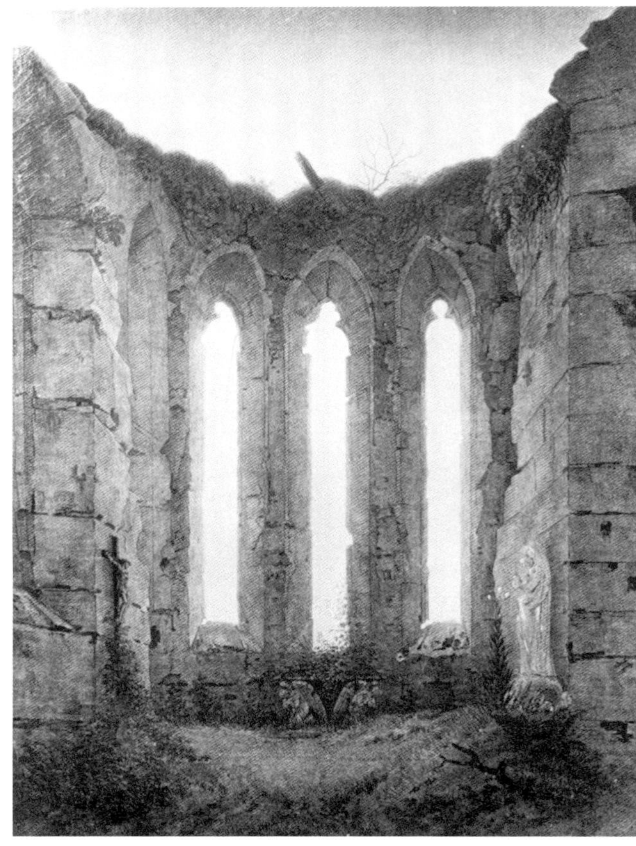

54. *Ruins at Oybin*,
c. 1812, oil on canvas,
65.7 x 46.7 cm (25⅞ x 18⅜ in.).
Private collection.

55. *Hutten's Tomb*,
1823–24, oil on canvas,
93 x 73 cm (36⅝ x 28¾ in.).
Staatliche Kunstsammlungen, Weimar.

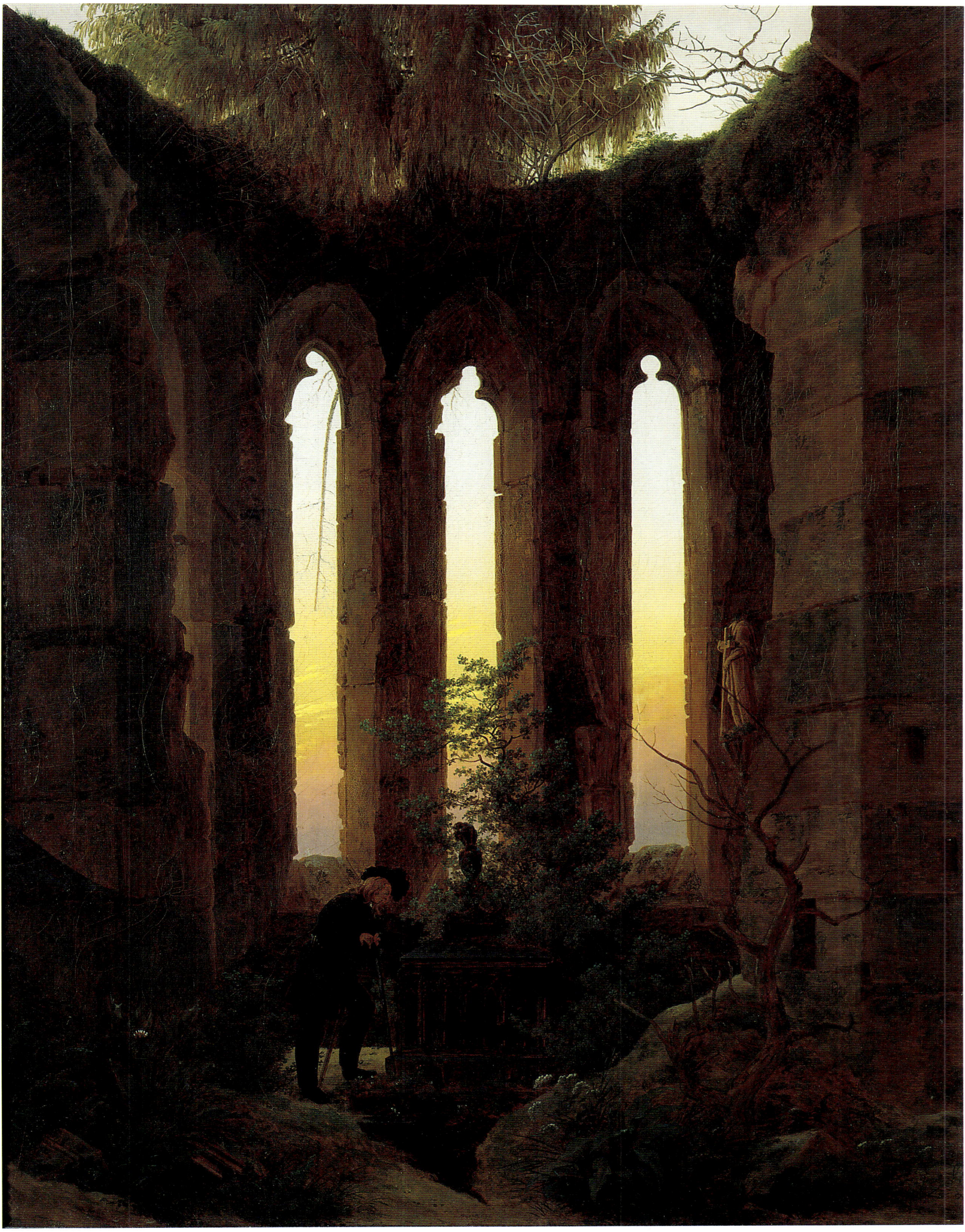

here of the holy anger that Friedrich poured, with apparent spontaneity, into his 'prayer' following the French forces' retreat.

'They hasten back to their home, fleeing, pursued by the sword of the North,
Smitten by the curse of the Almighty.'

The chasseur is not in haste, for he knows he will not see his home again. Neither will he be struck down by any sword of the North, but will instead succumb to the superior power of nature. It is for the viewer to choose whether or not to see the 'curse of the Almighty' in that. What can be observed in the picture, however, does not demonstrably involve the judgment of God. If the chasseur is removed, the wintry scene becomes a fatal landscape casting an irresistible spell over any human being who enters it. The viewer has no difficulty in recognizing the formal elements exerting the attraction. The track is framed by trees forming the 'funnel' with which we are now familiar. In the centre of this opening stands a pine tree, seemingly weightless and suggesting something of the world beyond, like a tabernacle – perhaps a discreet reminder of the salvation awaiting mankind. Admittedly, this allusion departs somewhat from the unambiguous message of, for example, *The Cross in the Mountains* (ill. 21).

A decade later, after restoration of the old order had taken control of public life, Friedrich painted an elegiac epilogue to the wars of liberation, *Hutten's Tomb* (ill. 55). The immediate occasion for the picture was the third centenary of the death of Ulrich von Hutten (1488–1523), the poet-knight, follower of Luther (and author of a version of *Arminius*), driven into exile for his political activities, who was hailed as a hero of resistance to royal tyranny and clericalism. In the painting, the tomb marked with his name stands neglected, half buried in vegetation, in a Gothic chancel which, according to Günther Grundmann, is based on the ruined monastery church at Oybin near Zittau in Saxony. On the right a bracket bears a headless figure of Fides. The ruin and the mutilated statue represent the current sorry state of a world that once was whole. The wounds suffered in the present day are marked by the five names engraved on the near side of the sarcophagus: 'Jahn 1813', 'Arndt 1813', 'Stein 1813', 'Görres 1821' and 'Scharnhorst' – four who spoke up for the cause of liberty, only to be persecuted or hounded into exile, and one unpopular reformer (Karl, Baron vom Stein). It is hard to imagine a more discreet homage to five witnesses to a secular belief, or a more abstract one, since, in good Protestant style, the Word has replaced the Image.

Hutten's Tomb also commemorates the tenth anniversary of the outbreak of the wars of liberation. The man bending over the tomb is a veteran of that heroic epoch, wearing the black uniform of the Lützow Volunteers, a battle-hardened troop, legendary for their death-defying exploits. Yet there is no sign of that past in this man. Immersed in his thoughts, he does not see what the viewer sees, which would help him draw hope and consolation from the picture. The three lancet windows discreetly counteract the effect of the derelict stone monuments below them. Their eloquent outlines suggest the forms of hovering saints, as if in photographic negative. Rather than bodies, we see three segments of a cloudless sky, three gaps containing nothing but the blue, pink and yellow variegation of the distance. By this means, the narrow, ruinous chancel opens up into a timeless space where ruin and destruction are unknown. The intact space is like a promise, albeit a distant one. As in *The Abbey in the Oak Wood* (ill. 23), the difference between the Catholic cult of images (the broken Fides) and the Lutheran rejection of images (the perfect sky) is unobtrusively expressed here and settled in the latter's favour. There is a hint of this in an earlier picture showing the ruined chancel at Oybin with a crucifix, a statue of the Virgin Mary and an altar table borne by two angels (ill. 54).

Börsch-Supan discovered that *Hutten's Tomb* was exhibited in 1826 in Berlin and Hamburg, with the note that the proceeds from its sale would be donated to those who had suffered in the Greek struggle for independence. It was presumably then that the picture was bought by Karl August, Duke of Saxe-Weimar, friend, patron and employer of Goethe.

In the meantime, the preoccupation with tombs and their symbolism led Friedrich to a subtler semiotic language. In *The Sea of Ice* (ill. 159) he invented an apparently harmless symbol for the frozen, paralysed condition of Germany (see page 228).

We have seen Friedrich's perception of his position in the contemporary world: a Protestant who wanted to enhance his church's beauty and status in the public eye, and a patriot who expressed his views of the oppression and suppression of his nation in landscape allegories. At the same time a change of scene took place in his private life. The work for the church in Stralsund and the choice of patriotic subject matter in his pictures show that he thought of himself as part of a community and wanted to help it attain self-expression. A member of an academic 'community' since 1816 (the Dresden Academy, although he did not hold a teaching post there), he now decided to give up his bachelor status and in 1818 married a much younger woman, Caroline Bommer. Entering conventional bourgeois life changed the direction of his art: pensive quietude became more contemplative and loneliness gained a degree of relaxation.

A town square, where the bourgeois life is lived and artlessly puts itself on public view (ill. 56). Mothers with children, women taking a stroll, four stately men in earnest discussion. Scattered among them, representatives of the lower classes: a coachman and his carriage, a man pushing a handcart. This solid world is made of similarly solid buildings, which obviously serve the common weal, and the street leading off the square ends at a town gate. We are looking at an apparently well-ordered urban idyll. Anyone who enters the town museum in Greifswald and stops in front of this large watercolour will recognize the scene at once, for he has just seen some of these very buildings in the marketplace outside, and he can compare the town hall, the pharmacist's shop and the tower of the Jakobikirche with their originals. But while the topographic orientation gives the viewer the pleasure of recognition, reading the artist's name gives a jolt. Can this be by Friedrich? It is a disorienting challenge to anyone familiar with the artist's oeuvre. The idyllic townscape does not fit within the frame of our expectations, seeming to contradict everything we associate with him and everything said about him on these pages so far. We see society, not isolation; a place with streets, not a remote or hostile environment; intact and inhabited buildings, not abandoned, overgrown ruins.

This is what has led commentators to call it, forbearingly, an 'occasional' work, and 'isolated' in the oeuvre as a whole (Börsch-Supan). Isolated it may be, but it is a symptom and merely an extreme formulation of a theme which frequently preoccupied the painter in the decade that began with *The Monk by the Sea* and ended with *Monastery Graveyard in the Snow*. This was no peripheral tendency; on the contrary, it produced some of his most felicitous (in every sense) paintings. The theme was an interest in the relationship between the sexes and in woman as an individual, set in a frame of familial intimacy and domesticity. Biographically speaking, the choice of a delimited, sheltered world was decided upon, at

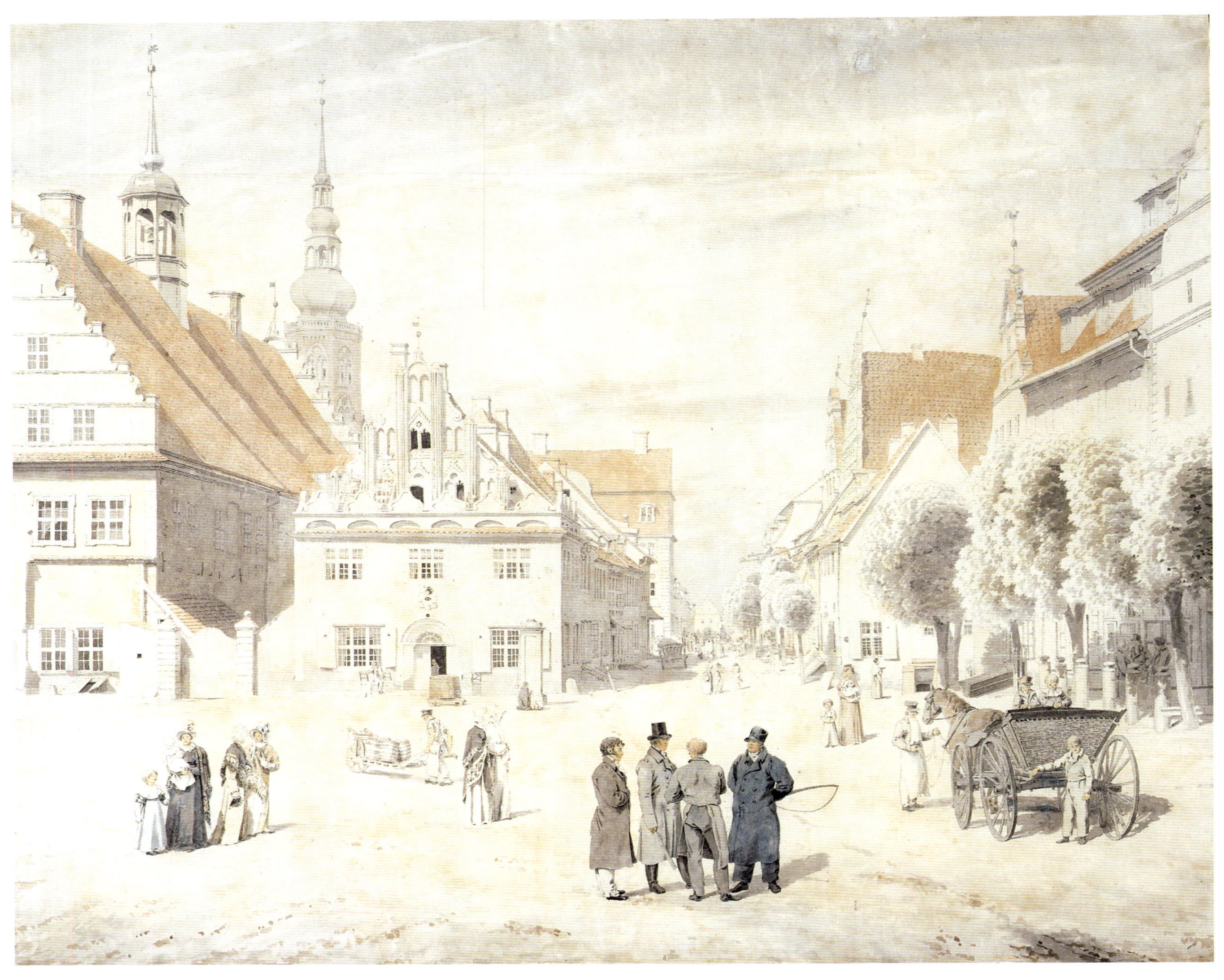

56. ***The Marketplace in Greifswald,***
1818, ink and watercolour,
54 x 76 cm (21¼ x 29⅞ in.).
Pommersches Landesmuseum, Greifswald.

least at first, when Friedrich married Caroline on 21 January 1818. The marriage came as a complete surprise to his family and friends, but for us, looking at his oeuvre, it is possible to make out the line that led to it.

The Greifswald watercolour, which combines a portrait of the town and a family group, is not our only source of information about a different Friedrich: a sociable fellow, not a loner. His letters to his brothers bear witness to his close relationship with his family, and they in turn also benefited from his artistic taste. In 1816 he designed a secretaire for one of his sisters-in-law, and at a later date a complete set of fittings for his brother Christian's shop. He took such mundane work just as seriously as a commission to decorate a church.

A contemporary, the painter Wilhelm von Kügelgen, described Friedrich's quarters in his bachelor days: 'Friedrich's studio ... was so absolutely bare that Jean Paul might well have compared it to the gutted corpse of a dead prince. It held nothing but the easel, a chair and a table, above which hung the room's only ornament, a T-square, although no one could understand how it came to be so honoured. Even the justifiable paintbox, phials of oil and paint rags were banished to the next room, for Friedrich was of the opinion that all external objects disturb the pictured world within.' The austerity of this cell, given over wholly to meditation, perhaps owes something to the writer's imagination, for when Friedrich's friend Georg Friedrich Kersting painted the studio in 1811 it is shown equipped with at least the essential tools of the painter's craft (ill. 57). But it is still spartan enough. Friedrich is depicted at work on a rocky landscape (not found among the surviving oeuvre), but whatever he is painting is in his head. Kersting testified to his friend's 'inner eye', and he seemed quite happy to acknowledge this routine seclusion, just as he probably did not mind when, in 1812, the *Morgenblatt für die gebildeten Stände* said of Kersting's picture that Friedrich's studio was as 'strange and inhospitable as his pictures'.

After the marriage, this ambience soon changed. Friedrich described it to his relatives in Greifswald in the whimsical letter he wrote a week after the wedding to let them know he was married. 'It's a droll business, when a fellow has a wife; it's droll having a household, be it ever so small; it seems droll to me when my wife summons me to the table at noon.... Much has changed now I have a wife. My old, simple domestic arrangements are in several ways no longer recognizable, and I am pleased to say my house looks cleaner and neater now. Only in the room where I work is everything still as it was. Everywhere else, window curtains are now required. The following are also now needed: coffee roaster, coffee grinder, coffee strainer, coffee bag, coffee pot, coffee cups, everything – everything is now needed. Big pots and little pots, big bowls and little bowls, big pans and little pans, everything – everything is now needed. Everything has changed; formerly my room was my spittoon, now I am directed to spit in little dishes put there for the purpose. But my love of cleanliness and neatness is happy to comply.'

Earlier in his life Friedrich had recognized woman's ability to guide man, although then it was not within the confines of the narrow domestic scene, but out in the boundless expanses of nature, where her role is to lead her partner onwards and upwards. This is depicted in *Morning in the Riesengebirge* (1810–11; ill. 58). A contemporary critic took exception to Friedrich's merging of two planes of meaning: 'The lady beside the crucifix, holding out her weak hand to a gentleman in this inaccessible place, is another thing I do not altogether care for, because the modern and the personal become insignificant in the midst of the great simplicity of nature.' Contemporary viewers were perplexed by 'the personal' because they assumed that Friedrich had portrayed himself in the man, being pulled up to the cross where she stands by a woman endowed with amazing strength. But this feat could be attributed only to an allegory – of faith, presumably, since it is faith which not only moves mountains but evidently makes them climbable as well.

The two figures, which are small but not insignificant, have their eyes fixed on the cross, but the painter and the viewer gaze out across an unbounded and distant landscape, which rises up out of the morning light and simultaneously sinks back down again. The sky and the earth meet at a horizon that divides the picture exactly in two, yet this division is more like a merging or a marriage. With a subtlety of brushwork close to bravura (which he famously despised), Friedrich paints a morphology consisting purely of transitions, a melody which can be read in two ways. In one direction, the banks of cloud and mist are firmed into floating, gliding outlines, which solidify and fill the foreground with a heavy corporeality; in the other, the rocky masses are dissolved into a sea of gentle waves that seems to vanish gradually into the pale sky. When the painter's imagination returned to the Riesengebirge in later work, it would simply take in the vast dimensions of elemental, uninhabited nature, to which the mists add a breath of nascent energy (ill. 59). But never again did Friedrich paint the forces of nature in such all-encompassing harmony as he did in the earlier picture, and never again did he imbue the relationship of man and woman with such cosmic aspirations. Nonetheless, the desire for light and harmony, and for peaceful, undisturbed happiness persisted, and went on to inspire a whole series of Friedrich's most significant pictures.

In Goethe's novel *Elective Affinities* (1809), there is a minor character, a nameless architect's assistant, into whose mouth the author puts some striking views on women and womankind; these he expounds to Charlotte, the more mature of the novel's two main female characters. He favours variety in dress, not in order to satisfy a desire for personal adornment but so that every woman can acquaint herself with her own individual style, since she is destined 'to stand alone, and act alone, throughout her life'. It is a remarkable thought to find expressed in a novel about relationships and their variations. Charlotte thinks it paradoxical, so he explains himself: 'Whether we look on a woman as a lover, a bride, a wife, or a housewife and mother, she always stands in isolation; she is always alone and wants to be alone. It is the same even for a vain woman. Every woman excludes other women by her very nature, for each one is required to do everything that it is the duty of the entire sex to accomplish. It is not the same for men. A man needs another man; he would invent a second man if there wasn't one. A woman could live an eternity without thinking of making another of her own kind.'

The passage describes something of the view of women that we find in Friedrich's pictures. Their contained figures have a power and meaning of their own. *The Garden Terrace* (1811–12; ill. 60) is an early example. While the experiential world is elevated into allegory in *Morning in the Riesengebirge*, here womankind is represented on two planes: as a woman reading in the foreground and as a classical goddess in the middle ground. The plinth supporting the statue (Flora?) is scarcely any higher than the garden wall behind it, so that the figure extends its gesture of blessing to both areas, the shady park and the sunny landscape, whose central peak crowns the sculpture from afar. The statue is both near and distant, a real work of art and a remote apparition, an allegory through which the experiences imagined by the young woman reading are turned into solid stone, a visible altar to culture and art. This duality affects the whole

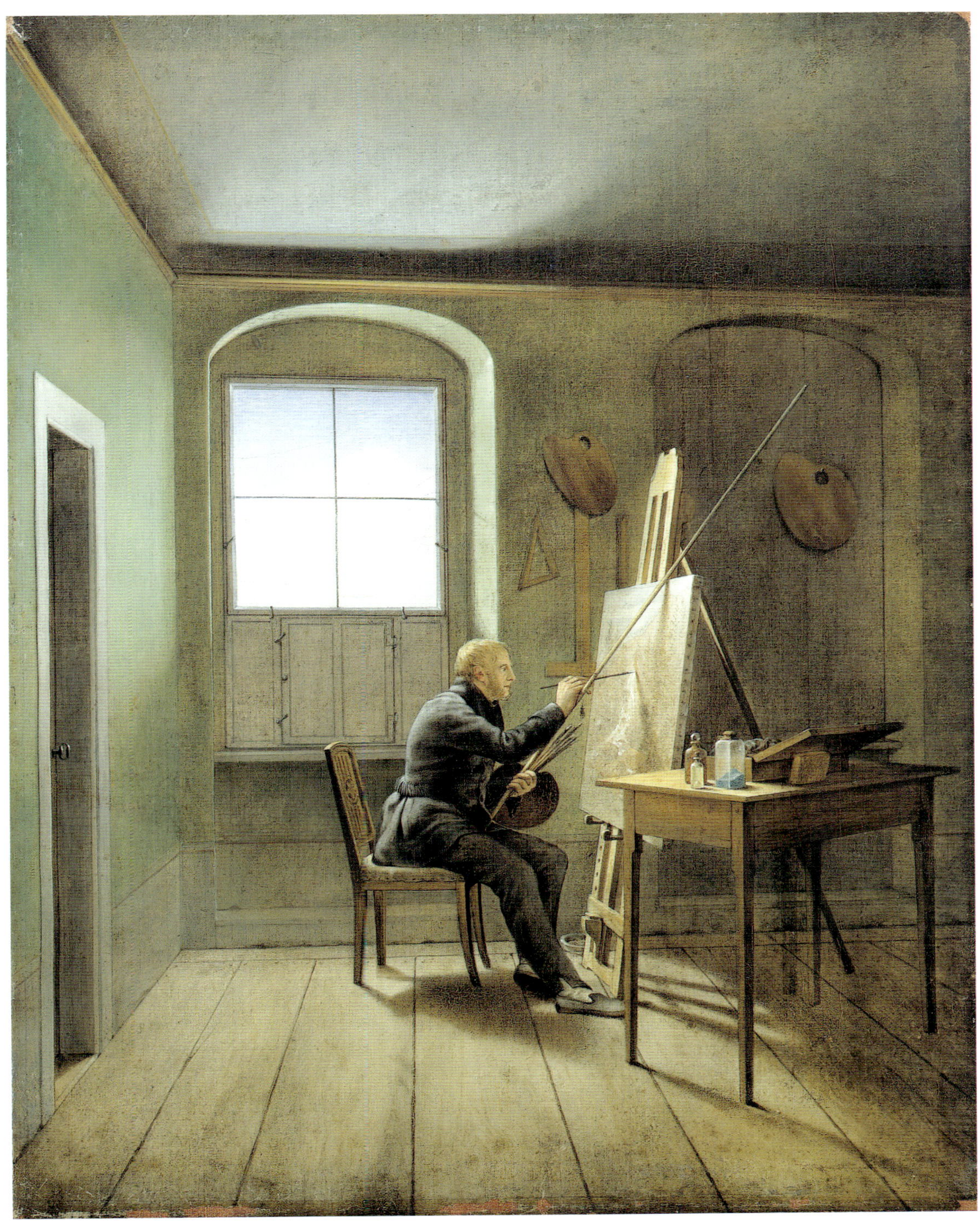

57. Georg Friedrich Kersting,
Friedrich's Studio,
1811, oil on canvas, 54 x 42 cm (21¼ x 16½ in.).
Hamburger Kunsthalle, Hamburg

Overleaf:
58. *Morning in the Riesengebirge* (*The Cross in the Mountains*),
1810–11, oil on canvas,
108 x 170 cm (42½ x 66⅞ in.).
Nationalgalerie, Berlin.

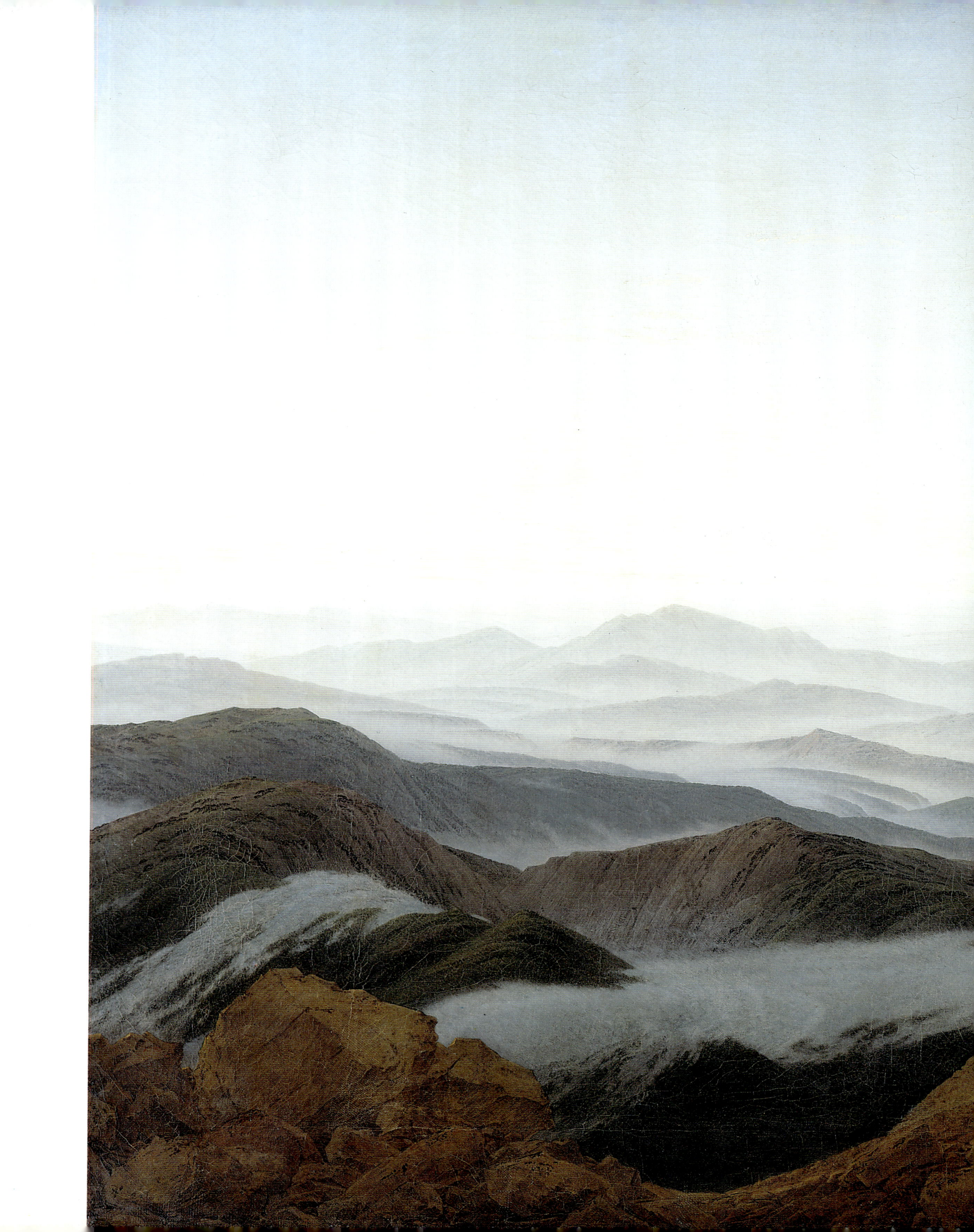

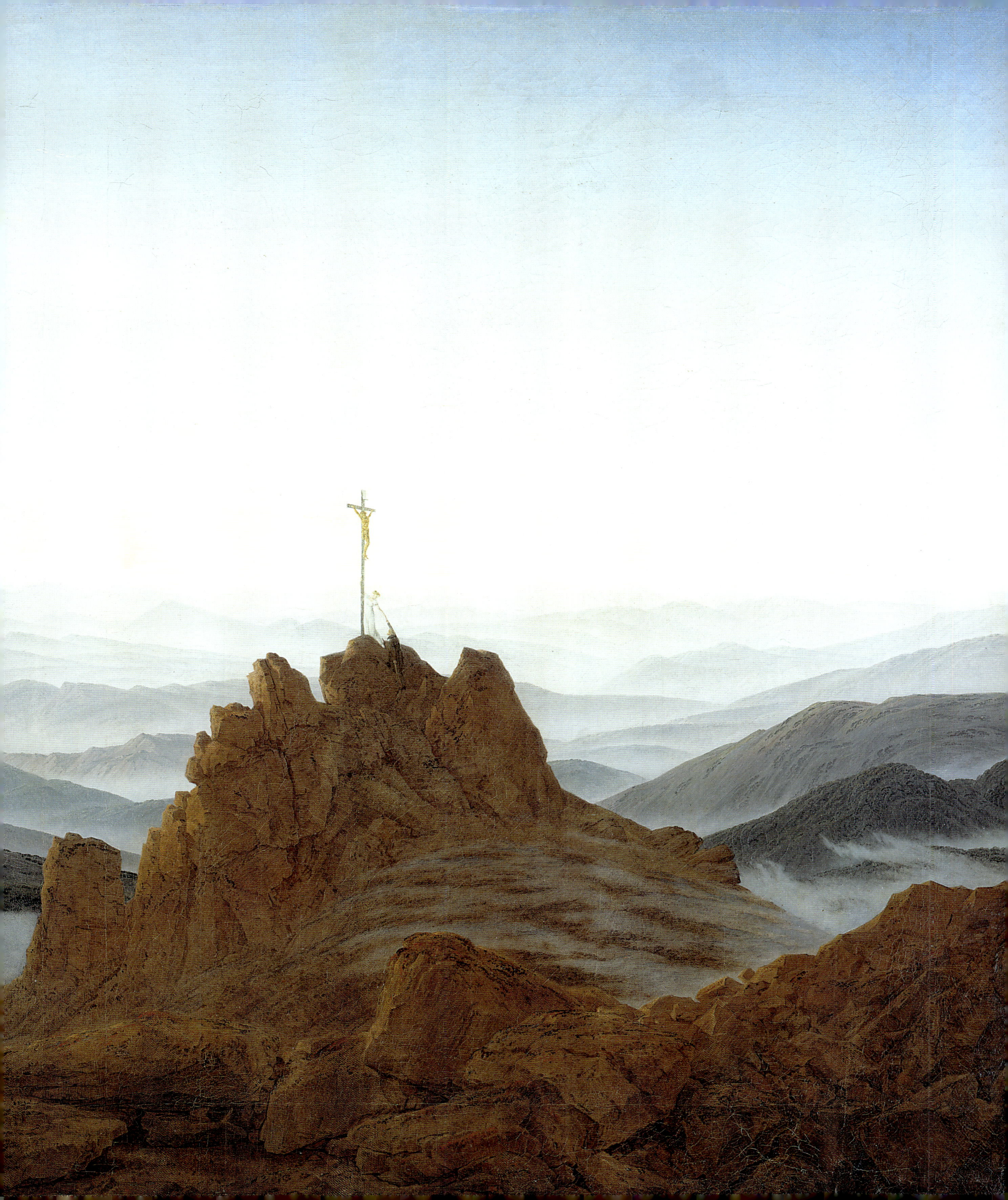

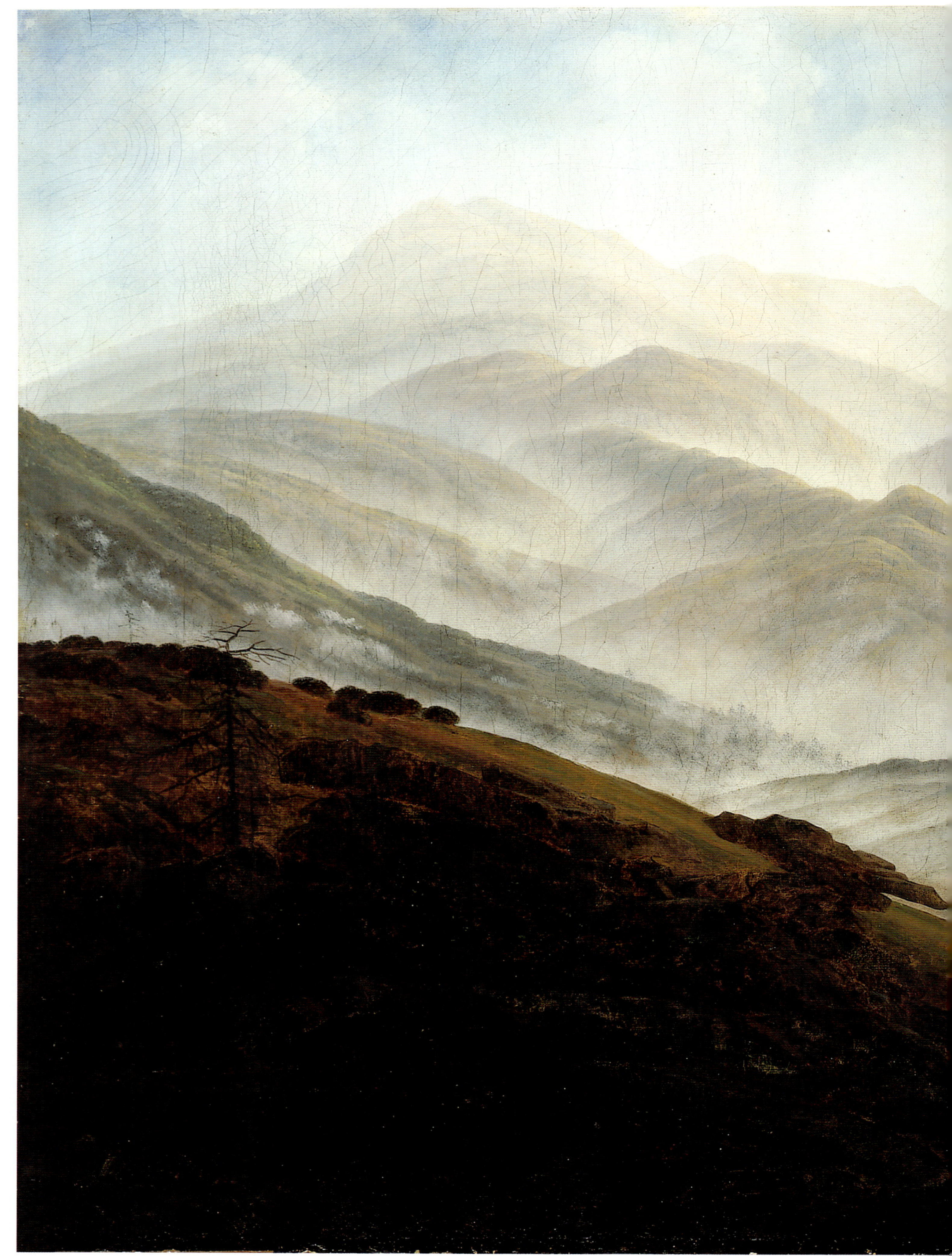

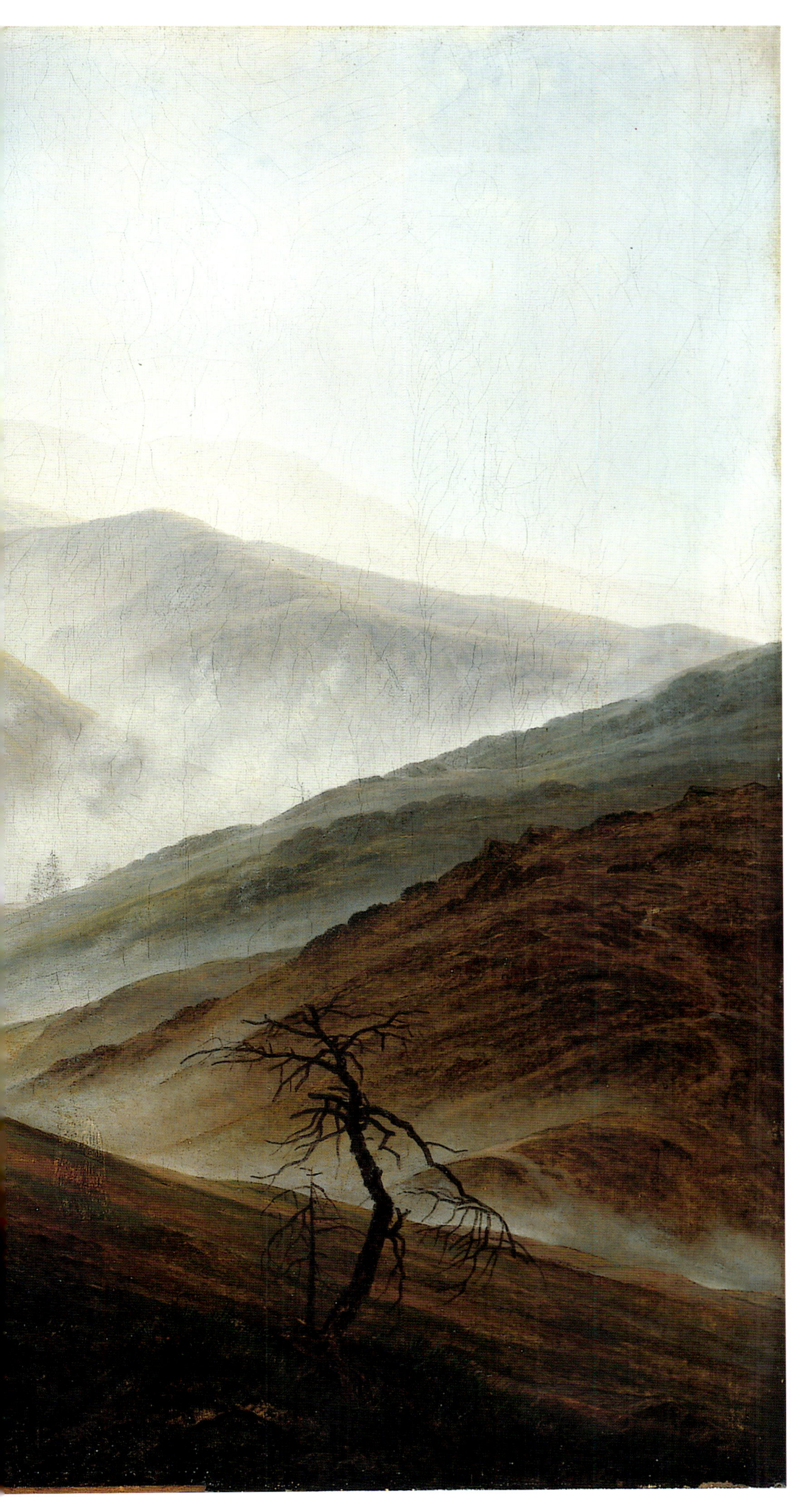

59. *Landscape in the Riesengebirge with Mist Rising*,
c. 1820–21, oil on canvas,
54.9 x 70.3 cm (21⅝ x 27¾ in.).
Neue Pinakothek, Munich.

structure of the picture. Although the low garden wall provides a horizontal caesura it does not form a spatial barrier. The two zones it creates are not alien to one another but interdependent, like breathing in and breathing out. Two huge chestnut trees give the surface space the structure of a triptych. The middle field, nearly twice the width of either of the 'wings', contains the most important of the picture's 'expressive' motifs, but these conform only partly to the symmetry prescribed by the trees. The statue occupies the central axis, as befits an altar, and so does the distant hill in the background, but the fact that the garden gate and the woman are not on this axis creates a subtle tension. Order and freedom are harmonized in a calculated yet seemingly unforced equilibrium. A composition in several movements, the picture emerges as the transparent sum of its convergent and divergent elements.

The Garden Terrace shows Friedrich engaged in a dialogue with his alter ego, whose sombre testimonies dominate our overall opinion of his art. One of his aphorisms states: 'Anyone who does not perceive Nature in the most delicate of harmonies, who knows her spirit only in the starkest of contrasts – that person's spirit is closed to art.' In *The Garden Terrace*, Friedrich counters his own images of contrast with 'the most delicate of harmonies'.

Marriage brought a woman into Friedrich's life, and womankind into his work. When he married in January 1818, he was forty-three, nineteen years older than his bride. He painted her, but not in a formal portrait; instead protecting her from inquisitive stares by showing her from behind or in *profil perdu*. It gives her quiet grace a radiance we might call aura, if the word had not been exhausted. She does not assume an outspoken individuality but bears the hallmarks of a prototype, a mystery on to which each viewer can project his own wishful notions. In accordance with the ideas of Goethe's assistant architect, Friedrich's young woman sheds the distinguishing marks of her humble background and stands ready to play different roles, while still remaining entirely herself, whether there is a man in the picture or not. Even if we think we recognize Caroline beside the sea, by the window or in sunlight (ill. 63), a slight doubt as to her identity remains. The woman in the sailing boat (ill. 77), meanwhile, is clearly not Caroline, but through Friedrich's deliberate transformation she could be made to represent her. Perhaps each of Friedrich's female figures is both his own Caroline and another that he seeks in his imagination: a dual figure.

As in *Garden Terrace*, space in these pictures is articulated by the tension between nearness and distance. Nearness is embodied in interiors and the foreground, and countered in the distance by things outside and in the background. The close can even absorb the distant to form a single whole; this occurs in the painting *Woman before the Rising Sun* (1818; ill. 63). The figure is reminiscent of an icon but seen from behind; her *orante* pose is directed towards the natural phenomenon, not us. The size and central position of the statue-like figure give it the leading role in the painting's action. Everything relates to her, everything derives from her. It could be said that she accommodates the entire landscape with a minimum of gestural drama, entirely unforced, as if the outlines of the hills were the formal upbeat to her outstretched arms or their continuation. All the relationships are carefully thought out but do not give the impression of calculation. Börsch-Supan thinks the picture represents a sunset rather than a sunrise, and although his argument is not very convincing, it must be admitted that no one interpretation of the sun's state can claim absolute certainty. Given that we continually find the same kind of uncertainty as a

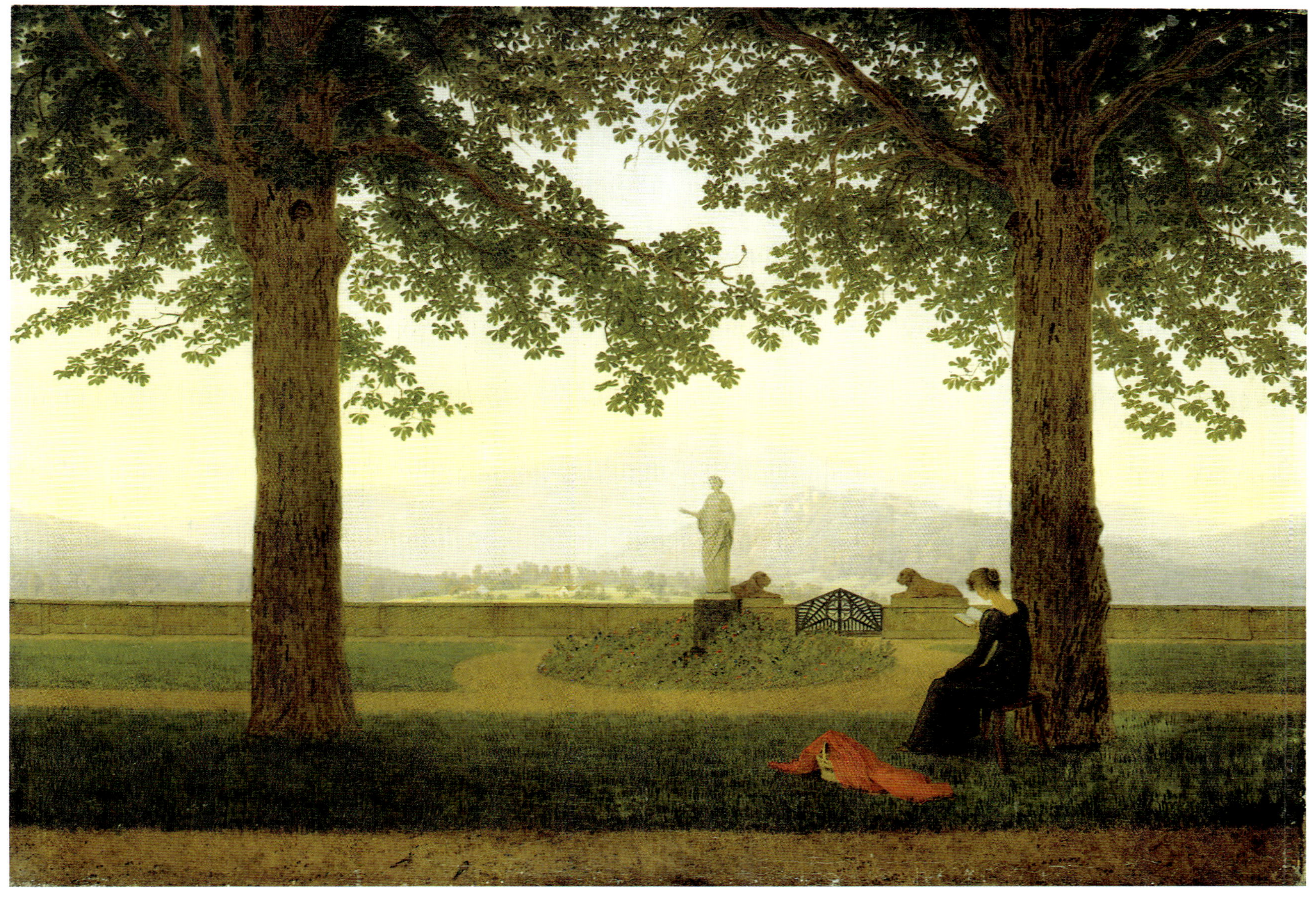

60. *The Garden Terrace*,
1811–12, oil on canvas,
53.5 × 70 cm (21 × 27⅝ in.).
Schloss Sanssouci, Potsdam.

distinguishing characteristic in Friedrich's paintings, the sun's ambivalence was probably intended. Concealment goes hand in hand with the desire to mystify.

The extent to which Caroline was part of him and his four walls is clear from a letter he wrote for her birthday when she was away visiting their friends, the Kerstings, in Meissen. The silence was like emptiness: 'If I tried to describe to you, precisely and in full detail, each and every thing which happens or is said around me throughout the livelong day, as you did, dear Lina, then you would receive not a letter but a big sheet of blank paper. Everything is quiet, quiet, quiet here; this quiet is good for me, to be sure, but I would not wish to have so much quiet around me always. I eat my breakfast alone.... I have my midday meal alone, my supper alone.' Only on his evening walks through nature does he cease to feel so abandoned: 'He who made heaven and earth is around me, and His love sustains me, and may His love sustain you and all our friends in that little place.'

Woman at the Window (ill. 66) dates from around the time of that letter. The room might be the same one in which Kersting portrayed Friedrich in 1811; the small bottles on the window sill suggest as much. There is no sign of any of the household goods the artist described in his letter to his family (see page 101); Caroline has not invaded this bare room. Instead, her husband has integrated her into his holy of holies, his cell-like studio. But this is not a prison cell, as Jensen believed, reading into the figure a longing for freedom and therefore interpreting the picture as representing a conflict between despair and hope. In my view, Friedrich's conception rests on the dialectics of picture and non-picture. The window plays an important role in this. As in the two Vienna sepias (ills 67 and 68) the interior frames and distances the exterior view. Meanwhile, in one of the Hermitage sepias (ill. 65) the bare-walled room is contrasted with the luxuriant landscape of a park. Opulent as it is, the organic world is framed by the six square windowpanes and turned it into a two-dimensional pattern. Similarly, in *Woman at the Window*, all the horizontals and verticals in the room come together in the window. Its lower part is closed by wooden shutters, forming a triptych ('in disguise', as Panofsky says). The middle shutter is open, and the

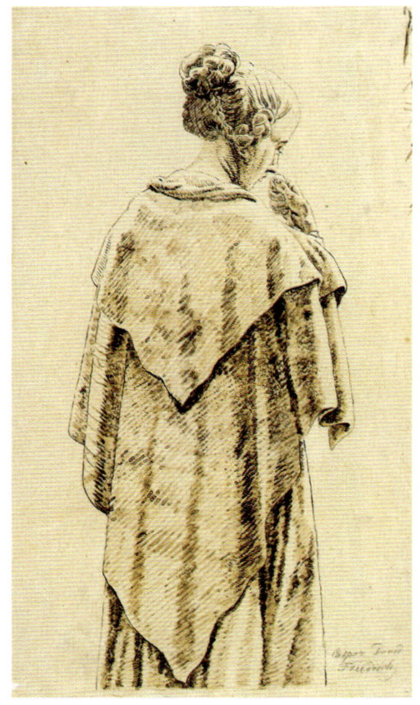

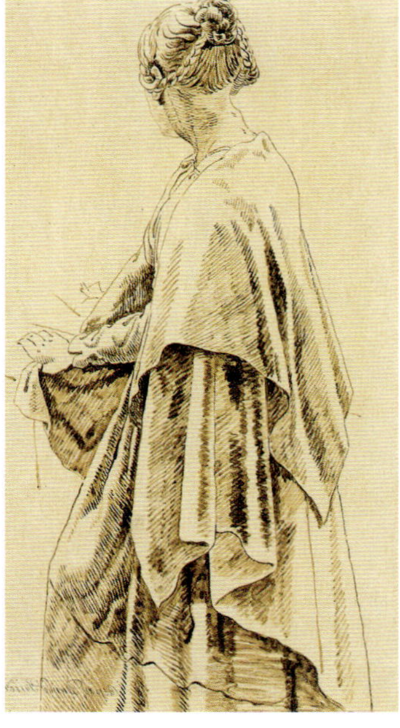

61. *Woman in a Shawl*, c. 1818–20, brush and sepia, 32.5 × 18.5 cm (12¾ × 7¼ in.). Kupferstichkabinett, Berlin.

62. *Woman in a Shawl*, c. 1818–20, brush and sepia, 35.3 × 20.7 cm (13⅞ × 8 in.). Kupferstichkabinett, Berlin.

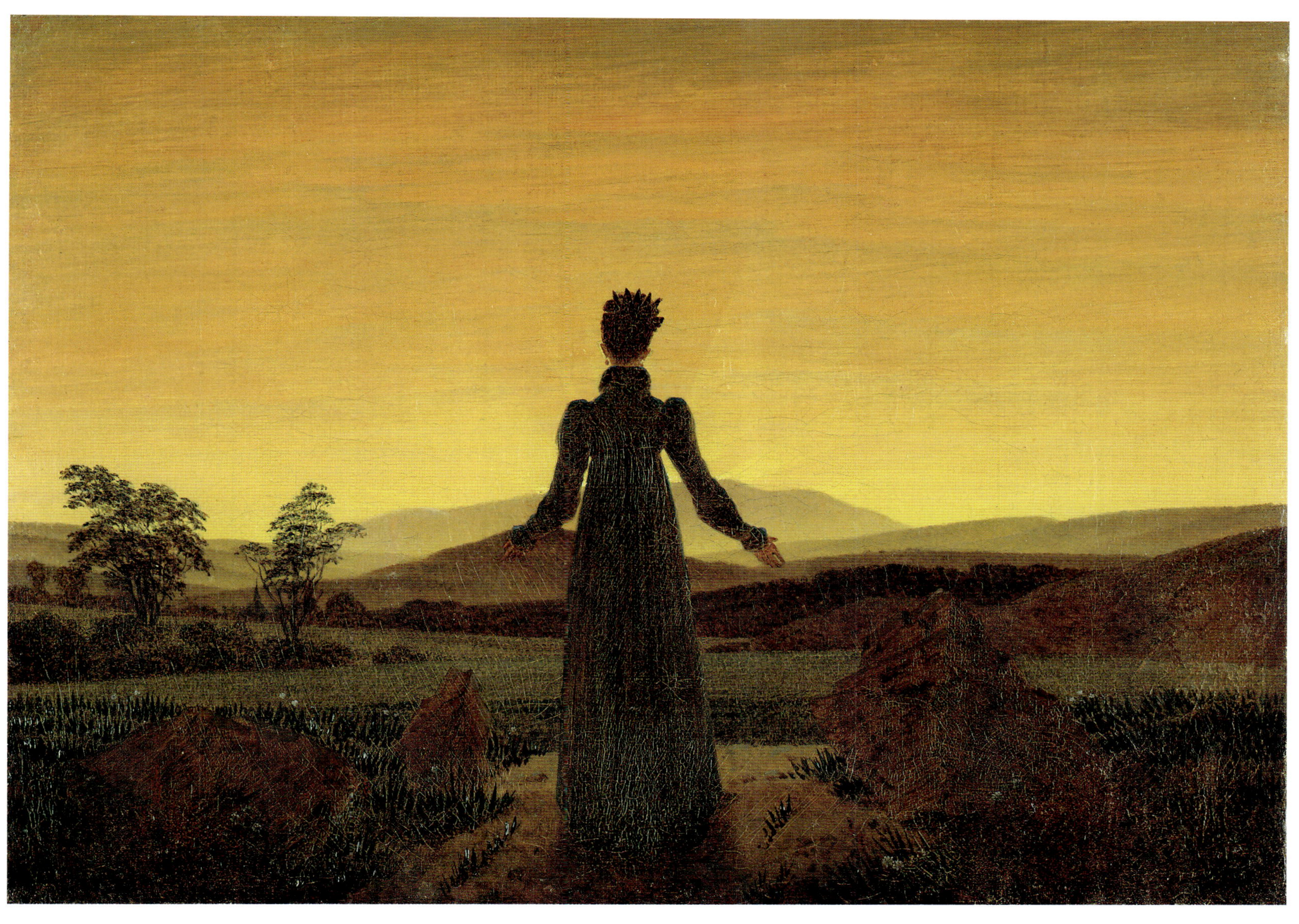

63. *Woman before the Rising Sun*,
1818, oil on canvas,
22 x 30 cm (8⅝ x 11¾ in.).
Museum Folkwang, Essen.

woman has a full view of what lies beyond, while we, the viewers, can see only a small segment: a river with poplars and two sailing boats. We guess more than we actually see. The mast of the nearer boat extends into the upper part of the window, which is subdivided by window bars forming a cross. Such windows were often called 'religious windows' in New England at that time. Why should not Friedrich, too, have spiritualized the formal analogy? (In a similar vein, he once said of *The Cross beside the Baltic* (ill. 69): 'To those who see it, a comfort, to those who do not see it, a cross.') It is also conceivable that he associated the window and its shutters with a small folding altarpiece. In that case, the abstract symbol which contains and articulates the vastness of the sky would represent contrast to the lower part of the picture, which conveys empirical reality at its most transient. The woman takes an interest in what is happening outside and leans forward in a definite way, but she is standing inside the house, where the cross in the window lifts the spatial axes into a higher, dematerialized sensory region. The message in the picture appears to be the spiritual liberation which this symbol promises to those who can see it.

A summerhouse or arbour is an area where a constructed interior space is extended into an exterior world of organic growth. In about 1818 Friedrich painted a married couple, friends of his, as figures in a summerhouse (ill. 70), turned away from the viewer and anonymous: once again he paints prototypes, rather than portraits. This painting is probably the first 'Summerhouse' (*Gartenlaube*) in German art. It represents a distillation of a garden scene with a triptych structure that Friedrich painted in about 1817, according to Börsch-Supan, in memory of the physician Johann Emanuel Bremer (ill. 71). There, the triple rhythm we already know from *The Garden Terrace* is duplicated, and distributed on two planes. It is articulated in the foreground by the two bare poles supporting the pergola, and in the plane behind by the four leafy trees on either side of the garden gate (which bears the inscription 'Bremer'). The randomly distributed poplars are like a third melody, lying beneath the essential pattern of the twofold triple rhythm. The vision of a Gothic town rises far away in the moonlit background, on the furthest bank, with the silhouettes of filigree towers and the rigging of sailing ships.

In *The Summerhouse*, the Nikolaikirche in Greifswald is visible in the background. From their shelter in the front of the picture, near the viewer, the two figures gaze out of the window towards the centre of their faith, which has retreated to the realm of contemplation, beyond prayer and preaching. Their religion is reified in the church, but while the building still means something to the individual, it allows him to remain in the privacy of his domestic setting. The picture anticipates a subject which later grew into a banal cliché of nineteenth-century German genre painting. Stripped of the religious dimension that it had for Friedrich, this intimate scenario shrinks to what later made the summerhouse an emblem of ideological self-identification: rejection of all public (social) obligations, and retreat into the cosy home and undisturbed togetherness ('just the two of us'). This was a theme previously taken up in Goethe's *Hermann and Dorothea* (1796–97), where German townspeople shrink from being touched by the 'terrible movement', whether of revolutionary ideas or of refugees, that streams across the Rhine into their quiet lives.

Friedrich was also an influence on another of the defining markers of bourgeois taste in art. *Marketplace in Greifswald* (ill. 56) is a portrait of his hometown and family, which contains in its realism the germ of the frame of mind which Ludwig Richter, Moritz von Schwind and Carl Spitzweg would exploit much more fully a generation later. What they would depict, with anecdotal embellishments, as a

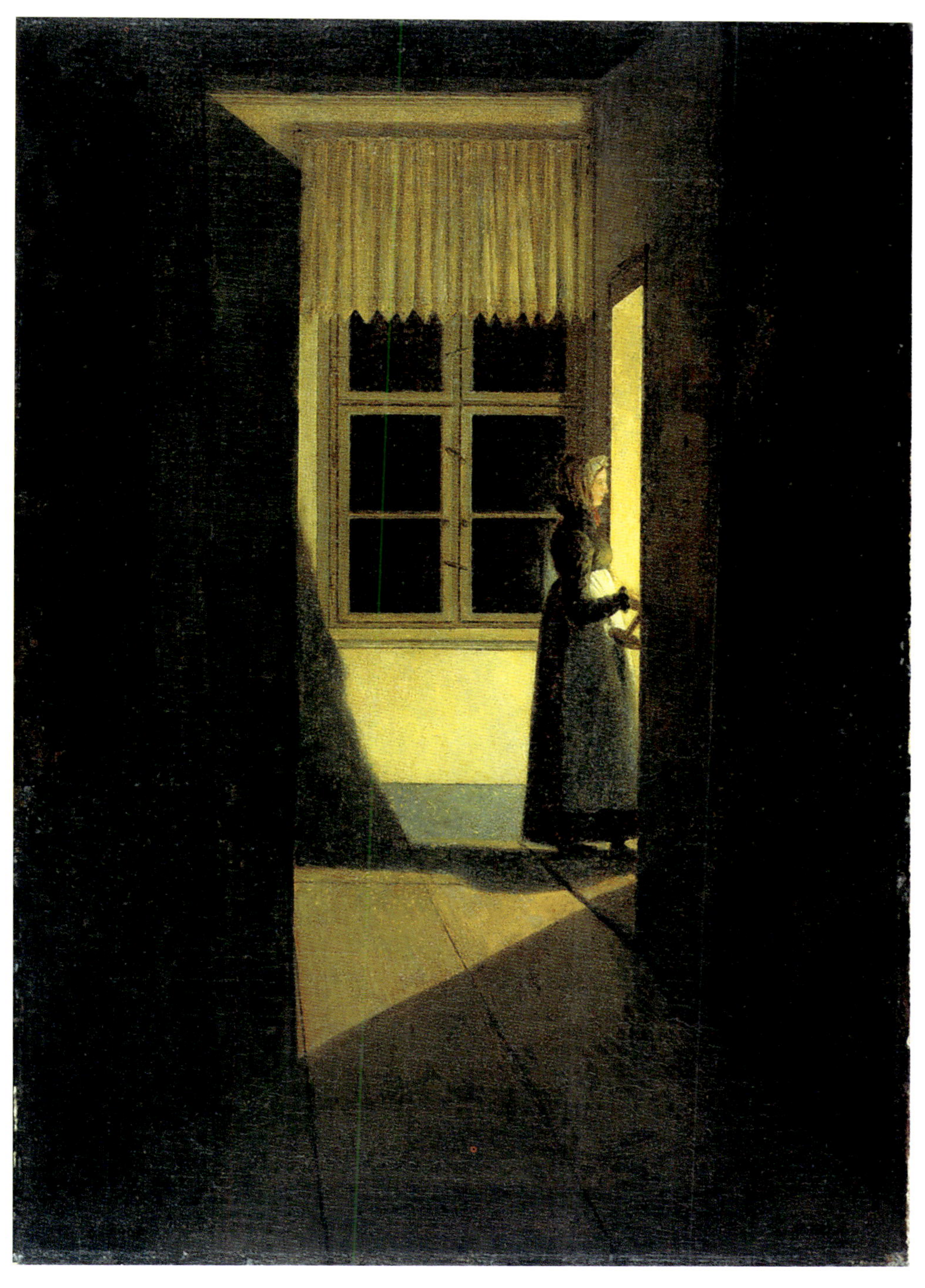

64. *Woman with Candlestick*,
1825, oil on canvas,
71 x 49 cm (28 x 19¼ in.).
Private collection.

safe, complacent world, is treated by Friedrich in a sober and objective way. The self-contained pleasure of a life spent in doing good does not yet show the signs of self-righteousness that would restrict this world's horizons to home and family. Moreover, Friedrich's town square contains none of the picturesque little oddities who would later people Spitzweg's quaint, old-Franconian, gabled streets.

Friedrich loved the towns and the countryside of his homeland, but as a painter he never reduced them to anything approaching a cosy little world. He carried the image of the North German Gothic of Greifswald, Eldena, Stralsund and Neubrandenburg in his heart, and used it in urban views (ills 72, 73, 74 and 75), but ultimately it provided him with the material for poetic paraphrases, set in Nowhere. One example is the dream architecture of *Picture in Remembrance of Johann Emanuel Bremer* (ill. 71). Another is the town like a mirage on the horizon, on which the couple in *On the Sailing Boat* (ills 46, 77) fix their gaze. The latter is an archetypal example of Friedrich's ability to intentionally invest a painting with multiple meanings, and it has received several different and contradictory interpretations. Antonina Isergina, writing in 1956 about the then 'unknown' Friedrich in the Soviet Union, related the picture to the painter's wedding trip to Rügen in the autumn of 1818, and interpreted the town in the morning light as a promise of future happiness. Gerhard Eimer associated it with a political ideal, perhaps one inspired by the urban vision in Ernst Moritz Arndt's poem *Auf dem Rugart* (1811), which is carried along by a definite and vigorous motion:

'Schimmernde Thürme
Stattlicher Städte

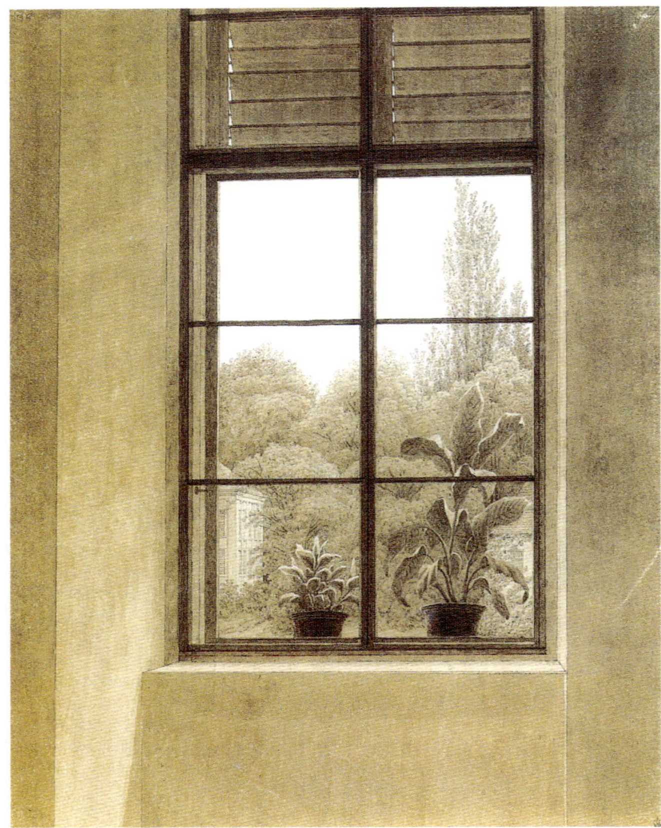

65. *Window and Garden*, 1806–11, pencil and sepia, 39.8 x 30.5 cm (15⅝ x 12 in.). Hermitage Museum, St Petersburg.

66. *Woman at the Window*, 1822, oil on canvas, 44 x 37 cm (17⅜ x 14⅝ in.). Nationalgalerie, Berlin.

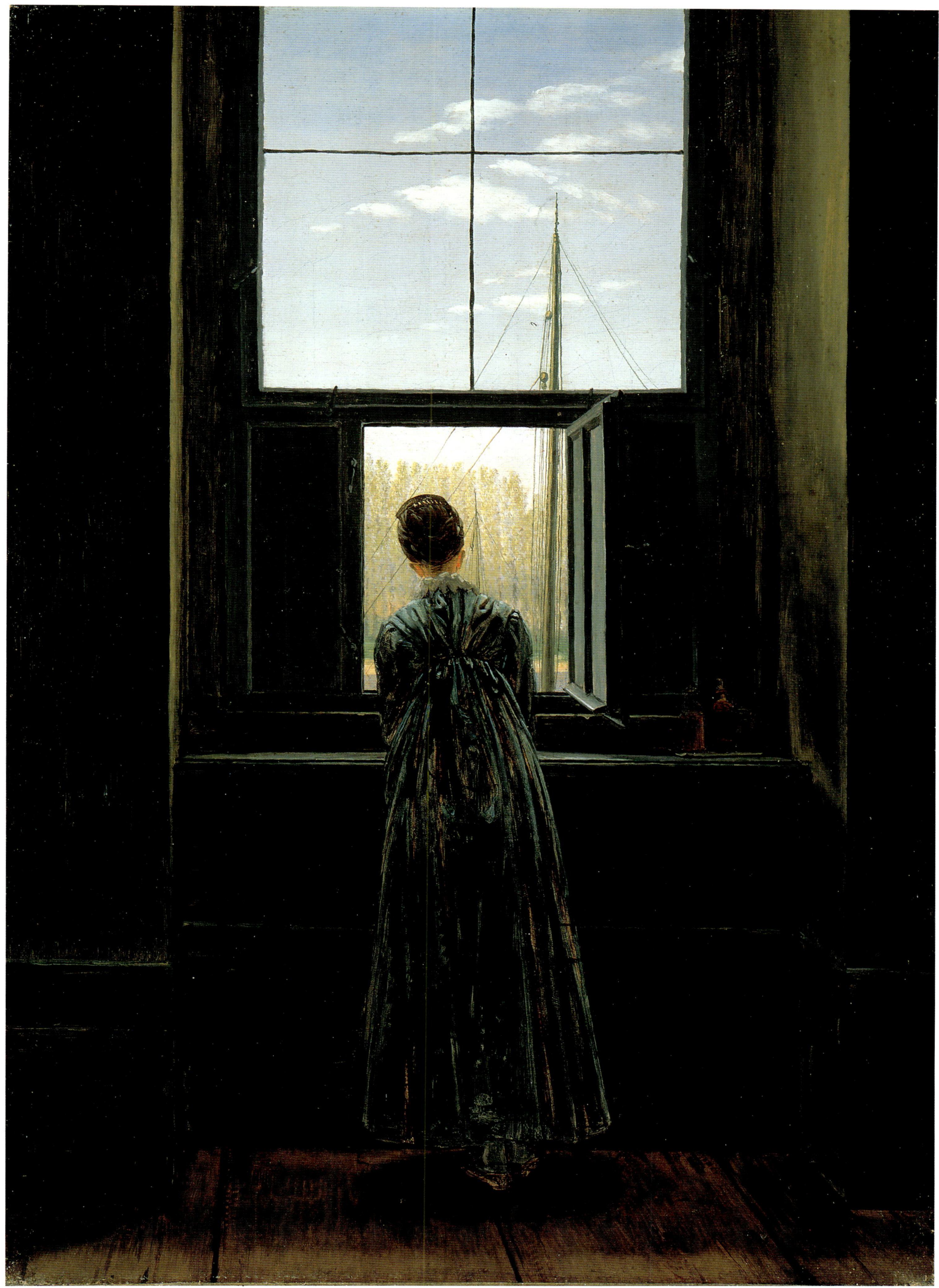

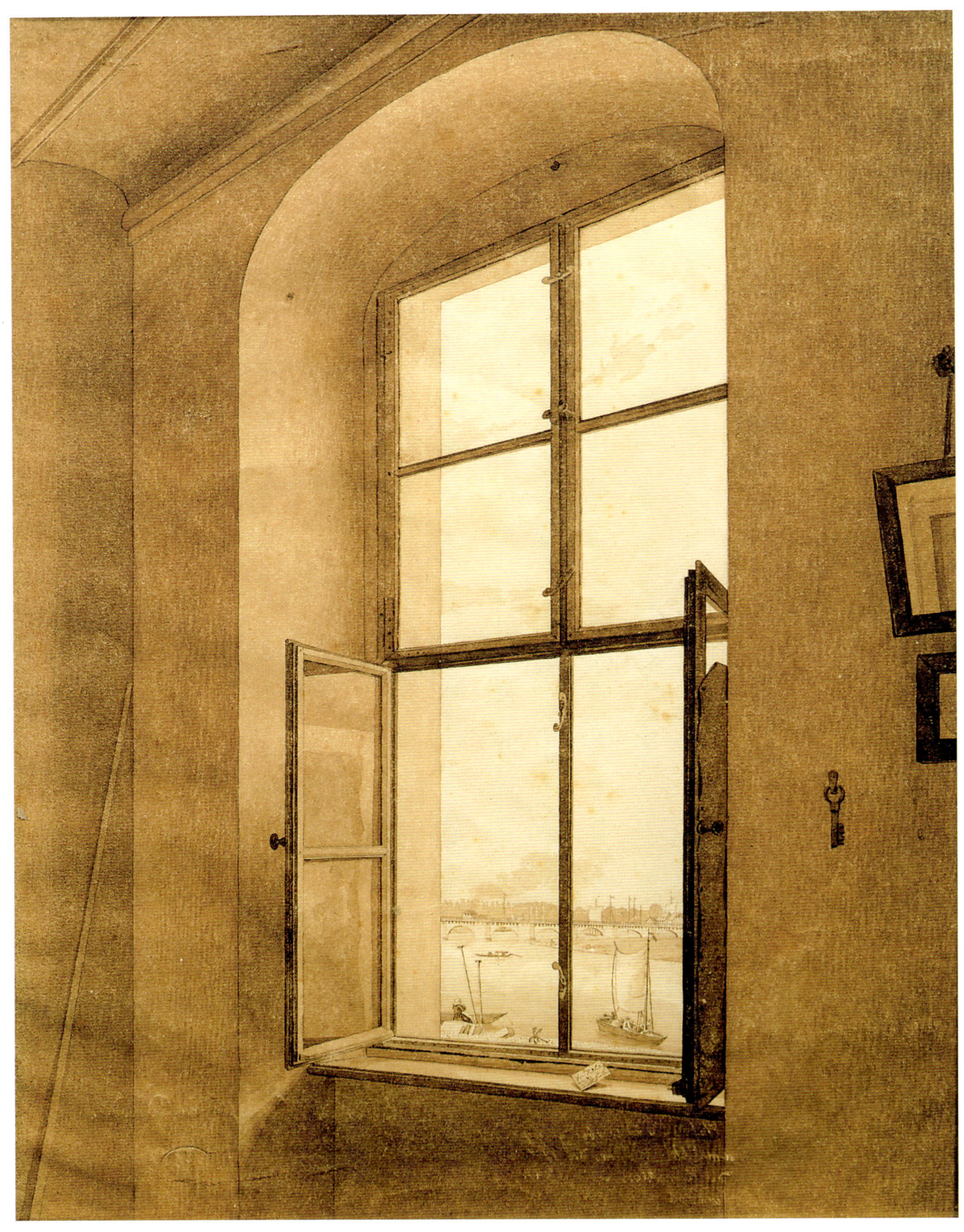

67. *View from the Artist's Studio (left-hand window),*
1805–6, pencil and sepia.
31.4 × 23.5 cm (12⅜ × 9¼ in.).
Österreichische Galerie im Belvedere, Vienna.

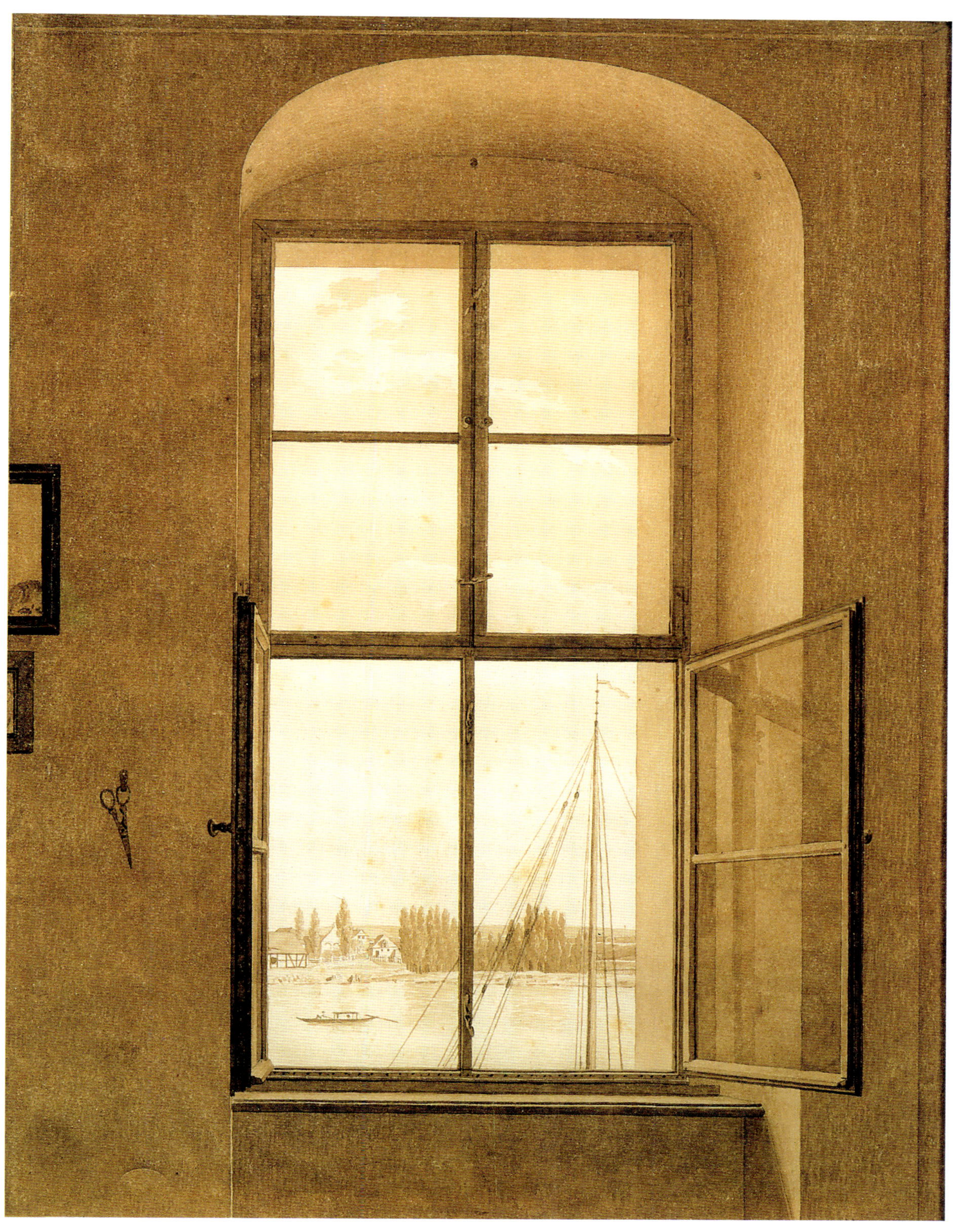

68. *View from the Artist's Studio (right-hand window)*,
1805–6, pencil and sepia,
31.2 x 23.7 cm (12¼ x 9⅜ in.).
Österreichische Galerie im Belvedere, Vienna.

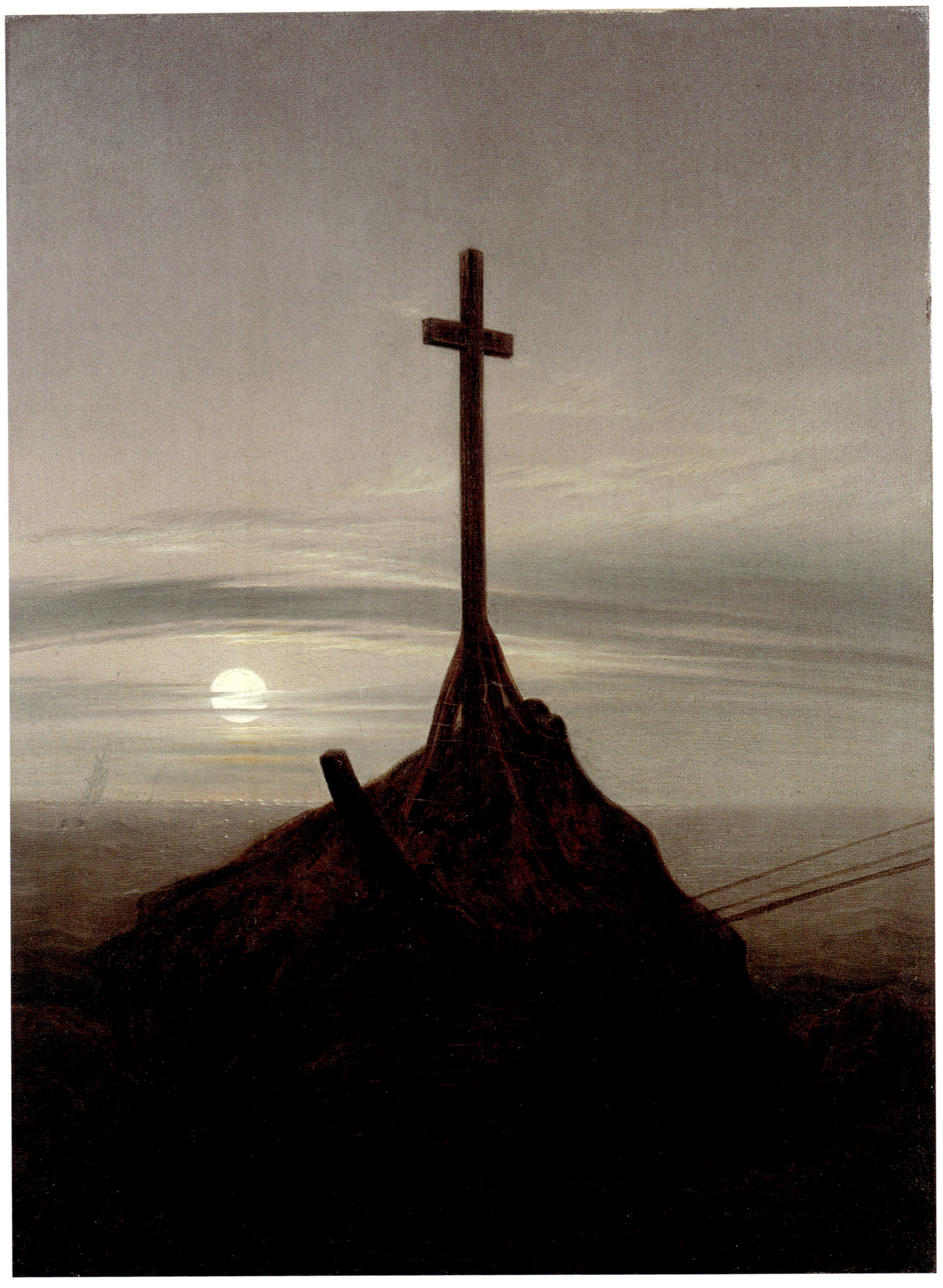

69. *The Cross beside the Baltic*,
1815, oil on canvas,
45 x 32 cm (17¾ x 12⅝ in.).
Schloss Charlottenburg, Berlin.

Scheinen zu tanzen
Jenseits im Blauen'
('Shimmering towers / of stately towns / seem to dance / yonder in the blue.')

Eimer regards the buildings as fantasy structures, and finds English neo-Gothic elements in them. Börsch-Supan, meanwhile, sees it as an evening scene, with the town as an eschatological symbol. He interprets the boat as representing married life, 'moving towards death, while the couple, unable to influence its course, are lost in contemplation of the vision of the Beyond'.

On the Sailing Boat provides a rare opportunity to consider not only the views of the art historians but also the opinions of those who bought the painting and lived with it. What moved the Russian Grand Duke Nikolay Pavlovich to buy it when he saw it in the painter's studio in 1820? Married to Princess Charlotte of Prussia since 1817, he was certainly already acquainted with Friedrich's work. It is highly likely that he knew *The Monk by the Sea* and *The Abbey in the Oak Wood*, bought at the urging of his brother-in-law, Charlotte's brother Frederick William. A few years after their wedding, Nikolay and Alexandra Feodorovna (the names she assumed in Russia) might have seen themselves in the young couple in the boat's bows – but where were they sailing from, and where to? Even if we refrain from interpreting the painting as a parable of fate, the young Grand Duchess may have recognized Stralsund, Greifswald and Dresden in the silhouetted buildings, and her husband might perhaps have seen another city: St Petersburg.

Is there any evidence to support this association? Yes: the place where the picture was eventually hung, in the so-called Cottage at Peterhof, the royal palace to the west of St Petersburg. It went on the east wall of the large salon, above a 'Gothic' doorway which led out on to a covered veranda. The painting paraphrases the view presented to the (privileged) observer, across the park to the shore of the Gulf of Finland and from there eastwards to a distant prospect of St Petersburg. The picture's composition depends on the contrast of near and far, the moment and the eternal, the solid and the illusory. Tilting slightly, the boat reacts to the rhythm of the waves. The moment determines its position. It could not be more solidly or meticulously constructed. Every detail is the product of careful study (as a watercolour testifies: ill. 76). Although every part of the boat is plainly recognizable and functional, the faces of the couple in the bows belong to an intermediate zone, where portrait moves closer to prototype. Lastly, the distant town appears wholly removed into the realm of the marvellous. The boat may be heading towards this insubstantial vision and its promise, but it is unlikely ever to reach it. Nikolay Pavlovich and Alexandra Feodorovna could thereby experience a German-Russian architectural conglomerate and transcend it in a parable.

Friedrich's admirer was the same man who, immediately after ascending the Russian throne as Tsar Nicholas I, had to confront the Decembrist uprising of young army officers, in December 1825. Its bloody suppression was his first act as Tsar. On the day five officers were executed, he retreated to his other palace near St Petersburg, Tsarskoye Selo, and arranged to be informed of events by couriers. Fleeing reality, the autocrat could also seek refuge in Friedrich's picture.

Formally and conceptually, the culmination of the paintings in which women have a central role is undoubtedly *The Chalk Cliffs on Rügen* (ills 79, 80). Today's visitors to the cliffs near Stubbenkammer follow a worn and well-fenced path to a point near where Friedrich set his three figures on the brink of the

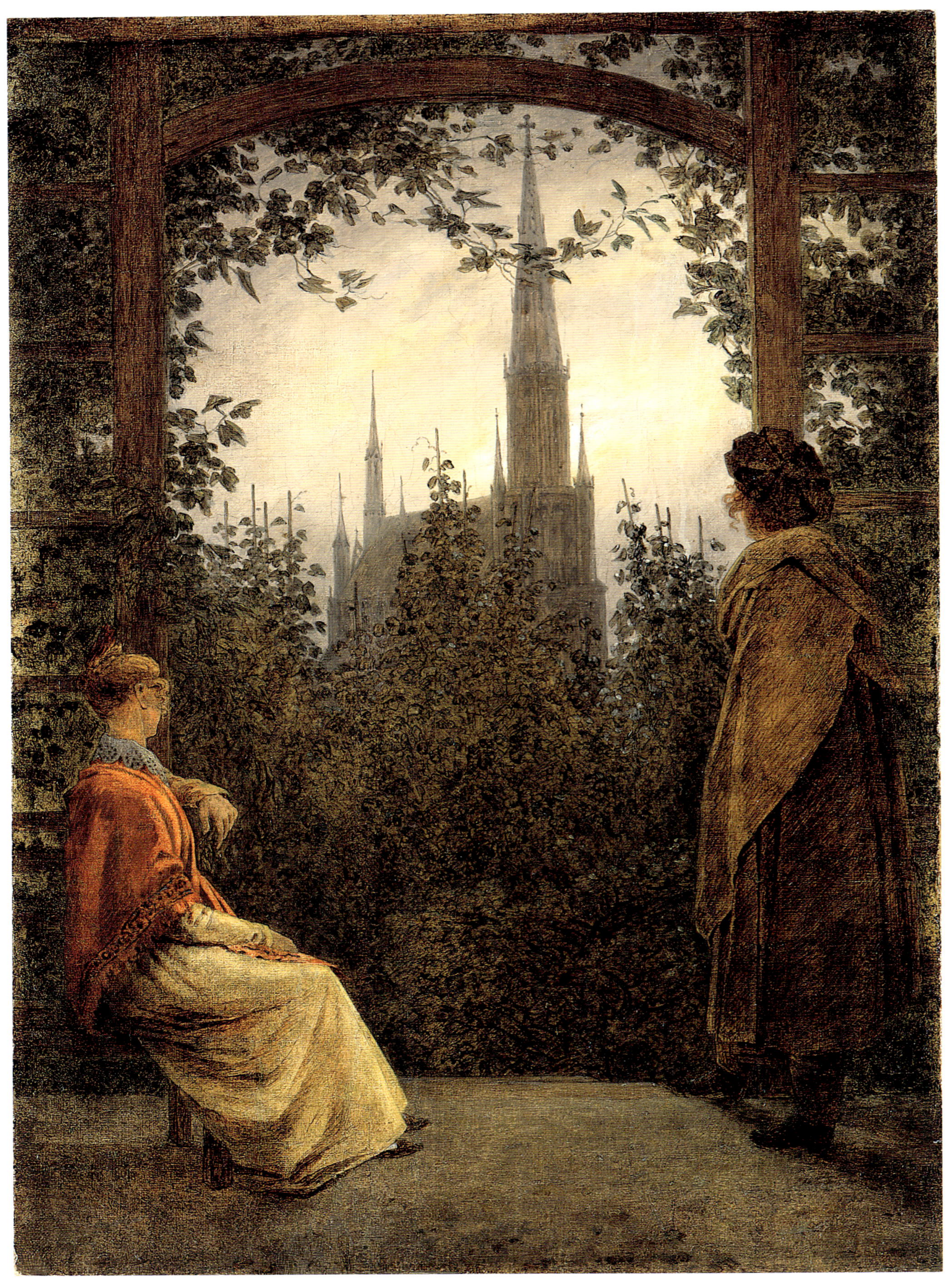

70. *The Summerhouse*,
1818, oil on canvas,
30 x 22 cm (11¾ x 8⅝ in.).
Neue Pinakothek, Munich.

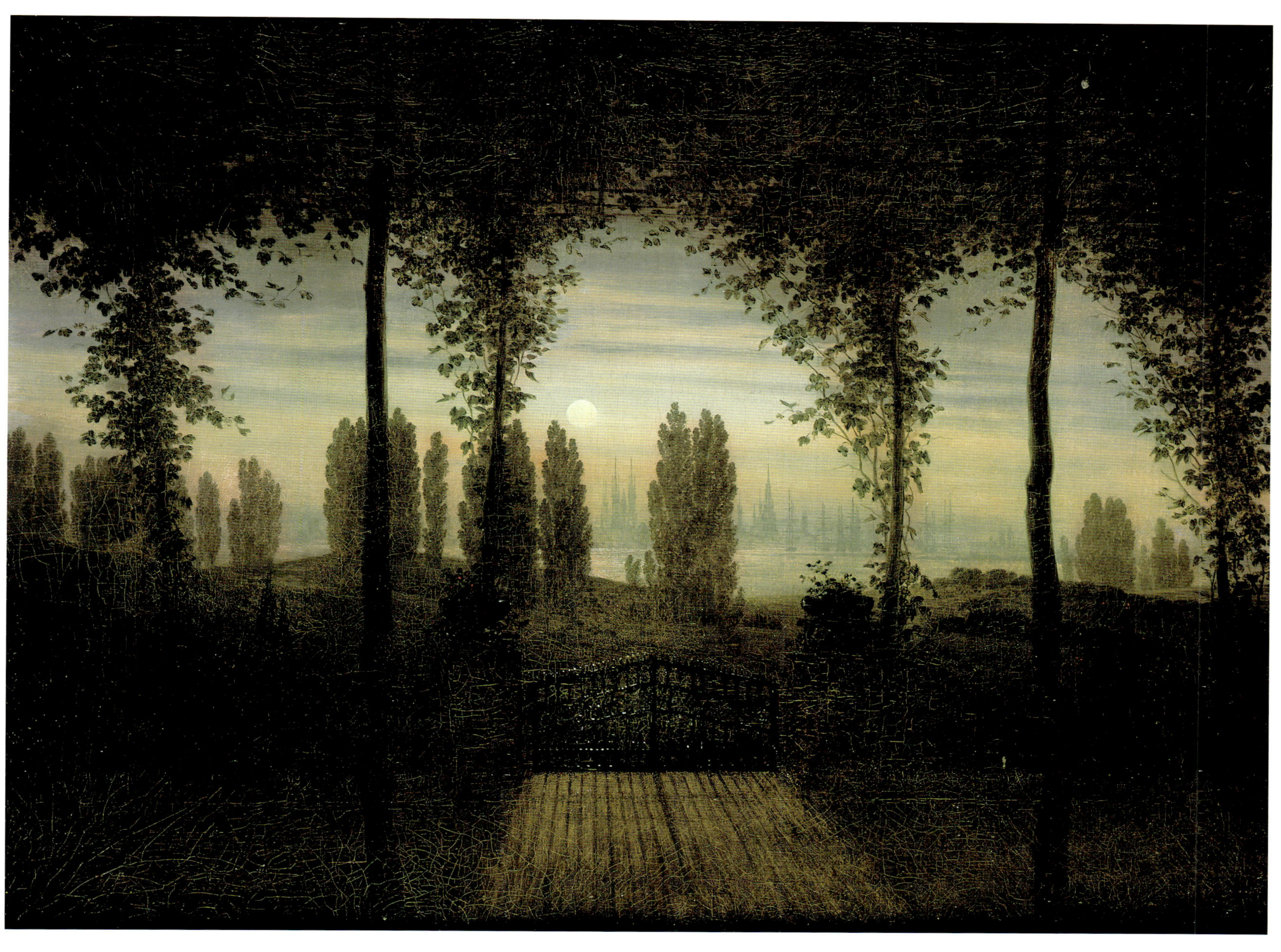

71. *Picture in Remembrance of Johann Emanuel Bremer,*
1817, oil on canvas,
43.5 × 57 cm (17 × 22½ in.).
Schloss Charlottenburg, Berlin

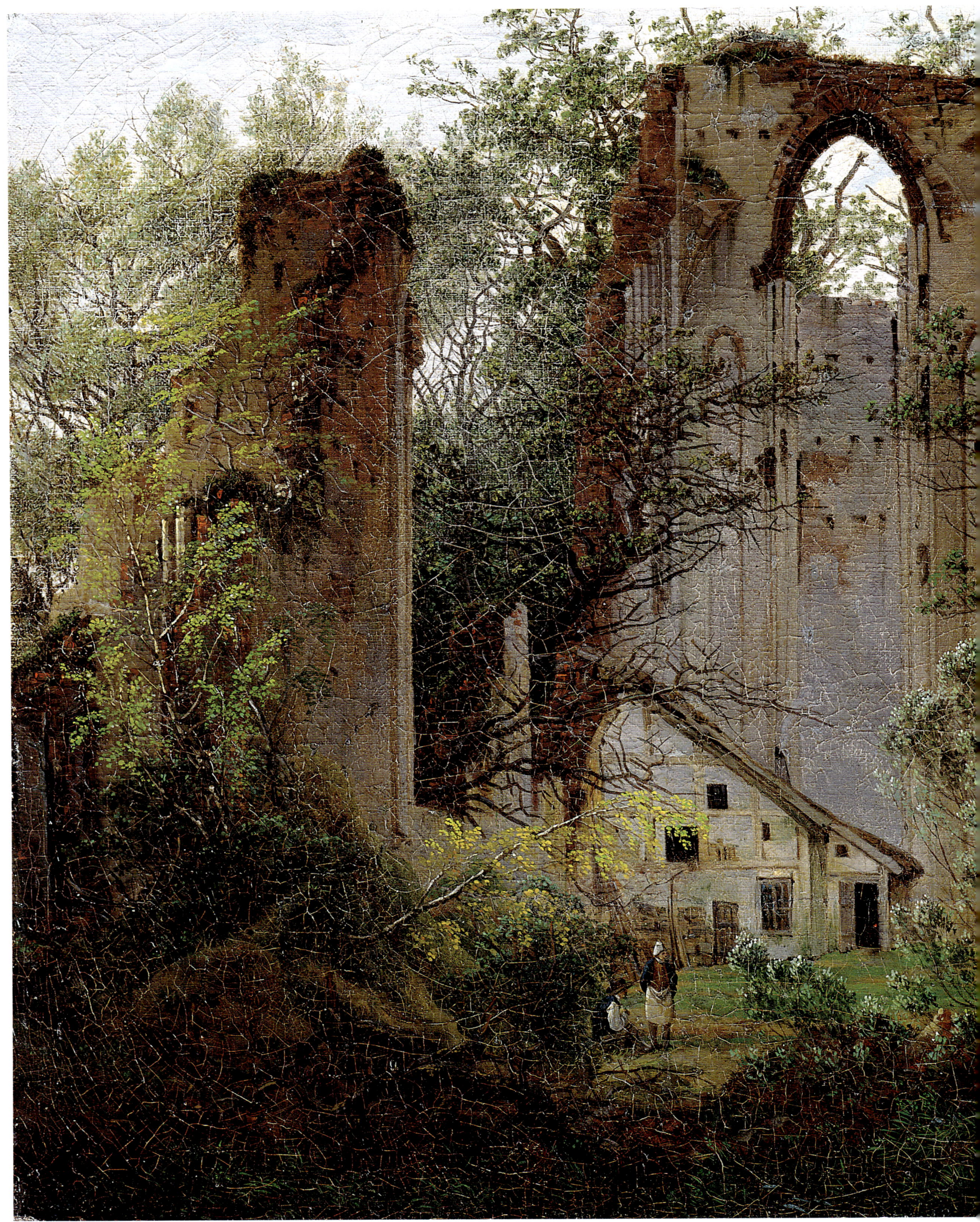

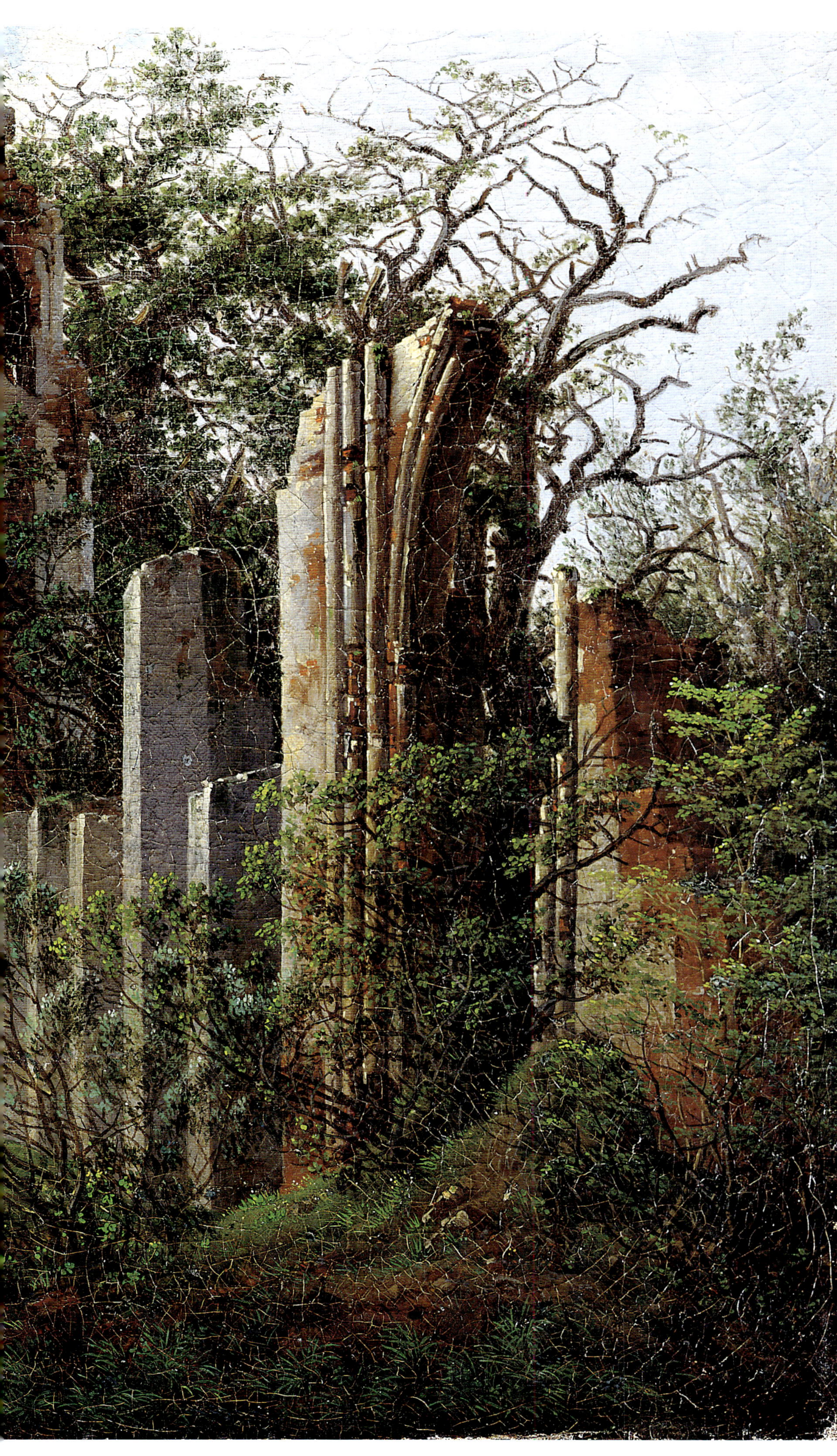

72. ***The Ruins at Eldena,***
c. 1825, oil on canvas,
35 x 49 cm (13¾ x 19¼ in.).
Nationalgalerie, Berlin.

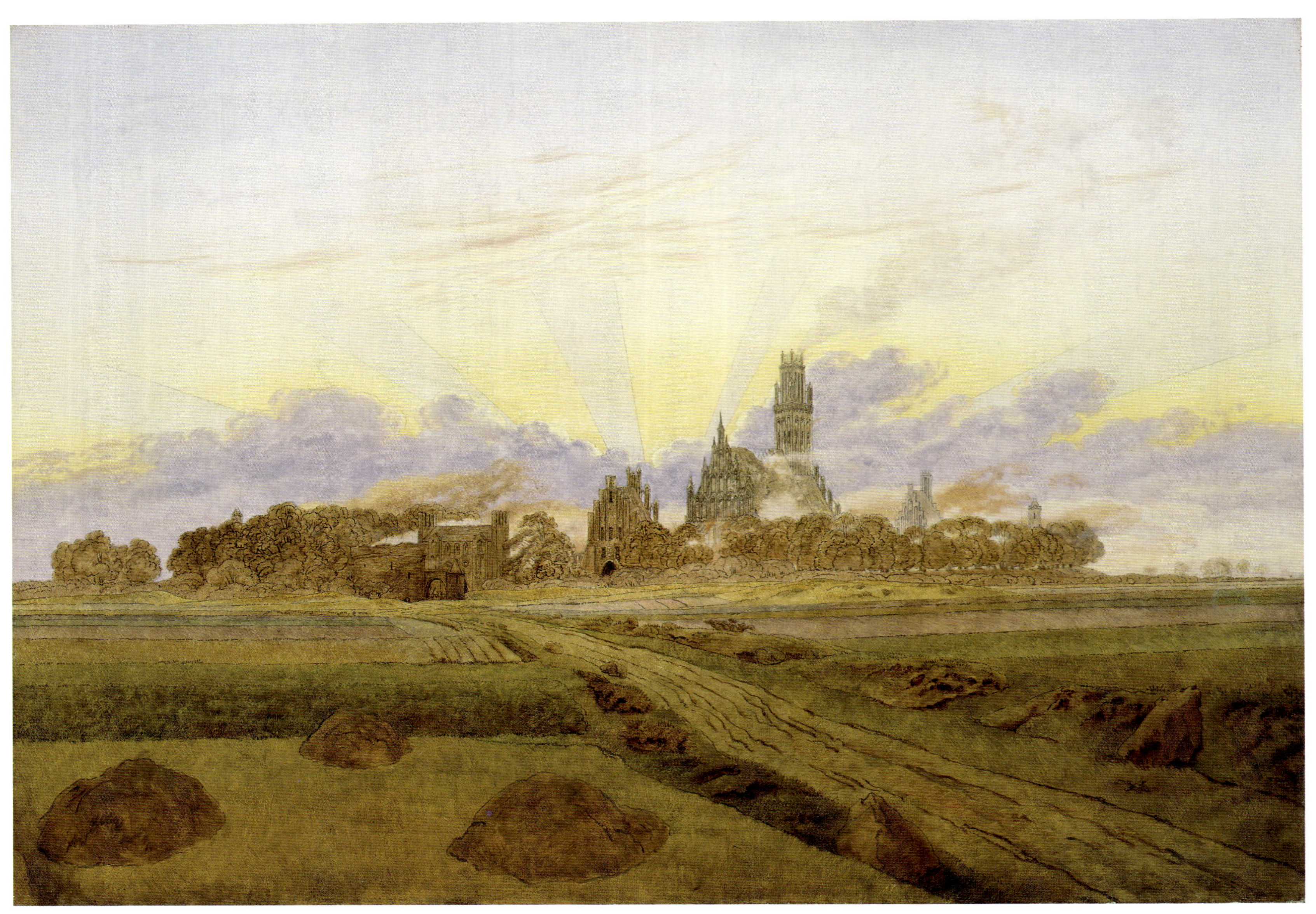

73. *Sunrise: Neubrandenburg in Flames*, 1835, oil on canvas, 72.2 x 101.3 cm (28½ x 39⅞ in.). Hamburger Kunsthalle, Hamburg.

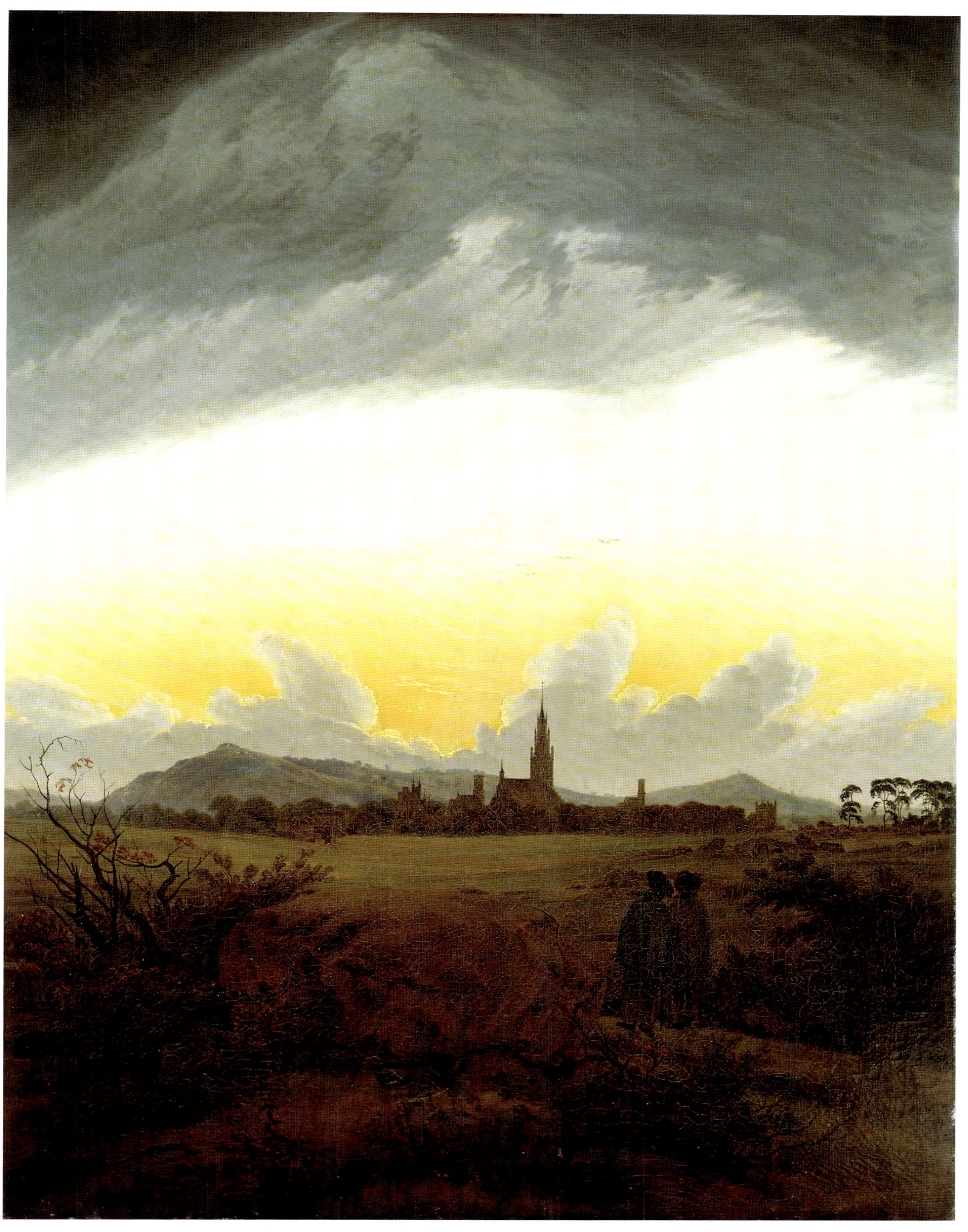

74. *Neubrandenburg in Morning Mist*,
1816–17, oil on canvas, 92 × 71.5 cm (36¼ × 28¼ in.).
Stiftung Pommern, Gemäldegalerie und Kulturgeschichtliche Sammlungen, Kiel.

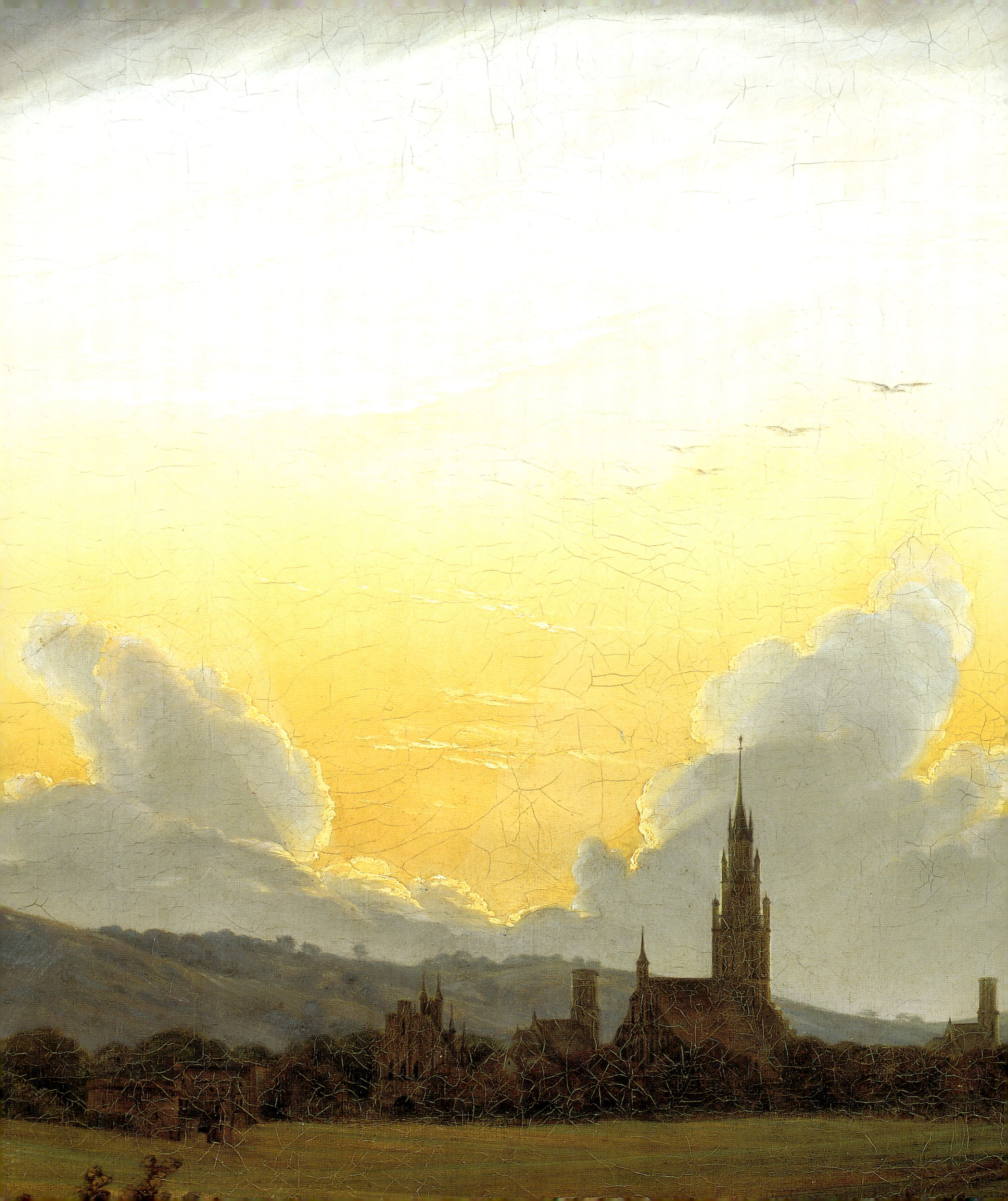

precipice. It goes without saying that the stillness and quiet of their cliff-edge experience is denied to the thousands who now flock to the place. A hackneyed tourist attraction, the real-life scene falls some way short of what Friedrich was able to make of it.

Instead of using perspective depth, the tension between near and far is expressed in a bold vertical construction. The sensation of depth results not from the gaze gradually moving on one plane towards a distant horizon, but from its sudden plunge into an abyss. This is due to the precipitous rise and fall of the chalk cliffs beyond the curve of the dangerously narrow strip of grass. The sea appears behind their jagged edges with equal abruptness, countering their vertical descent with a steep climb. Because it fills the funnel outlined by the cliffs, the sea does not stretch away into the depths of the picture but rises towards the top of the space, turning paler where it reaches the branches. The two tiny sailing boats provide an important clue to the vertical force: they are exactly the same size, as if one was directly above the other. The verticalization of the structure is achieved at the cost of the illusion of three-dimensionality, but it does create some astonishing formal equivalences. The sharp outline of the funnel has the effect of a silhouette, emphasizing the two-dimensional nature of the picture plane. If we turn the picture on its head, we find that the negative shape of the downward-pointing funnel is transformed into the positive shape of a bizarre mountain peak. To use Goethe's words, this painting really could 'just as well be looked at upside down'.

The unique and radical articulation of the picture surface is not an end in itself. It is also clear that the three human figures are not merely staffage; instead they represent three different ways of confronting nature. The woman points down into the abyss, the man crawling on hands and knees appears to be examining the blades of grass, the other man gazes out to sea. Nearness and distance are again thematicized, this time in association with human expectations. The knowledge that the picture records a memory of Friedrich's honeymoon prompts the question: how do these three people relate to one another, conceptually and biographically? Börsch-Supan interprets them as allegorical representations of the three cardinal Christian virtues. The woman's red dress stands for love, the standing man's green (?) coat for hope, and the crawling man's blue coat for faith. Recently Jensen proposed a different hypothesis: 'While the standing man in German costume shows Friedrich as artist ... he has also introduced himself into the picture in the older ... man, cautiously and courageously crawling towards the edge, as one who is integrated into social constraints, in their dependencies and anxieties.'

Independently from Jensen, my interpretation of Friedrich's dual vision had led me to believe that the two men do indeed represent a twofold self-portrait, but the conclusions I draw from it target, not the artist's self-doubt – presaging his later jealousy – but his artistic philosophy. The standing man is the painter looking at nature in its immensity (and saying 'How vast, how mighty, how glorious!'). The man peering near-sightedly at the blades of grass (on the very edge of the cliff, no less!) is the other Friedrich, who said 'Every flower, every stalk, considered on its own, is admirable and beautiful'; for whom the divine was present in everything, even grains of sand, and who denied that anything was secondary in importance: 'Nothing is secondary in a picture, everything belongs inescapably to the whole, and may therefore not be ignored.'

Seen thus, the two men are counterparts of the near and the distant. And the woman? She is not excluded from their relationship but gives her own pointer to the experience of nature with her gesture.

75. *Neubrandenburg in Morning Mist*, detail,
1816–17, oil on canvas, 92 × 71.5 cm (36¼ × 28¼ in.).
Stiftung Pommern, Gemäldegalerie und Kulturgeschichtliche Sammlungen, Kiel.

She draws attention to the depth of the abyss between the nearness of the grass and the distance of the sea. Her eyes are closed, as if she is obeying her husband's instruction to 'close your physical eye'. This connects her to the standing man, who is ignoring that advice for the moment. Jensen saw a coded link between the two figures: the trees and the branches meeting above can be seen as a heart.

The pairing of Friedrich's pictures creates double references which are mutually illuminating. *The Chalk Cliffs on Rügen* also has its pair, but it forms a sombre epilogue to the honeymoon memory. It is a watercolour from the 1820s that may have been painted on a return visit (ill. 78). Once again the man stands on a rocky ledge, but the magic has gone. This scene has neither the overriding unity nor the abrupt caesura of the cliff-edge. Jensen comments that the shrinking of the trees to stalks means that the outline of a heart is no longer complete: 'The heart has been broken.' The watercolour was the work of a man prematurely aged, isolated and tormented by jealousy.

Friedrich's own destiny is part of the psychological landscape of his age. In almost every one of the poems by Wilhelm Müller that Schubert set in his *Winterreise*, there are lines that seem to mirror the painter's distraction and dread of human contact:

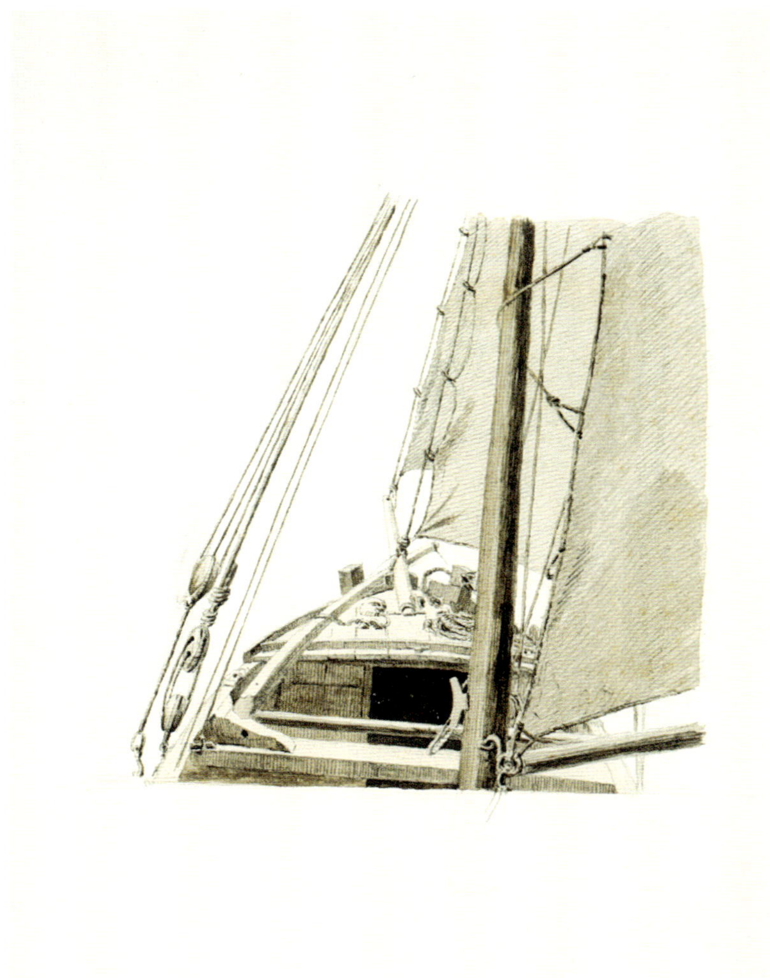

76. Study for *On the Sailing Boat*, 1818, pencil and wash, 36 x 26 cm (14⅛ x 10¼ in.). Nasjonalgalleriet, Oslo.

77. *On the Sailing Boat*, 1818–19, oil on canvas, 71 x 56 cm (28 x 22 in.). Hermitage Museum, St Petersburg.

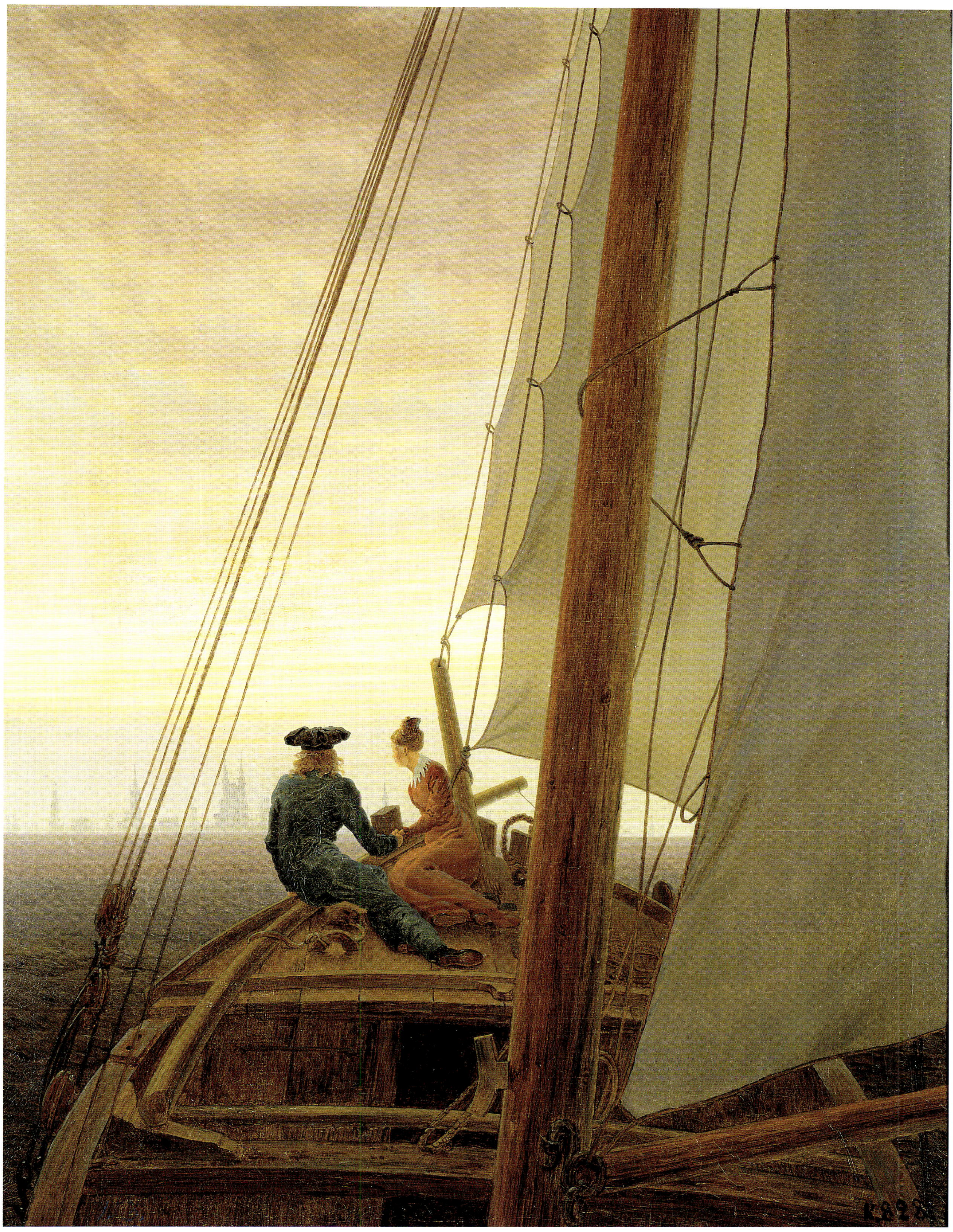

Durch des Bergstroms trock'ne Rinnen
Wind ich ruhig mich hinab –
Jeder Strom wird's Meer gewinnen
Jedes Leiden auch sein Grab. (*Irrlicht*)

('Down the mountain stream's dry gullies
I calmly pick my way
Every stream will reach the sea,
Every sorrow finds its grave.')

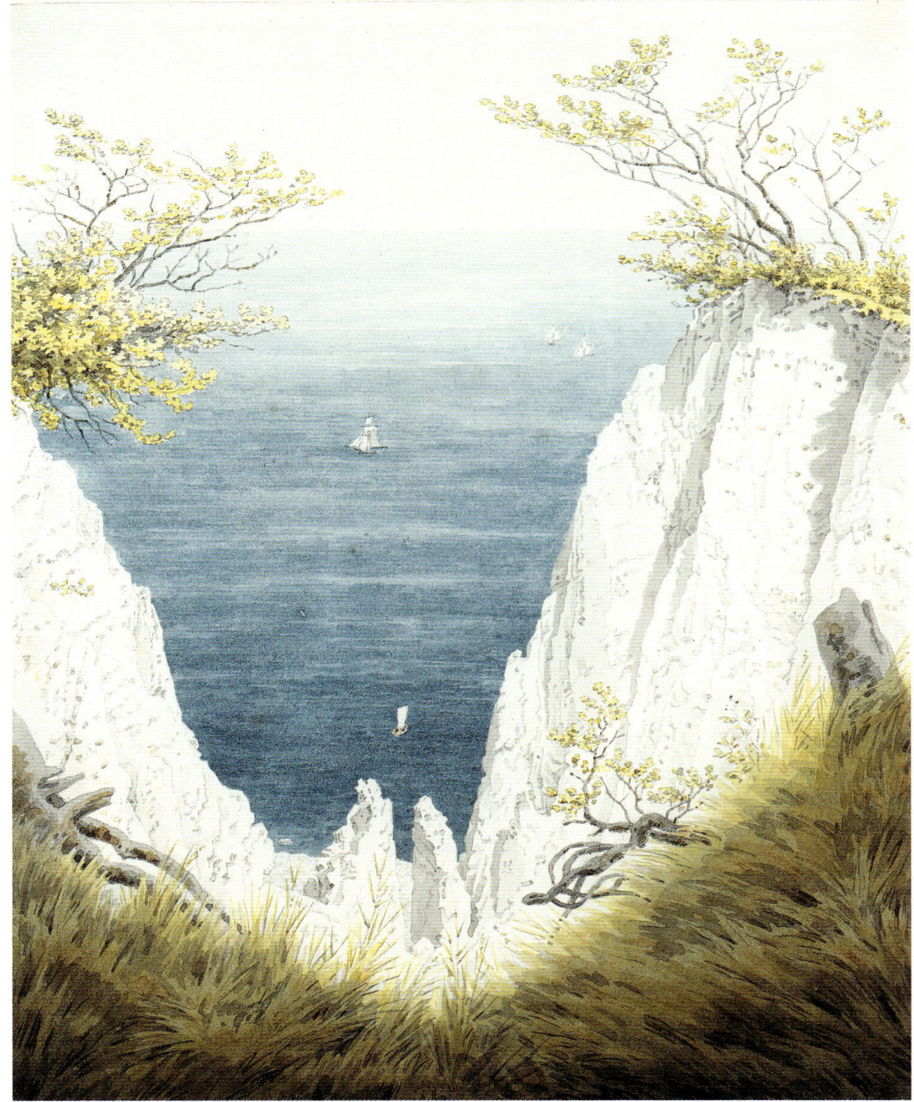

78. ***The Chalk Cliffs on Rügen,***
c. 1825–26, pencil and watercolour,
31.7 x 25.2 cm (12½ x 9⅞ in.).
Museum der bildenden Künste, Leipzig.

79 and 80. (overleaf)
The Chalk Cliffs on Rügen,
after 1818, oil on canvas,
90.5 x 71 cm (35½ x 28 in.).
Museum Oskar Reinhart am Stadtgarten, Winterthur.

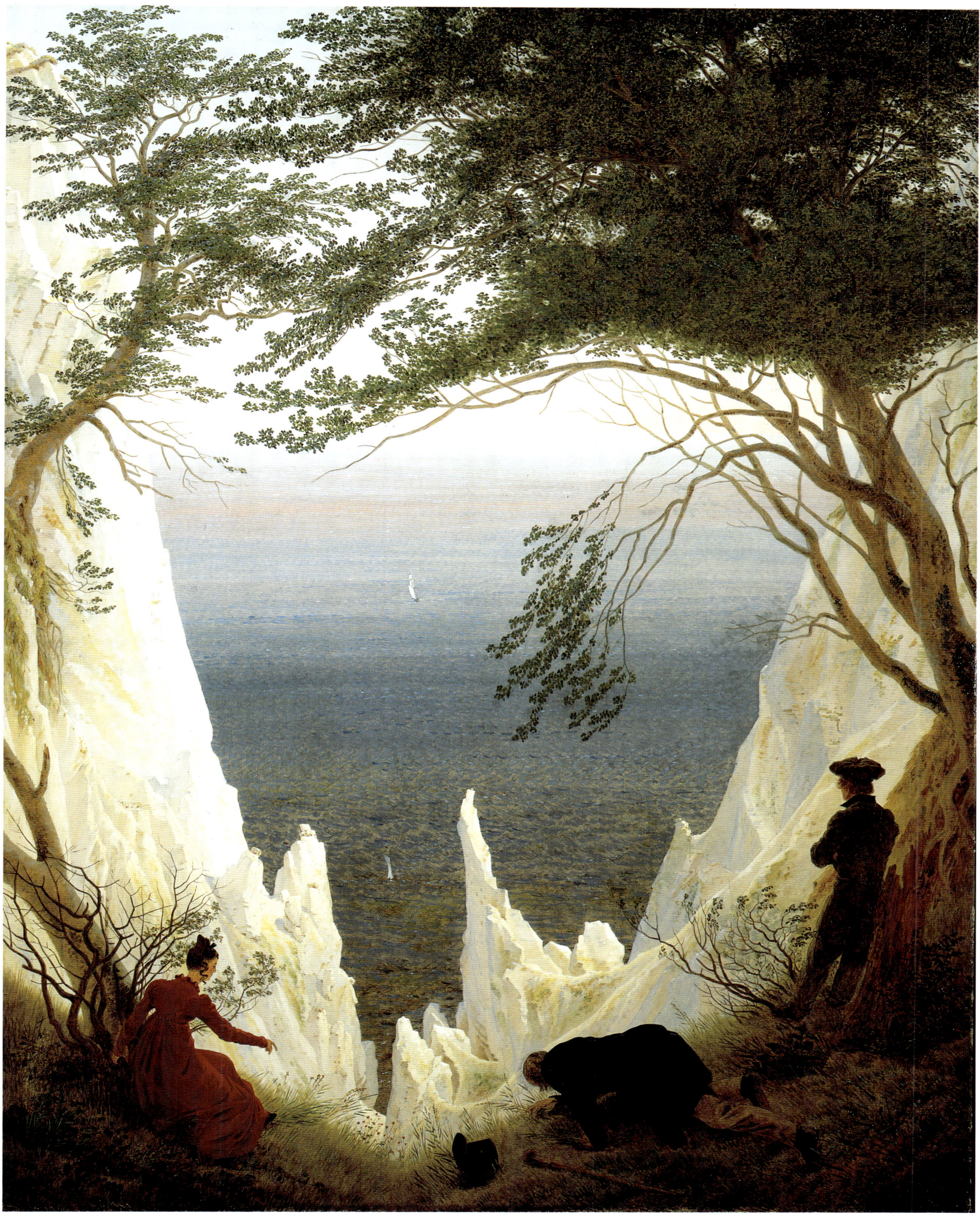

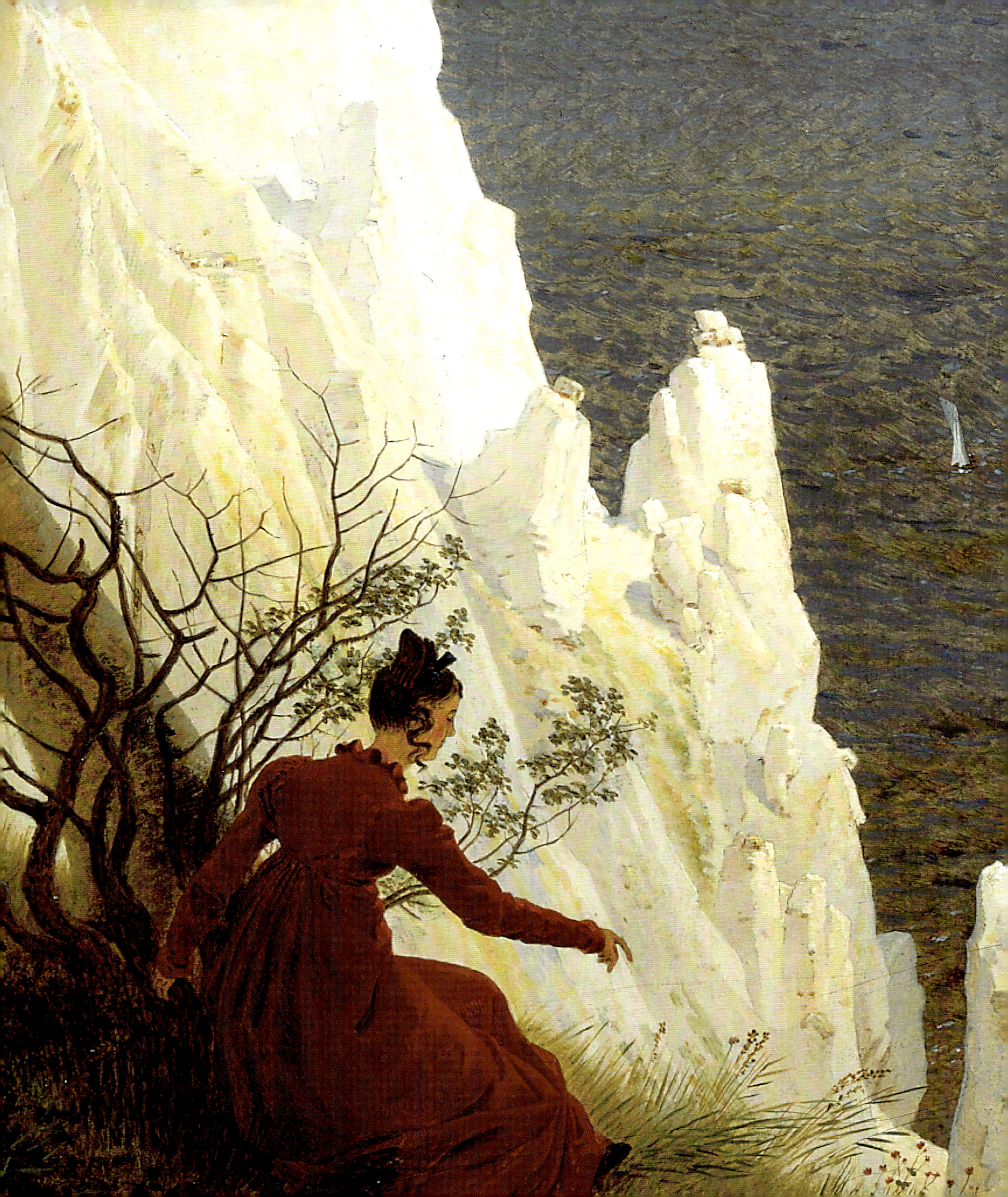

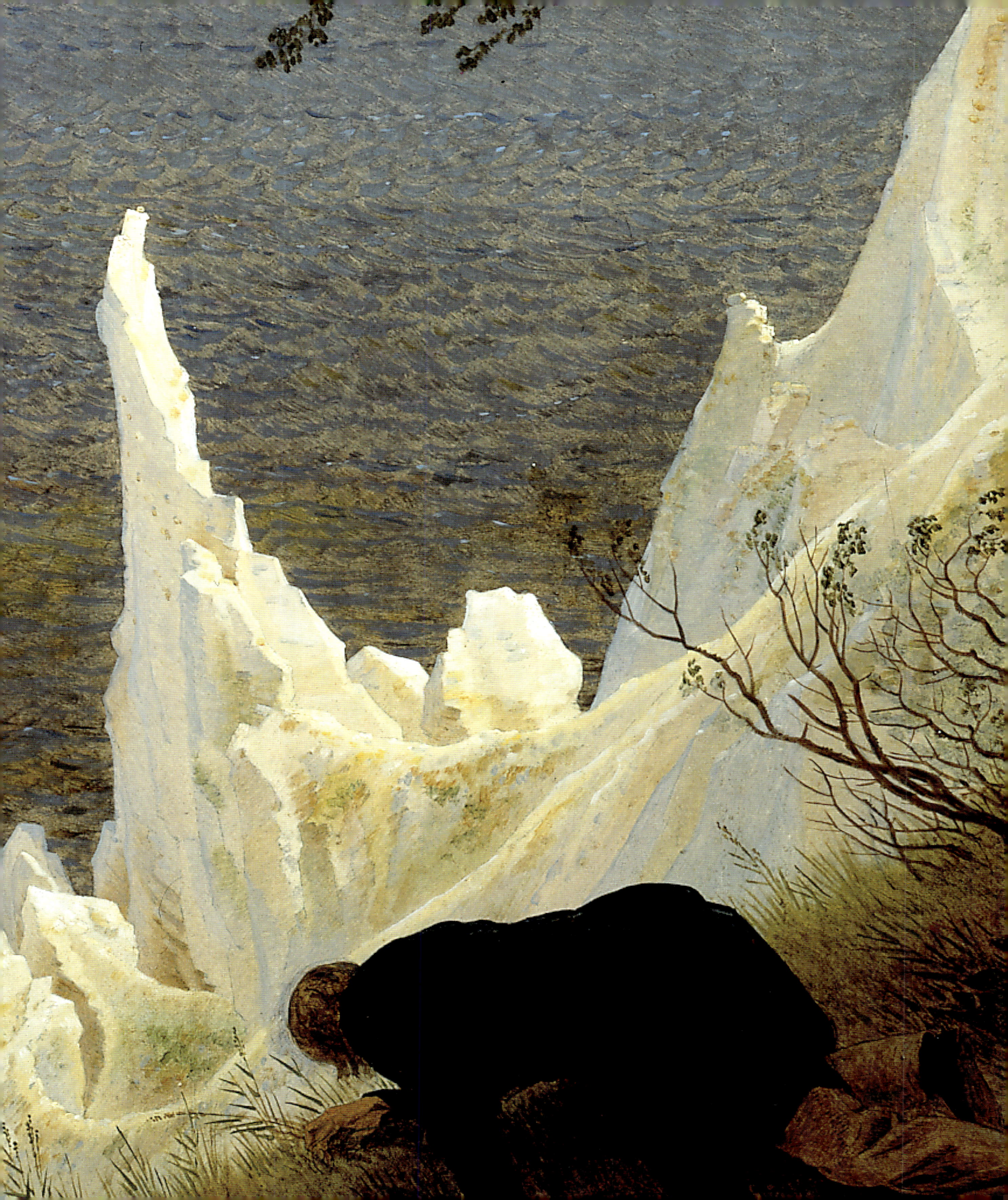

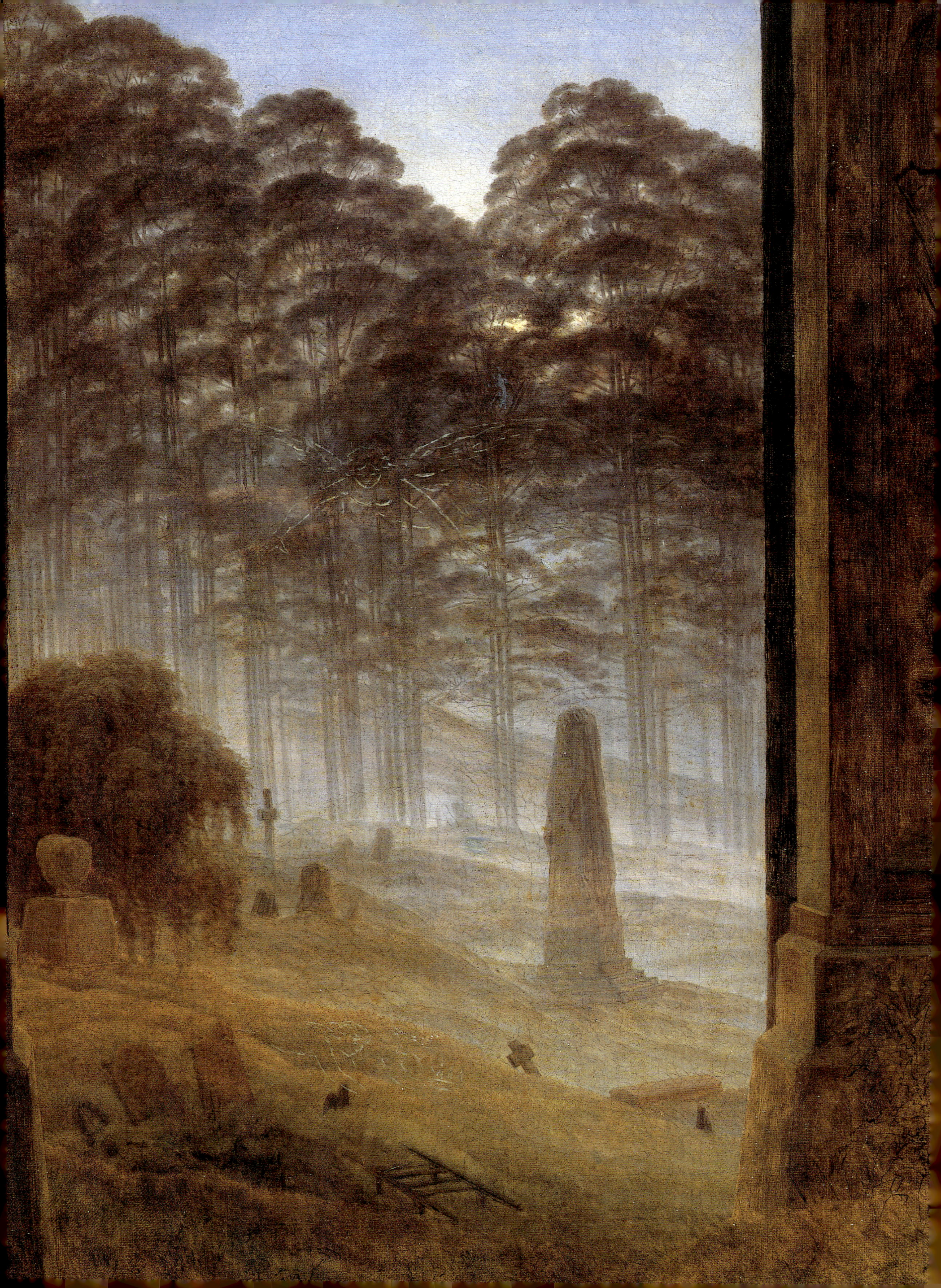

IV

THE 'OBSCURE TOTAL IDEA'

Behind us lies the decade from 1810 to 1820, when Friedrich's art achieved its greatest breadth and depth, and when he painted the key works that established his reputation. In discussing these, we examined three significant categories of subject matter: an overt concern with religion, the influence of patriotism, and the role of Woman both as an autonomous being and as the partner of Man. We have seen that the painter was not merely a loner, burrowing away obsessively at *la tragédie du paysage*. To see him as such would be to recognize the most obvious characteristic of his art, but this is merely one of many possibilities. The full spectrum is richer and more varied: it embraces isolation and companionship, faith in this world and expectations of the world beyond. But we are underestimating Friedrich's real contribution to the paradigm shift in painting if we restrict ourselves to its most important aspect, the iconization of landscape, and overlook what that step meant for the representation of man in nature. What Friedrich developed were entirely new levels of expression. In place of the traditional figures of nymphs and shepherds or heroic and mythological role-players, the painter depicted himself, and his friends and contemporaries, in still surrender to the experience of nature (ill. 82). Their meditations are consistent with the idea of sacralized nature; they are focused on the Creator. This is expressed through the use of rear-view figures. Friedrich did not invent this topos but he elevated it to an expressive dramatic formula and continued to find new variations on it (see Appendix II, page 256).

At this stage I want to take stock provisionally, and so will change direction. Up until now Friedrich's formal concepts have only been briefly mentioned in connection with his treatment of pictorial space. Since the publication of Helmut Börsch-Supan's dissertation on structure in Friedrich's paintings (1960), terms like 'spatial leap' (*Raumsprung*) and 'spatial barrier' (*Raumsperre*) have been used to describe the formal devices that Friedrich invented to portray such concepts as alienation, withdrawal and man's accord with nature. Nearness and distance are the coordinates on which everything turns. Within this field of reference, tensions are generated by figures and objects or masses, by rocks, trees, mountains, ships and boats, churches, tombs and fences. Through these objective attributes, space becomes something we can experience and a metaphor with multiple meanings.

The key to Friedrich's compositional procedure lies in space–mass relationships, which usually follow one of two paths. One approach involves a vertical arrangement of the picture space into grids or strips (*The Abbey in the Oak Wood*); in the other, space is arranged horizontally in bands, which the eye glides over (*The Monk by the Sea*). The following discussion will examine the syntactical characteristics of

81. *The Graveyard Gate*, detail,
1824–26, oil on canvas,
143 x 110 cm (56¼ x 43¼ in.).
Gemäldegalerie Neue Meister, Dresden.

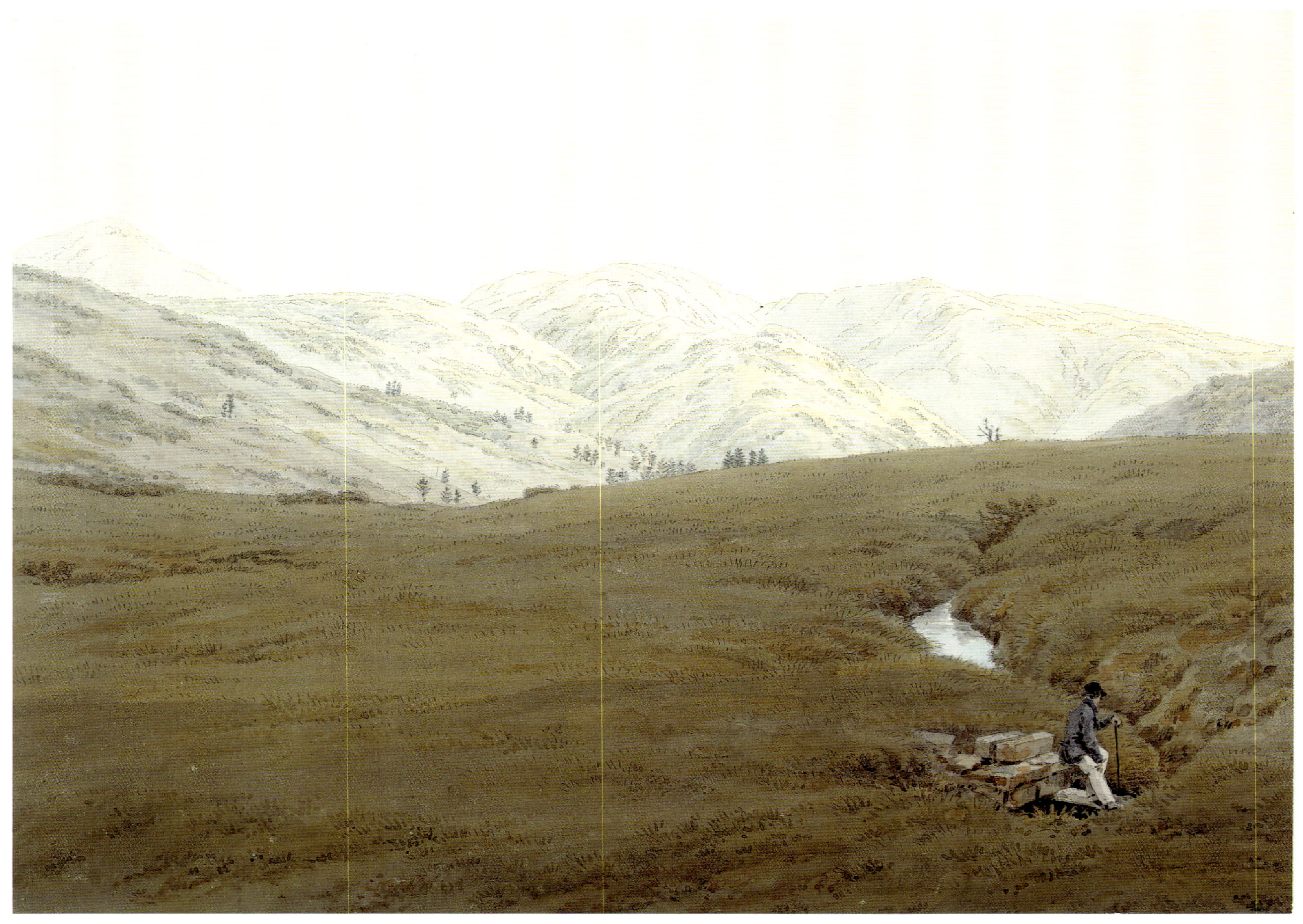

82. *The Source of the River Elbe*, *c.* 1830, pencil and watercolour, 25 × 34 cm (9⅞ × 13⅜ in.). Private collection.

these two methods of structuring space; not with a view to compiling a systematic catalogue, but with the intention at least of addressing all the important aspects of Friedrich's pictorial spaces as well as the transitions between them.

The first use of vertically ordered spaces is found in the idealized *View of Mountains with Waterfall* (ill. 4). It contains the underlying pattern, the *prima idea*, so to speak, of the manifold ways in which spaces and volumes can interact. In the foreground, on the central axis, there is an empty space between two rock massifs. These rocks, together with the gorge they frame, set up a three-beat rhythm: mass – space – mass, or rise (*arsis*) – fall (*thesis*) – rise. This is the rhythm of a triptych. In a triptych, of course, the central panel usually takes the main stress while here it has the falling accent, as the gap between the other two elements. Or does it? If the viewer raises his gaze above the gorge, the empty space unexpectedly turns into the mass of the steep mountain. The near and its constriction are transformed into the distant, where there is breadth in plenty. The upright spatial funnel of the gorge turns itself inside out to produce its own physical conclusion: a circumflex accent, whose volume completes the opening but does not close it.

When described as a calculation, Friedrich's management of form seems devoid of poetry and symbolism. Is this the work of some pedant wielding a set square? To counter that charge, I will point out the advantages of objective, prosaic formal language: it avoids superfluous use of symbols and lays down a framework that gives structure to the spaces. Concealed triptychs are often used to brace these frameworks, and a few examples will illustrate the wide range that this model permits.

Friedrich took the gorge of that early painting as a model and varied it in a series of landscapes, including *The Chalk Cliffs on Rügen* (ill. 79), *Landscape in the Riesengebirge with Mist Rising* (ill. 59), *Morning in the Mountains* (ill. 84), *High Mountains* (ill. 83), *Rocky Ravine* (ill. 85) and *Northern Lights* (ill. 164). The Vienna painting *Rocky Ravine* reverts to the elaborate descriptiveness of the earlier *View of*

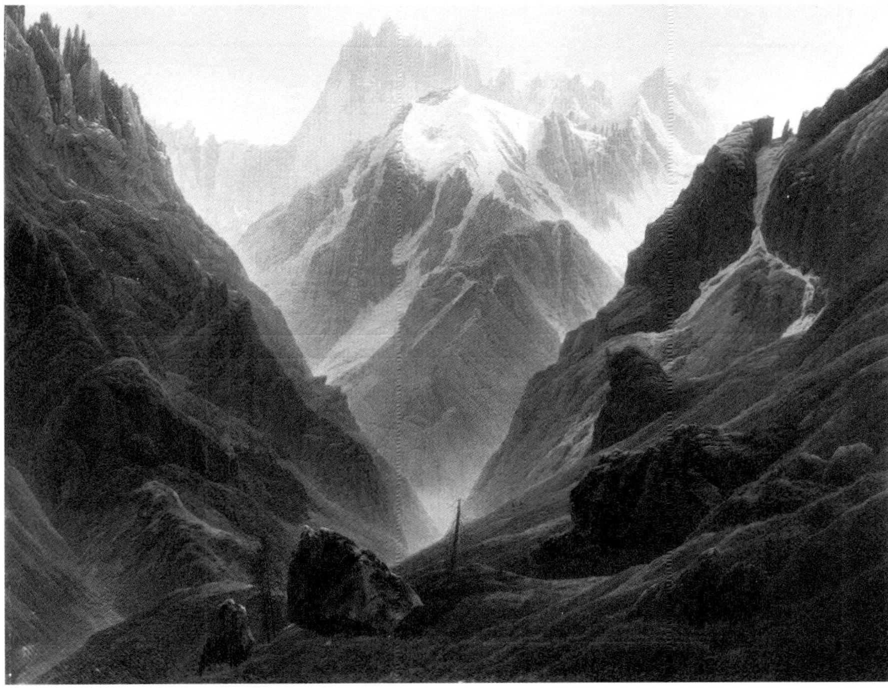

83. *High Mountains (Swiss Landscape)*,
1824, oil and canvas,
132 × 167 cm (52 × 65¾ in.).
Formerly Nationalgalerie, Berlin (destroyed 1945).

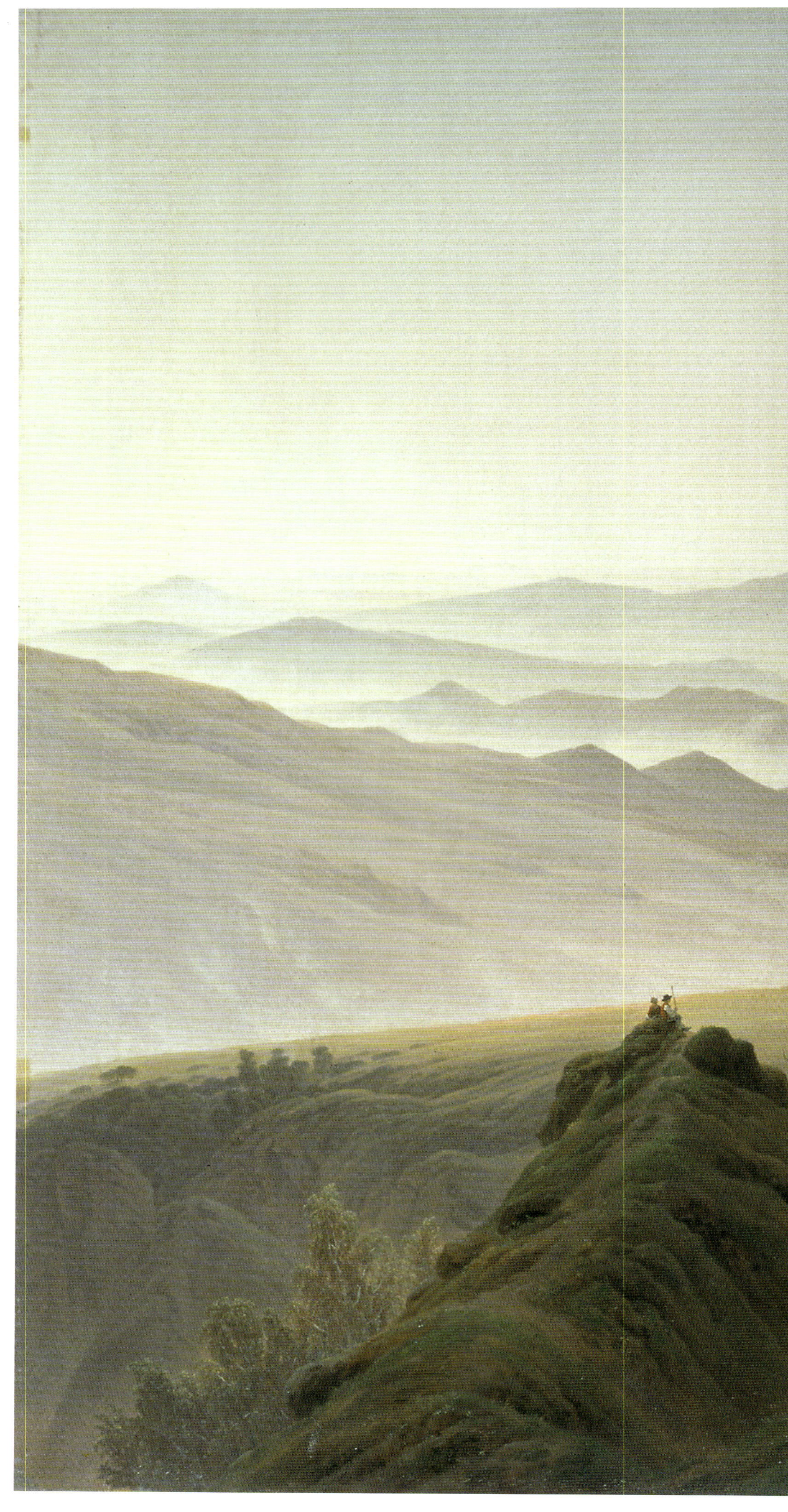

84. *Morning in the Mountains,*
1822–23, oil on canvas,
135 x 170 cm (53⅛ x 66⅞ in.).
Hermitage Museum, St Petersburg.

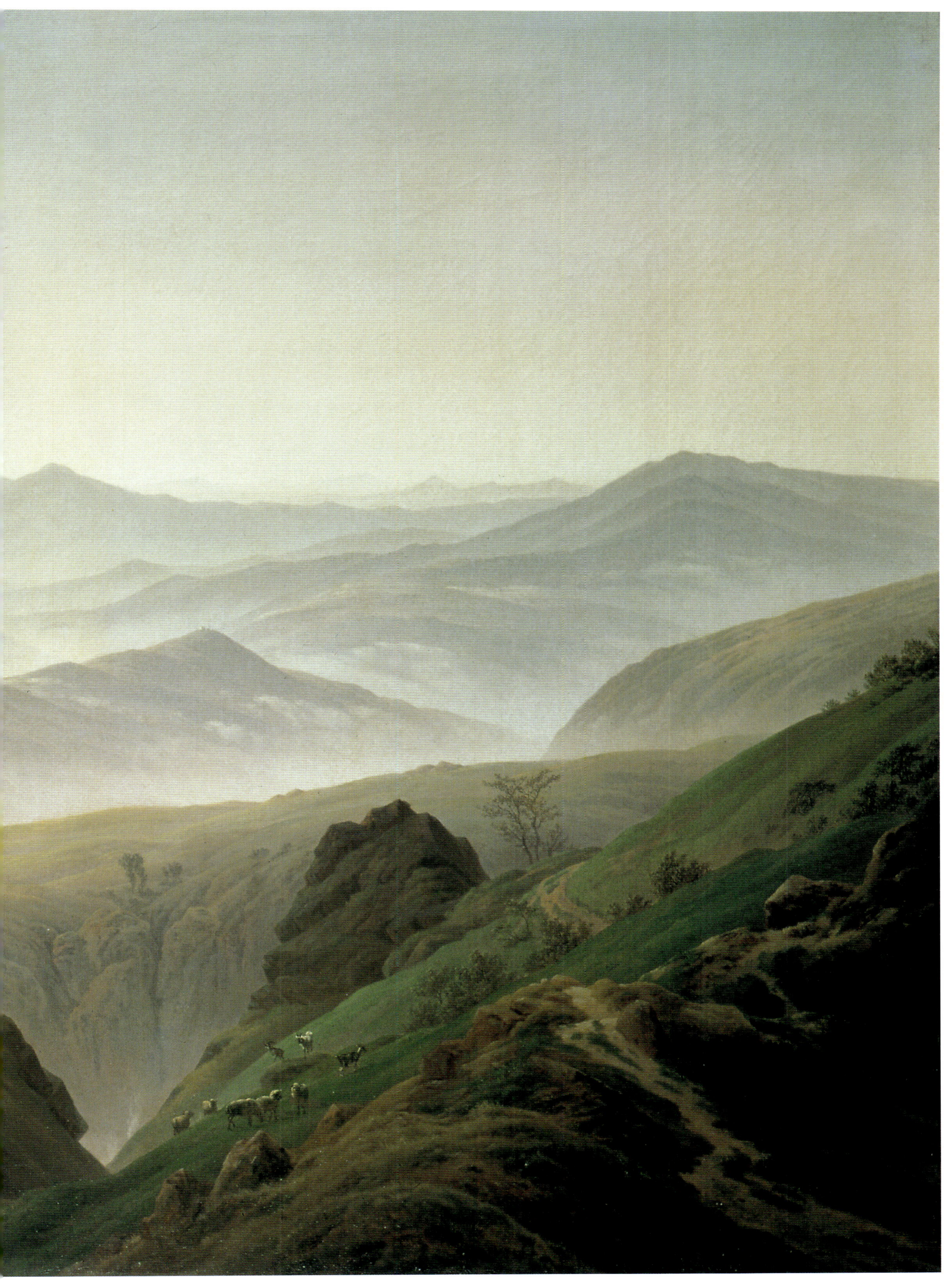

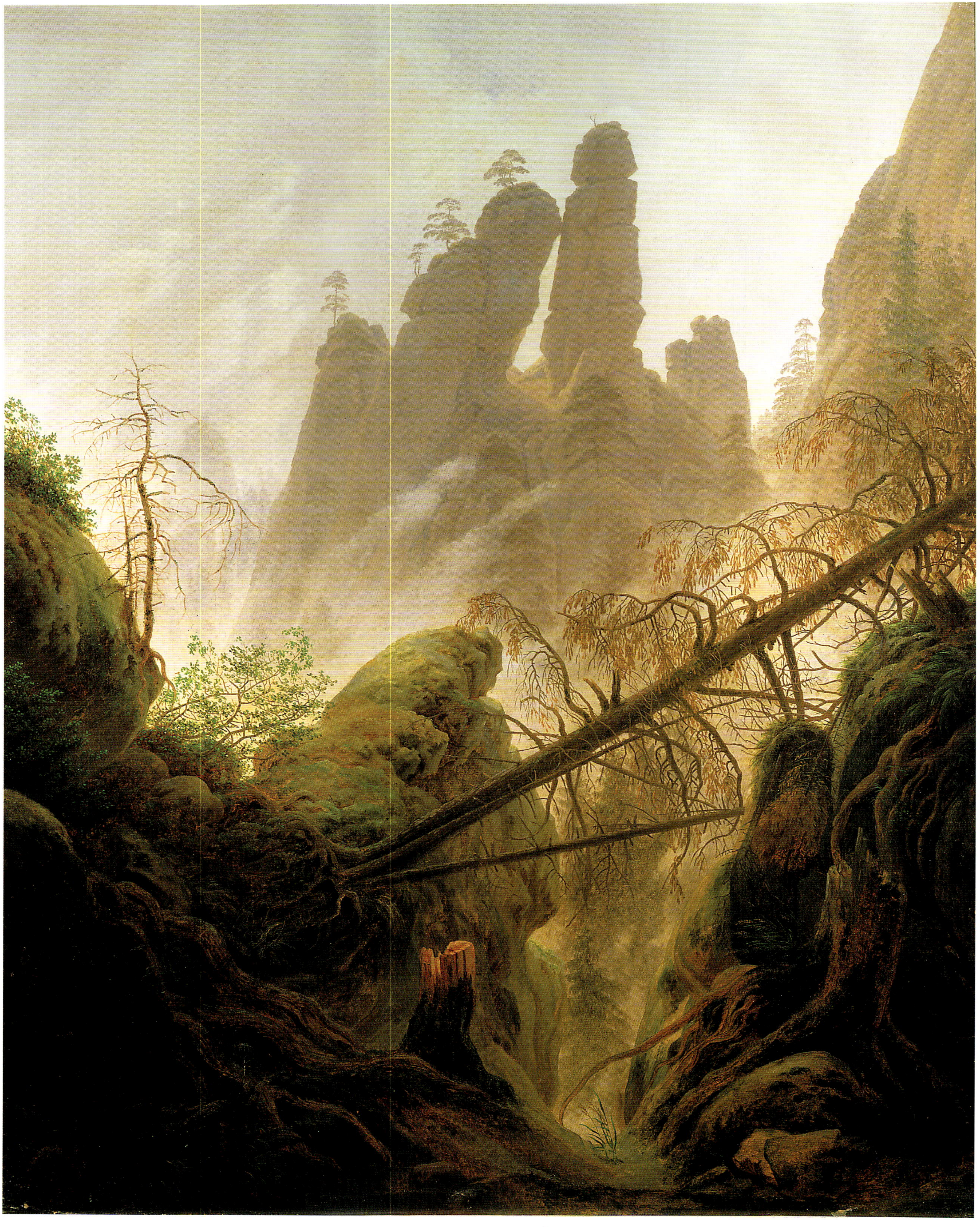

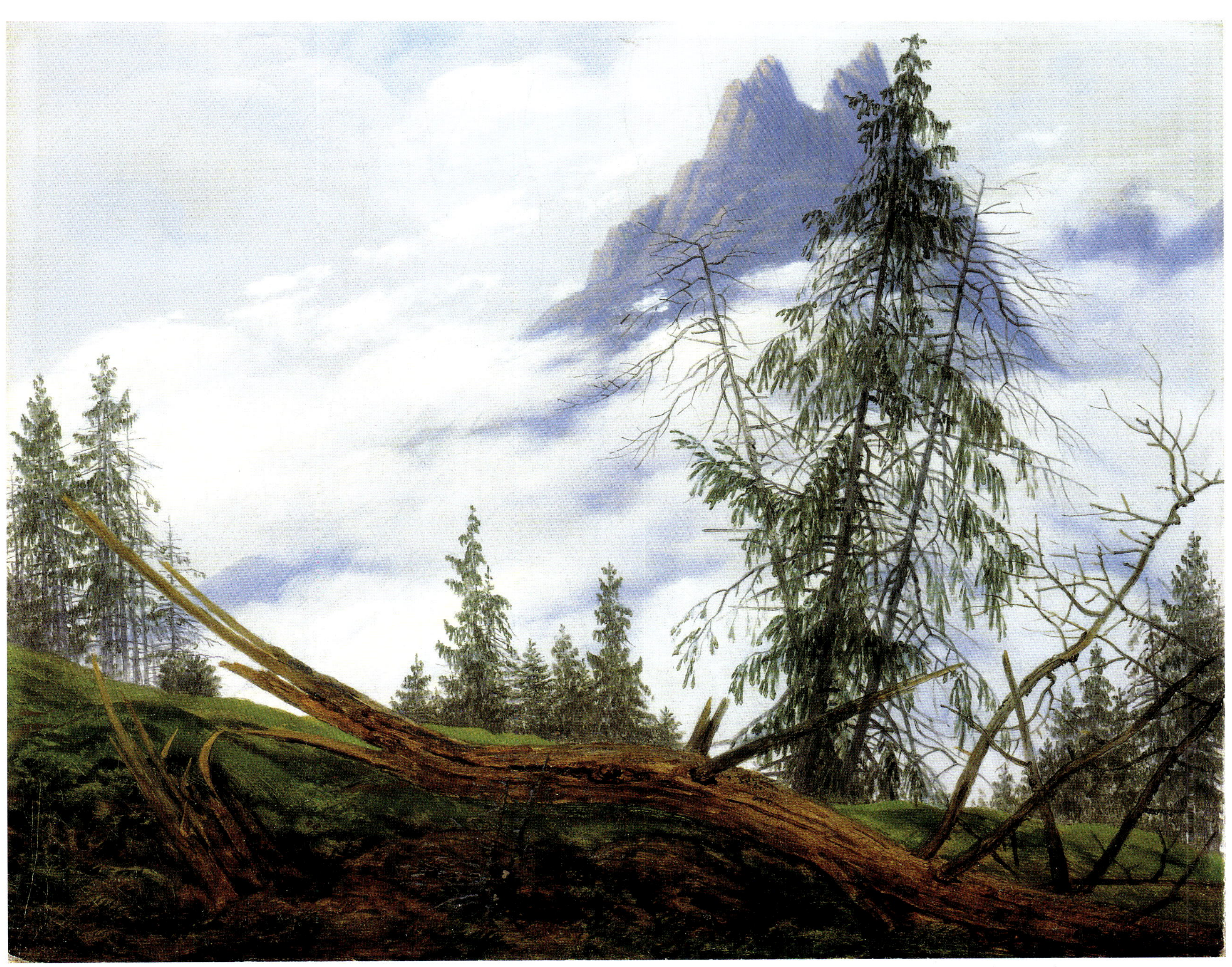

85. *Rocky Ravine,*
1822–23, oil on canvas,
94 x 74 cm (37 x 29⅛ in.).
Österreichische Galerie im Belvedere, Vienna.

86. ***Mountain Peak with Drifting Clouds,***
1835, oil on canvas,
25.1 x 30.6 cm (9⅞ x 12 in.).
Kimbell Art Museum, Fort Worth.

Mountains and its melodramatic pattern of *arsis* and *thesis*, and is reminiscent of late sixteenth-century landscape painting. The fallen fir tree provides an oblique bar, separating the gorge from the mountain peaks within the picture plane, but also linking foreground and background. *Mountain Peak with Drifting Clouds* (ill. 86) offers a variation on this structural model. The fallen and standing trees meet diagonally at a point in the right foreground, and the mountain peak rising up behind the mist provides a counterpoint. The slit formed by the asymmetrically converging tree trunks could indicate constraint and a feeling of oppression if a person is caught in it, as seen in the Schwerin *Winter Landscape* (ill. 33). Reading the trunks as materialized rays of light recalls the sunset in *The Tetschen Altar* (ill. 21). *The Cross beside the Baltic* (ill. 69) has a similar structure, with the circumflex shape of the rock blending into the V-formation of the objects in the foreground.

In the Essen *Landscape with Lunar Rainbow* (ill. 99), two groups of trees curve towards each other. From the gap between them rises a dark, rounded mountain top, but it occupies a distant spatial plane. The rainbow reaches across horizontally, crowning the material world with its ethereal curve of light. Like the curving necks of swans (ill. 87), two trees may come together, forming a natural archway or portal (ill. 142), to which the circumflex accent of a distant mountain is sometimes added (ill. 88). The flanking articulation is most apparent in *The Abbey in the Oak Wood* (ill. 23) and *Monastery Graveyard in Snow* (ill. 31), which are discussed in an earlier chapter. *Village Landscape in Morning Light* (ill. 89) inverts the relative weights of the elements in the triple rhythm. The main stress falls on a huge oak tree on the central axis, and the distant mountains are no more than unaccented silhouettes. The sky is hauled down to the meagre pond where it is mirrored in the accessible foreground. Friedrich makes similar use of reflection in the painting's pair, *Moonrise by the Sea* (ill. 90), where it occurs between the solid matter of the large rock on the shore and the equally wide oval of the moonlit bank of cloud. Nearness and distance echo each other's shapes, as in the two landscapes with rainbows (ills 98 and 99), in which heaven and earth fit together like a basin and its lid.

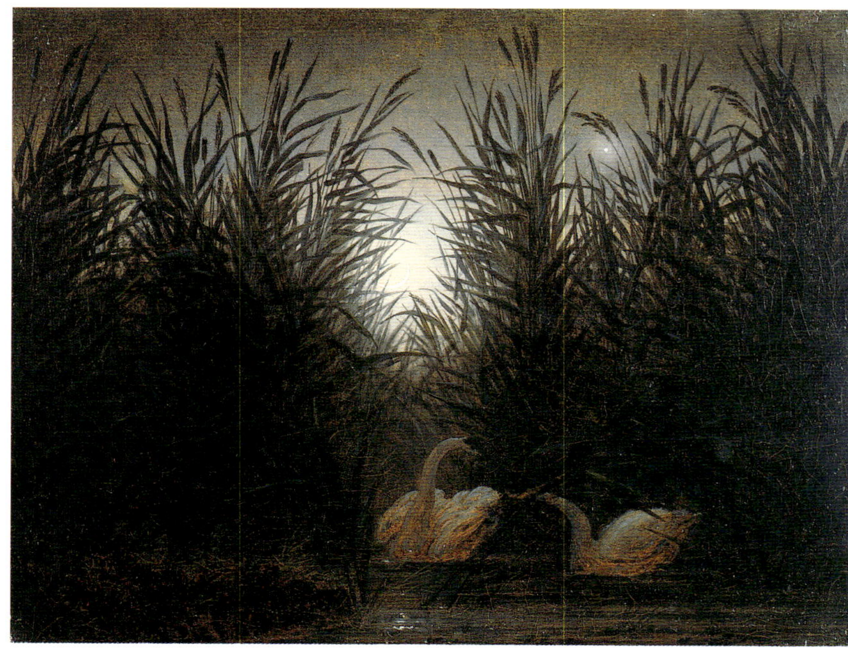

87. *Swans in the Rushes*, 1820, oil on canvas, 35.5 × 44 cm (14 × 17⅜ in.). Goethemuseum, Frankfurt.

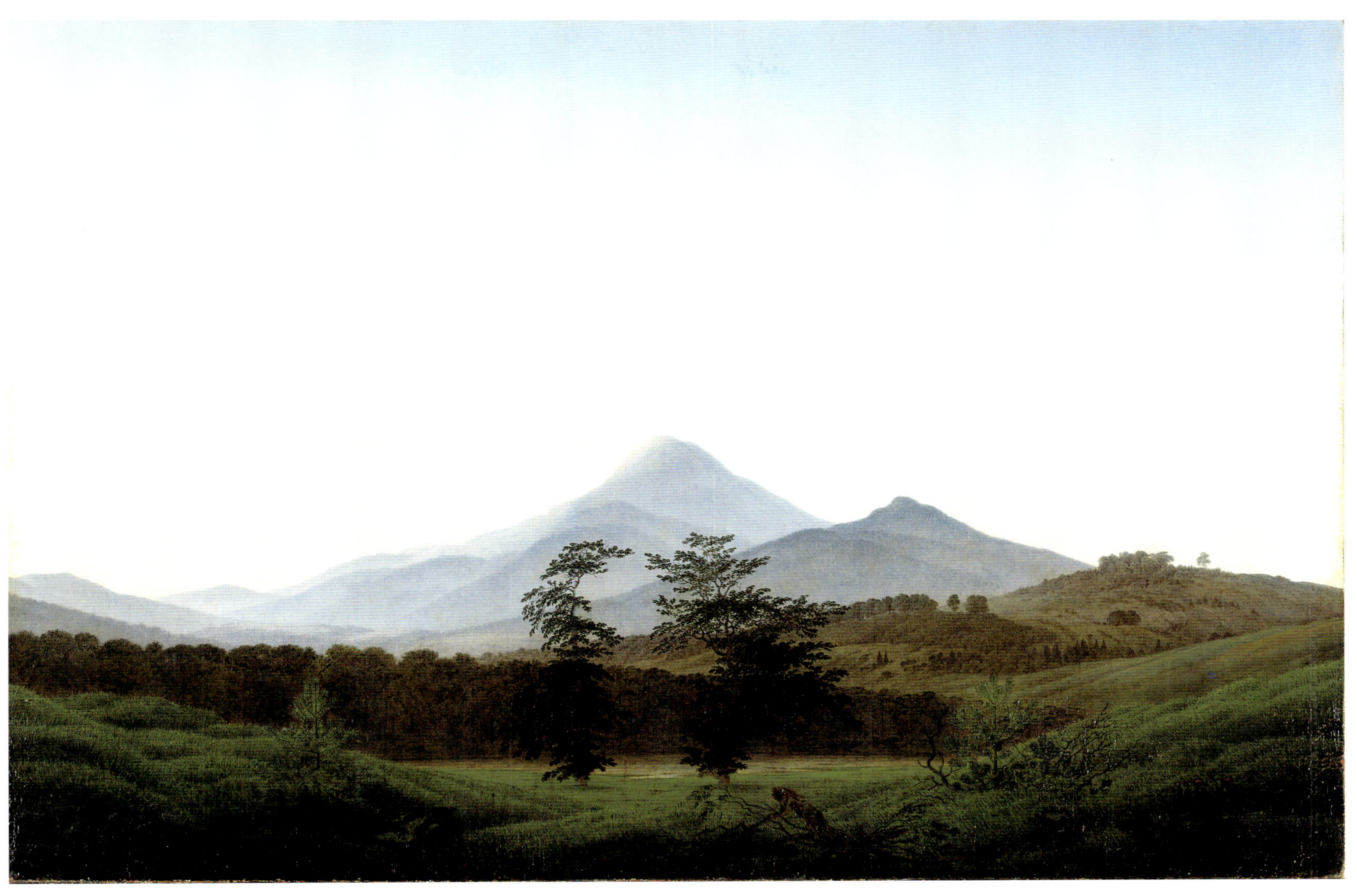

88. *Bohemian Landscape*,
1810, oil on canvas,
70 × 104.5 cm (27⅝ × 41⅛ in.).
Staatsgalerie, Stuttgart.

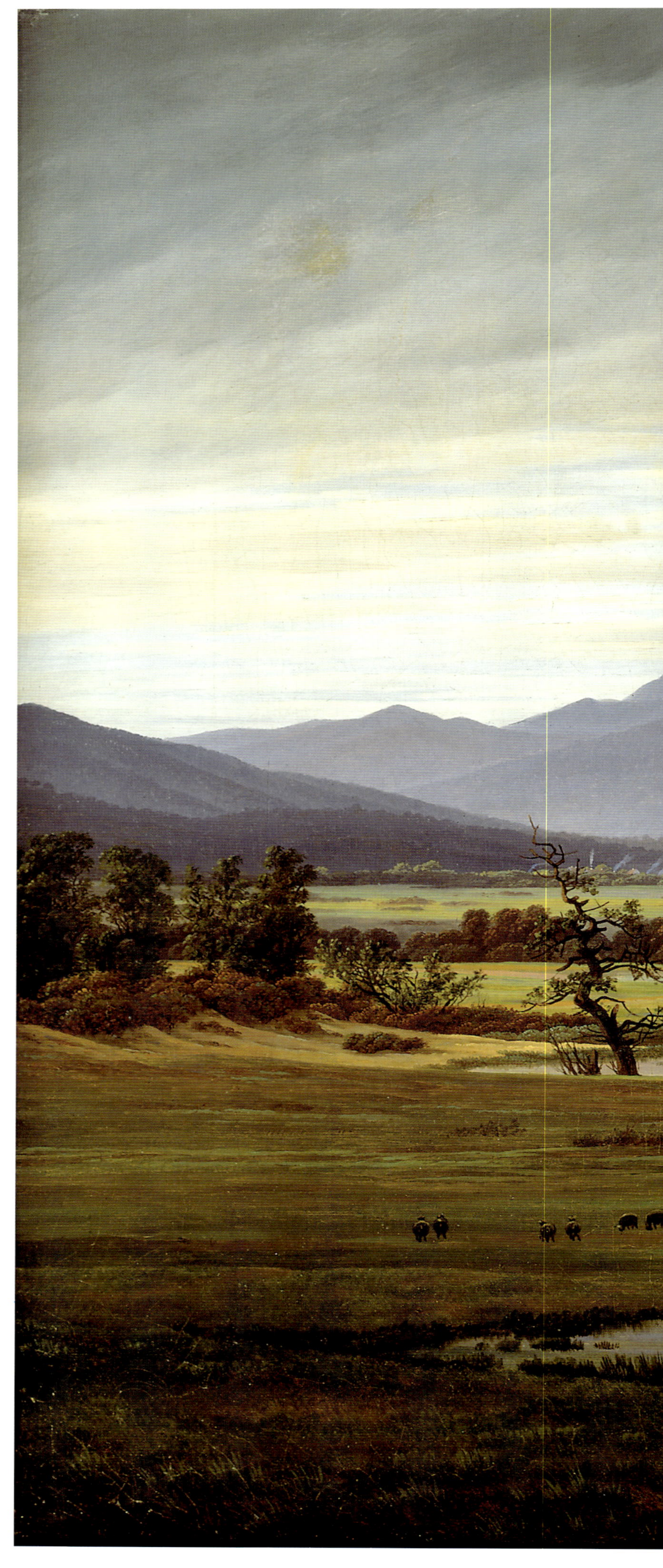

89. *Village Landscape in Morning Light,*
1822, oil on canvas,
55 × 71 cm (21⅝ × 28 in.).
Nationalgalerie, Berlin.

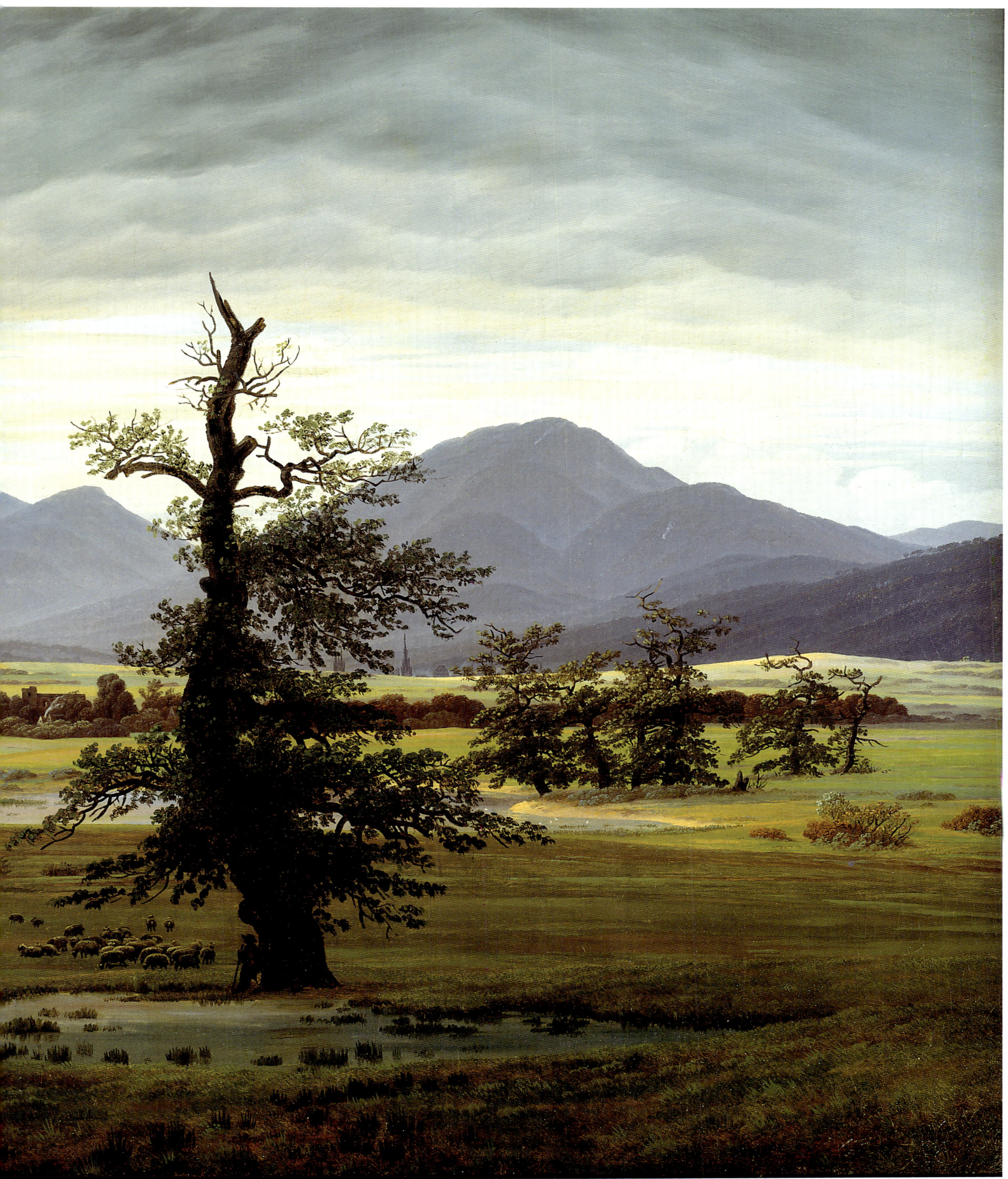

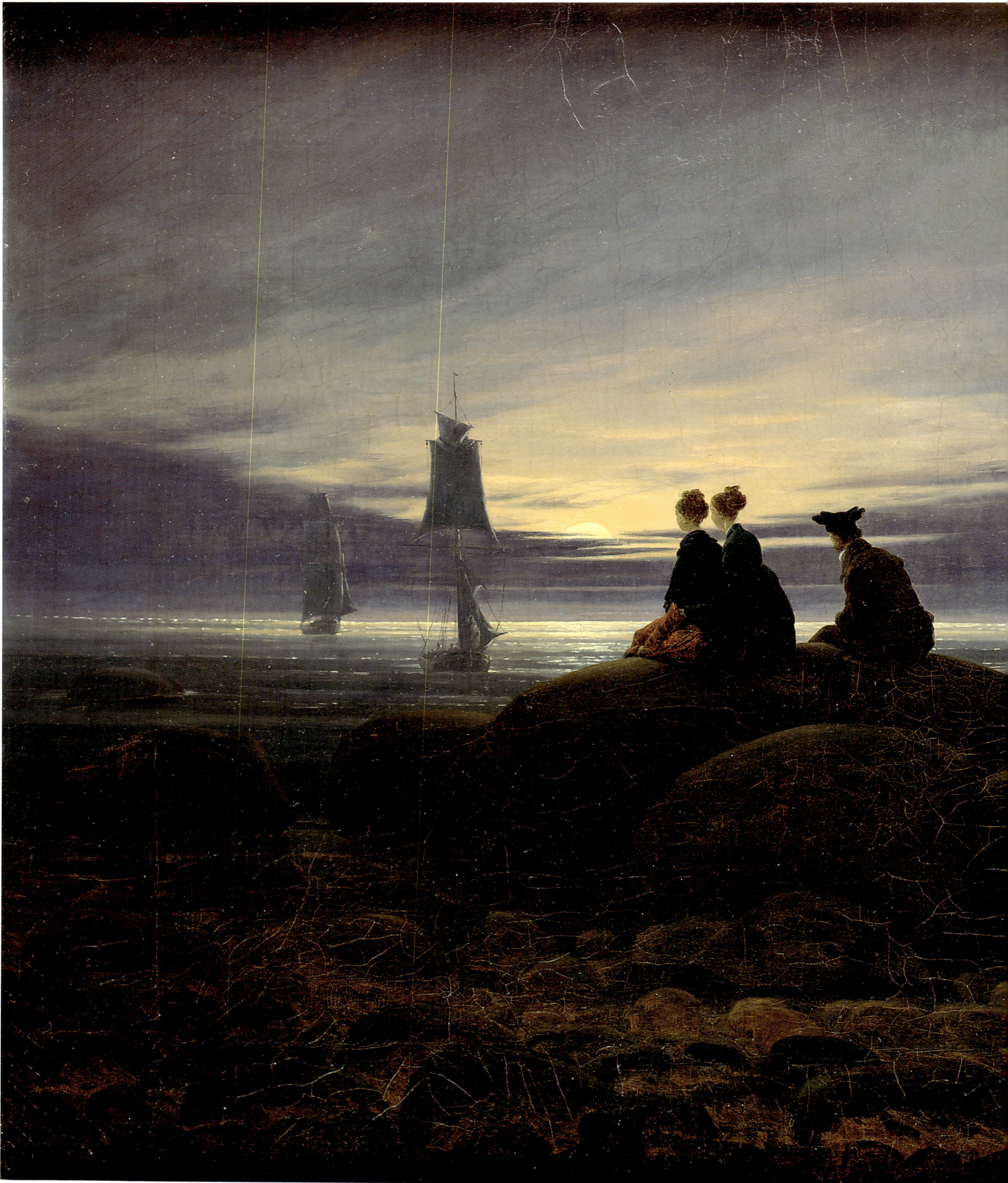

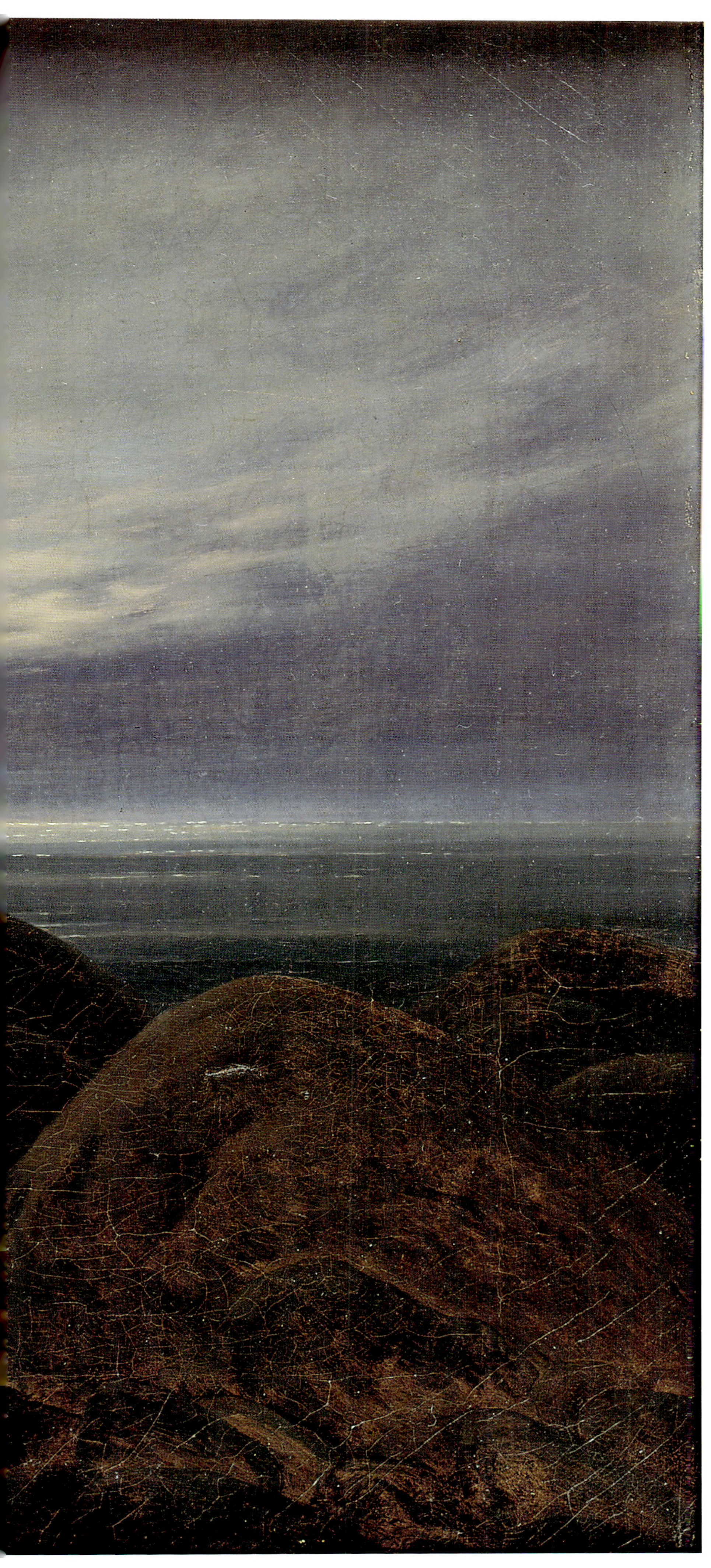

90. *Moonrise by the Sea*,
1822, oil on canvas,
55 x 71 cm (21⅝ x 28 in.).
Nationalgalerie, Berlin.

In other concealed triptychs, the articulation is provided by architectural elements. *The Graveyard Gate* (ills 81, 93) is one example. The exaggeratedly high pillars frame the view of the graveyard, over which floats the merest outline of an angel. Christ's crown of thorns adorns the gateway: the symbols that were placed in the frame of *The Tetschen Altar* are now reintegrated into the painting itself. At the same time, however, the place of prayer occupies a space that lies between this world and the world beyond. The Bremen *Churchyard* (ill. 94) uses another variant. A broken gate fills the round arch, with an obtuse circumflex accent created by two diagonal bars. The acute angle of the slit between the two wings exactly anticipates the outline of the church spire. Modified remnants of the triptych schema can be made out in *Hut under Snow* (ill. 91) and *Graveyard under Snow* (ill. 92). The hut is like a hummock of earth, a shrunken version of the topos of the distant mountain, and the dilapidated doorway is a vestige of the space we encountered in the early painting of a rocky gorge. The tension between nearness and distance has dwindled into the foreground, with the mass of the hut suppressing the spatial components.

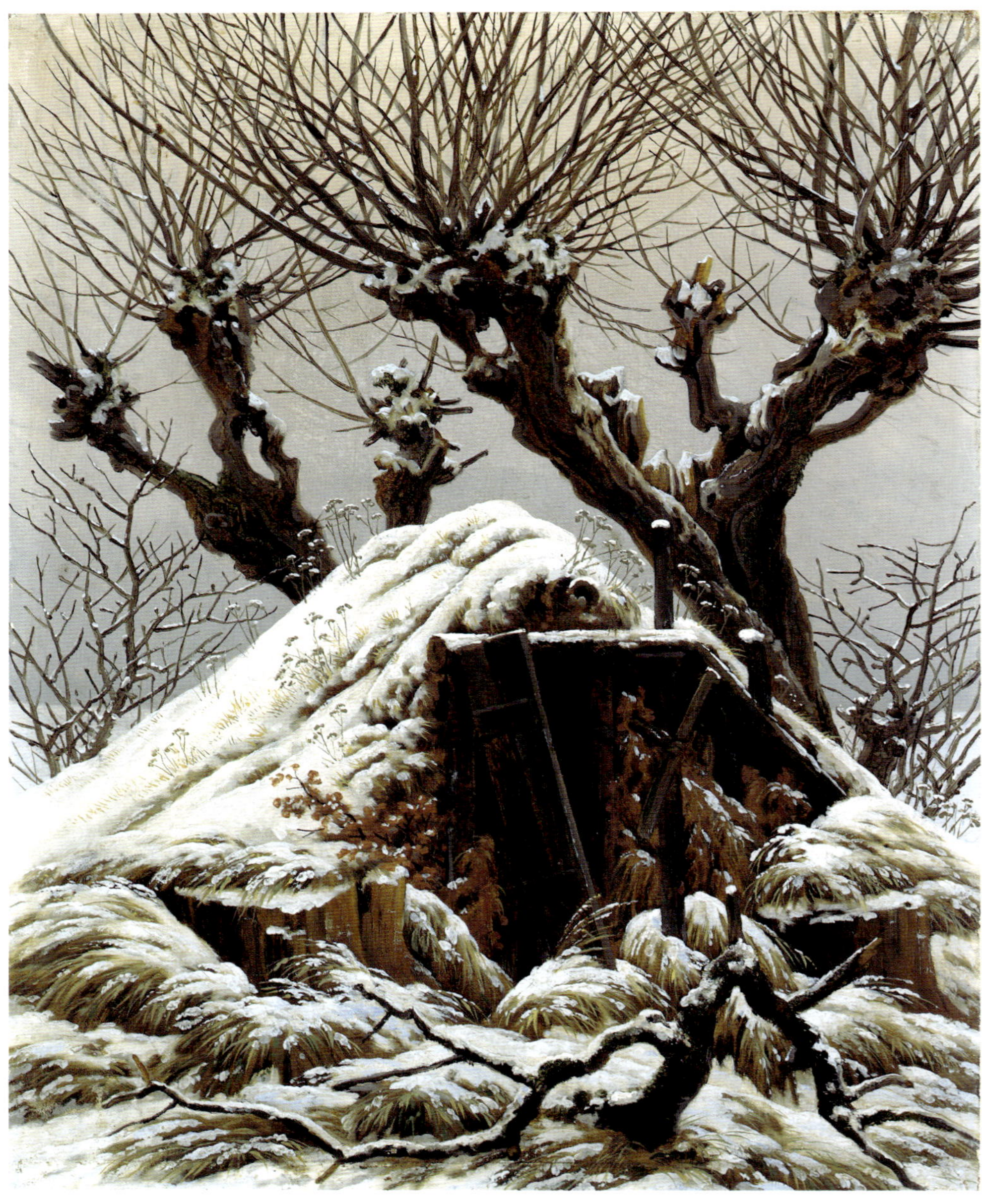

91. ***Hut under Snow,***
1827, oil on canvas,
31 × 25 cm (12¼ × 9¾ in.).
Nationalgalerie, Berlin.

Displacements of stress also occur when the thinking behind the picture is more complex. In *Two Men Contemplating the Moon* (ill. 95) and *Man and Woman Contemplating the Moon* (ill. 96), the figures stand on the edge of a V-formation, beyond which an empty chasm appears to open. The rocks in the foreground are near and accessible, however rough their surface. Their counter-stress does not lie out in the empty distance but instead in the proliferating, outstretched arms of the fallen tree's torn-out roots. Their bizarre shapes are nearby objects transmuted into something uncanny, and in that sense distant.

In *The Chalk Cliffs on Rügen* (ill. 79) Friedrich devised a breathtaking confrontation to bring about the switch from nearness to (inaccessible) distance. It takes place close to the abyss. Is the deep notch carved in the white cliffs a rising accent or a falling one? It is both, simultaneously. If we turn the picture upside down, the chasmic notch becomes the steep outline of several mountain peaks. The structure that Friedrich orchestrates here, with his artistic powers at their height, was prefigured in the early *View of Mountains with Waterfall* (ill. 4).

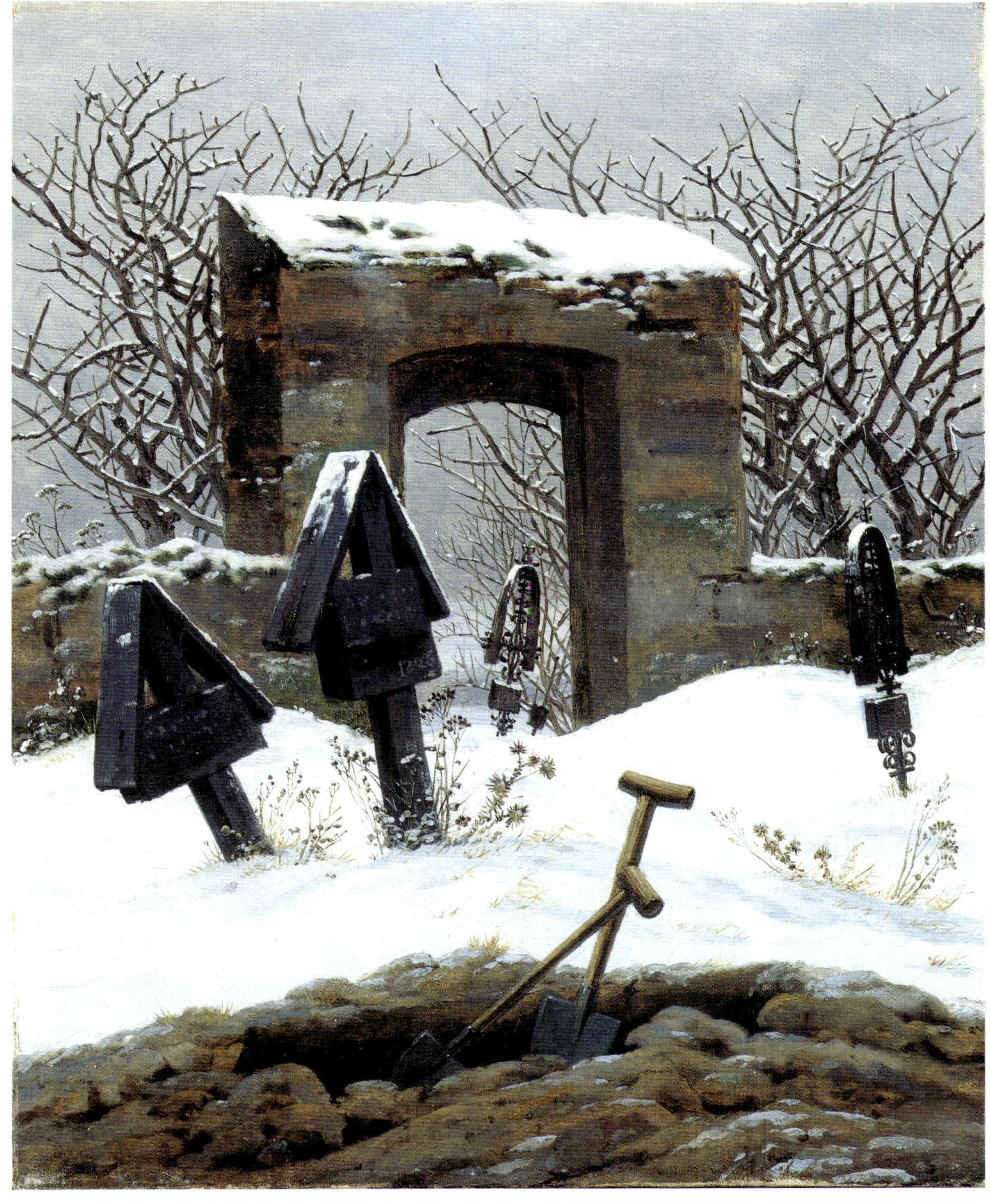

92. ***Graveyard under Snow*,**
1826–27, oil on canvas,
30 x 26 cm (11¾ x 10¼ in.).
Museum der bildenden Künste, Leipzig.

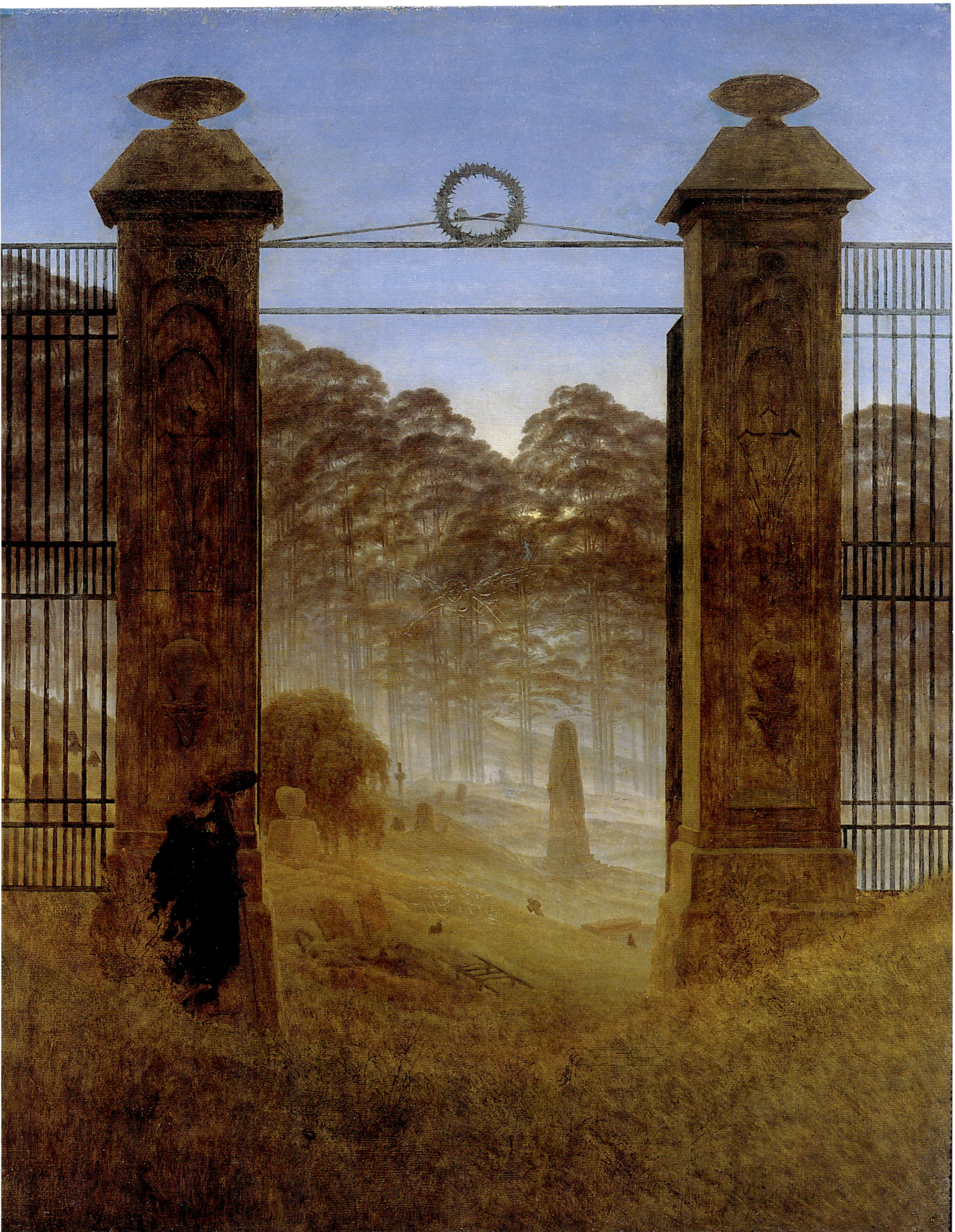

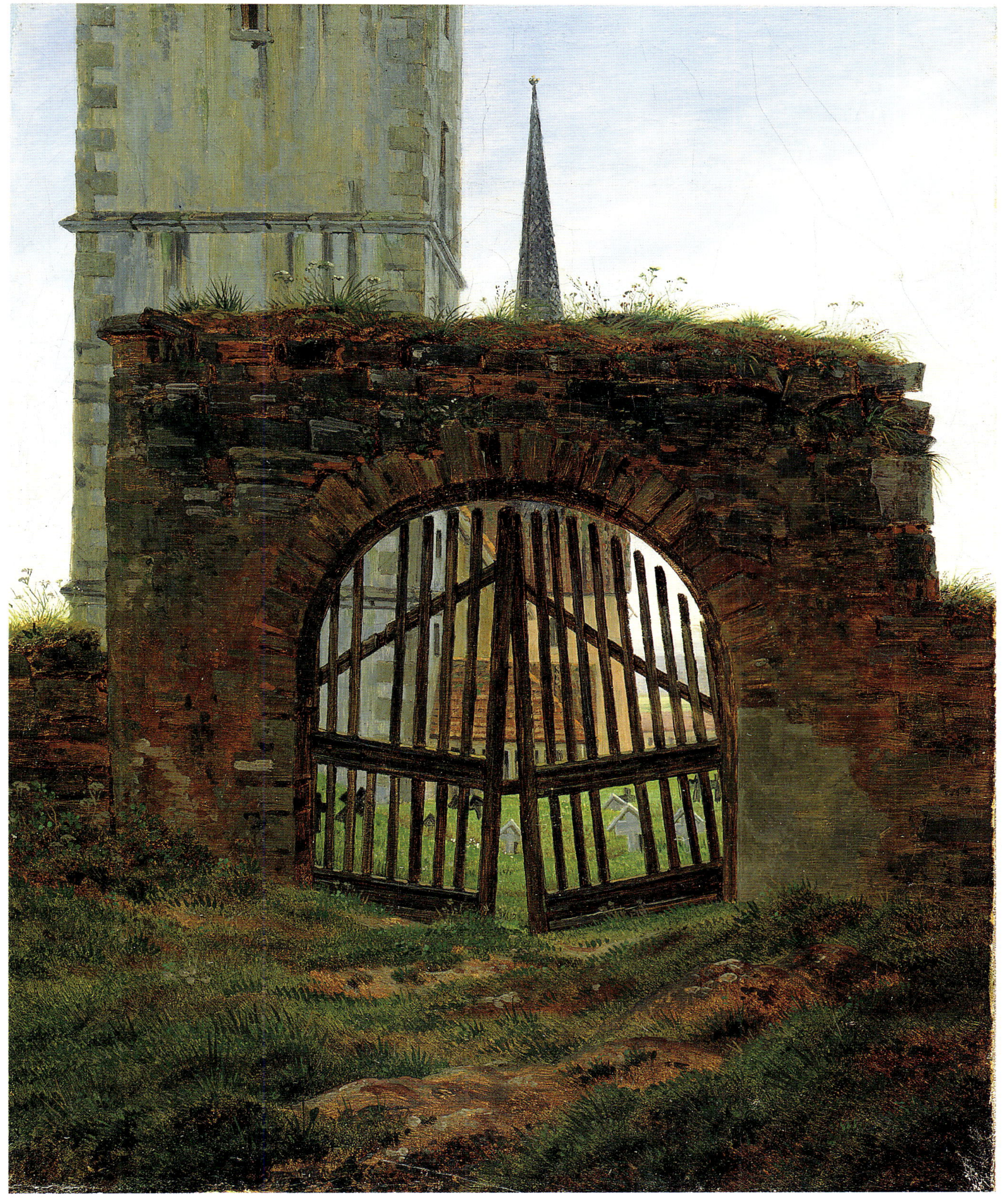

93. *The Graveyard Gate*,
1824–26, oil on canvas,
143 x 110 cm (56¼ x 43¼ in.).
Gemäldegalerie Neue Meister, Dresden.

94. *The Churchyard*,
c. 1828, oil on canvas,
31 x 25.2 cm (12¼ x 9⅞ in.).
Kunsthalle, Bremen.

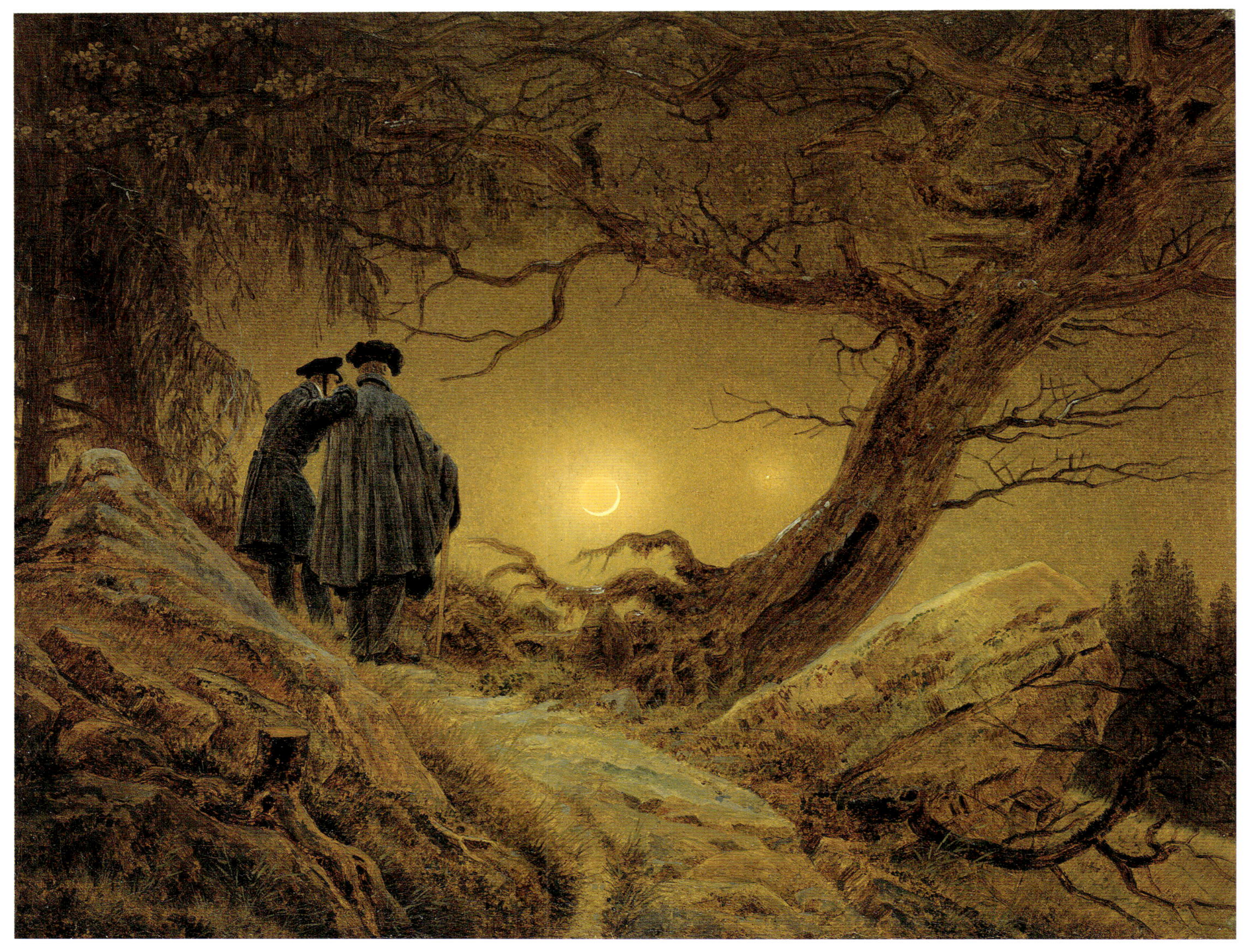

95. *Two Men Contemplating the Moon,*
c. 1819–20, oil on canvas,
35 × 44 cm (13¾ × 17⅜ in.).
Gemäldegalerie Neue Meister, Dresden.

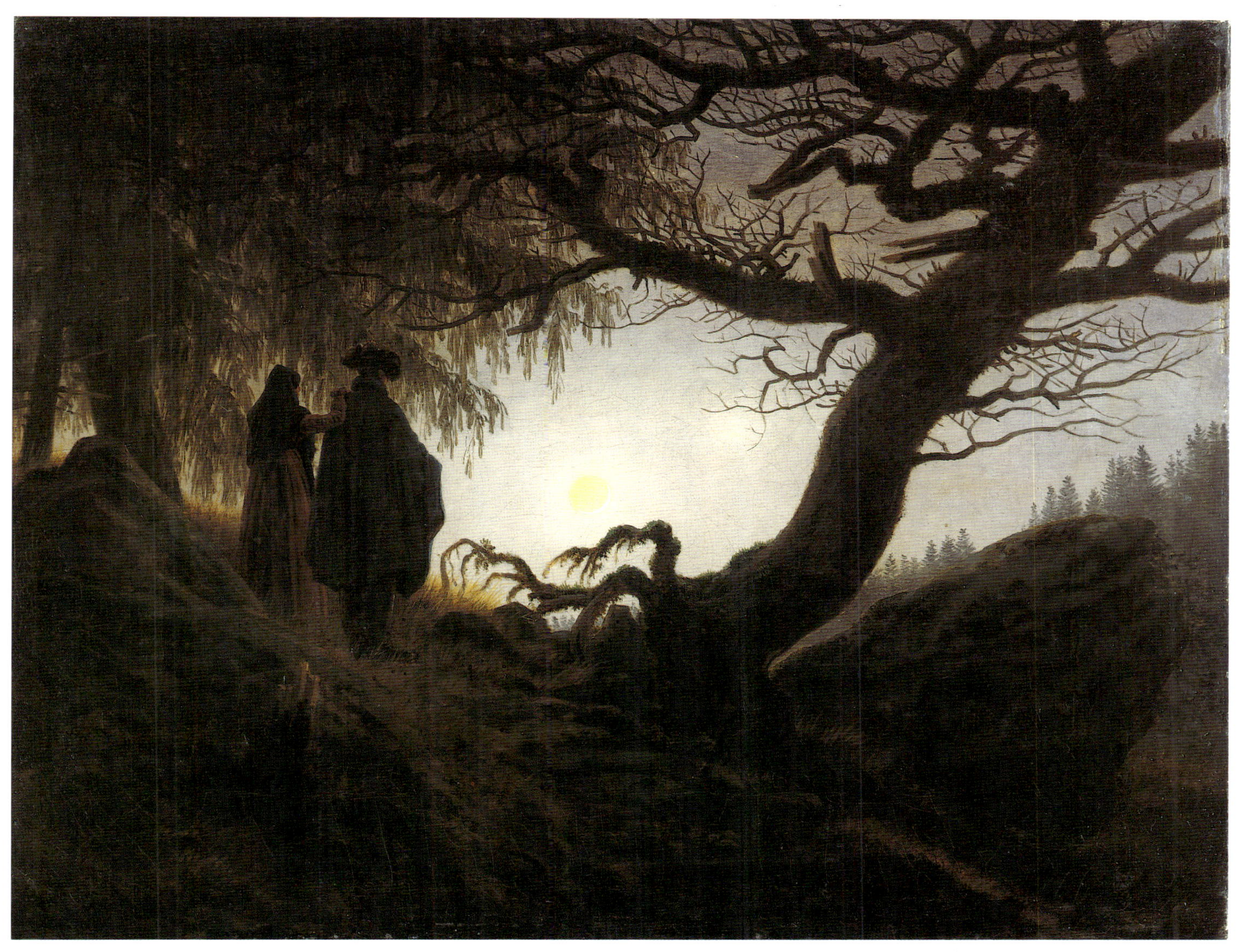

96. *Man and Woman Contemplating the Moon*,
late 1820s, oil on canvas,
34 x 44 cm (13⅜ x 17⅜ in.).
Nationalgalerie, Berlin.

Once we have learnt to recognize these space–mass codes, we can see that they fit together into loose chains of variations on the same formal idea. Whether concealed or overt, the triptych represents, as it were, the *basso continuo* underlying the axial structures. Here we find what I call the iconization of landscape. It occurs when the creativity of the picture is tautened by symmetries, when the sensory information is elevated from the prose of its random physical order into the poetry of a rhythmically structured work of art. These compositions, open to religious interpretation, are not a discrete category but a means of transition to the compositions where the space is arranged in horizontal bands. Compare the two landscapes with rainbows, for example (ills 98 and 99). The Essen painting displays the classic triple rhythm, while the Weimar painting has a tree on one side and a shepherd on the other with the arc of the rainbow stretching between them, forming a dome-shaped lid over the concave basin of the earth's surface. Nearness and distance are brought together in the picture plane; the triptych is transformed into horizontal bands.

These shifts sometimes lend Friedrich's pictorial structure a floating lightness (ill. 97 for instance), arising from the fact that the painter has braced the hieratic weight of the symmetry from the side, thereby changing verticality into horizontality. There is an example of this in *Greifswald in Moonlight* (ill. 101), where Friedrich depicts the gradual transformation of solid matter into a diaphanous vision. The dark foreground is occupied by stones and lumps of rock, while a sailing boat and poles on the left and right act as 'wings' to the 'centre stage'. In the middle ground, these structures are adapted and absorbed into the shapes of the fishing nets hung up to dry, their arabesque forming a suspended basin. The artistic construction poeticizes and exoticizes the mundane function of these everyday objects. The silhouette of the town appears in the remotest spatial plane, seeming to belong in another world. It both closes off the horizontal arrangement of the space and simultaneously transcends it. The central axis of symmetry then reasserts itself.

The view depicted in *Town at Moonrise* (ill. 100) recalls Greifswald and its church towers, but is actually an invention. The two dominant towers stand close together, as pairs of human figures frequently do in Friedrich's landscapes or seascapes. The two verticals continue downwards into the V-shape formed by the anchor in the foreground. This downward hollow, extended into a point, is countered by the contoured layer of cloud which extends across the pale sky like a shallow dome. Once again, Friedrich has made the iconic vertical space interact with the horizontal arrangement.

Meadows near Greifswald (ills 103 and 104) is another similar example. Horizontal spatial bands lead the gaze not in steps but in a smooth transition from the dark earth of the foreground into the pale distance. The foremost band suggests a basin, whose curve matches the silhouette of the town. Friedrich complements this horizontal correspondence of nearness and distance by a vertical correspondence: an axis leading from the two bushes on the edge of the ditch, across the two leaping horses, and up to the two churches (Sankt Nikolai and Sankt Jakobi). If the gaze travels back again, it seems that the depression is centred around the axis of the two towers. The vertical axis does not lie in the centre of the canvas, so the iconic drama is consciously underplayed. In *Hill and Ploughed Field near Dresden* (ill. 105), Friedrich boldly redistributed his vocabulary, as he also did in *Evening* (ill. 102) and *The Evening Star* (ill. 106). The curved outline of the Dresden hill corresponds to that of the cloud banks; the foreground rises like a wall and stops abruptly. Buildings spring into view directly behind it – or do they drop away? At the same time

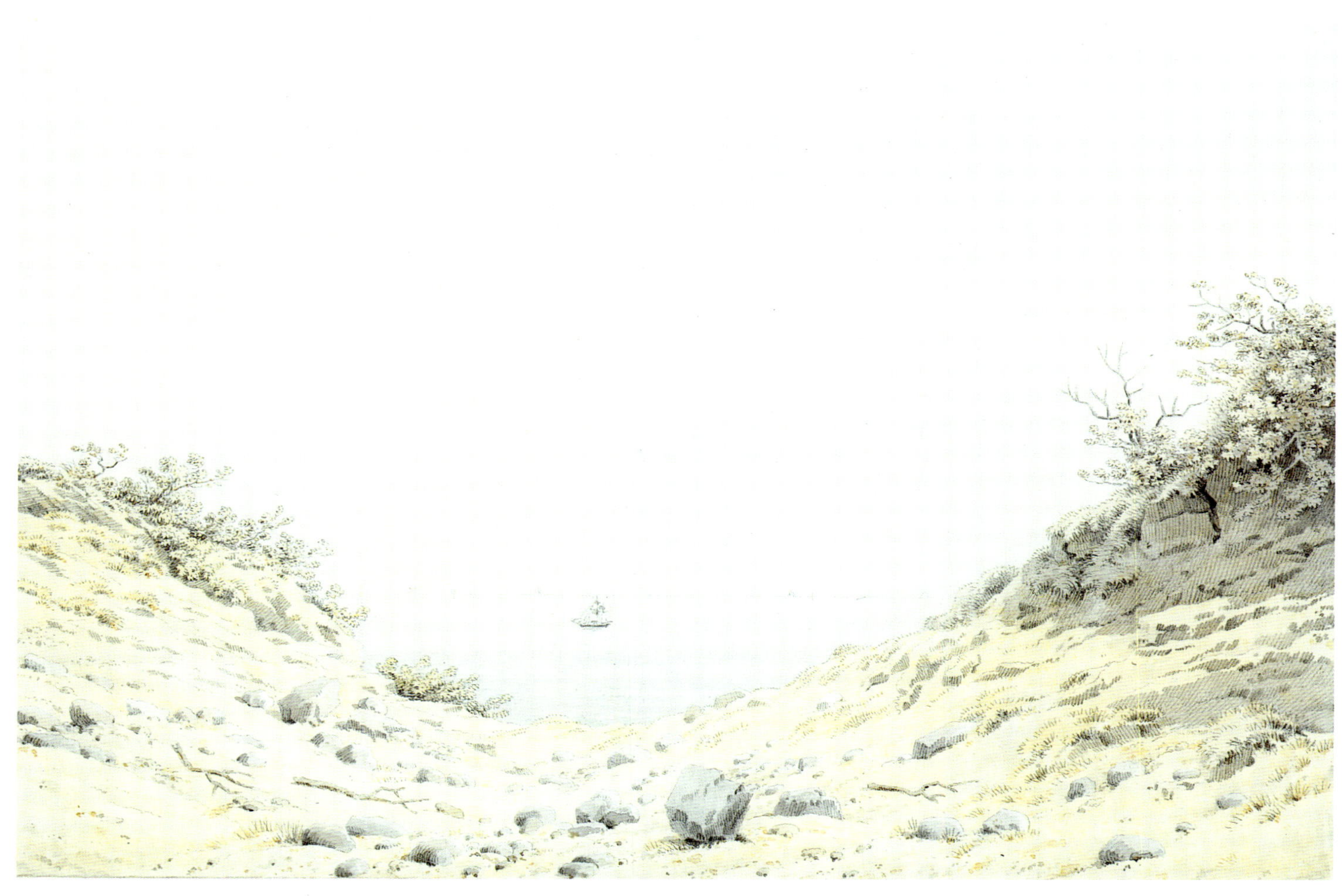

97. *Dune by the Sea,*
c. 1824, pencil and watercolour,
24.7 × 36.5 cm (9¾ × 14⅜ in.).
Kupferstichkabinett, Berlin.

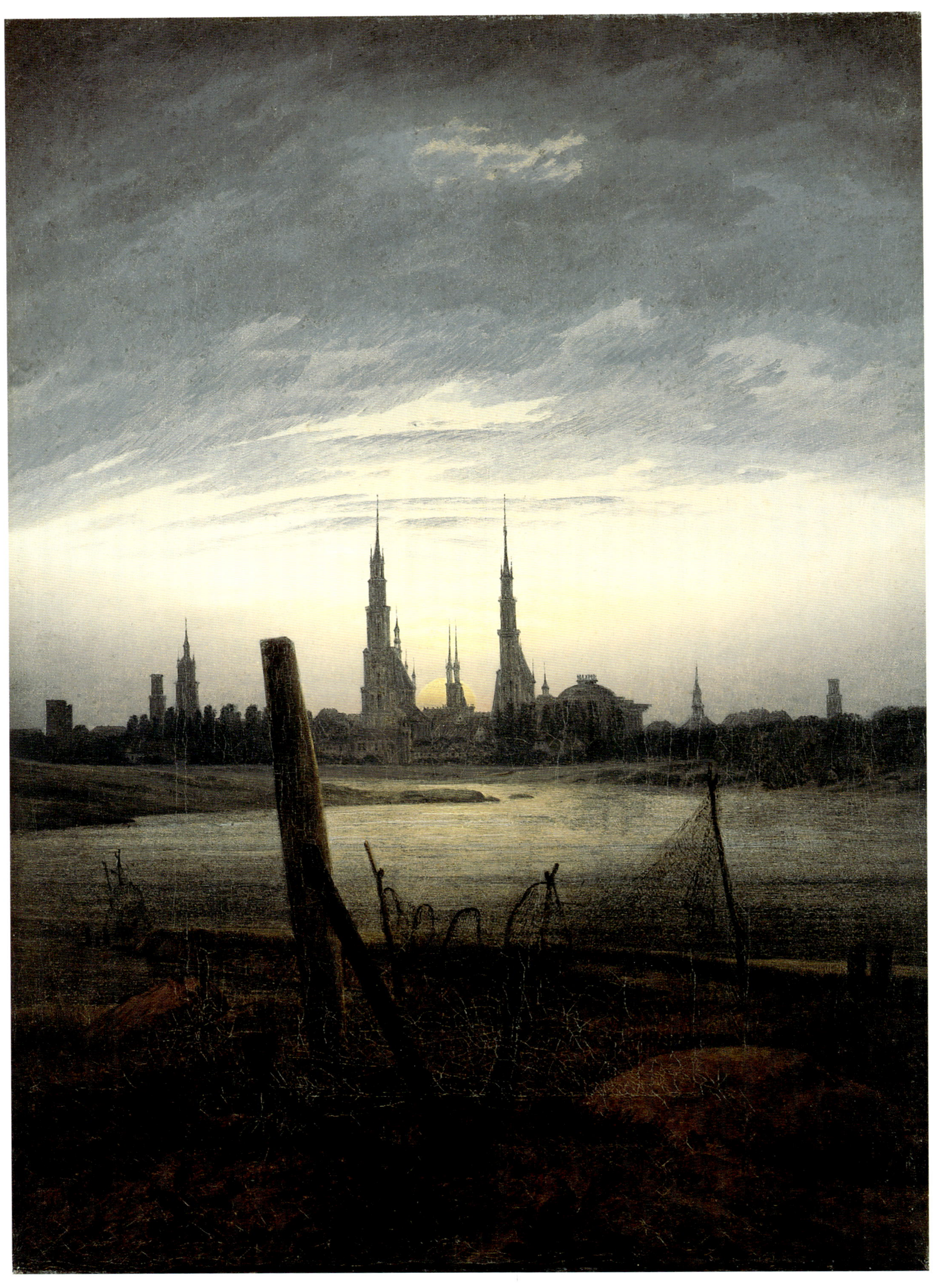

100. ***Town at Moonrise,***
1817, oil on canvas,
45.8 x 33 cm (18 x 13 in.).
Museum Oskar Reinhart am Stadtgarten, Winterthur.

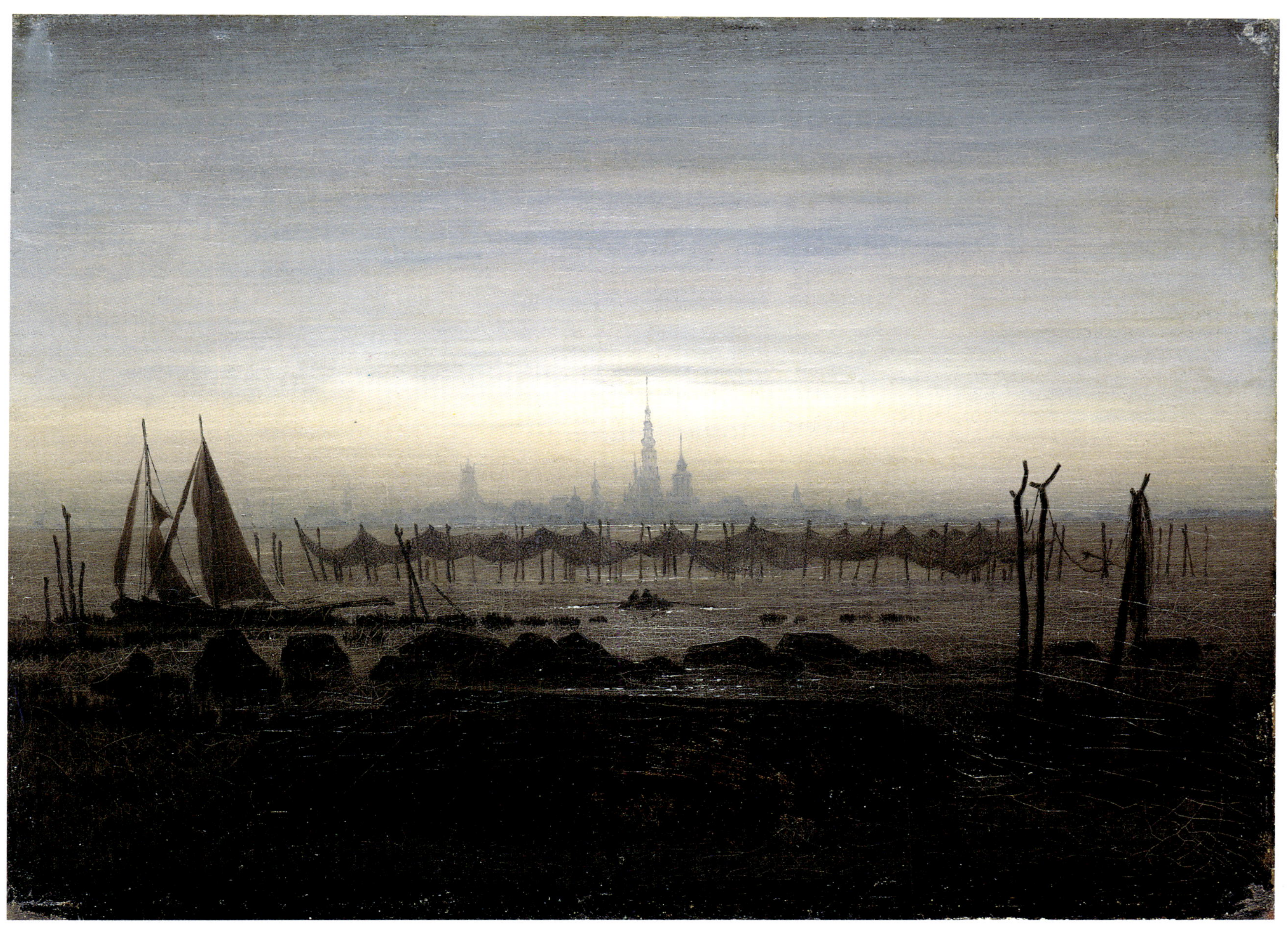

101. *Greifswald in Moonlight*, c. 1817, oil on canvas, 22.5 × 30.5 cm (8¾ × 12 in.). Nasjonalgalleriet, Oslo.

as he alludes to traditional viewpainting, Friedrich robs it of its informative value. He shows us something, yet at the same time whisks it away, and its removal awakens a desire to follow it into the distance. The bare trees are traces of a triptych formation, framing the landmarks of Dresden – the Frauenkirche and Schlossturm – like a pergola or an arbour.

The view of *The Augustus Bridge in Dresden* (destroyed in 1931; ill. 107) is made up entirely from horizontal spatial bands. The foremost level consists of the flagstones on the Brühl Terrace; then comes the railing where two men stand. They emphasize the centre of the picture and are remnants of a triple rhythm. Beyond them lie the river Elbe and the round arches of the bridge, which seems to support a distant landscape. The bridge lies parallel to the railing; in this way Friedrich suppresses the fact that the terrace and the bridge are at right angles to one another, with the bridge beginning on the left bank, where the terrace is, and ending on the other side of the river. He was obviously concerned to achieve strictly parallel layering of the levels from foreground to background. There is no axial perspective leading into the depth of the painting; instead, we perceive the picture space by means of confrontation, and as a confrontation. This lends uncertainty to the spatial dimensions, moving nearness away and bringing distance nearer. The backdrop of trees and mountains lies above rather than behind the bridge.

The two basic models for treatment of the third dimension – space ordered vertically in strips, and horizontally in bands – come face to face in Friedrich's most famous pair of paintings, *The Monk by the Sea* and *The Abbey in the Oak Wood*. Is this by chance or by design? It is tempting to see it as an intentional declaration of principle, staking out the terrain of future invention. Whatever the case, the confrontation demonstrates the many different ways in which spaces can be experienced as displaced and estranged. The space in *The Monk* is horizontally ordered, in bands which could continue indefinitely to either side. Lacking the axial depth that would close it and draw it together, it seems detached and separated from our

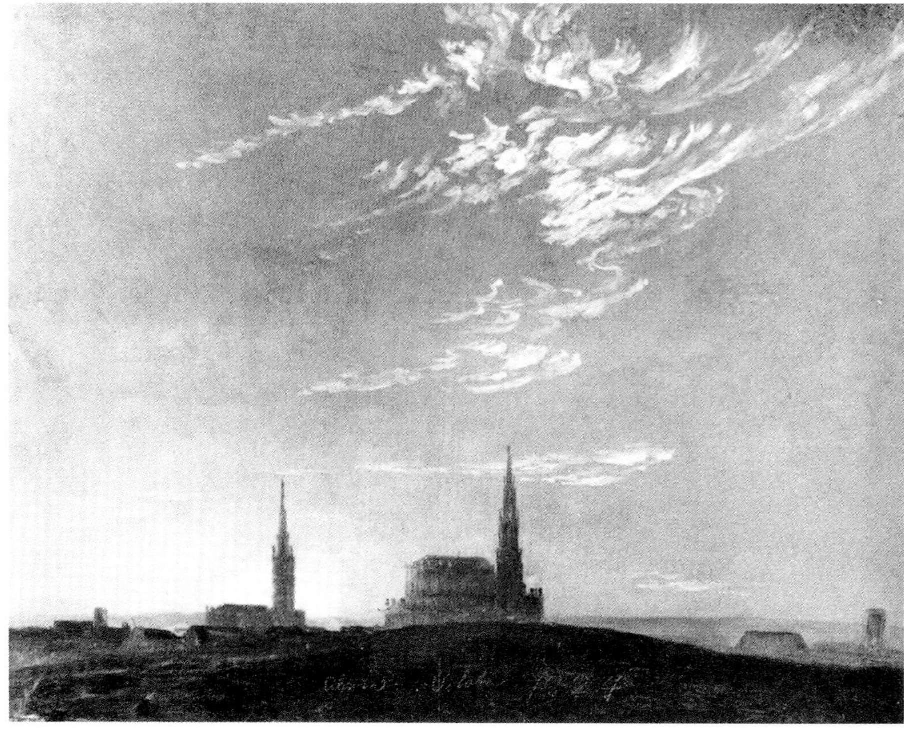

102. *Evening,*
1824, oil on canvas,
20.8 x 24.7 cm (8 x 9¾ in.).
Henke Collection, Essen.

103. *Meadows near Greifswald*, detail,
1820–22, oil on canvas,
35 x 48.9 cm (13¾ x 19¼ in.).
Hamburger Kunsthalle, Hamburg.

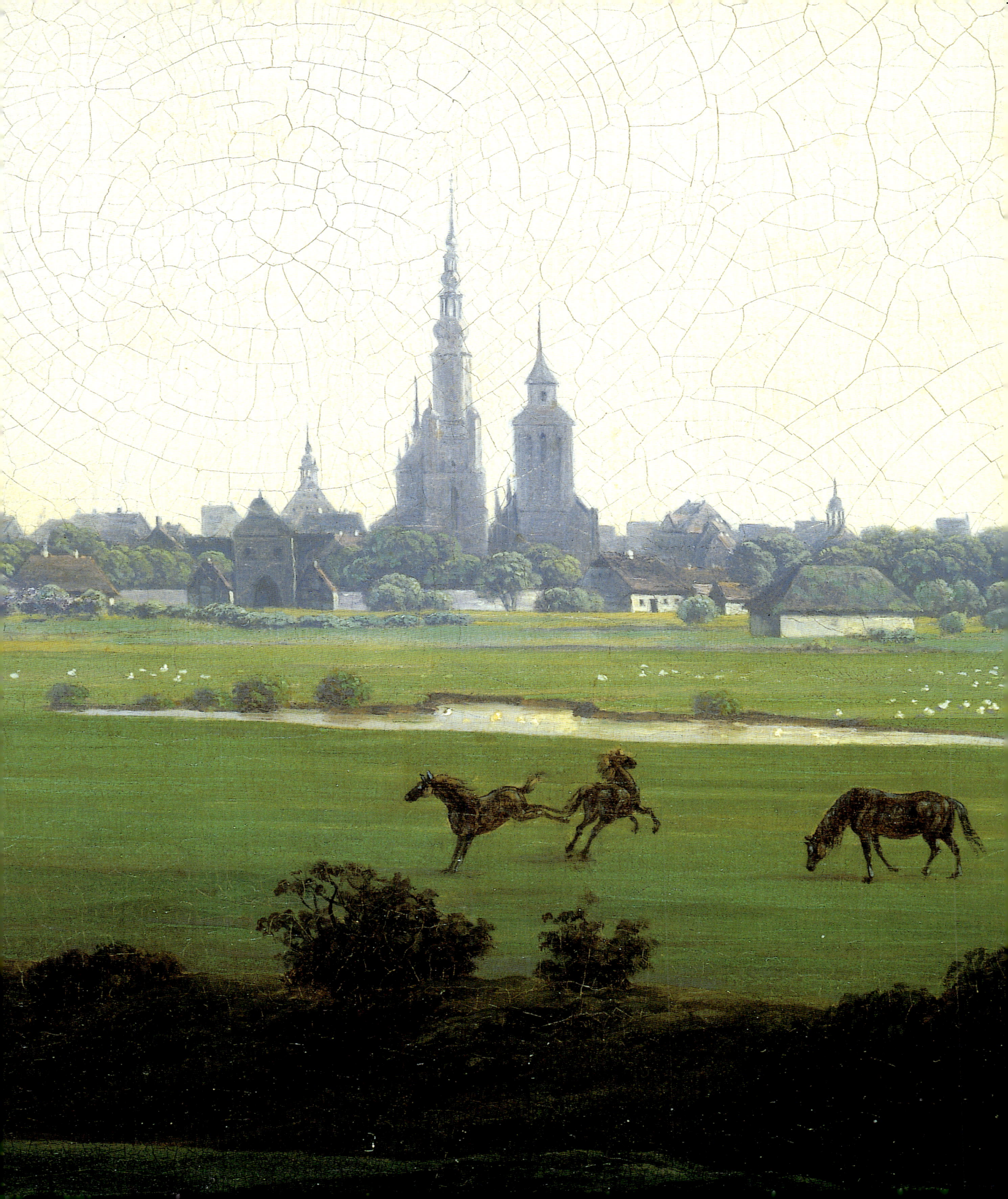

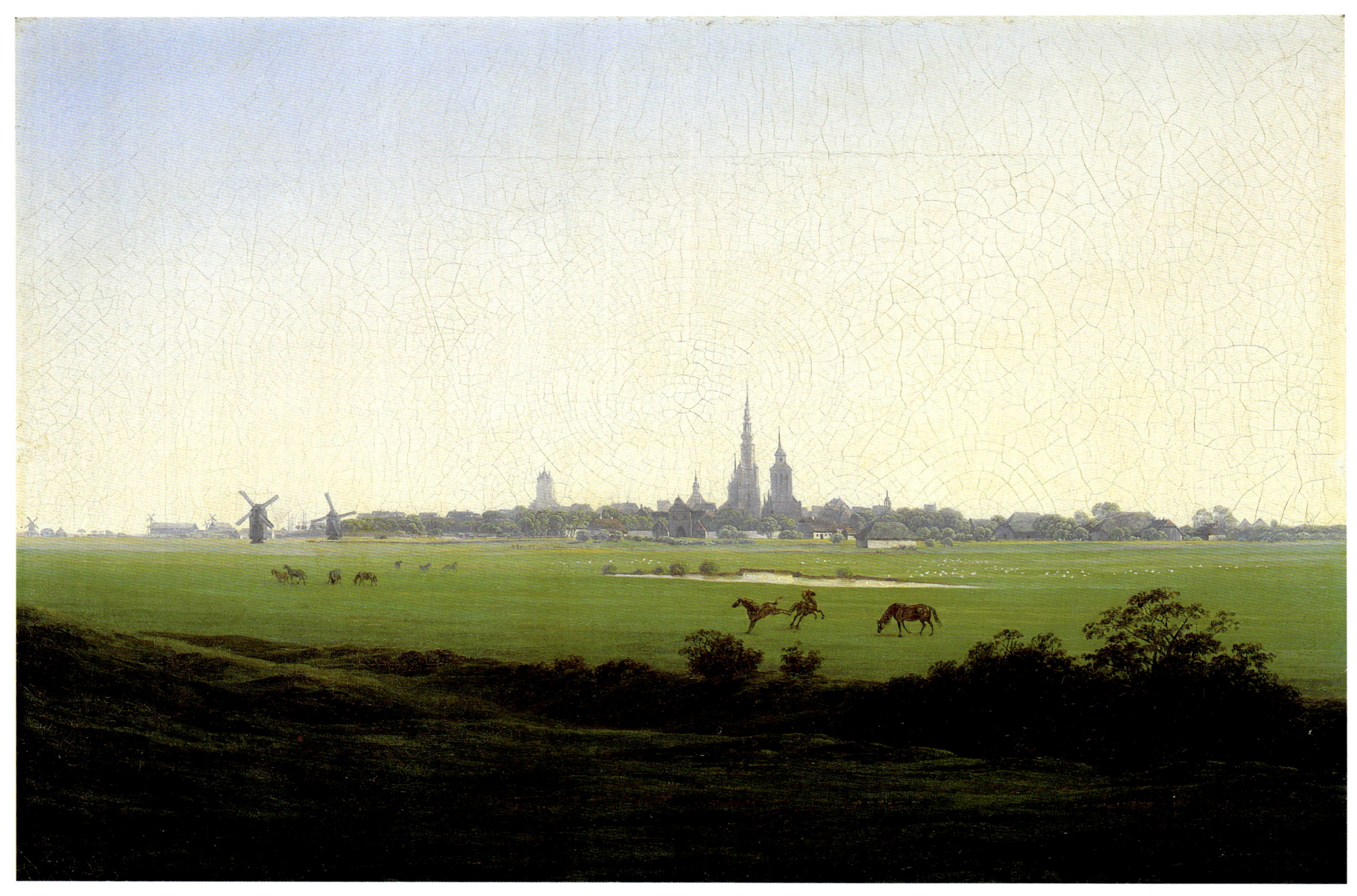

104. *Meadows near Greifswald*, 1820–22, oil on canvas, 35 × 48.9 cm (13¾ × 19¼ in.). Hamburger Kunsthalle, Hamburg.

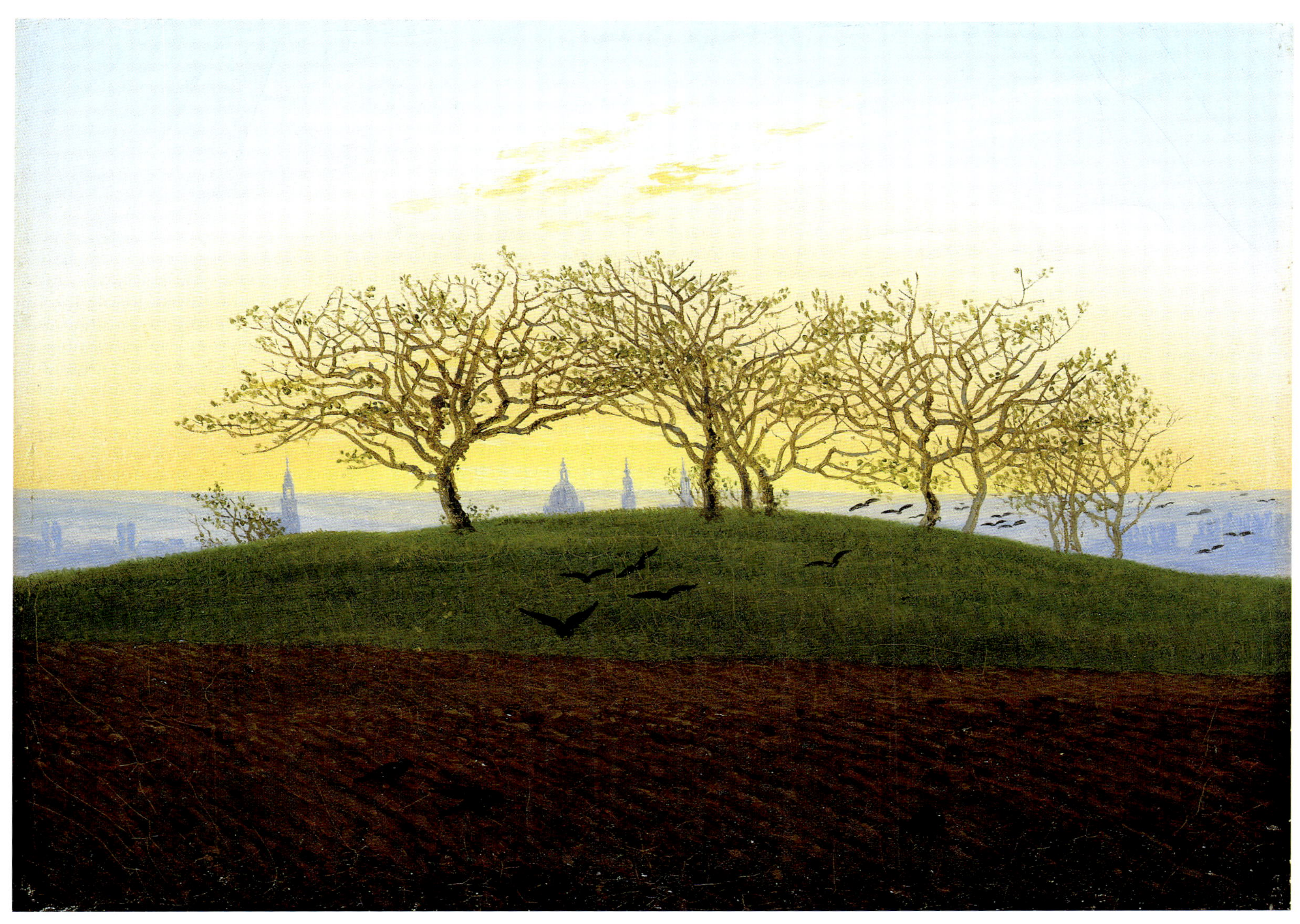

105. *Hill and Ploughed Field near Dresden,*
1824, oil on canvas,
22.2 × 30.5 cm (8¾ × 12 in.).
Hamburger Kunsthalle, Hamburg.

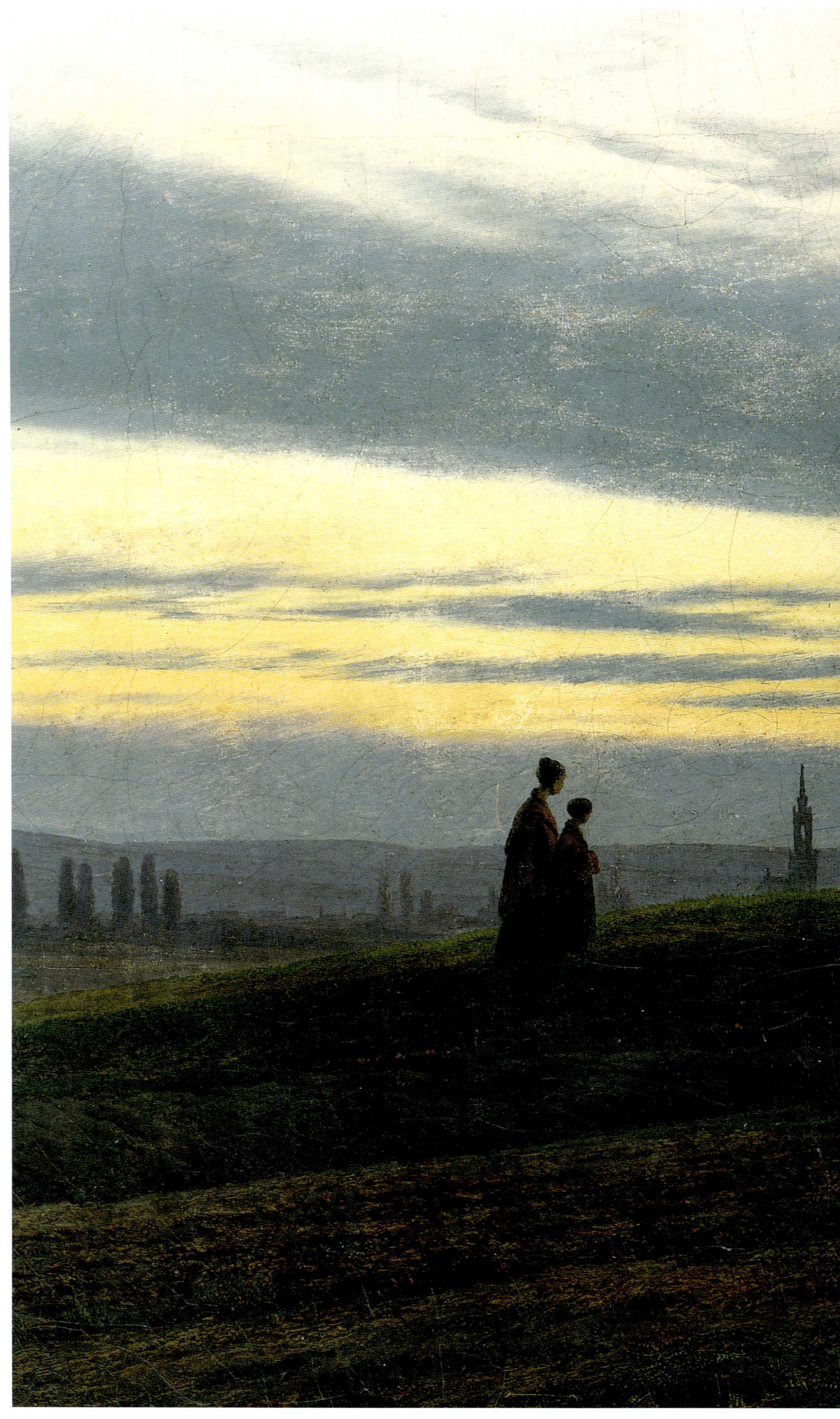

106. *The Evening Star,*
1830–35, oil on canvas,
32.5 x 45 cm (12¾ x 17¾ in.).
Freies Deutsches Hochstift, Frankfurt.

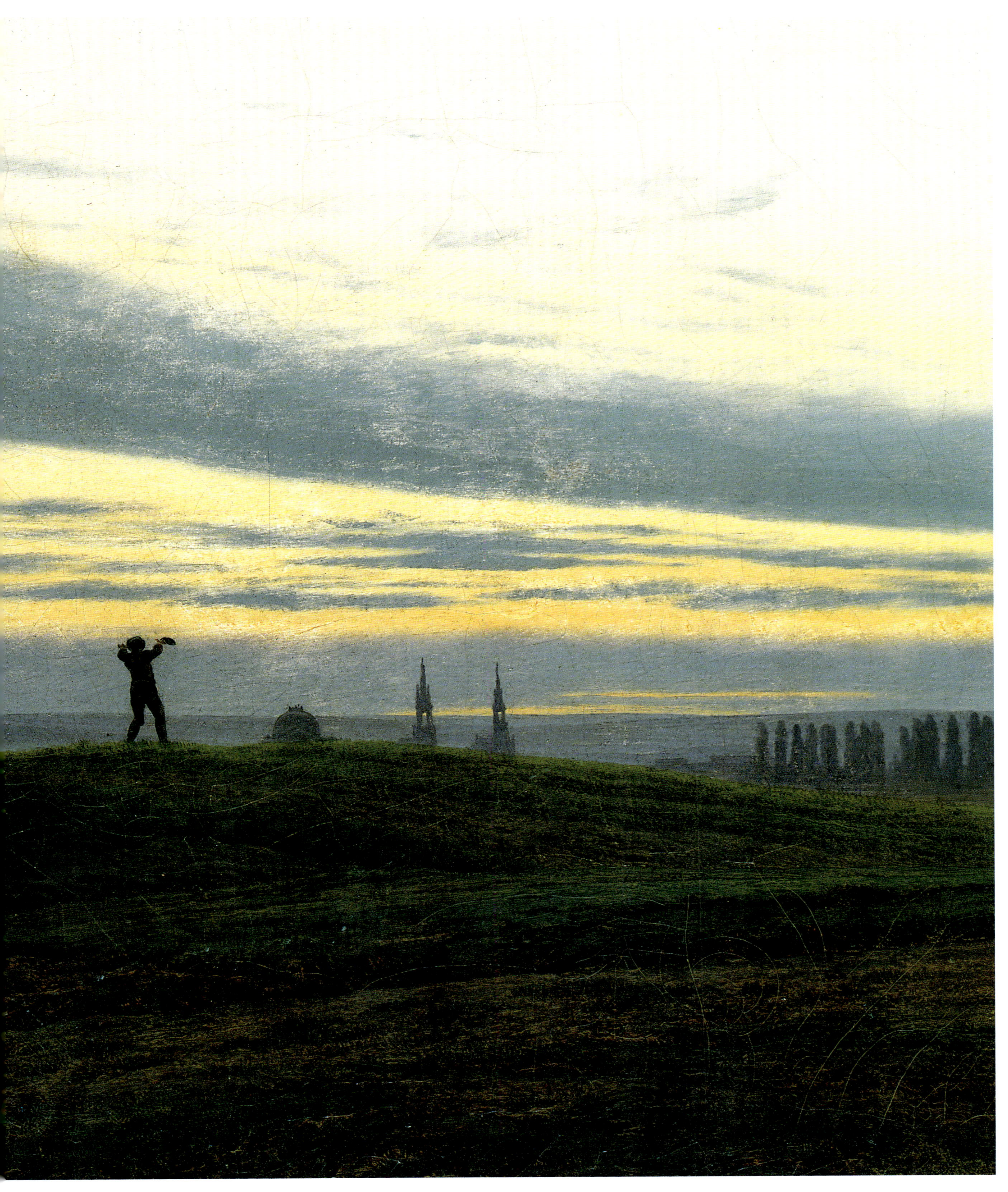

[illegible]
35 x 48.8 cm (13¾ x 19⅛ in.).
Hamburger Kunsthalle, Hamburg.

THE 'OBSCURE TOTAL IDEA'

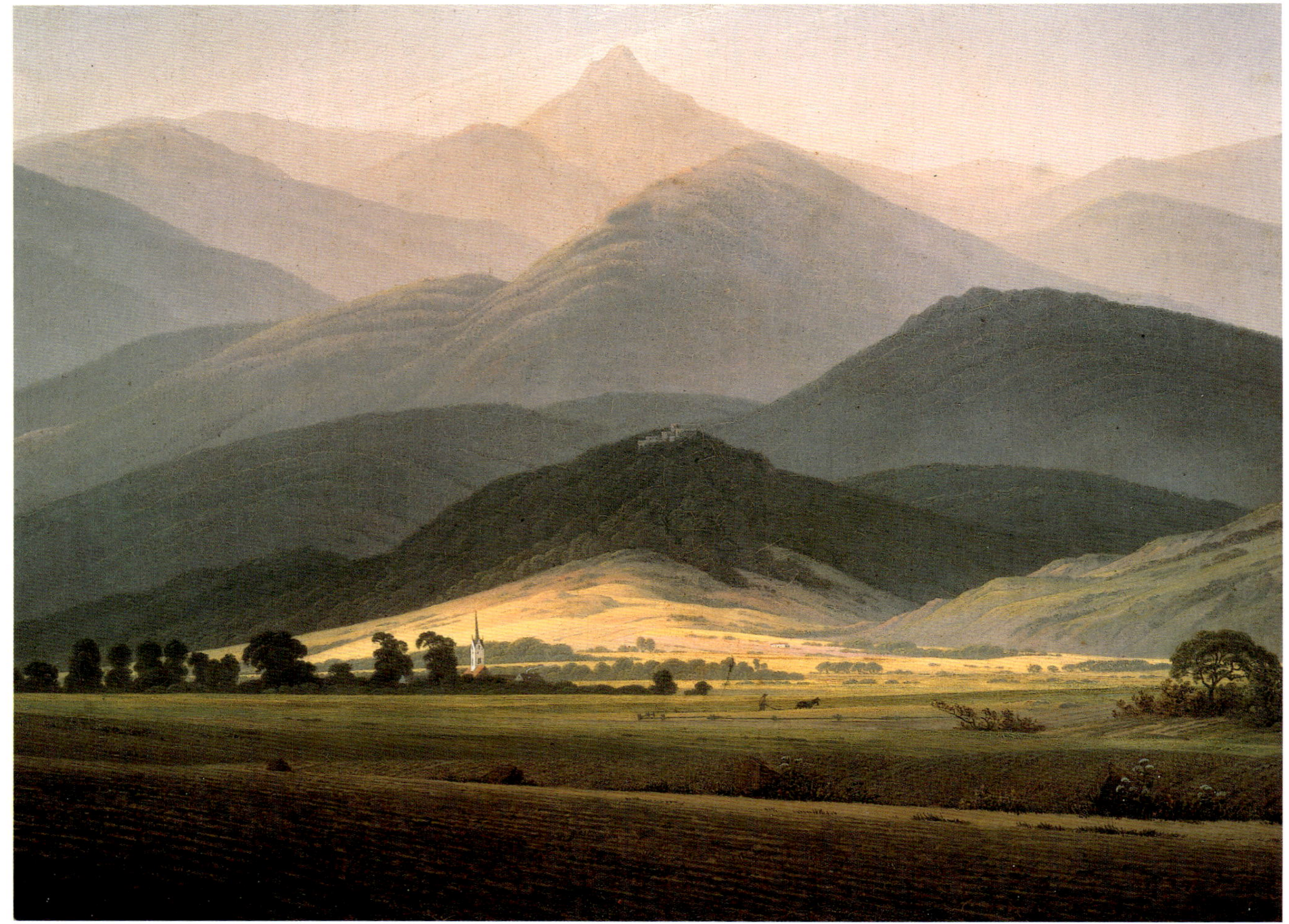

110 and 111. *Landscape in the Riesengebirge*, 1810, oil on canvas, 45 × 58.3 cm (17¾ × 23 in.). Pushkin Museum, Moscow.

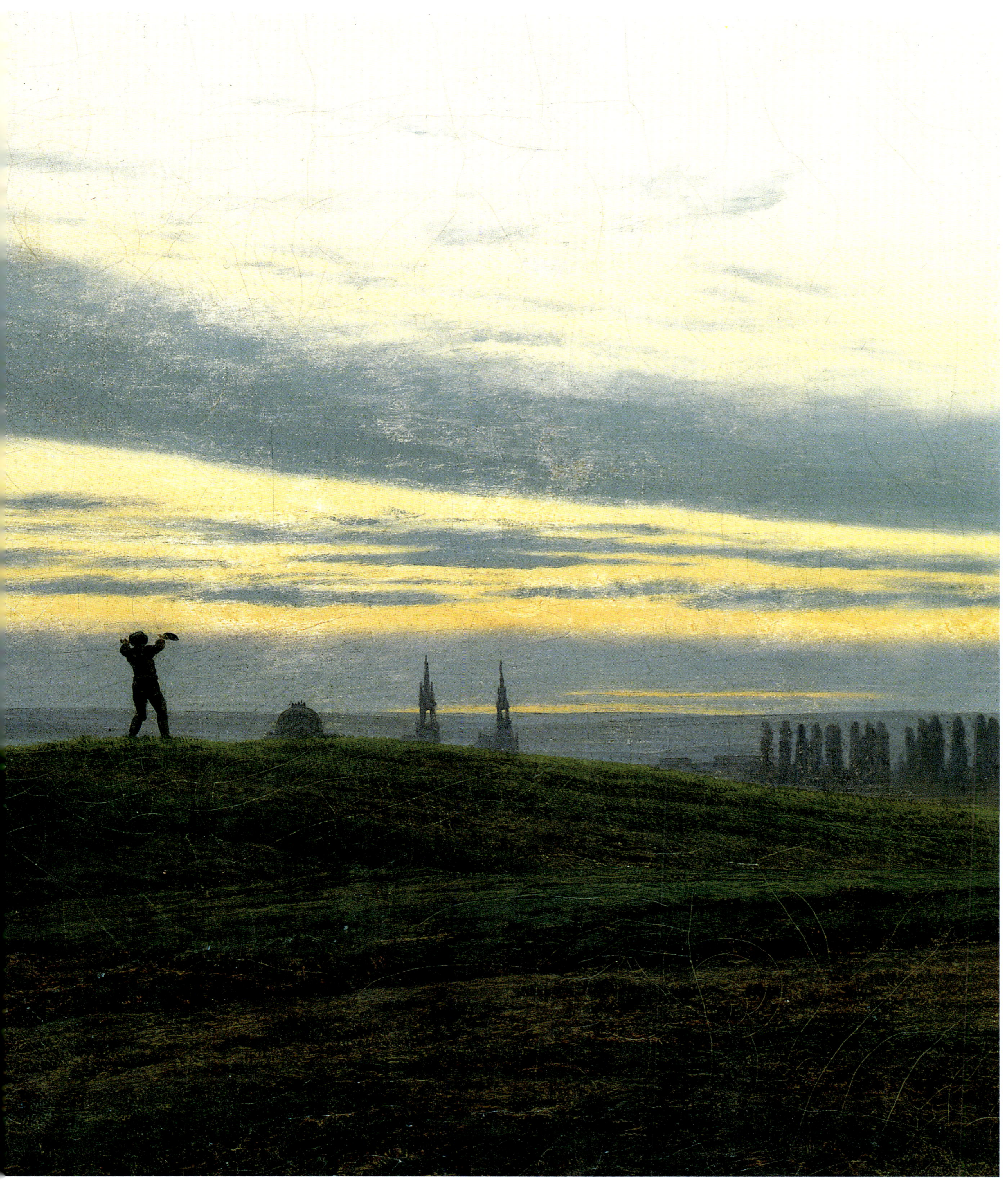

experiential world as if by an invisible barrier. We cannot withdraw from this boundless space; it exerts the compulsion that Kleist recognized when he wrote of having one's eyelids cut off. The narrow gateway opening in the centre of *The Abbey in the Oak Wood* draws in the eye like a funnel, but this attraction ends in the enveloping brown-black sea of fog, whose dimensions our experience has not equipped us to judge. In other paintings where the formal burden is less heavy, horizontal ordering of space carries landscapes past us as if we were sitting in a fast car, a sensation that was unknown to Friedrich and his contemporaries (ills 108, 109, 110 and 111). The vertically ordered pictures are mostly broken up into discontinuous strata and require the viewer to perform visual leaps from one spatial level to another. The horizontally ordered paintings have a temporal dimension, while this seems to have been removed in the triptychs. Their dominant quality is the timelessness of the true icon.

How can a formal fantasy contain all these variations and permutations? These creations involve fantasy in the best sense of the word, even if the analyses above may sometimes have given the impression that the pictures are nothing more than an assemblage of pieces of scenery that can be rearranged and combined in different ways to suit the artist's whim. In fact, these paintings are the precise opposite of whimsical. Friedrich's field of artistic invention was based on the fundamental models which Schiller designated by the term 'obscure total idea' (see page 26). Indistinct but powerful, it preceded 'everything technical' and the conception of specific subject matter. Schiller wrote the following to his friend Christian Gottfried Körner (25 May 1792): 'I believe that it isn't always the vivid imagining of his [the poet's] material that generates an inspired piece of work, but often only a need for material, an indistinct urge to pour out turbulent emotions.' More often he has only a vague idea of 'the musicality of a poem', rather than a 'clear conception of content'. Nevertheless, the poet is influenced by his store of language, and the painter by his hoard of remembered images, gathered through observation and perception. In concrete terms,

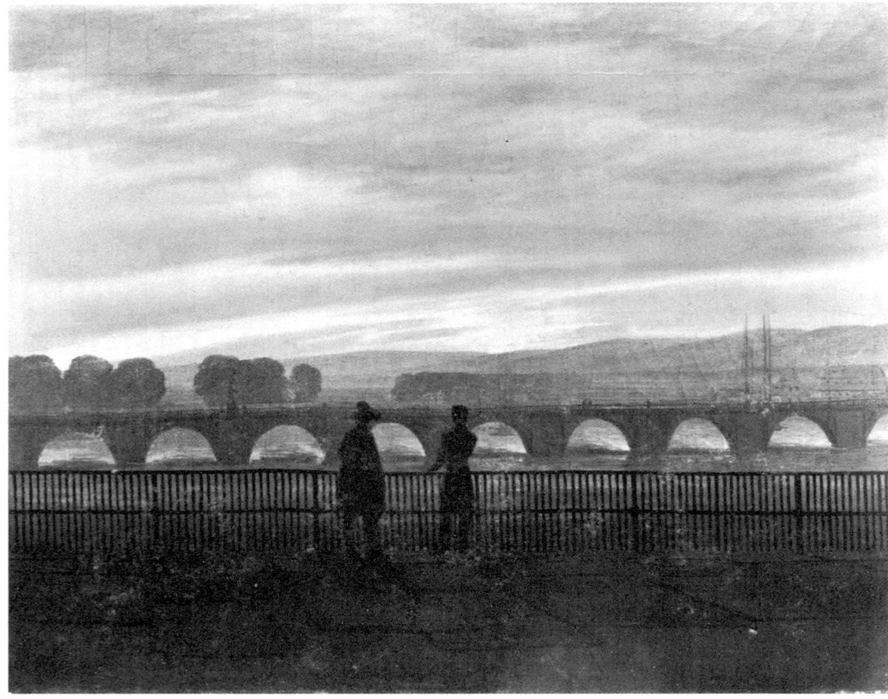

107. ***The Augustus Bridge in Dresden,*** 1826, oil on canvas, 28 × 35.2 cm (11 × 13¾ in.). Formerly Hamburger Kunsthalle, Hamburg (destroyed 1931).

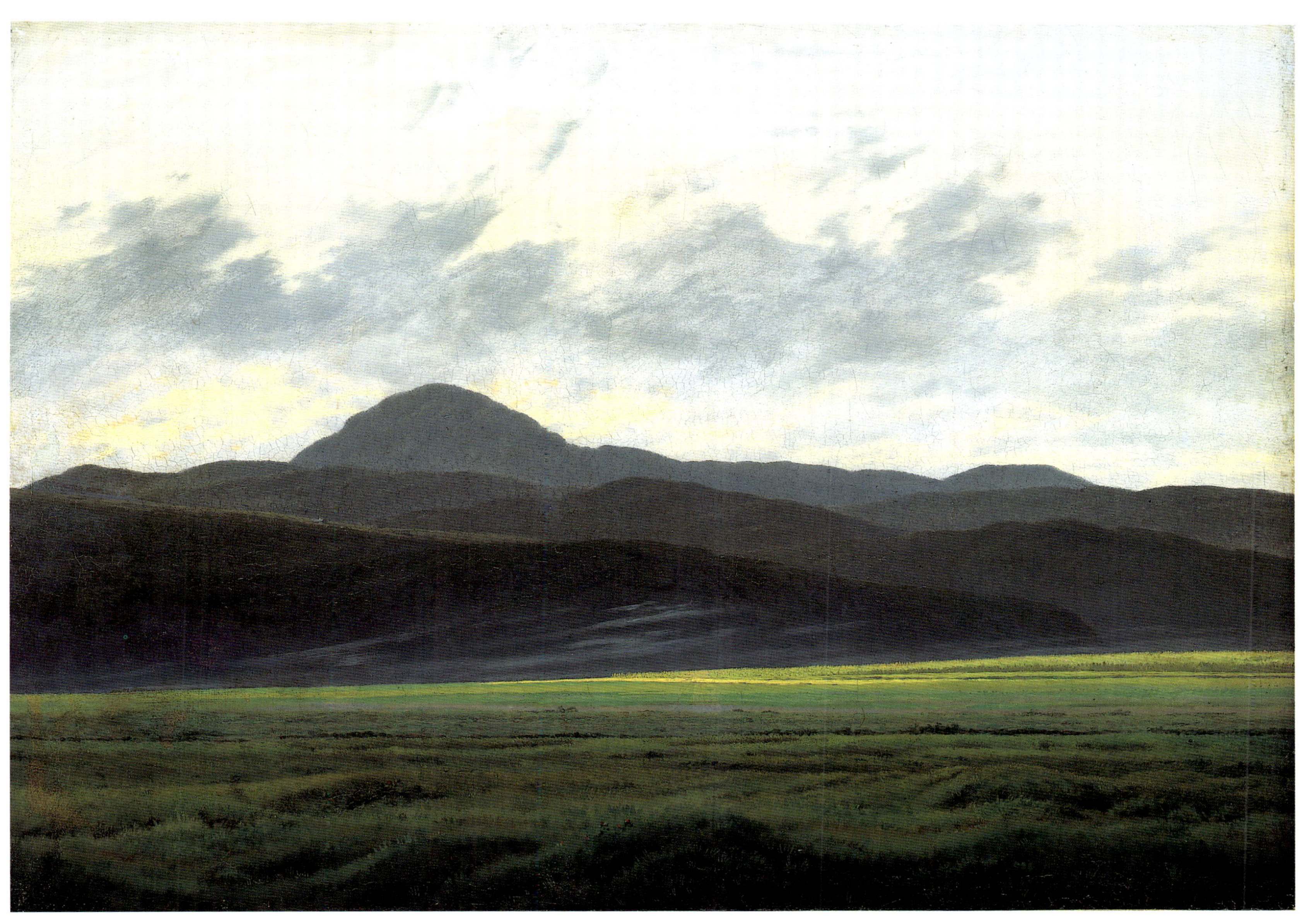

108. *Landscape in the Riesengebirge*, 1823, oil on canvas, 35 x 48.8 cm (13¾ x 19¼ in.). Hamburger Kunsthalle, Hamburg.

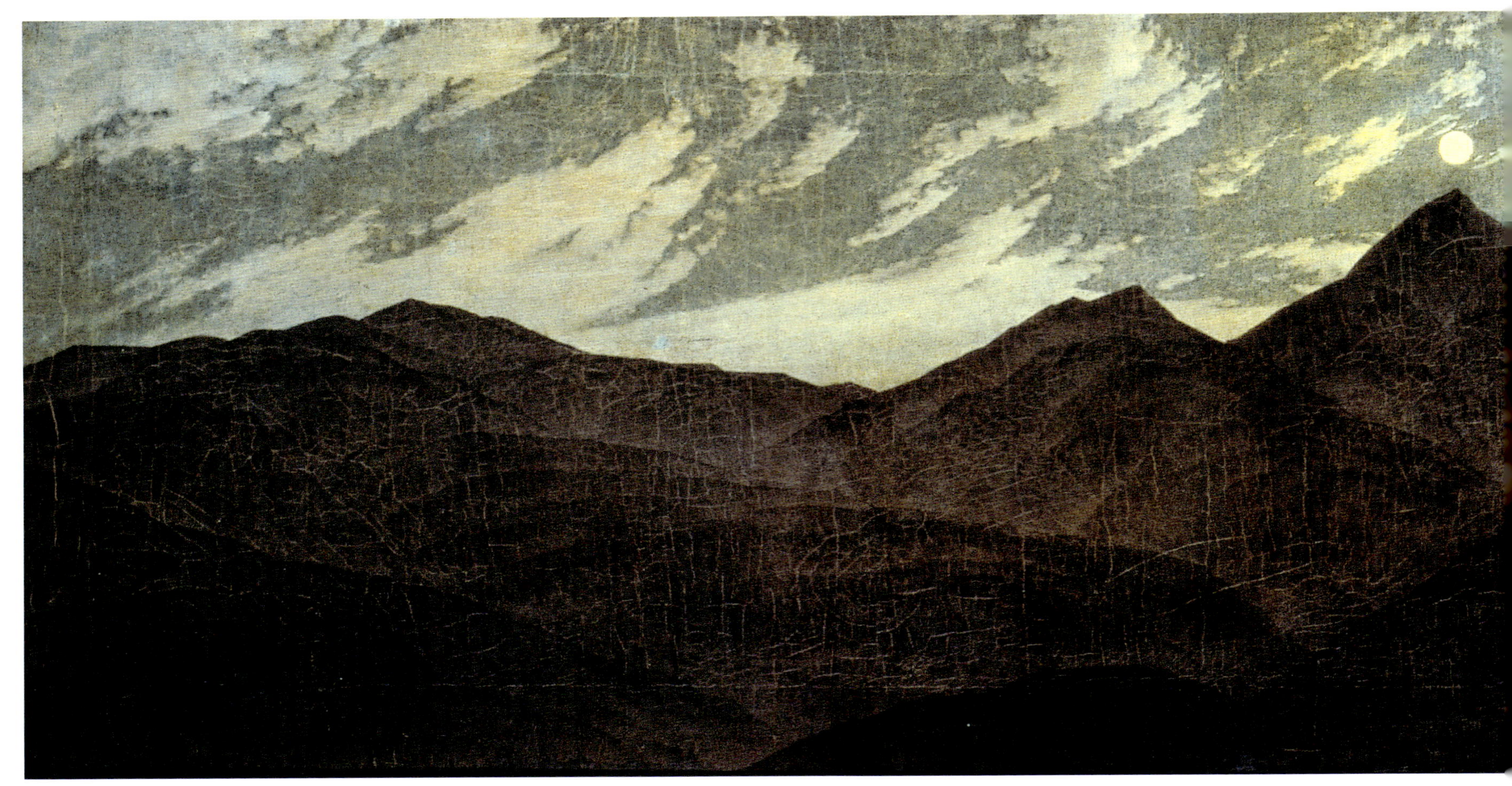

109. *Moon above the Riesengebirge,*
1810, oil on canvas,
47.5 x 167 cm (18⅝ x 65¾ in.).
Staatliche Kunstsammlungen, Weimar.

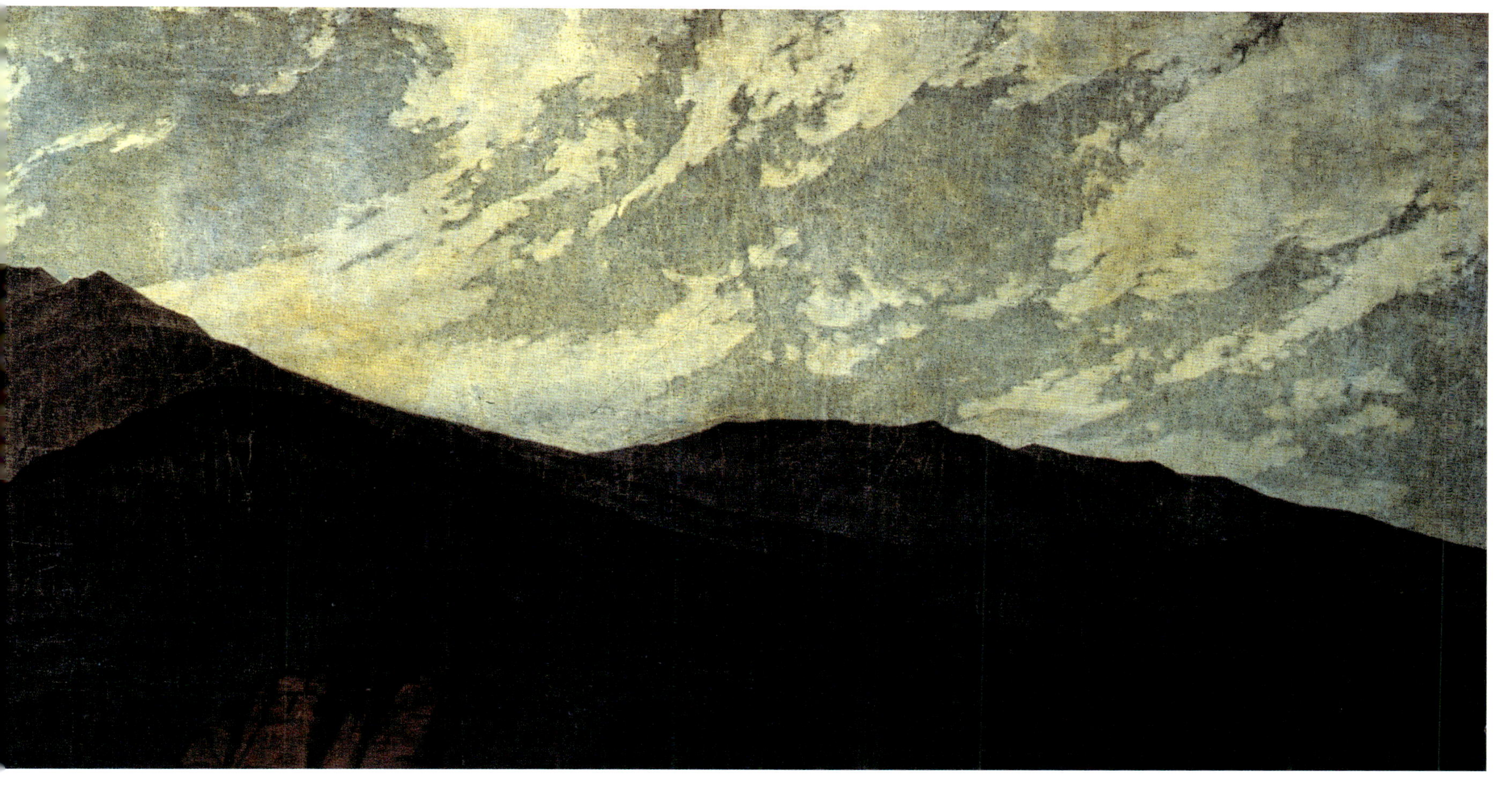

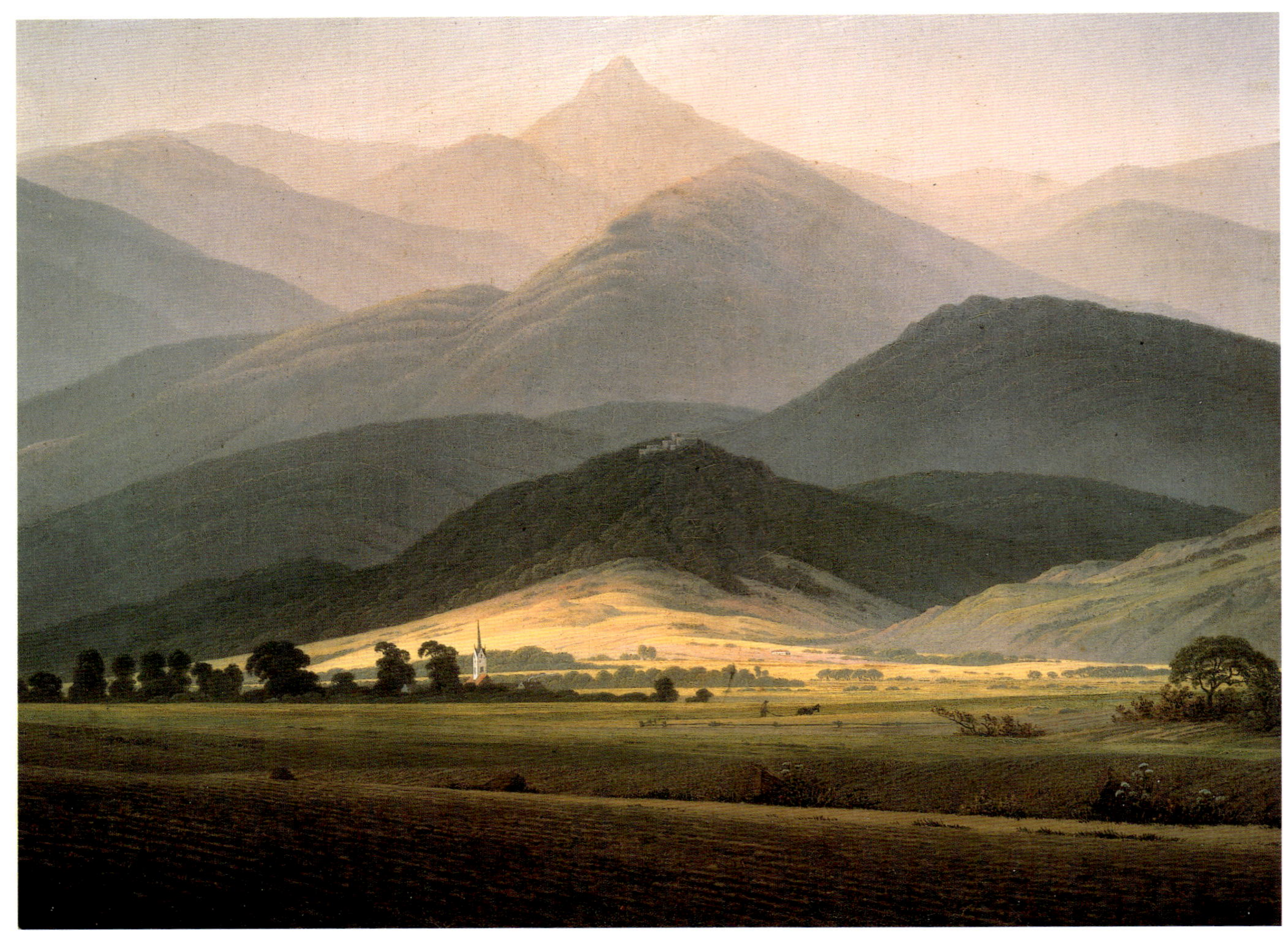

110 and 111. *Landscape in the Riesengebirge*,
1810, oil on canvas,
45 × 58.3 cm (17¾ × 23 in.).
Pushkin Museum, Moscow.

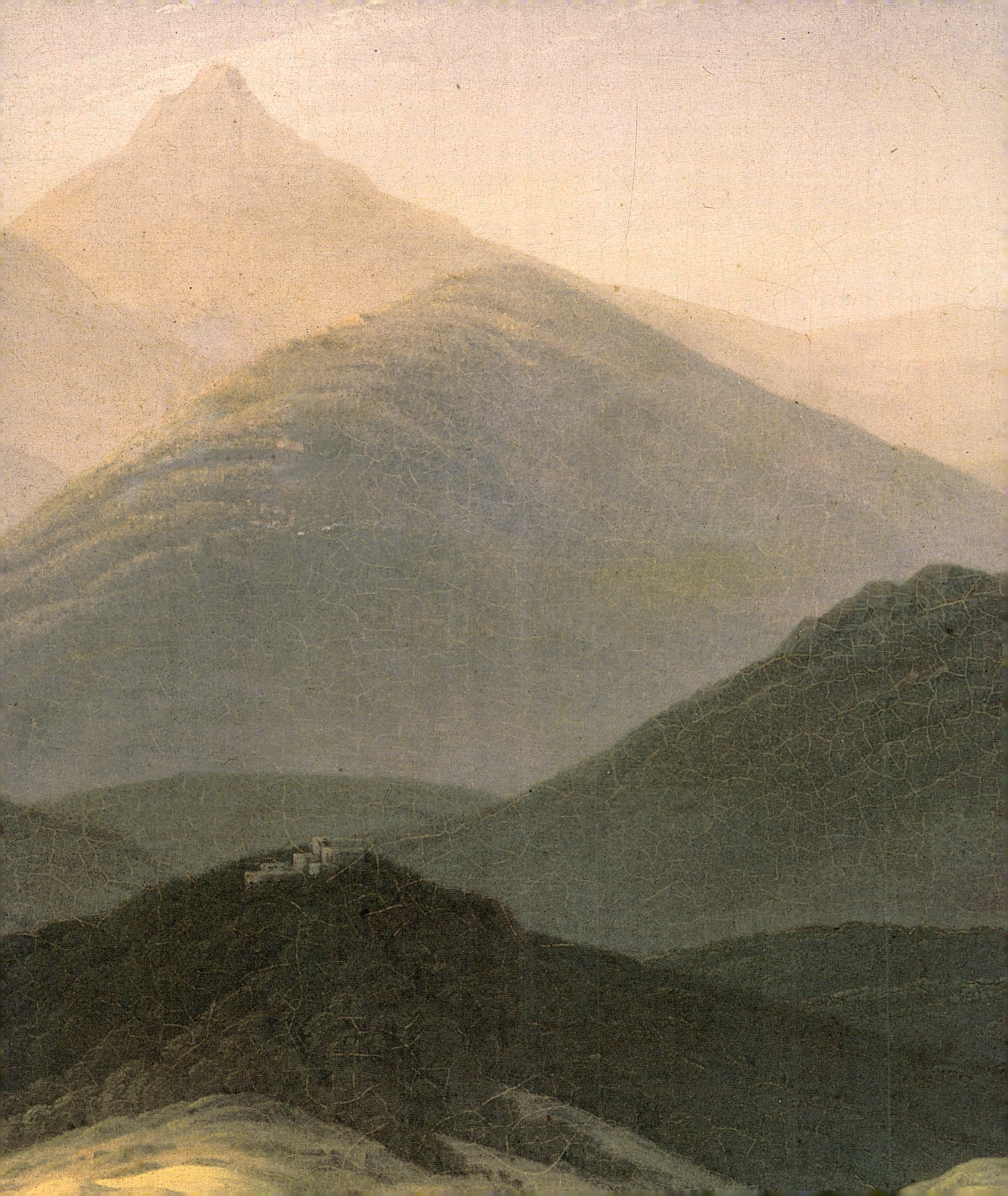

Friedrich's lifelong familiarity with sailing boats (ills 113, 114, 116 and 117), sea coasts, rocks and solitary trees structured his creative drive even before it reached out for specific 'factual content' (what Jacob Burckhardt called *Sachinhalt*), which in turn modified the 'total idea'. This is therefore a simplified description of the processes that trigger the creative act and steer its course.

The components of the 'total idea' are assumed to lie in each artist's mental constitution. Schiller located them in the unconscious mind, and regarded it as the job of poetry to express them, translating them into an objective form. He described this in a letter to Goethe (27 March 1801; see page 26), and Goethe returned to the idea years later when he wanted to distinguish the abilities of the 'true artist' from those of the dilettante: 'Their inner creative strength must by force of will, without predetermined intent, bring forth living images, idols left in the brain, memory and imagination; they must unfurl, grow, expand and contract, in order to change from cursory patterns into truly objective beings.' Championing the 'decisiveness of innate talent', Goethe had no time for the sketchy and the vague: 'The greater the talent, the more definitely the picture being produced takes shape from the first.'

The primary impulse of the 'total idea' should not be confused either with the search for an embodied ideal nor with tentative casualness; it does not legitimize either the cheerful confusion of a capriccio or the slavish imitation of reality. Instead, intelligently manipulated, it concentrates on meaningful transformations of certain fundamental models. Delacroix's definition of the cardinal point of this process remains unsurpassed, and this passage from his diary (26 March 1854) cannot be cited too often when demystification of the creative process is required. Delacroix's equivalent to the 'total idea' is *le moule consacré*: 'There are sacred moulds into which one throws all ideas, the good and the bad; the greatest and most original talents automatically bear their stamp.' This observation is augmented by another, concerning the *prima idea*, which complements Goethe's remarks about decisiveness. 'The first strokes with which a master outlines his ideas contain the germ of everything that will be in the eventual work.' Neither does this procedure merely produce the high points; Delacroix also took into account the inevitable moments when intensity drops, and spoke of intervals and necessary resting points, 'which allow the spirit to come to rest and lead to new ideas'. Friedrich's work, too, has such intervals when intensity diminishes.

View of Mountains with Waterfall (ill. 4) does not yet display the terse syntax which projects so strong an attraction in the later works, and it lacks Goethe's 'decisiveness', but nevertheless the *basso continuo* makes itself heard, and a kind of 'mould' can be distinguished. The wealth of painterly detail on offer shows how much rhetoric Friedrich had to shed and learn to do without, in order to free his central theme – nearness versus distance – from formulas and flourishes and make it his own. Did he perhaps, after all, follow the precepts of classical art school teaching, which made it the artist's duty to choose only the most beautiful and the most perfect from the available material? Friedrich had little respect for those precepts, preferring to be guided by another authority, his 'spiritual eye'. This was closely allied to the 'total idea', with the two concepts empowering and strengthening each other. The authority of his spiritual eye or inner gaze not only served Friedrich as a support for his formal vocabulary, but also allowed him to reuse and recombine his impressions of the outside world, recorded with scrupulous exactitude in his sketchbooks (ills 118, 119 and 120). However, unlike Zeuxis who painted the supreme beauty of Helen from many lesser beauties, Friedrich did not work with the intention of extracting an

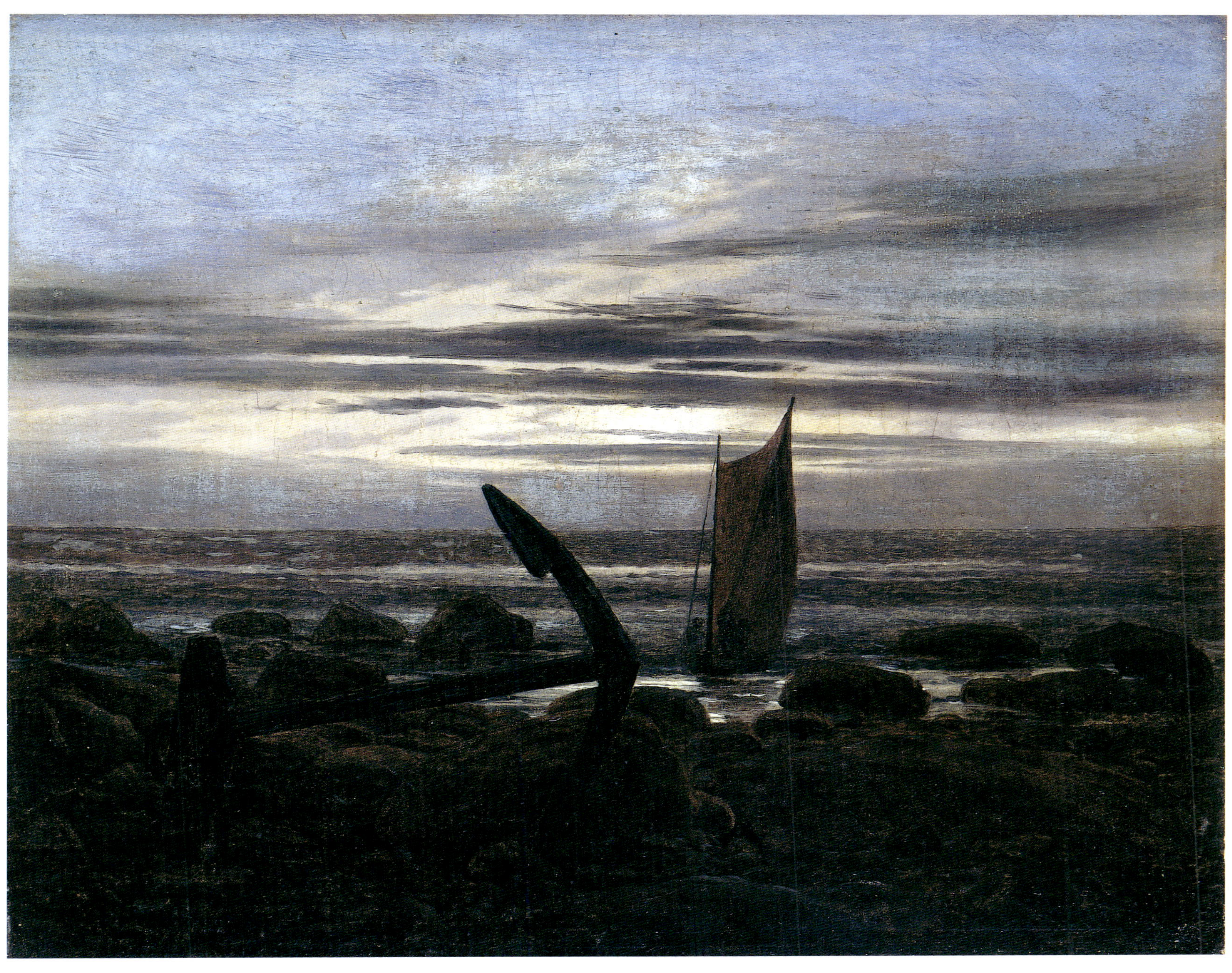

112. *Evening on the Baltic Sea*,
1826, oil on canvas,
25 x 31 cm (9⅞ x 12¼ in.).
Georg Schäfer Collection.

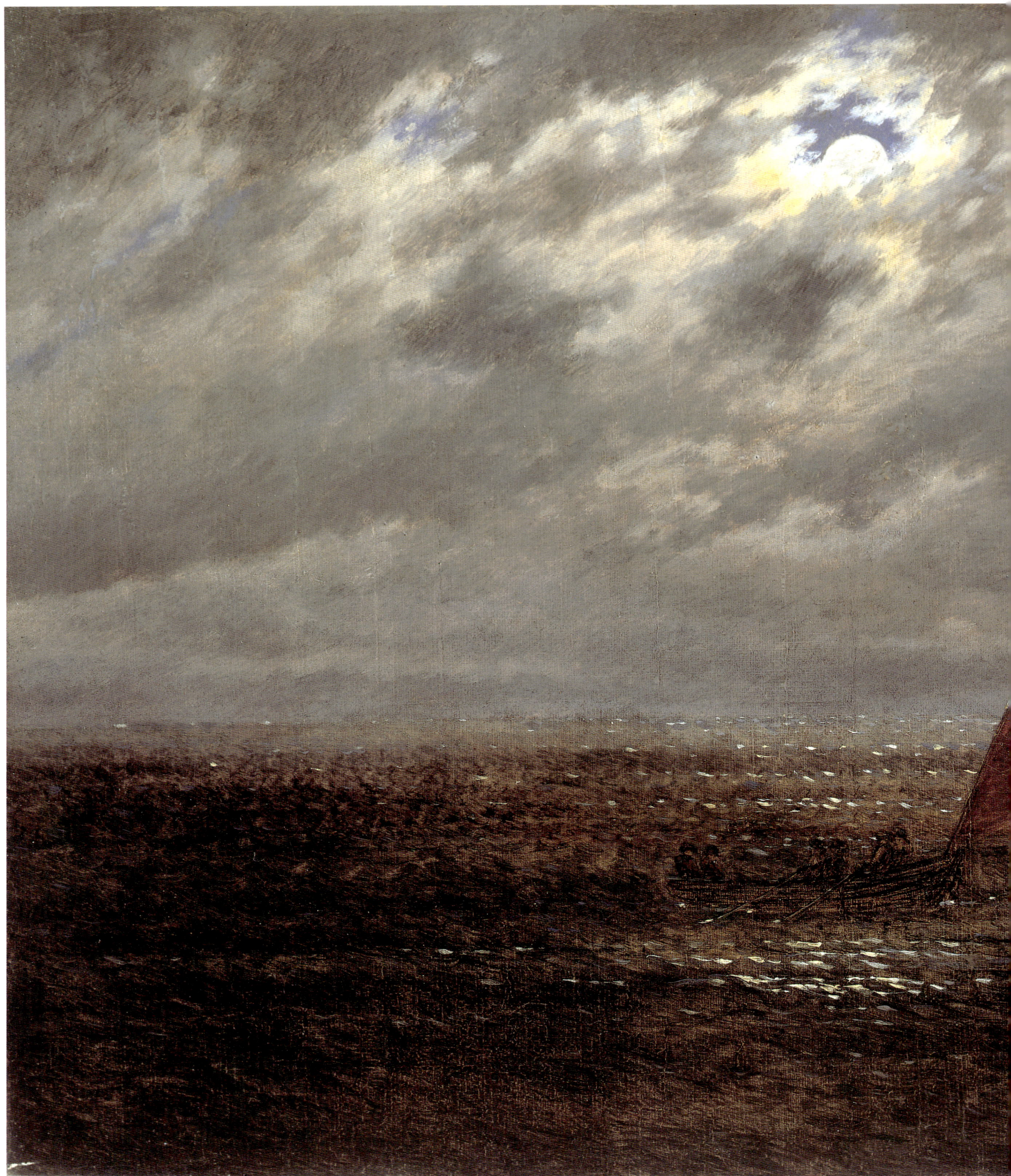

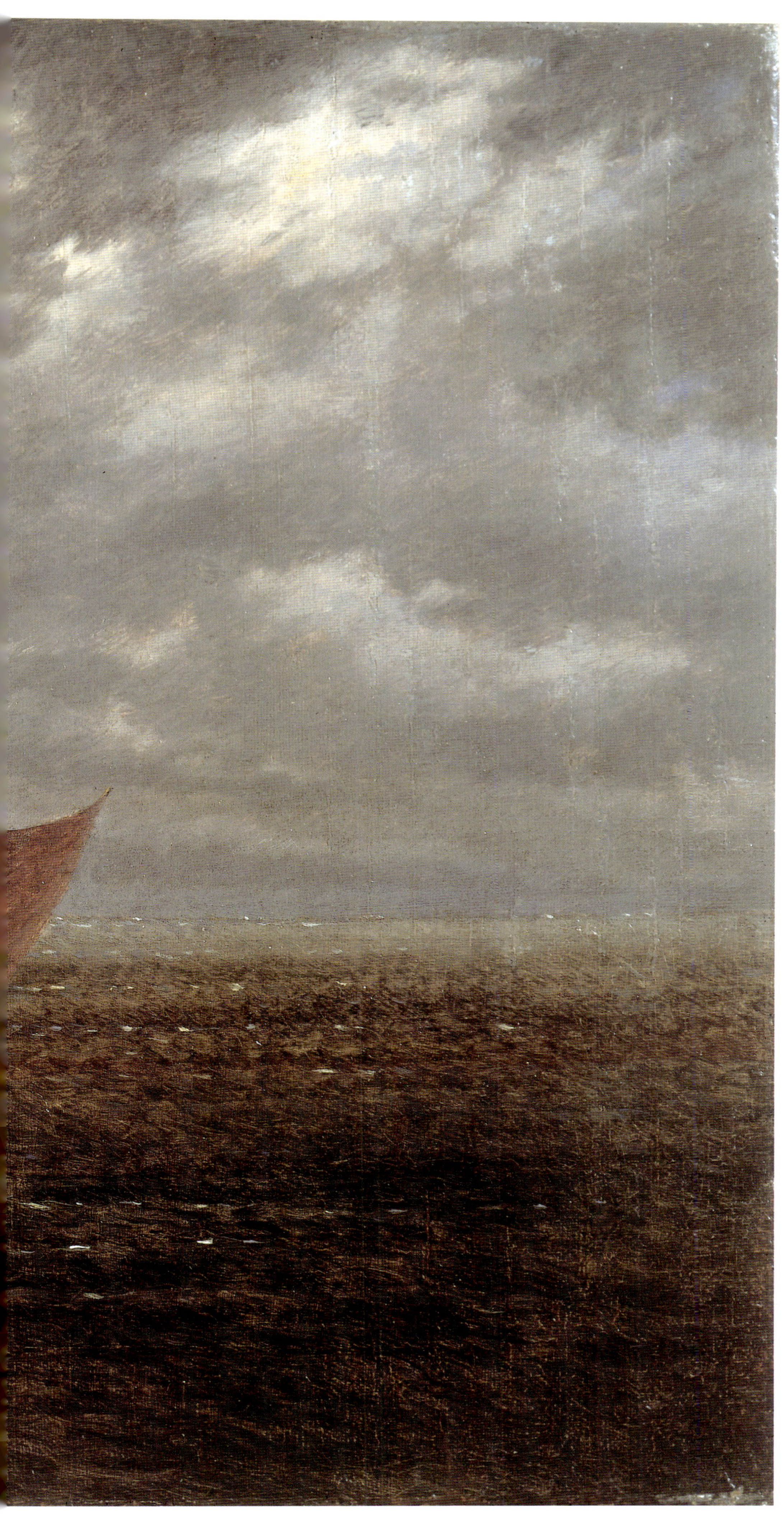

113. *Night*,
1816–17, oil on canvas,
22 x 30 cm (8⅝ x 11¾ in.).
Galerie Nathan, Zurich.

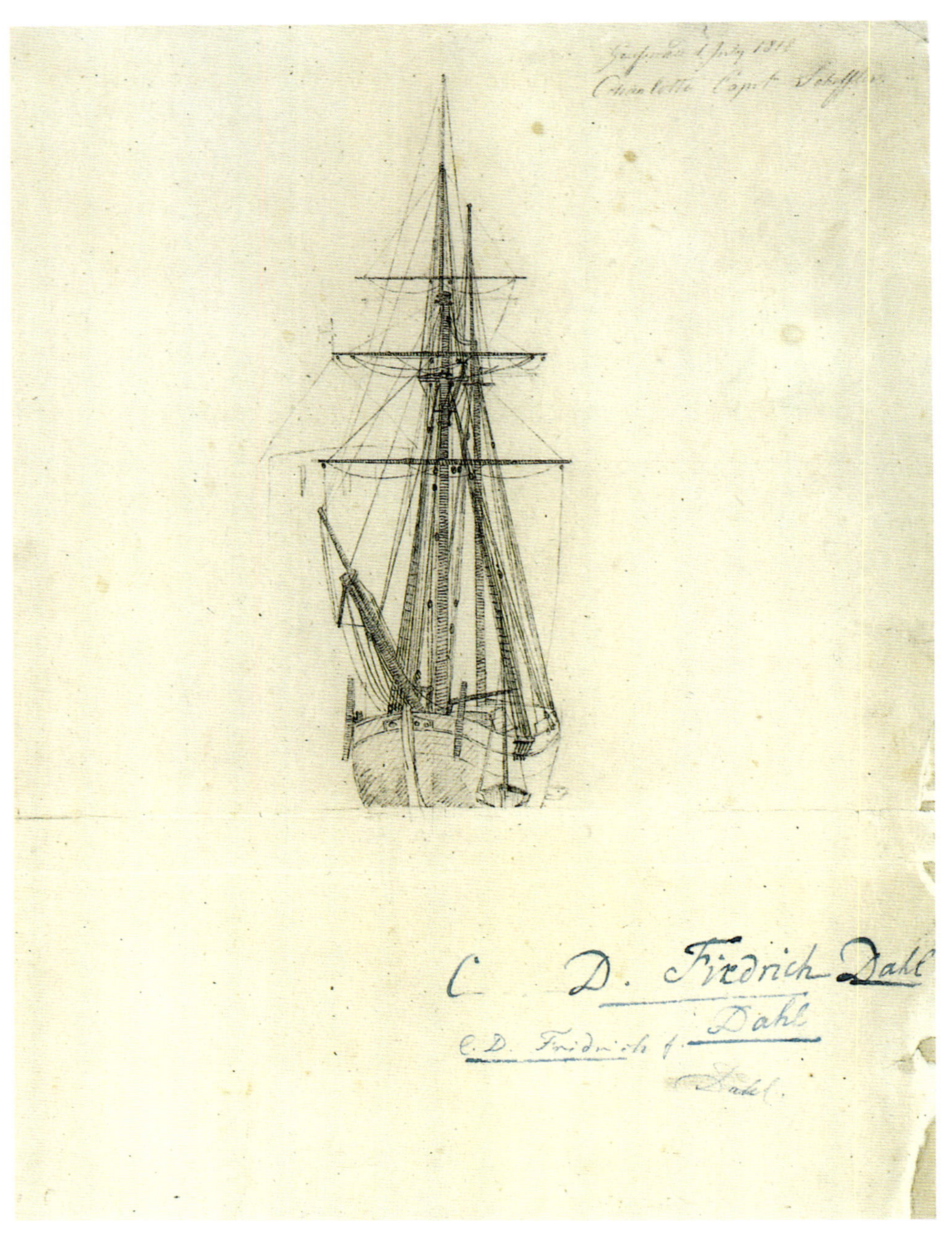

114. ***Sailing Boat,***
1818, pencil,
33.1 x 24.7 cm (13 x 9¾ in.).
Kupferstichkabinett, Berlin.

ideal but relied on his obscure total idea. This has similarities with the *certa idea* to which Raphael referred in his letter to Count Castiglione: 'In order to paint a beautiful woman, I should really see more beautiful women ... but as there are so few beautiful women, or qualified judges, I make use of a certain idea that comes into my head. Whether it has any artistic value, I cannot say.' (The last part of that confession, with its broad wink, is also reminiscent of Friedrich.)

Friedrich's motto is well-known: 'The painter should not paint merely what he sees in front of him but also what he sees within him. If he sees nothing within him, however, then he should refrain from painting what he sees in front of him.' Nonetheless, this was not a recommendation to withdraw from the empirical world into an arbitrary 'curiosity shop, where many things lie heaped together but nothing goes with anything else'. The things an artist observes should not, he believed, serve as an excuse for demonstrating subjective skill ('brush-wagging'). Instead, Friedrich wanted to reorder their components and accommodate them in his 'total idea'. In this, he seems to echo a concept that Goethe formulated in the introduction to *Die Propyläen*, his shortlived periodical on aesthetics (1798–1800): 'The genuine, law-making artist strives for artistic truth, while the lawless one, following a blind urge, strives for the reality of nature. Through the former, art rises to its highest pinnacle; through the latter, it falls to its lowest depth.' Friedrich's 'artistic truth' does not altogether coincide with what Goethe had in mind, of course, but the goal was the same: the reordering of the 'reality of nature'. Friedrich did not put any trust in dry rules; he was not content to produce the patchwork that others called 'composition', and 'aping' was never his motive for creating symmetry. In the same spirit, he rejected the idea of reusing elements of his original pictures like 'playing cards', which always remain the same, no matter how well-shuffled they are. To put it another way, he had no desire to serve up a 'ragout of leftovers'.

Friedrich's practice of his art, however, contradicted his own theoretical recommendations and warnings. We have seen that he based his formal repertoire on certain basic models (Delacroix's *moules*)

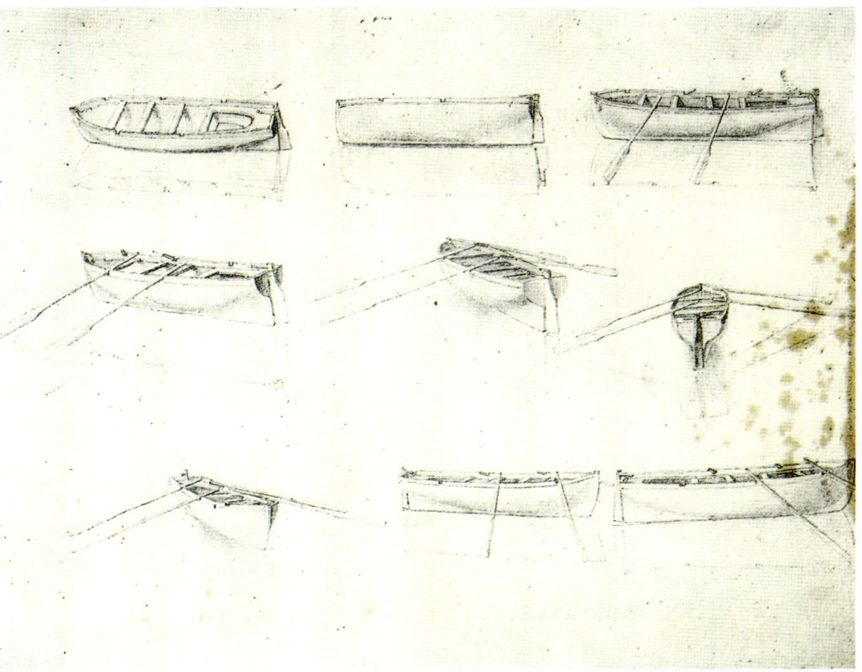

115. ***Studies of Rowing Boats,***
1818, pencil,
19.4 x 24.3 cm (7⅝ x 9⅝ in.).
Kupferstichkabinett, Berlin.

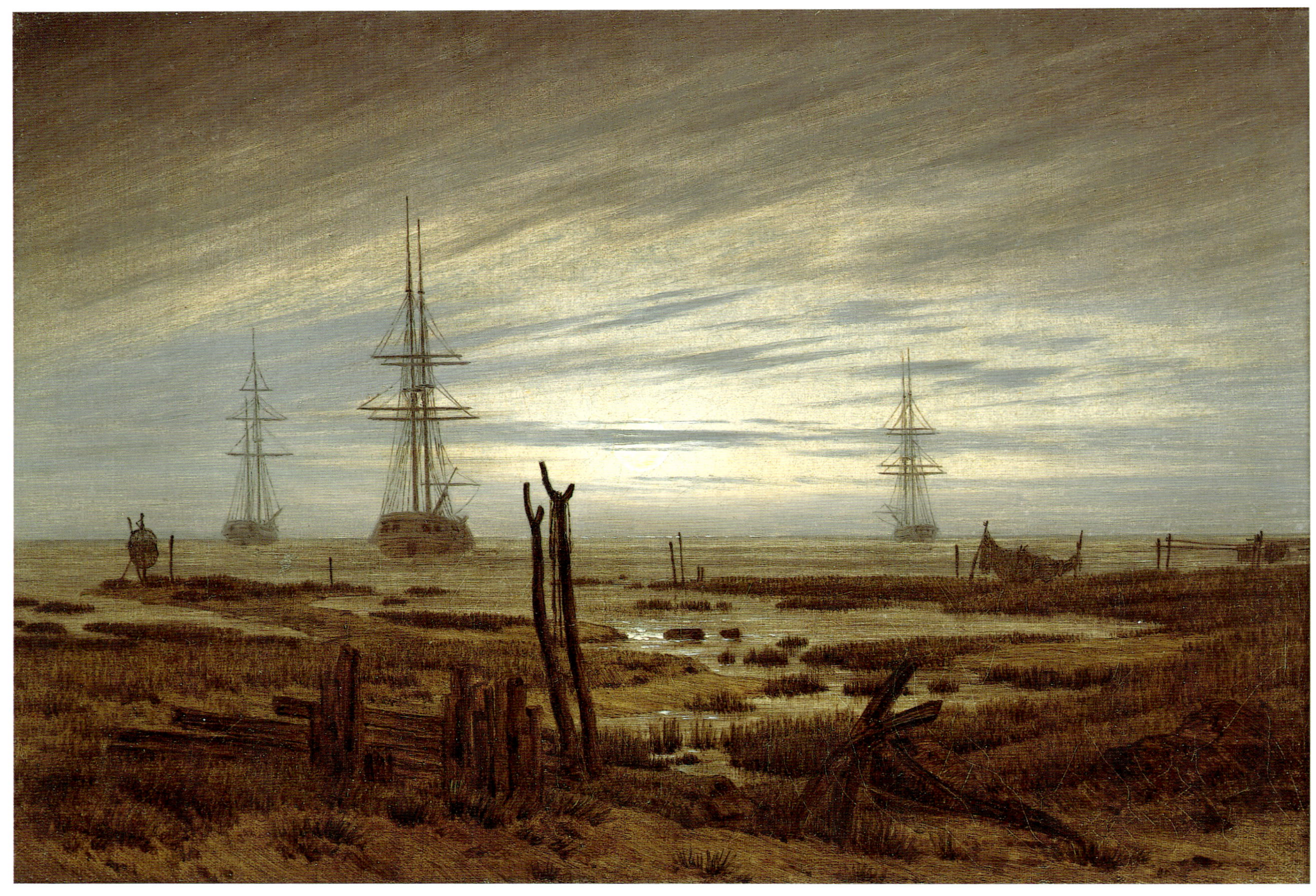

116. *Ships at Anchor,*
1815, oil on canvas,
21 × 30 cm (8¼ × 11¾ in.).
Private collection, on loan to Nationalgalerie, Berlin.

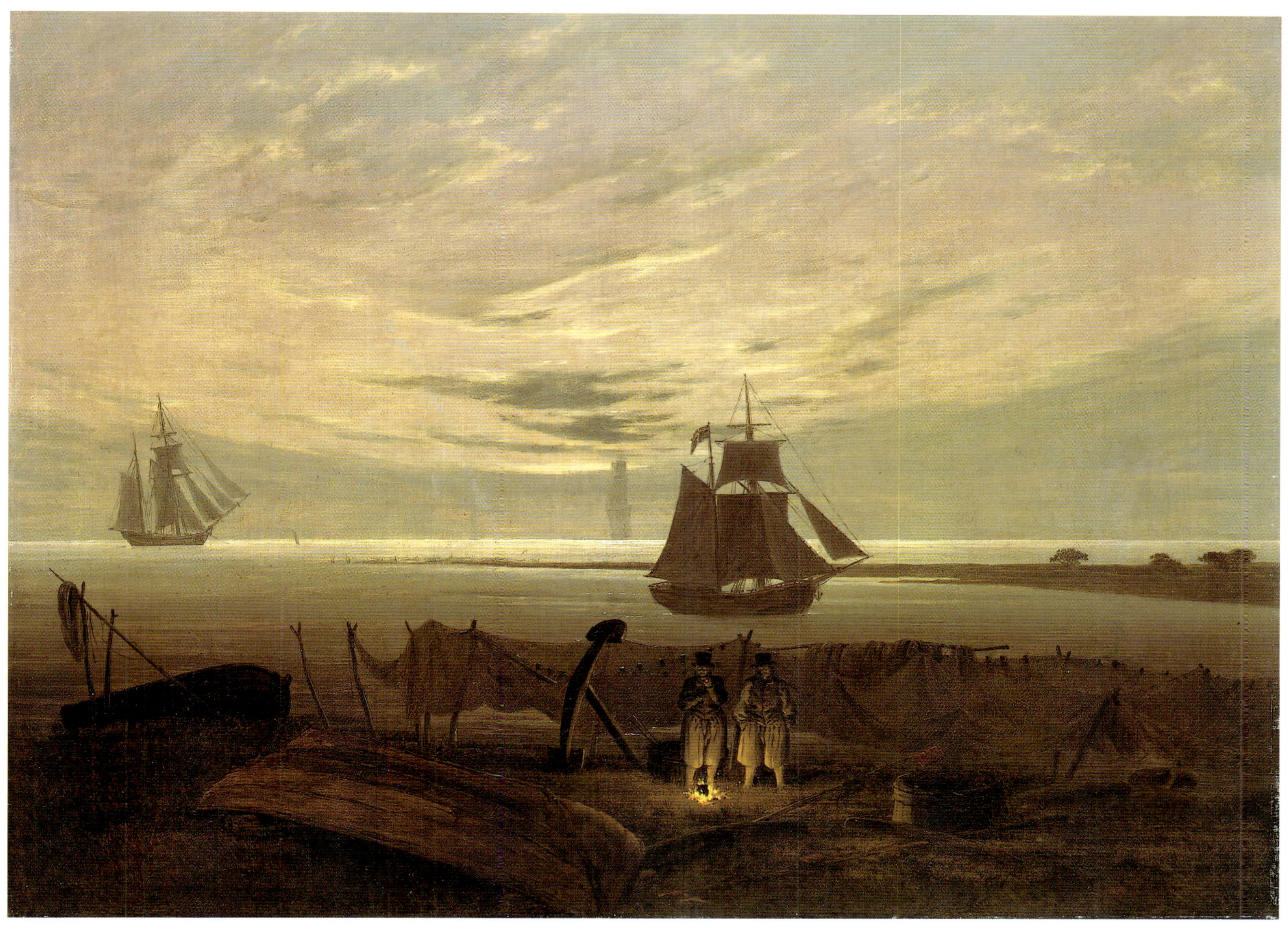

117. *Evening on the Baltic Sea,*
c. 1831, oil on canvas,
54 × 71.5 cm (21¼ × 28⅛ in.).
Gemäldegalerie Neue Meister, Dresden.

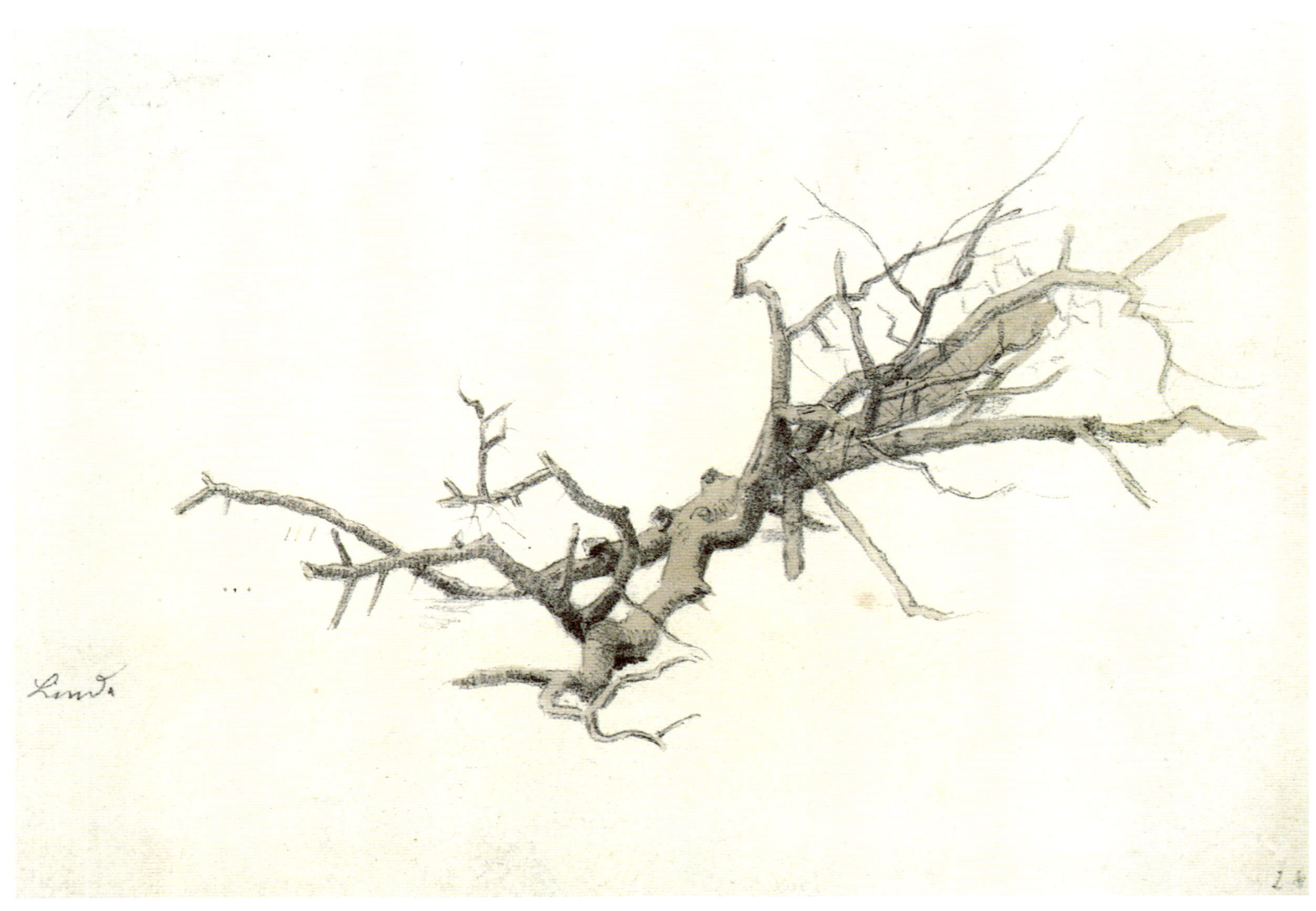

118. *Limetree Branch,*
c. 1812, pencil, wash,
12.8 × 18 cm (5 × 7⅛ in.).
Nasjonalgalleriet, Oslo.

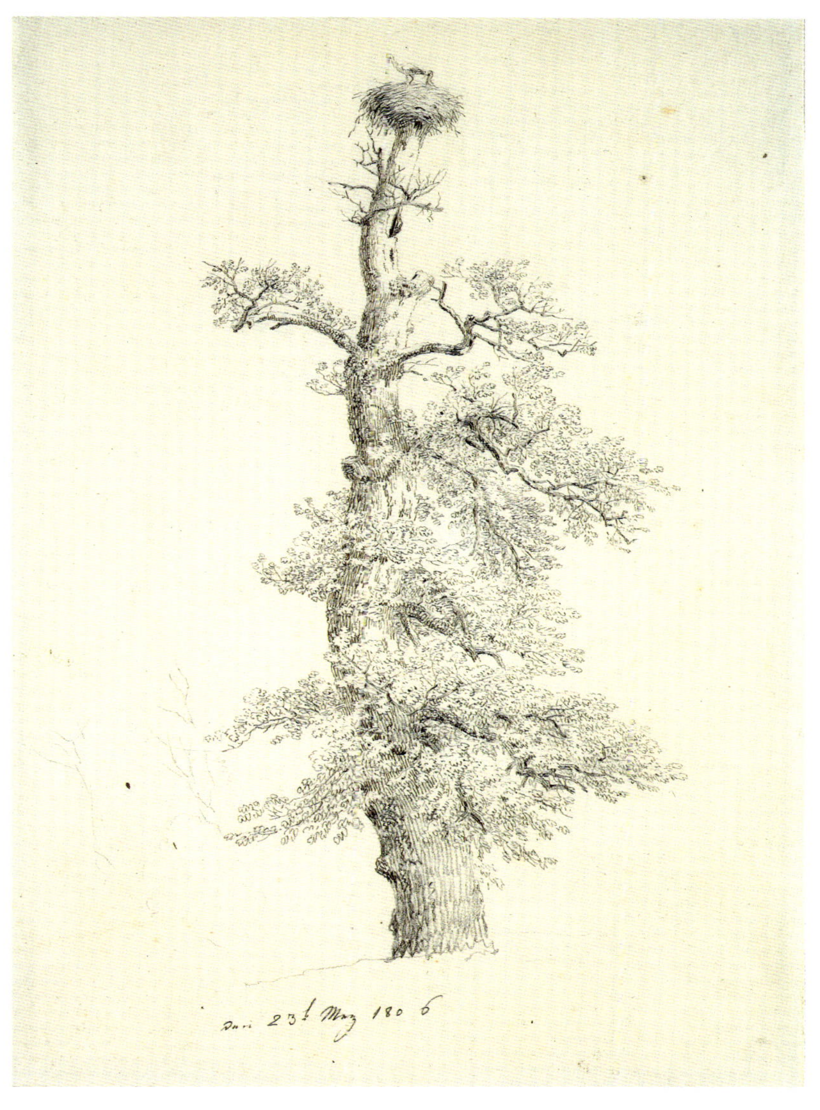

119. *Oaktree with Stork's Nest,*
23 May 1806, pencil,
28.6 x 20.5 cm (11¼ x 8 in.).
Hamburger Kunsthalle, Hamburg.

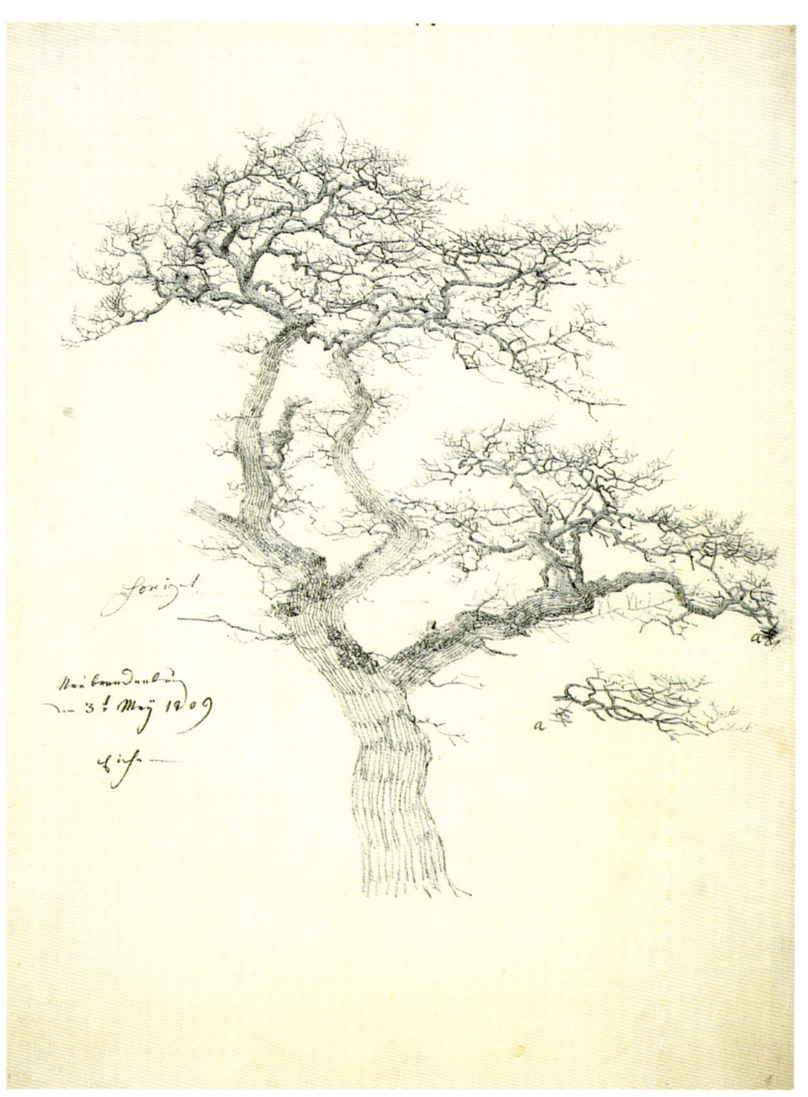

120. *Bare Oaktree,*
3 May 1809, pencil,
36 x 25.9 cm (14⅛ x 10¼ in.).
Nasjonalgalleriet, Oslo.

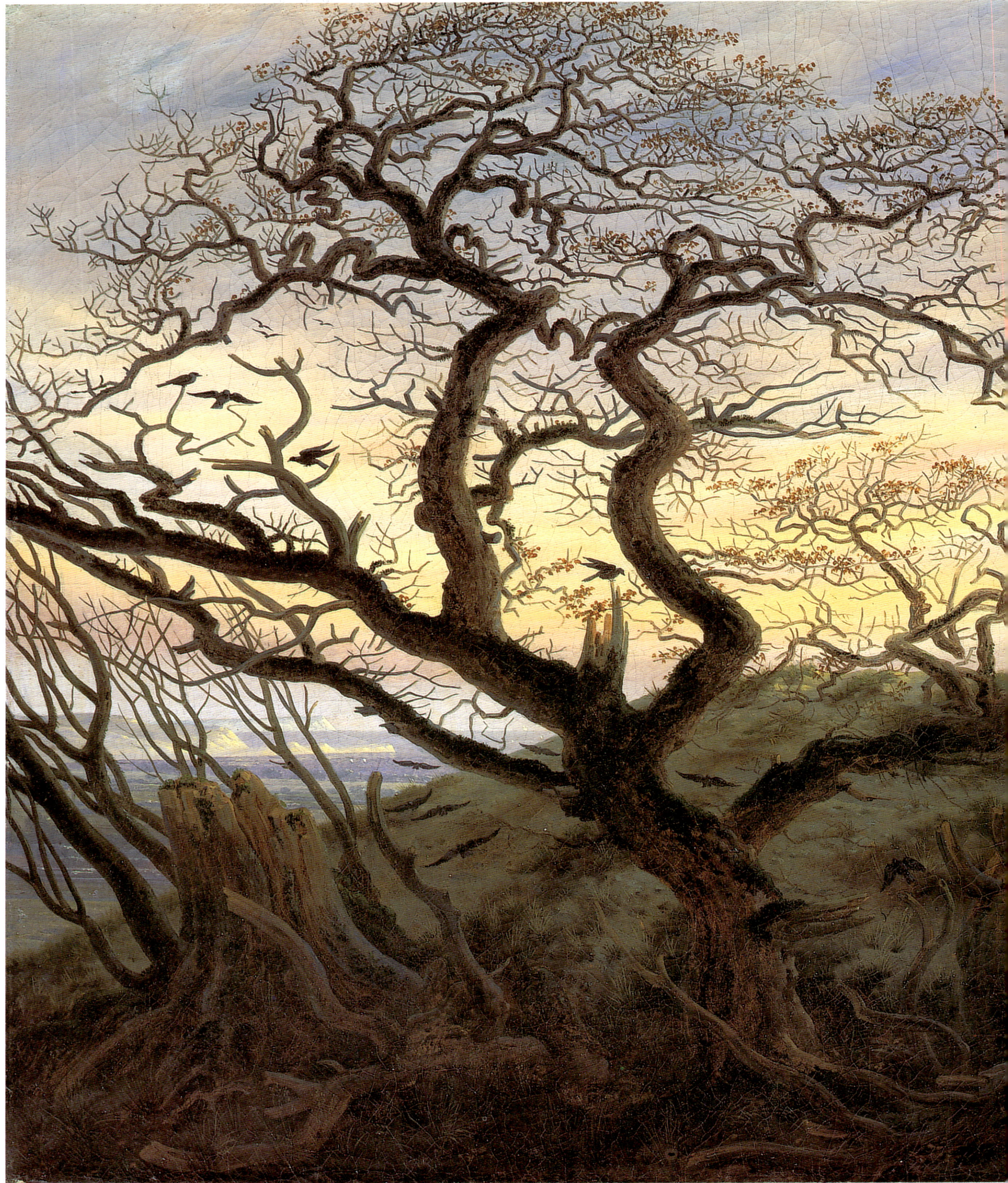

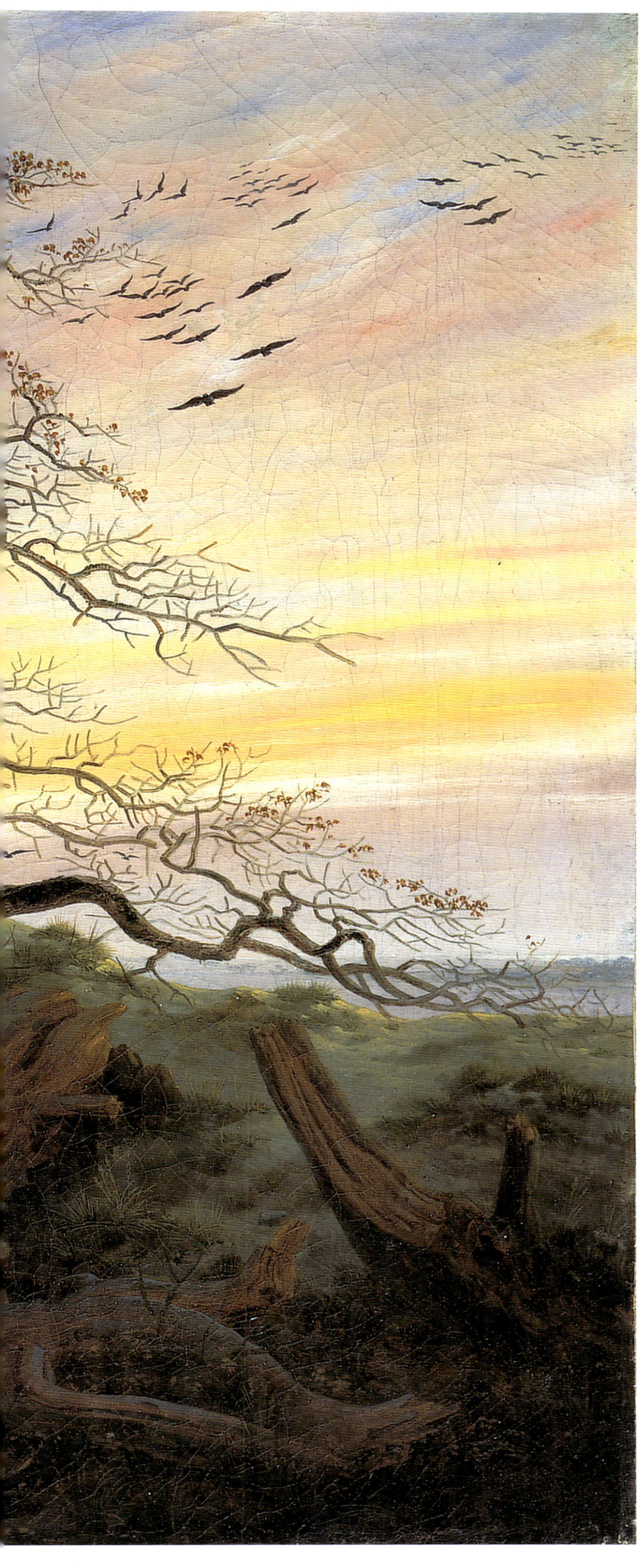

121. *The Raven Tree*,
1822, oil on canvas,
54 x 71 cm (21¼ x 28 in.).
Musée du Louvre, Paris.

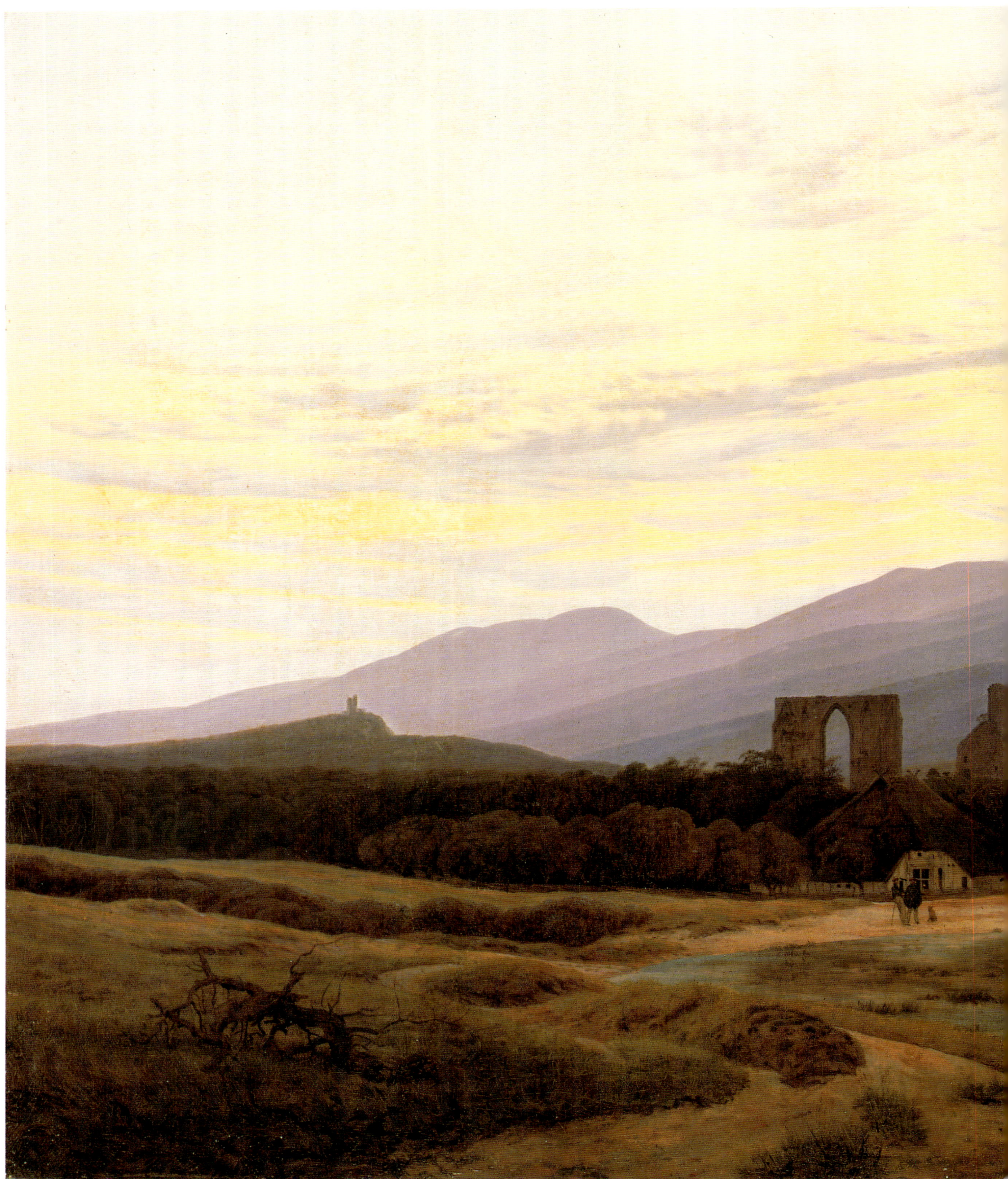

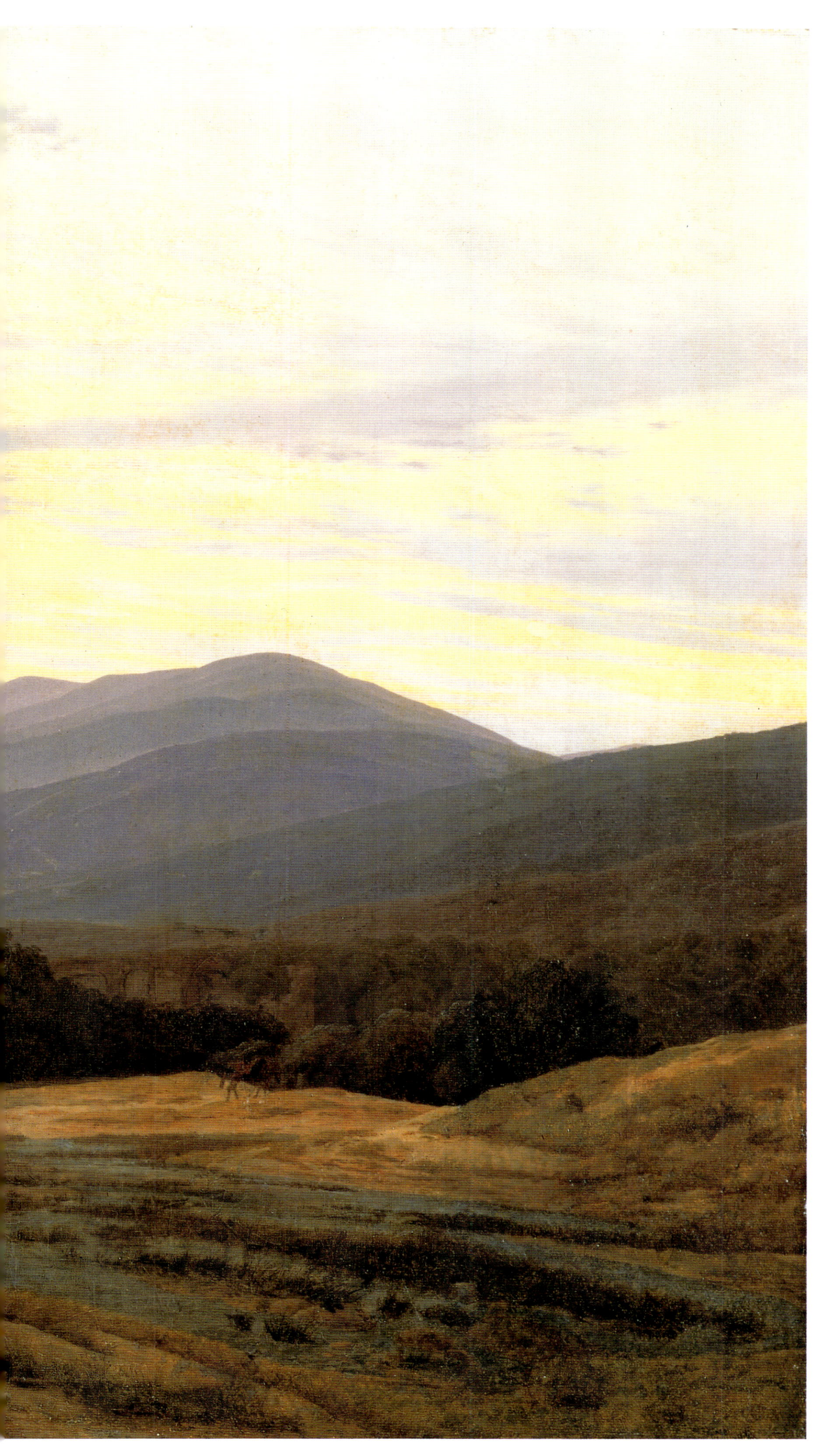

122. *Ruins in the Riesengebirge,*
1830–34, oil on canvas,
72 x 101 cm (28⅜ x 39¾ in.).
Pommersches Landesmuseum, Greifswald.

which he varied in different combinations and permutations. It has long been known that he frequently reused the trees, rocks and mountains recorded in his numerous sketchbooks in different paintings, swapping one for another just like 'playing cards'. The practice ensured both the literal fidelity of his pictures and the freedom of his thinking, which put artistic truth above reproduction. It also illustrates his economy, the conscious limitation of his lucid artistic reasoning to a manageable vocabulary of signs. His way of using these, in a manner that surpasses the boundaries of time and space, has been demonstrated by Otto Schmitt, who took *Ruins in the Riesengebirge* (ill. 122) as his example. Schmitt found three 'playing cards' in this puzzle. For the background, Friedrich used the 1810 drawing of a landscape in the Riesengebirge, but reversed it. There is a note on the drawing: 'The lines should stretch further.' Then for the ruins he used a drawing of 1815, and for the broken branch in the left foreground a study of 1808–10. He had done something similar when he took a realistic nature study (ill. 118) and later transformed it into a tree with monstrous, devouring branches (ill. 121). This compilation of discrete matter was also a spatial and temporal journey into his own past. The outcome of the poetic 'transplantation' is completely harmonious and betrays nothing of the topographical origins of the ruins and distant mountains; this fact distinguishes it from the architectural capriccios of the eighteenth century. Friedrich did not intend to trick anyone by putting these heterogeneous features together, but he may have wanted to create a visual equivalent for the spiritual eye's ability to visit two distant places, and to combine a feature from his first home on the Baltic (at Eldena) with another from the second homeland (Riesengebirge) he found for himself on his rambles from Dresden.

Having identified the processes of Friedrich's formal invention and organization, we come to the question of their poetic content. If he frequently produced 'montages', shuffling and dealing the elements of his formal vocabulary like playing cards, how then could he dissociate himself from the idea of a 'ragout'? The answer, and justification, are found in the writings which remained unpublished during his lifetime. He was aware, to a certain extent, that his art walked a tightrope, and his reflections were often self-critical. Copying his own work, he admonished, would put a stop to 'free, spiritual re-creation of nature'. But does not the 'free, spiritual re-creation of nature' imply the freedom to combine different experiences? Friedrich was obviously thinking to some extent of the correspondence between facts and their spiritual transformation that Goethe called 'artistic truth'. Nevertheless, he saw a relationship between artistic truth and its cause, the sheer reality of nature: 'Nothing in a picture is secondary....' He could as well have said 'Nothing in nature is secondary', and the next part of the sentence is even more true of nature: '... everything belongs inalienably to the whole, and therefore may not be neglected.' The reciprocal relationship of art and nature arises from their mutual ignorance of which is primary and which is secondary.

This is confirmed in Friedrich's landscapes. He follows his own advice not to confine himself to sublime scenes, such as lofty mountains, bottomless chasms and the boundless ocean: 'just a cornfield would be enough'. 'Every flower, every stalk, considered on its own, is admirable and beautiful.' And more firmly still: 'The noble person [painter] recognizes God in everything, the common fellow [painter] sees only the form, not the spirit.' In conversation with his celebrated contemporary Peter von Cornelius, Friedrich said of *Swans in the Rushes* (ill. 87): 'The divine is everywhere, even in a grain of sand, so for once I depicted it in the rushes.' All his thinking, feeling and painting turned on the dictum that the

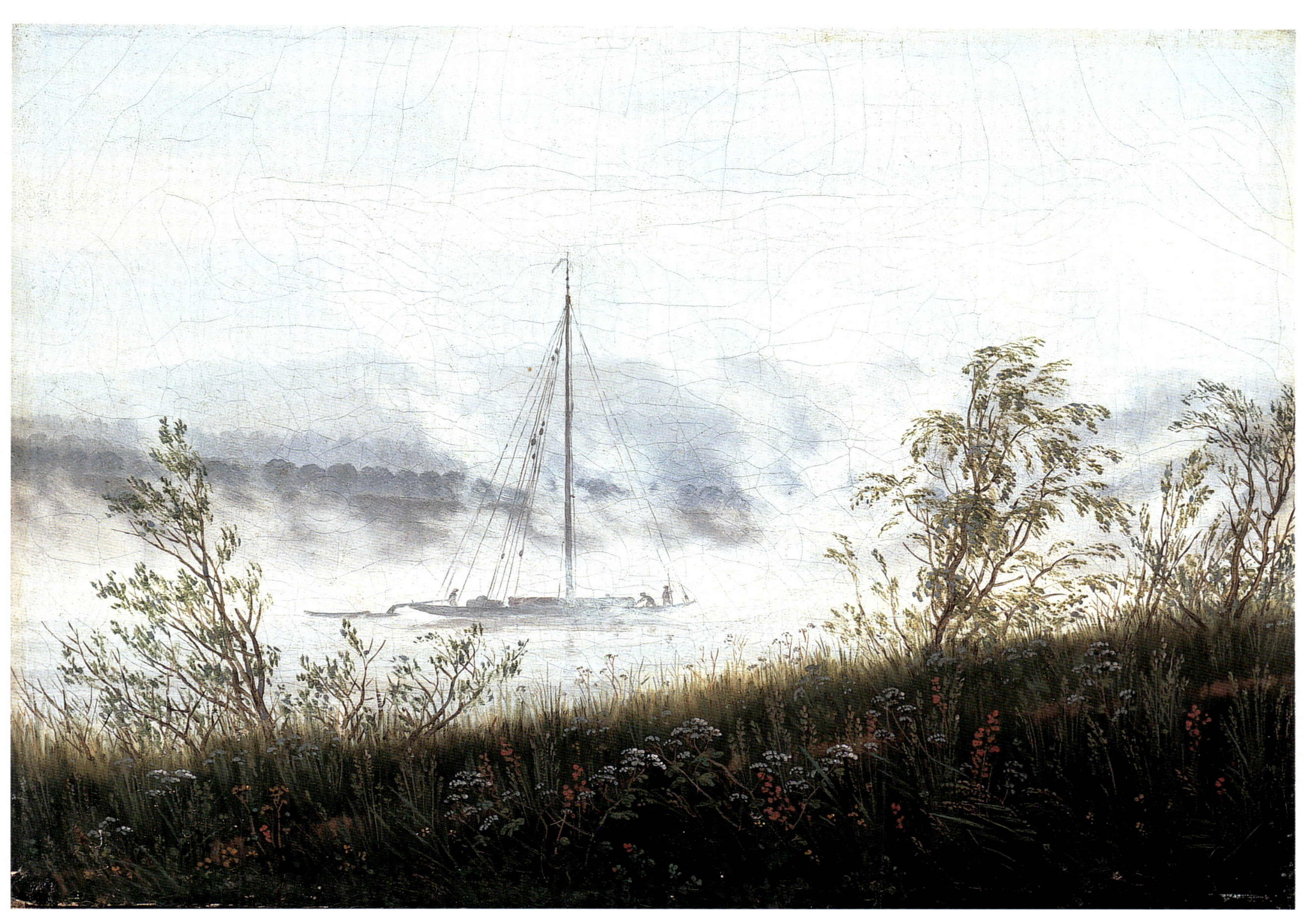

123. *Ship on the River Elbe in the Early Morning Mist,*
1820–25, oil on canvas,
22.5 x 30.8 cm (8¾ x 12 in.).
Wallraf-Richartz-Museum, Cologne.

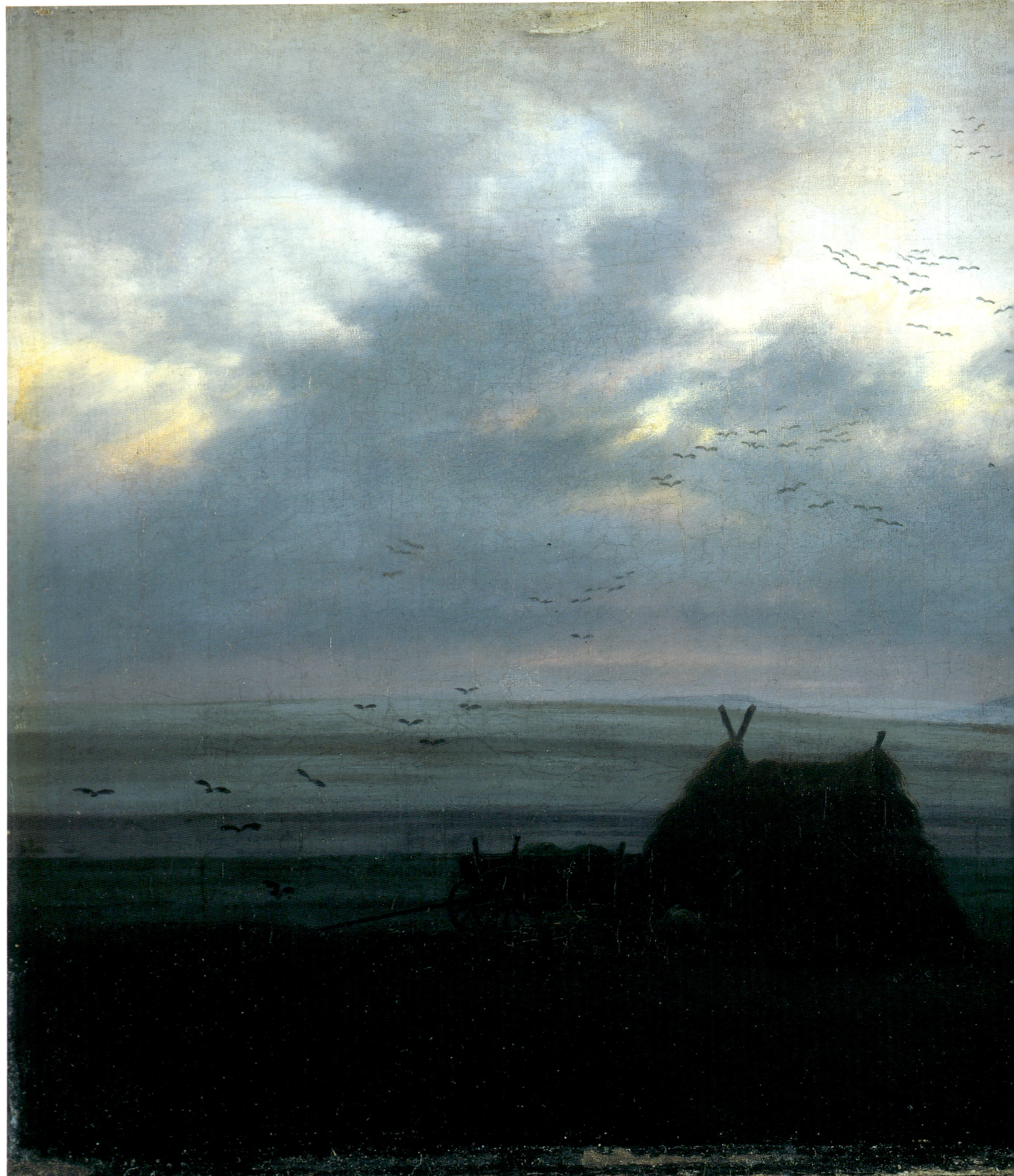

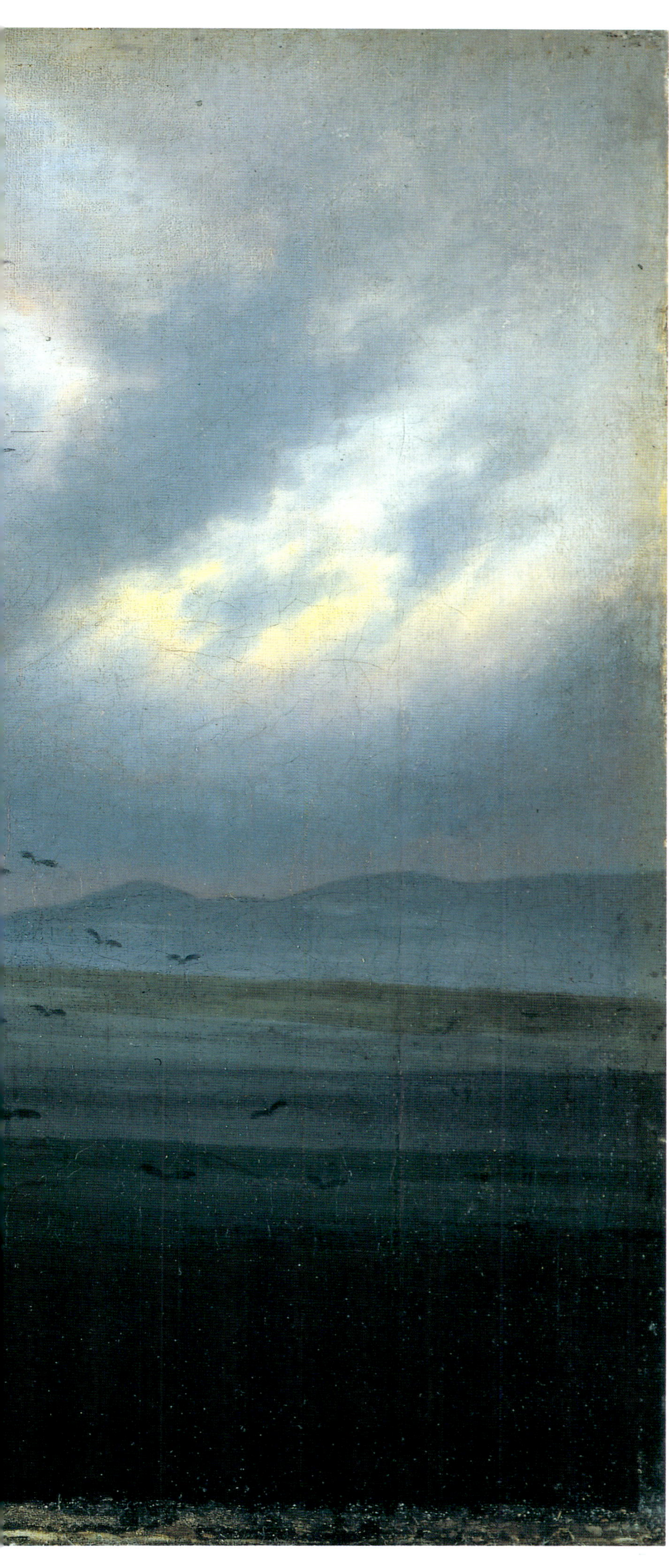

124. ***Ribbons of Mist,***
1818–20, oil on canvas,
32.6 × 42.5 cm (12¾ × 16¾ in.).
Hamburger Kunsthalle, Hamburg.

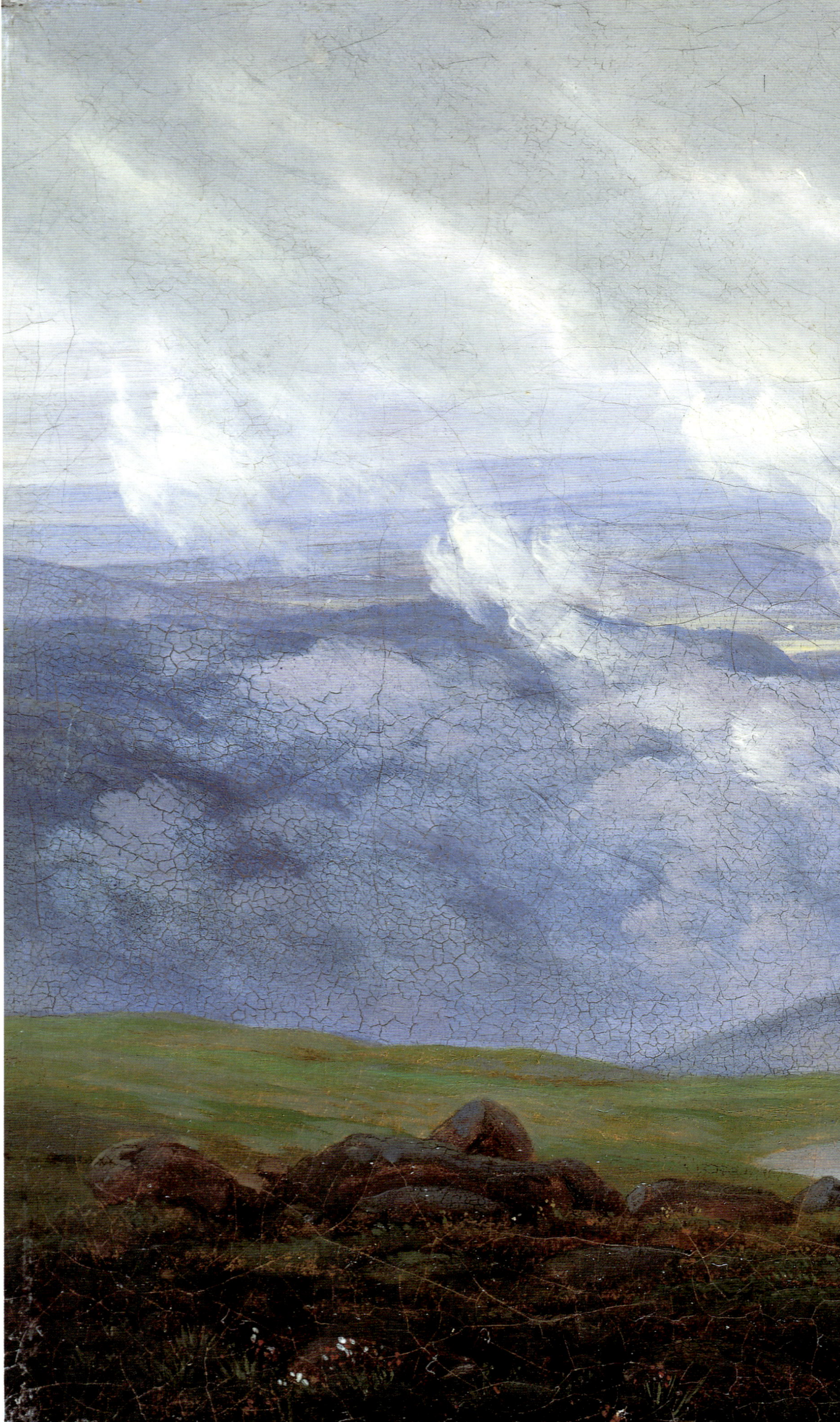

125. ***Clouds,***
1821, oil on canvas,
18.3 × 24.5 cm (7¼ × 9¾ in.).
Hamburger Kunsthalle, Hamburg.

Overleaf:
126. ***Evening*****, enlarged,**
1824, oil on board,
12.5 × 21.2 cm (5 × 8¼ in.).
Österreichische Galerie im Belvedere, Vienna.

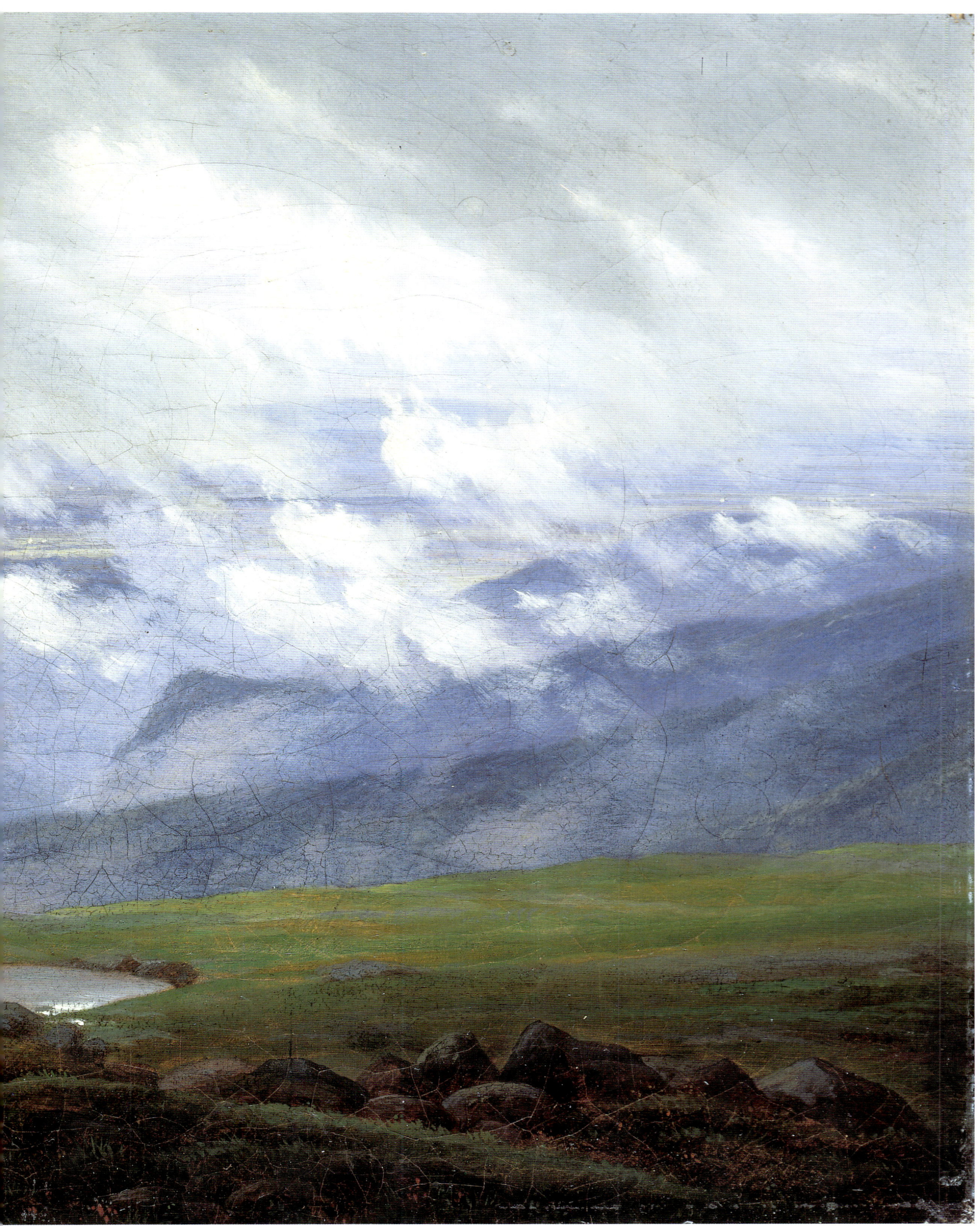

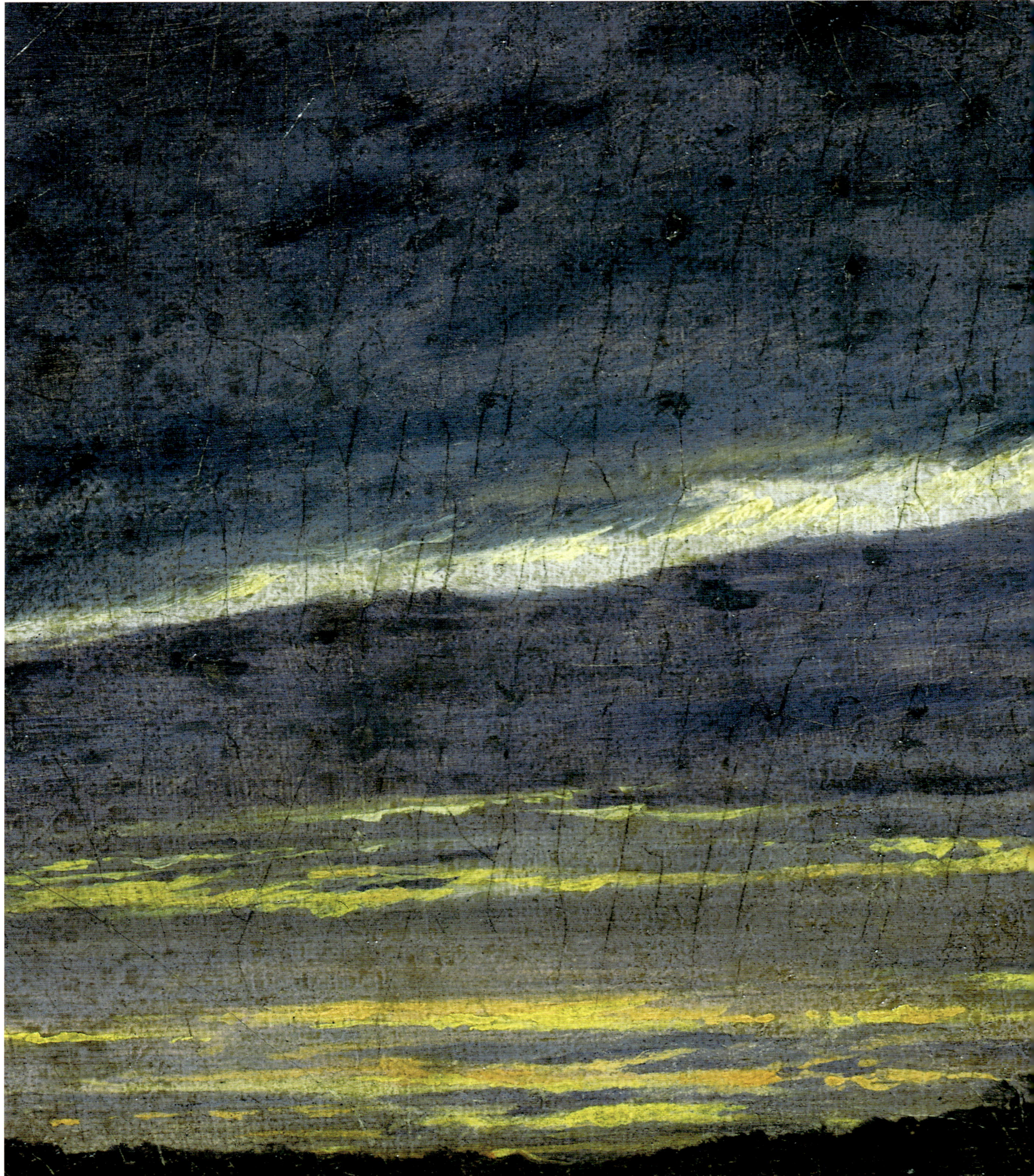

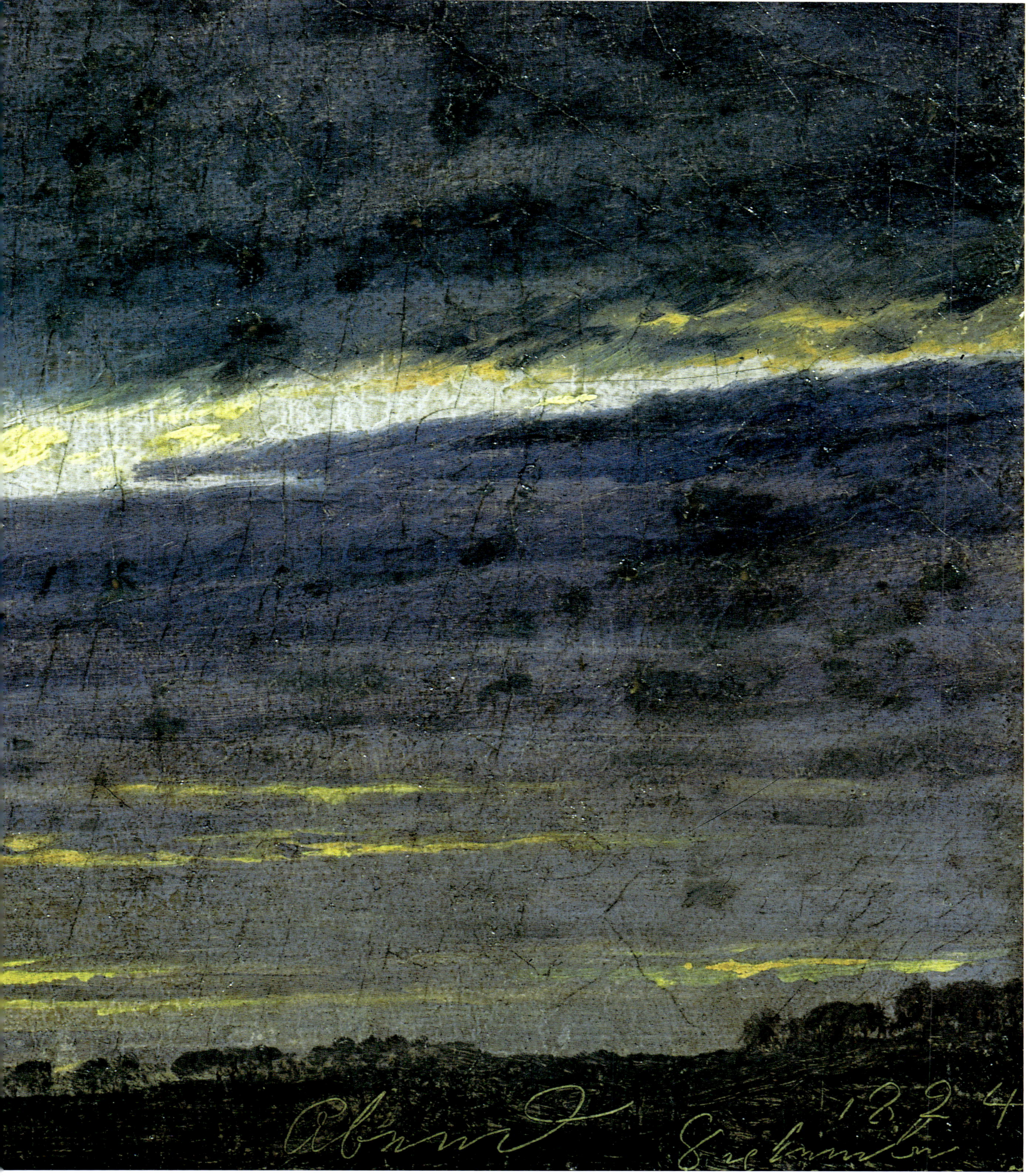

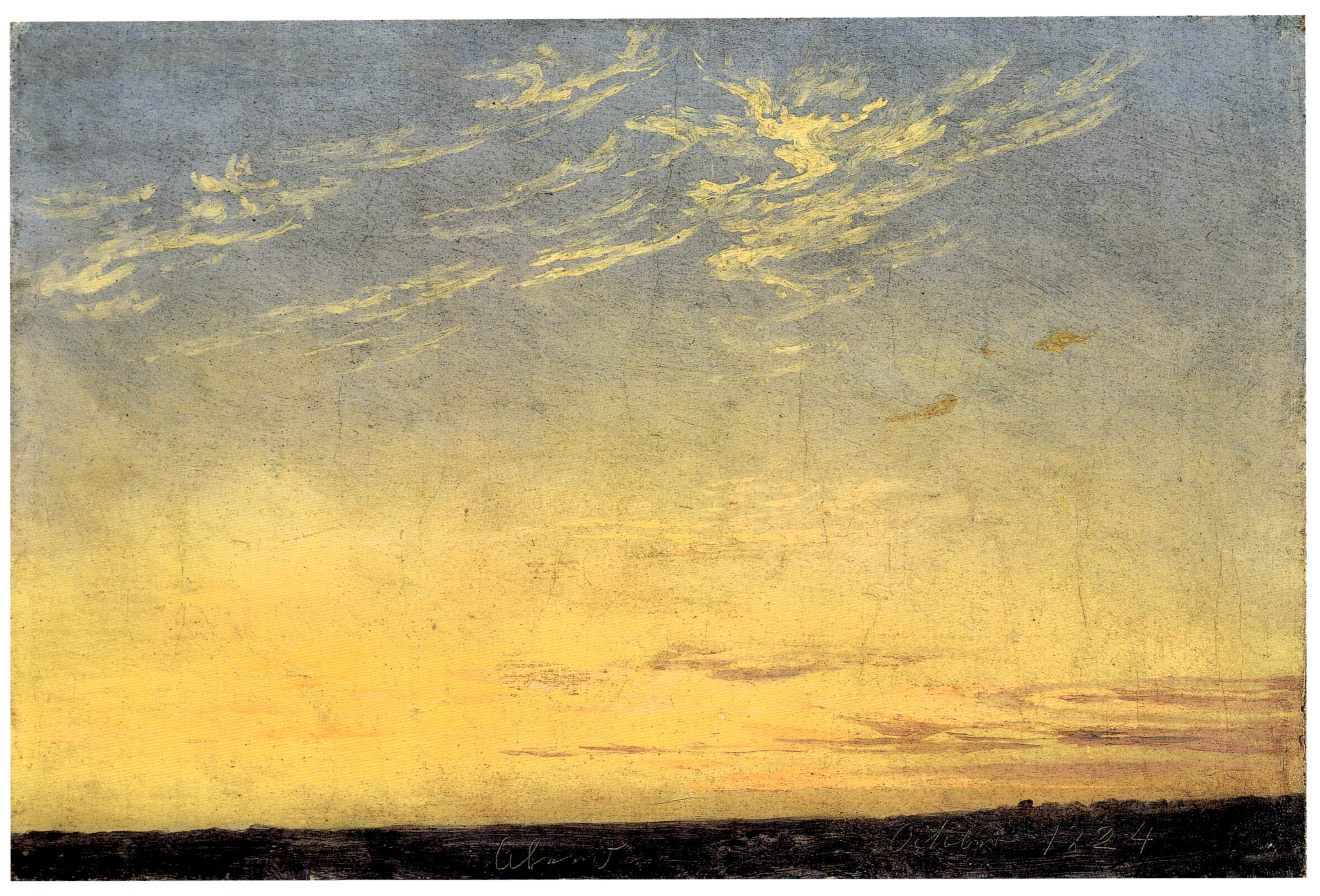

127. *Evening,*
1824, oil on board,
20 × 27.5 cm (7⅞ × 10¾ in.).
Kunsthalle, Mannheim.

divine is everywhere. In *The Chalk Cliffs on Rügen* (ills 79, 80) he finds it in both the tufts of grass in the foreground and the depths of the sea, in the near and the distant. Just as the omnipresence of the divine in creation knows no degrees of rank, so Friedrich does not accord secondary status to anything in his own act of creation. Within that fabric, everything is connected with, and dependent on, everything else.

This is a different concept from the immutable *concinnitas* (harmony) envisaged by Leon Battista Alberti, who wrote in *De re aedificatoria* (1485) that every physical form consists of its own specific set of individual elements. 'If but one is taken away, made larger or smaller, or put in the wrong place, then naturally everything harmonious in that goodly form will be spoilt.' But alterations and transpositions of that kind are exactly what Friedrich was attempting with his formal vocabulary. Alberti's rules for ideal beauty served the principle of structure based on central perspective, which Friedrich was intent on overcoming. His method of formal thinking allowed him to change empirical proportions, transforming them into bewildering morphological ambivalences in which the large and the small, the near and the distant meld into one another indistinguishably. 'Observe form closely, the smallest and the large alike, and do not separate the small from the large, but do remove the petty from the whole.' It is a concrete application of the Biblical injunction: 'He that is least among you all, the same shall be great' (Luke 9: 48).

Friedrich's precise study of nature was the continuation of an artistic practice that stretched back to the early fifteenth century. Cennino Cennini wrote in his treatise *Il Libro dell'Arte* (*c.* 1400): 'If you seek a suitable means of painting mountains so that they look natural, equip yourself with a few large, rough and unhewn stones and paint them from nature, using light and shadow.' Salomon Gessner advised in his *Brief über die Landschaftsmahlerey* (*Letter on Landscape Painting*, 1772; a well-known manual in its day): 'A stone can show me the finest dimensions of a rock: it is in my power to hold it in the sunlight and thereby observe the best effects of shadow and light, and half-light and reflection.' On 16 September 1849, in the forest of Champrosay, Delacroix noted: 'Nature is singularly consistent. I remember having drawn pieces of rock beside the sea at Trouville, whose features just happened to be so proportioned as to give on paper the impression of an immense cliff.... A piece of coal or a flint, or of any kind of stone could represent a huge rocky form on a smaller scale.' Finally, Paul Valéry on Edgar Degas: 'He is said to have made studies of rocks in his room, using heaps of coke from his stove as models.'

The link in this tradition could be termed an alienating perception: something small is regarded as potentially large and distant, and conversely something distant is brought close. This kind of approach operates differently from the one aspiring to Alberti's *concinnitas*; in the latter, sensory information is actually altered. Alberti says that with a tree or a clod of earth, one begins 'to experiment, adding or removing something here or there, to see if one might achieve what seemed still to be wanting in order to obtain a complete likeness' (*De Statua*, after 1464). Friedrich's procedure was more complicated, with the observation of nature, the 'total idea' and the inner eye all working together within him. His lofty ideals made it impossible for him to execute some 'cloud commissions' which Goethe asked of him. The task of illustration in a neutrally scientific spirit would not satisfy him; he preferred to paint clouds that fit with his goal of artistic truth (ills 126 and 127).

Friedrich thematicized the morphological correspondences which Delacroix and Gessner both observed but never transferred to canvas. For Friedrich, they were incentives to reveal the astonishing resemblances, reflections and symmetries in the world of phenomena, moulded and worked by God.

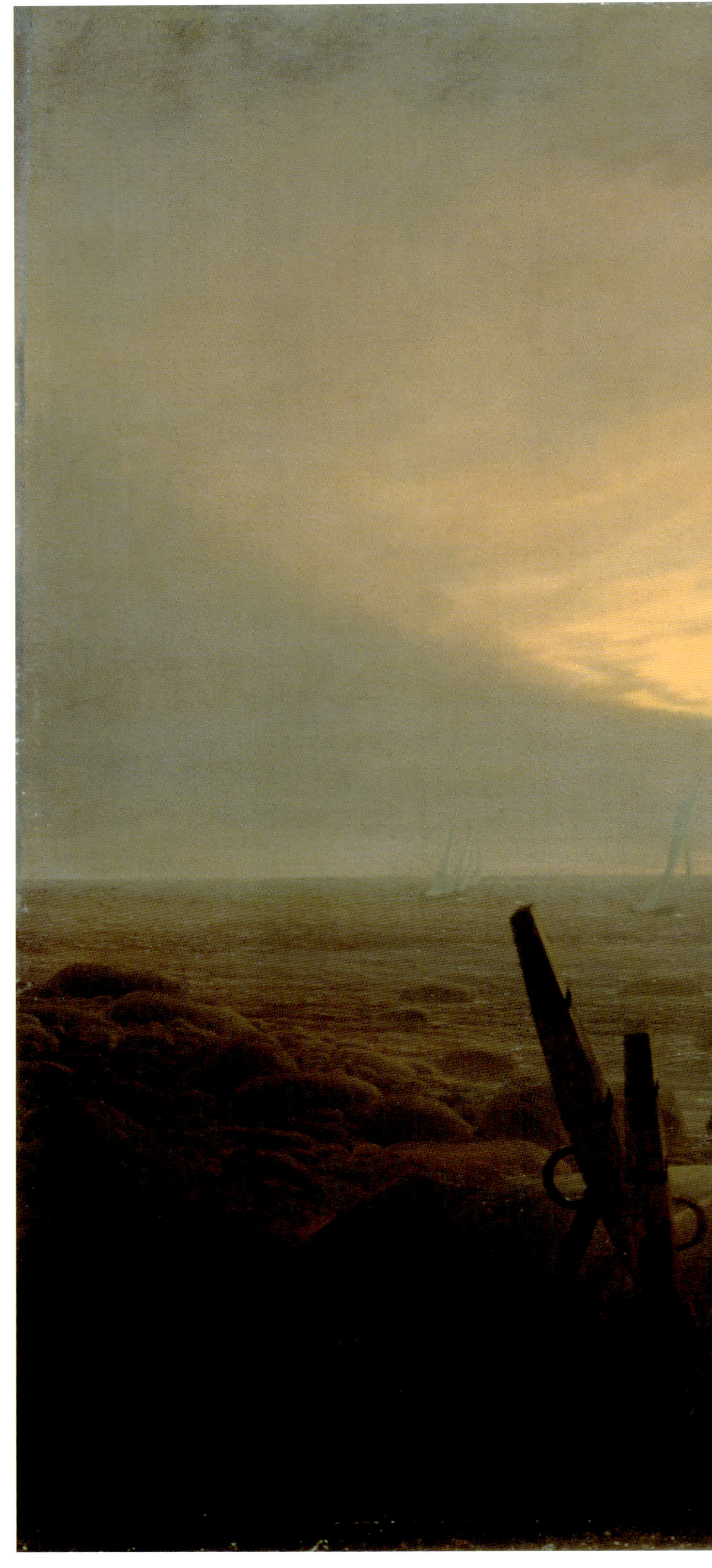

128. *Moonrise by the Sea,*
1821, oil on canvas,
135 × 170 cm (53⅛ × 66⅞ in.).
Hermitage Museum, St Petersburg.

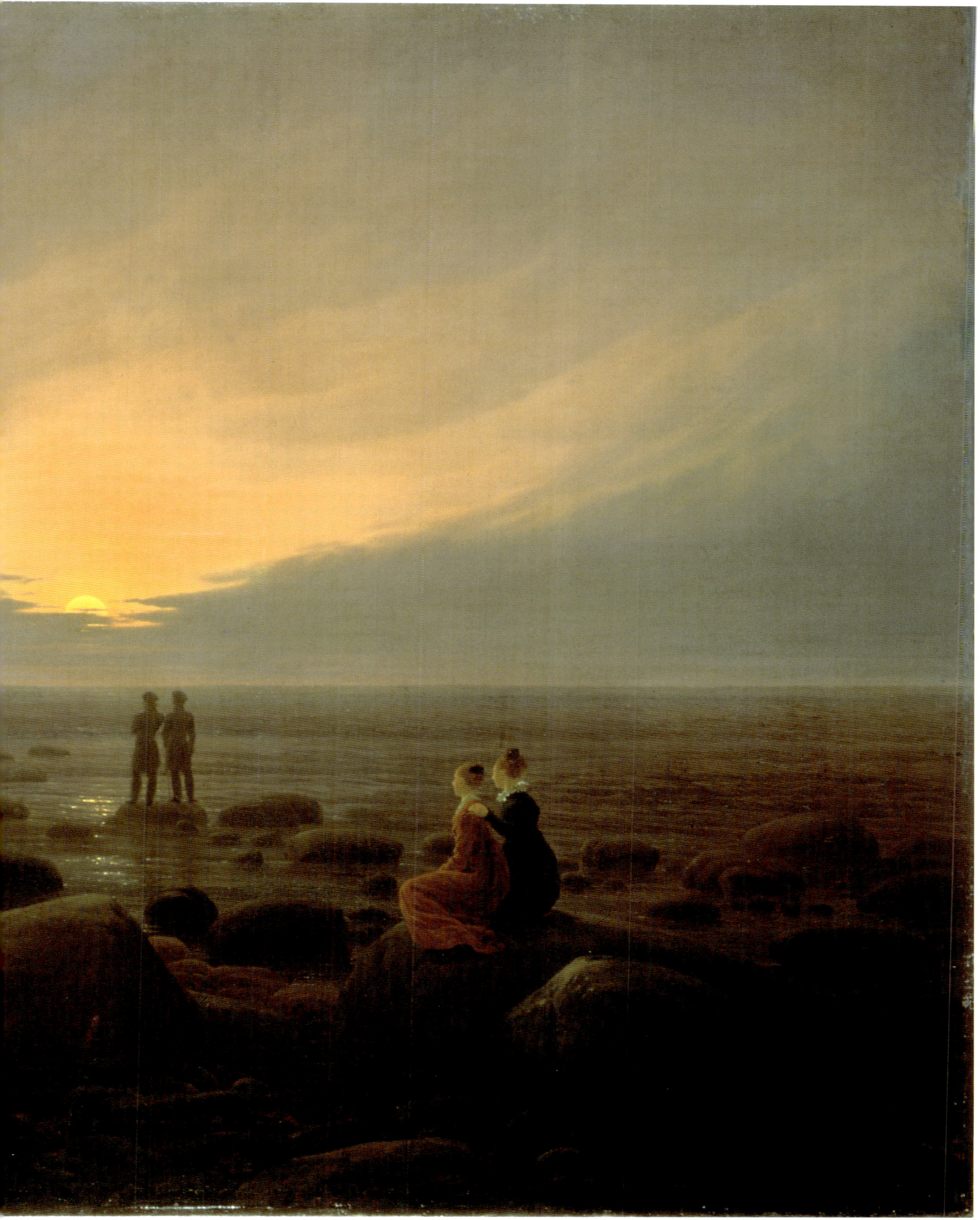

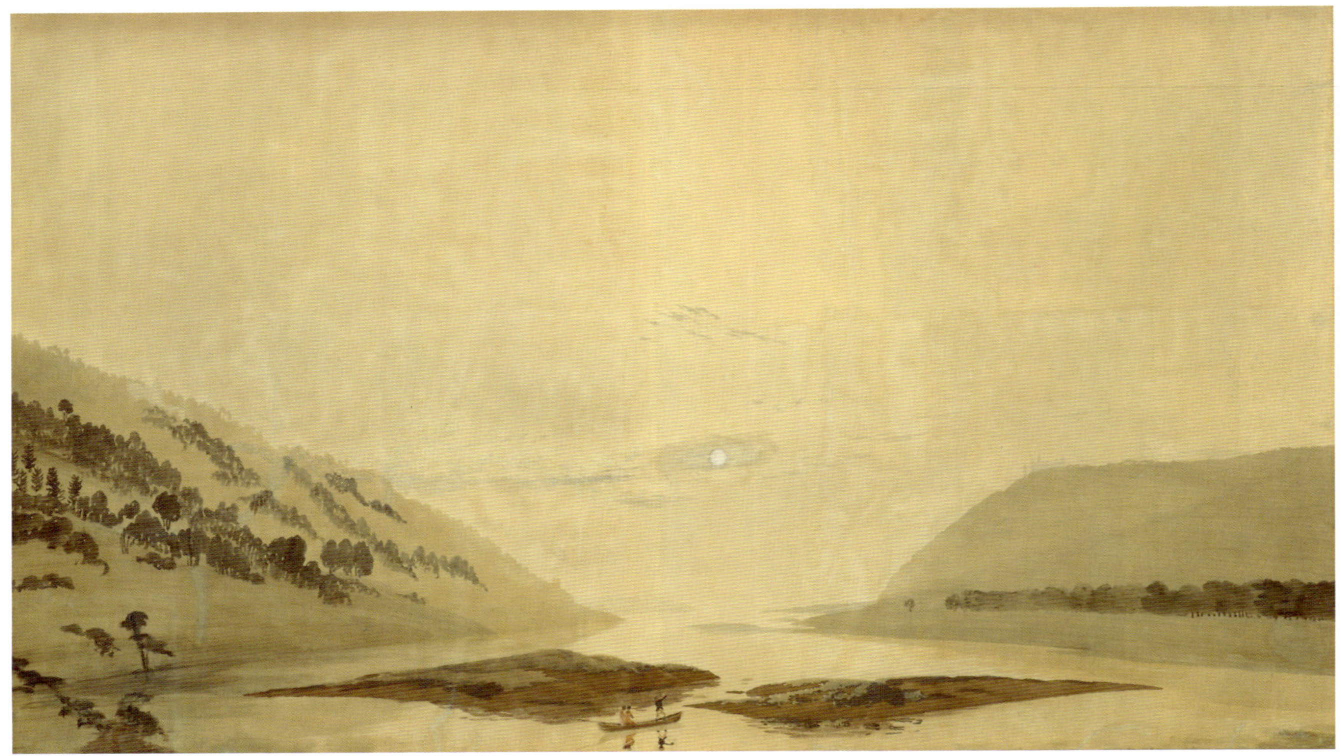

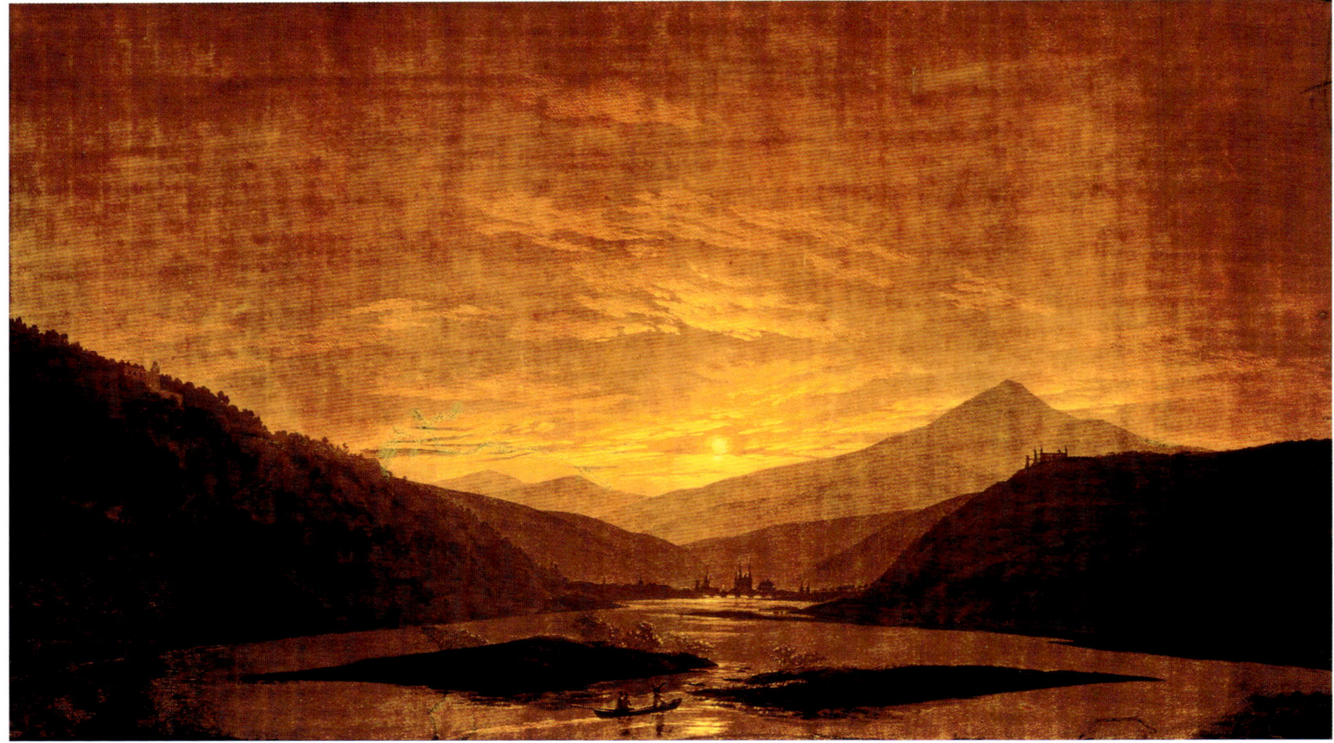

129 and 130. ***Mountainous River Landscape,***
1830–35, watercolour and tempera on paper,
74 × 124 cm (29⅛ × 48⅞ in.).
Staatliche Museen Neue Galerie, Kassel.

That is the essence of Friedrich's unmistakable metaphorical language. He mirrors waterside rocks in banks of cloud, the near in the distant, the solid in the intangible (ill. 132). He also turns the sharp edge of a precipice into open sea (ill. 125); links two trees in a formula of greeting with a mountain rising beyond them (ill. 88); places a rainbow over a dip in the ground like a lid over a basin, and puts a tree and a shepherd on either side at the points of connection (ill. 98). He piles up hay in the form of a funnel, and crowns it with mountain peaks (ill. 131). The luridly lit mouth of a limestone cave (ill. 147) looks like the jagged edge of a rocky reef. It is the negative image of the mountain in *The Tetschen Altar*: what is solid there has now become a fissure in space.

The most subtle alienation of this kind is found in *The Sea of Ice* and *The Large Enclosure*. The Hamburg Kunsthalle owns some small oil sketches (ills 157 and 158) which Friedrich painted in Dresden in 1821 when he saw the ice floes ramming into one another as the frozen Elbe broke up. The three sketches give no indication of the actual size of the blocks of ice. If they were small, they nevertheless give the impression of great size. Friedrich was able to reuse these later in *The Sea of Ice* (ill. 159) with only minor changes – making them harder and more cuboid – so that the empirical reality of nature became an artistic truth with multiple meanings.

The foreground of *The Large Enclosure* (ill. 162) presents several puzzles: looked at alone, the pale watercourses and shallow pools are strange and unfamiliar enough to be the surface of a distant planet. Then when we make out the sailing boat in the middle ground, the cosmic landscape turns into waterlogged earth. When our eyes finally reach the sky we see the harsh, uninhabited and inhospitable landscape mirrored in the clouds, simultaneously distanced and dematerialized.

The same basic principles recur again and again, up until the late works: hollows below humps, basins with lids, funnels topped by circumflexes, falls flanked by rises. Friedrich's dual vision does not only couple different levels of meaning in one and the same picture, objectifying the pairing of his different

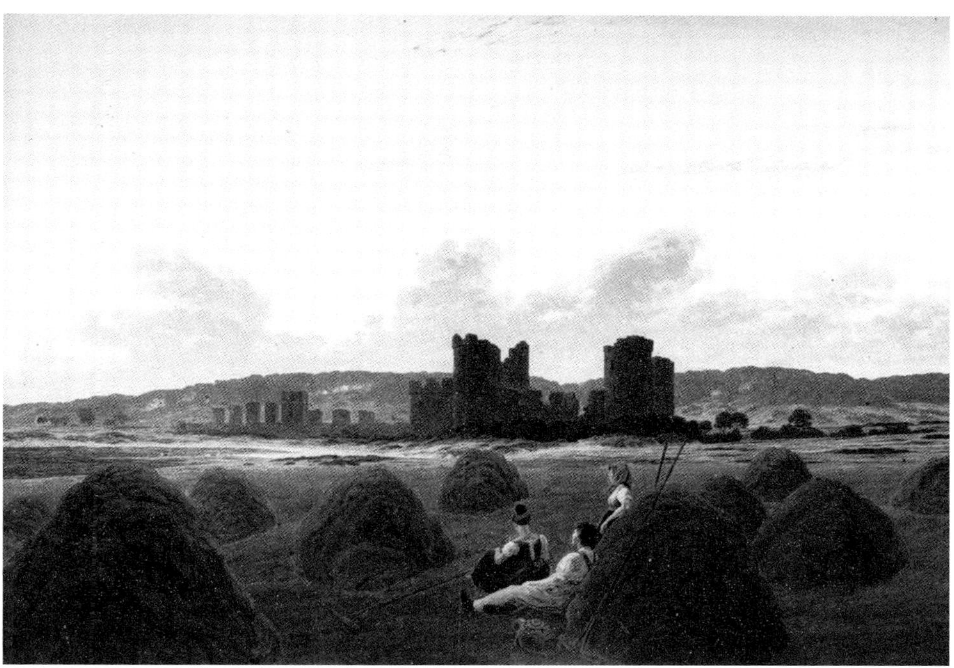

131. ***Rest during Haymaking,***
1834–35, oil on canvas,
75.5 x 102 cm (29¾ x 40⅛ in.).
Gemäldegalerie Neue Meister, Dresden.

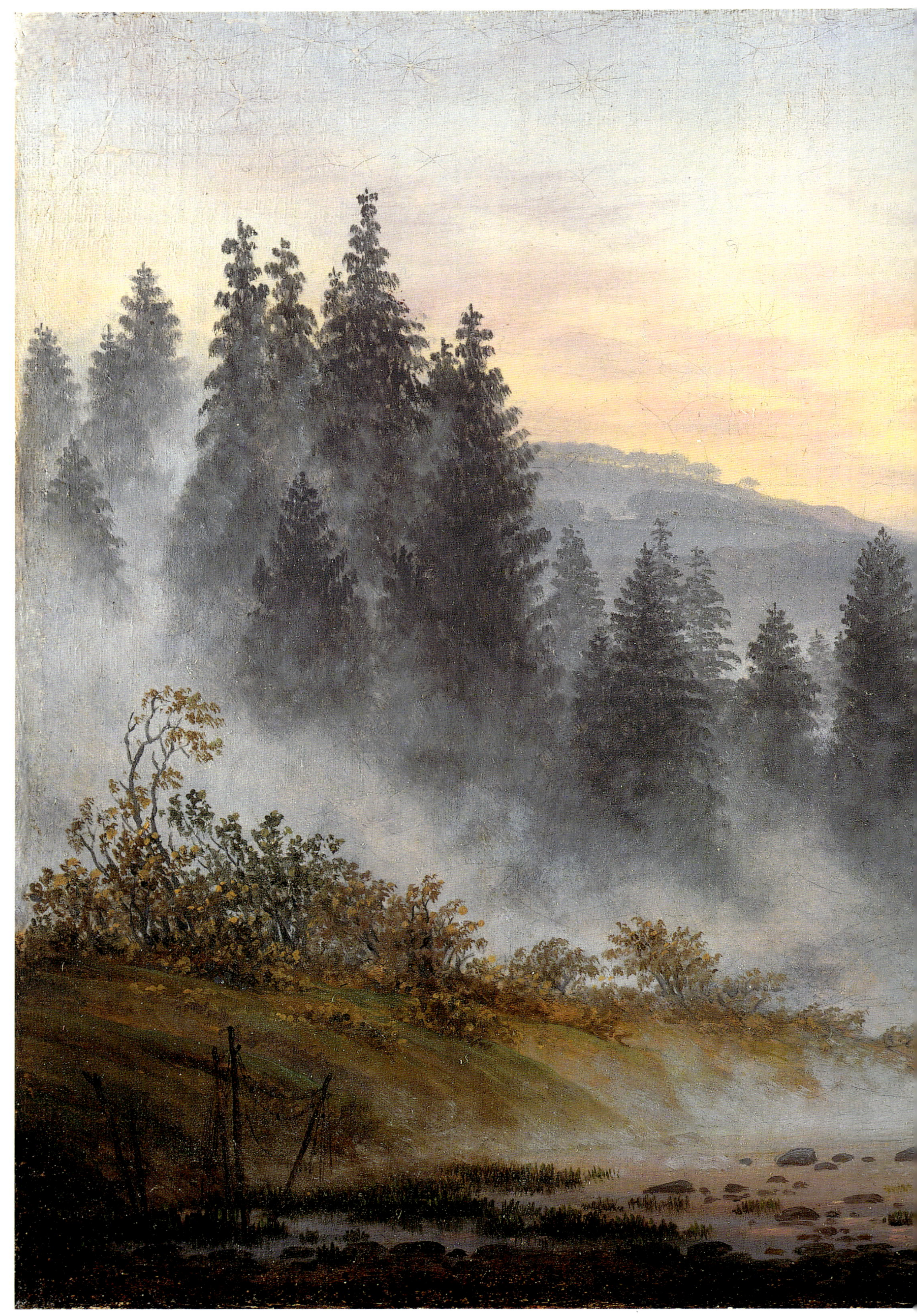

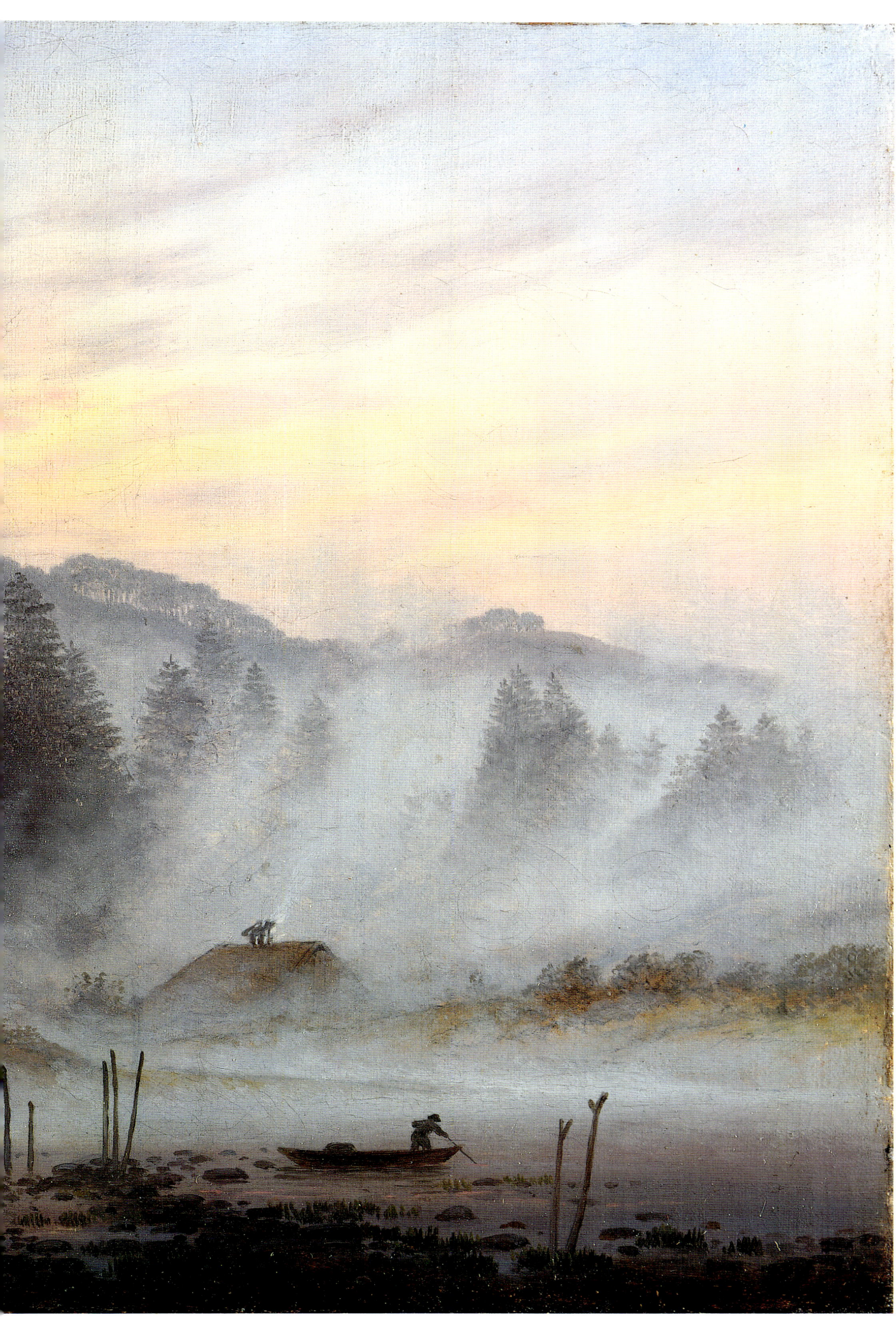

132. *Morning*,
1820–21, oil on canvas,
22 × 30.7 cm (8⅝ × 12 in.).
Niedersächsisches
Landesmuseum, Hanover.

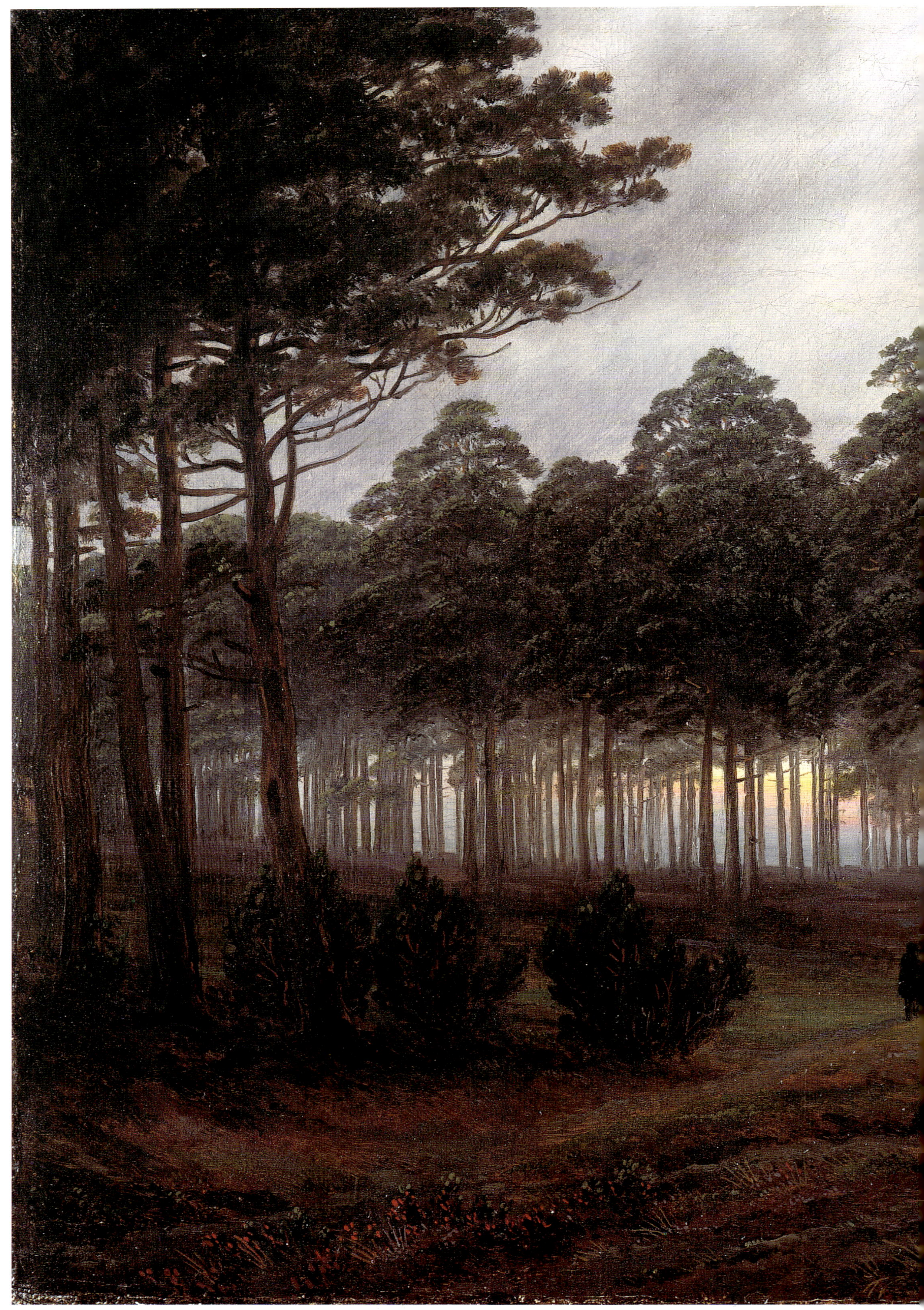

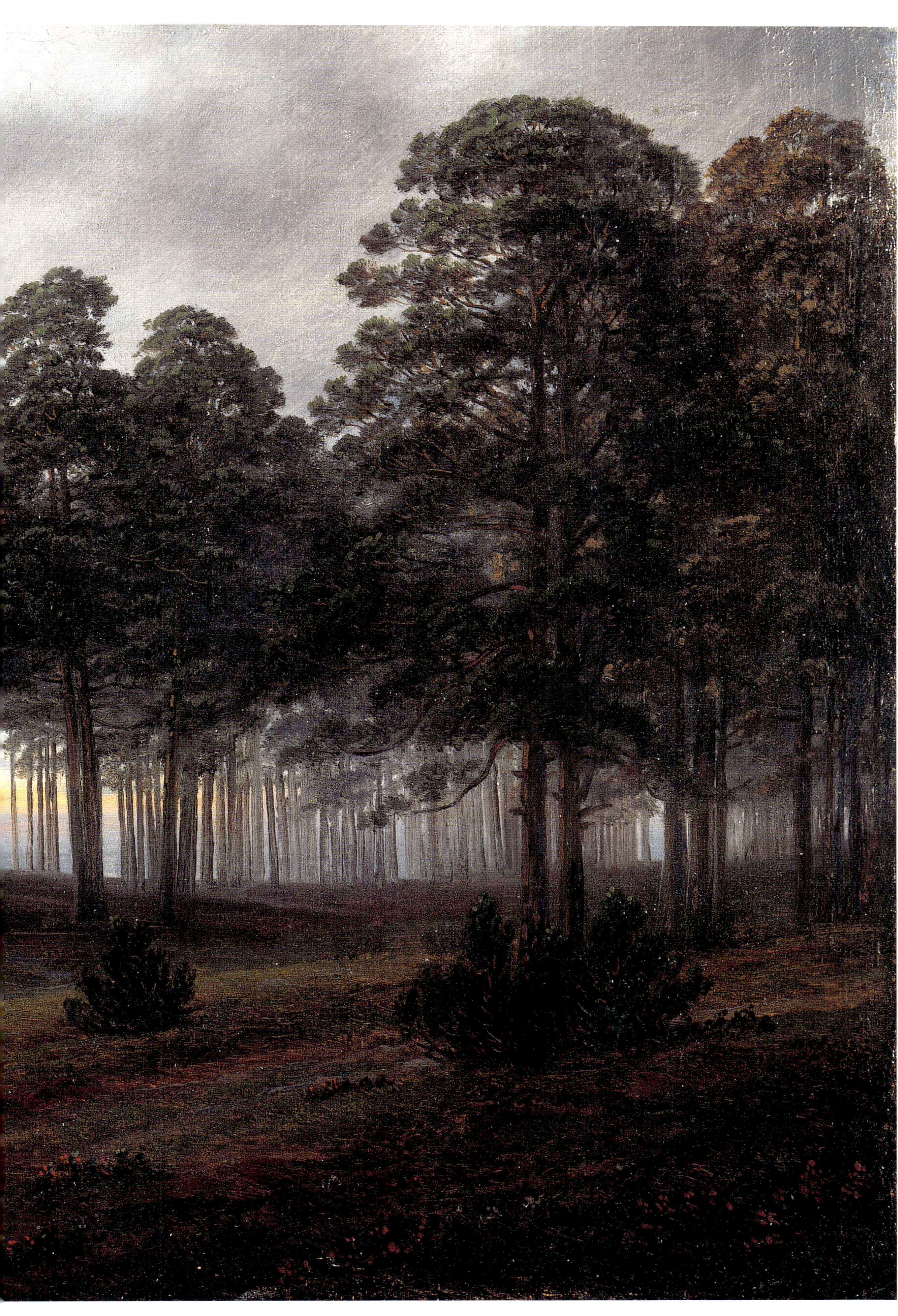

133. *Evening*.
1820–21, oil on canvas,
22.3 × 31 cm (8¾ × 12¼ in.).
Niedersächsisches
Landesmuseum, Hanover.

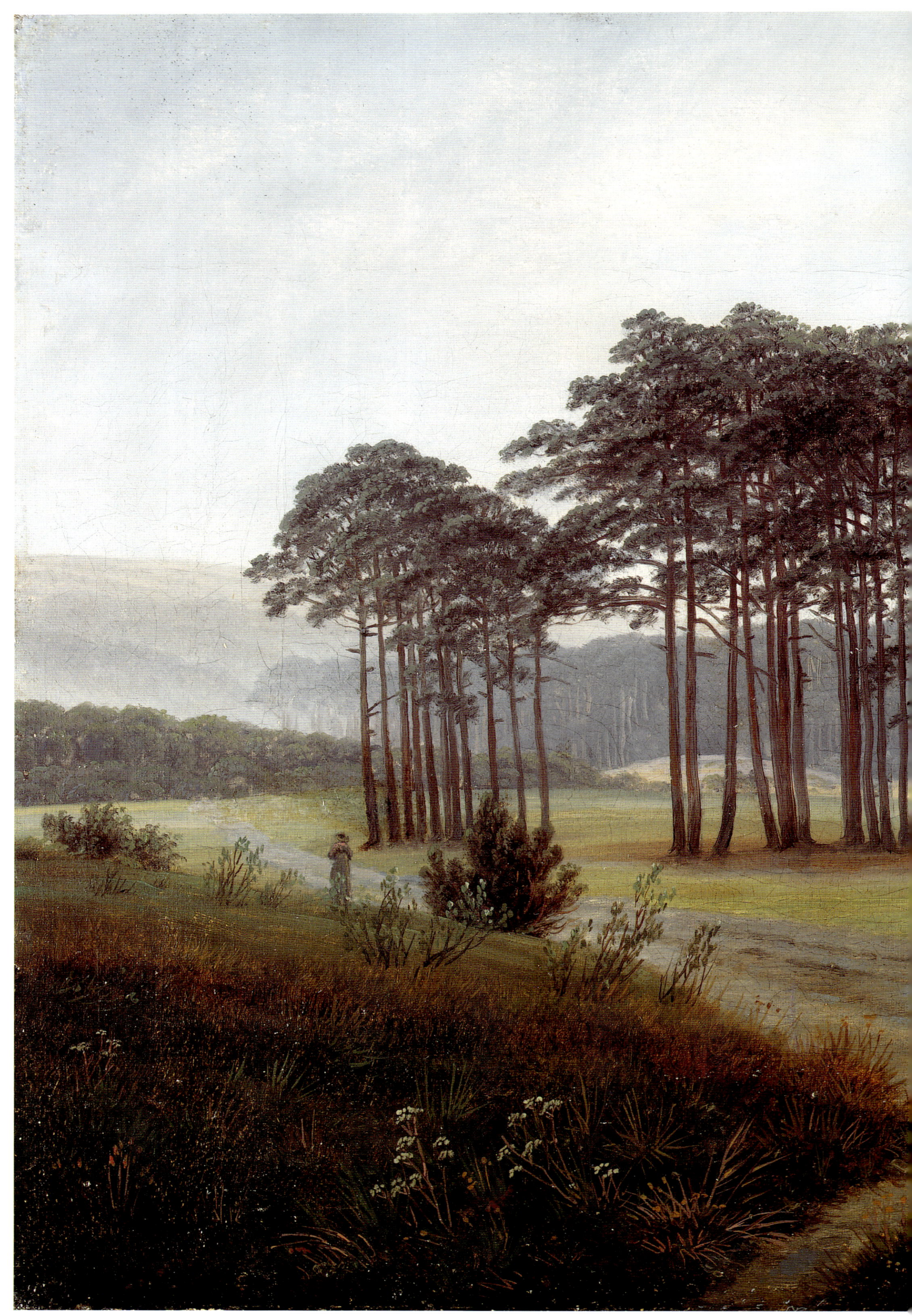

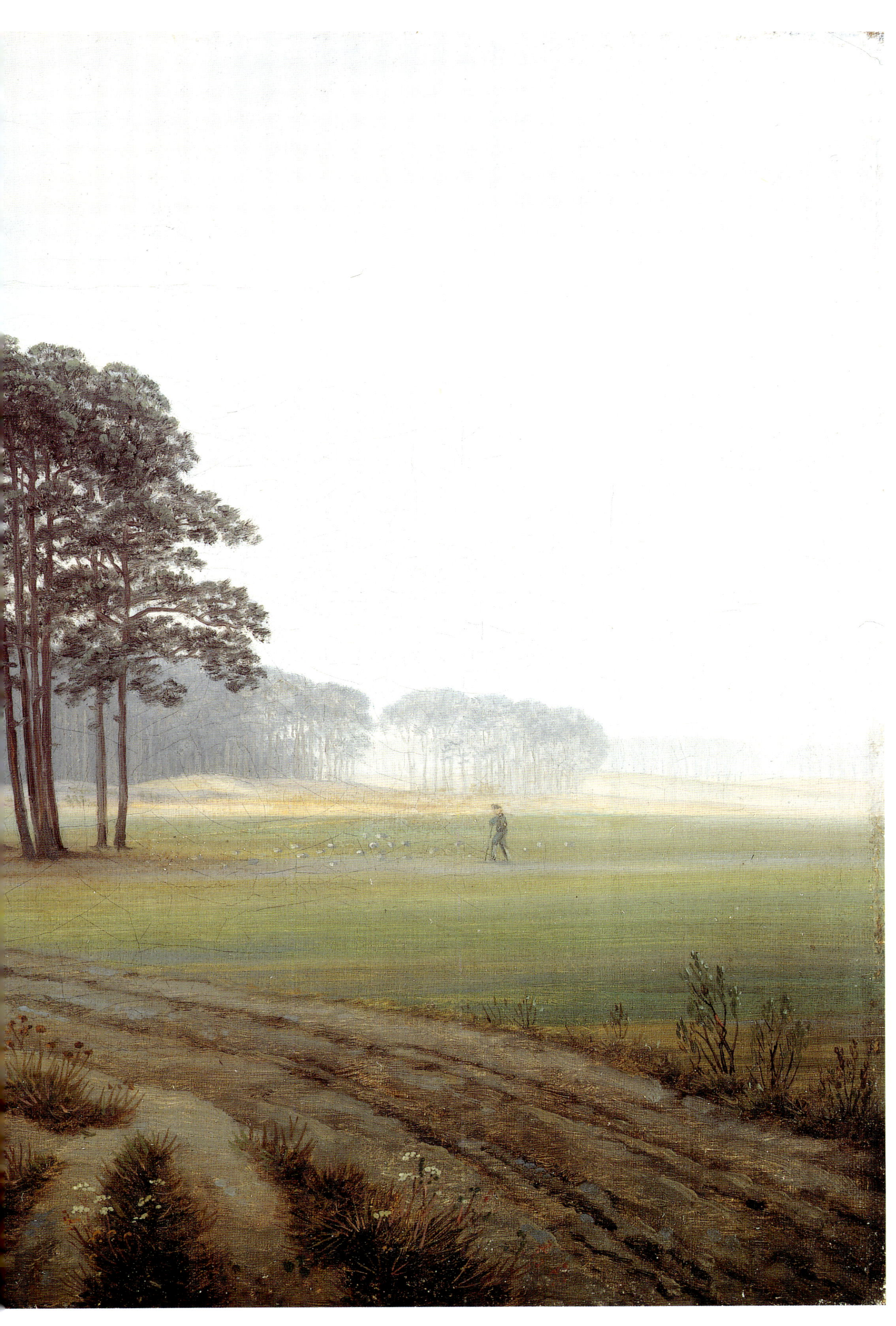

134. ***Midday,***
1822, oil on canvas,
20 x 30 cm (7⅞ x 11⅞ in.).
Niedersächsisches
Landesmuseum, Hanover.

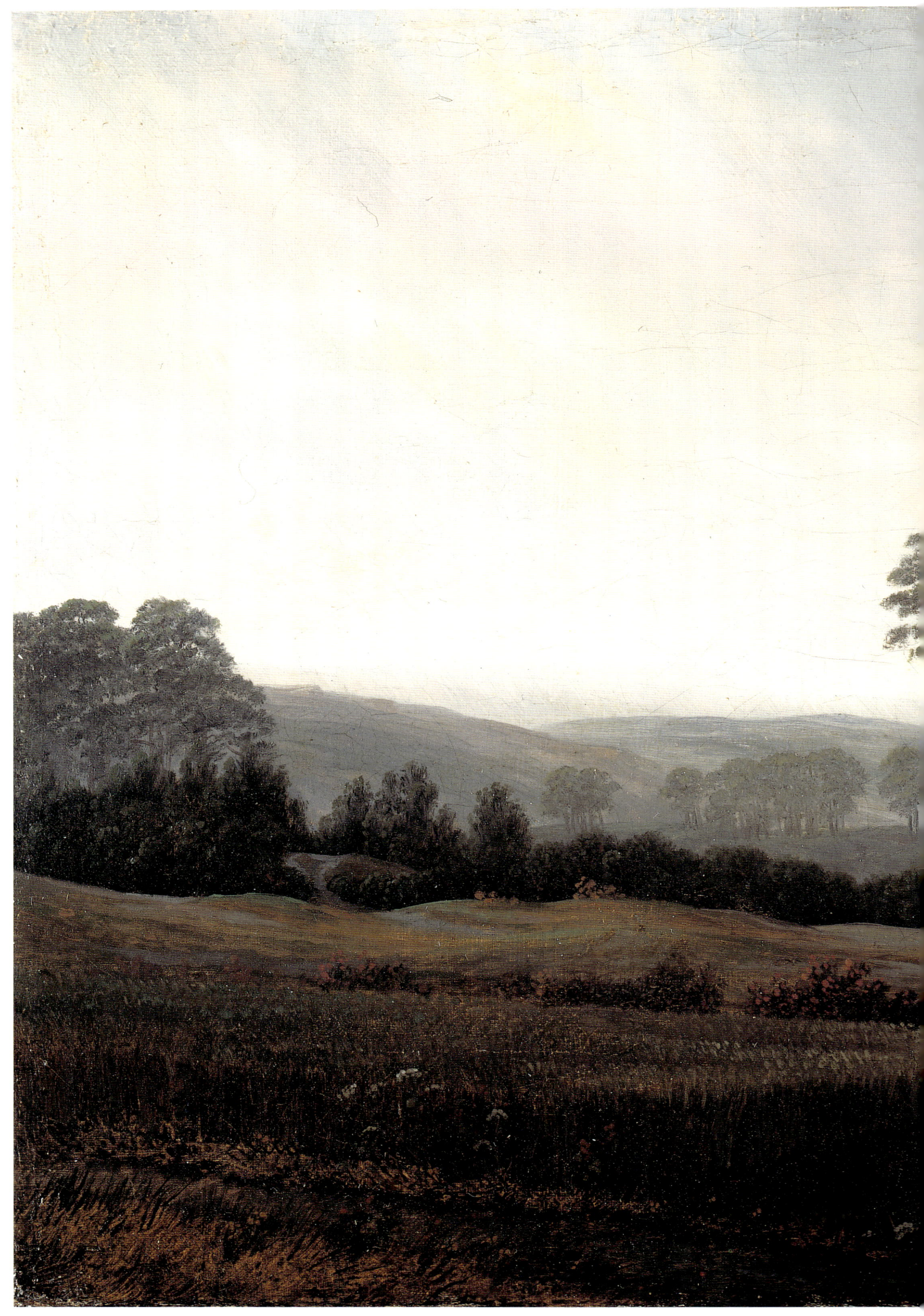

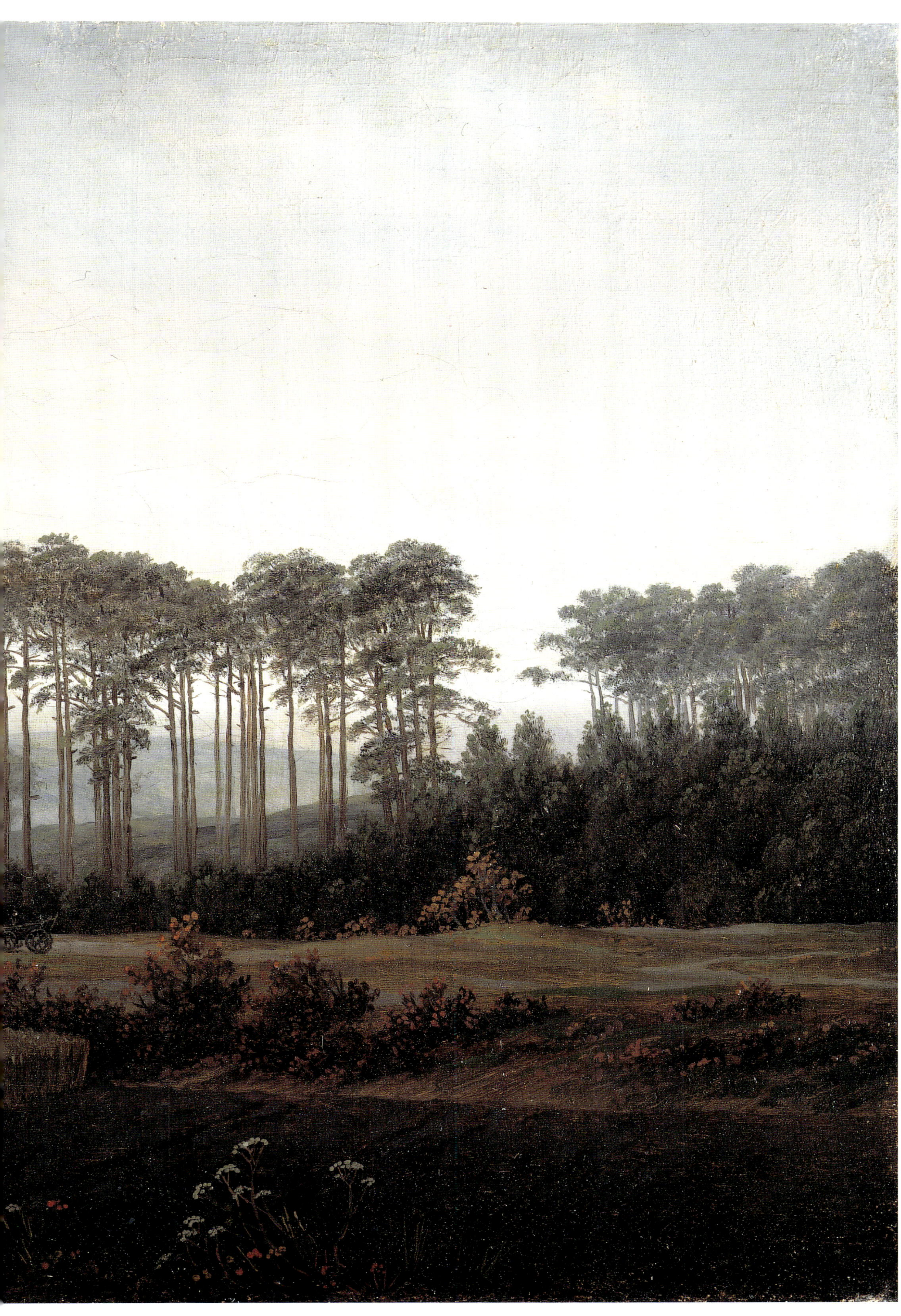

135. ***Afternoon,***
1822, oil on canvas,
22 x 31 cm (8⅝ x 12¼ in.).
Niedersächsisches
Landesmuseum, Hanover.

temperamental states, but it also holds the key to the regular pairing of pictures. As a rule (though not always, as the two Vienna views of the artist's studio windows show) the pairs contain contrasts; this begins in the two woodcuts (ills 10 and 11) and the sepias submitted for the Weimar prize (ills 8 and 9), where the principle is still dialectically inconclusive. The painter also used pairs in order to demonstrate the polarities possible in his artistic language, most persuasively in *The Monk by the Sea* and *The Abbey in the Oak Wood* (ills 22 and 23). Finally, in the early 1830s, he painted a pair of pictures in a compressed form, which we could call single and double at the same time, echoing Goethe's description of a gingko leaf. Friedrich recorded the same landscape at two different times of day, using the then-popular technique of transparency (ills 129 and 130). One side of the translucent parchment shows a river scene in the pale morning light. The reverse side requires a light source; when a candle is placed behind the parchment, the mirror image of the landscape is seen by the light of a full moon. The view and its reverse render two different experiences of space and time.

By adding the intermediate times of day to morning and night, and spring and autumn to summer and winter, the pairing of contrasts becomes a continuum of transitions, as the Hanover pictures of the four seasons (ills 132, 133, 134 and 135) illustrate. Friedrich was not content with one level of meaning, and thinking about the multiple meanings of natural development gradually led him to the idea of merging the times of the day, the seasons of the year and the ages of human life into one another. A common feature of these three cyclic processes is that they give an epic breadth to landscape. Iconization, Friedrich's great formal achievement, was now abandoned and relativized. Icon and narrative, the timeless and the temporal, are meshed together, and a hieratic state of being is added to a current of events in which man's journey through life and the organic cycle of nature overlap.

The formal consequences of the three-tier narrative can be seen in the cycle of seven sepias (ills 137, 138, 139, 143, 146, 147 and 148), in which the ages of man, the times of day and the seasons form an iconographic amalgam. David d'Angers saw five of the seven sepias when he visited Friedrich in his studio in 1834:

'He has just finished several large drawings representing the four seasons, which are also the four ages of human life. What a fine concept this beautiful work is, very poetic and very philosophical. The first picture shows nature in the infancy of creation; the sun is about to rise; the trees are white with fruit blossom, and a child is playing beside a little stream, whose banks are covered with flowers. In the second the trees are laden with fruit; the stream has grown into a river; the child is now a man and has found a wife. In the next, nature is imposing; the hills are mountains that threaten the sky; the trees are grandiose; the sun is being slowly hidden by clouds bringing up a storm; and the river, finally, has become a torrent; the man is seen wearing armour and bidding farewell to a woman who points out to him a cross on a mountain. In the fourth, the man and woman are seen as skeletons lying in a cavern beneath a rock; the form and colour of these rocks is very impressive; there is nothing to illuminate them except a mysterious light. In the last, we see Heaven: the earth is not visible; the clouds lie below; light shines above them, but it does not come from the sun, and the man and woman are angels, rising up towards this light.'

Friedrich's friend Gotthilf Heinrich von Schubert also discerned a philosophical idea which he described as an 'allegory representing the life cycle of the human soul, depicted through the life cycle of nature'. The seven drawings also illustrate the stages of another life cycle: the painter's own development as an artist, combined in a montage of remembered images. They even hark back to the four lost drawings of 1803 in which Friedrich first depicted the seasons (ill. 140). Three motifs from the earlier sequence can be seen paraphrased in the later one: spring, summer and winter (ills 138, 139 and 146).

This context of Friedrich's artistic life includes the influence of Philipp Otto Runge's *The Times of Day* (1803). Runge and Friedrich got to know each other in 1801, and often met in Dresden, where Runge lived until 1803. Runge himself often referred to the multiple meanings in his cycle, and his brother Daniel identified five different layers in it. As well as the times of day, the seasons and the ages of human life, he named the fourth as the stages of world history: the birth, growth and decline of nations, or 'youth, blossoming, ripening and decay – and transfiguration'; and the fifth as 'time and eternity, or the religious perspective over the whole'. Concerning himself with cosmic and religious laws, Runge devised symbolic tableaux, filled with plants, children, genii and three allegories of the Great Mother. The strictly iconized action takes place in an ideal space. Each of the four compositions is based on sophisticated symmetrical relationships, which give the picture field and the frame perfect equilibrium, and the many constants ensure stability throughout the cyclical changes. Friedrich, on the other hand, made the seasons principally a foil to the cycle of human life and his emphasis on the physical world gave his four drawings an immediate legibility comparable to that of lyric poetry and Lieder. Runge's hermetically encoded symbolic figures lacked this transparency and his contemporaries had good reason to refer to them as 'hieroglyphs'.

What more can we learn about Friedrich's development from his seven sepias? *Sunrise over the Sea* (ill. 137) represents a sublime moment from Genesis. Friedrich interprets the Bible literally: it is not God but His spirit that moves above the waters, still seeking a form for itself. At the start of his *Creation*, Joseph Haydn depicted chaos by analogy, in music that only gradually acquires form. One obvious difference between this picture and *The Monk by the Sea* is that here the sea and the space are experienced without the support of any foreground. The dry land has not been omitted; rather, it does not yet exist. In *Spring* (ill. 138), Friedrich moved Runge's children from their geometric framework into the plain context of awakening nature. In *Summer* (ill. 139) he made some alterations from his 1803 drawing (ill. 140) and the 1807 painting derived from it (ill. 14): the trees and vegetation form a frame about the pair of lovers and their passionate embrace is changed into a more tentative, symmetrical encounter. *Autumn* (ill. 143) introduces a new feature into Friedrich's formal repertoire. I interpret it as a reference to the two paths between which the Christian must choose: 'Enter ye in at the strait gate: for wide is the gate, and broad is the way, that leadeth to destruction, and many there be which go in thereat' (Matthew 7: 13). The broad way is seen leading into the valley of earthly pleasures. The knight is drawn towards it, but the woman – whose authority we know from *Morning in the Riesengebirge* (ill. 58) – wants him to go with her along the narrow and difficult path 'which leadeth unto life'. With this moral appeal, Friedrich allied himself with the edifying Protestant iconography of the nineteenth century, beloved of the publishers of tracts. The motif of the forking path first appears in an early watercolour, *Landscape with Pavilion* (ill. 141) from the Copenhagen period, where it perhaps has overtones of the Jacobin slogan 'Guerre aux châteaux, paix aux hameaux' ('War on the castles, peace to the villages').

A sepia from the 1830s (ill. 142) shares some spiritual similarities with *Autumn.* If human life is a pilgrimage leading to a crossroads of decisions, then this landscape offers a choice between the two

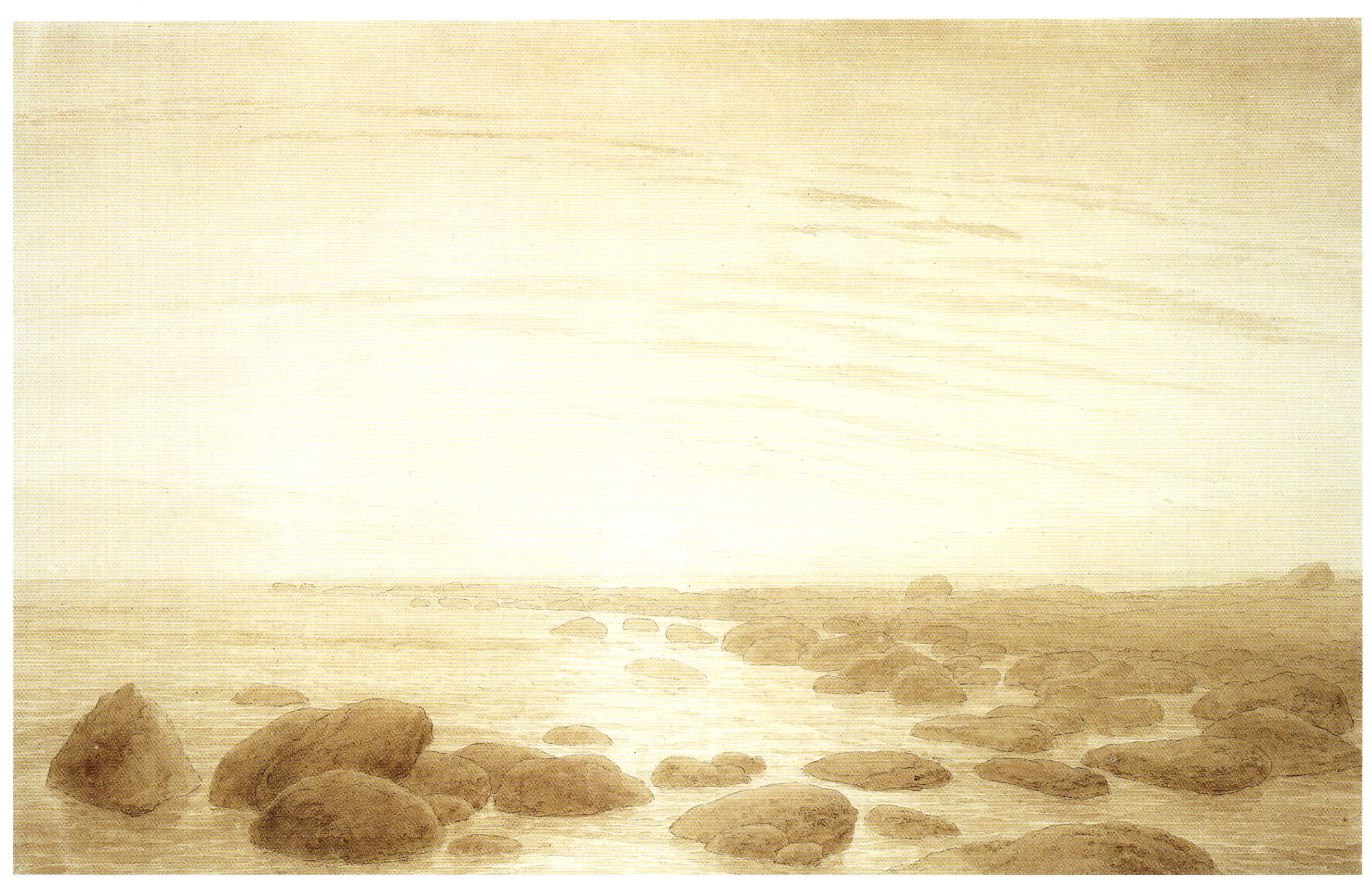

136. ***Moonrise over the Sea,***
c. 1837–39, pencil and sepia,
25.6 x 38.5 cm (10⅛ x 15⅛ in.).
Hamburger Kunsthalle, Hamburg.

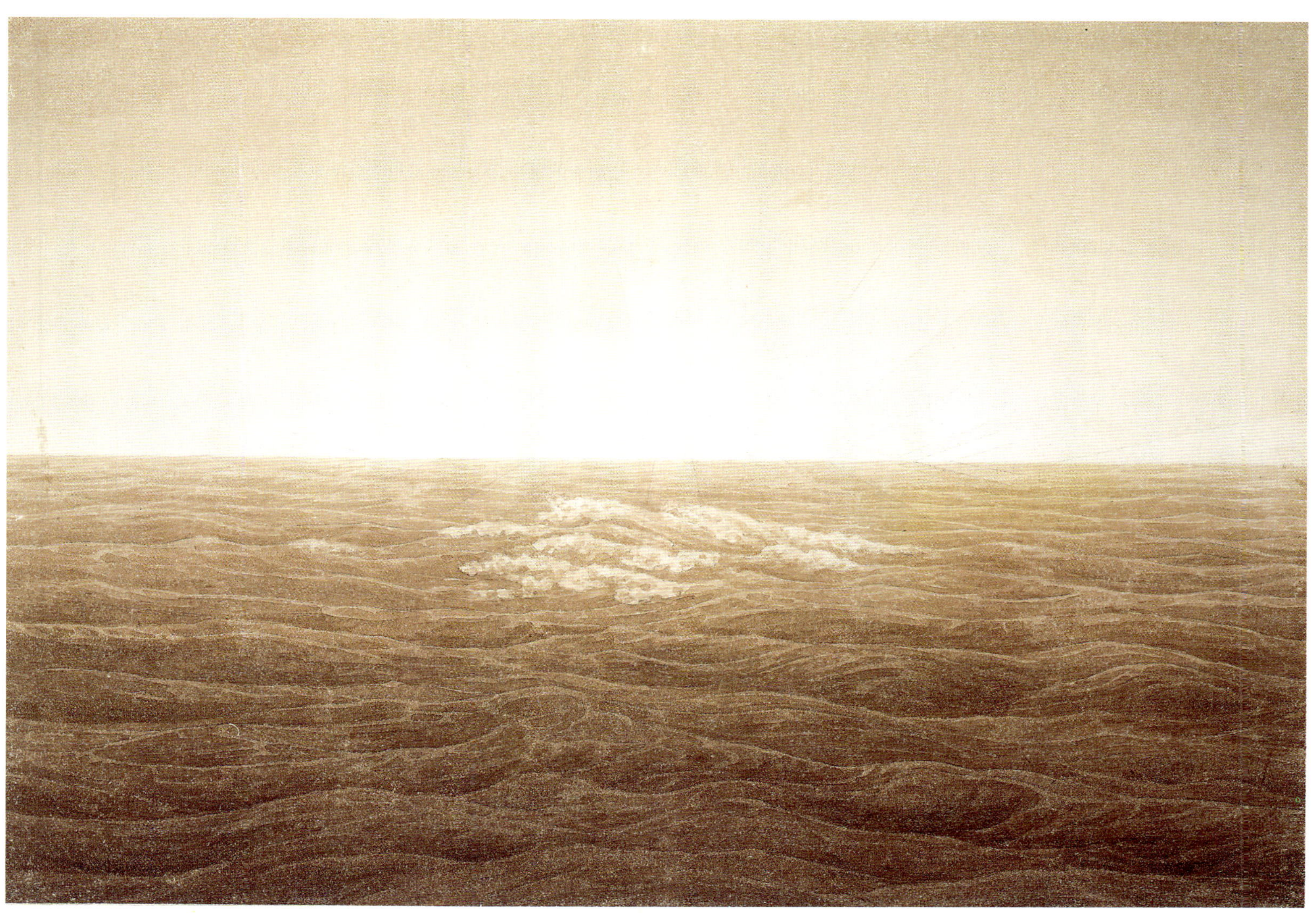

137. ***Sunrise over the Sea,***
c. 1826, sepia,
18.7 × 26.5 cm (7⅜ × 10½ in).
Hamburger Kunsthalle, Hamburg.

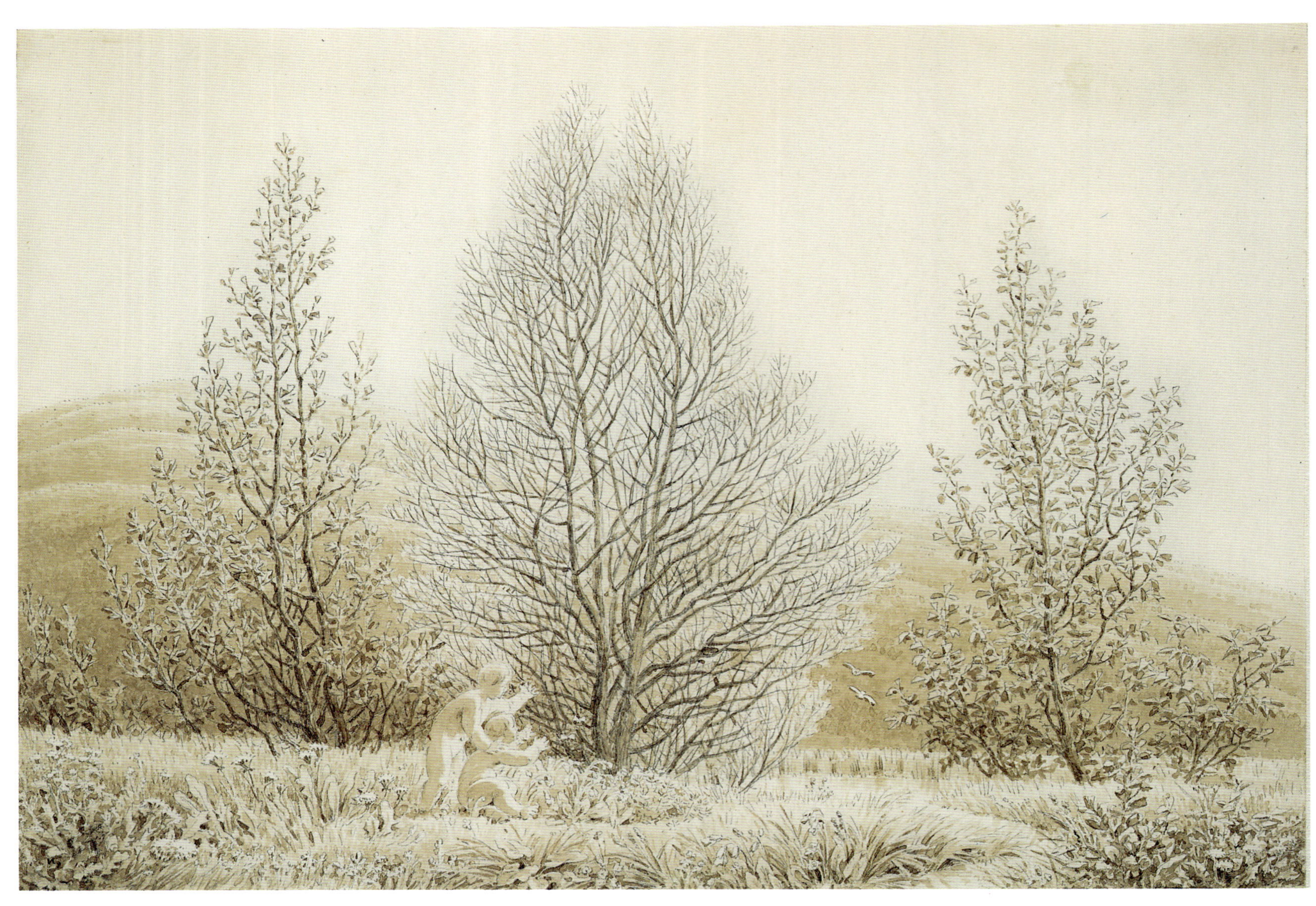

138. *Spring*,
c. 1826, sepia,
19.1 × 27.3 cm (7½ × 10¾ in.).
Hamburger Kunsthalle, Hamburg.

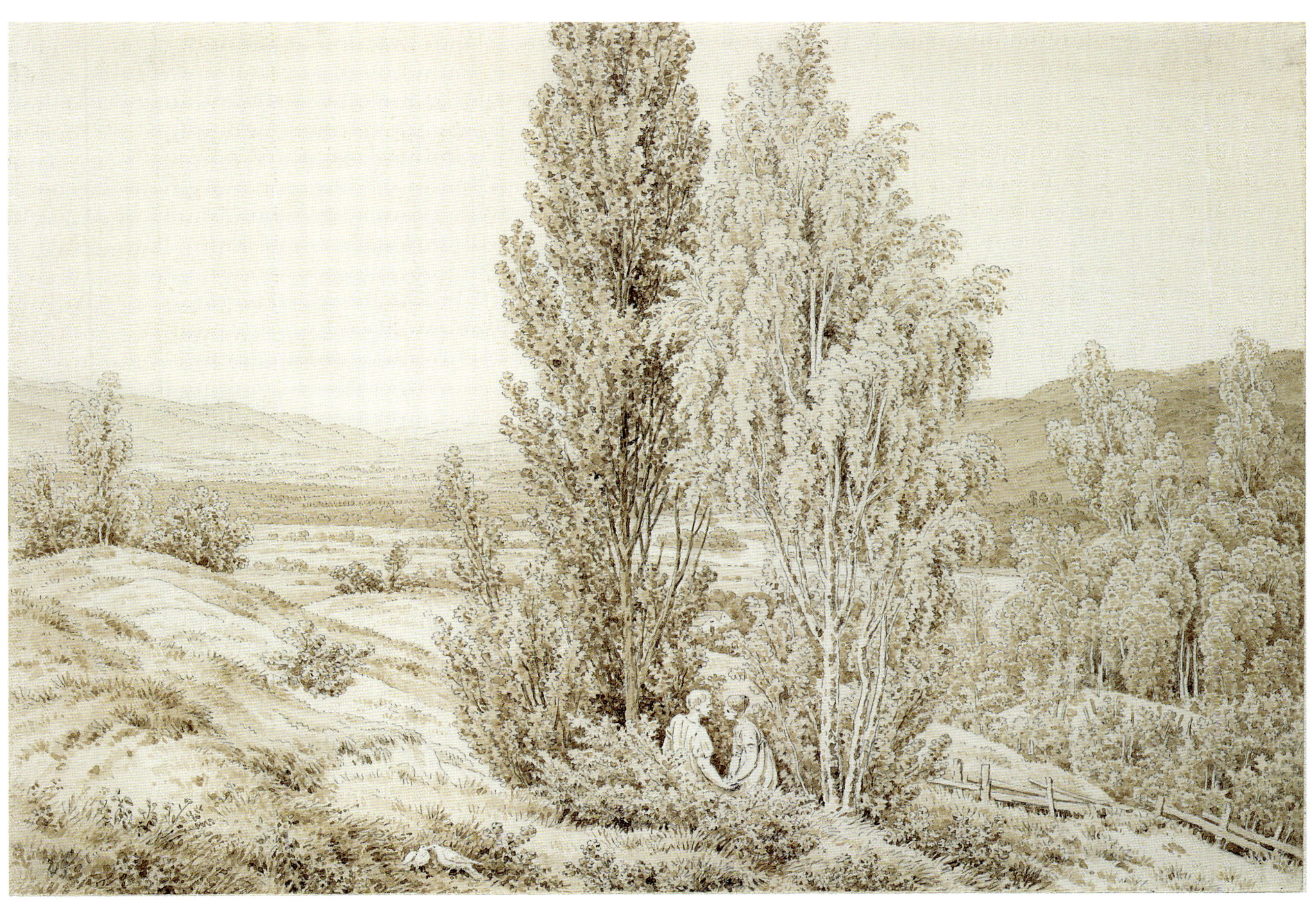

139. *Summer*,
c. 1826, sepia,
19 × 27.1 cm (7½ × 10⅝ in.).
Hamburger Kunsthalle, Hamburg.

Christian traditions. The hooded statue in the foreground stands in the shadows (of the past) and might represent Catholic idolatry, while the cross stands in broad daylight at the centre of the composition and represents true faith. The two trees on either side of it form a transparent frame; their curve recalls a Gothic window, and is a reminder of the frame of *The Tetschen Altar*. In this picture, Friedrich does without the body of Christ and settles for a plain cross, but overall the relaxed rhythm of this landscape lacks the rigour of the more famous *Altar*.

Winter (ill. 146) differs from the earlier version in one significant detail: originally the old man was alone and digging his own grave (ill. 145), but in the new version he and his wife contemplate the evening of their lives together. Taking into account the next sepia, the stony cave (ill. 147), the couple can be seen to be making ready to return to prime matter, as Georg Syamken has said. To show this, Friedrich reapplies the metaphor of the first sepia, and places the ruined church (Eldena) on the seashore. The cave, meanwhile, is an equivalent of *The Sea of Ice* (ill. 159), a variation on its syntax of sharp, jagged edges, intensified into a chiaroscuro contrast which allows a ghostly life to emerge amid the petrifaction. The dark teeth of stalactites and stalagmites tear a wound in the earth's body, and a harsh light pours out, consuming the skeleton. Friedrich was clearly influenced by baroque reliquaries. The two winged souls in the final sepia (ill. 148) are derived from the angelic choir in *The Cathedral* (ills 42, 149). With them, as Syamken comments, 'the circle closes'. 'The light, here the object of eternal veneration, was the object of creation itself on the first day of creation. The prime matter ... is returned here to the water cycle in the form of steam. The spirit which moved above the waters on the first day of creation ... has once more withdrawn into luminous ineffability.'

A new feature in this cycle, dated somewhere between 1826 and 1834, is the role assigned to man and woman as a couple. Obviously Friedrich wanted to use the six couples he depicted to tell the tale of human morphology – 'single and double at the same time' – in a new way. The sea is a cosmic prelude to the six-part journey of transformation, representing the source of all life, still malleable and carrying that

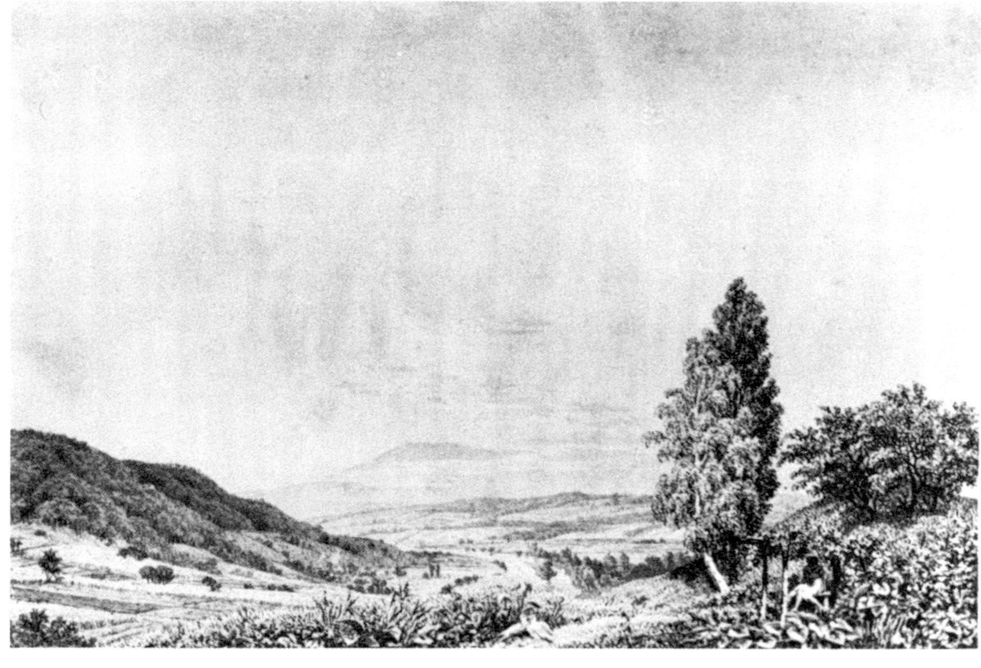

140. *Summer,*
1803, sepia,
19 x 27.5 cm (7½ x 10¾ in.).
Formerly Reichskammer der bildenden Künste, Berlin (destroyed).

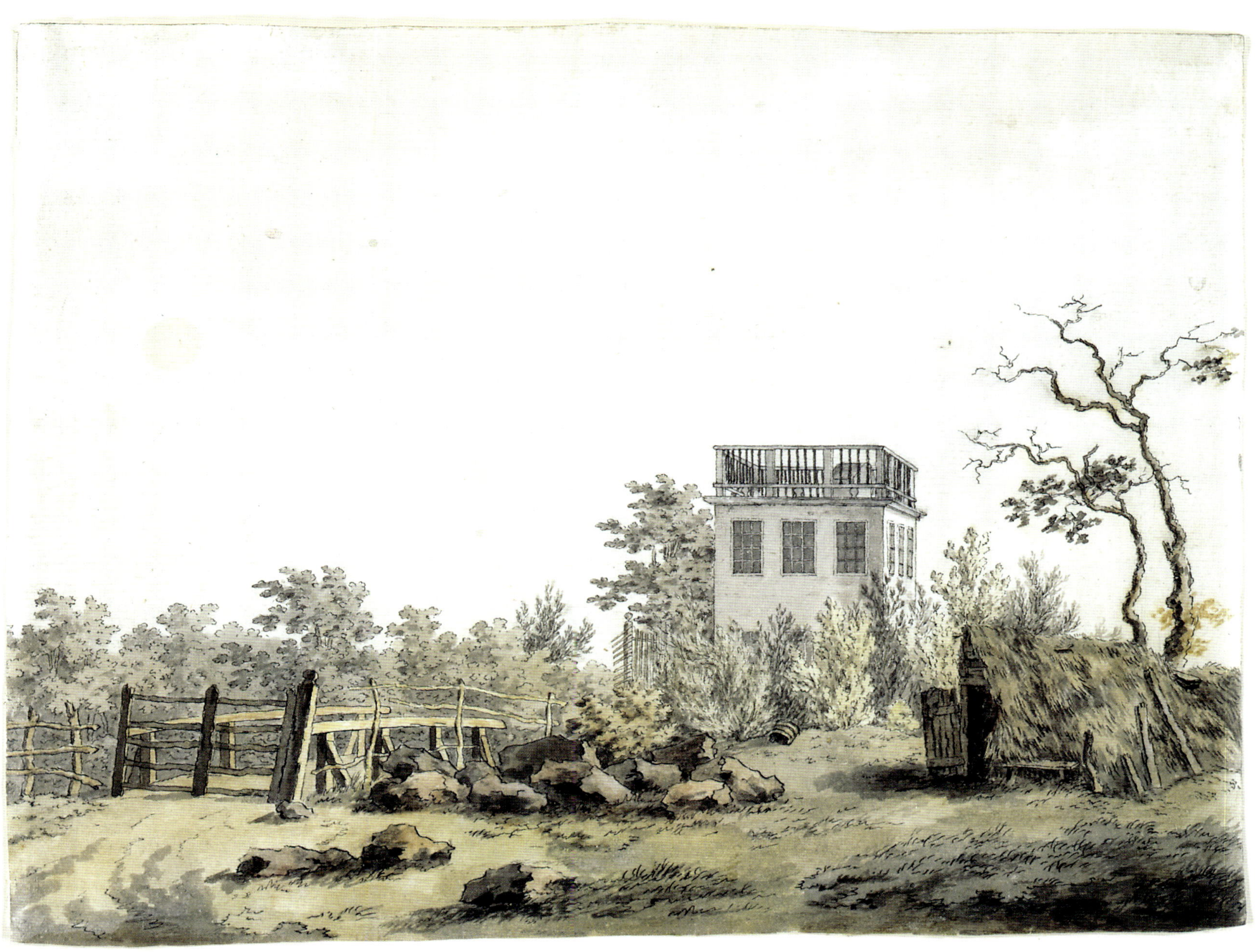

141. ***Landscape with Pavilion,***
1797, ink and watercolour,
16.5 × 22 cm (6½ × 8⅝ in.).
Hamburger Kunsthalle, Hamburg.

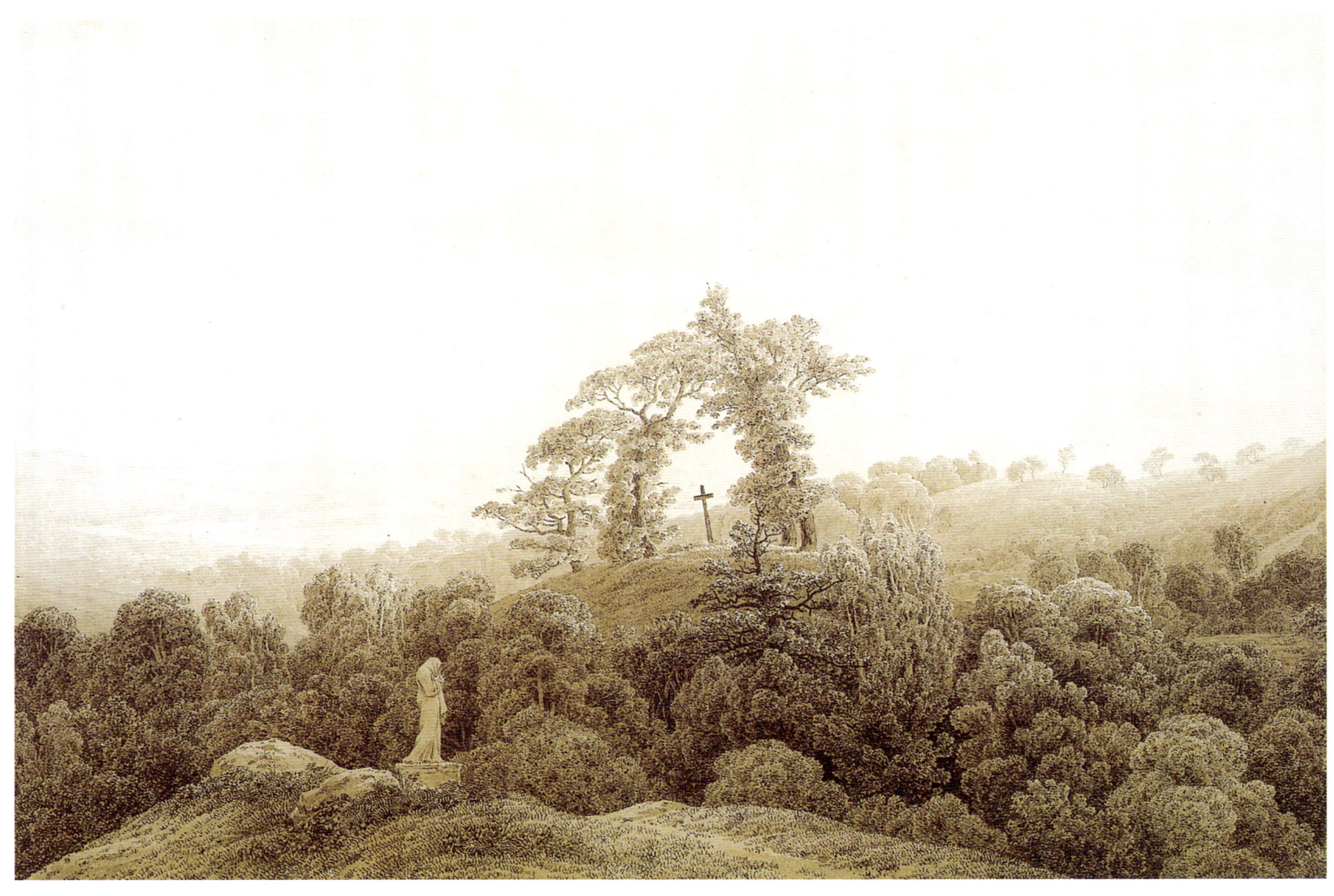

142. *Coastal Landscape,*
c. 1830, sepia,
40 × 58 cm (15¾ × 22⅞ in.).
Kupferstichkabinett, Berlin.

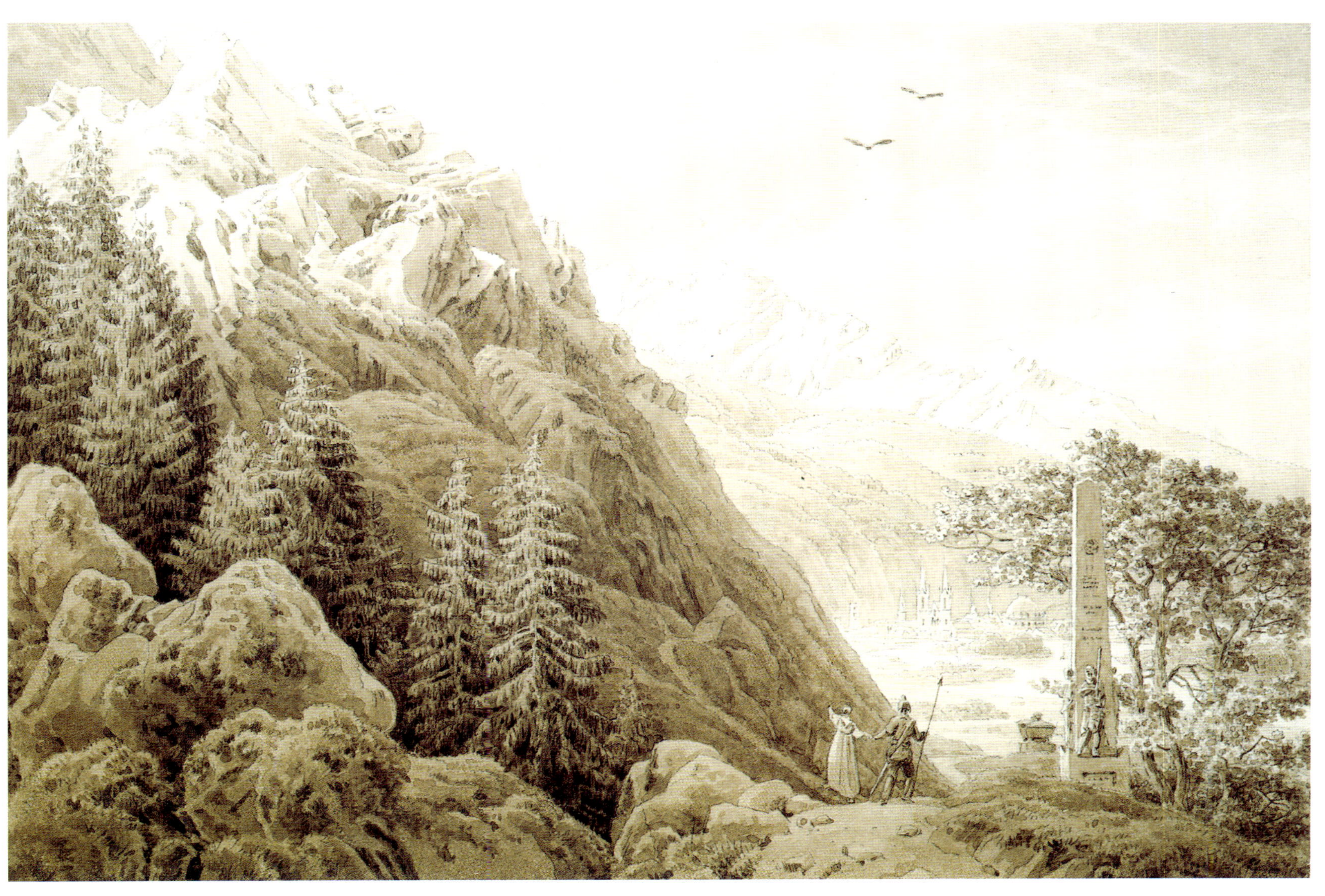

143. *Autumn,*
c. 1826, sepia,
19.1 x 27.5 cm (7½ x 10¾ in.).
Hamburger Kunsthalle, Hamburg.

living potential within itself. As early as 1828, Karl August Böttiger wrote that 'fermenting matter seems to swirl chaotically amid the waves, struggling to find form'.

'Forming, transforming, the eternal entertainment of the eternal mind' is the dual impulse which spurs Goethe's crafty Mephisto into phantasmagorical action (*Faust Part Two*, Act I, In a Dark Gallery). But for Friedrich it is nothing of the kind. He was no all-powerful conjuror and for him formation and transformation took place within a relatively narrow formal terrain. He had no intention of confusing or deceiving, and nor was he concerned with the constancy of nature's recurring cycle. Therefore, his human life cycle does not coincide with that of nature in the end, as G. H. von Schubert thought. It ends, not with man's return to the dust from which he was created (Ecclesiastes 3: 20), but with transubstantiation, metamorphosis into a glorious angel.

The changes between the first and second pictures entail a caesura, as do those between the sixth and seventh pictures. *Autumn*, the central piece of the series, has more than one register. There is also a caesura between the pairs Spring/Summer and Autumn/Winter. Two idyllic scenes of nature are followed by scenes of self-examination, as if someone had fashioned a collage from Haydn's *Creation* and *Seasons* or by combining the songs of Schubert's *Die schöne Müllerin* with those of *Winterreise* and *Schwanengesang*. Was this discontinuity intentional on Friedrich's part? Or did he merely accept it because he could not wrest any more transformational power (or harmony) from his means of expression?

These two questions pinpoint the ambiguous impression that the series makes. Friedrich tried to find an elevated vocabulary for this multi-part cycle; in doing so he skirted close to 'ideal' landscape, and in the last image he adorned 'artistic truth' with the mundane props of a piety that still believed in 'miraculous images' (see page 48). His last works, painted after a stroke, are similar in their meditation on graves, crosses, coffins and birds of the night (ills 150, 151 and 152), and seem to hark back to eighteenth-century poetry's taste for graveyards. Admirers of the innovative aspects of Friedrich's art will prefer to concentrate on the simplicities of the 'reality of nature', such as his *Doorway in the Fürstenschule, Meissen*

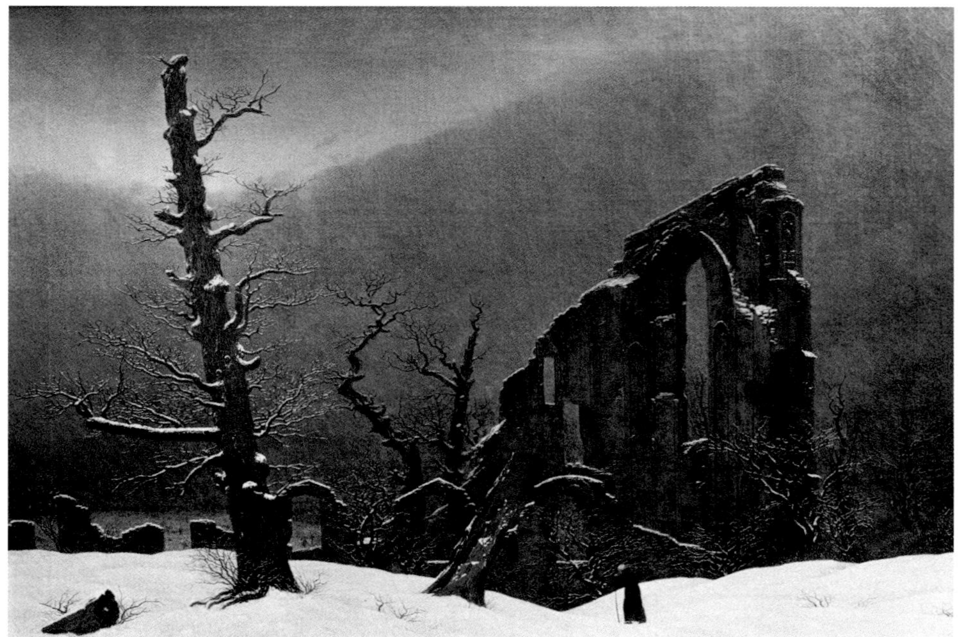

144. *Winter (Monk in the Snow)*, 1808, oil on canvas, 73 x 106 cm (28¾ x 41¾ in.). Formerly Neue Pinakothek, Munich (destroyed 1937).

(ill. 153) and *Landscape with Crumbling Wall* (ill. 154), which date from between 1826 and 1834. In the latter, the wall facing the viewer is in shadow, separating the foreground from the spatial depth which dissolves into light. Only a narrow gate (reminding us of Matthew 7: 14) gives access to the distant scene which Börsch-Supan identifies as the Elbe valley and Dresden. Furthermore, he suggests that it represents a vision of a paradise beyond this world, into which death casts its shadow. Friedrich was undoubtedly working once more with artistic distancing, but not at the cost of darkening the world near at hand. The wall is not a caesura, since the immediate foreground is also filled with light, a first hint of the earthly paradise which may also have been glimpsed by Friedrich's 'inner eye' in the *Spring* and *Summer* of his seven-part cycle.

Delacroix's concept of 'sacred moulds' is particularly helpful when applied to two of Friedrich's favourite artistic techniques: the vertical ordering of space into straight strips or a grid, usually with an axis of symmetry, and horizontal ordering of space into bands that the eye glides over. These two modes are exemplified in his most famous contrasting pair, *The Monk by the Sea* and *The Abbey in the Oak Wood*, but he also returned to the same contrast in two later masterpieces, *The Sea of Ice* (1823–24; ill. 159) and *The Large Enclosure* (*c.* 1832; ill. 162). They illustrate how he could remain faithful to his 'moulds' while adapting them to accommodate new dimensions of content.

Within Friedrich's spatial morphology, *The Sea of Ice* shows the vertically ordered, strip-like structure disintegrating before the viewer's eyes. We are looking at a scene of frozen devastation – the concentrated essence of two other northern landscapes of the same period (ills 160 and 161). The rocks and reefs of the two small paintings are in a setting that is still accessible, but they seem to await the formative intervention which will compress and intensify them into the monumental wastes of *The Sea of Ice*. In the Hamburg painting, it is as if nature has abandoned its normal organic processes of decay and regeneration and been visited by a final catastrophe, which has also extended to the works of man: we

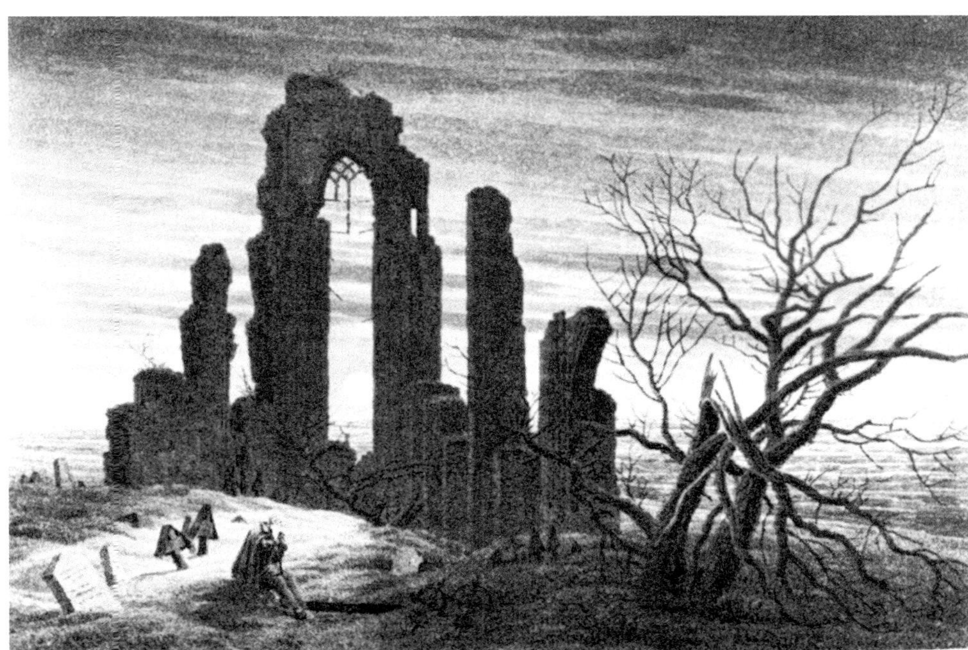

145. ***Winter,***
1807, sepia,
19 × 27.5 cm (7½ × 10¾ in.).
Formerly Reichskammer der bildenden Künste, Berlin (destroyed).

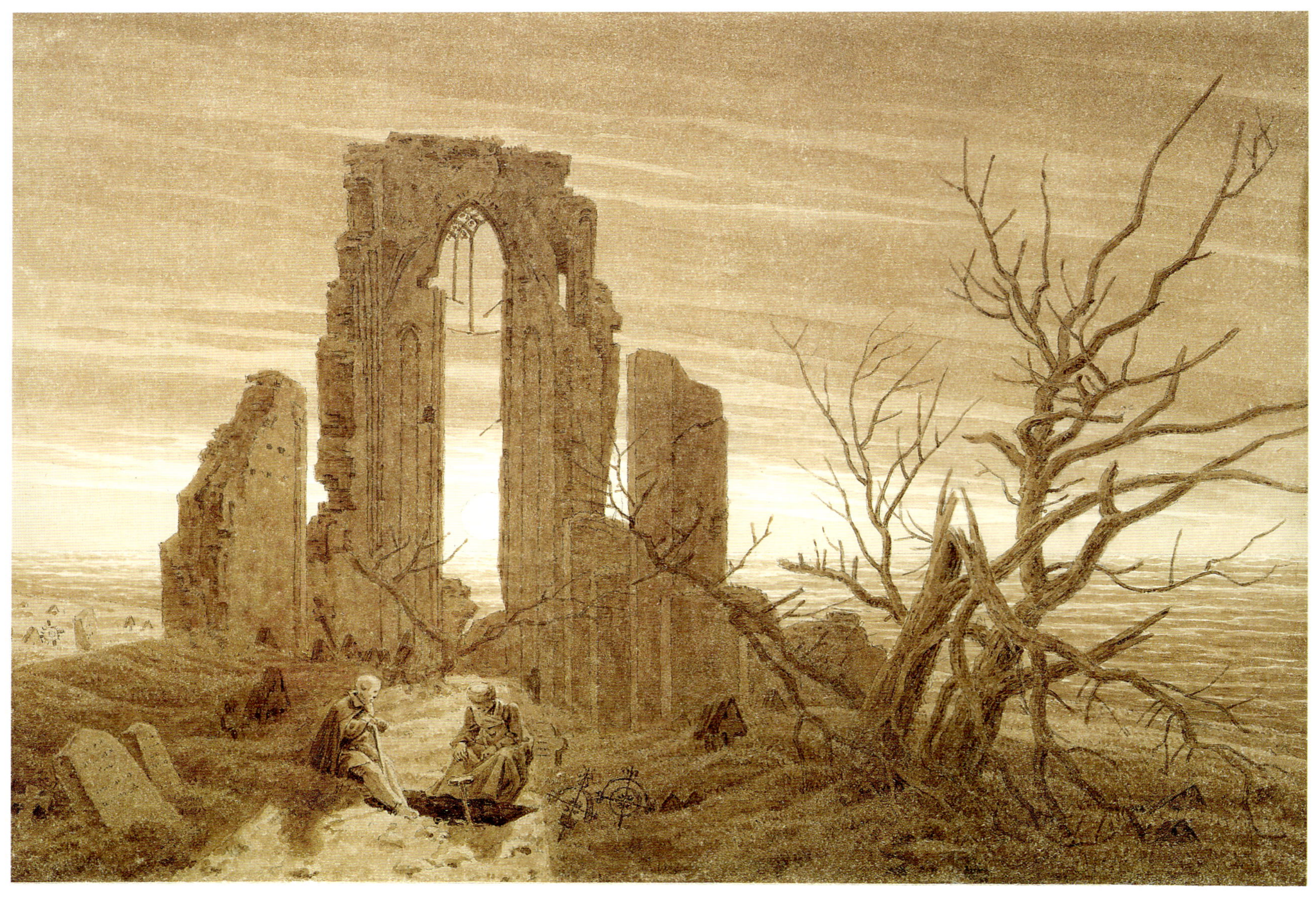

146. *Winter,*
c. 1826, sepia,
19.2 x 27.5 cm (7½ x 10¾ in.).
Hamburger Kunsthalle, Hamburg.

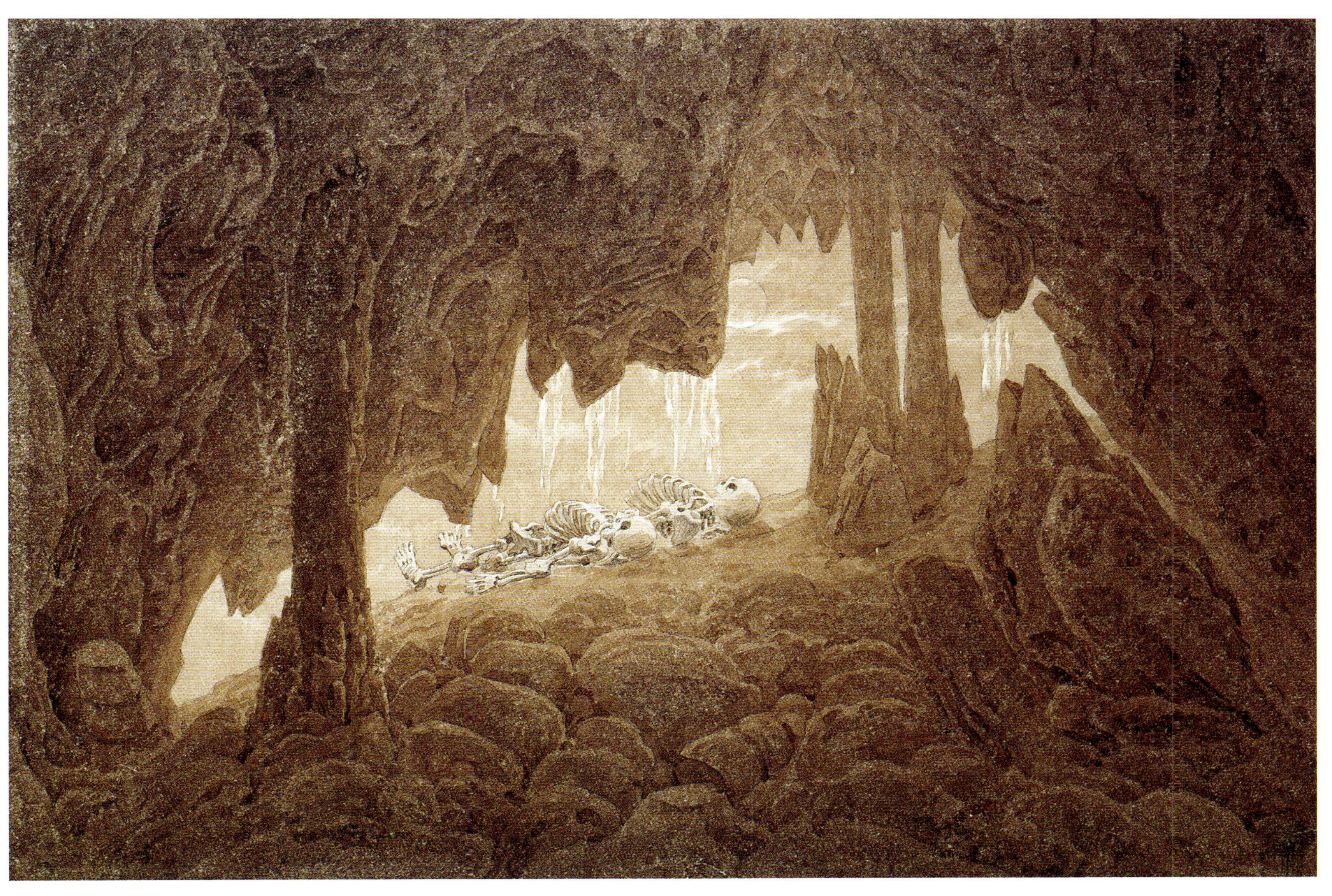

147. *Skeletons in a Cave with Stalactites,*
c. 1826, sepia,
18.8 × 27.5 cm (7⅜ × 10¾ in.).
Hamburger Kunsthalle, Hamburg.

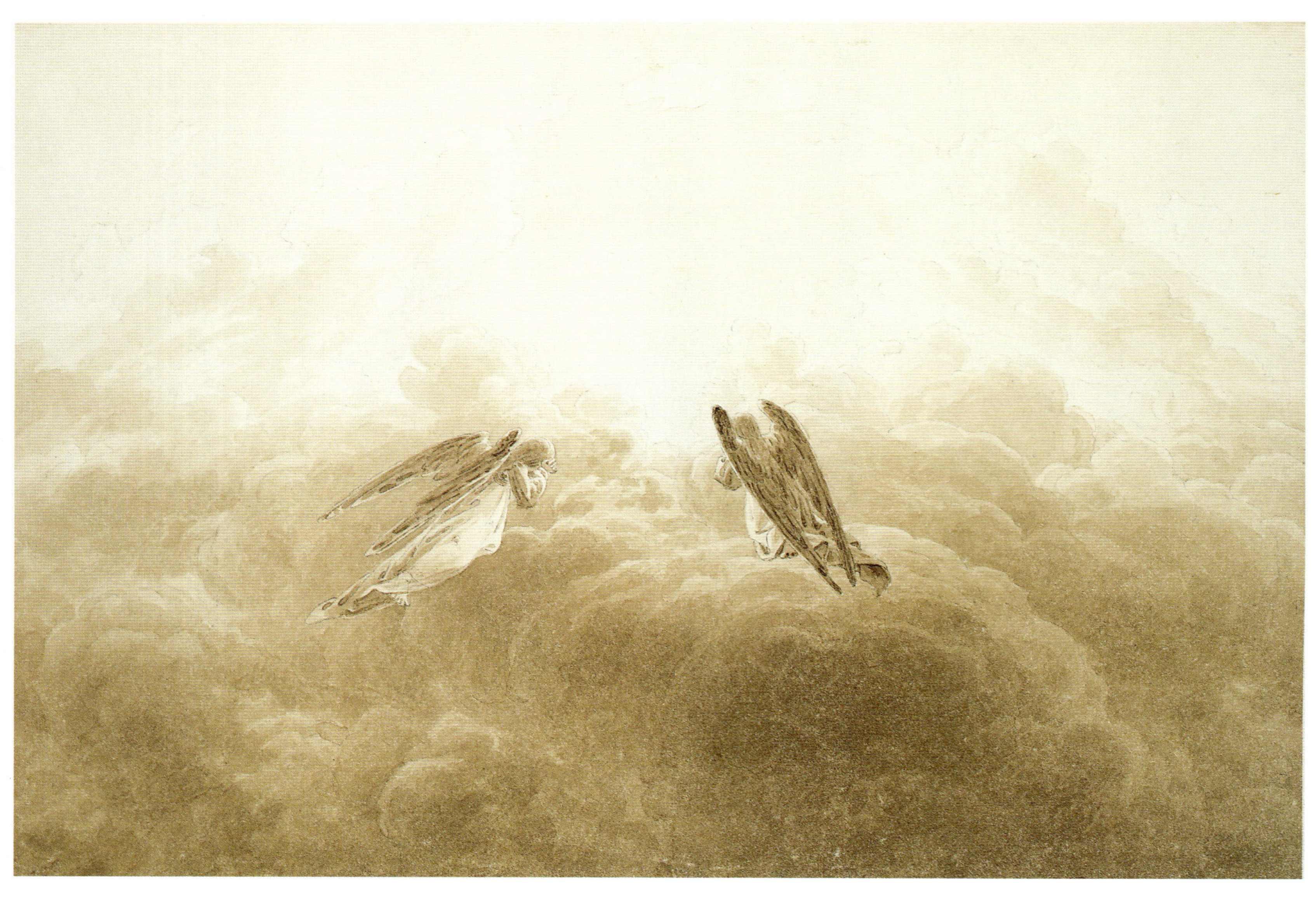

148. *Angels in Adoration,*
c. 1826, sepia,
18.5 × 26.7 cm (7¼ × 10½ in.).
Hamburger Kunsthalle, Hamburg.

149. *The Cathedral*, **detail,**
c. 1818, oil on canvas,
152.5 × 70.5 cm (60 × 27¾ in.).
Georg Schäfer Collection.

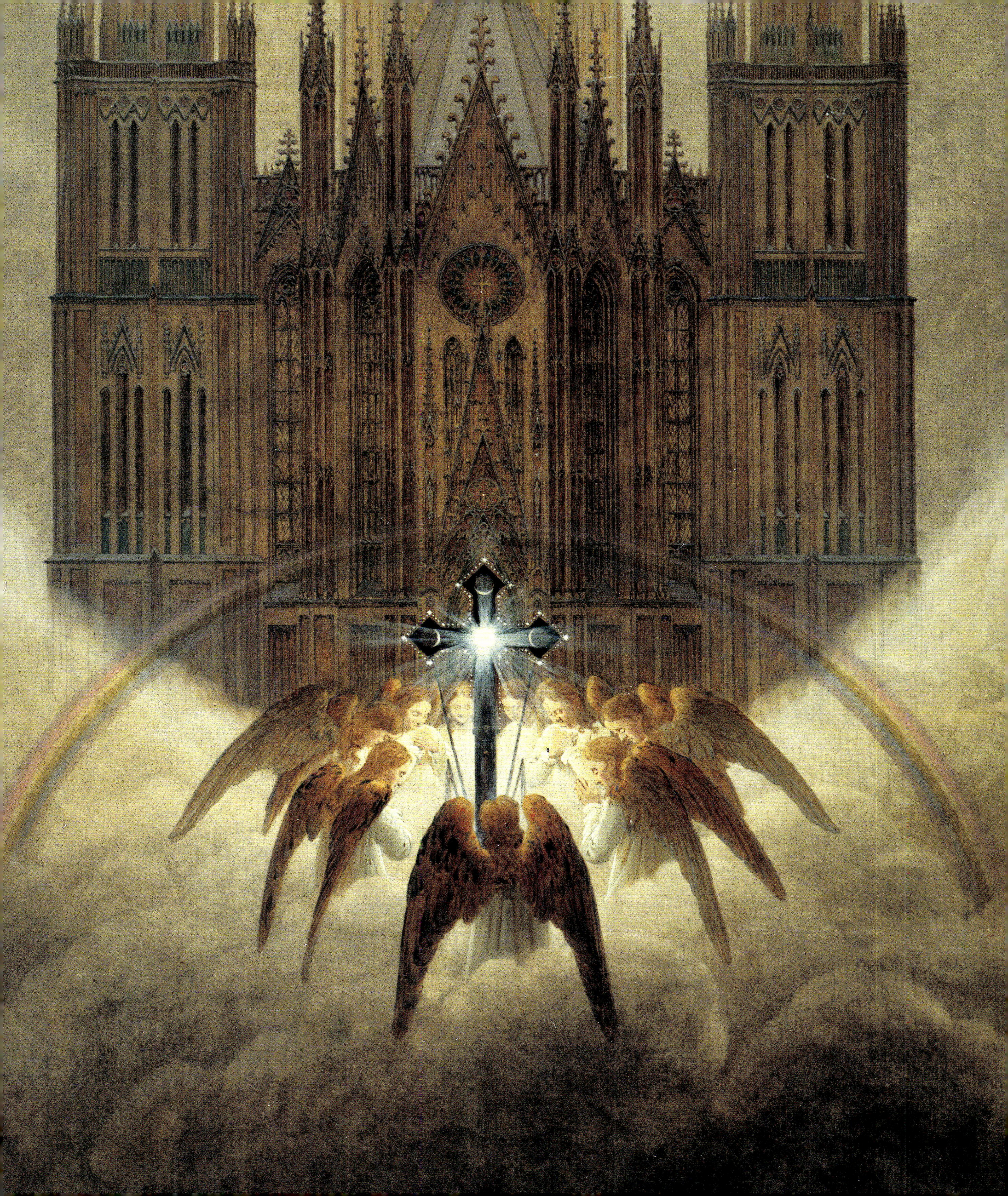

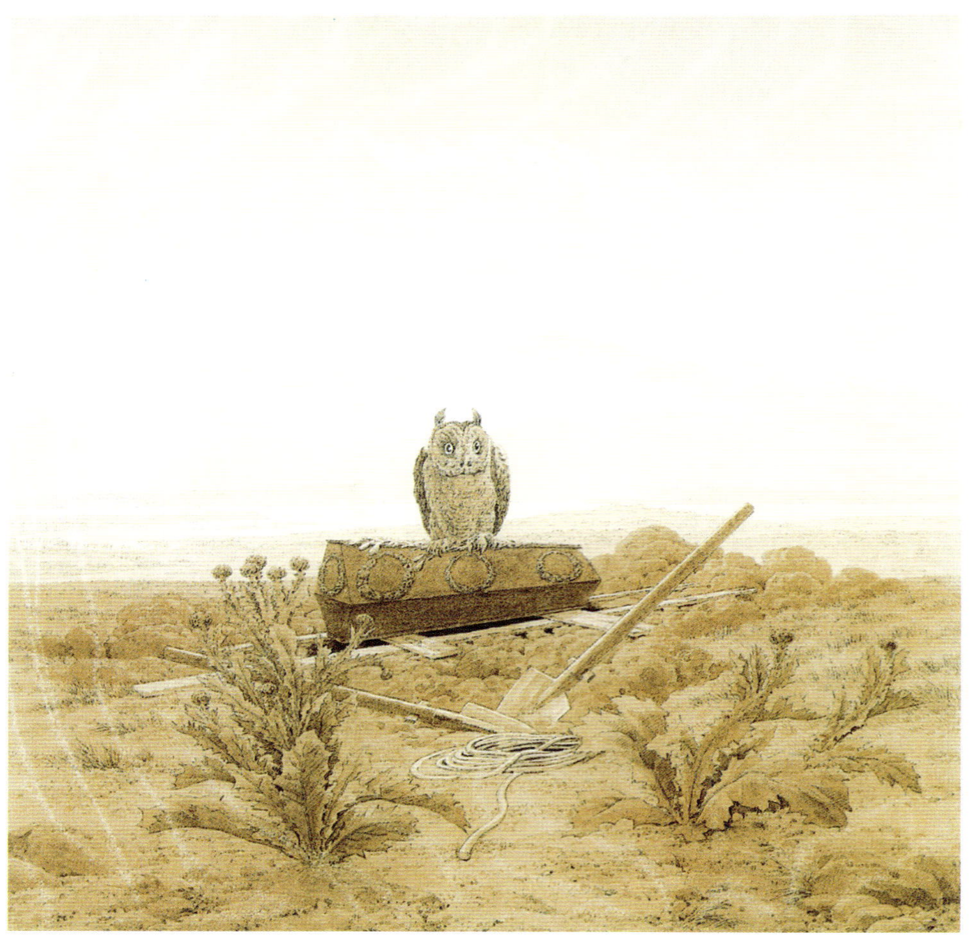

150. *Landscape with Grave, Coffin and Owl,*
c. 1836–37, pencil and sepia,
48.5 × 38.5 cm (19 × 15¼ in.).
Hamburger Kunsthalle, Hamburg.

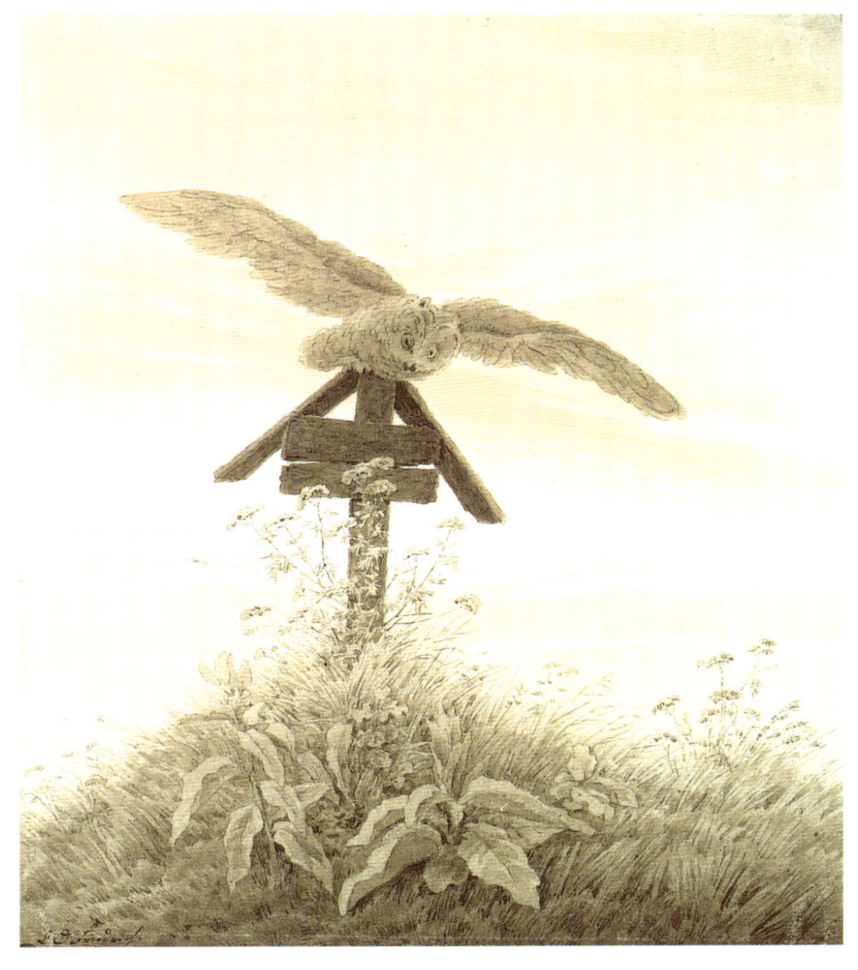

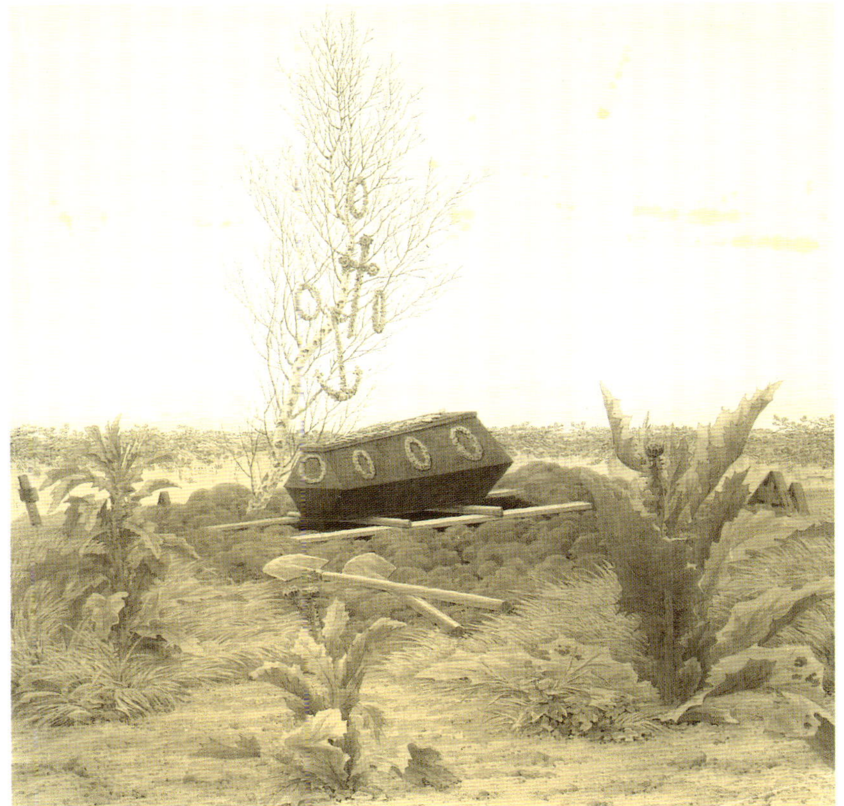

151. ***Owl on a Grave,***
1836–37, sepia,
25.9 x 22.2 cm (10¼ x 8¾ in.).
Pushkin Museum, Moscow.

152. ***Coffin and Grave,***
c. 1836, pencil and sepia,
39.2 x 39.4 cm (15⅜ x 15½ in.).
Pushkin Museum, Moscow.

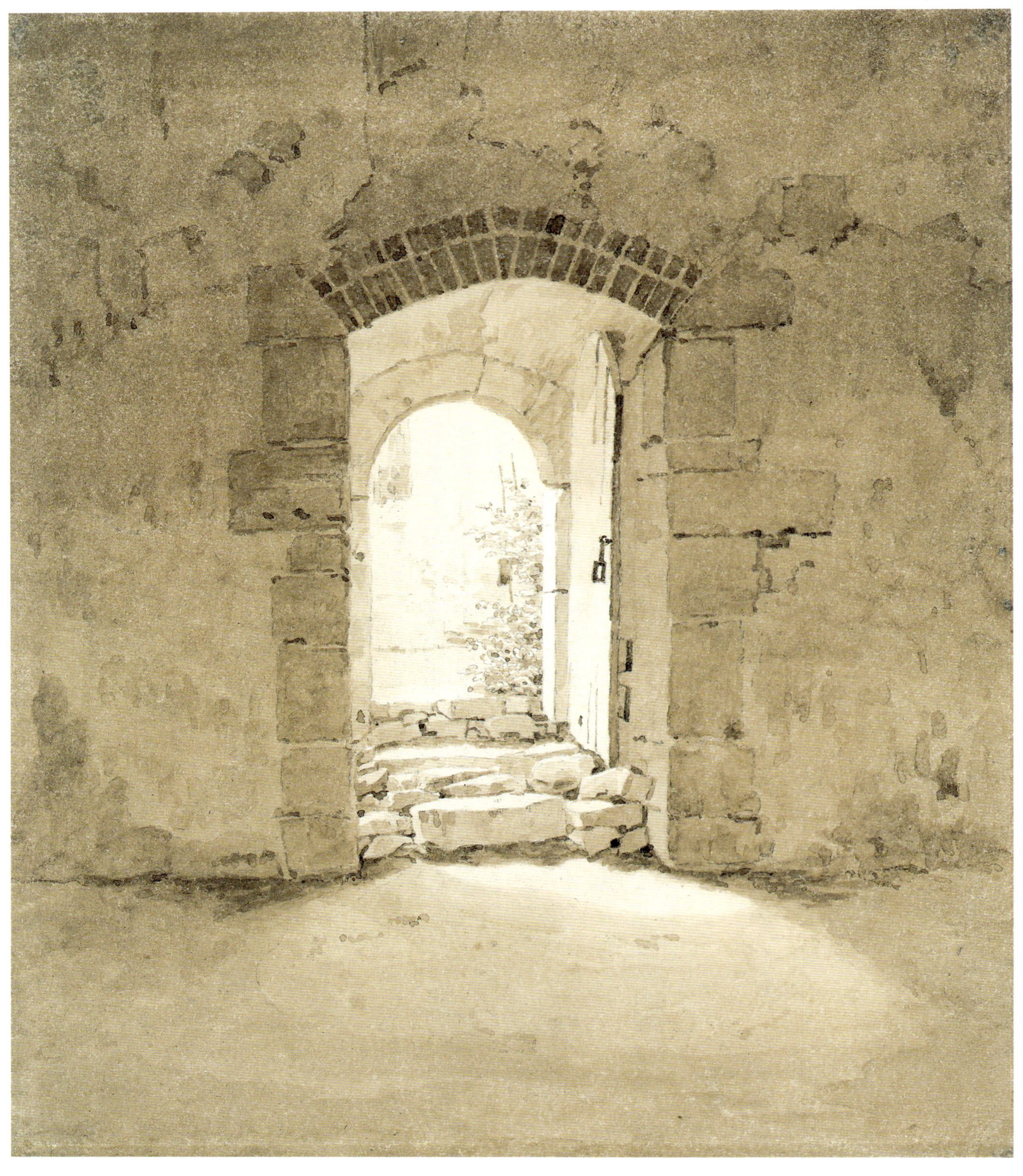

153. *Doorway in the Fürstenschule, Meissen,*
after 1835, pencil and sepia,
22.8 × 19.3 cm (8⅞ × 7⅝ in.).
Private collection.

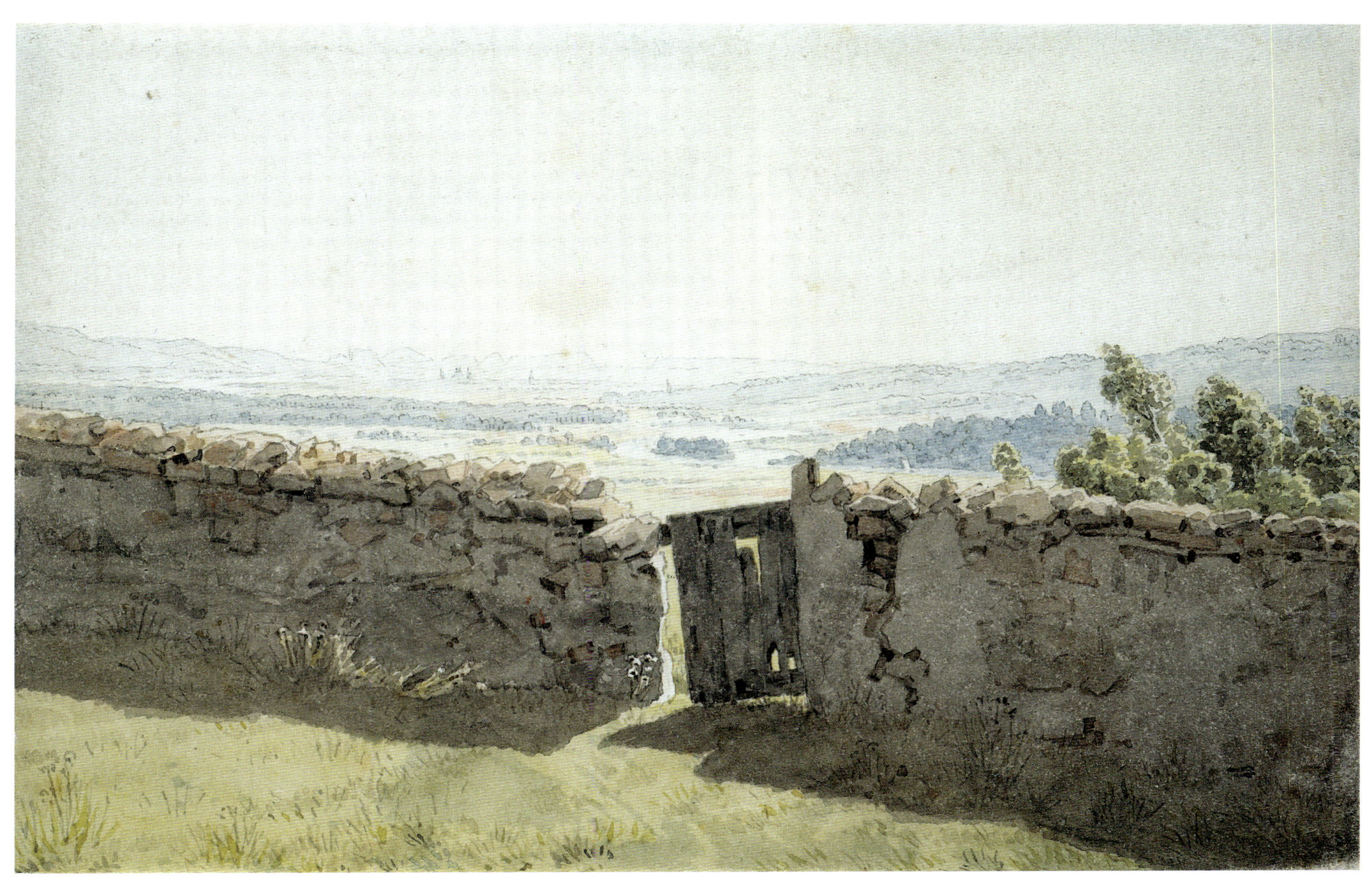

154. *Landscape with Crumbling Wall*,
c. 1837–40, pencil, Indian ink and watercolour,
12.2 × 18.5 cm (4¾ × 7¼ in.).
Hamburger Kunsthalle, Hamburg.

slowly become aware of a wrecked ship, crushed by the ice near the right-hand edge of the painting. In themselves, the formal cells of this relentless pressure seem constricted and forced, but we can see that, in relation to the whole, Friedrich secretly controls the devastation and transforms it into a harsh staccato. He does not leave the blocks of ice at the level of the 'reality of nature' which he had encountered and recorded in his oil sketches of broken ice on the Elbe at Dresden (ills 157 and 158) but elevates them to the plane of 'artistic truth'. He achieves this by varying one single item in his formal vocabulary: the entire content of the picture consists of nothing but sharply broken volumes or splinters – mere fragments, but nevertheless in complete syntactical accord. In this way, Friedrich stabilizes destruction in a synthesis whose dissonances are not veiled but preserved. We first discern a slight rise in the bottom floes from left to right, where an upright, ochre wedge suddenly opposes the drift; the battle is fought out in the heap of ice in the centre, with the left half of the picture winning the day. This zigzag course contains many potentially unifying elements which convert the jumble of blocks of ice into a 'harmonious' artistic construction. The structure is right in front of the viewer, for the foreground has been broken off, a device anticipating the zoom of a camera.

Raised to emblematic status, the frozen 'chaos' is open to many levels of interpretation. The painting used to be known as *The Wrecked 'Hope'*, which appeared to refer to an actual shipwreck, albeit fictionalized; this reportage seemed to be a comment on the dangers of human enterprises. Böttiger wrote in 1825 that the ship in question was the *Griper*, which took part in several Arctic expeditions, and for a long time it was not determined whether Friedrich was referring to actual events or not. However, since Wolfgang Stechow proved in 1965 that the title referred to another, lost painting, the case for pseudo-reportage with metaphysical overtones has been lost. All that remains for discussion is the picture itself and its formal substance, which has been variously interpreted as an emblem of existential inevitability, a symbol of 'God's unapproachable majesty' (Börsch-Supan) or of the 'general paralysis in Germany' (Jensen) – that is, a parable of the state of Germany in the decades when Metternich was in charge of public order.

The initial impression of rigid, frozen matter is succeeded (and corrected and modified) by the insistent impact of the angles of the central pile of ice, all pointing left and upwards. They proclaim escape from the grip in which they are held. An appeal or protest of some sort could be read into this, and it is certainly possible that the painting contains a hidden political message, as Georg Schmidt suggested (1949). In my view, that interpretation is indirectly strengthened by the memorial that Walter Gropius

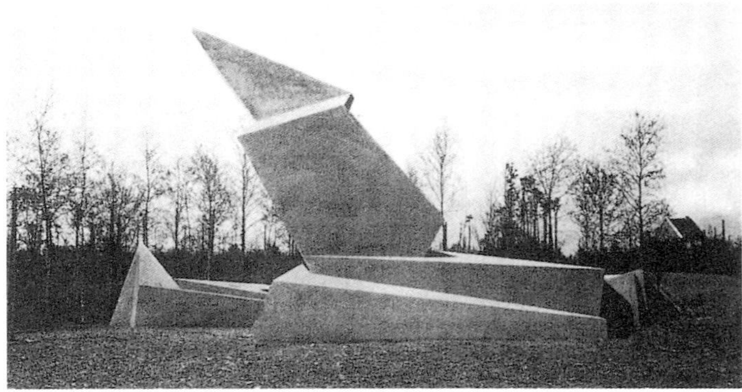

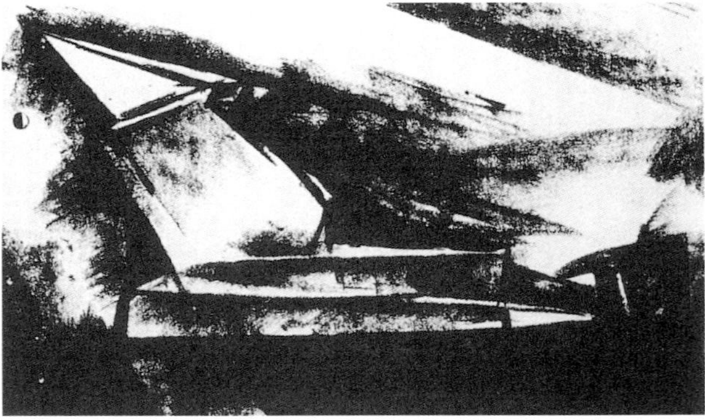

155 and 156. Walter Gropius, *Monument to the March Dead*, sculpture and sketch, 1922.

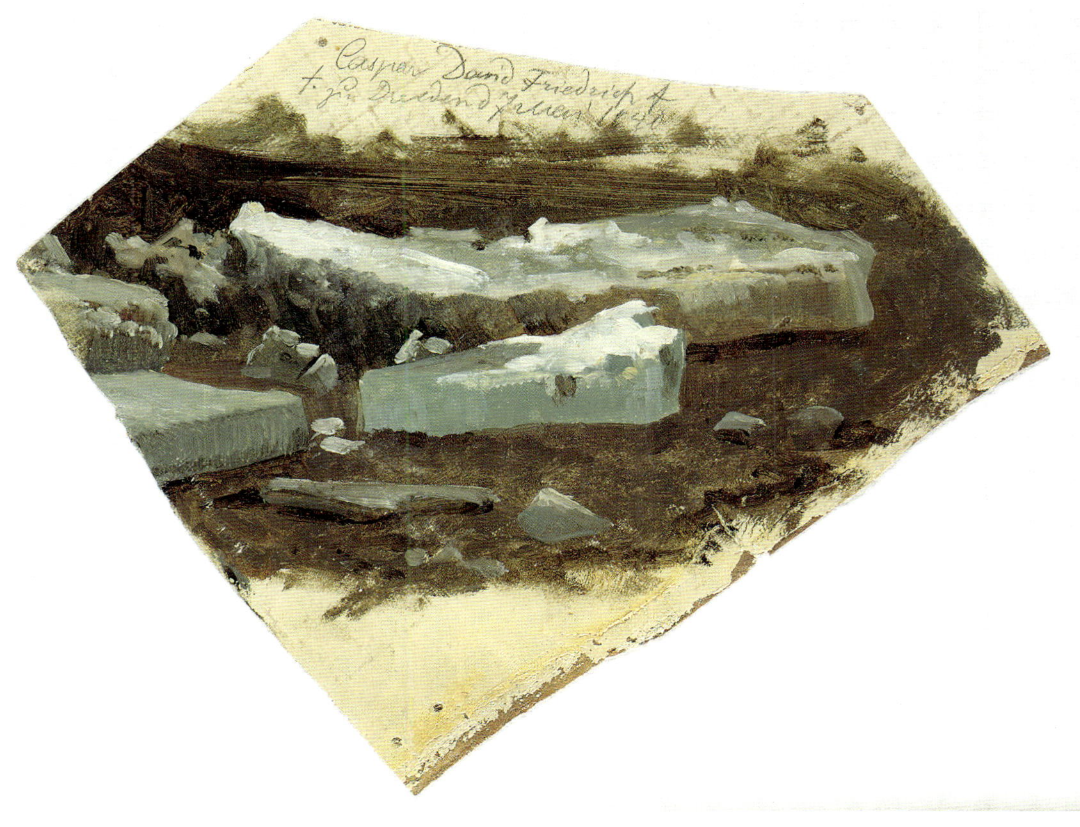

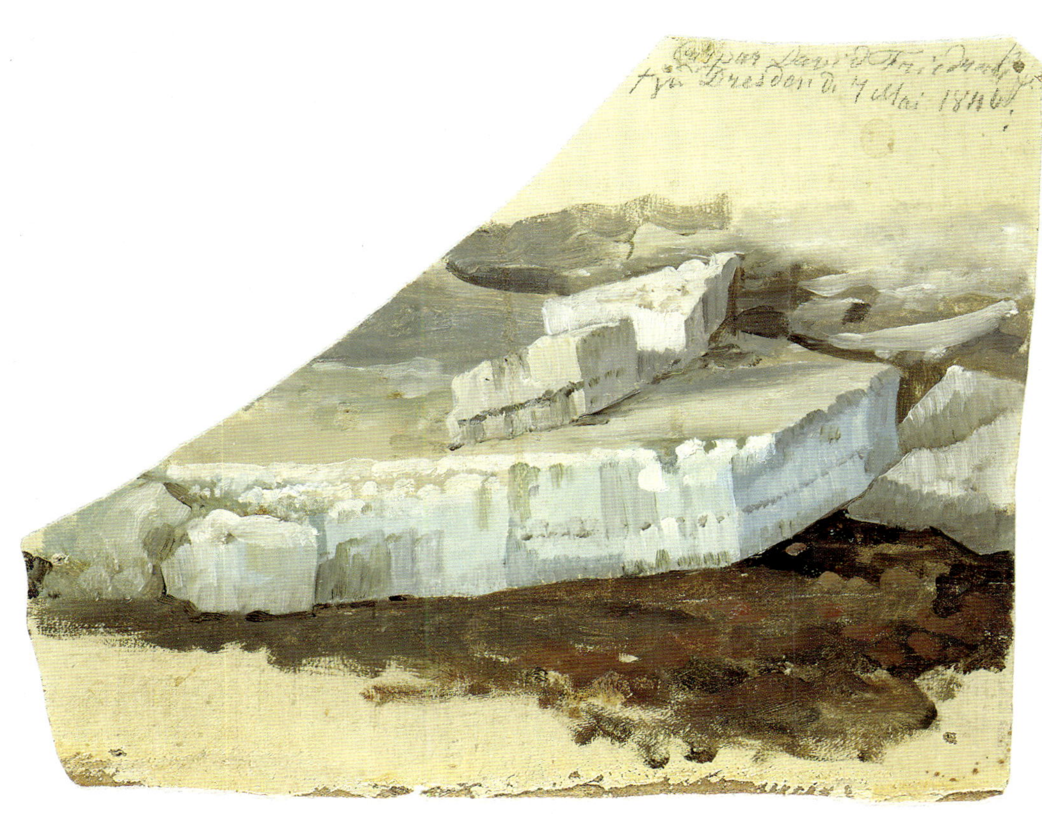

157 and 158. ***Blocks of Ice,***
1820–21, oil on canvas,
14 × 18 cm (5½ × 7⅛ in.) and 15.2 × 20.6 cm (5⅞ × 8 in.).
Hamburger Kunsthalle, Hamburg.

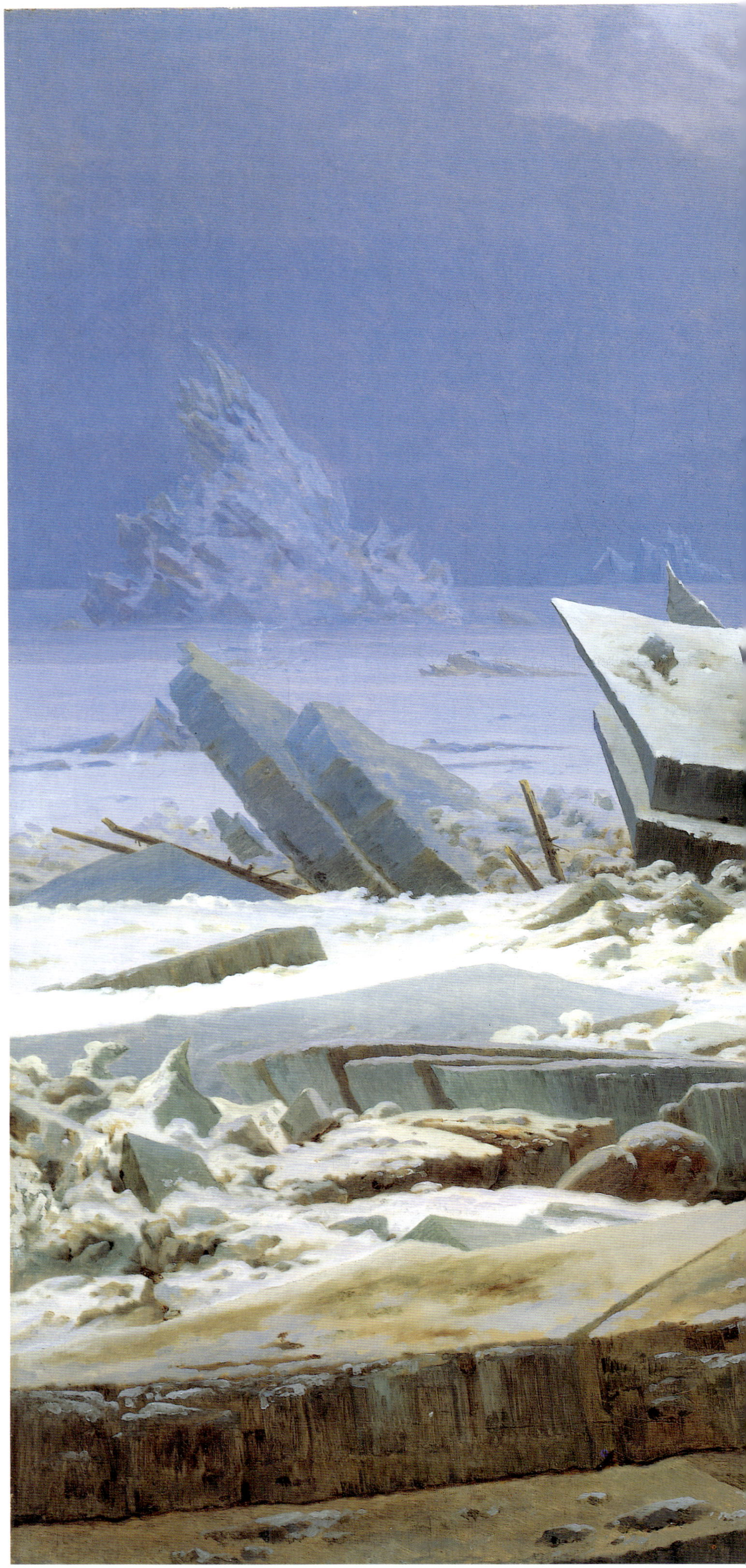

159. *The Sea of Ice (Arctic Shipwreck),*
1823–24, oil on canvas,
96.7 × 126.9 cm (38 × 50 in.).
Hamburger Kunsthalle, Hamburg.

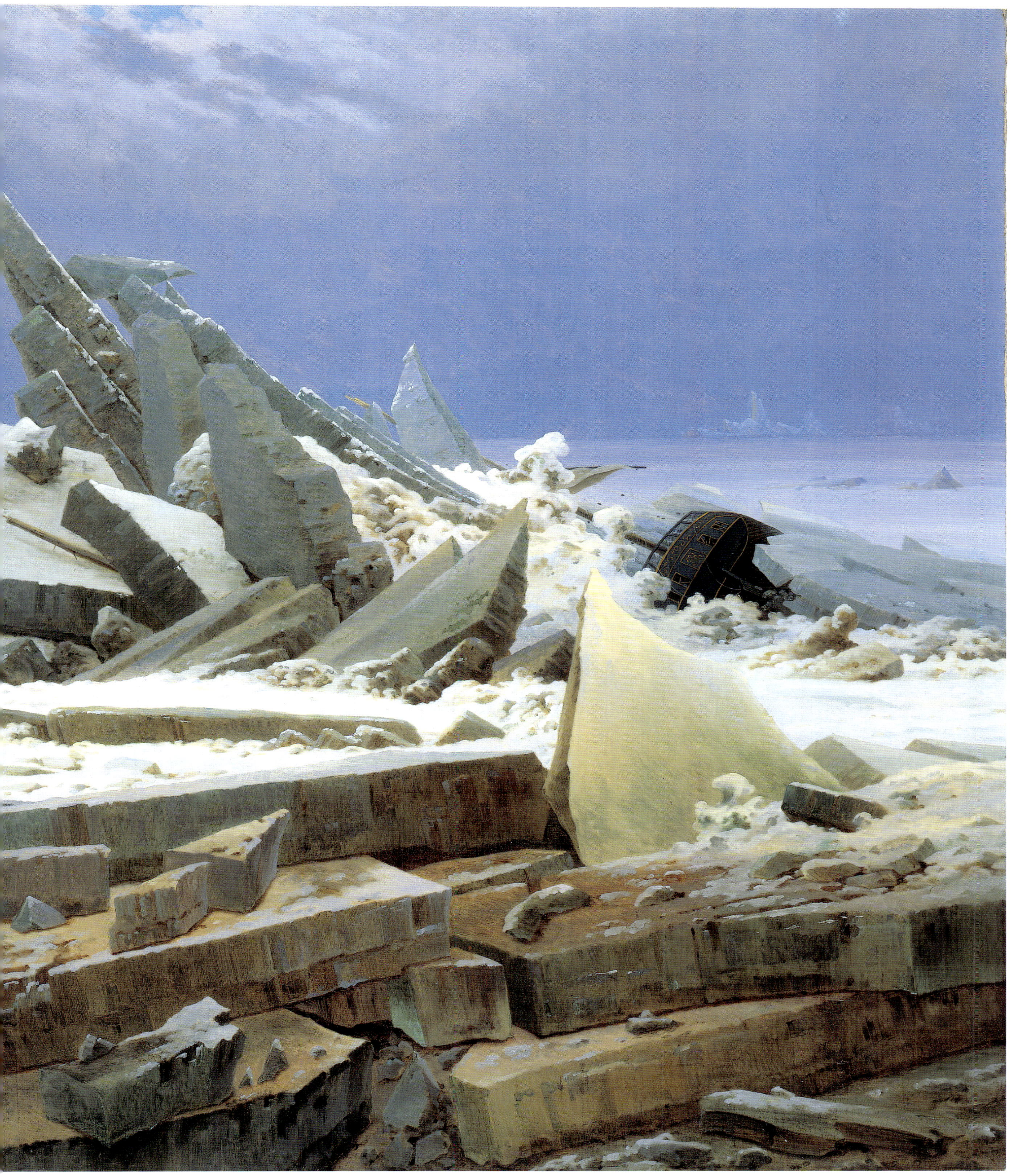

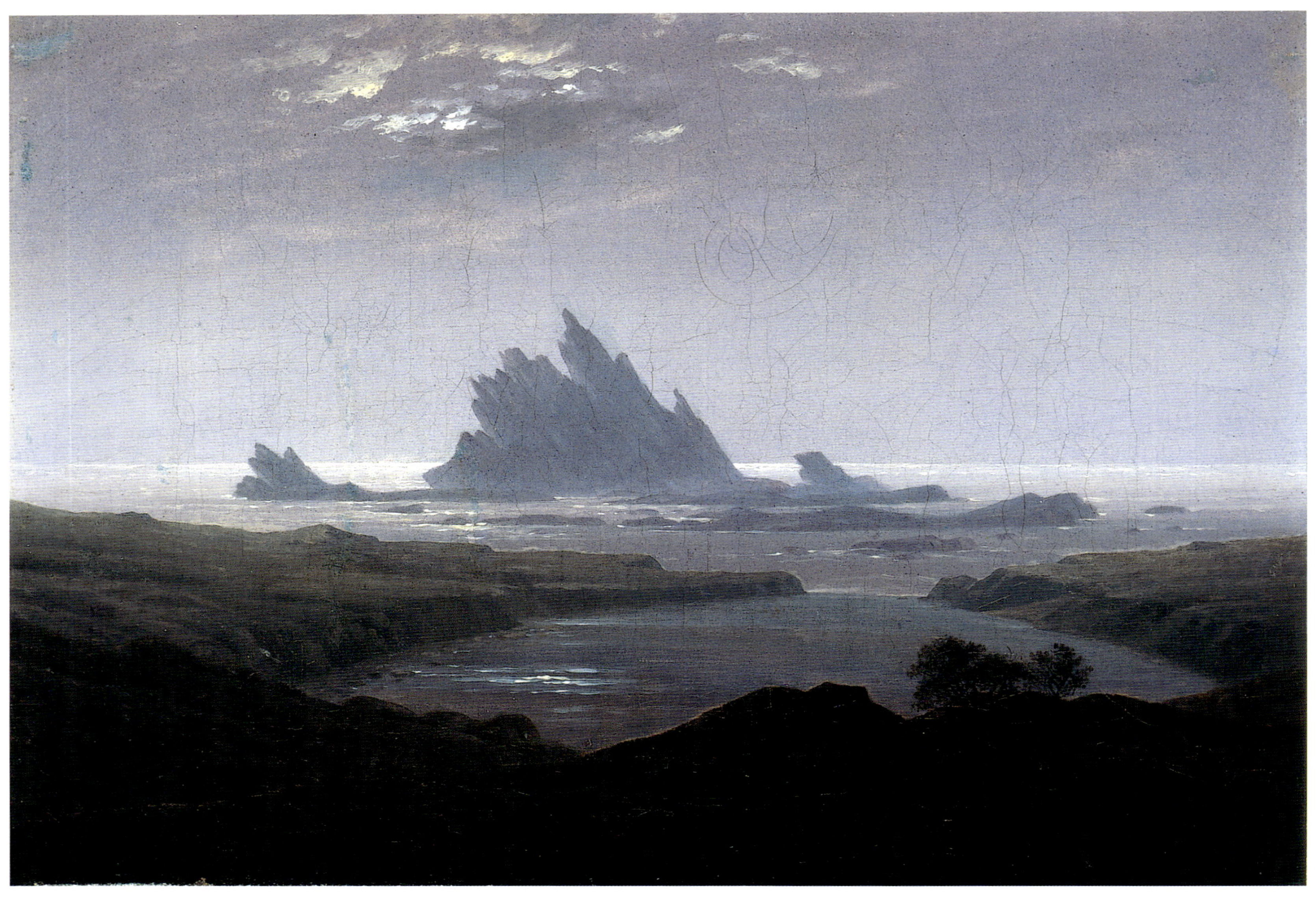

160. ***Rocky Reef on the Seashore,***
1824, oil on canvas,
22 x 31 cm (8¾ x 12¼ in.).
Staatliche Kunsthalle, Karlsruhe.

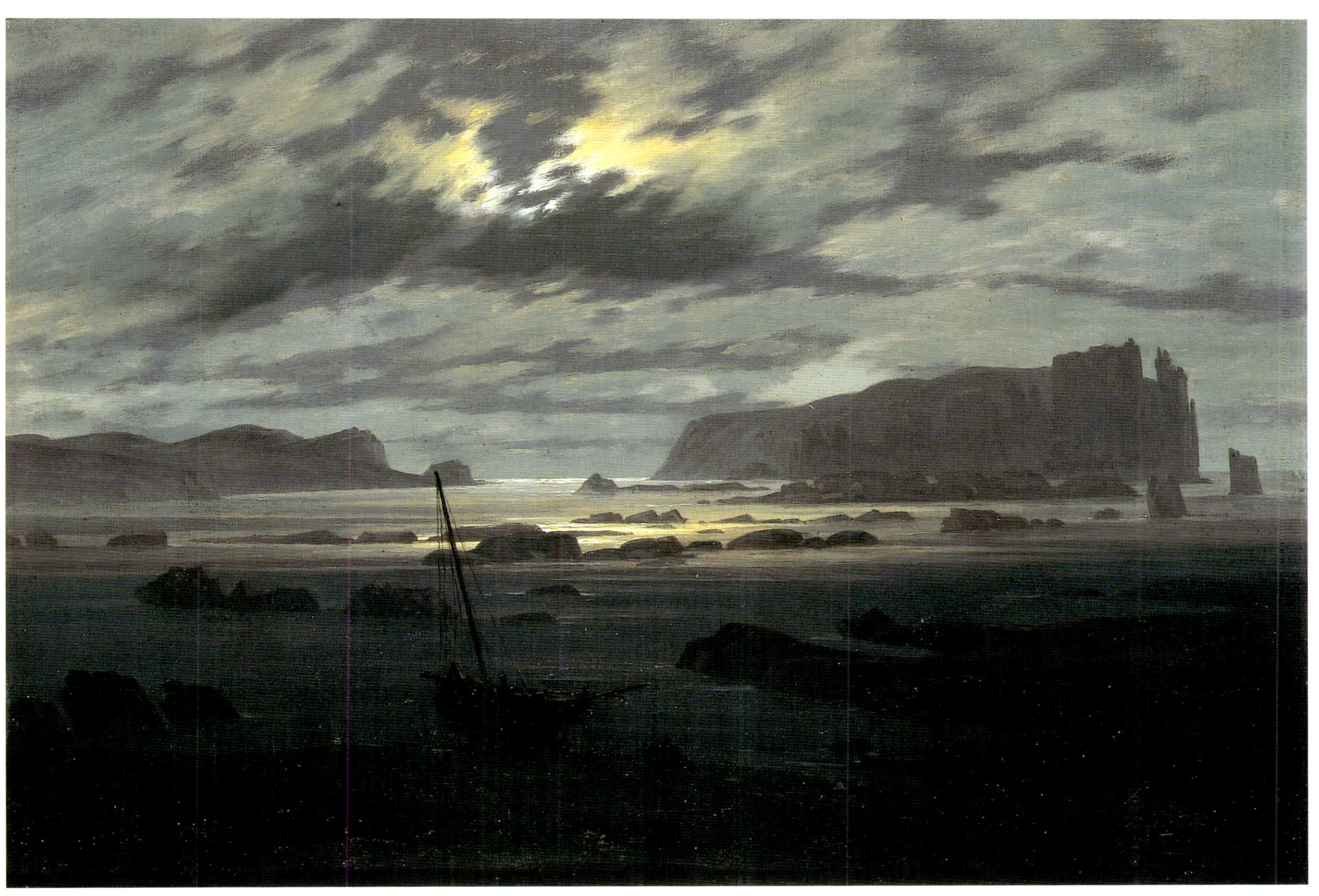

161. *Northern Sea in the Moonlight,*
1823, oil on canvas,
22 x 30.5 cm (8⅝ x 12 in.).
Národní Galerie, Prague.

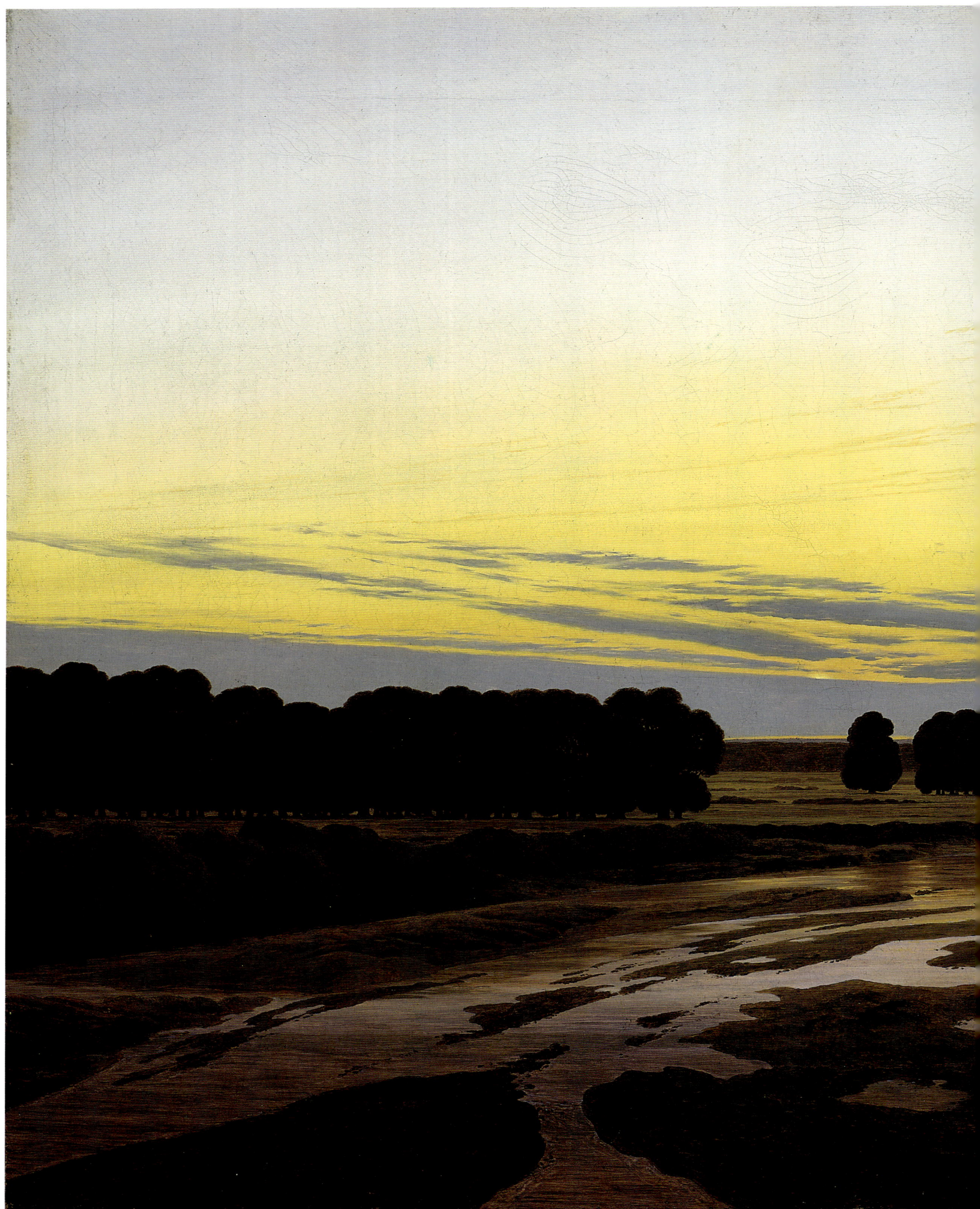

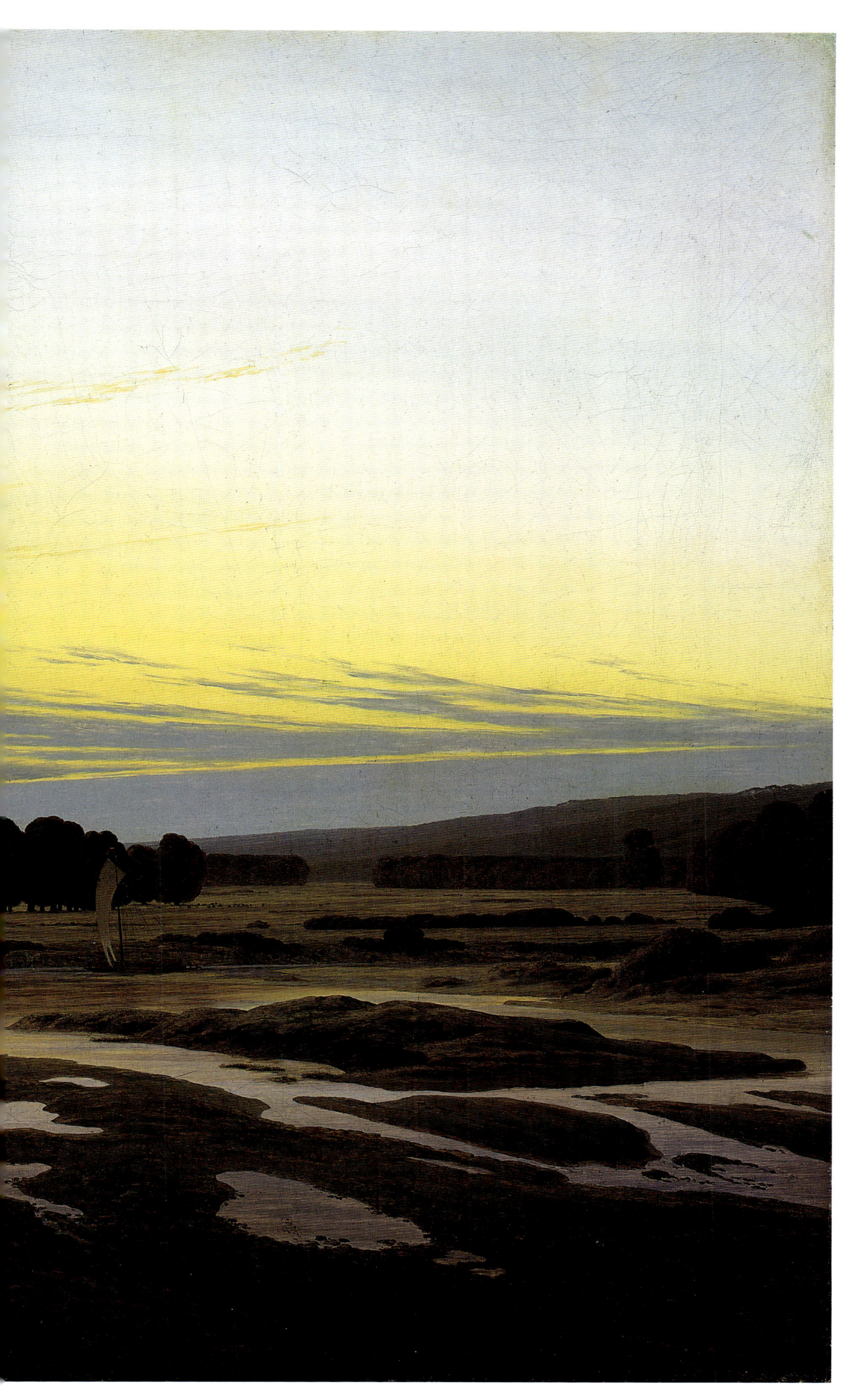

162. ***The Large Enclosure,***
c. 1832, oil on canvas,
73.5 x 103 cm (29 x 40½ in.).
Gemäldegalerie Neue Meister, Dresden.

created for Weimar in 1922, commemorating the left-wing victims of the Kapp Putsch of March 1920 (ills 155 and 156). Gropius used pointed, angular blocks, shaping them into an aggressive signal that marked not defeat but resistance. This idea may have been suggested to him by *The Sea of Ice.* If Friedrich's painting contains a concealed appeal, might it then fall outside the bounds of the fundamental model of the icon? An icon invites the viewer to meditation, a painting that makes an appeal incites the viewer to action. Both these things happen in *The Sea of Ice.* The destruction of stable, balanced order makes it an anti-icon, but at the same time its dynamic appeal initiates a long-term conscious process, rather than calling for spontaneous action. Lasting endurance is the quality of the icon which takes it beyond the vicissitudes of change.

The Sea of Ice is often compared to Théodore Géricault's *Raft of the Medusa*, but a comparison only makes sense if confined to the observation that both paintings exhibit the interlinking of registers characteristic of innovative painting of the nineteenth century. An event is given a paradigmatic aura without sacrificing any of its realism. In his great painting of the shipwrecked, marked equally by despair and hope, Géricault was also depicting the absence of a hand on the political helm of his country, just as Friedrich's angular blocks represent both anti-democratic hardening and the secret hope that the ice would one day break.

The Large Enclosure (ill. 162) – depicting a real location to the northwest of Dresden – is one of Friedrich's horizontally ordered compositions. However, that is a rather summary and imprecise categorization, since the dominant feature perceived by the viewer is not the horizontals in the middle ground but the double curves of the sky above them, and the lobed, chiaroscuro patches of water and earth below them. Willi Wolfradt saw the shallow curves of cloud as being mirrored, first in the outline of the bushes, then 'repeatedly, intensified by the greater curvature, in the shapes of the sandbanks', meaning that all the individual outlines conform to these curves. But where Wolfradt saw 'undulating ripples crossing the sky', I would describe the mirror image in terms of the geometrical figure of the hyperbola. The vertices of the two extended branches of the 'cones' come closest to each other around the picture's central axis. However, these curves do not lie two-dimensionally within the picture plane but bend through space. They correspond, but do not create any linear axes of central perspective. Friedrich leaves a gap to peer through (an isomorphic, Euclidean space, to be more precise), and invents an airy space which moves simultaneously towards us and away from us.

The foreground is bare of vegetation, which renders it alien and perplexing. As its curves slide towards and beneath us, the picture loses its grounding. How great or small is the distance from which we see this landscape? Are we standing on a bridge, as it has been suggested the painter did, or are we (and the artist) up in a balloon, floating above it all? These uncertainties give the picture the airy harmony that exists between all its zones. The waterlogged, lunar sandbanks are echoed by the pale green meadows where the river may well wind on, and this slow, constant sliding eventually becomes floating in the sky. As early as *Moonrise by the Sea* (ill. 90), two shallow curves are suggested: the sky encloses an oval space which is echoed by the huge rock. In *The Large Enclosure*, the curves have become the branches of a hyperbola. The sky is a single, all-embracing sweep of clouds, spread out over the earth as its echo and counterimage. Man has shrunk to a marginal element in this dialogue, and the sailing boat stranded in the shallow water – like the monk in *The Monk by the Sea*, it divides the picture by the Golden Section –

serves only as a reminder of human insignificance. The painter, however, marrying the earthly with the cosmic, is excepted from that marginality, as are we who follow him in experiencing the twofold wake of the double curve. Friedrich takes us into the picture, but does not build up any confidence in the world we see there. Instead he uses perhaps the most paradoxical of all his spatial constructions to create his fundamental theme: withdrawal from the world.

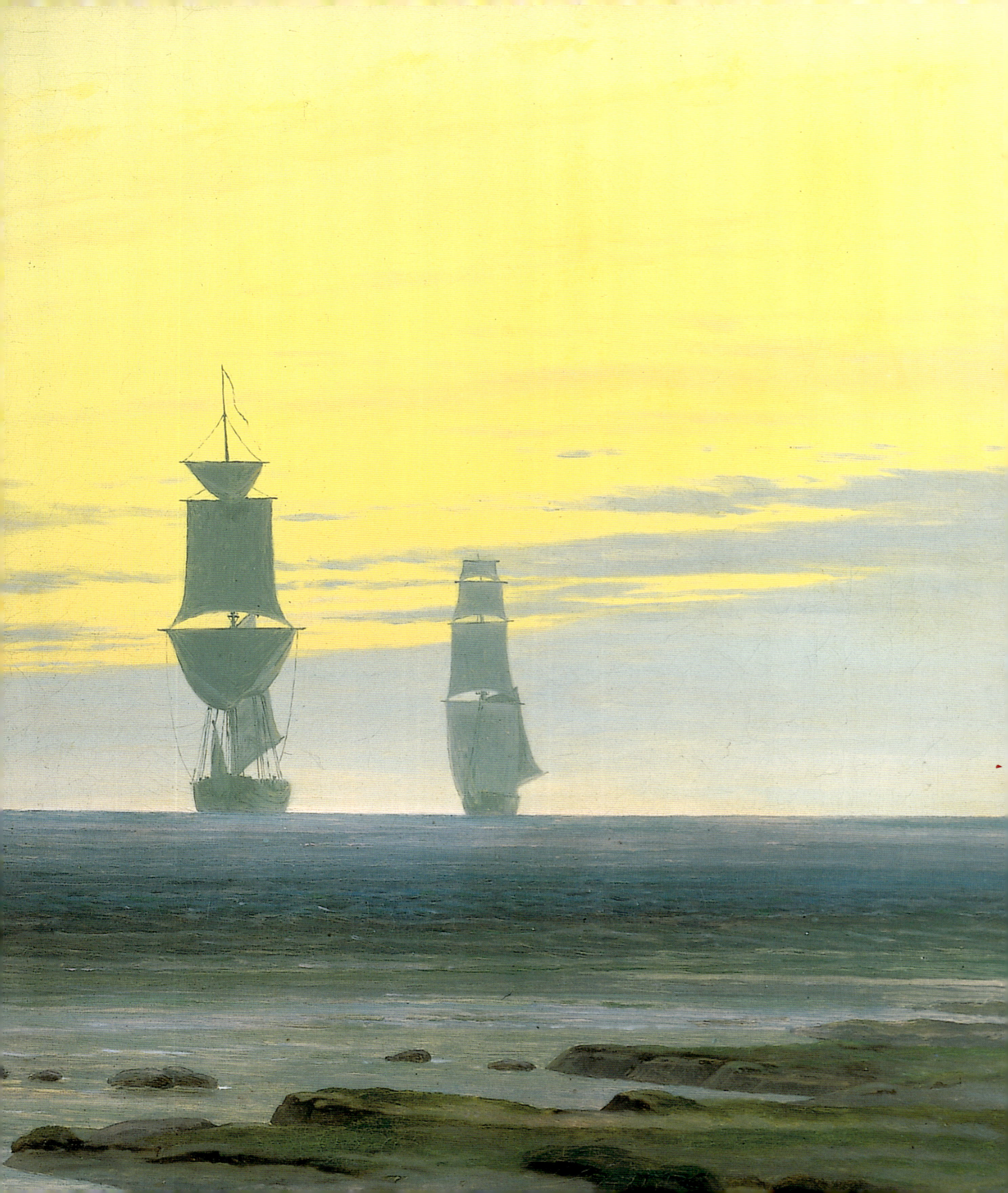

V

FROM RELIGIOUS INTENTION TO FREE INTERPRETATION

If an analytical study has managed not to overpraise its subject, but has affirmed his highly developed understanding of art and his careful, considered handling of expressive techniques, it should not then be expected to marshall works of art as evidence for biographical facts. Likewise, an author must avoid condensing an artistic intelligence that operates with multiple meanings into a code in which every sign has only a single meaning, and which purports to possess the invariably correct interpretation for every detail. Friedrich himself gave viewers the right to make their own choices from among the multiple meanings of his pictures, for he believed that possibly the greatest gift of an artist was 'to stimulate the spirit, and arouse thoughts, feelings and sensations in the viewer, even if they are not his own'. It is an unmistakable plea for the 'interpretative openness' (Hilmar Frank) which we regard today as the hallmark of his art.

Yet the man who stands behind these works of art (without intentionally hiding) should not be overlooked, nor should he be denigrated for sharing their multiplicity of meaning. What we see of him contains as many levels of meaning as the semiotic language of his paintings, yet no conclusive case can be made for the existence of reciprocal correspondences. His art and his life do not follow congruent paths. G. H. von Schubert's comment on Friedrich's 'strange pairing of temperamental states, tending to the deepest seriousness and the most lighthearted jesting' was cited in an earlier chapter, but while the works demonstrate the seriousness they contain no traces of the jesting. In any case, it would be out of the question to associate deep seriousness in a painting with the painter's temperamental state. What do the pictures betray of the darkening of the soul which his close friend Carl Gustav Carus perceived in Friedrich in the last decade of his life? Carus, a physician and amateur painter, wrote in a memoir about the 'unsettled states of mind, like a dark cloud, which led him to commit cruel injustices to those close to him'. 'In his distrust,' Carus wrote, 'he tortured himself and his family with ideas about his wife's infidelity, which were wholly figments of his imagination but were nonetheless enough to consume him entirely. These were followed by fits of brutal harshness against those close to him. I made the most earnest entreaties, and tried to make an impression on him as his physician, but all in vain.' A single work serves as the visual equivalent of this diagnosis: as Jensen argued, the watercolour version of *The Chalk Cliffs on Rügen* painted in the mid 1820s (ill. 78) can probably be interpreted as evidence of personal disturbance, which appears also to have affected the formal language and cast the uncertainty of self-doubt over the strict syntax of the original painting of 1818 (ill. 79).

163. *The Stages of Life*, **detail,**
1834–35, oil on canvas,
72.5 x 94 cm (28½ x 37 in.).
Museum der bildenden Künste, Leipzig.

The 'unsettled states of mind' Carus observed did not diminish the wide range of Friedrich's formal syntax in his last decade. *Northern Lights* (ill. 164) and *The Stages of Life* (ills 3, 163, 165) provide a clear demonstration: both were painted at about the same time, in the middle of the 1830s. Friedrich left *Northern Lights* unfinished after his stroke. Even disregarding the evidence of its incomplete state, such as the roughness of brushwork which would have been painted over, there still remains the impression of a turbulence in the elements comparable to little else in Friedrich's oeuvre. The two clumps of rock seem larger than they actually are, as a comparison with the two rear-view figures shows. The blocks have an elemental roughness which matches the 'wasteland' of the landscape. The narrow funnel is countered by the circumflex-shaped canopy of the sky, which transforms the devastation at ground level into a cosmic conflict, where some luridly coloured celestial gullet gapes wide, threatening to consume and destroy everything. A natural spectacle has become an apocalypse.

The Stages of Life shows some of the people who suffered the painter's 'fits of brutal harshness', depicted in a kind of family idyll. The two children playing with the Swedish flag have been identified as Friedrich's son Gustav Adolf (born 1824) and daughter Agnes (born 1823). The young woman watching them is thought to be their sister Emma (born 1819): their mother is not pictured. The man in a top hat may be the painter's nephew Johann Heinrich, and we can probably interpret the old man with a stick as a self-portrait. As early as 1816, when he was only forty-two, Louise Seidler had remarked in a letter to Goethe: 'I must say again how sorry I feel for Friedrich, already walking with a stick like an old man, and so gloomy and joyless from his own stubborn nature!'

There is no trace of gloominess in *The Stages of Life*, either in the old man or in the scene as a whole, which has something of a momentarily paused play about it. The title leaves no room for doubt about roles assigned to the five figures, but the certainty is relativized and given an enigmatic quality, because Friedrich does not arrange his allegory in the usual linear order but sets it out on an imaginary gameboard where old and young are intermingled. The sense of frozen time is reinforced by the five sailing boats, which also add to the mystification. The largest stands in the centre like a high tower and so establishes an axis of symmetry, although several things on either side detract from it. Just as the largest ship is flanked asymmetrically by the two boats close to the shore, so there is a lack of balance in the framing of the two children aligned with it (at the very centre of life!). Furthermore, the two boats are just as asymmetrical in their relationship with the old man as they are with the larger ship. The result is a kind of parallelogram which connects the old man to the tall ship: each is the largest in its category. This dual, or quadruple, relationship begins to dissolve when we look at the two ships near the horizon, which gives rise to new weightings. It brings to mind the title of one of Paul Klee's paintings: *boldly weighing*.

The five ships form an arrangement of verticals that recall musical notes; they seem to hang, light as air, above the calm, mirror-like surface of the sea, while the five human figures remain earthbound. However, the elements in this contrast are so enmeshed in the reciprocal relationships explained above that no polar tension arises. They do indeed represent stages of life, but are interwoven in a way that shows that Friedrich ultimately thought and composed in terms of formal relationships. While the old man is surveying the scene in front of him, the skilfully established artistic balance is, like the underlying barbs, seen only from the viewer's perspective. The symmetries, so essential in an icon, are shown to be disturbed asymmetrically by opposing forces, so that the resulting harmony is left unresolved and can be revoked.

However sombre Friedrich's attitude towards his family and friends may have been in the last ten years of his life, he could still summon up his wry humour. It sustained him when he suffered a stroke on 26 June 1835, which seems to have robbed his painting hand of its strength. He went to Teplitz (Teplice in Bohemia) to take the cure for six weeks, and from there he wrote to thank a friend for the gift of ten bottles of the 'very best wine': 'Perhaps the noble grape will also have a beneficial effect on my Better Self (!) and will result in new pictures, as different from those I have done up till now as wine is from beer.'

One such picture is *Seashore by Moonlight* (ill. 166), painted after the stroke. When Carus proposed that the Saxon Art Association purchase it in December 1837 (they agreed), he suggested that it might well be the last work from the artist, as he was 'stricken by paralysis'. Friedrich eventually died in May 1840, in his sixty-sixth year. Taking these circumstances into account, it seems impossible to avoid seeing premonitions of death in the picture (Helmut Leppien). But the memento mori is no more obvious here than it is in *Sea Piece by Moonlight* (ill. 167), where a mighty sailing ship – it could be a ship of the dead – fills the centre of the picture. What makes the later picture different is not the proximity of death but the disabled artist's newly refined orchestration of his well-tried structural elements. He combined a triptych

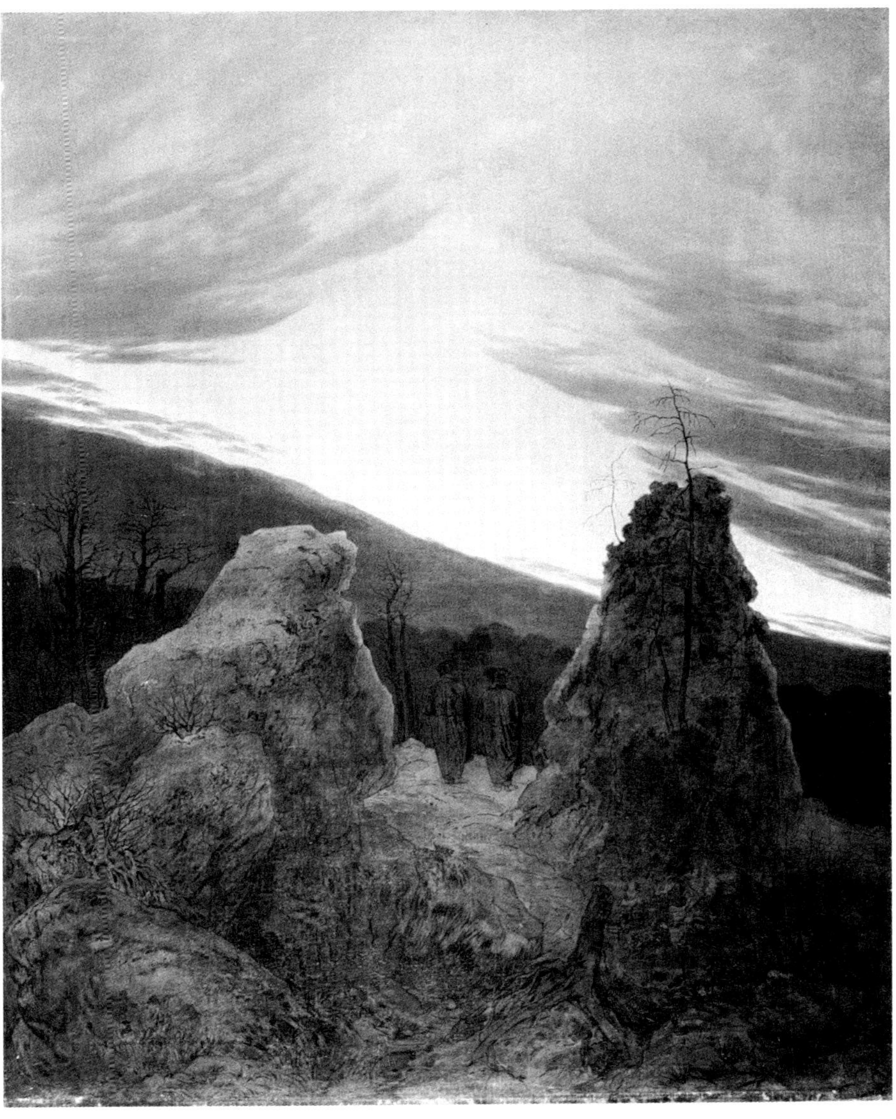

164. *Northern Lights,*
1834–35, oil on canvas,
143 x 108.5 cm (56¼ x 42¾ in.).
Formerly Nationalgalerie, Berlin (destroyed).

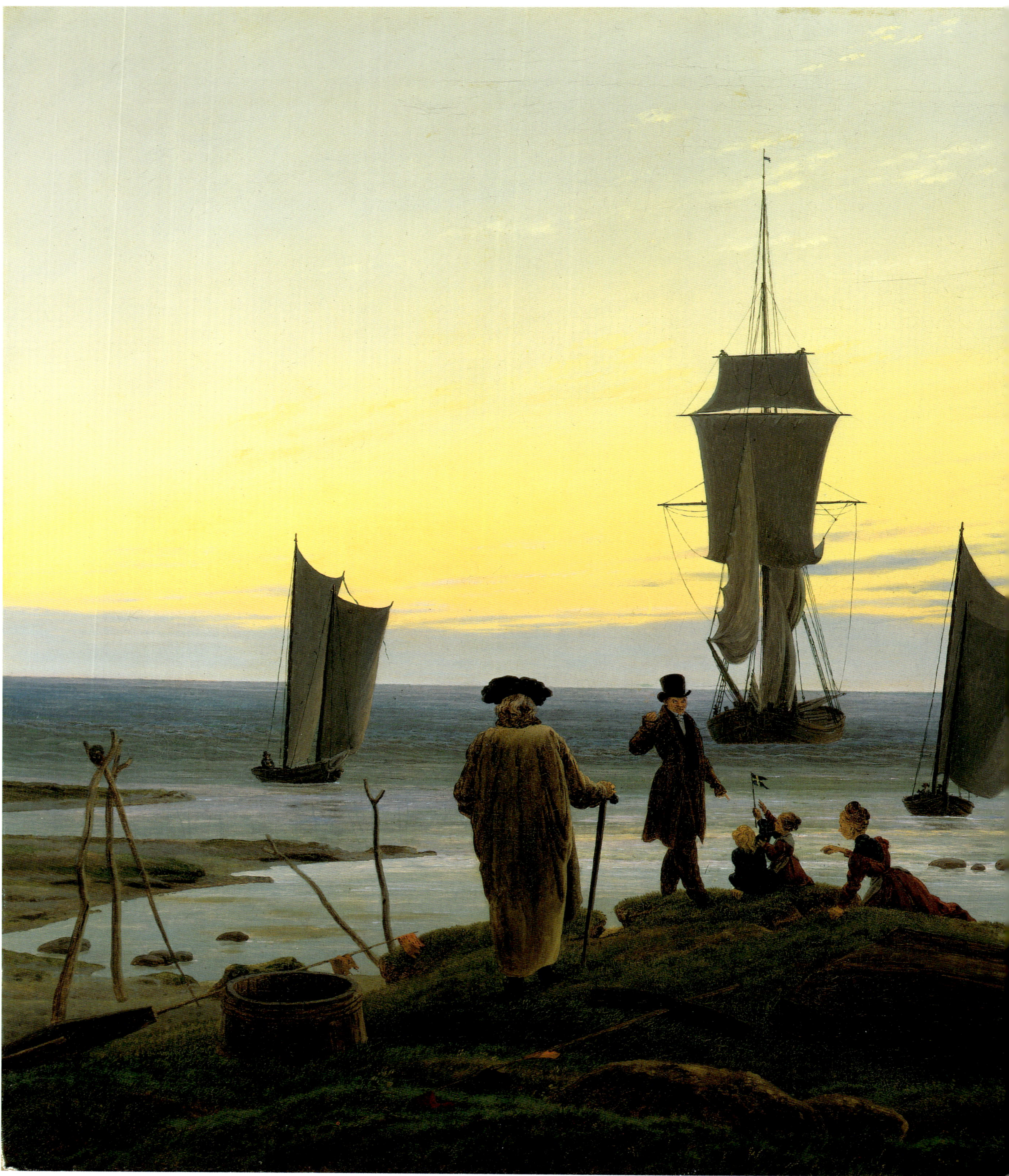

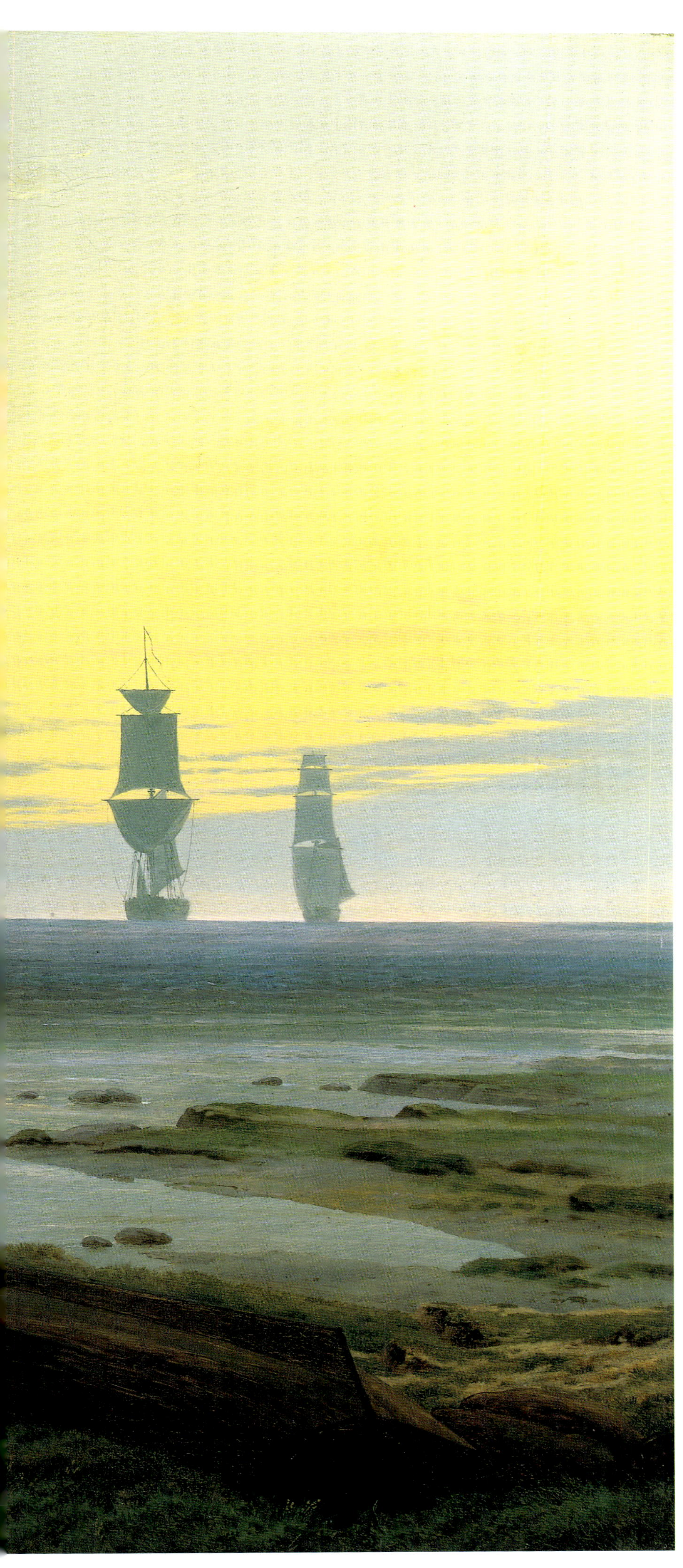

165. ***The Stages of Life,***
1834–35, oil on canvas,
72.5 x 94 cm (28½ x 37 in.).
Museum der bildenden Künste, Leipzig.

scheme with a vertical reflection, and the resulting axial cross creates a very high degree of symmetry. The triple rhythm comes from the vertical lines of two sailing boats. Dividing the picture into three balanced sections, they frame the central field, which is lit by the moon (visible just below the edge of the picture). The calm sea lets the reflection stretch as far as the stones on the shore. The brightest patch of light is in the immediate foreground. The vertical central axis marked by the moon and its reflection is crossed by the line of the horizon which divides the picture area in half. The two sailing boats and the moon's reflection form a depression, which is countered in the sky by the canopy of clouds – an extended circumflex accent. The density that this axial cross gives to the construction can be seen if we look at the picture upside down. The sea then becomes the sky, and the clouds become a floating bank of fog, lit by the moonlight.

Friedrich died in Dresden on 7 May 1840. The register of deaths lists the cause as 'pulmonary failure'. The following obituary was published in the *Leipziger Zeitung* on 13 May: 'In the late Professor Friedrich, whose funeral on the 10th, in the new Altstadt Cemetery, drew so large an attendance, the city's art lovers honoured the master who was the first among present-day artists to bring about proper recognition of the significance of landscape as a hieroglyph of all-powerful nature, by means of acclaimed works of art. We may therefore rejoice to learn that, only a few weeks before his death, some drawings – the only things remaining from his oeuvre – found a generous buyer in the Grand Duke [later to become Alexander II of Russia]. Illness of many years' duration made this honour particularly welcome for the sake of his family: a widow and three children.'

The artist's contact with the Russian court, which had begun with the purchase of *On the Sailing Boat* (ill. 77), was strengthened by Vasily Andreyevich Zhukovsky, who had become a friend of Friedrich in 1821 and took drawing lessons from him. As a State Councillor he acted as intermediary in the sale of several paintings to St Petersburg, and also arranged for a pension for his friend when he became ill. Unfortunately, payment was delayed by labyrinthine bureaucracy so that it was Friedrich's widow who eventually received it. Zhukovsky mentioned his last visit to Friedrich in his diary, on 19 March 1840: 'To Friedrich. Sad ruin. He wept like a child.'

The obituary, probably written or suggested by Carus, represents the first posthumous assessment of Friedrich's position as an artist. It runs counter to the taste of the times, which no longer wanted 'deeply felt, spiritual saturation ... with nature' from artists, but only 'faithful aping of objects, that is, their length, breadth and height, and forms and colours'. This was Friedrich's critical comment on an age which could no longer learn anything from his art, as it did not know what to make of a 'hieroglyph of all-powerful nature'. The word 'hieroglyph' came from the language used to express the most secret realms of German Romanticism. As a symbol of obscurity – the Rosetta Stone had only been deciphered in 1822 – the hieroglyph embodied the distinction of mythical mystification.

How obscure, Romantic or hieroglyphic was Friedrich? The most seductive definition of Romanticism was formulated by Novalis: 'By giving higher meaning to the mundane, a mysterious appearance to the ordinary, the distinction of the unknown to what is known, the guise of infinity to the finite, I romanticize it. The operation is reversed for those things that are higher, unknown, mystical and infinite: they are elucidated by the association, gaining a colloquial means of expression.'

Both of these are applicable to Friedrich: the imbuing of every sensory impression with depth and spirituality ('the divine is everywhere') and also the reverse operation, which perceives mystery and infinity in the finite and finds a 'colloquial means of expression' for this objectification. Another idea expressed by Novalis, 'reciprocal raising and lowering', was one of the most fruitful reciprocal relationships in nineteenth-century art, and is connected with the questioning of traditional iconographic conventions. From this point onwards, the profane and everyday could be ennobled or even sanctified, and likewise a mystical event could be clothed in the everyday. Delacroix's Liberty secularized the Church Militant but at the same time raised the nameless warrior woman to the status of allegory. This kind of reciprocity created the category *allégorie réelle*, the oxymoron coined by Courbet to describe his *Atelier* (1855). The genre of 'real allegory' was pioneered by Friedrich in his iconization of landscape.

Another passage from Novalis underlines the fact that Friedrich was a contemporary of the Romantics: 'Now we see ... that there is also an external world inside us, which is joined with our inner being in the same way as the external world outside us is tied to our outer being; the former and the latter are associated in the same way that our inner and outer beings are. We can therefore perceive the inner being and soul of nature only through thought, just as we perceive the outer being and physical form of nature only through sensations.'

An earlier chapter refers to Friedrich's common ground with the philosophy of Schleiermacher, but here I am more concerned to show how his image of the world fits into the tradition of thought and art stemming from the Reformation, for it was from his Lutheran-Evangelical faith that he derived the basic tenets that determined his artistic decisions. The man who appeared on the cover of *Der Spiegel*, surveying the calamities and catastrophes of twentieth-century Germany (ill. 2), was a trivialization of the image. Friedrich's *Wanderer above a Sea of Mists* (ill. 1) gazes out questioningly at a mountain landscape. He belongs to a species favoured by Friedrich: men and women – usually seen from behind – who are confronted with a choice or have already made one. With his own religious and philosophical choices made, Friedrich himself participated in the decision-making processes of his protagonists. The making of choices is an essential component of his art and his formal strategies.

The forking of the ways was one of the simplifying formulas already used by artists in Luther's time who were enlisted into the cause of the Reformation. They had chosen their own side and they wanted to persuade the public to join it too. In the thirteen pairs of pictures making up his *Passional Christi et Antichristi* (1521), Lucas Cranach the Elder compared the abuse of faith in the perverted Roman church with the new, true faith (ill. 186). His son Lucas Cranach the Younger undertook a similar confrontation in his *Difference between the true religion of Christ and the false idolatrous teaching of the Antichrist* (ill. 185). The papal church is depicted as a market; business is brisk, power and influence are in dispute – the priests huddle together and pay no heed to the wrath of God, who rains down hailstones upon them. There is no pomp or vain hierarchy on the opposing side; Luther shows his congregation the direct path to heaven. There is however one mediating factor, represented by a 'cross in the mountains' which foreshadows the one in *The Tetschen Altar*. The mountains are a place where God may be experienced: there is no need to go by way of the church, either as an institution or a building. Meanwhile, Hans Holbein juxtaposed the true and false forgiveness of sins (1523–24; ill. 187). False absolution is the work of wily priests, who profit from the trade in indulgences; true forgiveness is dispensed by God Himself, reaching down from

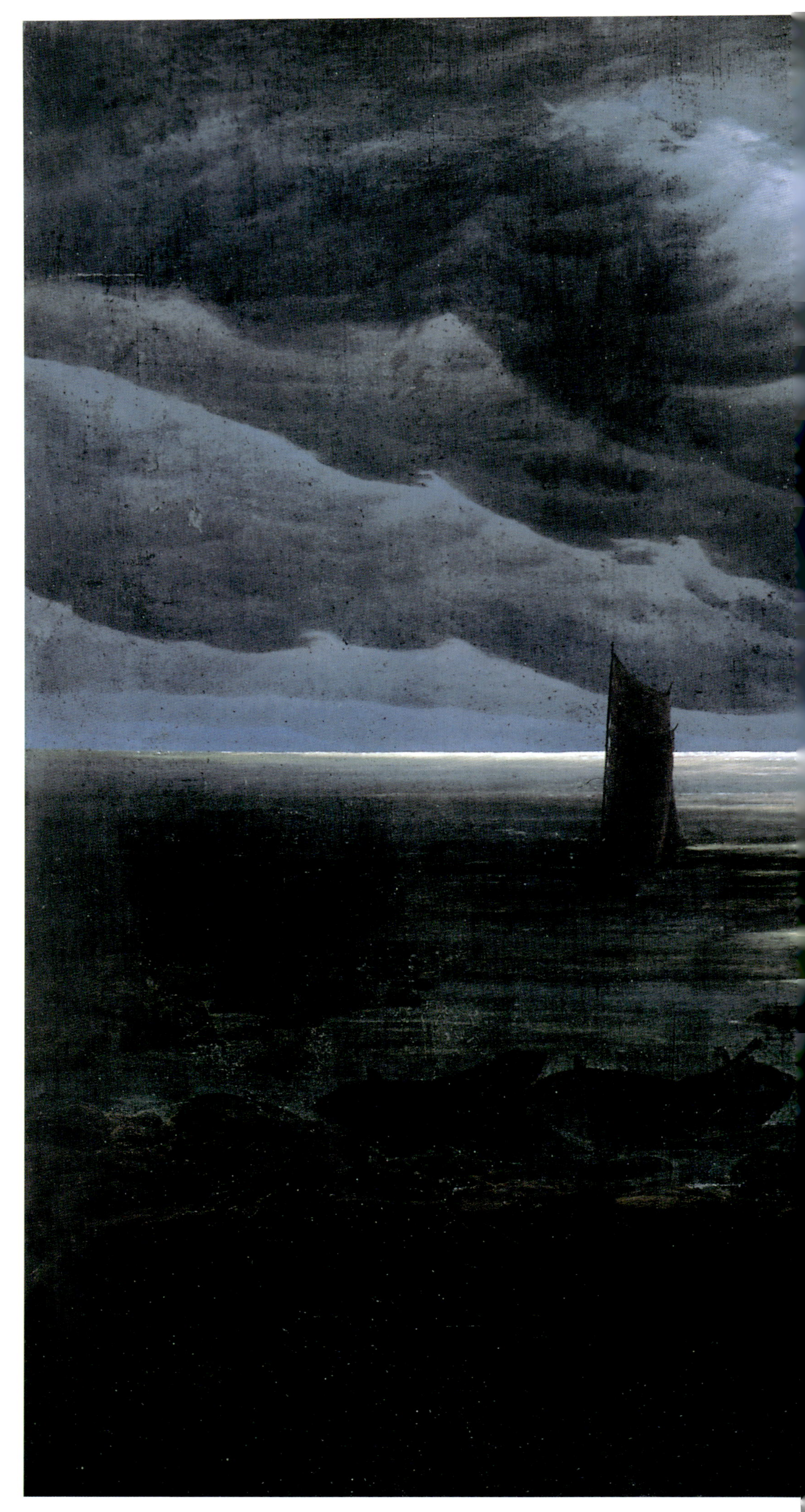

166. ***Seashore by Moonlight,***
1835–36, oil on canvas,
134 × 169.2 cm (52¾ × 66½ in.).
Hamburger Kunsthalle, Hamburg.

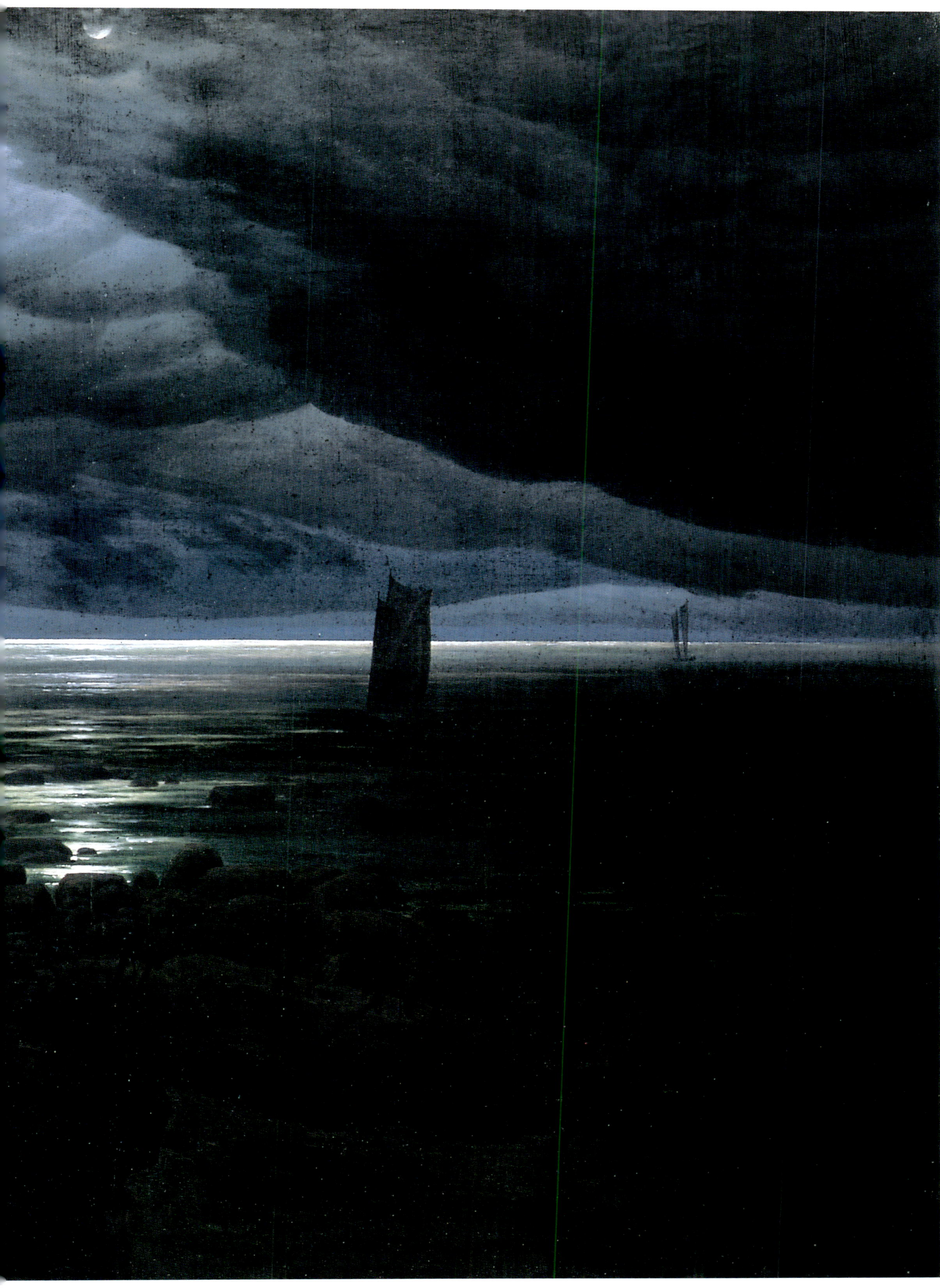

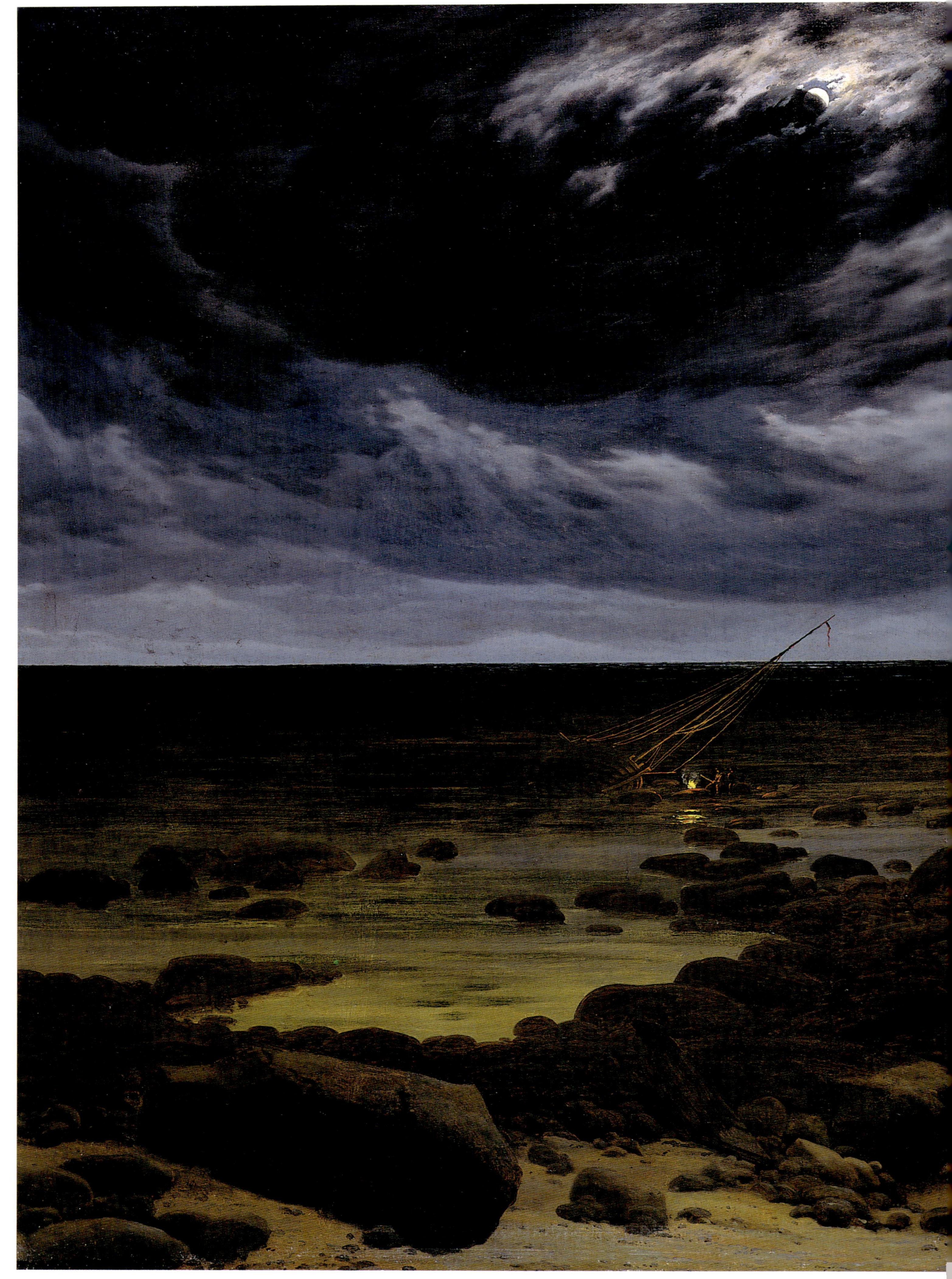

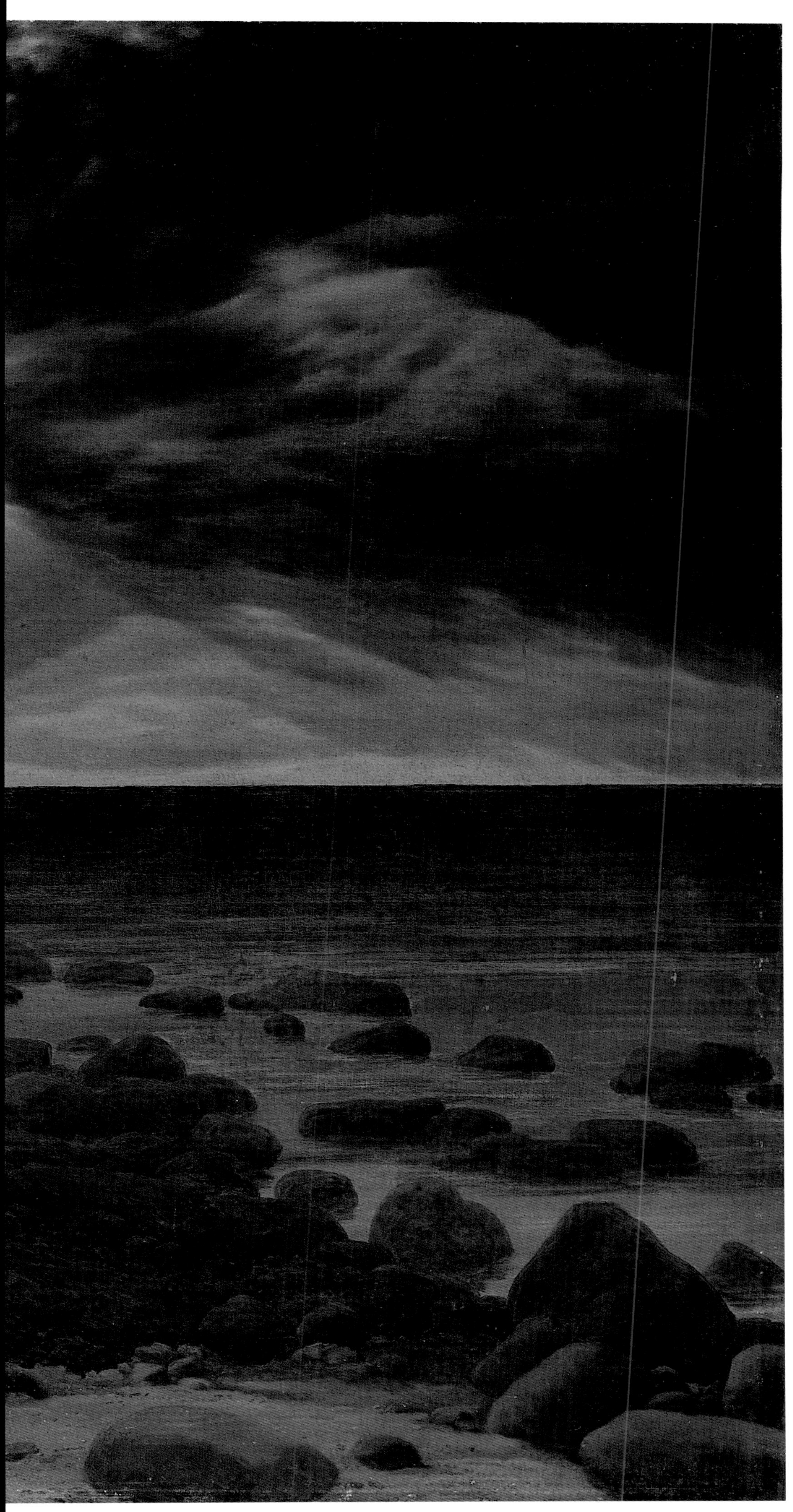

167. ***Sea Piece by Moonlight,***
1830, oil on canvas,
77 x 97 cm (30¼ x 38¼ in.).
Nationalgalerie, Berlin.

the clouds to famous sinners such as adulterous David and idolatrous Manasseh and also to the anonymous repentant sinner. Once again, the open air stands for the immediacy of true belief, and the enclosed building of the Roman church represents its falsification.

Friedrich's pictures were not tracts, but his absorption of the arguments of Lutheran propaganda was total. His artistic philosophy made an absolute distinction between right and wrong, between true and feigned sensation, especially where the errors of his contemporaries were concerned, and in particular the Nazarenes with their Catholic sympathies. It is as if he believed that popery was the cause of all their weaknesses, from the formal splendour and pomp to the illusionism and empty virtuosity, and above all behind the so-called 'simplicity' of those who painted 'Mary with her milk dried and a starving Christ-child in her arms'.

Friedrich also thematicized decision-making in the subject matter of his pictures. *Autumn* (ill. 143) shows the believer at a forking of the ways, and uses the schematic opposition of good and evil which Protestant propagandists employed in pictorial form until well into the nineteenth century. His paintings of ruined churches predict the end of 'the time of the glory of the temple and its servants', and proclaim 'a different desire for clarity and truth'. In the mingling of dark and light he finds a painterly metaphor for the end of the old and the dawn of the new.

The figures Friedrich painted with their backs to the viewer are also the products of a didactic iconography. Their devout concentration contains the religious idea of true contemplation of nature which Daniel Chodowiecki contrasted with 'modish sensibility'. The philosopher Georg Christoph Lichtenberg wrote in 1780 of Chodowiecki's couple watching a sunset (ill. 176): 'An artist would be hard put to express more emotion in figures who turn their faces almost entirely away from us, while everything about them is stable and restful; it shines forth here from the innocent gaze of the girl and the way the man holds his head. They are enjoying the sight of the setting sun with the calm feeling that slowly fills the whole soul without taking it by storm, just as the ripples gently lapping in the distance will fill the crimsoned surface of the water in which the sun's fire is reflected.' An heir of the Enlightenment, Lichtenberg did not want to utter the words 'God' or 'Creator', but the indefinable quality of the emotion moved him so strongly that he refrained from drowning these 'mysteries' in words.

Chodowiecki worked with the moralist's admonitory finger, but Friedrich did not, so it would be wrong to reduce his pictorial structures to dialectical confrontations. Even in a pair of pictures on a religious theme, exploring the opposition between the old church and the new faith, he avoids polemics and accommodates the confessional theme in the manifold context of his human figures' sense of the world and sense of self. The artist in Friedrich prefers the potential for many meanings and multiple interpretations to any unambiguous, polemical partisanship. The two Weimar sepias (ills 8 and 9) present a choice between two religious positions: the real-world faith of the elderly couple, based on useful activity, and the corporate, solemn procession of monks, making their way not to a church, admittedly, but to a crucifix in the open air.

The Monk by the Sea and *The Abbey in the Oak Wood* (ills 22 and 23) are also visual metaphors for different religious points of view, but that is not all. We can regard them as formal manifestos, prototypes of the painter's spatial structures, his horizontal and vertical methods of organization. The monk is a wanderer without a goal; he is open to the experience of the sublimity of nature, but God the Creator is concealed from him, for He is everywhere, in the grains of sand just as much as in the clouds. On the other hand, the procession of monks take a path which is man-made yet loses itself in the labyrinth of gravestones, bare trees and the ruins of the church. The funeral party are following a ritual, and perhaps that is what is being borne to its last resting place.

The Schwerin and Dortmund *Winter Landscapes* (ills 33 and 34) form a pair. The first picture shows a wanderer caught in a tight space between two trees; in the second he has freed himself and prays to a crucifix sheltered by a tree, paying no attention to the Gothic church which appears like a vision in the background. The praying man has no need of the building but the painter does, for he makes it participate in a dialogue. The outline of the church echoes the shape of the pine trees; an accord which enhances the vision and suggests that Friedrich wanted to leave the reciprocal relationship in the balance. This church does not seem to represent the end of 'the time of the glory of the temple'.

Friedrich's language is at its most powerful when it does not express an either/or relationship but instead offers several levels of interpretation. In *The Chalk Cliffs on Rügen* (ill. 79), the foreground is depicted as intensely as the distance, allowing the painting to be interpreted as a dual self-portrait. In *The Sea of Ice* (ill. 159) the destructive force of nature is a symbol of resistance, yet it remains ambivalent. The fascination of *The Large Enclosure* (ill. 162) also rests on a formal paradox. We are drawn into curving, airy space but never reach a vanishing point. Anyone who studies Friedrich's pictures intending to discover their structures – this text contains numerous pointers to them – will understand the artist's words, quoted earlier in this chapter, as an invitation to read more than one meaning in them: he wrote that it is 'an artist's gift, perhaps his greatest, to stimulate the spirit, and arouse thoughts, feelings and sensations in the viewer, even if they are not his own'.

We have seen how Friedrich's thinking followed a path leading from the iconographic contrasts of painting of the Reformation era to subtle 'not-only-but-also' alternatives, and that he ultimately gave up himself, and his own words, to the judgment of the viewer, allowing them a free choice. Perhaps this explains how the public came to identify with *The Wanderer above a Sea of Mists*, on T-shirts, coffee mugs and CD covers. The Wanderer's own stance as a viewer is open to receive many subjects, interior and exterior, and his inner eye is as likely to be contemplating the nightmares that *Der Spiegel* showed passing before him as anything else.

The possible interpretations that Friedrich offers to the viewer are all directed at the viewer's ability to use works of art to question himself. The artist himself does not present us with unshakeable certainties. His work fits in line with the tradition leading from German Romanticism to Parisian Surrealism, as Albert Béguin traced it just before the outbreak of the European disaster that was depicted from a German standpoint on the cover of *Der Spiegel*. In *L'âme romantique et le rêve* (1938), cited in the first chapter of this book, Béguin wrote that the followers of those movements knew that 'human dignity resides precisely in the desperate devotion, the absurd hope which feeds even on the depths of uncertainty'.

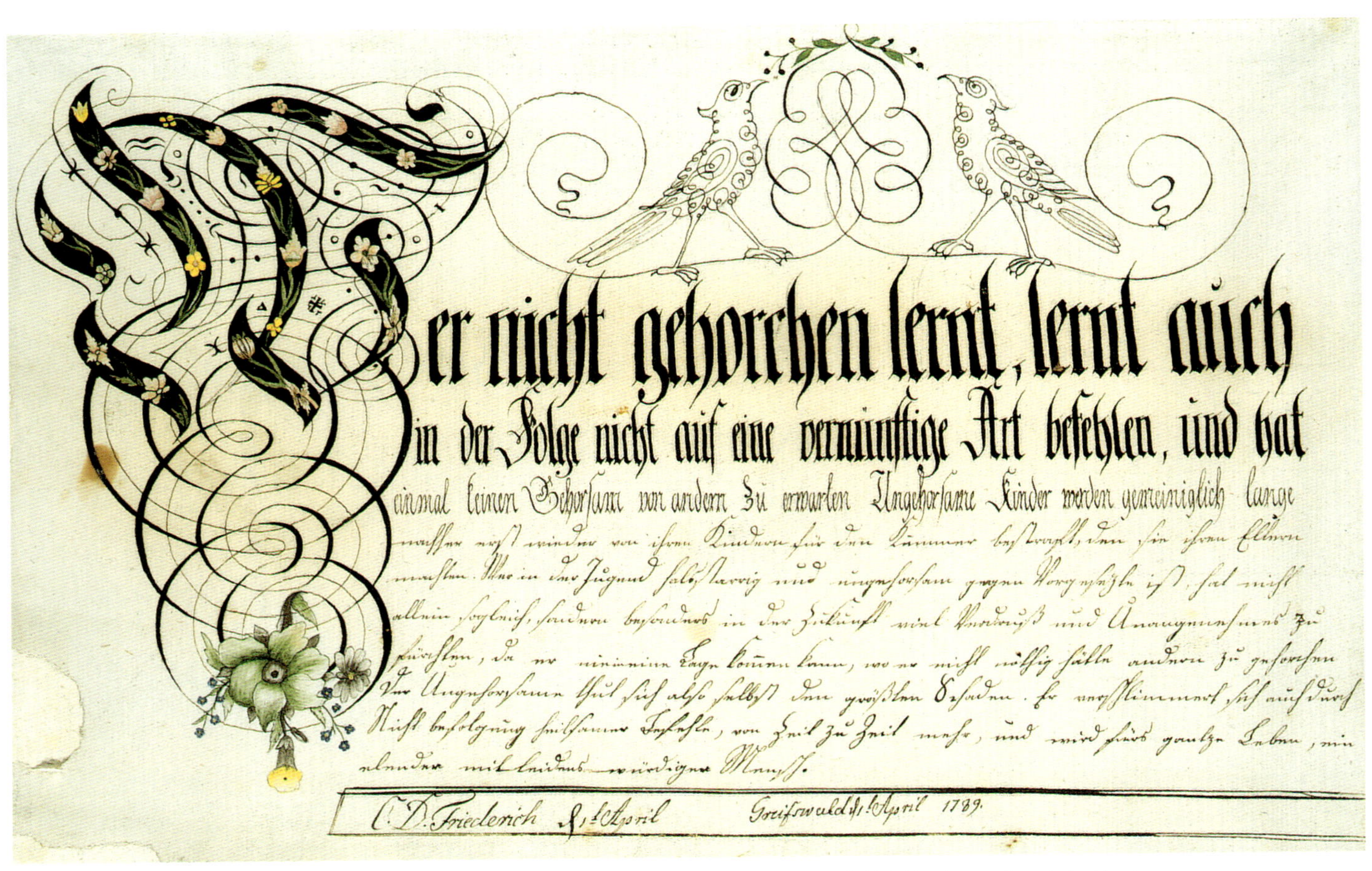

168. Page of writing, 1789, Indian ink, ink and watercolour, 20.2 × 31.8 cm (7⅞ × 12½ in.). Hamburger Kunsthalle, Hamburg.

APPENDICES

I Friedrich and Jens Juel

II Rear-view figures

III The 'emptiness' of Friedrich and the 'fullness' of his contemporaries

IV The 'emptiness' of Friedrich and the 'fullness' of didacticism

APPENDIX I

Friedrich and Jens Juel

The influence of Jens Juel on Friedrich, a student of his, was considerable. It was particularly strong as regards the fundamental models of Friedrich's spatial articulation, his vertically and horizontally ordered structural schemes, as Danish scholars (Anders Kolb, Kasper Monrad) have well established. Friedrich could have encountered the same juxtaposition in a pair of Juel's best known paintings. *View Across the Little Belt from Hindsgavl* (ill. 169) has a symmetrical structure. The central depression is framed vertically by the trees at the side, and directs the gaze inescapably into the distance. Like the balanced sides of this basin, the human figures stand in paired relationships to one another.

In the second painting (ill. 170), the sense of distance is reduced. The horizontal planes are forerunners of Friedrich's horizontally organized landscapes. The two horsemen are also subject to this scheme, and do not come forward from the depths of the space.

In Juel's *Landscape with Northern Lights* (ill. 171), nature is closely observed from the realm of rapt withdrawal that always fascinated Friedrich. The hour is uncertain: the sky is still light, but the darkness of night already lies across the land, which is ceremonially enhanced by the Northern Lights. However, the peasant by the fire is oblivious to this phenomenon, which is reserved for the painter and the viewer of his picture. This world is given an otherworldly quality. The fence in the centre of the picture separates the dull, material 'here' of the foreground from the 'there' of the Lights and also directs our eyes towards them. The tension thus created anticipates Friedrich's work.

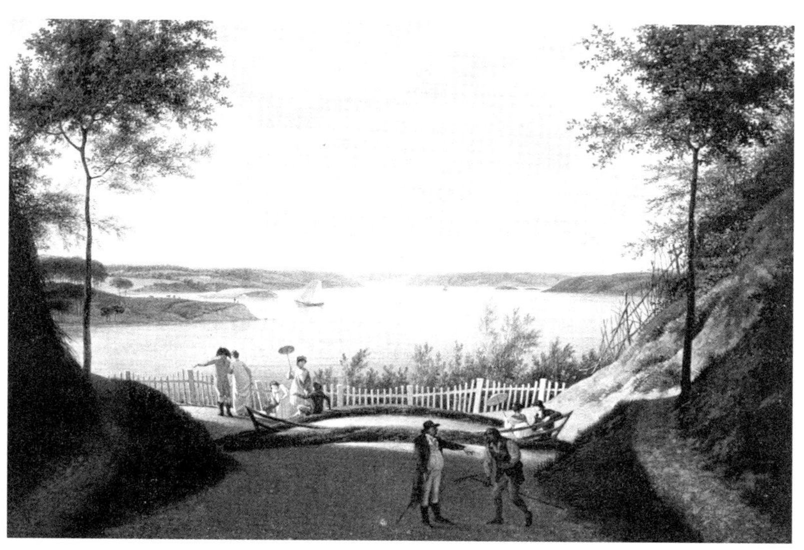

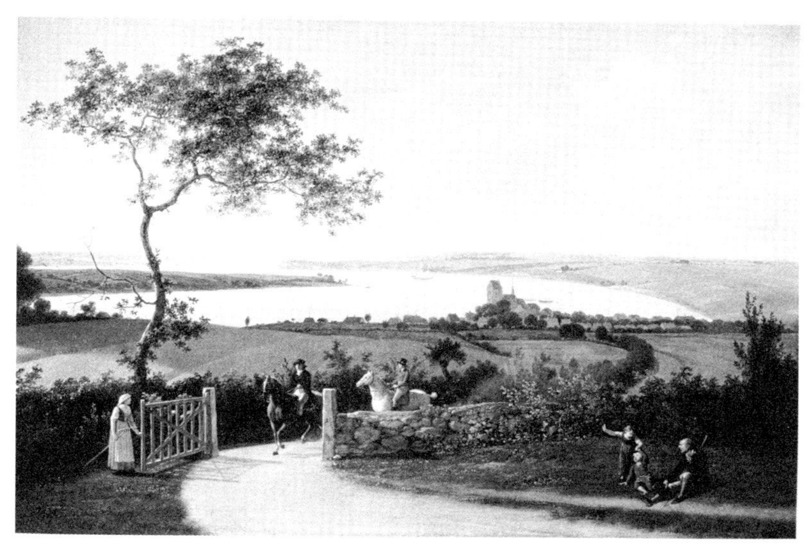

169. Jens Juel,
View across the Little Belt from Hindsgavl,
c. 1800, oil on canvas, 42 × 62.5 cm (16½ × 24½ in.).
Thorvaldsens Museum, Copenhagen.

170. Jens Juel,
View of the Little Belt, seen from a height near Middelfart,
c. 1800, oil on canvas, 42.3 × 62.5 cm (16⅝ × 24½ in.).
Thorvaldsens Museum, Copenhagen.

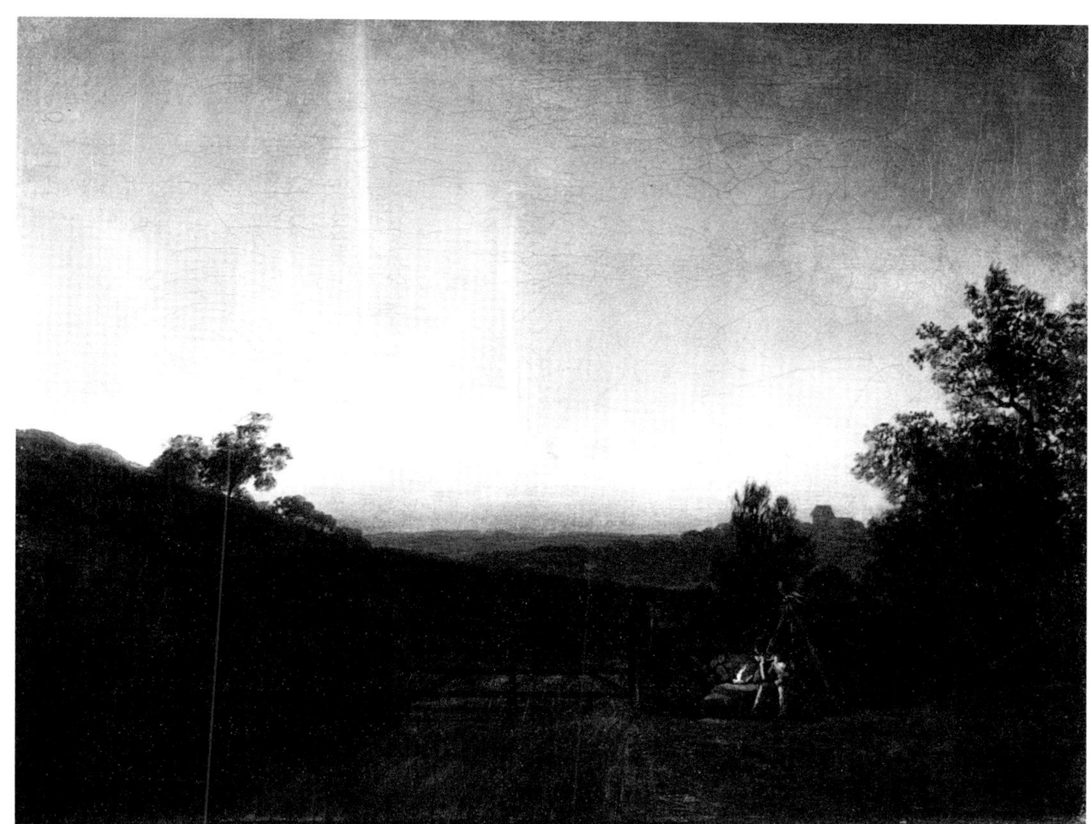

171. Jens Juel,
Landscape with Northern Lights,
c. 1790, oil on canvas, 31.1 × 39.5 cm (12¼ × 15½ in.).
Ny Carlsberg Glyptothek, Copenhagen.

APPENDIX II

Rear-view figures

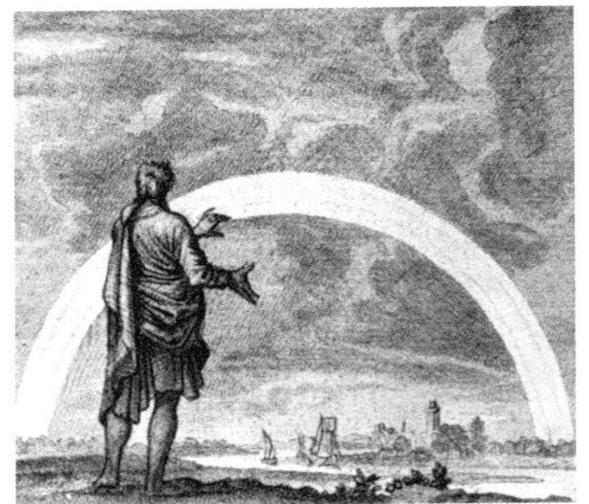

172. Jan Luyken,
The Rainbow,
1700, etching, 10.3 × 11.9 cm (4 × 4¾ in.).
Kupferstichkabinett, Hamburger Kunsthalle, Hamburg.

173. Michelangelo di Pace,
Rear View of a Man,
ink and wash, 32.5 × 22.4 cm (12¾ × 8¾ in.).
Graphische Sammlung Albertina, Vienna.

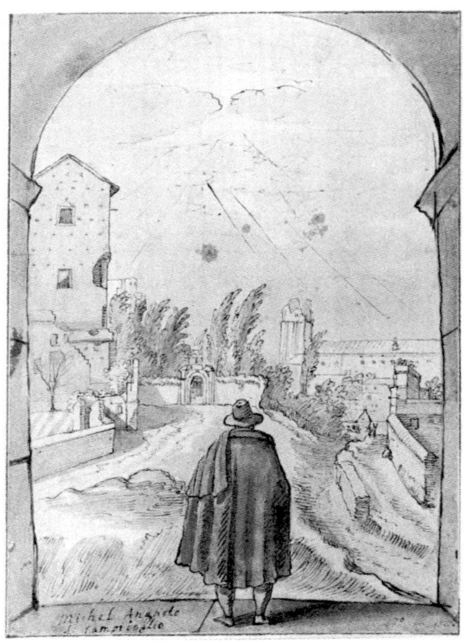

Friedrich's figures seen from behind are innovations in as much as they embody expressive formulas (*Pathosformeln*, in Aby Warburg's term) for which there are no precursors. Herbert von Einem long ago drew attention to the engravings made by the Dutch artist Jan Luyken for an *Ethica naturalis*, published around 1700 (ill. 172). The self-confident, explanatory or didactic gestures of Luyken's figures is never encountered in any of Friedrich's. His rear-view figures are not confronted with spectacular views, or involved in a dialogue with them; instead, they communicate admiration in a still and wordless way. Nor have they made a decision to walk out into the world, like the figure placed exactly in the middle of an archway by Michelangelo di Pace (ill. 173). Johann Christian Reinhardt (1761–1847) later realized the potential in this figure by copying the original drawing, but turning the stationary man into one who has already set off on his journey.

Johann Heinrich Wilhelm Tischbein's *Goethe at the Window of his Lodgings in Rome* (ill. 174) is also very different from any of Friedrich's rear-view figures. Like a snapshot, it spontaneously captures a moment when Goethe was attracted by the light and life in the street below. Tischbein drew his own impression of those impressions, and no sense of tension between interior and exterior is created. But the drawing does share some similarities with Friedrich's painting *Woman at the Window* (ill. 66): we see nothing or almost nothing of what is happening outside, and the room indoors is bare and empty in both cases. That changes as soon as emotions are visibly expressed, as seen in Schwind's woman at a window (ill. 175); here, description takes the place of suggestion. The interior is made comfortable, and the world outside is inviting.

In Friedrich's depiction of couples, Enlightenment worldliness is transformed into silent contemplation, a step that was prefigured in Chodowiecki's pictures of a man and woman watching a sunset (ills 176 and 177). The expansively gesturing couple made another appearance in 1783, when the engraver Johann W. Meil put them on the title page of Bernard de Fontenelle's *Entretiens sur la pluralité des mondes* (ill. 178).

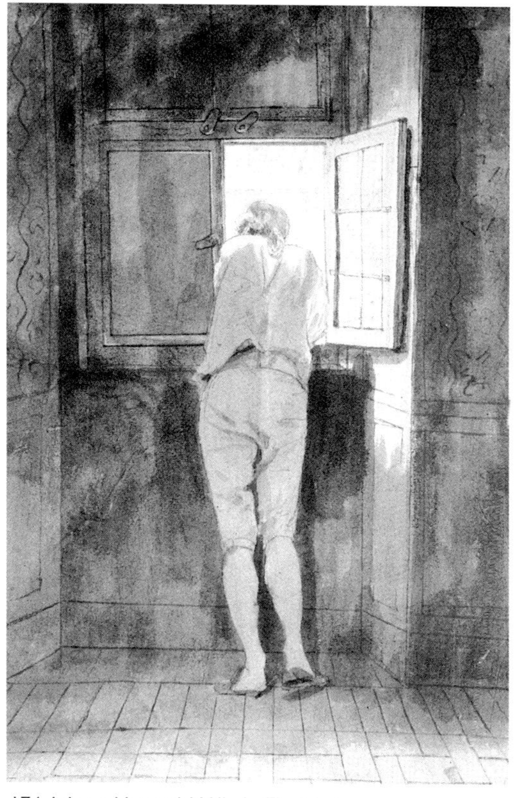

174. Johann Heinrich Wilhelm Tischbein,
Goethe at the Window of his Lodgings in Rome,
1787, watercolour, pencil and ink,
41.5 x 26.6 cm (16¼ x 10½ in.).
Freies Deutsches Hochstift, Frankfurt.

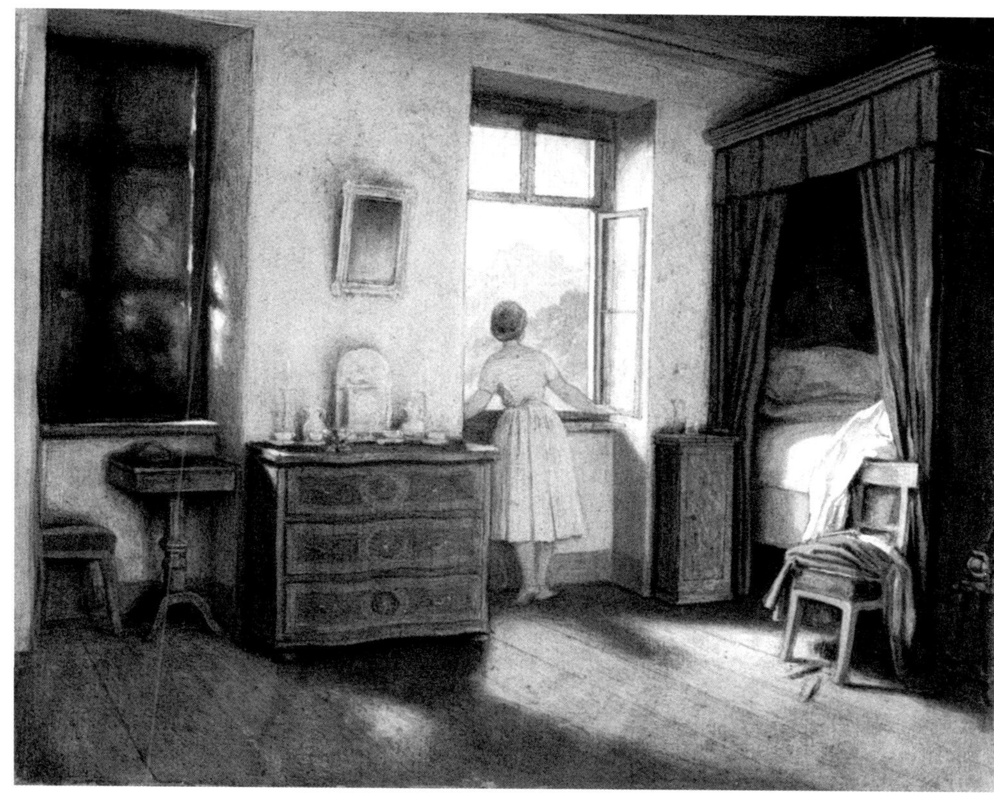

175. Moritz von Schwind,
The Morning Hour,
c. 1860, oil on canvas,
34.8 x 41.9 cm (13⅝ x 16½ in.).
Schack-Galerie, Munich.

176 and 177. Daniel Nicolas Chodowiecki,
True Feeling and Affected Feeling,
engravings taken from *Actions naturelles et affectées de la vie*, 1780.

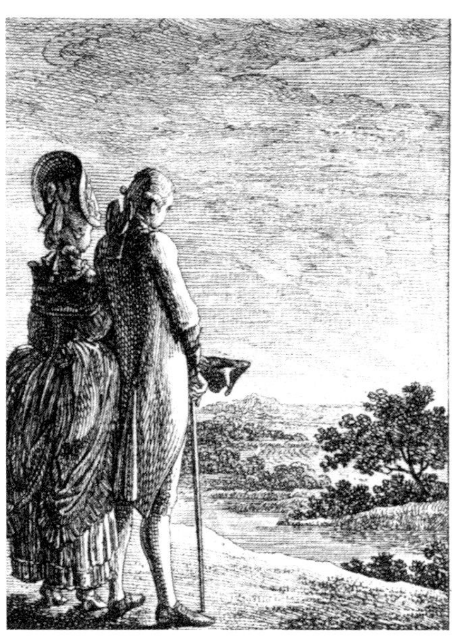

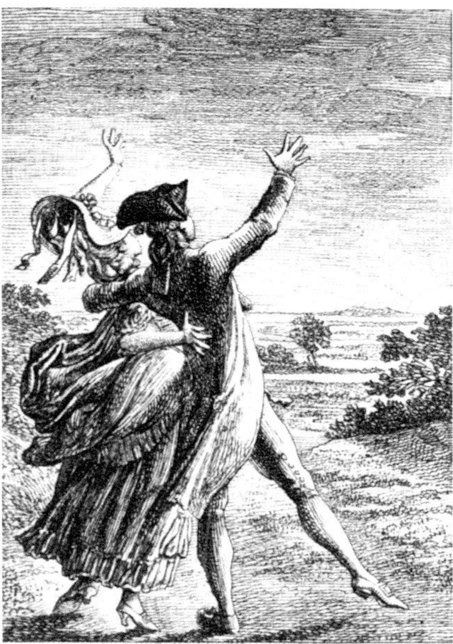

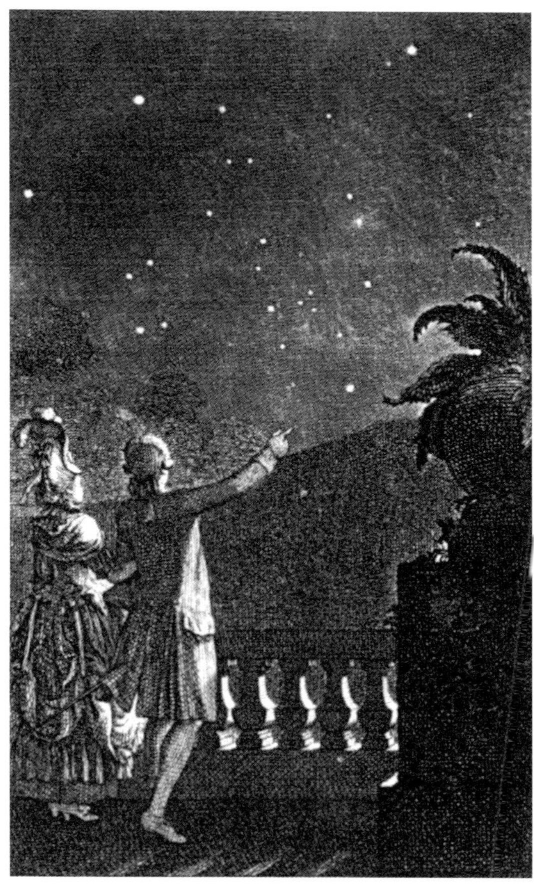

178. Johann Wilhelm Meil, Frontispiece from *Entretiens sur la pluralité des mondes,* by Bernard de Fontenelle, Berlin, 1783.

APPENDIX III

The 'emptiness' of Friedrich and the 'fullness' of his contemporaries

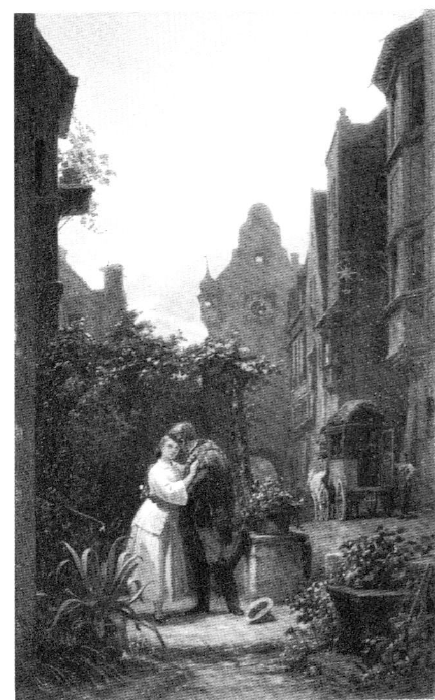

179. Carl Spitzweg, *The Farewell*, c. 1855, oil on canvas, 53.9 x 32 cm (21¼ x 12⅝ in.). Schack-Galerie, Munich.

Friedrich's conception of the transitory quality of human creations leaves the last word to nature: she takes possession of buildings by smothering them in her abundance. This topos, which has an association with the elegiac poetry of graveyards, goes back to the eighteenth century (ill. 182). Friedrich was to simplify it and put emptiness in the place of the picturesque abundance of allusions.

Friedrich's diatribe against a painter of overfilled 'curiosity shops' may have been aimed at Joseph Anton Koch, who squeezed as many elements of natural scenery into his landscapes as he could (ill. 180). The abundance of detail prevents space from entering the picture at all, and the multitude of incident claims so much of the viewer's attention that the eye cannot rest and find the hidden places to which Friedrich wanted to guide his viewers.

Runge's series of etchings, *The Times of Day*, are also essentially conglomerates, whose convolutions draw upon ever new fields of reference (ill. 181). Goethe and his adviser on artistic matters, J. H. Meyer, called it 'a true labyrinth of obscure associations, making the viewer well-nigh giddy with almost unfathomable meaning'. Friedrich had no aspirations to construct such complicated syntax.

Finally, in Biedermeier painting we encounter a theatre where interconnecting episodes, stories within stories, are displayed in detailed architectural sets. The outcome is a overall impression of an intimate, intricate and self-contained world (see page 271). Spitzweg was just one devotee of this sentimental idiom (ill. 179). Its core metaphor is the arbour or summerhouse, which in proverbial German usage meant a place of seclusion, hidden away from the public world and its discords. Dissemination and consolidation of this bourgeois ideology was served by the wide-circulation 'family magazine' *Die Gartenlaube* (*The Arbour*), which began publication in 1853 and ran until 1944 (re-named *Die neue Gartenlaube* in 1938).

181. Philipp Otto Runge,
Noon,
1803, engraving,
31.3 × 26.1 cm (12⅜ × 10¼ in.).
Hamburger Kunsthalle, Hamburg.

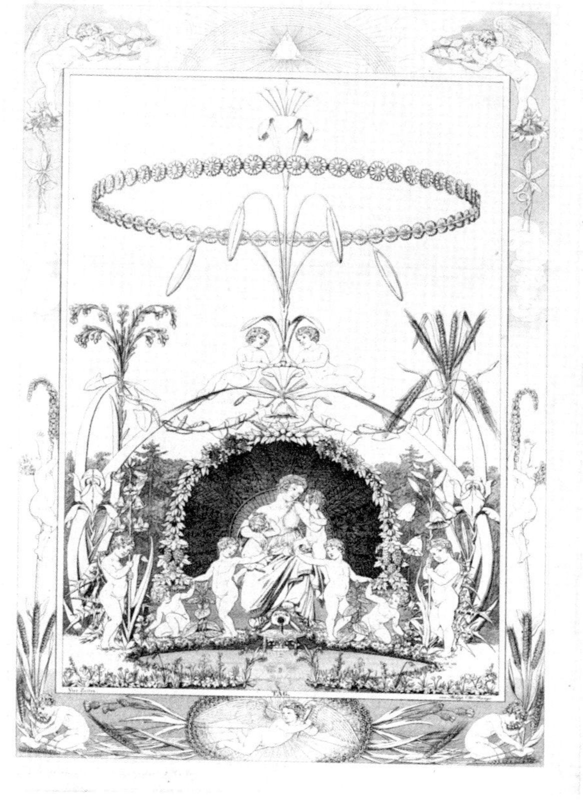

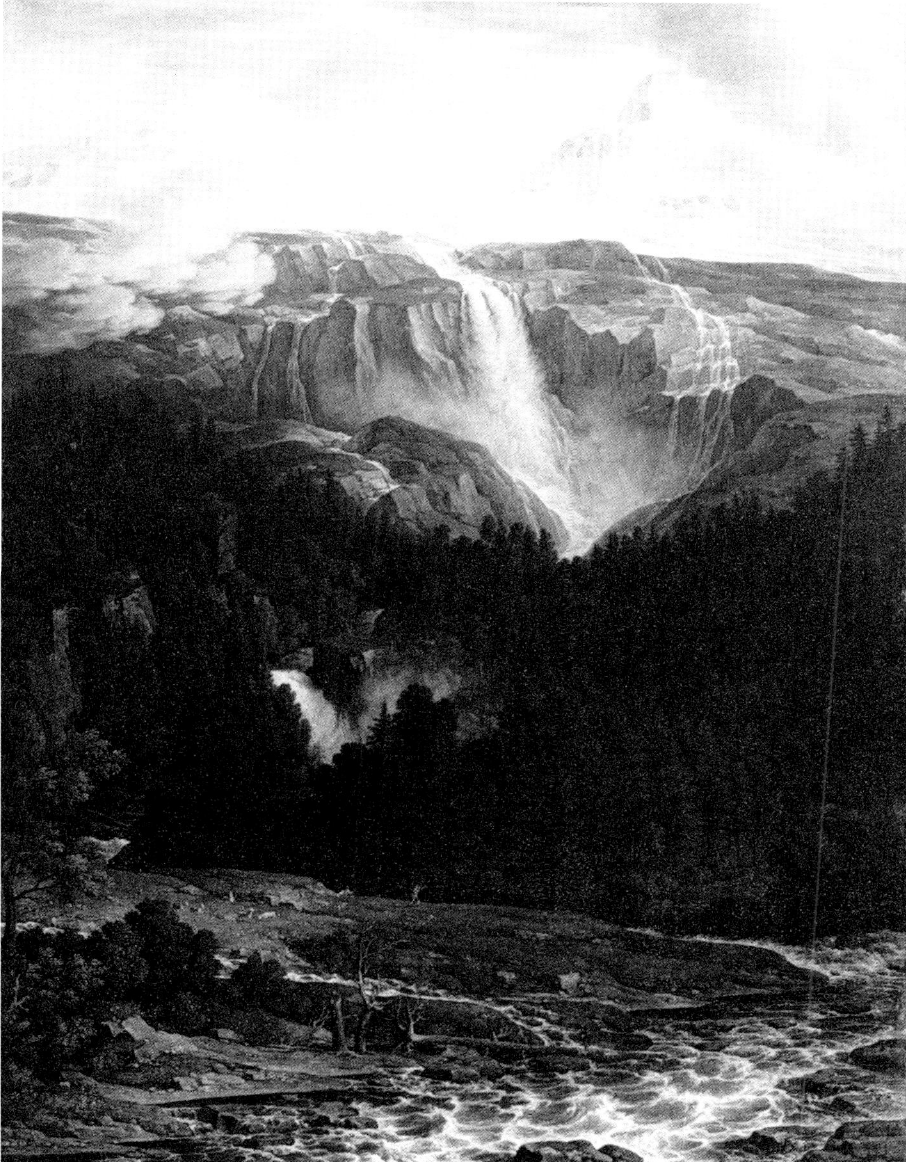

180. Joseph Anton Koch,
The Schmadribach Waterfall,
1811, oil on canvas, 123 × 93.5 cm (48⅜ × 36¾ in.).
Museum der bildenden Künste, Leipzig.

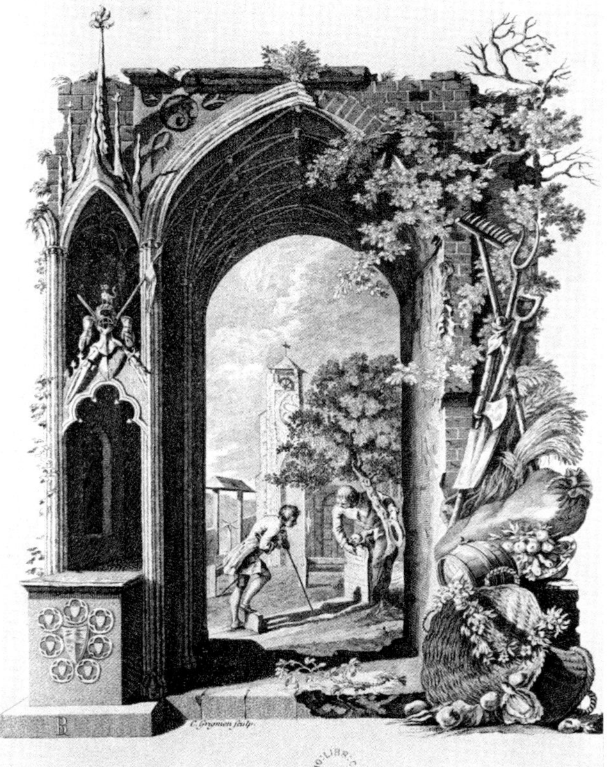

182. Richard Bentley,
engraving from
Poems, by Thomas Gray,
London, 1753.

APPENDIX IV

The 'emptiness' of Friedrich and the 'fullness' of didacticism

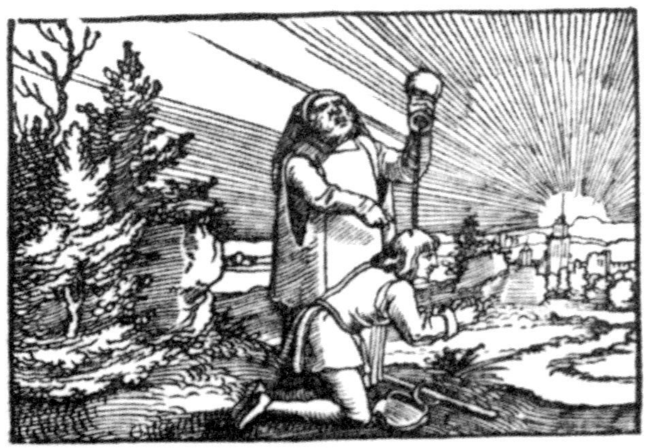

183. Sebald Beham,
The Anointing of David by Samuel,
woodcut from *Bible Stories*, Frankfurt, 1533.

184. Anonymous,
The Broad Way and the Narrow Way (Matthew 7: 13–14),
engraving, Museum der Kulturen, Basel.

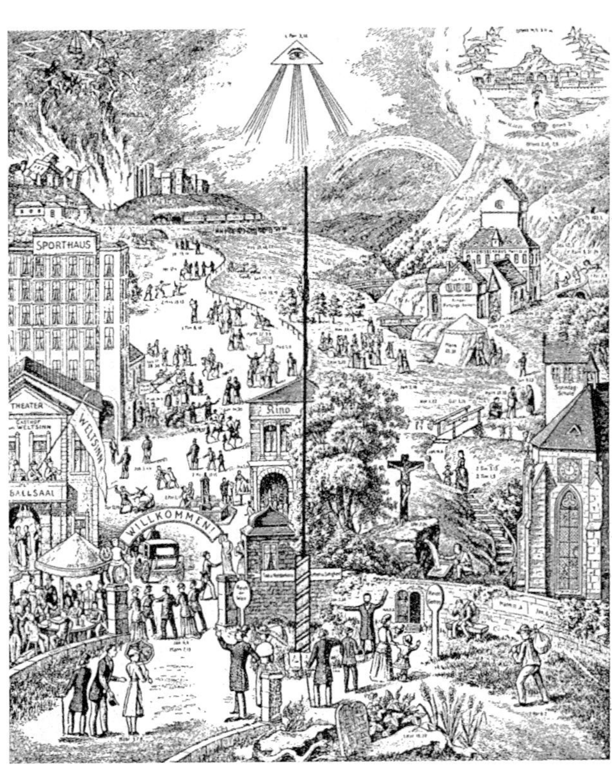

Friedrich's work follows the tradition of Lutheran imagery (see pages 209 and 245). The God he saw revealed in landscape is the same God who takes the form of the rising sun in a woodcut by Sebald Beham (ill. 183), the God in whose light David kneels in prayer after his anointing by Samuel. Three centuries later, Friedrich placed his human figures in nature in the same spirit.

Nature is on the side of true belief, while the Church of Rome asserts its power over the faithful in pompous buildings. Lucas Cranach the Younger depicted a crucifix standing on a hilltop (ill. 185), which anticipates *The Tetschen Altar*. Cranach's picture also presents an argument by antithesis: Luther's teaching is the true religion, secure in the knowledge of its immediate relationship with God, while papal dogma is the teaching of the Antichrist.

This antithesis is the source of the warnings and instruction expressed in the iconographic motif of the forking path (ill. 184). The broad, easy path leads to worldly pleasures and ends in the 'everlasting fire which was prepared for the devil and his angels' (Matthew 25: 41), while the narrow, difficult path leads to salvation. I would suggest that Friedrich's *Autumn* (ill. 143) is an indirect allusion to this doctrine.

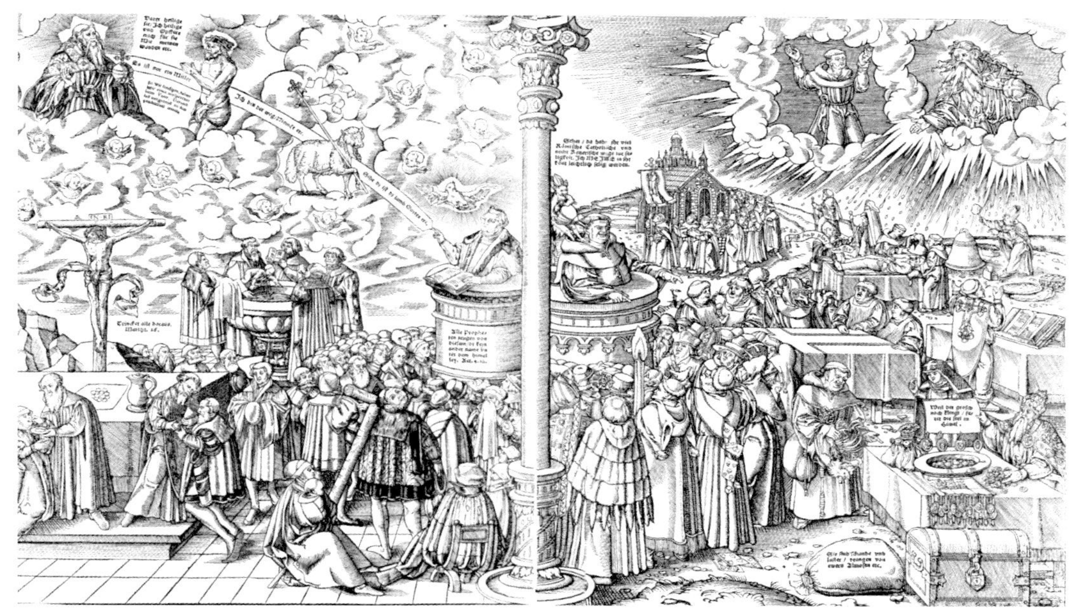

185. Lucas Cranach the Younger, *The Difference between the true religion of Christ and the false idolatrous teaching of the Antichrist*, 1546, woodcut, 35.1 × 58.5 cm (13¾ × 23 in.). Hamburger Kunsthalle, Hamburg.

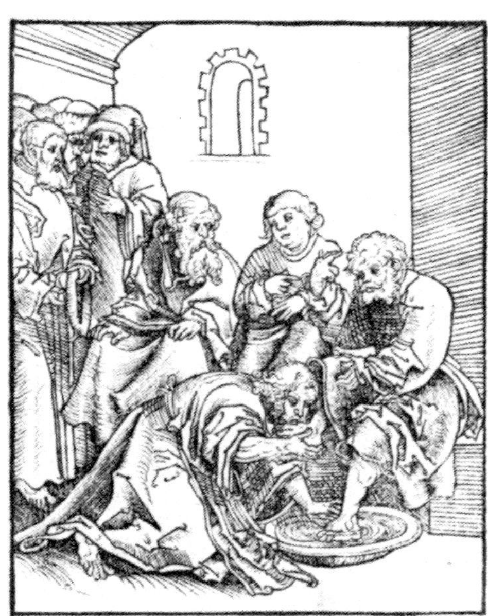

186. Lucas Cranach the Elder, *The Washing of Feet (John 13: 1–20).*

187. Hans Holbein the Younger, *The Sale of Indulgences,* 1523–24, engraving, 8 × 27 cm (3⅛ × 10⅝ in.). Fitzwilliam Museum, Cambridge.

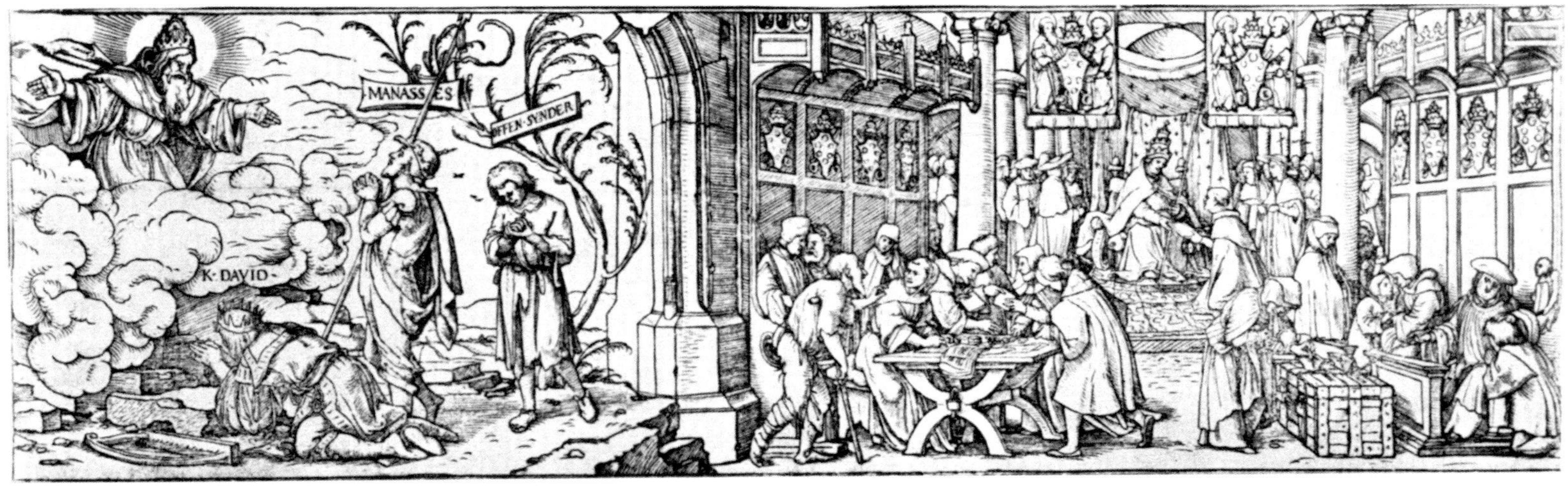

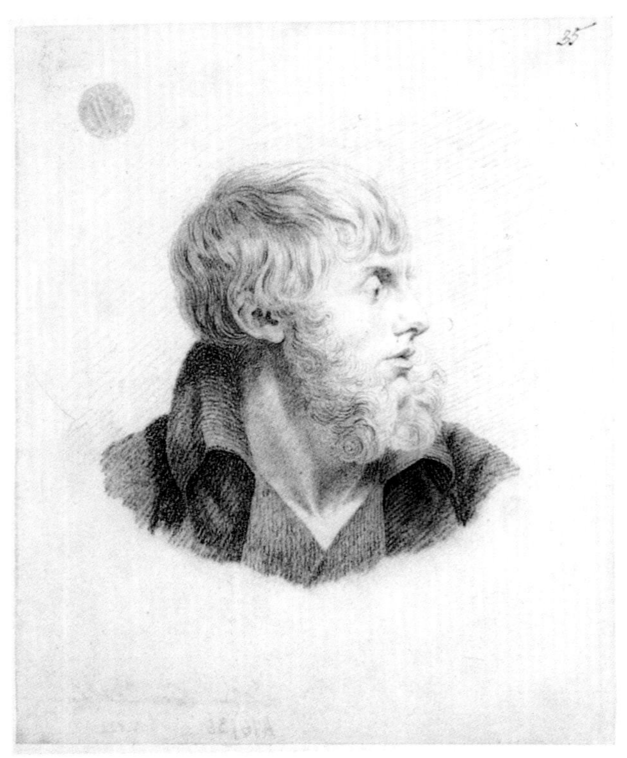

188. ***Self-portrait,*** c. 1806–9, black chalk,
22.6 × 18 cm (10½ × 7⅛ in.). Stadtmuseum, Dresden.

LETTERS AND WRITINGS

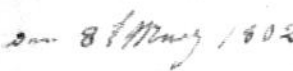

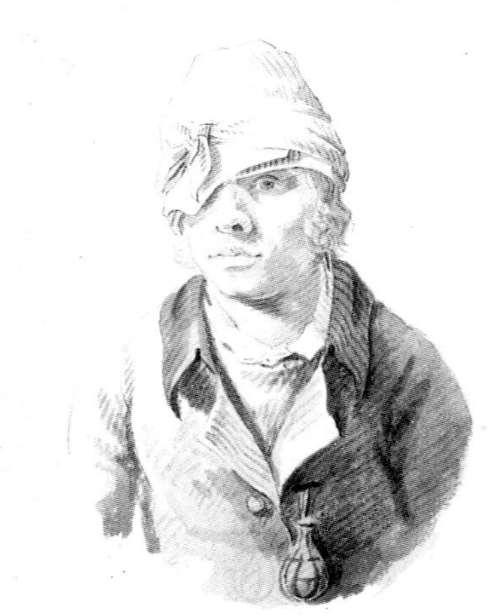

189. *Self-portrait with Cap,*
1802, pencil and Indian ink, 17.5 × 10.5 cm (7 × 4⅛ in.).
Hamburger Kunsthalle, Hamburg.

LETTERS

Caspar David Friedrich to Ernst Moritz Arndt
Dresden, 12 March 1814

Esteemed fellow countryman!

I have received your letter and the associated drawings. I am not in the least surprised that no monuments are being erected to mark either the great cause of the people, nor the high-hearted deeds of individual Germans. Nothing great of that kind will happen as long as we live in thrall to princes. Where the people have no voice, they are also not allowed to respect or have any sense of themselves as a people.

I am busying myself at present with a picture in which a monument stands in the public square of an imaginary town. I intend to dedicate this monument to noble Scharnhorst, and would like to ask you to write an inscription for it. It should not be much over twenty words, however, or else I will not have enough room for it. I await your kind consent to my request.

Your fellow countryman, Friedrich

Caspar David Friedrich to the painter J. L. G. Lund
Dresden, 11 July 1816

... Thank you for the kind invitation to Rome, but I freely confess that I have never wanted to go there. Now, however, having leafed through some of Mr Faber's sketchbooks, I have almost changed my mind. I can now see that it might be very fine to go and live in Rome. But I could not contemplate without horror the thought of returning to the North again; that, I imagine, would be like burying oneself alive. I'm content to stay in one place, without grumbling, if fate so wills; but turning back is against my nature, my whole being revolts against it. I've been lazy for a while, and felt utterly incapable of doing anything. From within, nothing would emerge, the spring was dry, I was empty; from without, nothing appealed to me, I was dull, and so I thought the best thing for me to do was nothing. What is the use of working, in the end, if nothing comes of it; the seed must lie in the earth a long time, if we want to be sure of getting anything from it....

CASPAR DAVID FRIEDRICH TO HIS BROTHER CHRISTIAN [1817]

... You call what I wrote jagged, and you are right. But mark my words: to work stone you need toughened steel. And beware of baring your heart to cold, heartless people of that kind, wrap it in a rind of ice to protect it against them, but only them. Invite my teacher and Professor Schildener to see the drawings....

CASPAR DAVID FRIEDRICH TO HIS RELATIVES IN GREIFSWALD
Dresden, 28 January 1818

... It's a droll business, when a fellow has a wife; it's droll having a household, be it never so small; it seems droll to me when my wife summons me to the table at noon. And lastly, it's droll staying at home in the evenings instead of roaming around out of doors as I used to. And it's especially droll that everything I do now is always done, and must be done, with my wife in mind. If I but knock a nail into the wall, it mustn't be as high as I can reach but only as high as my wife can reach in comfort. In short, since I became We, many things have changed....

VASILY ANDREYEVICH ZHUKOVSKY TO GRAND DUCHESS ALEXANDRA FEODOROVNA
Karlsbad, 23 June 1821

... Anyone who knew Friedrich's paintings of mist, and who, because these pictures show only the gloomier side of nature, expected to find him meditative and melancholic, with a pale face and poetic rapture in his eyes, would be quite wrong. Friedrich's face would not startle anyone who saw him in a crowd. He is a man of medium build, fair, with pale, beetling eyebrows; his most striking facial feature is the expression of innocence, and his character matches it: you sense innocence in every word he speaks. He talks without eloquence but with lively and sincere feeling, especially if one broaches his favourite subject, Nature, which he treats like a member of his family. He talks about it as he paints it, without rapture but with originality; there is no rapture in his paintings, either; on the contrary it is their truth that appeals to us, for each of them awakens the memory of something we know. If we find in them more than meets the eye, the reason is that the painter does not look at nature like an 'artist' who is seeking only a subject for his brush, but like a human being of feeling and imagination, who finds a symbol of human life everywhere in nature. Friedrich pays little heed to the rules of art: he does not paint his pictures for connoisseurs of painting but for friends of nature; critics may be displeased with him, but the best critic, open-minded feeling, is always on his side. That is the standard by which he judges other people's pictures; I have been to the gallery with him several times. In many cases he could not tell me the painters' names, and he knows little, altogether, of what is found in textbooks on painting. In compensation, he found qualities

or weaknesses in many paintings, such as only someone who has studied nature's textbook would notice....

CASPAR DAVID FRIEDRICH TO VASILY ANDREYEVICH ZHUKOVSKY
Dresden, 9 February 1830

... These paintings, which can only be seen by lamplight, require some special provision, which I would begin to arrange here, however, so that they could be hung with little trouble on arrival. The subjects are these: beside a pointed Gothic window, a harp stands unused, with two girls on either side of it, singing and playing mandolin and guitar, as if they are waiting for the harpist. The view through the window stretches only as far as a wooded hill, with a full moon shining above. But the girls await their friend in vain: she is in the second picture, standing on a balcony that overlooks a square; from the lighted church nearby comes the sound of the organ, which the girl accompanies on her harp. The moon rides higher in the sky, shedding its bluish light on the sleeping town far below. In the third picture, a young musician is sitting, asleep and dreaming, under some tall flowers (hollyhocks). The mandolin has slipped from his hand. From clouds, three winged beings lean over the sleeper, singing and playing. Radiant light pours down to earth from on high. The fourth picture is different: a scene in a wood, where through magic power, a treasure is extracted from the earth and heavenly goods are exchanged for earthly ones. These pictures must be seen to the accompaniment of music. The first with singing and guitar; the second with singing and harp; the third with glass harmonica; the fourth to the accompaniment of sonorous music heard from afar....

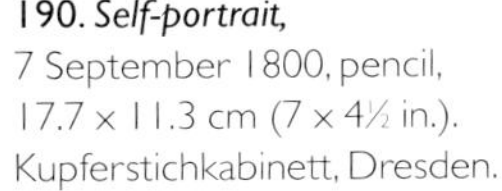

190. ***Self-portrait,***
7 September 1800, pencil, 17.7 × 11.3 cm (7 × 4½ in.). Kupferstichkabinett, Dresden.

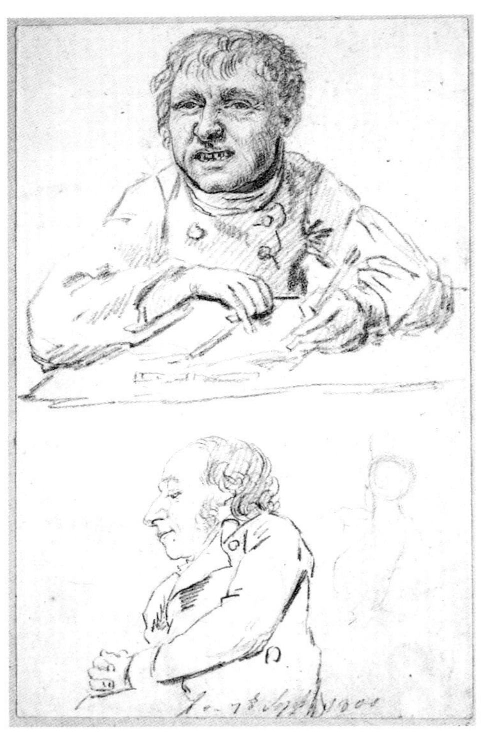

CASPAR DAVID FRIEDRICH TO HIS THREE BROTHERS IN GREIFSWALD
Dresden, 11 September 1830

... At ten we went to bed, at eleven I was woken by the sound of fire, shortly after that the citizens' alarum was beaten, and we also heard a frightful 'Hurrah! Hurrah!'. Before long I heard dreadful shouting from the people making for the guard headquarters (which I can see from my windows); about eight or ten shots were fired, at which the noise stopped but only for a few moments. Then the noise and shouting began again all the louder; this was when the crowd gave the soldiers a drubbing to drive them out of their headquarters so that the citizens could occupy it, I heard later. While this was happening, some people had broken the windows of the city hall and thrown papers out of the windows and set fire to them, on the ground floor and the next. When they wanted to do the same thing on the next floor up, a man came forward and told the enraged crowd that they ought to think about the great misfortune they would cause, because a lot of the money that was stored there belonged to widows and orphans. Upon hearing this, they withdrew at once. Don't you agree that when people are so agitated, yet still let themselves be persuaded by a

few words, you cannot help but respect them? Next they forced their way into the police station, smashed doors and windows and burnt anything and everything, and broke windows in several other places, including the house of the Catholic bishop Mauermann. But the good people were not satisfied with the destruction they had wrought in the police station, and so they started more fires and burnt anything and everything, on every floor, even the roof was completely destroyed, and no one was allowed to put the flames out; it was four o'clock in the afternoon before anyone put a stop to these people....

CASPAR DAVID FRIEDRICH TO V. A. ZHUKOVSKY
Dresden, 14 October 1835

... they are painted transparently on paper. These pictures can only be seen in special conditions, in a room where the light falls through a small opening and the rest of the room is dark. But they are not like the pictures in a peepshow. Three of them can be regarded as belonging together ...

[From the description, these resemble the three described in the letter to Zhukovsky of 9 February 1830.]

ROBERT KRÜGER, FRIEDRICH'S SON-IN-LAW, TO V. A. ZHUKOVSKY
Dresden, 24 December 1841

Your Excellency, Honoured State Councillor!

As it pleased Almighty God to end the earthly life of my father-in-law (Professor Friedrich, landscape painter in this city) almost two years ago, and as he was prevented during the last three years of his life from earning anything by his art, I venture now, on behalf of my mother-in-law (the widow of the deceased), to approach you with the following humble request, which you, Honoured State Councillor, will excuse the more graciously because the request is founded on gracious words His Majesty, now reigning Emperor of Russia, himself personally uttered some years ago to my father-in-law, saying that he might reckon on assistance from the imperial funds in case of need arising out of unhappy circumstances. As the widow of the deceased is now without means, and also is burdened with the upbringing of a younger daughter and a son (who dedicates himself to art), the surviving family of the late artist would be most profoundly grateful if it would please His most gracious Majesty the Emperor to let the gracious bounty of which he spoke to my father-in-law be conveyed to his widow.

Robert Krüger, Bathing Superintendent

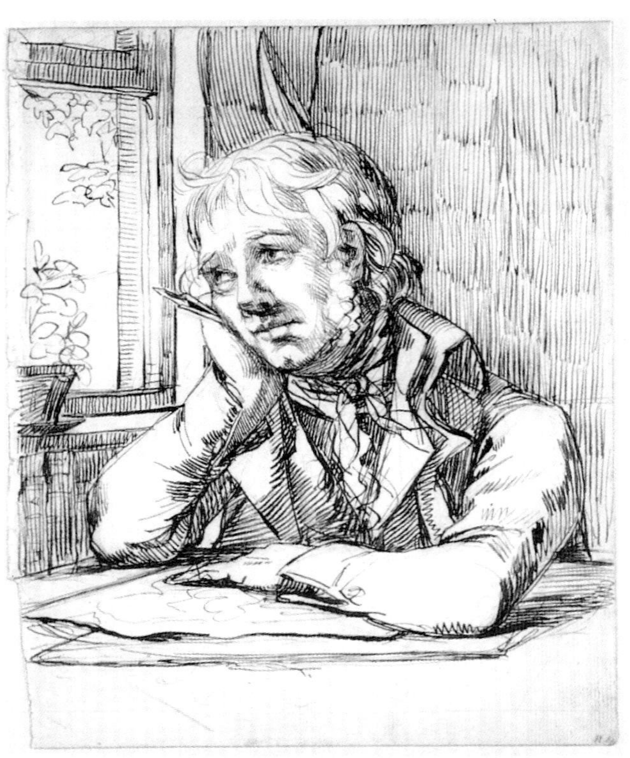

191. ***Self-portrait with Raised Arm,*** c. 1802, pencil and ink, 26.7 × 21.5 cm (10½ × 8½ in.). Hamburger Kunsthalle, Hamburg.

FROM FRIEDRICH'S JOURNAL (1803)

... Gently rising hills prevent any further view, exactly as children desire; they enjoy the precious present time, wishing for nothing else, nor for what may lie further away. Flowering bushes, nourishing herbs, sweet-smelling flowers enclose the still, clear stream which mirrors the pure blue of an unclouded sky, just as the souls of children mirror the glorious image of the godhead. Children are playing, kissing and enjoying themselves, and one of them claps his hands to greet the rising sun. Lambs are grazing in the valley and on the hillsides. Not a stone to be seen. Not a sombre twig, not a fallen leaf. All nature breathes peace, joy and innocence and life.

You know my house and the wonderful view. But today for the first time the normally glorious countryside cries out to me of decay and death, where before it has only smiled to me of joy and life. The sky is overcast and stormy, and today it casts its monochrome winter coat over the lovely coloured mountains and fields for the first time. All nature lies before me drained of colour.

ON ART AND THE SPIRIT OF ART

I hope I may be permitted to explain once more, and very briefly, my views on art and the spirit of art in man.

You must harken more to God than to man. Each bears within himself the law of right and wrong; his conscience says to him: do this, do not do that. The holy Ten Commandments are the pure, lucid statement of what we all know of truth and goodness. Every one of us recognizes them unconditionally as the voice of his inner self, no one can rebel against them. So if you wish to dedicate yourself to art, if you feel a calling to consecrate your life to it, oh, pay good heed to the voice of your inner self, for it is the art within us.

Beware of the superficial knowledge of cold facts, beware sinful ratiocination, for it kills the heart, and when heart and mind have died in a man, there art cannot dwell.

Preserve a pure and childlike understanding within yourself, and follow the voice of your inner self unconditionally, for it is the Divine in us and does not lead us astray.

Regard every pure mental impulse as holy, honour every devout presentiment as holy, for it is the art within us! In the hour of inspiration it takes on visible form, and this form is your picture....

Little is given to many, and much to a few. The spirit of nature reveals itself differently to each of us, and therefore no one should impose his doctrines and rules on another as an infallible law. No man is the yardstick for all, each is the yardstick only for himself and for minds more or less kindred to his....

This is secondary? That is secondary? Nothing in a picture is secondary; everything belongs inalienably to the whole, and therefore may not be neglected. If someone is incapable of giving worth to the most important part of his picture, except by neglecting other, subordinate aspects, then there is something wrong with his work. Everything must and can be executed with care, without every part clamouring to be seen on an equal footing. True subordination does not lie in neglect of secondary things in favour of the most important thing but in the ordering of things and the distribution of light and shade.

REMARKS ON A COLLECTION OF PAINTINGS, MOSTLY BY LIVING OR RECENTLY DECEASED ARTISTS

... What excess of objects, and yet, how empty and dead is the whole! What an expense of colours, yet without agreement among themselves or tone as a whole! What calculation of effect, or rather, miscalculation of effect; light versus dark in harsh opposition is not enough to produce a beautiful effect! But however large the heap of things supposed to make an effect here, they cannot hide the wretched nakedness and spiritual barrenness. This picture is like a curiosity shop where many things lie heaped together but nothing goes with anything else. The painter X, to judge by this picture, may well give himself airs and know a thing or two, but lacks the feeling which is the life-giving soul of all knowledge....

Who would claim to know what alone is beautiful, and who could teach it? And who would set limits to things of a spiritual nature and lay down laws about them? O, you dry, leathery, mundane people, go on thinking up rules! The crowd will praise you for the crutch they provide, but those with a will of their own will scorn you and laugh....

How great is the number of those who call themselves artists without having the least notion that it calls for something quite different from mere dexterity. Some people think it foolish to say that art must issue forth from within a man and depends, indeed, on his moral, religious worth. For just as only a pure, unclouded mirror can give back a pure image, so too a true work of art can issue only from a pure soul....

Close your physical eye, so that you see your picture first with the spiritual eye. Then bring what you saw in the dark into the light, so that it may have an effect on others, shining inwards from outside....

Painters exercise themselves in invention, in composition, as they call it. Is that not the same as saying they exercise themselves in patching and piecing together? A picture must not be invented, it must be felt....

The judges of art have extracted rules from pictures, rules that the painters themselves probably never thought of, and then they believe that more pictures can be made out of this froth. What fools!...

Every flower, every stalk, considered on its own, is admirable and beautiful. But in a flower garden, where everything stands crowded together, one flower works against another, and competes in form, colour and scent. I am against all heaping together of works of art in one place. Such collections can perhaps be useful to the practising artist but they can only be disturbing to a man of feeling....

It may be a great honour to have a large public on one's side. But it is certainly a greater honour to have a small, select public on one's side.....

If you can, make machines which nurture a human spirit inside them, and pour it forth from themselves; but you must not make people who are like machines, without will or energy of their own....

[On painter XX] At one moment, this is his opinion, among his many opinions: strict imitation of nature in every detail is what art requires. But then, at another moment: strict, slavish imitation of nature and excessively detailed execution are art that has failed. Art must never seek to deceive, and such detailed execution restricts the viewer's imagination;

the picture should only suggest, but above all it should excite the spirit and create room for the play of fantasy; the picture should not aspire to represent nature itself but only bring it to mind. The painter's task is not the faithful representation of air, water, rocks and trees, but his soul, and his feelings should be reflected therein. Perceiving the spirit of nature, penetrating, absorbing, and reproducing it with the whole of one's heart and mind: that is the task of a work of art....

XXX's representation of the Last Supper is ... nothing but an evening meal, where the good folk are enjoying their food, and that fat man seems to have undertaken to empty his cup at a single draught, and even to demonstrate that he has done so, for he would surely not need to hold the cup quite so high otherwise. They are all absorbed in eating and drinking, and none of them turns towards their Lord and Master, although he is shown to be speaking....

At first sight this painting represents the remains of a ruined monastery as a memento of a sombre past. The present time illuminates the past. In the breaking day, one can still perceive the dispersing darkness. In the picture, the eye is led from light into twilight, from twilight further into the dark, from the dark even deeper into darkness. Perhaps the painter is a Protestant, and it may be that something of what I have just said was in his mind as he painted the scene....

The lowliest, even the grubbiest object in nature or reality can be represented pleasingly to the eye in a picture, if an artist chooses. But a noble object represented in a beautiful and pleasing manner, as in poetry or painting, seizes the attention and remains attractive even if the execution is inferior; these two pictures by XX and XXX testify to this....

If you sobersides had ever experienced true feeling, your pictures would not be like corpses, without sensation or feeling, without warmth. One would do well to use the words of Holy Scripture here: Though thou hast all the knowledge in the world, and hast not love, thou art as sounding brass or a tinkling cymbal. Or perhaps: Though thou understandest the art of brush-wagging better than any other in the whole round world, and hast not the feeling that giveth life, all thy skill is so much dead lumber....

A man should never lose faith in himself and the talent God gave him, or he sins against his human nature and his time. If we are honest therefore, is there not something perverse, even disgusting, in the sight of Mary with her milk dried and a starving Christ-child in her arms, in threadbare clothes? And more so when the pictures contain deliberate and distorted offences against both linear and aerial perspective? People repeat all the errors of the past in the wish to deceive, but the good in those works, the deep, devout, childlike temperament that really gives these pictures their soul – that is not so easily imitated by the hand alone, and hypocrites will never succeed at it, not even if they have gone so far with the deceit as to become Catholic....

Yet another picture, like those of which there are so many here and everywhere, neither thought through, nor felt, nor experienced: all prettily done according to precept, and perhaps that's best for the dull of soul. People of that sort prefer to have a law for each and every thing in science, as in art, so as to be removed from all independent thought, feeling and sensation....

I spin myself a cocoon; let others do the same, and time will tell what comes out of the chrysalis, a bright butterfly or a maggot.

XX paints with words and often expresses his feelings in words with felicity. But when, purporting to be a painter, he tries to express himself in forms and colours, his efforts are in vain, as anyone can see. We may well ask whether his knowledge is not more of a hindrance to him than a help....

In every individual object lies an infinite number of interpretations, a multitude of representations. I recognize and honour the greatness of this when, as I have said, each recognizes the boundaries set him by nature and modestly remains within them and works according to his strengths, rather than wanting to force himself beyond his abilities....

Painter X is one of the many of our time whose studies, drawn or painted from nature, are quite excellent. However, when these studies are used for pictures, and the originals are no longer before the physical eye and the painter has to rely on his spiritual eye, then one no longer recognizes anything from the earlier studies he made. Other painters often draw from nature nervously or clumsily, but when they later use those drawings for pictures, everything gains life and soul....

How totally different are this painter's views on art, as I have heard them from his own lips. He says: 'Sensual beauty, that is, of course, purely elevated sensuality, is the first and only requirement one can make of a work of art. But it is by no means a requirement that a genuine work of art should awaken religious, sacred sensations in us, as Hegel's philosophy teaches; nor should landscape painting or any other branch of pictorial representation be excluded, for everything can hold a meaning for the sensitive person, and be interpreted from its beautiful side, putting the viewer in a more elevated frame of mind. A beautiful face', our speaker continues, 'or a beautiful bottom are both worthy subjects for the painter, for both are part of nature, and the Creator reveals himself to man in nature, through the beauty and variety of forms and the splendour of all kinds of colours'....

Finally, I would like to ask this question: does the man make the age, or does the age make the man? When contemplating a series of old and new works of art, I think it very pertinent to consider the way that every age has its boundaries, making even the greatest genius unable to surpass the aims of his own time, or the way that, when someone did succeed in going beyond the boundaries, the rest of the world would not recognize it, or even called it madness, so that only posterity recognized it. Is the human spirit truly free, or is it tied to a time and a place?...

Art should spread joy; that is what fashion wants. A few years ago, a painting of the severity of winter could give pleasure, but not any more. If a person's eyes and wits are too dull to appreciate the great white cloth with its delicate play of colours, the epitome of the utmost purity, under which nature is preparing new life, or if his imagination is so poor that he sees mist as merely grey, then his distaste [for winter scenes] is understandable. When a region cloaks itself in mist, it appears larger and more sublime, elevating the imagination and rousing the expectations like a veiled girl. The eye and the imagination are generally more attracted by hazy distance than by what lies close and clear before the eye. But mist and winter are in the doghouse now, and who would guarantee that the same fate might not also threaten harsh, death-foretelling autumn before too long....

Manuscript preserved in the
Kupferstichkabinett, Dresden

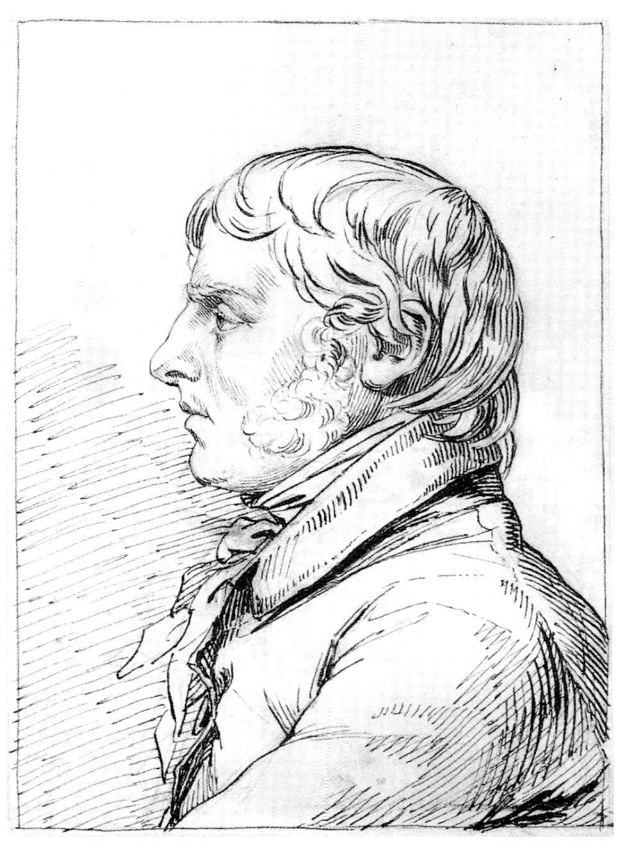

192. ***Self-portrait in profile,*** c. 1802, Indian ink, 13.1 × 9.2 cm (5⅛ × 3⅝ in.). Hamburger Kunsthalle, Hamburg.

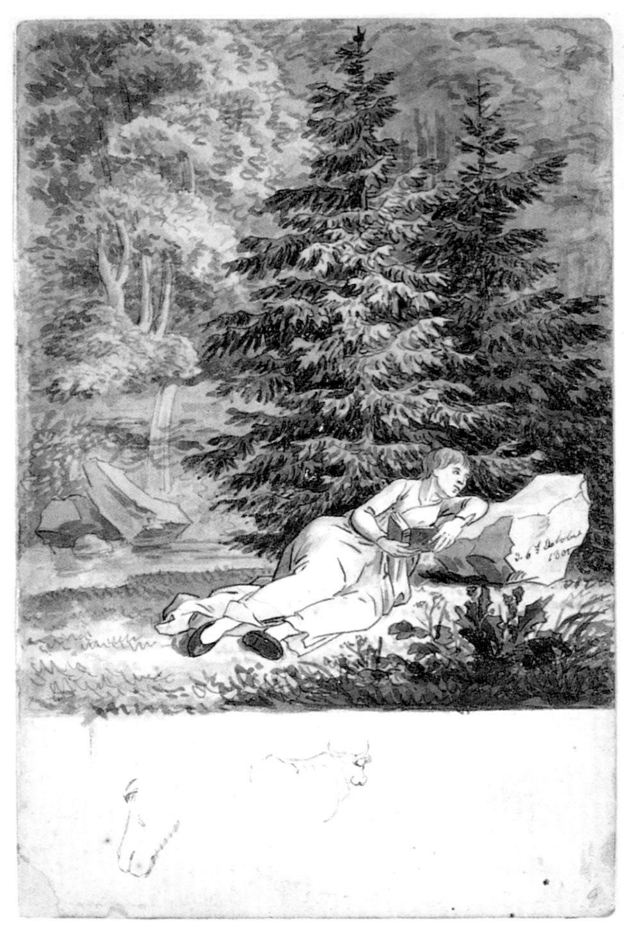

193. ***The Romantic Reader,*** 6 October 1801, ink and wash, 18.6 x 11.9 cm (7⅜ x 4¾ in.). Kupferstichkabinett, Dresden.

WRITINGS ON FRIEDRICH'S WORK

THE TETSCHEN ALTAR*

DESCRIPTION OF THE PICTURE

High up on the summit of the rock stands the cross, surrounded by evergreen fir trees, and evergreen ivy twines about the base of the cross. The radiant sun is setting, and the Saviour on the cross glows in the crimson light.

DESCRIPTION OF THE FRAME

The frame was made to Mr Friedrich's specifications by the sculptor Kühn. At the sides the frame has two Gothic columns. Palm branches rise from them and form a curve above the painting. There are five angels' heads in the branches, all looking down at the cross and worshipping. The evening star stands above the middle angel in purest shining silver. At the bottom, in an oblong panel, is the all-seeing eye of God, enclosed by the holy trigon, surrounded with rays. Ears of corn and vines on either side bow to the all-seeing eye and signify the body and blood of Him who is fixed to the cross.

INTERPRETATION OF THE PICTURE

Jesus Christ, nailed to the cross, turns towards the setting sun, image of the eternal Father, giver of all life. With the teachings of Jesus, an old world died, the time when God the Father walked directly on earth. The sun went down and the earth could no longer grasp the departing light. The Saviour on the cross shines in the gold of sunset with the purest, noblest metal, and reflects the light onto the earth with a gentler gleam. The cross stands on a rock, as unshakeably firm as our faith in Jesus. Fir trees grow around the cross, evergreen and everlasting, like the hope of men in Him, Christ crucified.

* Description and interpretation by Caspar David Friedrich, transcribed by Christian August Semler, and published in the *Journal des Luxus und der Moden*, Weimar, 1809, iii, p.239.

ON A LANDSCAPE PAINTING BY MR FRIEDRICH IN DRESDEN, INTENDED AS AN ALTARPIECE, AND ON LANDSCAPE PAINTING, ALLEGORY AND MYSTICISM IN GENERAL

F. W. B. von Ramdohr
[Chamberlain at the court of the King of Saxony]

It is with reluctance that I venture to publish any judgment of a work by the hand of a living artist. If only the altarpiece exhibited by the landscape painter Mr Friedrich in Dresden during the recent Christmas holiday were a work executed according to principles tested by lengthy experience and sanctioned by the example of great masters – no matter if the work were good or bad, I would remain silent. The commonplace and the bad topple unaided, and it is a prudent maxim not to stake one's peace of mind in a literary endeavour unless it is necessary. But Mr Friedrich's picture departs from the common path. It opens a new vista of landscape painting, one hitherto unknown, at least to me; it testifies to an artist of great imagination and feeling; it echoes the opinion of the public; it impresses the majority. Yet when I see that the tendency of this talent is a threat to good taste, that it robs the essence of painting, especially landscape painting, of its particular strengths, and that it allies itself with a spirit which is the unhappy offspring of the present times and the horrifying precursor of a rapidly approaching age of barbarism, then it would surely be pusillanimous to remain silent. Pusillanimous for any man who has a right to believe that he can halt the progress of art and science in an erroneous direction by explaining his reasoning, but especially pusillanimous for me, since having thrown off the bonds that previously tied me to whatever was locally expedient, I have devoted the brief remainder of my days to propagation of the good and the beautiful everywhere in their boundless domains.

I repeat it yet more distinctly and emphatically: my criticism is not directed against Mr Friedrich's picture, but against the system it reveals; against a host of ideas that appear to me to be insinuating themselves into art and science at present; against errors, some of which the picture itself does not display, but which are closely associated with those that it does make. The public will therefore excuse me, if I place such a discursive essay about a single picture in its hands.

The true position of the critic, the writer about art, is often misunderstood. He cannot tell the artist how to set about producing a good work of art. Not a single work has ever been written or painted in accordance with any theory of art. But the critic can be useful by acting as a warning, either to genius, when it wishes to turn on to new paths, or to the age, when either blind faith in prevailing practice has lulled it to sleep, or adventurous illusion or surprise has dazzled it. In this respect, there is no disputing the valuable contributions of the Winckelmanns, the Mengses, the Reynoldses. They drove out the ecclesiastical style, the boudoir style, and the rest of the insipid and bad tastes that prevailed in the first half of the eighteenth century. True, they may now responsible for the repugnant practice of piecing together a cold patchwork of timidly gathered and copied fragments from living nature, from works of great masters and from antiquity, or even for the colouring of marble, as well as for the equally erroneous striving for effect from great masses of form and light, and the production of illuminated sketches instead of finished works due to neglect of the truth of detail. But these errors of our time do not lie at the door of those worthy writers and their immediate intentions. Why would a painter wish to learn how to paint from them? The only thing they could teach him was how not to do it....

Now to the painting! It measures about three feet wide and four feet high. The lower part is occupied by a rocky mountain top. This is covered with fir trees, some with their tips sticking up from the far side of the summit, while on the near side only half a tree can be seen, for most of the lower half of the trunk is cut off by the frame. The firs standing on the far side are arranged fairly symmetrically on both sides of the mountain slope; at least they are not grouped together. They rise in steps to two rocky outcrops, which lean over like two mountains of the kind known as a 'Horn', leaving enough space to place a crucifix between them. The figure of Christ is bronze and is turned with its front in three-quarter profile facing the far side of the mountain, so that the viewer on the near side gets to see scarcely a quarter of it. The surface of the mountain has a few granite boulders and stony soil with a little moss growing here and there, and a few struggling young spruces and Scots pines.

This pyramidal mass of earth stands out distinctly against the sky, which is a dirty violet at the top, a little redder below, and eventually fades to a chilly yellow. There are some streaks of vermilion in the upper part. But the whole sky is transected by rays indicating that the sun is very low and moreover illuminating nothing on the ground except some parts of the figure of Christ on the cross: the head, the lower trunk and a knee. Everything else on the mountain, even the cross, suggests a dusk engaged in so unequal a struggle with the night that one must take it for darkness, especially from a distance.

The open-minded viewer can be in no doubt that an allegorical significance underlies the scene. The frame, whose symbols surround the picture and which I shall discuss in more detail below, points to that very conclusion, and the frame must have the approval of the artist since he exhibits the painting with it in place. The painting's designation as an altarpiece also leads to that conclusion, but this designation cannot justify the crucifix, two or three inches high, with its back towards the viewer. It leaves no doubt that behind the landscape depicted by the artist lies a hidden allegorical meaning, intended to put the viewer into a devout mood appropriate to partaking of Holy Communion....

Now, if it is true to say that every art does best to hold to the things that are its particular strengths, it follows that a fine landscape must represent several planes, the better to display the beauties of linear perspective, and that a single object in a landscape, such as a tree, a mountain peak, a house or a still sheet of water, definitely does not belong at the very front. It also follows that the landscape ought not to portray any one detail as if seen from close up, bereft of the haze of air; and that it ought not to represent twilight or darkness, in which aerial perspective and the sense of light are completely lost. Admittedly, such subject matter may turn out very agreeably in a drawing in sepia, for lovers of anything new and meticulously executed, but it nonetheless runs contrary to the serious nature of the finished work of art.

In his altarpiece, Mr Friedrich has positively and quite intentionally gone against all those principles. He has filled the whole lower part of his picture with a single rocky hilltop, without any noticeable indication of different planes, like a skittle. He has excluded all aerial perspective, and worst of all, he has even spread darkness over the face of the earth and thereby deprived himself of all the favourable effects that the influx of light can offer....

The execution of the picture illustrates all the consequences that invariably result from neglect of the principles I have outlined. The painter has not adopted, or was not able to adopt, any standpoint at all from which to express what he wanted to express. In order to see the mountain and the sky together from this angle, Mr Friedrich would have had to stand several thousand paces away at the same height as the mountain and in such a position that the horizon was in line with the mountain. From that distance he could not have seen any detail within the mountain's outline. No boulders, no moss, no trees encircling the mountain's near side. All those things would have vanished, and the whole mass would have stood out sharply against the sky like a black silhouette. And that is not all! Granted what cannot be denied, that the horizon runs parallel to the tip of the mountain, the light on the crucifix is completely contrary to the most basic rules of optics. For if the prism of the sun's rays as they cut across the sky is drawn together at the point from which they begin, namely at the sun, then this point is so low that it would have been impossible for Mr Friedrich, standing on the far side of the mountain, to have seen even the slightest hint of light from the sun falling on the figure of Christ, at least from below. In support of my assertion, I could refer to the best textbook on perspective, Valenciennes's *Traité de perspective*, chapter 7, section 4. But instead I will defer to the words of Lairesse, [whose manual] every artist has to hand....

What led Mr Friedrich to his offence against all the rules of optics is that he either placed an artificial light against a clay and wax model of the mountain or imagined himself standing beside the mountain and not behind it. In the latter case, admittedly, the light would have streamed towards the mountain, which would have been much lower than the sun; but in that case, not simply the crucifix but also everything else on the mountain would have been lit by parallel rays. From a position behind the mountain, Mr Friedrich would not have been able to see anything of the sun's rays at all, any more than if he held his hand horizontally before his eyes.

Another of the picture's faults is that the time of day is uncertain, due to this lack of multiple planes. The coldness of the air argues for morning, the absence of mist against it. The silver star on the uppermost angel's head in the frame is probably meant to compensate for this uncertainty: but Mr Friedrich might just as well have written up there 'This is morning'!

The earth has a bluish-brown, highly uniform tone. Completely bereft of light, it is flat and without any curvature. It stands in the most strident contrast to the bright sky, without any transition or harmony, except for that of effect: the division into a large light mass and a large dark mass wishes to be taken for chiaroscuro.

All these errors are largely due to the unfortunate choice of subject and standpoint. But others can be attributed to the execution....

What [the painting] does provide is aesthetic emotion, enabling us, while remaining aware of the distance from real life, to enjoy the game that art plays with our emotions. If it were possible for art to stimulate a true pathological emotion in us, the aesthetic would fall by the wayside: the work of art would turn into nature, our enjoyment of beauty into the enjoyment of sympathy. Would that be an advantage to the work? Not in the least! Every reliquary of a commonly revered saint, set upon an altar, can arouse pathological emotion far more powerfully than the most beautiful work of art, and the crudest caricatures have a much stronger claim to this advantage than the most beautiful painting.

But if the painting is not meant to be the actual reason for our emotion and true veneration, if the reason is instead supposed to lie in the devout rites we perform before the altar, if the work of art is meant only to *underpin* that mood by aesthetic emotion – how much closer history painting comes to serving that end! History painting depicts the veneration itself! We have grown up in the sure knowledge of the events it depicts, and the least allusion to them arouses a host of the most moving facts, character traits and words! Lastly, it can portray the Last Supper, which we mean to re-enact at the altar, and through depiction of the figures and facial expressions of the Saviour and his faithful followers can invite us to worthy celebration of that rite, just as powerfully as the figure and facial expression of Judas the betrayer can deter us from unworthy enjoyment of this commemorative act!

O you innovators! You could remind us a thousand times of the moving words 'Remember me!' without exhausting the character and feeling of Him who spoke them and of them who heard Him. In fact, it is truly an act of presumption if landscape painting tries to sidle into churches and creep on to altars. But let us move on from this to the most important question.

Does it befit the dignity of art, or that of the truly devout person, to invite the viewer to worship by such means as Mr Friedrich has adopted?

Here I must mention the frame surrounding the picture. It is closely related to the painting and is all the more integral for the fact that without it, the allegory would be utterly incomprehensible, and because the frame itself constitutes the retable. In any case, the carved and silvered morning star above the picture is an obvious reference to the time of day represented....

Let us add this emblematic content [of the frame] to the allegory of the painting and consider the tendency of the whole, while sacrificing truth and taste, to give sensory form to an idea of our religion which is worthy of respect in itself, and consoling, but not in the least aesthetic: a belief in the mysterious workings of Holy Communion. How then could we overlook the influence that a current trend has had on Mr Friedrich's composition – the mysticism which is insinuating itself everywhere at present and wafts towards us out of art as out of science, from philosophy as from religion, like a narcotic vapour! Mysticism which pronounces symbols and fantasies to be painterly and poetic images and would like to replace classical antiquity with Gothic carving, stilted Little-Mastery and legends! Mysticism which purveys wordplay instead of ideas, bases principles on far-fetched analogies and desires only to sense a thing instead of either knowing or perceiving it, rather than modestly holding its tongue. Mysticism for whose followers ignorance serves as a shibboleth in facts and literature! Mysticism which favours the times and the institutions of the Middle Ages over the age of the Medicis, Louis and Frederick! Mysticism which would prefer to replace the sturdy, vigorous inspiration that befits the true religion of Christ with swooning adulation of the cross! Mysticism, finally, which makes me tremble for what will follow our present times and reminds me of the times which ushered in the decline of true learning and taste in the last days of the Roman Empire! For then, as now, neo-Platonic sophists, gnostic and orphic shamans flourished; then, as now, men made play with legends, declamation, amulets and symbols; then, as now, men crippled art with the presumption of taking it back to its first simplicity.

Good Friedrich, and all you men of genius and talent whom fashion has temporarily led astray from the true path! Return to it, to the path which experience has shown you to be the safe one. Current fashion will find it hard to disseminate itself in places where history is taught thoroughly and classical antiquity is propagated with taste; wherever skill and knowledge are the main aims of artists and scholars. But in capitals, and near courts, distraction prevents people from making a thorough study of the things that lie outside the sphere of day-to-day affairs. Art and learning are generally material for light, social entertainment, while satiated sensuality looks to fantasy in its search for renewed stimulus and increased enjoyment. Those places will, I say, accept the doctrines that try to purvey wordplay, images and facts grasped from one side only and dressed in sonorous phrases as true knowledge and wisdom; doctrines that prate constantly of godliness and social harmony, especially with respect to art, but do not demand so much as the first requirements of both: truth and manual skill!

Dresden, 7 January 1809

Ramdohr's articles on art were written from a rigidly classical perspective. This critique and others were published in the *Zeitung für die elegante Welt*, (1809).

CASPAR DAVID FRIEDRICH, IN A LETTER ADDRESSED TO PROFESSOR SCHULZ OF THE DRESDEN ACADEMY*
8 February 1809

... Had Friedrich proceeded along the paved road, where every donkey bears his load and every dog and cat walks to be safe, because the famous artists of the past are exhibited there to serve as models for the millennia, then truly Chamberlain von Ramdohr would have remained silent. But those men did not choose to exhibit themselves as models; instead it was presumptuous judges of art who placed them before us as the sole, sure guide. Those admirable masters knew full well that an infinite variety of paths lead to art, that art is actually the centre of the world, the goal of the utmost spiritual striving, and that artists stand in a circle about that central point. And so it can happen very easily that two artists move towards each other from opposing directions, though both are heading for one and the same point. The difference in their standpoints is the difference between their temperaments, and both may reach the same goal along opposing paths. It is only in the restricted imagination of the heartless judges of art, whose writings have already stunted and frozen many a tender temperament, that there is only one path leading to art, namely the one laid down by them. If Friedrich's picture was devoid of value, no doubt the Chamberlain would have offered Friedrich his hand in friendship, and not have entered the ring as his opponent. The commonplace and the bad may topple unaided, but one must give a push to something that may be good.

But why did Friedrich not communicate his view of landscape painting to Chamberlain von Ramdohr earlier than this? Why did the painter not ask this illustrious connoisseur whether he knew of it or not? For therein lies the other question together with its answer: does he approve it or not? So let him now accept Ramdohr's threat of divine vengeance, as the consequence of his stubbornness. What use is it if the picture pleases the majority, if it does not please the Chamberlain!

How sad it must make a man like Chamberlain von Ramdohr when he sees the horror of our age, the precursor of approaching barbarism, black as night, bearing down upon him, treading contemptuously underfoot all the rules, all the fetters, all the chains which he would use to bind the spirit and keep it on the paved and bounded road. Does not the spirit of the art of our time depend, with foolish, lamentable faith, on an imagined spiritual being that knows no boundaries? Does it not follow every sacred impulse of its temperament with childlike or even childish trust? Does it not honour with blind devotion every devout presentiment, as if it were unconditionally the purest spring of art?

Friedrich does not recognize the Chamberlain's unconditional requirement that a landscape must represent several planes. Neither does he believe in the greatest possible alternation of form and colour; that a crooked line must necessarily lie next to a straight one; that while one line skips about, inviting the viewer to rejoice, the next crawls past slowly and sadly; that while one line gradually loses itself in the undergrowth the second offers us Ramdohr's 'Urania' in a friendly fashion, and the third well-meaningly serves up rules for art. In short, Friedrich is an implacable enemy of so-called contrast. He thinks it mad to try to express oneself through contradiction (which is what contrast means to fine but crude gentlemen). In his opinion, every true work of art must express a specific sense, and move the viewer either to joy or to sorrow, to melancholy or to mirth, but not attempt to combine all emotions in itself, as if whisked together. The work of art must want to be only one thing, and this single will must persist throughout the whole work. Each individual part of it must have the features of the whole, and must not hide itself behind flattering words and surreptitious malice as many people do.

Contrast, you say, is the rule of rules, the fundamental law of art, but it is only the case for you who are the contrast to spirit, you who are nothing but clay! You may keep it!

* Friedrich decided to refer to himself in the third person ('I don't really know why ...') in defending his painting against Ramdohr's criticism.

ON CRITICAL DESPOTISM AND ARTISTIC ORIGINALITY, IN RESPONSE TO MR VON KÜGELGEN'S REMARKS ON THE CRITIQUE, WRITTEN BY MYSELF, OF A PAINTING BY MR FRIEDRICH

F. W. B. von Ramdohr

... My words will be forgotten and his works will live. But if he believes he should strike out upon a different path, I am equally convinced by his noble way of thinking that he will thank me in ten years' time for having drawn his attention some years earlier to the wrong path that he would eventually have discovered for himself.

So Mr von Kügelgen accuses me of critical despotism. What does 'despotism' mean here? I know three varieties which are particularly prevalent in Germany. The worst is the despotism of anarchy of taste and its hallowed tenet: live and let live. According to this principle, we should tolerate and suffer every type of foolhardiness in art and science, either because genius might grow from chaos, after all, or else so as not to disturb the present peace and the earning of our daily bread. Then comes the despotism of partisanship. Woe betide anyone who doubts the excellence of any member of the select handful! Finally there is the despotism of the artist or author who possesses a certain celebrity....

VARIOUS IMPRESSIONS EXPERIENCED BEFORE A SEASCAPE WITH A MONK, BY CASPAR DAVID FRIEDRICH, 1810

Heinrich von Kleist, Clemens Brentano, Achim von Arnim

The best commentary on this 'palimpsest' has been written by Élisabeth Décultot*:

'On 13 October 1810, Kleist published an article entitled *Impressions before Friedrich's Seascape* in the *Berliner Abendblätter*, signed 'C. B.', the initials of Clemens Brentano. However, the article was in fact a considerably modified and cut version of an original piece by Brentano and Arnim, who no longer recognized their work. In a later issue of the paper, 22 October 1810, Kleist was obliged to publish an admission that he himself was the (re)writer of the article. The co-existence of these two versions is of great interest for the debate on landscape painting in the early nineteenth century.'

In fact, Kleist's view of the painting (his additions are given in italics below) is quite distinct from the jocular, satirical tone of the selection of 'quotations' from imaginary dialogues by Arnim and Brentano. The little dramatic scenes suppressed by Kleist were not published until 1852, when they were included in volume 4 of Arnim's *Collected Works.*

* Élisabeth Décultot, *Peindre le paysage. Discours théorique et renouveau pictoral dans le romantisme allemand,* Tusson (Charente), Editions du Lérot, 1996, p.412.

It is magnificent to stand in infinite solitude on the seashore, beneath an overcast sky, and to look out on an endless waste of water. Part of this feeling is the fact that one has made one's way there and yet must go back, that one would like to cross over but cannot, that one sees nothing to support life and yet senses the voice of life in the sigh of the waves, the murmur of the air, the passing clouds and the lonely cry of birds. Part of this feeling is a claim made by the heart and a rejection, if I may call it that, on the part of nature. But this is impossible in front of the picture, and what I should have found in the picture itself I found only between myself and the picture, namely a claim my heart made on the picture and the picture's rejection of me; and so I myself became the monk, and the picture became the dune, but the sea itself, on which I should have looked out with longing – the sea was absent. *There can be nothing sadder or more desolate in the world than this place: the only spark of life in the broad domain of death, the lonely centre in the lonely circle. The picture, with its two or three mysterious subjects, lies there like an apocalypse, as if it were thinking Young's* Night Thoughts *and since it has, in its uniformity and boundlessness, no foreground but the frame, it is as if one's eyelids had been cut off.*

Yet the painter has undoubtedly broken an entirely new path in the field of his art, and I am convinced that with his spirit, a square mile of the sand of Mark Brandenburg could be represented with a barberry bush, on which a lone crow might sit preening itself, and that such a picture would have an effect that rivalled Ossian or Kosegarten. Why, if the artist painted this landscape using its own chalk and its own water, I believe he would make the foxes and wolves weep: the most powerful praise, without doubt, that could be given to this kind of landscape painting.

Yet my own impressions of this wonderful painting are too confused, and so, before I venture to express them in full, I have decided to learn what I can from the remarks of the couples who pass before it from morning till evening. I listened to the remarks of the many viewers about me and now relay them as comments on this painting, which is surely a stage set before which a scene must be acted, for it allows no repose.

Enter a Lady (the wife of a senior official in the War Department) and a Gentleman (perhaps a great wit).
LADY *(looks in her catalogue)*: Painting Number Two: a landscape in oils. What do you think of it?
GENTLEMAN: Infinitely deep and sublime!
LADY: You mean the sea, yes, it must be amazingly deep, and the monk is also very sublime.
GENTLEMAN: No, Frau Kriegsrat, I mean the emotion felt by the one and only Friedrich before this painting.
LADY: Is it old enough for him to have seen it too?
GENTLEMAN: Ah, you misunderstand me, I refer to the painter Friedrich, not our great King Frederick. At the sight of this picture, Ossian strikes up on his harp. *(Exeunt)*

Enter two Young Ladies.
FIRST LADY: Did you hear that, Louise? It's Ossian.
SECOND LADY: No, surely you misunderstand. It's the ocean.
FIRST LADY: But he said he was striking his harp.
SECOND LADY: Well I don't see any harp. It's really gruesome. *(Exeunt)*

Enter two Connoisseurs.
FIRST CONNOISSEUR: Greysome, yes, it is all terribly grey. How he insists on painting such dry stuff.
SECOND CONNOISSEUR: You mean, how he insists on painting such wet stuff so drily.
FIRST CONNOISSEUR: I suppose he paints it as well as he can. *(Exeunt)*

Enter a Governess and two Young Ladies.
GOVERNESS: This is the sea near Rügen.

FIRST YOUNG LADY: Where Kosegarten lives.
SECOND YOUNG LADY: Where groceries come from.
GOVERNESS: Why did he paint nothing but dull skies? How lovely it would be if he had painted some men gathering amber on the seashore.
FIRST YOUNG LADY: Oh yes, I'd like to fish for a nice amber necklace for myself. *(Exeunt)*

Enter a Young Lady with two Fair-haired Children and a few Gentlemen.

GENTLEMAN: Magnificent, magnificent! This is the only artist who expresses a soul in his landscapes. There is a great individuality in this picture, high truth, solitude, the overcast, melancholy sky – he knows what he's painting all right.
SECOND GENTLEMAN: And he also paints what he knows, and feels it, and thinks it, and paints it.
FIRST CHILD: What is that?
FIRST GENTLEMAN: That is the sea, my boy, and a Capuchin who is taking a walk along the shore and feeling sad because he hasn't got a good little boy like you.
SECOND CHILD: Well, why isn't he dancing at the front of the picture? Why doesn't he waggle his head like in a shadow-play? That would be more fun!
FIRST CHILD: I suppose he predicts the weather, like the Capuchin outside our window.
SECOND GENTLEMAN: That's a different kind of Capuchin, my boy, but he does predict the weather, he is the one within the wholeness, the lonely centre in the lonely circle.
FIRST GENTLEMAN: Yes, he is the soul, the heart, the whole picture's reflection in itself and on itself.
SECOND GENTLEMAN: How divinely the figure is chosen, it is not merely a device to show the height of the other objects, as in the work of the common run of painters. He is the subject itself, he is the picture; and as he seems to dream himself into this setting, as if into a sad mirror of his isolation, so the shipless, enclosing sea, which binds him like a vow, and the bleak, sandy shore, as friendless as his life, seem symbolically to make him spring up again like a lonely dune plant prophesying its own fate.
FIRST GENTLEMAN: Magnificent, certainly, you are right. *(To the Lady)* But, my dear, you have not said a word.
LADY: Oh, I felt so at home in front of the picture, it truly touched me. It is truly lifelike, and when you were talking like that, it was all hazy, just like when I went for a walk beside the sea with our philosophical friends. I only wish that a fresh sea breeze was blowing and a sail was coming in, and that there was a glint of sunlight and the water was lapping. As it is, it's like a dream, having a nightmare or feeling homesick – let's move on, it's making me feel sad. *(Exeunt)*

Enter a Lady and a Gentleman as her guide.

LADY *(stands for a long time without speaking)*: How grand, how immeasurably grand! It is as if the sea was thinking Young's *Night Thoughts.*
GENTLEMAN: You mean, as if they had occurred to the monk here?
LADY: If only you wouldn't make jokes all the time, and spoil the impression. Secretly you feel the same but you want to mock in others what you yourself reverence. What I said was, it is as if the sea was thinking Young's *Night Thoughts.*
GENTLEMAN: Yes, I agree, particularly the Karlsruhe second edition, and Mercier's *Bonnet de nuit* as well, and then [Gotthilf Heinrich von] Schubert's *View of Nature from its Dark Side* on top of that.
LADY: The best answer I can give you is a similar anecdote. When the immortal Klopstock wrote the line 'Dawn smiles' in a poem for the first time, Madame Gottsched read it and said 'Did she pout as well?'
GENTLEMAN: Surely not as prettily as you when you say that.
LADY: You are beginning to annoy me.

GENTLEMAN: And Gottsched gave his wife a kiss for her bon mot.
LADY: I could give you a *bonnet de nuit* for yours, but a wet blanket might be more appropriate.
GENTLEMAN: Surely I am more like a view of your nature from its dark side.
LADY: You are teasing.
GENTLEMAN: Ah, if only we were both standing there, like the monk!
LADY: I would leave you and go to the monk.
GENTLEMAN: And ask him to make us one.
LADY: No, to throw you in the water.
GENTLEMAN: And then you would be alone with the holy man, and you would seduce him, and spoil the whole picture and his night thoughts; you see, that's what you women are like, in the end you destroy what you feel, in your very lying you tell the truth. How I wish I was the monk, forever gazing out alone over the dark, foreboding sea which spreads out before him like the apocalypse. I would forever yearn for you, dear Julia, yet would be without you forever, for longing is the only magnificent feeling in love.
LADY: No, no, my dear, it is true in this picture too; if you talk like that, I will jump in the water after you and leave the monk by himself. *(Exeunt)*

All this while, a tall, forbearing man was listening with some signs of impatience; I came close to treading on his foot and he answered me as if in so doing I had asked his opinion. 'It's a good thing the pictures can't hear, or else they'd have veiled themselves long ago; people treat them in a very ill-mannered way and are firmly convinced that they're standing in the pillory here for some secret offence which onlookers must at all costs discover.'

'But what is your own opinion of the picture?' I asked. 'I am glad', he replied, 'that there is still one landscape painter who pays attention to the strange conjunctures of the seasons and the sky, which produce the most striking effects in even the poorest regions. True, I would prefer it if he also had the gift and the technique to represent it truthfully; in this respect he is as far inferior to some of the Dutch School who have painted subjects similar to this as he is their superior in his overall approach. It would not be difficult to name a dozen pictures where the sea and the shore and the monk are better painted. From a certain distance the figure looks like a brown smudge; if I had wanted to paint a monk I would sooner have shown him lying down asleep, or set him lower to pray or look about him in all modesty, so as not to spoil the view for the visitors, on whom the outspread ocean obviously makes a greater impression than the little monk. Anyone who looked around later for the people of the coast would still find in the monk every reason to say what several of the visitors have said effusively and confidently, loud enough for all to hear.'

These words pleased me so much that I at once went home with the gentleman, where I still reside, and where you will be able to find me in future.

CHRONOLOGY

1774
5 September: Caspar David Friedrich born in Greifswald.

1781
Death of his mother.

1787
His brother Johann Christoffer drowns while skating.

1788
Lessons with the 'academic drawing master' Johann Gottfried Quistorp.

1791
Death of his sister Maria.

1794–98
Studies at the Copenhagen Academy, in the freehand drawing class until 1796, then in the plaster and modelling classes.

1798
May: returns to Greifswald. By October he is in Dresden, where he meets Philipp Otto Runge, Gotthilf Heinrich von Schubert and Ludwig Tieck.

1799
Takes part in the Dresden Academy Exhibition for the first time.

1800
Publication of Christian August Semler's *Untersuchungen über die höchste Vollkommenheit in der Landschaftsmalerey (Enquiry into the Greatest Perfection in Landscape Painting).*

1801
Runge visits Friedrich in Greifswald; frequent visits to Rügen.

1803
Friedrich spends the summer in Loschwitz near Dresden. He shows some sepias in the Academy Exhibition. Runge buys two and writes to his brother Daniel: 'Here's the young Fridrich [sic] from Greifswald, a landscape painter, who's showing a few views of Stubbenkammer, sepia drawings of a respectable size, beautifully lit, composed and executed; they are earning general praise and deserve it.' (6 April; *Hinterlassene Schriften*, II, 208)

1805
Friedrich enters the Weimar competition.

1806
Illness. Spends time in Greifswald and Neubrandenburg and on Rügen.

1807
Travels to northern Bohemia.

1808
Second journey to northern Bohemia. *The Tetschen Altar* is exhibited in Friedrich's Dresden studio. 'It cast a spell on everyone who entered the room. The loudest chatterboxes lowered their voices as if they were in church' (Helene von Kügelgen to her husband).

1809
Death of Friedrich's father.

1810
Walking tour of the Riesengebirge with Georg Friedrich Kersting. Receives visits from Johanna Schopenhauer, and from Goethe and Heinrich von Kleist. *The Monk by the Sea* and *The Abbey in the Oak Wood* are shown at the Berlin Academy. Carl Gustav Carus calls *The Abbey* 'perhaps the most profoundly poetic work of art in recent landscape painting', but the sculptor Johann Gottfried Schadow mocks its 'nightwatchman tone'.

1811
Friedrich is elected to the Berlin Academy. Walking tour of the Harz Mountains with the sculptor Gottlieb Kühn. Short stay in Jena, meeting with Goethe.

1812
King Frederick William III buys *Morning in the Riesengebirge.*

1813
Becomes acquainted with Ernst Moritz Arndt in Dresden. The French army occupies Dresden, and Friedrich goes to the Elbsandsteingebirge in July in search of peace and quiet.

1814
Friedrich shows *Tombs of Ancient Heroes* at an exhibition of patriotic art organized by the Russian governor.

1815
Elected to the Dresden Academy.

1817
Meets the physician and scientist Carl Gustav Carus, and the Norwegian landscape painter Johan Christian Clausen Dahl. Both of them become friends and pupils.

1818
21 January: marries Caroline Bommer. Honeymoon in Greifswald, Stralsund and Rügen.

1819
Visit from Prince Christian Frederick of Denmark. Birth of Friedrich's daughter Emma.

1820
The Friedrich family moves to a house by the river (An der Elbe 33). Visit from Grand Duke Nikolay Pavlovich (later Tsar Nicholas I).

1821
Friedrich makes the acquaintance of the Russian poet and state councillor Vasily Andreyevich Zhukovsky.

1822
The writer Friedrich de La Motte-Fouqué visits Friedrich.

1823
Dahl moves into Friedrich's house. A second daughter, Agnes Adelheid, is born.

1824
Friedrich is appointed professor (annual salary 200 ducats) but not given the vacant directorship of the landscape class. His son Gustav Adolf is born. Friedrich falls ill.

1826
A stay on Rügen to improve his health. Zhukovsky writes to the Tsarina Alexandra Feodorovna: 'I see the painter Friedrich here from time to time ... He has started a large landscape which will be delightful if the execution matches up to the idea.'

1828
Friedrich takes a rest cure in Teplitz (Teplice), Bohemia.

1830
He receives a visit from Crown Prince Frederick William of Prussia.

1834
7 November: the sculptor David d'Angers visits Friedrich.

1835
26 June: Friedrich suffers a stroke. Goes to Teplitz to take the cure. He does not entertain a 'hope ... of ever recovering fully from the paralysis' (letter to Zhukovsky, 19 November).

1840
7 May: Friedrich dies in Dresden.

1843
His widow receives a gift of 150 thalers from Tsar Nicholas I, originally intended for Friedrich but delayed by bureaucracy; her receipt for it is dated 28 February.

BIBLIOGRAPHY

Asvarishch, Boris,
(see Rewald)

Bailey, Colin J.,
(see Leighton and Monrad)

Börsch-Supan, Helmut and Jähnig, Karl Wilhelm,
Caspar David Friedrich: Gemälde, Druckgraphik und bildmäßige Zeichnungen (catalogue raisonné), Munich, Prestel, 1973

Décultot, Élisabeth,
Peindre le paysage. Discours théorique et renouveau pictural dans le romantisme allemand, Tusson (Charente), Éditions du Lérot, 1996

Eimer, Gerhard,
Zur Dialektik des Glaubens bei Caspar David Friedrich, Frankfurt am Main, Kunstgeschichtliches Institut der Johann Wolfgang Goethe-Universität, 1982

Frank, Hilmar,
'Die mannigfaltigen Wege zur Kunst. Romantische Kunstphilosophie in einem Schema Caspar David Friedrichs', in *IDEA, Jahrbuch der Hamburger Kunsthalle,* X, 1991, pp. 165 ff.

Grundmann, Günther,
'Schlesien und Caspar David Friedrich', in *Schlesische Monatshefte,* VII, 1930, pp. 421 ff.

Hinz, Sigrid (ed.),
Caspar David Friedrich in Briefen und Bekenntnissen, Munich, Rogner & Bernhard, 1974

Hoch, Karl-Ludwig,
Caspar David Friedrich – unbekannte Dokumente seines Lebens, Dresden, Verlag der Kunst, 1985

Hofmann, Werner (ed.),
Caspar David Friedrich, exhibition catalogue, Hamburger Kunsthalle, Hamburg, 1974

Hofmann, Werner,
'Art – Nature – Histoire', in *La Peinture allemande à l'époque du romantisme,* exhibition catalogue, Musée de l'Orangerie, Paris, 1976–77

Hofmann, Werner (ed.),
Caspar David Friedrich: Pinturas y dibujos, exhibition catalogue, Museo nacional del Prado, Madrid, 1992

Howoldt, Jenns E.,
Caspar David Friedrich: seine Zeichnungen in der Hamburger Kunsthalle, Hamburg, Kunsthalle, 1990

Jäger, Hans-Wolf,
Politische Metaphorik im Jakobinismus und im Vormärz, Stuttgart, J. B. Metzler, 1971

Jensen, Jens Christian,
Caspar David Friedrich: Life and Work, Woodbury, NY, Barron's, 1981

Kellein, Thomas,
Caspar David Friedrich: Der künstlerische Weg, Munich, Prestel, 1998

Koerner, Joseph Leo,
Caspar David Friedrich and the Subject of Landscape, London, Reaktion, 1990

Leighton, John and Bailey, Colin J.,
Caspar David Friedrich: Winter Landscape, exhibition catalogue, The National Gallery, London, 1990

Leppien, Helmut R.,
Caspar David Friedrich in der Hamburger Kunsthalle, Hamburg, Kunsthalle, 1993

Mehring, Franz,
Deutsche Geschichte vom Ausgange des Mittelalters, Berlin, J. H. W. Dietz, 1952

Monrad, Kasper and Bailey, Colin J.,
Caspar David Friedrich øg Danmark, Copenhagen, Statens Museum for Kunst, 1991

Neidhardt, Hans J.,
'Caspar David Friedrich und Ludwig Richter', in *Jahrbuch der Staatlichen Kunstsammlungen,* Dresden, 1970–71

Panofsky, Erwin,
Perspective as Symbolic Form, New York, Zone Books, 1991

Reitharová, Eva and Sumovski, Werner,
'Beiträge zu Caspar David Friedrich', in *Pantheon,* XXXV/1, 1977

Rewald, Sabine (ed.),
The Romantic Vision of Caspar David Friedrich. Paintings and Drawings from the USSR, exhibition catalogue, The Metropolitan Museum of Art, New York, 1991 (with contributions by Robert Rosenblum and Boris Asvarishch)

Rosenblum, Robert,
(see Rewald)

Schmied, Wieland,
Caspar David Friedrich: Zyklus, Zeit und Ewigkeit, Munich, Prestel, 1999

Schmitt, Otto,
'Die Ruine Eldena im Werk von Caspar David Friedrich', in *Kunstbrief* 25, Berlin, 1944

Stechow, Wolfgang,
'Caspar David Friedrich und der "Griper"', in *Festschrift für Herbert von Einem,* Berlin, 1965

Sumovski, Werner,
Caspar David Friedrich-Studien, Wiesbaden, F. Steiner, 1970

Sumovski, Werner,
(see also Reitharová)

Syamken, Georg,
Luther und die Folgen für die Kunst, exhibition catalogue, Hamburger Kunsthalle, Hamburg, 1983–84 (see cat. 342–348)

Wolfradt, Willi,
Caspar David Friedrich und die Landschaft der Romantik, Berlin, 1924

LIST OF ILLUSTRATIONS

Works by Caspar David Friedrich are listed alphabetically by title; works by other artists are listed separately at the end. The illustration number is given for all works.

BS references refer to:
Börsch-Supan, Helmut and Jähnig, Karl Wilhelm, *Caspar David Friedrich : Gemälde, Druckgraphik und bildmäßige Zeichnungen* (catalogue raisonné), Munich, Prestel, 1973.

Kellein references refer to:
Kellein, Thomas, *Caspar David Friedrich : Der künstlerische Weg*, Munich, Prestel, 1998.

Cross in front of a Rainbow in the Mountains, The,
c. 1817, ink and watercolour,
27.2 x 20.8 cm (10⅝ x 8 in.).
Kupferstichkabinett, Dresden.
ILL. 45; BS 229.

Cross in the Forest, The,
c. 1820, oil on canvas,
42 x 32 cm (16½ x 12⅝ in.).
Staatsgalerie, Stuttgart.
ILL. 37; BS 450.

Cross in the Mountains, The,
1811–12, oil on canvas,
44.5 x 37.4 cm (17½ x 14¾ in.).
Kunstmuseum, Düsseldorf.
ILL. 36; BS 201.

Cross in the Mountains, The (The Tetschen Altar),
1807–8, oil on canvas,
115 x 110.5 cm (45¼ x 43½ in.).
Gemäldegalerie Neue Meister, Dresden.
ILL. 18 AND 21; BS 167.

Design for the Marienkirche, Stralsund,
1817, pencil, ink and watercolour,
56.6 x 43.7 cm (22¼ x 17⅛ in.).
Germanisches Nationalmuseum, Nuremberg.
ILL. 44; KELLEIN 126.

Dolmen by the Sea,
1807, pencil and sepia,
64.5 x 95 cm (25½ x 37⅜ in.).
Staatliche Kunstsammlungen, Weimar.
ILL. 28; BS 147.

Dolmen in the Snow,
1807, oil on canvas,
61.5 x 80 cm (24¼ x 31½ in.).
Gemäldegalerie Neue Meister, Dresden.
ILL. 29; BS 162

Doorway in the Fürstenschule, Meissen,
after 1835, pencil and sepia,
22.8 x 19.3 cm (8⅞ x 7⅝ in.).
Private collection.
ILL. 153; BS 458.

Dune by the Sea,
c. 1824, pencil and watercolour,
24.7 x 36.5 cm (9¾ x 14⅜ in.).
Kupferstichkabinett, Berlin.
ILL. 97; BS 324.

Early Snow,
1828, oil on canvas,
43.8 x 34.5 cm (17¼ x 13½ in.).
Hamburger Kunsthalle, Hamburg.
ILL. 52; BS 363.

Evening,
1820–21, oil on canvas,
22.3 x 31 cm (8¾ x 12¼ in.).
Niedersächsisches Landesmuseum, Hanover.
ILL. 133; BS 275.

Evening,
1824, oil on board,
12.5 x 21.2 cm (5 x 8¼ in.).
Österreichische Galerie im Belvedere, Vienna.
ILL. 126; BS 318.

Evening,
1824, oil on board,
20 x 27.5 cm (7⅞ x 10¾ in.).
Kunsthalle, Mannheim.
ILL. 127; BS 319.

Evening,
1824, oil on canvas,
20.8 x 24.7 cm (8 x 9¾ in.).
Henke Collection, Essen.
ILL. 102; BS 320.

Evening Landscape with Two Men,
1830–35, oil on canvas,
25 x 31 cm (9⅞ x 12¼ in.).
Hermitage Museum, St Petersburg.
ILL. 49; BS 406.

Evening on the Baltic Sea,
1826, oil on canvas,
25 x 31 cm (9⅞ x 12¼ in.).
Georg Schäfer Collection.
ILL. 112; BS 350.

Evening on the Baltic Sea,
c. 1831, oil on canvas,
54 x 71.5 cm (21¼ x 28⅛ in.).
Gemäldegalerie Neue Meister, Dresden.
ILL. 117; BS 391.

Evening Star, The,
1830–35, oil on canvas,
32.5 x 45 cm (12¾ x 17¾ in.).
Freies Deutsches Hochstift, Frankfurt.
ILL. 106; BS 389.

Fallen Rocks,
19 June 1813, watercolour over pencil,
21 x 17.4 cm (8¼ x 7 in.).
Kupferstichkabinett, Berlin.
ILL. 50; BS 22.

Garden Terrace, The
1811–12, oil on canvas,
53.5 x 70 cm (21 x 27⅝ in.).
Schloss Sanssouci, Potsdam.
ILL. 60; BS 199.

Graveyard Gate, The,
1824–26, oil on canvas,
143 x 110 cm (56¼ x 43¼ in.).
Gemäldegalerie Neue Meister, Dresden.
ILLS 81 AND 93; BS 335.

Graveyard under Snow,
1826–27, oil on canvas,
30 x 26 cm (11¾ x 10¼ in.).
Museum der bildenden Künste, Leipzig.
ILL. 92; BS 353.

Greifswald in Moonlight,
c. 1817, oil on canvas,
22.5 x 30.5 cm (8¾ x 12 in.).
Nasjonalgalleriet, Oslo.
ILL. 101; BS 224.

High Mountains (Swiss Landscape),
1824, oil on canvas,
132 x 167 cm (52 x 65¾ in.).
Formerly Nationalgalerie, Berlin (destroyed 1945).
ILL. 83; BS 317.

Hill and Ploughed Field near Dresden,
1824, oil on canvas,
22.2 x 30.5 cm (8⅝ x 12 in.).
Hamburger Kunsthalle, Hamburg.
ILL. 105; BS 321.

Hutten's Tomb,
1823–24, oil on canvas,
93 x 73 cm (36⅝ x 28¾ in.).
Staatliche Kunstsammlungen, Weimar.
ILL. 55; BS 316.

Hut under Snow,
1827, oil on canvas,
31 x 25 cm (12¼ x 9⅞ in.).
Nationalgalerie, Berlin.
ILL. 91; BS 355.

Landscape in the Riesengebirge,
1810, oil on canvas,
45 x 58.3 cm (17¾ x 23 in.).
Pushkin Museum, Moscow.
ILLS 110 AND 111; BS 187.

Landscape in the Riesengebirge,
1823, oil on canvas,
35 x 48.8 cm (13¾ x 19⅛ in.).
Hamburger Kunsthalle, Hamburg.
ILL. 108; BS 304.

Landscape in the Riesengebirge with Mist Rising,
c. 1820–21, oil on canvas,
54.9 x 70.3 cm (21⅝ x 27¾ in.).
Neue Pinakothek, Munich.
ILL. 59; BS 264.

Landscape with Crumbling Wall,
c. 1837–40, pencil, Indian ink and watercolour, 12.2 x 18.5 cm (4¾ x 7¼ in.).
Hamburger Kunsthalle, Hamburg.
ILL. 154; BS 496.

Landscape with Grave, Coffin and Owl,
c. 1836–37, pencil and sepia,
48.5 x 38.5 cm (19 x 15¼ in.).
Hamburger Kunsthalle, Hamburg.
ILL. 150; BS 460.

Landscape with Lunar Rainbow,
1810, oil on canvas,
70 x 102 cm (27⅝ x 40⅛ in.).
Museum Folkwang, Essen.
ILL. 99; BS 183.

Landscape with Pavilion,
1797, ink and watercolour,
16.5 x 22 cm (6½ x 8⅝ in.).
Hamburger Kunsthalle, Hamburg.
ILL. 141; BS 12.

Landscape with Rainbow,
1810, oil on canvas,
59 x 84.5 cm (23¼ x 33¼ in.).
Formerly Staatliche Kunstsammlungen, Weimar.
ILL. 98; BS 182.

Large Enclosure, The,
c. 1832, oil on canvas,
73.5 x 103 cm (29 x 40½ in.).
Gemäldegalerie Neue Meister, Dresden.
ILL. 162; BS 399.

Letter to Louise Seidler,
1814, ink,
19.4 x 26.2 cm (7⅝ x 10¼ in.).
Kupferstichkabinett, Dresden.
ILL. 26.

Limetree Branch,
c. 1812, pencil, wash,
12.8 x 18 cm (5 x 7⅛ in.).
Nasjonalgalleriet, Oslo.
ILL. 118; KELLEIN 49.

Man and Woman Contemplating the Moon,
late 1820s, oil on canvas,
34 x 44 cm (13⅜ x 17⅜ in.).
Nationalgalerie, Berlin.
ILL. 96; BS 404.

Marketplace in Greifswald, The,
1818, ink and watercolour,
54 x 76 cm (21¼ x 29⅞ in.).
Pommersches Landesmuseum, Greifswald.
ILL. 56; BS 251.

Meadows near Greifswald,
1820–22, oil on canvas,
35 x 48.9 cm (13¾ x 19¼ in.).
Hamburger Kunsthalle, Hamburg.
ILLS 103 AND 104; BS 285.

Midday,
1822, oil on canvas,
20 x 30 cm (7⅞ x 11¾ in.).
Niedersächsisches Landesmuseum, Hanover.
ILL. 134; BS 296.

Mist,
1807, oil on canvas,
34.2 x 50.2 cm (13⅜ x 19⅝ in.).
Österreichische Galerie im Belvedere, Vienna.
ILLS 15 AND 16; BS 159.

Monastery Graveyard in Snow,
1817–19, oil on canvas,
121 x 170 cm (47⅝ x 66⅞ in.).
Formerly Nationalgalerie, Berlin.
ILL. 31; BS 254.

Monk by the Sea, The,
c. 1809, oil on canvas,
110 x 171.5 cm (43¼ x 67½ in.).
Nationalgalerie, Berlin.
ILLS 22 AND 25; BS 168.

Moon above the Riesengebirge,
1810, oil on canvas,
47.5 x 167 cm (18⅝ x 65¾ in.).
Staatliche Kunstsammlungen, Weimar.
ILL. 109; BS 186.

Moonrise by the Sea,
1821, oil on canvas,
135 x 170 cm (53⅛ x 66⅞ in.).
Hermitage Museum, St Petersburg.
ILL. 128; BS 281.

Moonrise by the Sea,
1822, oil on canvas,
55 x 71 cm (21⅝ x 28 in.).
Nationalgalerie, Berlin.
ILL. 90; BS 299.

Moonrise over the Sea,
c. 1837–39, pencil and sepia,
25.6 x 38.5 cm (10⅛ x 15⅛ in.).
Hamburger Kunsthalle, Hamburg.
ILL. 136; BS 485.

Morning,
1820–21, oil on canvas,
22 x 30.7 cm (8⅝ x 12 in.).
Niedersächsisches Landesmuseum, Hanover.
ILL. 132; BS 274.

Morning in the Mountains,
1822–23, oil on canvas,
135 x 170 cm (53⅛ x 66⅞ in.).
Hermitage Museum, St Petersburg.
ILL. 84; BS 300.

Morning in the Riesengebirge (The Cross in the Mountains),
1810–11, oil on canvas,
108 x 170 cm (42½ x 66⅞ in.).
Nationalgalerie, Berlin.
ILL. 58; BS 190.

Morning Mist in the Mountains,
1808, oil on canvas,
71 x 104 cm (28 x 41 in.).
Staatliche Museum Schloss Heidecksburg, Rudolstadt.
ILL. 19; BS 166.

Mountain Landscape,
1804–5, sepia,
12.2 x 18.2 cm (4¾ x 7⅛ in.).
Goethe Nationalmuseum, Weimar.
ILL. 5; BS 122.

Sea Piece by Moonlight,
1830, oil on canvas,
77 x 97 cm (30¼ x 38⅛ in.).
Nationalgalerie, Berlin.
ILL. 167; BS 392.

Seashore by Moonlight,
1835–36, oil on canvas,
134 x 169.2 cm (52¾ x 66½ in.).
Hamburger Kunsthalle, Hamburg.
ILL. 166; BS 453.

Seashore with Fisherman,
1807, oil on canvas,
33.5 x 50.8 cm (13¼ x 20 in.).
Österreichische Galerie im Belvedere, Vienna.
ILL. 17; BS 158.

Self-portrait,
7 September 1800, pencil,
17.7 x 11.3 cm (7 x 4½ in.).
Kupferstichkabinett, Dresden.
ILL. 190; BS 37.

Self-portrait,
c. 1806–9, black chalk,
22.6 x 18 cm (10½ x 7⅛ in.).
Stadtmuseum, Dresden.
ILL. 188; BS 142.

Self-portrait,
1810, chalk,
23 x 18.2 cm (9 x 7⅛ in.).
Kupferstichkabinett, Berlin.
ILL. 24; BS 21.

Self-portrait in Profile,
c. 1802, Indian ink,
13.1 x 9.2 cm (5⅛ x 3½ in.).
Hamburger Kunsthalle, Hamburg.
ILL. 192; BS 73

Self-portrait with Cap,
1802, pencil and Indian ink,
17.5 x 10.5 cm (7 x 4⅛ in.).
Hamburger Kunsthalle, Hamburg.
ILL. 189; BS 72.

Self-portrait with Raised Arm,
c. 1802, pencil and ink,
26.7 x 21.5 cm (10½ x 8½ in.).
Hamburger Kunsthalle, Hamburg.
ILL. 191; BS 75.

Ship on the River Elbe in the Early Morning Mist,
1820–25, oil on canvas,
22.5 x 30.8 cm (8¾ x 12 in.).
Wallraf-Richartz-Museum, Cologne.
ILL. 123; BS 283.

Ships at Anchor,
1815, oil on canvas,
21 x 30 cm (8¼ x 11¾ in.).
Private collection, on loan to Nationalgalerie, Berlin.
ILL. 116; BS 241.

Skeletons in a Cave with Stalactites,
c. 1826, sepia, 18.8 x 27.5 cm (7⅜ x 10¾ in.).
Hamburger Kunsthalle, Hamburg.
ILL. 147; BS 343.

Source of the River Elbe, The,
c. 1830, pencil and watercolour,
25 x 34 cm (9⅞ x 13⅜ in.).
Private collection.
ILL. 82; BS 386.

Spring,
1803, sepia, 19 x 27.5 cm (7½ x 10¾ in.).
Formerly Reichskammer der bildenden Künste, Berlin (destroyed).
ILL. 12; BS 103.

Spring,
c. 1826, sepia,
19.1 x 27.3 cm (7½ x 10¾ in.).
Hamburger Kunsthalle, Hamburg.
ILL. 138; BS 339.

Stages of Life, The,
1834–35, oil on canvas,
72.5 x 94 cm (28½ x 37 in.).
Museum der bildenden Künste, Leipzig.
ILLS 3, 163 AND 165; BS 411.

Studies of Rowing Boats,
1818, pencil,
19.4 x 24.3 cm (7⅝ x 9⅝ in.).
Kupferstichkabinett, Berlin.
ILL. 115; KELLEIN 18.

Study for *On the Sailing Boat,*
1818, pencil and wash,
36 x 26 cm (14⅛ x 10¼ in.).
Nasjonalgalleriet, Oslo.
ILL. 76; KELLEIN 22.

Summer,
1803, sepia,
19 x 27.5 cm (7½ x 10¾ in.).
Formerly Reichskammer der bildenden Künste, Berlin (destroyed).
ILL. 140; BS 104.

Summer,
c. 1826, sepia,
19 x 27.1 cm (7½ x 10⅝ in.).
Hamburger Kunsthalle, Hamburg.
ILL. 139; BS 340.

Summerhouse, The,
1818, oil on canvas,
30 x 22 cm (11¾ x 8⅝ in.).
Neue Pinakothek, Munich.
ILL. 70; BS 253.

Summer Landscape with a Dead Oak Tree,
1805, pencil and sepia,
40.5 x 62 cm (16 x 24⅜ in.).
Staatliche Kunstsammlungen, Weimar.
ILL. 9; BS 125.

Summer (Landscape with a Pair of Lovers),
1807, oil on canvas,
71.4 x 103.6 cm (28⅛ x 40¾ in.).
Neue Pinakothek, Munich.
ILL. 14; BS 164.

Sunrise: Neubrandenburg in Flames,
1835, oil on canvas,
72.2 x 101.3 cm (28½ x 39⅞ in.).
Hamburger Kunsthalle, Hamburg.
ILL. 73; BS 427.

Sunrise over the Sea,
c. 1826, sepia,
18.7 x 26.5 cm (7⅜ x 10½ in.).
Hamburger Kunsthalle, Hamburg.
ILL. 137; BS 338.

Swans in the Rushes,
1820, oil on canvas,
35.5 x 44 cm (14 x 17⅜ in.).
Goethemuseum, Frankfurt.
ILL. 87; BS 266.

Tombs of Ancient Heroes,
1812, oil on canvas,
49.5 x 70.5 cm (19½ x 27¾ in.).
Hamburger Kunsthalle, Hamburg.
ILL. 51; BS 205.

WORKS BY OTHER ARTISTS

INDEX

PHOTO CREDITS

Berlin, Bildarchiv Preussischer Kulturbesitz / Jörg P. Anders: ills 22, 23, 25, 32, 48, 50, 58, 71, 72, 89, 90, 96, 97, 116, 167.

Berlin, Bildarchiv Preussischer Kulturbesitz: ills 31, 83.

Bremen, Kunsthalle: ill. 94.

Cologne, Rheinisches Bildarchiv: ill. 123.

Copenhagen, Ny Carlsberg Glyptothek: ill. 171.

Dortmund, Museum für Kunst und Kulturgeschichte: ill. 33.

Dresden, Fotostudio Herbert Boswank: ills 190, 193.

Dresden, Sächsische Landesbibliothek / Deutsche Fotothek: ills 18, 21, 29, 95, 117, 131, 162.

Dresden, Stadtmuseum: ill. 188.

Dusseldorf, Kunstmuseum: ill. 36.

Essen, Museum Folkwang: ills 7, 63, 99.

Euerbach, Schäfer Collection: ill. 112.

Fort Worth, Kimbell Art Museum / Michael Bodycomb: ill. 86.

Frankfurt, Goethemuseum / Ursula Edelman: ill. 87.

Greifswald, Pommersches Landesmuseum: ills 56, 122.

Hamburg, Kunsthalle / Elke Walford: ills 1, 6, 10, 11, 20, 40, 51, 52, 57, 64, 73, 103, 107, 108, 119, 124, 125, 136, 137, 138, 139, 146, 147, 148, 154, 157, 158, 159, 166, 168, 172, 180, 181, 187, 191, 192.

Hanover, Niedersächsisches Landesmuseum: ills 132, 133, 134, 135.

Kassel, Staatliche Kunstsammlungen / Hensmanns: ills 129, 130.

Kiel, Stiftung Pommern, Gemäldegalerie und Kulturgeschichtliche Sammlungen: ills 74, 75.

Leipzig, Museum der bildenden Künste: ills 78, 182.

Mannheim, Kunsthalle / Margita Wickenhäuser: ill. 127.

Moscow, Alexander Burkatovski: ills 47, 49, 84, 110, 111, 128, 151, 152.

Munich, Engelbert Seehuber: ills 82, 153.

Munich, Shack-Galerie: ills 175, 179.

Munich, Neue Pinakothek: ill. 144.

Oslo, Nasjonalgalleriet / J. Lathion: ill. 101.

Paris, Réunion des Musées nationaux / Arnaudet: ill. 121.

Paris, Réunion des Musées nationaux / Michelle Bellot: ill. 39.

Peissenberg, Artothek: ills 53, 66, 70, 81, 93, 160.

Peissenberg, Artothek / Joachim Blauel: ills 14, 38, 41, 42, 59, 69, 149.

Peissenberg, Artothek / Sophie R. Gnamm: ills 46, 47.

Peissenberg, Artothek / Christoph Sandig: ills 3, 163, 165.

Potsdam, Stiftung Preussische Schlösser und Gärten Berlin-Brandenburg: ill. 60.

Prague, Národní Galerie / Milan Posselt: ill. 161.

Rudolstadt, Thüringer Landesmuseum Heidecksburg Rudolstadt: ill. 19.

Schwerin, Staatliches Museum / Elke Walford: ills 34, 35.

Stuttgart, Staatsgalerie: ills 37, 88.

Vienna, Albertina: ill. 30.

Vienna, Fotostudio Otto: ills 15, 16, 17, 67, 68, 85, 126.

Weimar, Goethe Nationalmuseum / Sigrid Geske: ill. 5.

Weimar, Staatliche Kunstsammlungen / Atelier Louis Held: ills 8, 9, 28, 55, 98, 109.

Winterthur, Museum Oskar Reinhart am Stadtgarten: ills 79, 80, 100.

Zurich, Galerie Nathan: ill. 113.